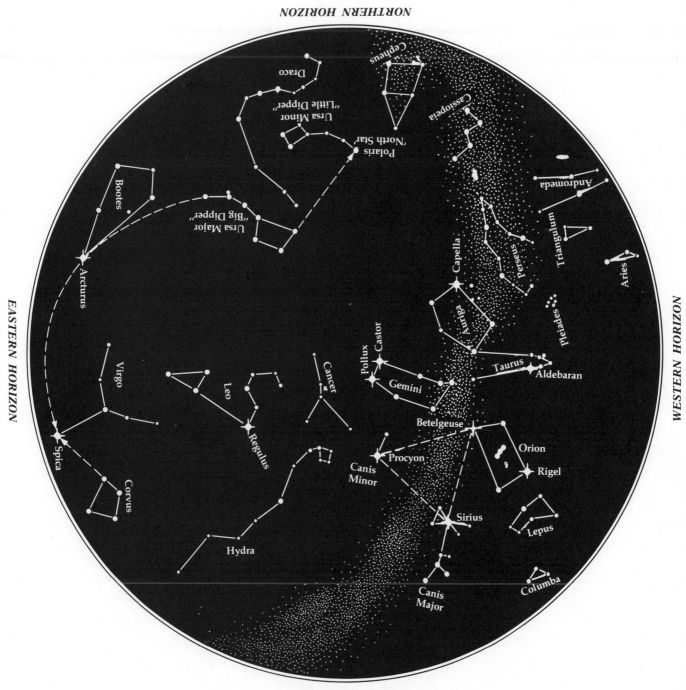

The night sky in MARCH

ASTRONOMY
The Evolving Universe

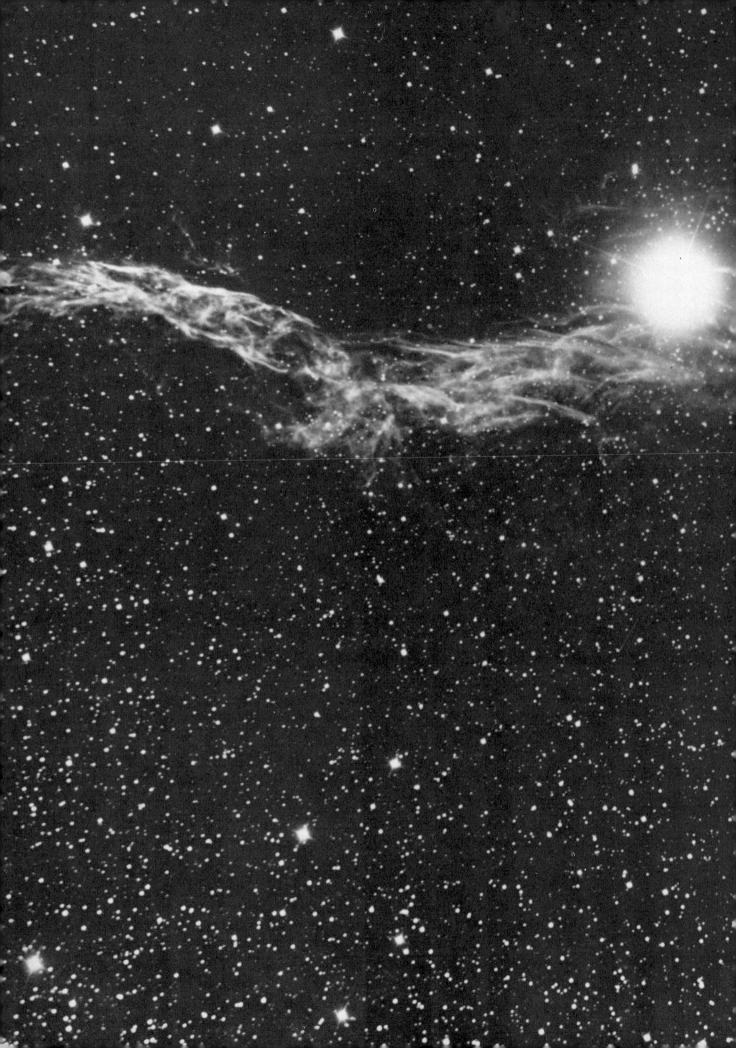

ASTRONOMY
The Evolving Universe

THIRD EDITION

Michael Zeilik
The University of New Mexico

1817

HARPER & ROW, PUBLISHERS, New York

Cambridge, Philadelphia, San Francisco,
London, Mexico City, São Paulo, Sydney

To my parents, Margaret and Michael

PHOTO CREDITS. Title spread: Hale Observatory. Part 1: Hale Observatory / Parts 2, 3: NASA / Part 4: Kitt Peak National Observatory. Chapter 1: Lick Observatory / Chapters 2, 3, 4: Yerkes Observatory / Chapter 5: Harvard College Observatory / Chapter 6: Cerro Tololo Inter-American Observatory / Chapter 7: Palomar Observatory, California Institute of Technology / Chapters 8, 9: NASA / Chapter 10: Palomar Observatory, California Institute of Technology / Chapter 11: NASA / Chapters 12, 13: Mt. Wilson Observatory, Carnegie Institute of Washington / Chapter 14: A. Hoag / Chapter 15: Harvard College Observatory / Chapter 16: Kitt Peak National Observatory / Chapter 17: Harvard College Observatory / Chapter 18: Kitt Peak National Observatory / Chapter 19: Palomar Observatory, California Institute of Technology / Chapter 20: Harvard College Observatory / Chapter 21: Harold E. Edgerton, Massachusetts Institute of Technology / Chapter 22: NASA.

Figures 8.3, 8.10, and 8.12 are adapted from figures in *The Earth Sciences*, Second Edition, by A. N. Strahler, Harper & Row, 1971.

The lines of poetry at the beginning of Chapter 17 are from *Prologue* by Edward Field. Reprinted by permission of Grove Press, Inc. Copyright © 1963 by Edward Field.

The star charts used on the endpapers are adapted from the *Griffith Observer* monthly magazine published by Griffith Observatory, 2800 East Observatory Road, Los Angeles, CA 90027.

ABOUT THE COVER

Stars form the nexus of cosmic evolution. And the key to understanding the stars is an understanding of our home star, the sun.

Total solar eclipses provide unique opportunities for earth-based astronomers to view the sun's outer atmosphere, called the corona. The full extent of the corona blossoms during a total solar eclipse—no artificial means can bring it out so clearly.

The cover photo of the February 26, 1979 total solar eclipse reveals the corona's complex beauty. It was taken by William H. Regan and Maxwell T. Sanford of the Los Alamos National Laboratory from an aircraft at an altitude of 40,000 ft over North Dakota. The clear, dark skies at this altitude permitted the photography of details in the corona out to about 5 solar radii from the sun.

To the east side (left) no activity is obvious. To the west (right) an explosive blast moves out through the corona. The streams in the corona show places where the sun's magnetic field threads out into space. Knots occur where the field is twisted and kinked.

The sun is the only star close enough for us to see the flux and flow in its atmosphere. Astronomers believe that stars similar to the sun undergo the same activity at distances too far for us to discern directly.

Sponsoring editor: *Malvina Wasserman*
Project editor: *Brigitte Pelner*
Text and cover designer: *Gayle Jaeger*
Production manager: *Jeanie Berke*
Compositor: *York Graphic Services, Inc.*
Printer and binder: *Kingsport Press*
Art studio: *J&R Art Services, Inc.*

ASTRONOMY: *The Evolving Universe,* *Third Edition*
Copyright © 1982 by Michael Zeilik

Library of Congress Cataloging in Publication Data
Zeilik, Michael.
    Astronomy, the evolving universe.
    Includes bibliographies and index.
    1. Astronomy.   I. Title.
QB43.2.Z44 1982   520   81-13187
ISBN 0-06-047376-2   AACR2

Contents

v

From the author

Everytime an astronomer speaks about the cosmos, he or she takes you on a journey in space and in time. This trip extends outward in space and backward in time. Whenever we view the universe, we see it as it was in the past. The long journey of light to the earth reveals the story of the past of the cosmos. From this image of how the universe was and our perception of it now, astronomers try to infer its future. So the expanse of cosmic evolution ranges from the fossil records of light to the active vision of human imagination.

The astronomer's cosmic vision arises from the fusion of past perception with present imagination. This book attempts to provide you with key facets of that vision—insights to the cosmic connections that tie us so deeply to the universe from which we were created. These connections mark the processes of cosmic evolution—the main theme of this book.

New technology brings us new images of the universe and so changes our cosmic vision. This third edition reflects those transformations in two main areas: the solar system and distant galaxies. I have incorporated these new ideas into the overall fugal structure of the first and second edition. This structure divides the book into four main parts, each one focusing on one key subtheme of cosmic evolution. And—like the cosmos—each part connects and relates to the others, so you can approach the parts in any order. They are:

Part 1: Changing Conceptions of the Cosmos / This part concentrates on the evolution of cosmological thought from the nonscientific ideas of the Babylonians to the mind-boggling visions of contemporary astronomy. It starts with the simplest observations that can be made from the earth and ends with the difficult observations of the farthest reaches of the visible universe. It also introduces the idea of scientific models, the conceptual core of scientific thought, used in the context of our changing ideas about the cosmos. The development and evolution of scientific models continues as a major subtheme throughout this book, and you'll see that they evolve because they are always subject to doubt.

Part 2: The Planets—Past and Present / Flyby spacecraft and gangly landers—along with the manned exploration of the moon—have provoked dramatic revisions in our picture of the planets in the solar system. This part focuses on the physical properties of the planets to infer their origin and evolution. It first takes a comparative look at what we now know about the planets, especially our moon and the others like the earth—Mercury, Venus, and Mars. These planets show the hallmarks of their evolution on their surfaces. The others—Jupiter, Saturn, Uranus, Neptune, and Pluto—have, in contrast, changed little since their birth. And Jupiter and Saturn are surrounded by systems of moons that are worlds unto themselves—mostly ice and rock, some scarred by violence in the past. I then turn from evolution to origin—the birth of the solar system from an interstellar cloud of gas and dust. This model implies that many other stars have planetary systems and that, perhaps, these other worlds resemble the local planets in general ways.

Part 3: The Universe of Stars and Galaxies / Where are we in the cosmos? The sun and the planets swing around in a vast island of stars called the Milky Way Galaxy. The sun is the nearest star to the earth in the Galaxy, so this part first investigates the sun as a model star. From our knowledge of the sun, we generalize about the natures of the stars in the Galaxy—some hundreds of billions of them. Almost all stars and planets reside in galaxies, some like the Milky Way Galaxy. Many do not—they show evidence of throes of violence in the past, which continues now. All these galaxies, violent or not, come in groups—clusters held in rein by gravity. Some clusters are gigantic—tens of millions of light years in size and containing thousands of galaxies. Oddly enough, clusters of galaxies tend to cluster. Beyond these lies the vast extent of the cosmos.

Part 4: Cosmic Evolution / Where do we fall in the grand scheme of cosmic evolution? This part connects the major theme of the other three parts. It reveals how physical, chemical, and biological evolution have interwoven from the time of the universe's creation to now to make the fabric of life on the earth. These cosmic connections then guide us to grapple with the question of life elsewhere in the Galaxy and the possible future of the human race—the evolution of an advanced, technological civilization. I point out that in the cosmic view we'll be forced to leave the earth—perhaps to travel to the stars.

I have designed this four-part structure so that you can investigate each part more or less independently of each other. Many cross-references, especially to basic physical and astronomical ideas, have been included to help you to read the parts intelligently in an order different from the one presented.

The focus sections can also help in linking together different parts of the text. They are numbered consecutively throughout the book for easy reference—either forward or backward. I have set the focus sections off from the main flow of the text because they deal in more detail (occasionally mathematically) with physical and astronomical concepts.

New to This Edition

Although I have not changed the overall structure, I have made two changes to make the presentation more concrete. In Part 2 I have taken out the chapter on the sun, moving it to the beginning of Part 3. So this part now begins with a chapter on the earth (Chapter 8), the planet we know the best. Our earth is also the planet that has evolved the most since its birth—so it serves as a model for the evolution of other planets like it—the moon, Mercury, Venus, and Mars. I have combined information about the moon and Mercury in the same chapter (Chapter 9) because these two planets are similar from an evolutionary view—they are both dead worlds. Chapter 10 deals with Venus and Mars as examples of worlds that have evolved more than the moon and Mercury but less than the earth. The revamping of these chapters emphasizes the comparative evolution of these earthlike planets. Part 3 now begins with the chapter on the sun (Chapter 13), presenting it as a concrete example of a star. The sun is the only star we see close up—the others are mere points of light. Yet they are suns in their own right, many quite different from our sun. Our understanding of stars begins with an understanding of the sun.

Other changes have been driven by the constant updating of astronomical knowledge and my striving to make matters clearer to you. In Part 1: Basic astronomical observations are presented more concretely; Chapter 2 now begins with a section on scientific models and includes a simplified explanation of Ptolemy's cosmology; Chapter 3 has a revision in the order of the

presentation of the Copernican model; Chapter 5 deals with spectra more concretely; and Chapter 7 incorporates more specific analogies to help in understanding cosmology. In Part 2: The material on the planets has been greatly updated; Chapter 10 includes the results of radar mapping of the surface of Venus; Chapter 11 presents the Voyager flyby results on Jupiter, Saturn, and the moons of these mighty worlds and also new information on Charon, the moon of Pluto; in Chapter 12, the presentation of the condensation sequence has been simplified. In Part 3: Chapter 13 on the sun opens this section; Chapter 15 includes new information about the interstellar medium; Chapter 16 has the new picture of the Milky Way Galaxy, more massive and larger than thought before; Chapter 17 contains expanded material on different types of galaxies and the controversy over the value of the Hubble constant; Chapter 18 has been radically revised to incorporate new radio observations, especially by the Very Large Array, of the nuclei of galaxies. These detailed radio pictures reveal the kind of violence going on in the cores of active galaxies. In Part 4: Chapter 19 has expanded material on the evolution of Population II stars, clusters of stars, and post-main-sequence evolution; Chapter 20 updates pulsars (including binary pulsars), black holes, and X-ray bursters; Chapter 21 presents new ideas about the evolutionary connections among galaxy types; and Chapter 22 includes new information about space colonization, the pessimistic view of life in the Galaxy, and speculations as to the future of humankind. The Appendixes and Glossary have been expanded and revised, reflecting the changes in the text.

I have strived to clarify and simplify the writing by making it more direct and concrete, and also to make the language as nonsexist as possible. To these ends, I often address the reader directly as "you" and use the first person "I" to speak directly to you and also to express my personal opinion.

The *Study Guide,* written by John Gaustad of the University of California, Berkeley, and myself, has undergone extensive revision to reflect the changes in the text. It is basically a self-study guide that has evolved from the use of the book in a Personalized System of Instruction (PSI) format in astronomy courses at Berkeley and the University of New Mexico. The

Study Guide supplements and amplifies the book and provides extra help with troublesome material. It also provides self-tests (with answers) for each chapter.

Richard Reif, the director of the planetarium of the Albuquerque Public Schools System, and I put together the *Instructor's Resource Manual.* We tried to provide teachers with specific hints for presenting the material in each chapter plus references, lists of audio-visual materials, and suggested answers to the book's study questions. We have included sample test questions that are keyed to the learning objectives of each chapters. We also provide suggestions for using the parts of the book in a different sequence.

Again, I thank many people who have helped me to make this a better book for learning. These include: Michael Shurman, Tom Harrison, Charles Tolbert, John Gaustad, Stu Vogel, John Evans, Dennis Schatz, Linda Kelsey, Darrel Hoff, Jack Burns, David King, Marc Price, Paul Heckert, Bob Anderson, Carl Bachhuber,

John Friedman, Chuck Long, Robert Boyle, and Owen Gingerich. Deborah Stark did the bulk of the typing. Lorene Deckert compiled the index.

I give special thanks to the students and tutors of Astronomy 10S at Berkeley during winter and spring quarters 1980 for their patience and comments. And, of course, I thank all my past students for their reactions and ideas.

If you have any comments on the book (especially if you find mistakes!), send them to me at the Department of Physics and Astronomy, The University of New Mexico, Albuquerque, New Mexico 87131.

Michael Zeilik

P.S. If you have picked up this book because you're curious about astronomy, you may be interested in taking a college-level course for credit by mail. Write to Independent Study, Continuing Education, UNM, 805 Yale NE, Albuquerque, NM 87131. Ask about Astronomy 101C.

Changing Conceptions
of the Cosmos

PART 1

I have often wondered what the first star-gazers felt as the heavens reeled above them. What magic did the dance of the planets weave for them? How did they picture the cosmos and their place in it?

I have found hints to answers to these questions. As part of my graduate work I traveled to Mt. Hopkins Observatory in Arizona. On the mountain I worked anxiously through sunset and dusk to set up my equipment at the telescope. The sky was visible to me only through the dome's slit. When my instruments were ready, I walked out to take a curious look at the sky.

I was stunned. With the blinders of the dome removed, I was struck by the entire sky. Faint constellations I'd never seen before formed an unfamiliar quilt of patterns. The planet Mars shone like a red searchlight—a steady beacon in a sea of stars. I sensed then how ancient people watched the sky and wondered.

The problem of the design of the cosmos and our place in it has intrigued people for centuries. The picture of the universe painted by a culture betrays many of its beliefs: religious, philosophical, and social. Astronomical observations set the outlines of the cosmic scheme by their demand for explanation. The evolution from fascinated stargazing to a design of the universe has happened in both ancient and contemporary cultures.

Part 1 presents the evolution of our conceptions of the cosmos, from ancient musings to modern speculations. It starts off with fundamental observations; then investigates how much astronomy motivated the development of ideas about the universe, and how well the cosmic schemes explained the known astronomy. I confine the investigation to Western civilizations and will describe critical episodes in the evolution of astronomy. This perspective will give some insight into the development of physical ideas that relate to cosmological ones and of the basis of scientific theories. It focuses on our conceptions of the cosmos from the ancients to Einstein. Such an evolution of human thought is one theme in the grand scheme of cosmic evolution.

From chaos to cosmos

1

LEARNING OBJECTIVES

After studying this chapter you should be able to:

1. Describe the motions of the sun and the moon, as seen from the earth, relative to the stars of the zodiac.

2. Describe the motions of the planets, as seen from the earth, relative to the stars of the zodiac with special attention to retrograde motion.

3. Describe the daily motions of the sun, stars, moon, and planets relative to the horizon.

4. Describe the seasonal motion of the sun relative to the horizon.

5. Tell what astronomical events or rhythms set the following time intervals: day, month, and year.

6. Describe the astronomical conditions necessary for the occurrence of a total solar and total lunar eclipse.

7. Argue, on the basis of naked-eye observations of planetary motion, an order of the planets from the earth.

8. Identify one astronomical achievement of prehistoric cultures.

Do the heavens have an order? Can you make sense of the objects and events in the sky? Early skywatchers, unhampered by air and light pollution, felt overwhelmed by what they saw. Then their wonder probably gave way to a desire to find some order in the apparent chaos of the sky.

This quest drove them to concepts of space and time naturally derived from astronomy. Space: the arching heavens, cushioned by the invisible air, are far removed from the earth. Time: the cycles of celestial motions serve as cosmic clocks. Watching the heavens for a long time allows you to pick out basic celestial cycles. Such cycles bring order to our ideas about the heavens. Early astronomers found an order in the heavens, a structure in space and a sequence in time. An orderly cosmos emerged from the initial chaos.

This chapter deals with observations you can make of the sky without optical equipment—the same observations made by early astronomers. From such observations you can easily sense the regular cycles of motions in the heavens. This chapter will not attempt to explain those motions. (That explanation will come in Chapters 2, 3, and 4.) But long-term observations can establish the periods of celestial cycles with amazing accuracy. The recognition of these rhythms marked a crucial step in the development of astronomy and early concepts of the cosmos.

1.1
The visible sky

Have you ever looked carefully at the night sky from a location far away from a city? Perhaps you have, from a mesa in New Mexico or the White Mountains of New Hampshire. (If you haven't, I recommend that you do!) You probably were amazed by the sparkle of stars set against the deep velvet of the sky. At first glance, you can't count the stars or find any order in them. You have no way to judge their distances, except to say that they are far away.

Constellations / Study the stars for a while. Their apparent chaos falls into patterns, designs imposed by your mind (Fig. 1.1). Ancient astronomers perceived stellar patterns and passed them on; such patterns are called *constellations*. Early constellations marked a convenient group of stars, with ill-defined boundaries, that out-

1.1

A time exposure of the stars of the constellation Orion and others nearby. The three bright stars making a diagonal line pointing to the top right make up Orion's belt. The very bright star right of center is Rigel. This photo shows many faint stars invisible to your eye. See the constellation end papers for winter to find Orion. (Courtesy Mt. Wilson Observatory, Carnegie Institution of Washington)

lined a mythological or realistic figure (Fig. 1.2). The oldest known constellations originated about 3000 B.C., somewhere in the Tigris–Euphrates valley of Mesopotamia. Here people enchanted by the heavens dreamed up stories about the celestial figures. (The end papers of this book show some modern constellations.)

If you observe the stars night after night, you will see that the shapes of the constellations do not change. In fact, if you were patient enough to watch for your whole life, you would notice no change. The stars appear to maintain fixed positions relative to one another.

1.2

The mythological figure of Orion, the hunter. This drawing is from a star atlas by Johann Bayer called Uranometria, *published in 1603. Albrecht Dürer made the engraving of the figure.*

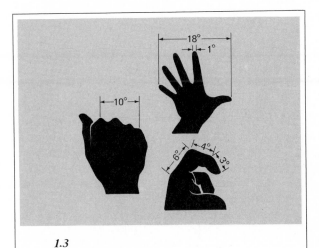

1.3

Angular measurements made with your hand. The indicated angles are those you see when you hold your hand extended at arm's length. They are typical for an average adult.

1.4

Measuring angular sizes in the sky with your hand at arm's length. The angular distance between the two pointer stars in the Big Dipper is about half a fist, or 5°.

Angular measurement / How can you measure how far apart stars appear in the sky? You need a convenient sighting device, such as the extent of your hand held at arm's length. You can then measure the angle between one star and another; this angle is the *angular separation* between two stars. Angular measurement is based on a counting system in which 60 is the basic unit (Focus 1). A circle is divided into 360 degrees, each degree into 60 minutes of arc, and each minute into 60 seconds of arc. At arm's length your fist covers about 10° of sky and each fingertip about 1° (Fig. 1.3). This crude but handy angular measuring instrument can mark out the angular size of the sun and moon (both about $\frac{1}{2}$°, or half a fingertip) and the separation of the pointer stars in the Big Dipper (about 5°, or half a fist; see Fig. 1.4). Try making such measurements sometime soon.

The celestial sphere / What about the sky that forms the backdrop to the stars? It's not hard to see the sky as a dome to which the stars are attached. Imagine another half to this apparent dome, the half below your horizon. If

you can imagine it, you have reinvented the *celestial sphere* (Fig. 1.5), a concept first devised by the Greeks. The celestial sphere appears to be centered on the earth, and the stars seem to be

focus 1

THE SEXAGESIMAL SYSTEM, ANGULAR MEASUREMENT, AND ANGULAR SPEED

The sexagesimal counting system is based on the number 60 rather than on the number 10 of our decimal system. Although not our standard counting system, the sexagesimal system survives in measuring angles and in part in measuring time (60 seconds equal one minute, 60 minutes equal one hour). The Babylonians developed this sexagesimal system, the system of angular measurement still used today.

For angular measurement a circle contains 360 degrees. Each degree amounts to 60 minutes and each minute, 60 seconds. The symbol for a degree is °, for a minute ', and for a second ". To distinguish angular minutes and seconds from units of time, we refer to minutes of arc or seconds of arc. (An arc is any segment of the circumference of a circle.)

Whenever I talk about the angular size (or diameter) of some object, keep in mind the following relation among the actual size of the object, its distance from you, and its angular size: The farther away an object is, the smaller is its angular size. For example, suppose someone stands 10 meters (m) from you. You can measure the person's angular size. Now imagine the person moves away to 100 m from you. The angular size would be only one-tenth as much as before. Note that you must know the distance to an object in order to determine its actual size from its angular size.

The concept of angular speed is related to the concept of angular size. When you see an object in the sky—an airplane, for example—you typically do not know how fast it is actually traveling in miles or kilometers per hour. All you can observe directly is how many degrees that object covers in a certain period of time. That's the object's angular speed. You cannot determine its actual speed unless you know its distance.

Consider, for example, the moon's eastward motion relative to the stars. You can observe this motion to be about $\frac{1}{2}$° an hour. That's the moon's angular speed as seen from the earth. However, the moon's actual orbital speed cannot be worked out unless you know the earth–moon distance. It comes out to about 1000 meters per second for a distance of 384,000 km.

Note on focus sections: The material set off in the focus sections would break up the flow of main ideas if it were in the text. The focus sections contain (1) physical ideas developed in more detail, (2) astronomical ideas in more depth, (3) sidelights, and (4) speculations. A few of them, such as Focus 4 in Chapter 2, are essential to understanding later material, but most are not. Some focus sections deal with material at a deeper mathematical level than the text itself. These are not meant to scare you; rather, they are there for the readers who are curious about and can understand the material at such a level.

Your instructor may assign specific focus sections for you to read. Otherwise, check out each focus as it is referred to in the text and read it carefully if it interests you.

fixed to it. This picture of the cosmos, typical of older ideas, is *geocentric:* centered on the earth.

Stay out one night and watch the stars from dusk until dawn. You will notice that they move relative to your horizon: *The stars rise in the east, travel slowly in arcs against the celestial sphere, and set in the west* (Fig. 1.6). If you live in the Northern Hemisphere and observe the stars to the north, you will find that some stars never dive below your horizon. Instead, they trace complete circles above it (Fig. 1.7). The Egyptians called such stars "the ones that know no destruction"; today we call them *circumpolar stars.* As you watch the circumpolar stars swing around, they draw concentric circles like the rings of a bulls-eye (Fig. 1.7). The center of these rings marks the *celestial pole,* the point about which the stars appear to pivot. A

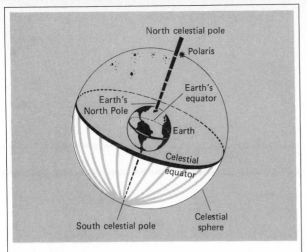

1.5

A simplified picture of the geo-centric universe viewed from outside. The earth, known to be round, rested in the center of a much larger sphere of stars, called the celestial sphere. The earth did not rotate; the celestial sphere did, resulting in the daily motion of the stars. The celestial poles lie on points directly above the earth's poles, and the celestial equator is a circle on the celestial sphere above the earth's equator.

1.7

The motion of stars looking north. On a clear night, face north and watch the stars for a few hours. They will appear to move **counterclockwise** *(east to west) about the North Pole star, Polaris. This time exposure shows Polaris, near the center, tracing a small arc; this indicates that it is not exactly at the north celestial pole. (Courtesy Lick Observatory)*

1.6

The motion of stars relative to your horizon. Face west on a clear night and pick out a group of stars just above the horizon. Wait a few hours and look again. You will see that the stars have moved closer to the western horizon; perhaps they have even set. This figure is a time exposure of the **east-to-west** *motion of the stars. (Courtesy Lick Observatory)*

moderately bright star called *Polaris* lies close to the north celestial pole. Polaris is now the North Pole star. (No bright star now falls close to the position of the south celestial pole.)

If you acquire a regular stargazing habit, you can discover that the constellations shift their positions relative to the sun with the change of seasons. Here's a way to see it: In winter, at midnight, you can see Orion due south. Look due south every night at midnight. Orion creeps slowly to the west toward the sun. In summers you can't see Orion at all because it's so close to the sun. In winter, a year later, Orion again lies due south at midnight. Every constellation takes one year to return to its initial place in the sky relative to the sun.

Warning. Don't confuse this gradual seasonal change *relative to the sun* with the daily motion, *relative to your horizon,* of the stars from east to west.

In summary: Over a human lifetime the stars do not move noticeably with respect to each other. They do move, daily, from east to west with respect to the horizon, as well as westward, annually, with respect to the sun.

1.2

The motions of the sun

The sun dominates all objects visible in the sky. It establishes the most fundamental cycle of our world: day and night. Every day the sun rises above the eastern horizon, traces an arched path across the sky, and falls below the western horizon. Midway between sunrise and sunset the sun ascends to its highest point relative to the horizon. This daily event defines *noon,* a fundamental reference in the measurement of time. The interval from one noon to the next sets the length of the *solar day.*

Motions relative to the horizon / Place a stick vertically in a flat place on the ground. You have then constructed an instrument to study the sun's seasonal motion in the sky relative to your horizon. (This device is called a *gnomon* and was first developed by the Babylonians. It is still used today in sundials.) Look at the shadow cast by the gnomon. The tip of the gnomon's shadow marks the end of a line that connects the shadow's tip, the top of the stick, and the sun (Fig. 1.8). The shadow points *opposite* the direction of the sun in the sky. Also, the shadow length tells you the height of the sun relative to your horizon. When the sun hangs low in the sky, the shadow is long. At noon the shadow has it shortest length for that day. Also, at noon in the northern latitudes, the shadow points north.

Here's an example: From Albuquerque, New Mexico, at noon on March 21 or September 21, the gnomon gives an angular height of the sun of 55°; on December 21 at noon, a height of only 31.5°; at noon on June 21, 78.5°.

Observe a gnomon's shadow throughout a year (Fig. 1.8). You will find that the height of the sun in the sky *at noon* varies from summer to winter. During the summer the shadow falls

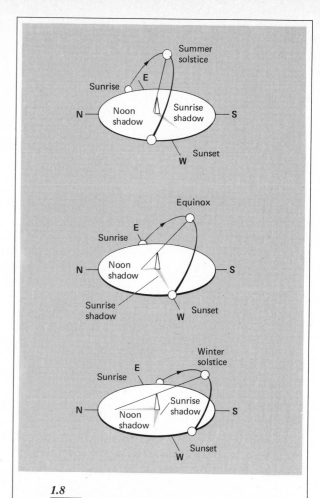

1.8

Gnomon shadows and the position of the sun in the sky for the northern hemisphere. (The view is from the west looking east.) The higher the sun relative to the horizon, the shorter the shadow at noon. The shortest noon shadow occurs on the day of the summer solstice (top), the longest on the winter solstice (bottom), indicating that the sun has dropped to its lowest point in the sky. At the equinoxes (middle) the length of the noon shadow falls between that for winter and summer.

the shortest at noon on the *summer solstice,* the day of the year with the greatest number of daylight hours. At the summer solstice the noon sun hits its highest point in the sky for the year. In winter at noon the shadow stretches longest on the *winter solstice,* the day of the year with the fewest daylight hours. The noon sun has dropped to its lowest point in the sky for the year. At the first day of spring and autumn the gnomon casts a shadow with a length halfway between its summer maximum and winter minimum. Those times are called the *equinoxes.* Note that the cycle of the gnomon's noon

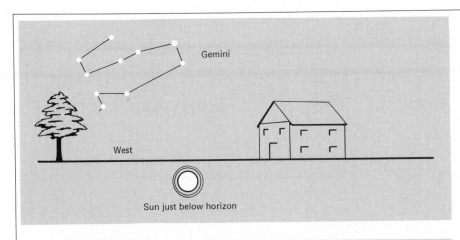

1.9

*The annual motion of the sun relative to the constellations. Find a zodiacal constellation (such as Gemini shown here) near the western horizon at sunset. About a week later look for the same stars again at sunset. They will appear closer to the western horizon. Eventually, they will set before the sun goes down. So the stars seem to move to the **west** with respect to the sun; or you can picture the sun as moving **east** with respect to the stars.*

Gemini

West

Sun just below horizon

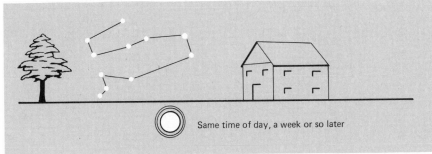

Same time of day, a week or so later

shadow defines a second fundamental unit of time: the year of seasons.

Motion relative to the stars / The sun not only moves relative to your horizon; it also moves with respect to the stars. This motion is hard to observe, for you can't see the stars during the day. Try this: Pick out a bright constellation visible just above your western horizon after sunset (Fig. 1.9). Look again at the same time about a week later; the constellation will be closer to your horizon and also to the sun (Fig. 1.9). So relative to the stars, the sun appears to move to the *east*. In one year the sun returns to the same position relative to the stars; that's 360° in a year, or about 1° a day *eastward*.

Imagine that you recorded the sun's position with respect to the stars for a year. If you drew an imaginary line through these points, you would trace out a complete circle on the sky; it is called the *ecliptic* (Fig. 1.10).

Warning. Are you sure you have this motion? The sun moves *eastward* with respect to the *stars* in a *year*. At the same time it moves *westward* with respect to the *horizon* in a *day*.

TABLE 1.1   The zodiacal constellations

Constellation	Astronomical symbol	Mesopotamian-Euphratean identity
Aries, the Ram	♈	Ram, Messenger
Taurus, the Bull	♉	Bull in Front
Gemini, the Twins	♊	Great Twins
Cancer, the Crab	♋	Workman of the River Bed
Leo, the Lion	♌	Lion
Virgo, the Virgin	♍	Proclaimer of the Rain
Libra, the Balance	♎	Life-Maker of Heaven
Scorpius, the Scorpion	♏	Scorpion of Heaven
Sagittarius, the Archer	♐	Star of the Bow
Capricornus, the Goat	♑	Goat-Fish
Aquarius, the Water Bearer	♒	Urn
Pisces, the Fish	♓	Cord-Place Joining the Fish

The constellations through which you see the sun move define the *zodiac*, the most ancient and coherent set of constellations (Table 1.1). The sun's position along the ecliptic is labeled with reference to the constellations of the zodiac. For instance, to say that the sun is "in Taurus" specifies the sun's approximate position along the ecliptic. The zodiac probably devel-

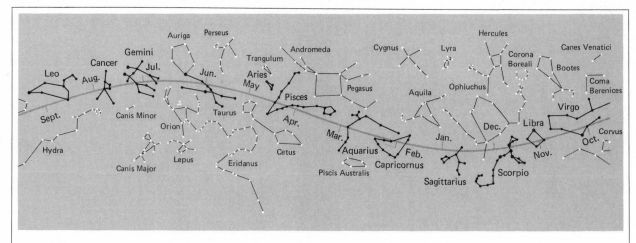

1.10

The ecliptic and zodiacal constellations. If the earth had no atmosphere, you could easily see the sun's changing position with respect to the stars during the day. The sun's path is called the ecliptic. This diagram indicates the sun's position by date along the ecliptic. Note that the sun moves from west to east among the stars. (A few of the constellations shown, such as Aquila, are not part of the zodiac, but are drawn in because the sun travels close to them.) The zodiacal constellations have the bold outlines.

oped from a desire to mark the sun's position with respect to the stars.

The sun's location in the zodiac also roughly indicates the time of year. Twice yearly, during spring and fall, day and night each has an equal number of hours. These times are called the *equinoxes.* At the *vernal equinox* in the spring and *autumnal equinox* in the fall, the sun at noon stands halfway between its highest and lowest positions in the sky. Taurus the Bull, called by the Babylonians "The Bull in Front," is probably the oldest zodiacal constellation. In Babylonian times the sun rose on the day of the vernal equinox with the stars of Taurus—the sun was "in Taurus." This astronomical event signaled the renewal of spring. (Today Taurus no longer marks the vernal equinox; now Pisces does. The positions of the equinoxes and solstices have shifted since Babylonian times. See Focus 2.)

Warning. It's standard practice to refer to the sun, moon, and planets, as previously noted, as being "in" certain constellations. For example, on March 21, when the sun is at the vernal equinox, it is in the constellation Pisces. But the stars that form the constellations are far from the sun and are not necessarily close to each other in space; they appear close together be-

cause they're all more or less in the same direction along our line of sight. So the statement "the sun is in Pisces" doesn't mean that the sun is within a clump of stars, just that it's *in the same direction in the sky* as that pattern of stars. Knowing that an object is "in" a particular constellation tells you where to look for it in the sky, but that's about all.

To sum up: As seen from the earth, the sun displays three motions: (1) daily, from east to west with respect to the horizon; (2) annually, from west to east through the zodiac; and (3) seasonally from higher to lower (summer to winter) with respect to the horizon at noon.

1.3

The motions of the moon

If you watch the moon throughout a warm summer's night, you can spot two of its celestial motions. First, like the sun and stars, the moon daily rises in the east and sets in the west. Second, the moon also journeys *eastward* against the backdrop of zodiacal stars. You can see this eastward motion for yourself in a few hours (Fig. 1.11). Wait until the moon appears just east of a bright star. Observe the moon and star again a few hours later. You will notice that the

focus 2

PRECESSION OF THE EQUINOXES

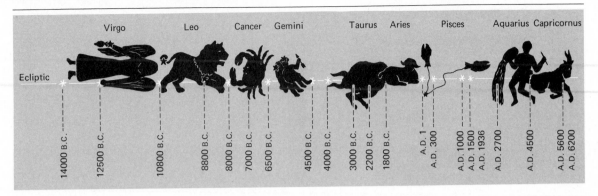

Virgo · Leo · Cancer · Gemini · Taurus · Aries · Pisces · Aquarius · Capricornus

Ecliptic

14000 B.C. · 12500 B.C. · 10800 B.C. · 8800 B.C. · 8000 B.C. · 7000 B.C. · 6500 B.C. · 4500 B.C. · 4000 B.C. · 3000 B.C. · 2200 B.C. · 1800 B.C. · A.D. 1 · A.D. 300 · A.D. 1000 · A.D. 1500 · A.D. 1936 · A.D. 2700 · A.D. 4500 · A.D. 5600 · A.D. 6200

1

The changing position of the vernal equinox with respect to the zodiacal stars as a result of precession. Note that the vernal equinox does not move into the constellation Aquarius until almost A.D. 3000. This event will mark the true dawn of the age of Aquarius.

In Sumerian times the sun appeared in Taurus at the vernal equinox. Today you see the sun in Pisces at the beginning of spring. In the passage of 5000 years the position of the vernal equinox in the zodiac has moved to the west out of Taurus, through Aries, and into Pisces. From this information you can estimate how long it would take the vernal equinox to circuit the zodiac. If in 5000 years it has moved through two constellations, or one-sixth of the zodiac, then to cover the entire zodiac takes six times as long, or about 30,000 years. (A more precise calculation gives 25,780 years.) This slow westward drift of the equinoxes is called the precession of the equinoxes.

The precession of the equinoxes changes the zodiacal location of the sun at the equinoxes and solstices (Fig. 1) Precession results in another, less obvious but important, effect: The celestial poles move in the sky, so the North Pole star changes (Fig. 2). The north celestial pole now lies near the star Polaris at the end of the handle of the Little Dipper. About 3000 years ago the north celestial pole was near the star Thuban (in Draco) rather than Polaris. Approximately 12,000 years from now precession will have carried the north celestial pole near the bright star Vega in Lyra.

Precession is hard to observe because it takes place so slowly. However, if a culture kept astronomical records for a few centuries, its astronomers could notice the shift of the equinoxes and solstices in the zodiac. Giorgio de Santillana and Hertha von Dechend argue in Hamlet's Mill that a few ancient cultures may have been aware of the precession. If so, it demonstrates a remarkable astronomical achievement and the serious attention paid to celestial motions by early skywatchers.

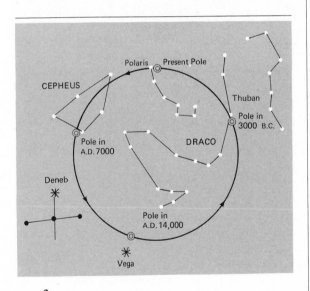

2

The changing position of the north celestial pole because of precession. The pole's motion moves in a complete circle in about 26,000 years. The pole is now near the star Polaris. About 12,000 years from now the pole will be near the bright star Vega, and this star will then be the North Pole star.

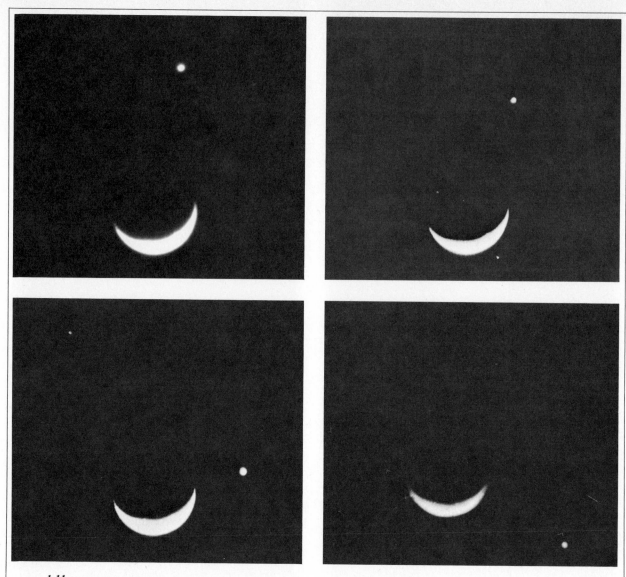

1.11

The motion of the moon with respect to the planet Venus. The time span is 2½ h. The moon moves about ½° per hour eastwardly. Note that east is to the top and west to the bottom of the photos. (Courtesy D. Hoff)

moon has moved farther east of the star at a rate of about ½° per hour. At this rate the moon completes a circuit of the zodiac in about 27 days. (*Note:* Although the moon's path does not lie along the ecliptic, it falls close to it and so the moon stays within the zodiac.)

You have probably been struck by the moon's changing appearance in the sky, its *phases,* which follow a regular sequence. When the moon rises at sunset, it glares as a full moon (Fig. 1.12). About 14½ days later the moon is "new." After this vanishing act, the moon reappears at sunset as a crescent moon. (The term "new moon" derives from legends in which the moon died at the end of its cycle of phases and was reborn. People did not recognize the moon as a reflector of sunlight until the fourth cen-

tury B.C.) A complete cycle of phases—say, from one full moon to the next—takes about 29½ days. It defines a third fundamental unit of time: the month of phases.

The different phases of the moon correspond to specific alignments of the sun and the moon in the sky. At new moon the sun and the moon are close together in angular separation. At first quarter the moon lies 90° *east* of the sun (Fig. 1.13). At full the moon is 180° from the sun; and at last quarter it is 90° *west* of the sun. (*Note:* First and last quarters refer to the position of the moon in the sky, one-quarter of a full circle away from the sun, and not to the degree of illumination of the moon; the moon at quarter-phase looks half full.) So the full moon lies opposite the sun in the sky.

(a)

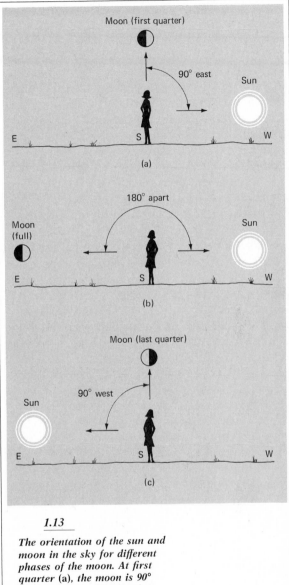

Moon (first quarter)

90° east

Sun

E   S   W

(a)

180° apart

Moon
(full)

Sun

E   S   W

(b)

Moon (last quarter)

90° west

Sun

E   S   W

(c)

1.13

*The orientation of the sun and
moon in the sky for different
phases of the moon. At first
quarter (a), the moon is 90°
east of the sun (due south as
the sun sets). At full (b), the
moon is 180° away from the
moon (in opposition, so the full
moon rises as the sun sets). At
last quarter (c), the moon is 90°
west of the sun (due south as
the sun rises). The view here is
facing south.*

(b)

1.12

(a) *A full moon rising over the
solar telescope at Kitt Peak
Observatory. At this phase the
moon rises in the east at sunset. (b) The face of the full
moon. (Courtesy Lick Observatory)*

To summarize: Daily, the moon rises in the
east and sets in the west with respect to the
horizon. Like the sun, the moon also moves
gradually eastward with respect to the stars and
takes about one month to make a complete circle around the sky.

1.4

The motions of the planets

If you observe the stars often enough, you can quickly pick out objects that don't belong to the familiar patterns. Five of these wander in regular ways through the stars; these are the *planets.* You can see them easily without a telescope: Mercury, Venus, Mars, Jupiter, and Saturn. These planets were known to the oldest civilizations that practiced astronomy or astrology. (Uranus, Neptune, and Pluto were discovered much later with telescopes.)

The planets display a peculiar celestial motion that sets them apart from all other objects in the sky. Let me give you a specific example. Suppose you observe Mars every night for a few months in a year when Mars appears brightest in the sky. First, you will notice that Mars moves through the zodiac close to the ecliptic. This motion is *eastward* (Fig. 1.14). At some time Mars falters in its eastward motion with respect to the stars and then stops. Next, for about three months Mars travels *westward,* opposite its normal motion. After that, Mars's westward motion slows down and stops. Then the planet resumes its normal eastward course. The planet's backward swing to the *west* is called *retrograde motion.* In the middle of its retrograde motion, Mars shines its brightest.

All planets loop along or near the ecliptic in retrograde motion but generally not at the same time or for the same duration. For instance, Mars takes about 83 days to go through its retrograde motion, but Saturn takes 139 days

	TABLE 1.2	**Fundamental observations of the visible planets**	
Planet		Typical duration of retrograde motion (days)	Period around ecliptic (years)
Mercury		34	1
Venus		43	1
Mars		83	2
Jupiter		118	12
Saturn		139	30

Note The lengths of retrograde motion (from start of westward displacement to renewal of eastward displacement) may vary a little from the above values from retrograde to retrograde. The period listed in the last column is the length of time, in terms of an earth year, that it takes the planet to cover 360° along the ecliptic.

(Table 1.2). In 1980 Mars was in the middle of a retrograde loop on February 25; and Saturn, on March 14.

Ancient astronomers were puzzled by the planets' retrograde motion. The moon and sun never exhibit such westward motion, and, in general, the planets travel eastward along or near the ecliptic, as do the sun and moon.

In addition to these motions, the planets have a daily motion from east to west with respect to the horizon. So the planets display three motions in the sky: (1) daily, rising in the east and setting in the west; (2) generally eastward in the zodiac near the ecliptic; and (3)

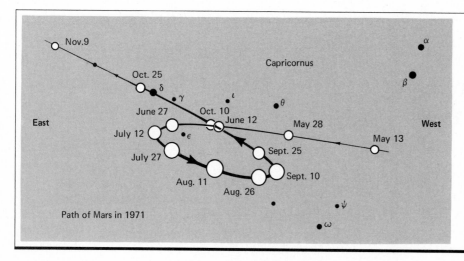

1.14

The retrograde motion of Mars during its August 1971 opposition. The position of Mars at different times is shown relative to the stars of Capricornus labeled by Greek letters. Note that from July 12 until September 10 Mars moved from east to west; this was the time of its retrograde motion. The size of the circles indicates how the brightness of Mars varied. In the middle of its retrograde (August 11), Mars lies in opposition to the sun, so it rises as the sun sets. Also, it reaches its maximum brightness.

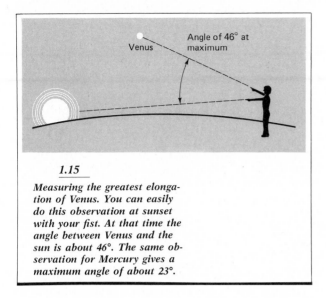

1.15

Measuring the greatest elongation of Venus. You can easily do this observation at sunset with your fist. At that time the angle between Venus and the sun is about 46°. The same observation for Mercury gives a maximum angle of about 23°.

Mercury and Venus make up one group. These planets never stray very far along the ecliptic from the sun. Because they stick close to the sun, they are visible only as morning or evening "stars." (But keep in mind that they are *not* actually stars.) Using your fist you can measure the maximum angular separation of Venus and Mercury from the sun. For Mercury the average maximum separation is 23° (about two fists), and for Venus it is about 46° (about $4\frac{1}{2}$ fists). When either planet reaches its greatest angular separation from the sun, it is at *maximum elongation* (Fig. 1.15). Mercury and Venus begin their retrograde motions shortly *after* they have swung farthest east of the sun as evening stars. They then move westward, pass the sun, and reappear as morning stars west of the sun at dawn (Fig. 1.16). When Venus and Mercury are close together with the sun in the sky, they are in alignment, called *conjunction*.

occasionally westward in retrograde loops. *Note:* A planet's changing position among the stars occurs much more slowly than its daily rising and setting.

One more point about retrograde motion. The alignment of the sun and planet, as seen from the earth, at the time of retrograde motion separates the visible planets into two groups.

The second group of planets includes Mars, Jupiter, and Saturn. In contrast to the first group, these planets freely move anywhere along the ecliptic with respect to the sun. They are not restricted to a region near the sun, as Mercury and Venus are. The planets of this group retrograde when they stand in *opposition*

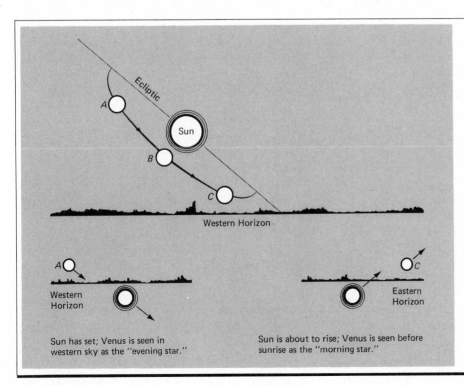

1.16

*Retrograde motion of Venus. The upper part shows how Venus appears to move (from **A** to **C**, east to west) with respect to the sun and ecliptic during retrograde motion. You can tell that Venus is going through its retrograde motion when it switches from being an evening "star" (**A**) to a morning "star" (**C**).*

to the sun, in an alignment opposite the sun in the sky as seen from the earth. At opposition the planet and the sun are separated by 180°. For example, Mars at opposition rises just as the sun sets. If you extended one arm to point at Mars and the other at the sun, your arms would be 180° apart (they'd make a straight line). When at opposition, each planet crosses the middle of its retrograde loop and shines its brightest.

To sum up: Mercury and Venus can *never* be in opposition to the sun; they retrograde at the conjunction after their greatest eastern elongation. Mars, Jupiter, and Saturn can be in opposition or conjunction, but they retrograde *only* at opposition.

Relative distances of the planets / The differing amounts of time that each planet spends in retrograde motion and that each takes to circle the zodiac provide a clue to the relative distances of the planets *from the earth*. Assume that the planets move at the same speed. Then, as seen from the earth, the slowest-moving planet must be the most distant from the earth; the swiftest, the nearest to earth.

Here's an analogy (Fig. 1.17): Suppose you were watching the flashing lights of two airplanes at night and wanted to estimate their relative distances from you. Assume both planes fly at the same speed. Then the one that appears to move faster must be the closer of the two. You can apply the same argument to the planets, sun, and moon: The fastest is the closest to the earth; the slowest, the farthest. And if one planet, for instance, moves half as fast as another, it is about twice as far away.

Greek astronomers during the third century B.C. applied this argument and established the order of Mercury, Venus, Sun, Mars, Jupiter, and Saturn. Because the moon moves more swiftly than any other heavenly body, the Greeks placed the moon between the earth and Mercury. This wondrous whirl of celestial bodies seemed to center on the earth, so ancient people naturally pictured the cosmos as geocentric. Simple observations led to the idea of ordering the cosmos.

But the retrograde motion of the planets posed a sticky problem to those who wanted a geocentric cosmos. The explanation of this contrary motion eluded astronomers for centuries. The evolution of our ideas about the motions of

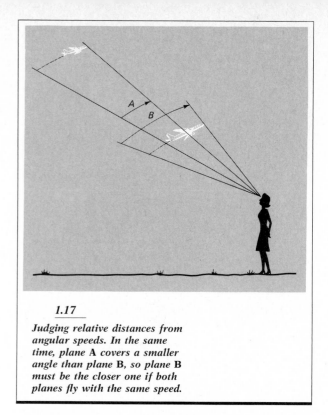

1.17

Judging relative distances from angular speeds. In the same time, plane A covers a smaller angle than plane B, so plane B must be the closer one if both planes fly with the same speed.

the planets is a central theme of the next three chapters.

1.5

Eclipses of the sun and moon

Eclipses, especially of the sun (Fig. 1.18), have always awed people. According to ancient historians, in 585 B.C. the armies of the Medes and the Lydians were locked in bitter combat. Suddenly the sun disappeared in an eclipse. This omen struck people so strongly that the armies ceased their fight and established a peace.

Solar eclipses occur when the moon, as seen from the earth, passes in front of the sun (Fig. 1.19). It's a remarkable fact that although the moon is actually smaller than the sun, it's closer by just the right amount so that the angular size of the sun and moon in the sky is almost the same—about $\frac{1}{2}$°. So the moon can just cover the sun's disk when it passes directly between the sun and earth, as it may do at new moon.

Why don't we have an eclipse each and every month?—mainly because the moon's path in the sky relative to the stars does *not* coincide with the ecliptic but is tilted at an angle of about 5° (Fig. 1.20). So only at or near the two points where the ecliptic and the moon's path intersect will the sun and moon be close enough for a solar eclipse to occur.

When a total solar eclipse does take place, the moon's shadow is at most 300 kilometers

1.18

A total eclipse of the sun (June 8, 1918). As seen from the earth, the moon covers the sun's visible disk, so it is possible to view the sun's outer atmosphere. (Courtesy Lick Observatory)

(km) wide on the earth. Only people in the narrow band as it sweeps across the earth can see a total solar eclipse. Those just outside this band get only a partial eclipse.

An eclipse of the moon occurs when the moon passes directly through the shadow cast by the earth (Fig. 1.21). Then the sun's illumination is cut off from the moon (Fig. 1.22). A total eclipse of the moon can take place only when the moon is full; that is, when the earth lies between the sun and the moon. Again, the moon must also be close to the ecliptic; otherwise it'll miss the earth's shadow.

Eclipses occur less frequently than the other celestial events described in this chapter. Their spectacular nature sets them apart and has motivated people to study them. The Greeks, for one, found that eclipses were predictable from the motions of the sun and moon in the sky. They also noted that solar eclipses demonstrate that the moon must be closer to the earth than the sun. Therefore the sun must be larger than the moon.

If you've been puzzled about why the sun's path relative to the stars is called the ecliptic, it should now become clear: Only when the moon lies on or close to the *ecliptic* can *eclipses* occur.

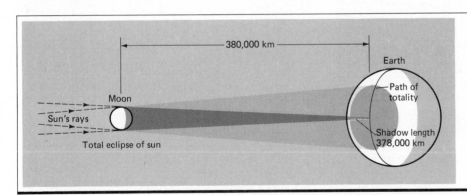

1.19

Alignment of moon, sun, and earth for a total solar eclipse to occur. The moon must be new and on or very close to the ecliptic as viewed from the earth. The length of the moon's central shadow is usually long enough to hit the earth. A total eclipse can be seen by people in the path where the central shadow hits the earth.

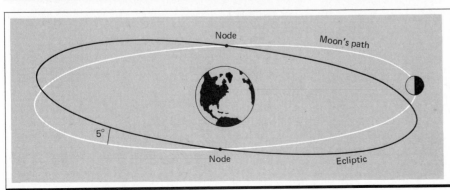

1.20

The path of the moon in the sky, relative to the ecliptic, as seen from the earth. The moon's path is tilted about 5° with respect to the ecliptic and intersects it at two points (called nodes*).*

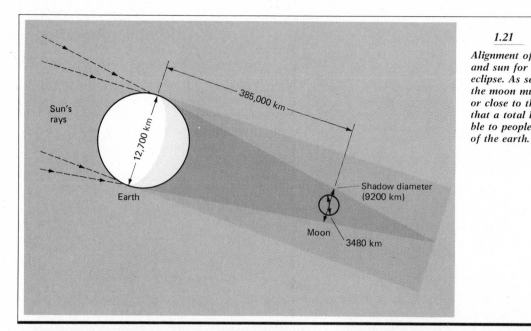

1.21

Alignment of the earth, moon, and sun for a total lunar eclipse. As seen from the earth, the moon must be full and on or close to the ecliptic. Note that a total lunar eclipse is visible to people on the night side of the earth.

1.22

Some aspects of a total lunar eclipse. At left, the moon is entering the earth's shadow. At right, the moon is immersed in the shadow and time exposures show the stars in the background. (Courtesy NASA)

1.6

Prehistoric astronomy:
The Anasazi achievement

How much astronomy did ancient peoples know? Certainly, they had dark skies unlit by local lights. And at night the celestial cycles presented one of the few entertainments available at that time. Yet, to define the subtle rhythms of the heavens, to see the long cycles, takes years of observations and the means to record them. Prehistory has left us few written records. How were these people informed about celestial motions?

This information was probably communicated by word of mouth in the form of symbolic stories, which leave no permanent records. Yet, fossils of oral traditions do exist: the Polynesian islanders knew how to navigate from Tahiti to Hawaii by stories of the sky, and in the pueblos of New Mexico, sun watchers still spin their seasonal tales. Ancient people had much more astronomical knowledge than we generally have credited them with. We are now uncovering many archeological sites that seem to have astronomical purposes. Let me describe one such site: Chaco Canyon in New Mexico.

The sun watchers of Chaco / Snow greeted me on my first night in Chaco Canyon: a late November storm that blew in a gray fury out of the San Juan mountains of Colorado to engulf the mesas of northwestern New Mexico. The next day I huddled in the ruins of Pueblo Bonito (Fig. 1.23(a)), the largest of the dwellings in the canyon. At its height in 850–1150 A.D., Chaco contained perhaps 10,000 inhabitants; two thousand in Pueblo Bonito alone. As I toured the fascinating ruins, I came upon an upper-story room with a corner window high upon the south wall (Fig. 1.23(b)). How strange! Why would the Anazasi ("Old Ones") have put in such an unusual design feature?

I didn't think about that window again until I came across an article by Jonathan Reyman, who argued that careful solar observations must have formed an important aspect of the farming strategy in prehistoric Chaco. As careful attention to the seasons was critical to successful crops, the former inhabitants of Chaco may have introduced astronomical alignments in their buildings. Reyman pointed out two rooms in Pueblo Bonito that had high, exterior corner

(a)

(b)

(c)

1.23

(a) *The ruins of Pueblo Bonito in Chaco Canyon.* (b) *and* (c) *Corner windows in Pueblo Bonito with winter solstice sunrise alignments. Both are located in the second story.*

1.24

Fajada Butte in Chaco Canyon, viewed from the northeast. The noon solar marker is at the top.

(a)

(b)

1.25

(a) The rock slabs, each about 3 m long, against the rock wall at the top of Fajada Butte. (b) The sunlight dagger viewed through the slabs at about noon. (Courtesy W. Wampler)

windows well placed for watching the sun rise on the winter solstice. (At the Zuni pueblo today the winter solstice marks the start of the seasonal year.) Note that on the winter solstice, the sun rises farthest south on the horizon—recall Fig. 1.8.

Reyman set up cameras to photograph the winter solstice sunrise from both rooms and discovered that the sun rose in the centers of both, parallel to the jambs, as the lower part of the sun just appeared to touch the horizon. So from these rooms early sun watchers in New Mexico could have spied the winter solstice and then announced the event to all.

A new discovery has recently come to light on a different aspect of Anasazi astronomy: a probable *noon* marker of the summer solstice. The sandstone mass of Fajada Butte (Fig. 1.24) erupts at the southern end of Chaco Canyon. In June 1977 Anna Sofaer, an American artist interested in Indian rock art (petroglyphs), climbed past the rattlesnakes to the top of the butte. There she found three large rock slabs (each about 3 meters (m) high) that allowed a dagger-shaped beam of sunlight to fall on a spiral petroglyph on the rock wall behind the slabs (Fig. 1.25).

1.26

The noon sunlight dagger on the day of the summer solstice, falling in the large spiral petroglyph. (Courtesy W. Wampler)

TABLE 1.3 *A summary of major celestial motions visible without optical aid*

Object	Motion	
	Daily	*Long-Term*
Sun	E to W in about 12 hours from sunrise to sunset. Day length varies from season to season.	W to E along ecliptic 1° per day. Height of sun in sky at noon maximum in summer, minimum in winter.
Moon	E to W in about 12 hours, 25 minutes from moonrise to moonset. Rises about 50 minutes later each day.	W to E within 5° of ecliptic. Takes 27.3 days to travel 360° relative to the stars. Phases repeat in cycles of 29.5 days.
Planets	E to W with about 12 hours from rising to setting.	W to E within 7° of ecliptic. Time around ecliptic varies, shortest for Mercury and longest for Saturn. Retrograde motion from E to W at a time specific to each planet.
Stars	E to W with about 12 hours from starrise to starset. Rise about 4 minutes earlier each day. Circumpolar constellations never set; their motion centers on the celestial pole.	Relative to the sun, a constellation returns to the same position in one year. In fixed positions with respect to each other. The position of the celestial pole changes slowly, returning to its initial position in about 26,000 years. (Focus 2)

The time was near noon (and close to the summer solstice). The dagger landed near the spiral's center. Suspecting this site a solstice marker, Sofaer informed Volker Zinser, an architect, and Rolf Sinclair, on the staff of the National Science Foundation. They hiked up the butte on the solstice and discovered that, at noon, the light dagger slashed through the center of the spiral (Fig. 1.26). The flat rocks and spiral make a precise marker of noon at the summer solstice.

I will return to Chaco Canyon in Chapter 20, where I show evidence of a possible astronomical record of the explosion of a star.

SUMMARY

Simple observational astronomy leads to ideas of space and time. The heavens appear far away from the earth in a distinct, eternal realm of their own. The motions of the sun and moon in regular cycles set the fundamental time periods of day, month, and year.

The stars appear fixed and unchanging; they form distinct patterns called constellations. This imprint of constellations marked an early important step toward establishing order in the heavens. The backdrop to the constellations is the celestial sphere, the apparent dome of the sky.

The most important constellations are the 12 through which the sun journeys each year; these make up the zodiac. With respect to these stars, the sun annually traces a complete circle in the sky. This path is called the ecliptic. The moon and visible planets hug the ecliptic as they travel eastward with respect to the stars. However, the planets regularly slow down, halt their eastward motion, and then move westward for a period. They eventually stop their westward motion and move eastward again. This contrary, westward motion of the planets is called retrograde motion. It is unique to the planets and so sets them apart from other celestial objects. In any picture of the cosmos the retrograde motion of the planets emerges as the most difficult motion to explain. The question of how the planets move baffled astronomers for centuries and will be dealt with as a central theme in the next three chapters. (See Table 1.3 for a summary of visible celestial motions.)

STUDY EXERCISES

1   Tell how you would find the ecliptic in the sky; the zodiac. (*Objectives 1 and 2*)
2   Draw a diagram showing the retrograde motion of a planet. (*Objective 2*)
3   What celestial bodies never exhibit retrograde motion? (*Objective 1*)
4   Into what two groups can the planets be divided on the basis of their retrograde motion? (*Objective 2*)
5   When Mars is at opposition, at about what time will the planet rise? set? (*Objective 2*)
6   What *two* reasons did ancient astronomers have for believing (correctly) that the moon

was closer to the earth than the sun? (*Objective 7*)

7   *a*   You go outside one night, about 9:00 P.M., and face south. The moon is up and off to your right, near the horizon. Is it rising or setting? What is its phase? (*Objective 3*)

b   The next night you go out again at 9:00 P.M.. Where is the moon? Is it higher, lower, or not up at all? Did it move east or west? Has its phase changed? (*Objective 3*)

8   Describe the changing position of the rising sun on the eastern horizon throughout the course of a year, highlighting the solstices and the equinoxes. (*Objective 4*)

BEYOND THIS BOOK . . .

Astronomy and *Sky and Telescope* magazines contain monthly star maps and planetary locations to help you observe.

Hamlet's Mill (Gambit, Boston, 1969) by G. de Santillana and H. von Dechend has an intriguing analysis of the astronomy of preliterate people incorporated in oral myths.

In *The Roots of Civilization* (McGraw-Hill, New York, 1972), A. Marshack argues that the need to keep track of time, especially the cycle of the month, led to the development of symbolic notation and language.

For a return to Stonehenge and a look at other possible ancient astronomical observatories, read *Beyond Stonehenge* (Harper & Row, New York, 1973) by G. Hawkins. An excellent summary about prehistoric sites in Great Britain and Europe is in *Sun, Moon, and Standing Stones* (Oxford University Press, New York, 1978) by J. E. Wood.

For articles on Chaco Canyon, see "Solstice-Watchers of Chaco" by K. Frazier, *Science News*, August 26, 1978, vol. 114, p. 148; and "Astronomy, Architecture and Adaptation at Pueblo Bonito" by J. E. Reyman in *Science*, September 10, 1976, vol. 193, p. 957; "The Anasazi Sun Dagger" by K. Frazier, in *Science 80*, Nov./Dec. 1980, vol. 1, p. 56.

Marduk bade the moon come forth;
entrusted night to her,
Made her creature of the dark, to measure time;
and every month, unfailingly, adorned her
with a crown.

From Enuma Elish;
translated by THORKILD JACOBSEN

The birth of cosmological models

2

LEARNING OBJECTIVES

After studying this chapter you should be able to:

1. List the important astronomical achievements of the Babylonians.

2. Illustrate the distinction between a mythical and a mechanical cosmological model with specific examples from ancient astronomy.

3. Use at least one specific case to show how geometrical and aesthetic concepts influenced Greek ideas about the cosmos.

4. Describe the Aristotelian cosmological model in terms of its physical reasoning and correspondence to astronomical observations.

5. State the assumptions and physical ideas behind Ptolemy's model for the cosmos.

6. Sketch the Ptolemaic model for Venus, the sun, and Mars, and show how the epicycle and deferent explained retrograde motion.

7. Evaluate the assets of the Ptolemaic model that led to its wide acceptance.

8. Describe the essential aspects of a scientific model and evaluate cosmological models in the context of scientific model-making.

CHAPTER 2

CENTRAL QUESTION *What is a scientific model, and how did early cosmological models explain and predict astronomical observations?*

How have people pictured the cosmos? Most ancient cultures viewed the cosmos as finite and geocentric, a boundary—usually a shell of stars—closed off the universe with the earth enthroned in the center. Ancient cosmologies generally paid little attention to the details of celestial motions, even if the cycles were carefully observed.

The Greeks first attempted to take their cosmological ideas beyond the skeleton of a finite, geocentric cosmos. Grappling with the problem of planetary motions, Greek philosophers fleshed out the bare cosmological structure with mechanical devices to account for the celestial cycle. These schemes marked the first earnest models: mental constructions that exhibited features like those observed in nature. These systematic efforts to explain the natural world culminated in the geocentric model of Claudius Ptolemy. His cosmological model marks the first careful effort to represent accurately the observed celestial motions. Ptolemy succeeded so well that no one seriously challenged his system for over 14 centuries.

This chapter examines Babylonian and Greek cosmologies to determine how closely early cosmological ideas related to actual astronomical observation.

1   We see how these cultures tried to make sense of what they saw in the sky.
2   We contrast cosmic ideas grounded in myths to those grounded in aesthetic, physical, and geometrical ideas—those that are scientific models.
3   We investigate the birth of the first comprehensive model of the universe—one that eventually forced the birth of the models used today.

2.1

Scientific models

Chapter 1 described naked-eye astronomical observations that you can make from the earth. As you read, you may have felt the urge to place these observations in a grand design, a model for the operation of the heavens. You probably felt this compulsion even though the observations were presented in a way that did not rely on any particular model to explain heavenly motions.

People in general share your urge to make sense of what they see. This natural drive prompted the birth of *scientific models*—conceptual plans that attempt to explain what is seen in nature. Scientific models lie at the heart of contemporary scientific thought.

But this conceptual framework did not always underpin people's ideas about the world. Like all natural things, the concept of a scientific model sprung from older visions and evolved as more was discovered about the world. Ancient models tend to be *mythical* rather than scientific. As such, they should not be faulted, for myths mark serious early attempts to understand the world. *The key point:* Astronomical observations naturally drove people to create models of the cosmos.

What is a scientific model? It is a mental picture based on geometrical ideas, physical concepts, and aesthetic notions, which attempts to explain by analogy what you see in nature. A model tries to come to grips with a seemingly chaotic world by casting it in familiar terms, striving to make sense of what is observed.

A few basic elements go into constructing a scientific model (Fig. 2.1). First, our sense impressions about the world provide the raw information that sparks our curiosity. Then the human mind attempts to interpret this input by using intuitive notions: geometry, physics, and aesthetics. Ideas from geometry establish a visual framework for the model. Physical ideas attempt to cope with the motions and interactions of the various parts of the model. And aesthetic ideas—a gut judgment of what appeals to you—select the simplest, most pleasing models from those that a fertile mind imagines. Then comes the crucial test: How well do the features of the model correspond to what is actually seen in nature? If this correspondence is good (within your errors of observation), you have a growing confidence that the model applies. If not, you change various features of the model to get a better fit.

A scientific model has two key functions: (1) It *explains* what is seen and (2) it *predicts* accurately what can be seen. The explanations must be anchored in basic physical ideas. A model's predictions must relate directly to observations and must do so with sufficient accuracy to be convincing. All good scientific models contain the aspects of explanation and predic-

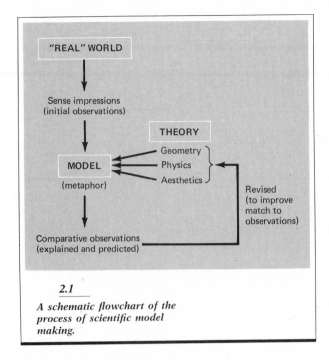

2.1

A schematic flowchart of the process of scientific model making.

tion. (One may, however, overshadow the other in any particular model.)

The power of prediction prompts the drive to confirm a model by investigating how well predictions fit observations. The search for confirmation can make or break a model, depending on how well observations and predictions agree. This endless search makes all scientific models tentative as they may contain their own seeds of destruction.

2.2
Babylonian skywatching— the start of a science

About 1600 B.C. the Babylonians compiled the first star catalogs and began making records of planetary motions. By 800 B.C. the Babylonian astronomers were able to fix planetary locations with respect to the stars. They kept records of planetary positions that compared a planet's position with that of recognized constellations. Their early observations included the motions of Venus, Jupiter, and Mars. From the ninth century B.C. the Babylonians kept continuous astronomical records on clay tablets.

Babylonian astronomy / For what reasons did the Babylonians become careful observers? In part, the development of astronomy was supported by the state. Astronomical information was needed for both the calendar and the prac-

tice of astrology (Focus 3). These problems stimulated the development of arithmetical techniques that the Babylonians used to predict planetary positions. In addition, observations preserved on cuneiform tablets enabled the Babylonians to find the daily, monthly, and annual cycles—the main themes of celestial motions. (These are listed in Table 1.3.)

Such permanent records indicate that the Babylonian astronomers also knew of the variations in the celestial cycles. For example, the angular size of a planet's retrograde loop and the duration of its retrograde motion vary from one synodic period to the next (Fig. 2.2). The *synodic period* of a planet is the interval between a planet's similar alignments with respect to the sun as viewed from the earth; for example, the period of time between one opposition and the next of a planet. The Babylonian astronomers had lists of these cycles on cuneiform tablets, with each major cycle represented by a table of consecutive numbers. A Babylonian astronomer could use these cycles to predict the next time of retrograde motion.

So Babylonian astronomers could predict future planetary motions from their tables of past cycles. This procedure did not require an explanation of the cycles, merely a knowledge of their existence over a long period. The Babylonians could predict but not explain.

Babylonian cosmology / As priests, the Babylonian astronomers occupied the holy ziggurats—towers that also served as observatories. To serve as both priest and astronomer had an advantage: It fostered the continuity of astronomical knowledge. However, it also divorced Babylonian cosmology from astronomy. In the cosmic picture the gods created, ordered, and controlled the world. These divine functions were far beyond human comprehension and consequently were not explicable except as religious myth.

The fantastic Babylonian tale of genesis, the *Enuma Elish* (literally, "when above"), dealt with the formation of the world from chaos. The Babylonian story (completed about 2000 B.C.) featured Marduk. From an unordered swirl of primeval waters Marduk fashions the constellations and sets the duties of the planets. He bids the moon to rule the night with her phases to provide a measure of time (see the quotation at the beginning of the chapter).

focus 3
ASTROLOGY

Some ancient cultures believed that the sun, moon, and planets were actually gods and that these gods had powers over people and events on earth. Such beliefs crystallized in the practice of astrology, which sought a reasonable connection between celestial and terrestrial events.

Both astronomy and astrology start with the recognition of cycles in celestial events (those in the previous sections). The early Babylonians practiced astrology to understand how the planets influenced the fate of rulers and nations. Later the Greeks gave birth to the ideas that each person—not just the mighty—fell under the influence of the stars, especially their positions at the time of his or her birth. This belief and practice is called natal astrology. *Today's popular astrology is usually natal astrology.*

As you have seen in this chapter, the famous astronomer Claudius Ptolemy devised a clever scheme to predict planetary positions, in part for astrological purposes. His writing, the Tetrabiblios, synthesized the astrological knowledge of the day and established the traditional horoscope interpretations that most Western schools of astrology rely upon. (The horoscope *charts the planetary and zodiacal positions for the time and place of an individual's birth and sets the keystone of natal astrology.)*

The list of astronomers who practiced astrology—whether for money, prestige, or personal curiosity—includes not only Ptolemy but also Tycho Brahe, and Johannes Kepler, among others. For Kepler, who divined the structure of the cosmos in the harmony of the spheres, astrology struck an inner chord to which he responded with mixed feelings of belief and skepticism. He thoroughly spurned customary rules of the astrology of his day, which derived from the work of Ptolemy. Although financial gain strongly motivated Kepler, personal beliefs also compelled him to cast over 1800 horoscopes. He wrote:

That the heaven does something in people one sees clearly enough; but what it does specifically remains hidden.

The scientific revolution in Europe in the seventeenth and eighteenth centuries demolished most scientists' belief in astrology. Almost all modern astronomers view astrology as a pseudoscience at best and an outright fraud at worst, if they bother to consider it at all. In the context of modern scientific attitudes, astrology cannot stand up as a science because astrologers must depend on unknown forces, exerted by the sun, moon, and planets in geocentric lineups, to influence the destiny of human beings. Since the time of Copernicus (Section 3.1) the earth has been removed from its former geocentric glory. Astronomers suspect geocentric claims because the universe, as they see it today, has no unique, central place for the earth.

In terms of scientific model making, traditional astrology lacks a physical basis. No astrological school I'm familiar with has demonstrated a clear link-by-link chain of physical influence between heavenly bodies and the individual's actions on the earth— using either known or unknown(!) forces. In addition, astrology has very poor predictive success. Traditional personality characteristics do not correlate well with sun signs, even for large, carefully selected populations. Astrology does not work as a scientific enterprise.

Don't take a denial of a scientific basis to modern astrology as a rejection of the idea that heavenly bodies have influences on the earth. They do. The most obvious are the natural cycles of day, month, and year to which all living creatures respond. Also, the moon produces tides, and the sun appears to affect our climate in direct and subtle ways that we are just beginning to understand.

Despite today's rejection of astrology by astronomers, the historical fact remains that astrology motivated the early development of astronomy. And certainly, the posture of astrology—to place us in an ordered universe, in a cosmos rather than a chaos—is akin to the cosmic perspective of modern astronomy.

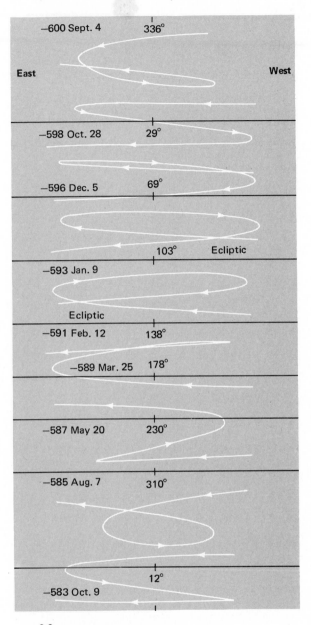

-600 Sept. 4   336°

East   West

-598 Oct. 28   29°

-596 Dec. 5   69°

103°   Ecliptic

-593 Jan. 9

Ecliptic

-591 Feb. 12   138°

-589 Mar. 25   178°

-587 May 20   230°

-585 Aug. 7   310°

12°

-583 Oct. 9

2.2

Retrograde motions of Mars in Babylonian times. This diagram shows the positions of Mars relative to the ecliptic (indicated in degrees) for nine different times of retrograde motion. Note that the size of the retrograde loop, and so its duration, vary. (Courtesy O. Gingerich)

Although *Enuma Elish* glosses over the science of astronomy, the poetic story carefully pictures the creation of space and the ordering of time by Marduk. The details of astronomical motions pale before the grand scheme. The actual predictions were purely arithmetical; no geometrical framework provided any skeletal support to the natural appearances. The Babylonian astronomers knew well the periods of the planets, sun, and moon around the zodiac and the occurrence of retrograde motion. They did not, however, attempt to account for the causes of these motions beyond a religious, mythical explanation. They were able to predict but not to explain, in a modern sense of a scientific explanation. Their ideas also lacked the notion of physical causes—a concept central to modern science. Instead, religious myths secured the structure of their world.

2.3
Greek models of the cosmos

The Greeks took number and geometry seriously but paid only passing heed to careful observational work as the Babylonians did. Yet the Greek philosophers accomplished what the Babylonian astronomers probably never dreamed of: They invented a geometrical, physical model of the universe. The Babylonians made sense of the world through myths. The Greeks had myths, too. But their philosophies drove them to develop models to get at reality.

A look at Greek astronomy and cosmology shows how the idea of a scientific model arose.

The music of the spheres / Number reveals the nature of things. This theme reverberates throughout Western thought. The Pythagoreans, for example, found harmony in numbers, especially 1 and 10. They believed that these sacred numbers generated all other numbers, which made up the *kosmos*, the "good array." The word we use today to describe an ordered universe—"cosmos"—derives directly from the Greek *kosmos* and conveys a sense of harmony and symmetry. These aesthetic notions are based on a faith of order in nature.

The Pythagorean picture of the cosmos (Fig. 2.3) first incorporated some aspects of a scientific model. According to the Pythagoreans, the earth had a spherical shape. This figure was supported by arguments from both symmetry and the observed shape of the earth's shadow

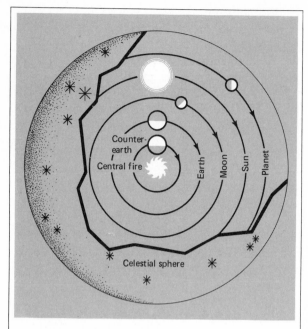

2.3

An artist's representation of the Pythagorean cosmos. From symmetry, the Pythagoreans argued that the shapes of the celestial bodies must be spherical, and so must be the entire cosmos. The earth was not set in the center of the cosmos; rather, it revolved around a central fire (not the sun) once in 24 h. (Adapted from a drawing by R. E. Ridley)

The ideas of the philosopher Plato (428–348 B.C.) derived from Pythagorean concepts. His questions concerning the cosmos—although he answered them in vague terms—initiated an influential cosmological picture. Plato saw the perfection of the universe in the form of a three-dimensional sphere: In keeping with this intuitive harmony, all motions of the heavenly bodies must be composed of *uniform, circular motions*. Plato succinctly described the problem of the planets: The goal of an astronomical model was to "save the appearances"—to devise a model that explained natural phenomena like the motions of the planets. This goal preoccupied astronomers for centuries.

A mechanical model / Eudoxus (c. 370 B.C.), a friend and student of Plato, devised the first mechanical system based on uniform circular motion to account for the celestial cycles. He synthesized Greek astronomical knowledge into a scheme that attempted to save the appearances, as Plato had demanded. He saw that just a few heavenly spheres could not account for the complicated behavior of the planets, especially their retrograde motions. His ingenious model required 27 moving spheres centered on the earth.

Although Eudoxus's scheme did not reproduce the actual retrograde patterns well, his model stands as the first serious effort to construct a mechanical cosmos that exhibited some imitation of actual planetary motions. Even more important, Eudoxus's spheres directly influenced the astronomical ideas of Aristotle (384–322 B.C.), the most famous of Plato's pupils.

Aristotle added 28 more spheres to Eudoxus's basic system. Even then, his model (Fig. 2.4) described poorly the intricate celestial ballet. Although Aristotle was unhappy with his model in this respect, he was pleased because the astronomical mechanisms fitted comfortably into his aesthetical and physical ideas about the universe.

Aristotle anchored his model in physical principles about motion. (This use of physics made his work more "scientific" in the modern sense of the word.) In *De caelo* (*About the Heavens*) he used the ideas that all corruptible bodies were made of the four basic elements: earth, air, fire, and water. Each of these elements had its own natural motion toward its natural place in the universe: the earth to the

on the moon during lunar eclipses (recall Fig. 1.22). A spherical shell bounded the universe and held the stars; other smaller spheres carried the planets around. The stellar sphere, conveying the other spheres with it, rotated daily east to west. At the same time, the planetary spheres rotated slowly within the star shell, west to east, with the period of each planet's circuit time around the zodiac (Table 1.2).

Note that this early model contains geometrical and aesthetic elements, but its correspondence to observations is crude and lacks physical ideas. For example, the model fails to account for the observed retrograde motion.

Despite its practical drawbacks, the Pythagorean model relied strongly on the aesthetic notions of harmony and symmetry. These principles recur in cosmology—the study of the universe—even today.

2.4

A geocentric cosmos in the tradition of Aristotle. This is a medieval picture of Aristotle's system of geocentric spheres. The earth is at the center, and above it lie the natural realms of water, air, and fire below the sphere of the moon. Beyond the moon are the heavenly spheres to which the planets and the stars were attached. Only one sphere is shown here for each planet; the actual scheme used a number of spheres to account for the motions. (Courtesy Yerkes Observatory)

the planets moving in their paths. In the terrestrial realm the nature of motion—except for the natural down motion of earth and up motion of water, air, and fire—was quite different, because motions required the application of a force to persist. For example, in order to keep a bicycle moving, a person must always be peddling it. Once this force ceases, the bike rolls a bit but will stop eventually because no force is being applied. Aristotle called such motion *forced motion* in contrast to the *natural motion* of the four elements. Aristotle's idea that forces were needed for terrestrial motions but not for celestial motions was the crux of his physical reasoning.

From this foundation Aristotle reasoned that the earth must be stationary and in the center of the universe. First, the natural motion of earthly material is to fall toward the center of the universe. This explains the location of the earth. Second, if the earth moved, bodies thrown upward would not fall back to their points of departure. Yet "heavy objects, if thrown forcibly upward in a straight line, come back to their starting place." So the earth must not move. (Note that these arguments spring from Aristotle's basic understanding of natural motion. He coupled physical ideas to aesthetic ones to arrive at a cosmological conclusion.)

A model gains belief when it leads to the explanation of observations. In this respect Aristotle's finite, geocentric universe was a successful model. Two important observations the model explained were the spherical shape of the earth and the lack of an annual parallax (Focus 4). Aristotle noted that if the earth moved around the sun, the stars (which are a finite distance away) must display an annual shift in position, called *parallax*. No one observed this change, so Aristotle concluded that the earth did not move around the sun. Following Pythagorean ideas, Aristotle argued that the earth must be spherical in shape. The actual measurement of the earth's size arose from the belief that the earth was, in fact, a sphere. Aristotle cited a diameter of about 5100 km. A later Greek, Eratosthenes, used a clever observation to find a diameter of about 13,400 km (Focus 5).

A contrary viewpoint: A heliocentric model / After the time of Alexander the Great, the scientific tradition, carried by the Greeks through the known world, centered upon the library at Alex-

center, the fire to the greatest heights, the air below the fire, and the water between the earth and the air. The corruptible region of the universe existed below the sphere of the moon; above was the incorruptible heaven made of the *quintessence*—the fifth essence—an immutable, transparent substance that formed the heavenly spheres. Note that Aristotle's model had two distinct realms—the heavens and the earth—in which different physical laws of motion applied. This split arose from the idea that the perfect heavens must have a different nature from the imperfect earth.

The natural motion of the heavenly spheres was to rotate. So *no forces* were needed to keep

focus 4

HELIOCENTRIC STELLAR PARALLAX IN A THIN-SHELL COSMOS

Stellar parallax is an apparent shift in the positions of stars. In a heliocentric model because it arises from the earth's revolution around the sun, it is usually called **heliocentric parallax.** *The details of heliocentric parallax differ depending on whether the stars in space are either confined to a thin shell (as in the Greek picture) or spread more or less throughout space (as in modern ideas).*

Consider what happens if the stars are stuck in a thin shell that closes off the universe, as in the heliocentric picture of Aristarchus (Fig. 1).

Pick out two stars close together on the celestial sphere (A and B in Fig. 1). Observe them at midnight (position 1 in Fig. 1); they will appear some angular distance α apart. Just after sunset three months later, observe the stars again (position 2 in Fig. 1). They will appear close together (angle β is less than angle α), partially because you're now seeing them at an angle, rather than face on. Now imagine you'd observed them six months later (position 3 in Fig. 1) at sunrise. Their angular separation is again β.

Now imagine you observed these stars in a regular six-month cycle: from positions 3, 1, and 2. You'd see the stars close together (3), then farther apart (1), and then closer together (2 again). This angular shift (from β to α to β) is the heliocentric parallax. Note that the greater the distance to the stars is, compared with the earth–sun distance, the smaller will be the observed parallax.

Greek astronomers did not *observe this annual back-and-forth motion of the stars. So the heliocentric model was inconsistent with the observations, and Greek astronomers re-*

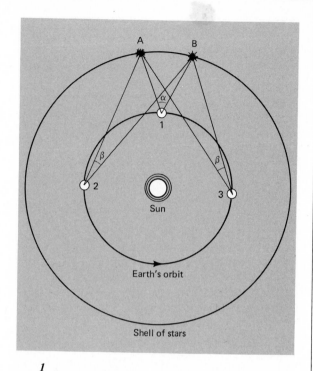

1

Parallax in a finite, heliocentric cosmos. As the earth goes around the sun (from 1 to 2 to 3), the angular distance between two stars (A and B) located the same distance from the earth and fixed to the celestial sphere should change with a yearly cycle.

jected the idea for good reason. We now know that they did not detect heliocentric parallax because the stars are so distant that the shift is too small to be seen without a telescope.

If the stars are spread out in space rather than attached to a thin shell, heliocentric parallax shows up as the shift in the positions of nearby stars compared with distant ones. See Focus 35.

focus 5

SURVEYING THE EARTH

Around 200 B.C. the Greek astronomer and geographer Eratosthenes, believing the earth to be round, measured its circumference. Eratosthenes worked in the great library in Alexandria, and while on a vacation trip in Syene, Egypt, on June 21 he noticed that sunlight fell directly down a well at noon. This indicated that the sun was directly overhead. At noon on the same date the following year, he observed that in Alexandria (located directly north of Syene) a gnomon shadow indicated that the sun was about 7° south of the zenith. Because the circumference of the earth encompasses 360°, he concluded that the distance from Syene to Alexandria must be $\frac{7}{360}$ of the earth's circumference (Fig. 1).

To determine the length of the circumference, Eratosthenes needed to know the distance from Alexandria to Syene. In the second century B.C. this information was not readily available, but as Herodotus recorded, the trip by camel took about 50 days. Because the average camel traveled about 100 stadia per day, it covered 5000 stadia for the entire journey. (The stadium was an ancient unit of length, about $\frac{1}{6}$ km, although its exact length varied throughout the ancient world.) Eratosthenes calculated the earth's circumference as $\frac{360}{7} \times 5000 \cong 250,000$ stadia. If we take the length of a stadium to be $\frac{1}{6}$ km, then the Alexandria–Syene distance as determined by Era-

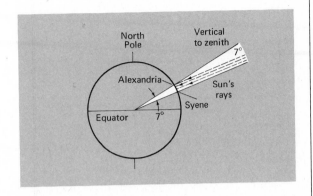

1

Eratosthenes' method of measuring the size of the earth. He noted that at the summer solstice the noon sun's light came down from directly overhead at Syene. Later, in Alexandria, he saw that at noon on the same date, the sun's rays came in at an angle of 7° from the vertical. If the sun is so far from the earth that the incoming rays are parallel, then the earth's curvature accounts for the difference in angle.

tosthenes was about 830 km, and the circumference of the earth, about 42,000 km, surprisingly close to the modern value of 40,030 km. (This numerical coincidence may be mere chance, because the precise length of the stadium is not known).

Knowing the circumference you can easily compute the earth's radius by dividing it by 2π; the result is about 6700 km.

andria. Eratosthenes, who worked in the library, was one of the astronomers in this new Hellenistic tradition.

Another of these, Aristarchus, who lived during the third century B.C., went so far as to propose a *heliocentric* (sun-centered) rather than geocentric model for the cosmos (Fig. 2.5). This heliocentric model explained the apparent daily motion of the stars by saying that the earth rotated on its axis once a day and that the sphere of the stars did not move. Because we stand on the earth and do not feel it moving, we think the heavens rather than the earth rotates. Aris-

tarchus argued that if the earth rotated from west to east, it would appear to us that the heavens moved east to west. In addition, Aristarchus believed that the earth also revolved around the sun in one year. The sun's motion along the ecliptic was then a reflection of the actual motion of the earth. In these ideas Aristarchus reached far ahead of his time.

Unfortunately, when the library in Alexandria was burned, the major writings of Aristarchus were lost, and we know his ideas only from comments made by others and his one surviving work. In this piece Aristarchus worked

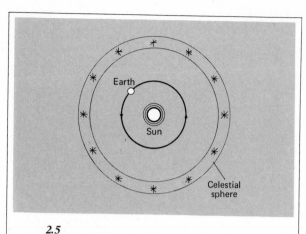

2.5

A simplified sketch of the helio-centric model of Aristarchus. With the earth rotating daily about its axis and, at the same time, revolving yearly around the sun, Aristarchus explained the most important observed celestial motions.

out the earth–sun distance relative to the earth–moon distance, and from this result inferred (correctly!) that the sun was a body much larger than the earth. But we have no evidence that Aristarchus worked out the details of planetary motions using his heliocentric model.

The heliocentric scheme was attacked during Greek times on two fronts: (1) it contradicted both common sense and Aristotle's physics in stating that the earth moved and (2) it required an annual parallax of stars that was *not*, in fact, observed (Focus 4). For these philosophical and observational reasons, and because of the influence of Aristotle's ideas, Aristarchus's model languished.

Expanding the mechanical, geocentric model / Another distinguished Hellenistic astronomer, Hipparchus, lived and worked at Rhodes from 160 to 127 B.C. His most useful accomplishment was the organization of the observations available from Babylonia. Hipparchus codified the ancient records because he wisely recognized that devising a better cosmological model required a careful accumulation of observations; these observations made up the raw materials from which a model could be constructed.

Although Hipparchus gathered relevant information, he did not assimilate it completely enough to develop a comprehensive model of planetary motion. He did, however, use geometrical devices called *eccentrics, deferents*, and *epicycles* (Focus 6), which enabled him to explain planetary motions with some accuracy. Each device accounted for some aspect of planetary motion: The epicycle and deferent explained retrograde motion: the eccentric, the nonuniform rate of motion of the planets through the zodiac.

Taking up a suggestion of Aristarchus, Hipparchus measured the earth–moon distance from observations during a total lunar eclipse. To do this he had to assume that the earth and moon were round and that the moon orbited the earth. This step at surveying the cosmos was crucial in establishing the size of the universe—a task continued by modern astronomers. Note the similarity here to Eratosthenes; both men accepted geometrical models of the universe and, because of these models, made fruitful observations. Without the models they had no reason to make such observations. In this sense scientific models channel what observations are made and what is expected from them.

2.4

Claudius Ptolemy: A comprehensive, geocentric model

Two-and-a-half centuries after Hipparchus, Claudius Ptolemy (Fig. 2.6) worked in Alexandria and so had access to the records in the famous library. Ptolemy molded the monumental records and ideas of the astronomy then known into a comprehensive model that would endure for centuries.

We know little of Ptolemy's personal life, not even the exact dates of his birth and death. From his observations, however, we know that he worked around A.D. 125. His most noted astronomical work was the *Almagest*. The original Greek title is translated as the *Mathematical Composition of Claudius Ptolemy*, but because the impact of this book on Western science came through the Arabic text, it is usually referred to as the *Almagest*, a transliteration of Arabic words meaning "the greatest."

Many of the technical devices that Ptolemy utilized did not originate with him, but he was

2.6

Claudius Ptolemy (with Astronomy). ". . . we shall only report what was rigorously proved by the ancients . . ." (Courtesy O. Gingerich)

the first person to design a complete system to describe and predict planetary motions. The *Almagest* was the first professional astronomy textbook. Most important, his model worked; Ptolemy's many circles whirled the planets around the ecliptic with an error of not more than 5° and sometimes less. The careful application of geometry explained the celestial motions.

A geometrical, geocentric model / In the opening pages of the *Almagest*, Ptolemy pays his respects to Aristotle and then defines the problem:

we wish to find the evident and certain appearances from the observations of the ancients and our own, and apply the consequences of these conceptions by means of geometrical demonstrations.

Note that Ptolemy is following Plato's dictum to "save the appearances." To start, he assumes that the earth is spherical, in the center

of the heavens, has no motions, and is much smaller than the sphere containing the stars. In addition, Ptolemy also requires that *uniform motion around the center of circles* be the aesthetically pleasing motion for the celestial spheres carrying the planets.

In practice, Ptolemy ends up violating this uniform, circular precept. For, if the planetary motion is in fact uniform along circles, how could he explain the *observed variations* in the motions? Remember (Section 1.4) that the planets have retrograde motion, and these retrograde motions vary. For example, Fig. 2.2 shows nine retrograde motions of Mars, all of which have different angular sizes, shapes, and durations.

You can think of the problem of planetary motion as a model-building puzzle that requires a different device for each aspect that needs explanation. The planets have two kinds of motion: (1) the general eastward motion along the ecliptic—with variations and (2) occasional retrograde motions—also with variations!

Ptolemy modeled the first with a planet moving around the earth in a circle at uniform speed. For the main variations he offset the earth from the center of the circle—this was the eccentric (Focus 6). For the second he used small circles moving on larger ones—epicycles (Focus 6). Then for the variations of the retrograde motions, Ptolemy devised a new, subtle device—the *equant*.

To see basically how the equant works, you start with an eccentric (Fig. 2.7(a)). Imagine a point in a circle placed the same distance away from the center as the eccentric point but located opposite from it (Fig. 2.7(b)). Ptolemy demanded that the planet move on the circle in such a way that an imaginary observer at this point (E' in Fig. 2.7(b)) sees uniform motion. This point is called the *equant point*. Note that the planet no longer moves along the circle with uniform speed around its center (Fig. 2.7(b)). The equant is a nonphysical, totally geometrical device and a significant break with astronomical traditions because the planetary motion was *no longer uniform about the center of a circle*.

Ptolemy violated the precept of uniform motion about the center of a circle in order to construct a model consistent with his aesthetic ideals about motion along circles and one that

focus 6

THE GEOMETRICAL DEVICES USED BY HIPPARCHUS

Hipparchus made use of three geometrical devices: the eccentric, the deferent, and the epicycle. Each of these was used to account for some aspect of planetary motion.

Following older ideas, Hipparchus demanded that the planets move at a constant speed along circular paths. Yet he knew from observations that the motion is not uniform but varies regularly such that the average angular speed of a planet is faster in one region of the ecliptic and slower in the opposite region. Hipparchus explained the variation in a planet's speed along the ecliptic by the eccentric (Fig. 1). The earth was displaced from the center of a planet's motion. Then as the planet moved, it appeared to go faster when closer to the earth and slower when farther away. However, the planet's angular motion

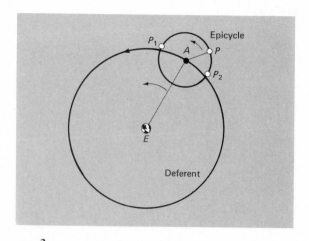

2

The epicycle and deferent. A planet (P) is attached to a small circle (the epicycle) whose center rides on a larger circle (the deferent). The earth (E) lies in the center of the deferent. The radius of the epicycle turns in the same direction as the radius of the deferent. So when the planet moves on the inside of the deferent (from P_1 to P_2), it moves opposite its normal (eastward) motion. This is the time of its retrograde motion (westward).

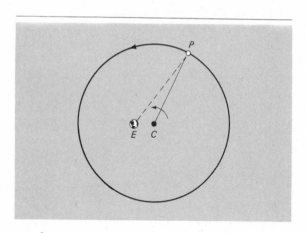

1

The eccentric. A planet (P) revolves with uniform circular motion about the center (C) of its path. The earth (E), however, is displaced from this center. So the planet's motion as observed from the earth is not uniform.

remained uniform when viewed from the center of its circular path.

The eccentric did not provide an explanation of retrograde motion. To cope with this peculiarity, Hipparchus used the epicycle and the deferent (Fig. 2). The **deferent** was a large circle centered more or less on the earth. (The deferent could be an eccentric; if so, then the earth was a bit off-center.) The center of a smaller circle called the **epicycle** moved around the circumference of the deferent. The planet moved on the epicycle, so its motion was a combination of circular motion about the epicycle and the epicycle's motion about the deferent. If the epicycle and deferent turn in the same direction, the combination seen from the deferent's center imitates retrograde

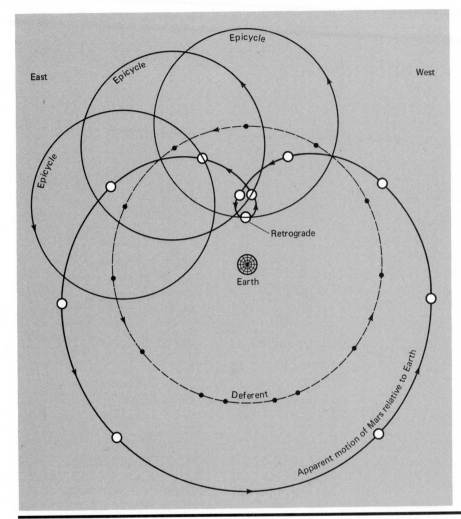

East West

3

The motion of Mars, as seen from the earth, produced by an epicycle and a deferent. The view is down on the earth's north pole.

motion. As the planet moves on the part of the epicycle interior to the circumference of the deferent, it moves opposite the deferent's motion. Hipparchus had the deferent represent the planet's general motion west to east along the ecliptic. The reverse swing on the epicycle then represented the east-to-west retrograde motion (Fig. 3).

The periods of the epicycle and deferent are set from observations. The average time it takes the planet to return to the same place in the zodiac (Table 1.2) is the period of the

deferent. Mars, for example, has a deferent period of a little less than two years. The period of the epicycles is just the average time between retrograde motions. For example, at the midpoint of its retrograde motion, Mars is at opposition. The next midpoint of retrograde motion takes place at the same relative alignment of the sun, earth, and planet; this period is the planet's synodic period. The epicycle's period equals the planet's synodic period. For Mars this time is 780 days, slightly more than two years.

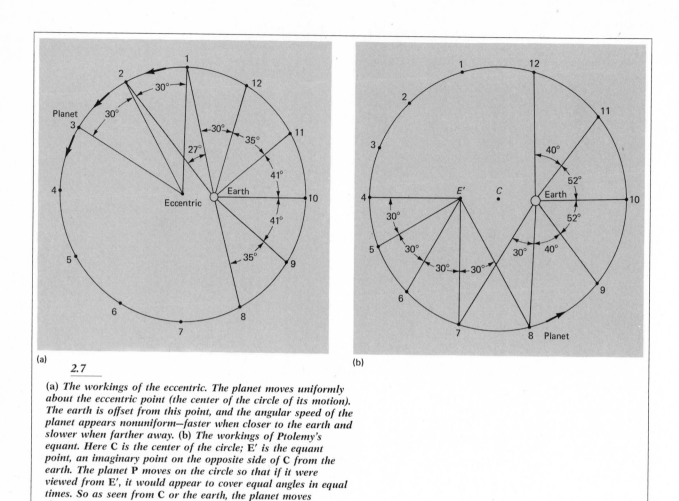

(a)

2.7

(a) The workings of the eccentric. The planet moves uniformly about the eccentric point (the center of the circle of its motion). The earth is offset from this point, and the angular speed of the planet appears nonuniform—faster when closer to the earth and slower when farther away. (b) The workings of Ptolemy's equant. Here C is the center of the circle; E′ is the equant point, an imaginary point on the opposite side of C from the earth. The planet P moves on the circle so that if it were viewed from E′, it would appear to cover equal angles in equal times. So as seen from C or the earth, the planet moves through different angular distances in equal times.

predicted planetary positions reasonably well. He put accuracy before esthetics.

How did the system look when completed? (A simplified diagram is shown in Fig. 2.8(a) and (b).) First consider the inner planets. Recall (Section 1.4) that Mercury stays typically within 23° of the sun and Venus, within 46°. Ptolemy could account for these observations by requiring that the size of the epicycle for Venus be larger than that for Mercury and by insisting that the centers of the epicycles always lie on the line connecting the earth and the sun.

For other planets the model is somewhat different. Recall (Section 1.4) that Mars, Jupiter,

and Saturn can be seen anywhere along the ecliptic with respect to the sun. So the centers of the epicycles can be anywhere on the perimeter of the deferent. But to ensure that the planets go through retrograde motion when at opposition (and only when they are at opposition), the model requires that the radii of the epicycles must all line up with the radius of the earth–sun deferent.

A key point: In Ptolemy's model the heavenly spheres are actual, physical (not imaginary) spheres made of the quintessence. The *natural* motion of these solid spheres—rotation—drives all of the planetary motions.

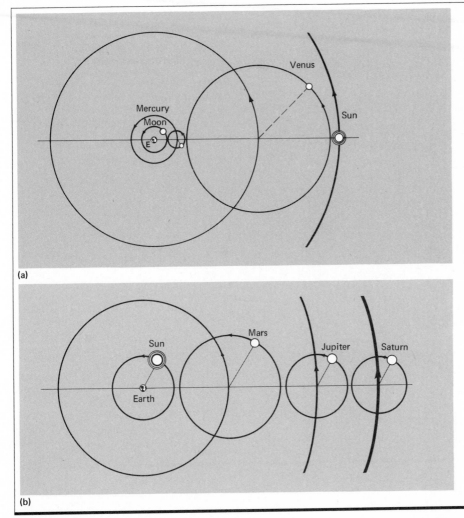

2.8

(a) *The Ptolemaic model for Mercury and Venus. The centers of the epicycles of Mercury and Venus are always in line with the sun to account for the observed range of maximum elongations. The size of each epicycle is related to the observed angle at maximum elongation. The period of the deferents for both planets was one year.*
(b) *The Ptolemaic system for Mars, Jupiter, and Saturn. To account for the observed sizes of retrograde loops, the epicycles of Mars, Jupiter, and Saturn decrease in size. The radii of these epicycles must align with the earth–sun radius for the system to work. The arrangement here emphasizes that point; in general, the planet's epicycles could be anywhere on their deferents.*

Although the Ptolemaic model (Fig. 2.9) lost acceptance some centuries ago, you should not condemn it as obviously wrong. This model remained in use for some 1400 years, because it incorporated useful technical methods for calculating and predicting planetary positions with some accuracy. Ptolemy's model also agreed in most details with the philosophical doctrines of the Greeks and had a commonsense geocentric appeal. It survived because no other comprehensive system was advanced to compete effectively with it.

The size of the cosmos / Ptolemy's cosmos was finite, but how large was it? For the sun and moon he gives the distances in terms of earth radii. Both were determined from the apparent angular sizes of the bodies and the lunar distance established by Hipparchus. To go farther out he assumed that no space is wasted between the heavenly spheres. Then with the earth–moon distance set at 59 earth radii, the distances out to Saturn can be laid out if all the spheres nest tightly together. The sphere of the fixed stars was then 20,000 earth radii from the earth. A small universe, only about the actual known distance of the earth from the sun! But it marked a reasonable attempt to establish the scale of the cosmos.

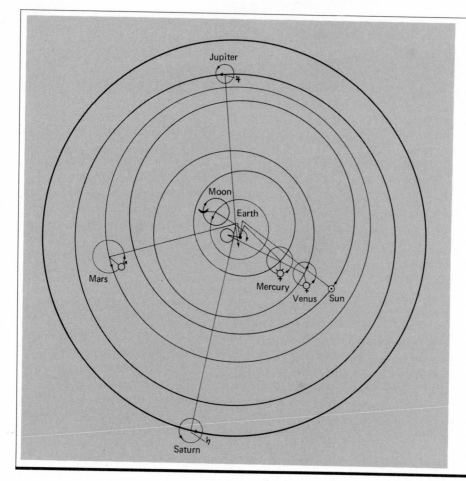

2.9

A view of the complete Ptolemaic model displaying eccentrics. Note that the centers of the deferents are offset from the earth; these are eccentrics. This figure does not show the proper sizes of the epicycles, nor their correct alignment (see Fig. 2.8). (Adapted from a diagram by W. Stahlman)

SUMMARY

This scan of astronomy from Babylonian to Greek times has picked out one important evolution of cosmological ideas: the birth of models of the universe. The invention of a model was lacking in the Babylonian astronomy, even though the Babylonians were excellent observers and developed arithmetical methods to predict planetary positions.

Greek ideas show the first models of the universe. In these attempts to "save the appearances," mechanical devices—usually with a simple geometry—were used to explain the actual observed motions of the planets. In addition, these models often sprang from aesthetic ideas.

Models lie at the heart of modern science, but model making was a new conceptual activity during Greek times. Ptolemy's geocentric model found favor because it was the first comprehensive scheme supported by philosophical and physical ideas (those of Aristotle) to describe in detail the motions in the sky (Table 2.1). Containing a practical approach, the Almagest provided the conceptual framework for the geocentric cosmos.

Scientific model making marked a critical turn in astronomy. Before its arrival, the cosmos was explained in terms of myths, such as the Babylonian Enuma Elish. The early cosmological model of the Pythagoreans included geometrical and aesthetic elements (spheres and the harmony of the spheres) but lacked physical ideas. Aristotle injected physics into his cosmological model but knew that the correspondence of his model with some observations—especially retrograde motion—just wasn't terribly good. Ptolemy put together the first comprehensive

TABLE 2.1   A summary of Ptolemy's model

Observation	Explanation
Motion of entire sky E to W in about 24 hours.	Daily motion E to W of the sphere of stars, carrying all other spheres with it.
Sun Motion yearly W to E along ecliptic. Non-uniform rate along ecliptic.	Motion of sun's sphere W to E in a year. Eccentric—earth displaced from center of sun's circle.
Moon Monthly motion W to E compared to stars.	W to E motion of the moon's sphere in a month.
Planets General motion W to E through zodiac.	Motion of deferent W to E; period set by observation of period of planet to go around ecliptic.
Retrograde motion	Motion of epicycle in same direction as deferent; its period is the time between retrograde motions.
Variations in speed through zodiac, in retrograde motions.	Eccentrics, equants.
Mercury, Venus Greatest elongations of 23° and 46°; appear fixed to sun.	Size of deferents set by those angles; centers of deferents on earth–sun line.
Mars, Jupiter, Saturn Retrograde at opposition, when brightest.	Radii of epicycles aligned with earth–sun radius.

Notes 1. Motions of heavenly spheres were natural motions and did not require a force.
2. Use of equants *violated* the precept of uniform, circular motion for all heavenly bodies.
3. Overall accuracy: usually 5° or less, occasionally larger.

cosmological model, one that incorporated all three key elements: geometry from the Greeks, aesthetics of his own, and physics from Aristotle. More important, his model conformed to observations within sufficient accuracy for his day. So Ptolemy's model worked well and was complete. That's why it survived for so long!

STUDY EXERCISES

1   What was an important observational achievement of Babylonian astronomers? (*Objective 1*)

2   Contrast Babylonian and Greek astronomy in terms of their observational achievements. (*Objectives 1, 2, and 3*)

3   How did the model of Aristotle explain the
  a   apparent lack of motion of the earth
  b   daily motion of the stars
  c   annual motion of the sun? (*Objective 4*)

4   How did Aristotle argue against a heliocentric system? (*Objectives 3 and 4*)

5   In the Ptolemaic system, how do observations establish the period of the epicycle? the deferent? (*Objective 6*)

6   Why and how did Ptolemy treat Mercury and Venus differently from Mars, Jupiter, and Saturn? (*Objective 6*)

7   How did Ptolemy violate his own precept of uniform motion about the center of a circle? (*Objectives 5, 6, and 7*)

8   What *observation* was Ptolemy attempting to explain with each of the following geometrical devices:
  a   epicycle
  b   eccentric
  c   equant?
(*Objectives 6 and 7*)

BEYOND THIS BOOK . . .

A classic work on the astronomical achievements of the Babylonians is *The Exact Sciences in Antiquity* (Dover, New York, 1969) by O. Neugebauer.

You can find an English translation of the *Almagest* in volume 16 of Great Books of the Western World (Encyclopaedia Britannica, Chicago, 1952).

Was Ptolemy a fraud? Did he make up observations to conform with his model? Read *The Crime of Claudius Ptolemy* (Johns Hopkins University Press, Baltimore, Maryland 1977) for an assertion of this view by R. Newton.

The new cosmic order
3

CHAPTER 3

CENTRAL QUESTION *How did Copernicus's sun-centered model explain the motion of the planets and ignite a revolution in cosmological thought?*

Astronomy languished with the decline of Greek civilization in the first few centuries after the work of Ptolemy. Most of the Greek astronomical works were unknown in Western Europe until the twelfth century, when Arabic manuscripts in Spain were translated into Latin. In the thirteenth century Alfonso the Great of Spain sponsored the publication of the *Alfonsine Tables*, handy tables of planetary positions based on the Ptolemaic model. The essential Ptolemaic model worked well for predicting planetary positions without any additional complications. Practicing astronomers had no reason to be unhappy with it.

Although medieval astronomers were generally satisfied with the Ptolemaic model, one of them was not—a quiet Polish monk, Nicolaus Copernicus (1473–1543). In the year of his death Copernicus's great work was published: *De revolutionibus orbium coelestium (On the Revolutions of the Heavenly Spheres)*, in which the earth was shaken from its static place at the center of the universe into an orbit around the sun—just another planet in the cosmos. The model of Copernicus was *heliocentric*.

Copernicus's view did not immediately wrench the minds of astronomers from their geocentric notions. Some, like the Danish observer Tycho Brahe, considered the Copernican claims but finally clung to a geocentric model. Others, like Johannes Kepler, found an essential harmony in Copernicus's model that led to the introduction of a physical force to understand the motions of the planets. The revolution in astronomy after Copernicus marked the first important shift in the popular concept of the earth's place in the universe: the shift from the geocentric to the heliocentric model. This revolution later injected a new concept into cosmological models: that of a physical force in operation in the heavens.

3.1

Copernicus the conservative

In the sixteenth and the seventeenth centuries in Europe a new model of the cosmos arose. Nicolaus Copernicus (Fig. 3.1) initiated this revolution. I highlight here some events in Copernicus's life that may have influenced him in developing a new model of the universe when the old one seemed adequate.

3.1

Nicolaus Copernicus. "In the center rests the sun." (Painting by Maxim Kopf, courtesy Harvard College Observatory)

Following the traditional liberal arts curriculum at the Collegium Maius in Krakow, Copernicus studied astronomy with more interest than the average student. His copy of the *Alfonsine Tables* still exists, with many notes in the margins. (These tables gave predictions of planetary positions based on the Ptolemaic model.) After leaving Krakow, Copernicus traveled to Italy, where he bought more astronomy books and enrolled to study canon law at the University of Bologna. Later he studied medicine in Padua for two years and finally received a law degree from the University of Ferrara. Eventually, he served as a canon at the cathedral at Frauenberg (in Poland), a position arranged for him by his uncle, who was the bishop.

Copernicus made observations from which he noted that some Ptolemaic predictions of planetary conjunctions were fairly inaccurate, especially those of Jupiter and Saturn, one of which occurred in 1504. (A *conjunction* occurs when two celestial bodies, such as two planets, pass very close together in the sky.) He found that the conjunction of 1504 took place at a time ten days different from the predicted time. These inaccuracies may have driven Copernicus to reconsider the Ptolemaic model and eventually to devise a heliocentric one.

How did the sun come to play a central role in his model? Copernicus had become familiar with Aristotle, Pythagoras, and Plato while in Italy. An offshoot of Plato's philosophy, Neoplatonism, asserted that the sun is the source of the godhead and of all knowledge. Copernicus may have first recognized the importance of the sun in Neoplatonic thought when he was at Krakow and read a new book by the editor of a new Latin edition of Plato's works in which the virtues of the sun were praised. These writings singled out the sun as a body quite different from the planets and perhaps encouraged Copernicus to consider a heliocentric system.

About 1529 Copernicus wrote a summary of his new model, which he circulated in manuscript copy to some of his friends. In this commentary he presented a general description of his heliocentric cosmology: The sun replaced the earth as the center of the cosmos, and the earth not only revolved around the sun but also rotated daily on its axis (Fig. 3.2). (Recall that these ideas were first outlined by Aristarchus; Section 2.3.)

Copernicus still asserted that all the celestial motions must be composed of uniform circular motions. Viewing the equant as a violation of this principle, Copernicus attacked the Ptolemaic model as "not sufficiently pleasing to the mind." His new model would reinstate the rule of uniform motion to its proper unadulterated status.

Just what compelled Copernicus to offer a new cosmological and computational model is still somewhat puzzling. The basic Ptolemaic model generally worked well enough to predict the planetary positions. Contrary to some stories, the Ptolemaic model did *not* require the continual addition of circles to match the observations and so did not grow to a monstrosity in medieval times. Copernicus would take 20 years to work out the details of his new model. Even then his predictions came out no better than those based on the old Ptolemaic picture.

However, Copernicus asserted that his model surpassed the Ptolemaic one from an aesthetic standpoint. He wrote

So we find underlying this ordination an admirable commensurability in the Universe, and a clear harmonious bond between the motion and magnitude of the spheres such as can be discovered in no other way.

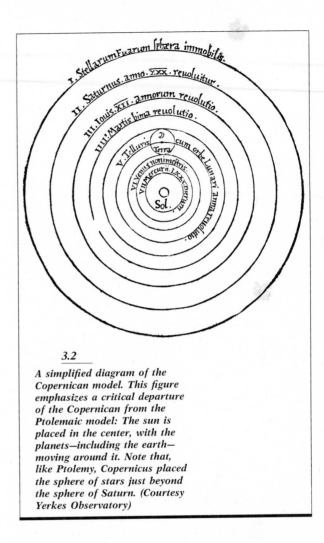

3.2

A simplified diagram of the Copernican model. This figure emphasizes a critical departure of the Copernican from the Ptolemaic model: The sun is placed in the center, with the planets—including the earth—moving around it. Note that, like Ptolemy, Copernicus placed the sphere of stars just beyond the sphere of Saturn. (Courtesy Yerkes Observatory)

Copernicus focused on the notions of harmony and commensurability. What were these new, aesthetically striking aspects of his model?

The writing of De revolutionibus / Long after Copernicus had privately distributed his ideas among his friends, his work became known to two astronomers at the University of Wittenberg, Georg Rheticus and Erasmus Reinhold. Fascinated by Copernicus's new cosmos, Rheticus visited the aging astronomer, who showed him the final manuscript copy for *De revolutionibus*. Rheticus begged Copernicus to allow it to be published for all to read. (Not until Copernicus's lifetime had printed texts, rather than manuscript copies, become common.) Copernicus agreed, and after much trouble with the printer the book was published around April 1543 (Fig. 3.3). Meanwhile Coperni-

NICOLAI CO
PERNICI TORINENSIS
DE REVOLVTIONIBVS ORBI
um coeleftium, Libri VI.

Habes in hoc opere iam recens nato, & ædito,
ftudiofe lector, Motus ftellarum, tam fixarum,
quàm erraticarum, cum ex ueteribus, tum etiam
et recentibus obferuationibus reftitutos: & no-
uis infuper ac admirabilibus hypothefibus or-
natos. Habes etiam Tabulas expeditifsimas, ex
quibus eofdem ad quoduis tempus quàm facilli
me calculare poteris. Igitur eme, lege, fruere.

3.3

Title page of De revolutionibus.
The words orbium coelestium
were probably added by
Osiander to emphasize that it
was the celestial *spheres that*
were moving and so play down
the motion of the earth. (Cour-
tesy O. Gingerich)

cus, who was then 70, suffered a stroke and was confined to his bed. Although the book was delivered to him before he died in June, he probably did not read it.

Copernicus would have been amazed to find that the final version of his life's work had been given a new title. The work was probably originally entitled *De revolutionibus* (*On the Revolutions*), but the published title sported two additional words: *De revolutionibus orbium coelestium* (*On the Revolutions of the Heavenly Spheres*). He would have been even more surprised to find a new but unsigned preface, which stated that the work contained a new hypothesis, of a heliocentric universe, proposed for the computation of planetary positions. It was not, however, to be taken as a statement of reality, because the astronomer "cannot by any line of reasoning reach the true causes of these movements . . . let no one expect anything in the way of certainty from astronomy, since astronomy can offer us nothing certain."

For some years this preface was attributed to Copernicus's belief that his model had no

basis in reality. However, Johannes Kepler—whom you will meet later in this chapter—discovered that the preface had been written by Andrew Osiander, a Nürnburg clergyman, who oversaw completion of the book's publication. Osiander had needed the disclaimer to elicit Protestant approval for the publication of a book by a Catholic. He may have changed the title in order to emphasize the motions of the heavens rather than those of the earth.

De revolutionibus took after the *Almagest* in style and outline as well as in basic intention: to explain the planetary motions using only combinations of uniform circular motions, the precept of the Greeks (Section 2.3). Copernicus thought that although Ptolemy's model was consistent with observation, it clashed with the Greeks' ideas about heavenly motions because it required equants. On an equant, a planet cannot move with uniform motion about the center of its deferent. Copernicus was offended by the equant, because it did not allow for uniform motion around the center of a circle. In a basically conservative mood he wished to devise a system that was faithful to the uniform circular motion of the Greeks and to eliminate the equant. To take this step, Copernicus had to discover a natural explanation for retrograde motion and a new fundamental harmony for the celestial spheres, which related the planets' distances to their periods around the sun.

The heliocentric model / In the introduction to *De revolutionibus* Copernicus, like Ptolemy, lays out his assumptions before looking at the details. First, he requires that the planets move in circular paths around the sun at uniform speeds. Second, the closer the planet is to the sun, the greater is its speed. For instance, Copernicus correctly placed Mercury closer to the sun than the earth, so its speed around the sun was faster than the earth's. Except for using the sun as the center of motion, this was identical to the ideas of Ptolemy. For the rest, however, Copernicus treads a different ground. Here's a short summary of the fundamental ideas for his heliocentric picture:

1   All the spheres revolve around the sun, and the sun is therefore the center of the universe. (In actual detail, Copernicus does not place the sun exactly at the center of the planetary paths.)

2   The distance from the earth to the sphere

of fixed stars is much greater than the distance from the earth to the sun.

3 The daily motion of heavenly bodies relative to the horizon results from the earth's motion about its axis.

4 The apparent annual motion of the sun relative to the stars is caused by the revolution of the earth around the sun.

5 The planets' retrograde motions occur because of the motion of the earth relative to the planets.

Let me expand upon these points to emphasize the key differences between the Copernican and Ptolemaic models.

In point (1) Copernicus asserts that the universe is heliocentric rather than geocentric. He comes to this conclusion for philosophical and aesthetic reasons. But as the Greeks before him realized in reaction to Aristarchus's heliocentric model, this model requires a stellar parallax (Focus 4), which had never been observed. Point (2) addresses this problem: If the stars are very far away, the parallax would be so small that no one could detect it by naked-eye observations. (Later observations with telescopes demonstrated that Copernicus's intuition about the vast distances to stars was correct.)

In point (3) Copernicus asserts that the daily rising–setting motions of all celestial objects result from the earth's rotation rather than from that of the celestial spheres. This idea has aesthetic appeal, for it replaces the rotations of many celestial spheres by the rotation of one sphere—the earth. You may wonder how the earth can rotate without objects on its surface flying off. This objection from physics was voiced against Copernicus's model, for which he had no good answer. (Now we explain it by gravity.) Copernicus suspected that the cosmos contained more than one center of attraction, but he could not prove it. Point (4) explains how, in a heliocentric system, the sun still appears to move around the earth. Here's an analogy. Imagine you're walking slowly counterclockwise in a circle around a lamppost (Fig. 3.4(a)). As you make your slow revolution, keep looking in the direction of the lamppost and note the background behind it. You will see the background slowly change; the lamppost appears to be moving counterclockwise with respect to background objects. Now imagine that the lamppost is the sun, that you are the earth

revolving around the sun, and that the background is the stars of the zodiac (Fig. 3.4(b)). Suppose looking out from the earth you see the sun in Leo. As the earth revolves counterclockwise, the background stars change; after one month the sun appears in Virgo. It seems to have moved, relative to the stars, counterclockwise. Actually, the earth has moved, and it's our line of sight from the earth to the sun to the stars that has changed.

The last point has an important consequence for the heliocentric model—it makes retrograde motion a *natural* result of the planet's revolutions. This result eliminates the need for epicycles and deferents to explain retrograde motion. Instead, retrograde motion arises from the planets chasing each other around, the faster inside planets regularly passing the outer ones because of their greater speed. For example, as the earth approaches Jupiter at opposition, it catches up to Jupiter, the slower outer planet, and passes it. At this time, Jupiter appears to move backward. An analogous situation occurs on the subway when an express train on the inner track passes a local train; if you are sitting in the express, the local train appears to go backward. Similarly, as the earth speeds by Jupiter, the planet seems to move westward in the sky against the backdrop of the stars. Let's look at this situation in more detail.

Retrograde motion in the Copernican model / In the Ptolemaic model, epicycles moving on deferents generated the retrograde motion of the planets (Section 2.3). In his heliocentric model, Copernicus eliminated epicycles for retrograde motion such that one circle—the earth's—replaced five Ptolemaic epicycles (one each for Mercury, Venus, Mars, Jupiter, and Saturn). Copernicus noted that the *relative motion* of the earth and planets produces retrograde motion.

Copernicus found that the *farther* a planet is from the sun, the *slower* it moves. For instance, Mars, Saturn, and Jupiter all lie more distant from the sun than the earth. So the earth moves faster than any of these, and when it passes any of them, we see these planets appear to move backward (westward) with respect to the stars.

Take Jupiter as a specific example (Fig. 3.5). The retrograde motion of Jupiter occurs at opposition, when the earth passes it. Imagine the

(a)

3.4

(a) *A concrete example of how the sun appears to move with respect to the stars, in a heliocentric model. Imagine moving in a circle* **counterclockwise** *(west to east) around a lamppost. Your line of sight to the lamppost and into the background constantly changes in the* **same** *direction (west to east) you are moving.* (b) *The sun's apparent motion through the zodiac in a heliocentric model. As the earth travels around the sun (counterclockwise), the line of sight to the sun and toward the background stars moves in the same direction. Here you would see the sun in Leo. A month later the earth would have moved eastwardly so that Virgo lies behind the sun. So the sun seems to have moved eastward.*

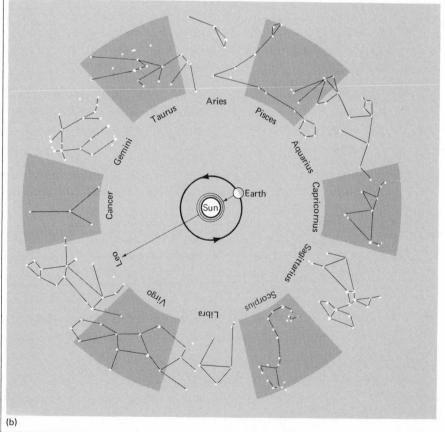

(b)

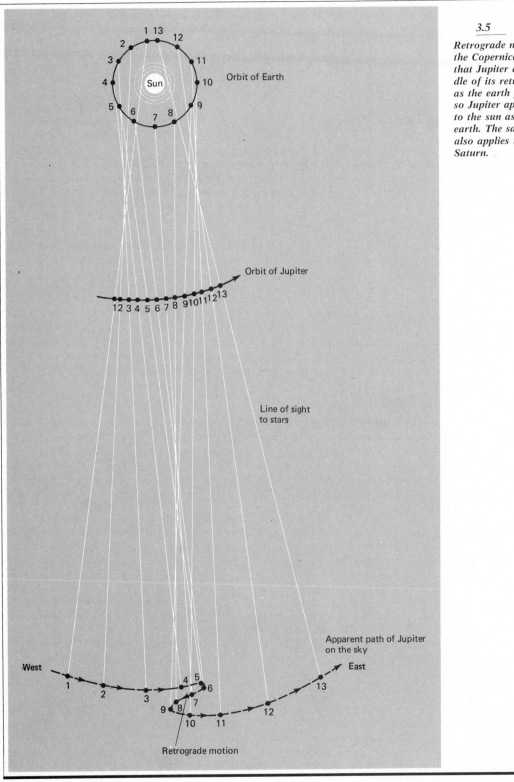

3.5

Retrograde motion of Jupiter in the Copernican model. Note that Jupiter appears in the middle of its retrograde loop just as the earth passes it (point 7), so Jupiter appears in opposition to the sun as viewed from the earth. The same basic diagram also applies to Mars and Saturn.

Sun

Orbit of Earth

Orbit of Jupiter

Line of sight
to stars

Apparent path of Jupiter
on the sky

West

East

Retrograde motion

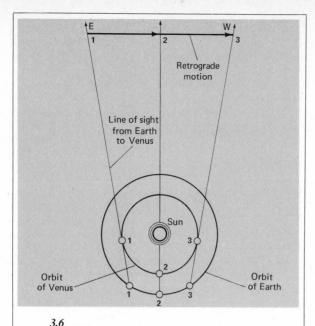

3.6

Retrograde motion of Venus in the Copernican model. As Venus passes the earth (along 1, 2, and 3), it appears to move westward, opposite its normal motion with respect to the stars. (Note that if you were on Venus, you'd see the earth undergo retrograde motion while in opposition to the sun.)

earth approaching opposition. Well before opposition, the line of sight toward Jupiter is swinging eastward. As the earth overtakes Jupiter, the line of sight to Jupiter changes direction and swings from east to west (westward) relative to the stars. As the earth moves on, the line of sight swings more slowly westward until it stops and then moves eastward once again. Jupiter appears from the earth to undergo retrograde motion as the earth passes it.

Note that the earth and Jupiter are closest together in the middle of the time of retrograde motion. So Jupiter should be brightest in the sky then, and it is.

The same chase-and-pass situation results in the retrograde motion of Venus and Mercury as seen from the earth. But in these cases it's the earth that is passed by. Let's consider Venus (Fig. 3.6). When Venus moves from greatest western elongation around the back of the sun, it appears to move normally eastward. However, as Venus catches up to the earth (from the east side of the sun) and passes it by, we observe Venus to move westward with respect to the stars (toward the west side of the sun). So for the inner planets, retrograde motion arises from the same relative motion as for the outer planets, but the role of the earth is reversed. Note

focus 7

SIDEREAL AND SYNODIC PERIODS IN THE COPERNICAN SYSTEM

From the earth you can directly observe the synodic period of a planet, that is, the time from a specific alignment of the planet and sun as seen from the earth to the next occurrence of the same alignment. For example, the time from one opposition of Jupiter to the subsequent opposition sets Jupiter's synodic period. In contrast, a planet's sidereal period is the interval from the time when the planet is in a specific location in the zodiac to the time when it returns to the same position as seen from the sun: in other words, how long it takes a planet to go around the sun once relative to the stars.

The synodic period is a geocentric property, while the sidereal period is a heliocentric one.

You are stuck on the earth, so you can observe only synodic periods, never sidereal ones. How can you transform synodic to sidereal periods? Assume, as Copernicus did, that the planetary orbits are circular and that the closer a planet is to the sun, the faster it moves in its orbit, that is, the shorter its sidereal period. The problem is then a chase situation. Suppose two adjacent planets start out lined up (the outer planet in opposition as seen from the interior one). How long will it be until they are aligned again? What is the relationship of the sidereal periods of both planets and their synodic periods? (Note that the time from the starting alignment to the next occurrence of that alignment is the synodic period between the two planets—Fig. 1.)

From the starting position, the inner planet, moving at $360°/P_i$ per day, travels faster than the outer one. (P_i is the sidereal

that it is the *passing* of two planets that causes the illusion of retrograde motion.

Planetary distances / Another fundamental achievement of Copernicus was the establishment of the order and distances in the planetary

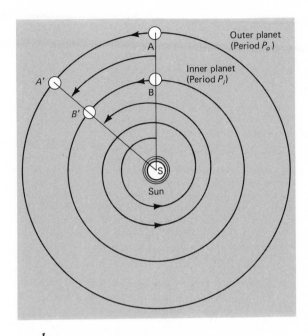

Synodic and sidereal periods in the Copernican model. If two planets start out lined up on the same side of the sun (A and B), the inner planet must come around a bit more (to B') than one revolution in order to catch up with the outer planet (at A').

period of the inner planet.) The outer planet, moving at the slower rate of $360°/P_o$ per day, lags behind the inner planet more and more each day. (P_o is the sidereal period of the outer planet.) For example, at the end of one day the inner planet has gained an angle of $(360°/P_i - 360°/P_o)$ on the outer one. This day's gain is equal to $360°/S$ (S is the synodic period of either planet seen from the other), because in S days it must gain a full 360°. In algebraic terms,

$$\frac{360°}{S} = \frac{360°}{P_i} - \frac{360°}{P_o}$$

or dividing by 360°,

$$\frac{1}{S} = \frac{1}{P_i} - \frac{1}{P_o}$$

Suppose the earth is the inner planet and Mars is the outer one. Then since the earth's sidereal period is one year, $P_i = 1$, and

$$\frac{1}{S} = 1 - \frac{1}{P_{Mars}}$$

where P_{Mars}, the sidereal period of Mars, and S, the synodic period of the earth and Mars, are in years.

Now imagine the case of the earth as the outer planet and Venus as the inner planet. Then $P_o = 1$ is the earth's sidereal period, and

$$\frac{1}{S} = \frac{1}{P_{Venus}} - 1$$

where all the quantities are in years. Let me work this one out completely. The synodic period of Venus is 585 days, or $\frac{585}{365} = 1.6$ years. Using the preceding equation, I get

$$\frac{1}{1.6} = \frac{1}{P_{Venus}} - 1$$

$$0.62 = \frac{1}{P_{Venus}} - 1$$

$$1.62 = \frac{1}{P_{Venus}}$$

and

$$P_{Venus} = \frac{1}{1.62} = 0.62 \text{ year, or 225 days}$$

This transformation from synodic to sidereal periods is important because the sidereal periods of the planets, from shortest to longest, place them in a natural order from the sun. This result holds true even for elliptical orbits.

system from the observed *synodic periods*. (The synodic period is the time required for a planet in a given alignment with the sun as seen from the earth—such as opposition—to move through the sky and return to the same position in the sky relative to the sun.) From the observed synodic periods Copernicus calculated the *sidereal periods*—the planet's period of revolution with respect to the distant stars, as seen from the sun (Focus 7).

To understand the difference between synodic and sidereal periods, consider this example: in February 1980 Jupiter was at opposition and in the constellation Leo. In March 1981 Jupiter was again at opposition (the synodic period is about 13 months), but it had moved to the constellation Virgo (one constellation eastward along the ecliptic). Moving at this rate, Jupiter will not come back to the same position on the ecliptic until 1992 (in Leo). In this 12-year-time interval (one *sidereal* period), Jupiter will have been at opposition 11 times, once every 13 months (its *synodic* period).

Copernicus found that the planetary order, from Mercury to Saturn, fell into a *natural* sequence, going from the shortest sidereal period (Mercury) to the longest (Saturn). He saw a harmony in this sequence, which later scientists such as Kepler and Galileo considered an essential elegance of the heliocentric model.

Copernicus calculated the order of the planets and their relative distances from the sun. He had no way to fix his model's distance scale in units like kilometers or miles from observations, for all he could do was observe angular speed and direction (Section 2.4 and Focus 1). But he could—and did—establish from observations the distances of the planets from the sun relative to the earth–sun distance, which is called the *Astronomical Unit* (Table 3.1 and Focus 8). Copernicus was extremely pleased with this result; here he found the "commensurability" in the motions of the planets and their distances from the sun.

TABLE 3.1 *Copernicus's relative distances of the planets*

Planet	Copernicus's value (AU)	Modern value (AU)
Mercury	0.38	0.387
Venus	0.72	0.723
Earth	1.00	1.00
Mars	1.52	1.52
Jupiter	5.22	5.20
Saturn	9.17	9.54

Note AU is the abbreviation for *Astronomical Unit,* the average earth–sun distance.

---

focus 8
THE RELATIVE DISTANCES OF THE PLANETS IN THE COPERNICAN MODEL

*The planetary distances from the sun relative to the earth–sun distance (known as one **Astronomical Unit**, or **AU**) can be directly determined in the Copernican model. The method differs, however, for the planets interior to the earth and for those exterior to it. It assumes the orbits are circular.*

For Mercury and Venus, the interior planets, the method is a direct geometrical one and rests on the observed maximum elongation angle of the planet from the sun. Recall from Section 1.4 that this angle is 23° for Mercury and 46° for Venus. Take Venus as a specific case.

In a heliocentric model, maximum elongation for Venus takes place when the line of sight from the earth to Venus is a line tangent to Venus's orbit (Fig. 1); that is, the radius of Venus's orbit is at right angles to the line of sight at the circumference of Venus's orbit. This makes a right triangle with the side opposite the observed elongation angle (side SV) the distance of Venus from the sun, and one other side (SE) the distance of the earth from the sun (1 AU). The ratio of side SV to side SE is the sine of angle α, the angle of elongation, so

$$\sin \alpha = \frac{SV}{SE}$$

$$\sin 46° = \frac{SV}{SE}$$

The angle is known from observation; the sine of 46° is in a table of trigonometric functions. It is approximately 0.72. So the ratio of Venus's distance from the sun (SV) to the earth's distance from the sun (SE) is about 0.72. Define the average earth–sun distance as 1 AU. Then Venus must be 0.72 AU from the sun. Similarly, you can find the size of Mercury's orbit if you use 23° as the maximum elongation angle. It comes to 0.39 AU.

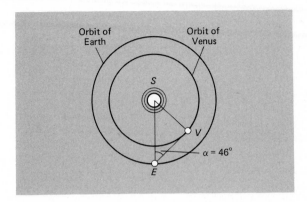

1

Determining the distance of Venus from the sun in the Copernican model. From the earth at the time of greatest elongation, Venus makes an angle (α) of about 46° from the sun. The line of sight from the earth then touches tangent to the orbit of Venus. So a radius of Venus's orbit drawn to this point makes a right triangle, with one side the sun–Venus distance (SV) and the other the earth–sun distance (SE).

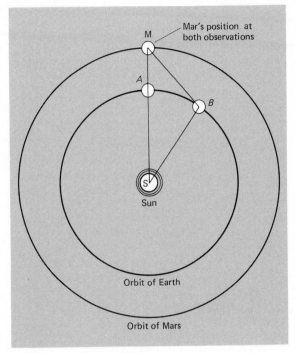

2

Finding the distance of Mars from the sun in the Copernican model. Start with the earth at (A) and Mars (M) at opposition. Wait one sidereal period of Mars. Then Mars returns to the same place (M) in its orbit (as seen from the sun), but the earth has gone around once and almost twice (B). The line of sight from the earth to Mars crosses the Martian orbit at the same spot that the earlier one did (from A). Suppose this diagram is drawn to scale where the earth–sun distance equals 1. Then the distance from earth to Mars is known to this scale because all the angles are known.

Note that one observation for each of the inner planets establishes their distances from the sun (relative to the earth–sun distance) in the heliocentric model.

For the outer planets the method of finding their distances is less direct. Let me use Mars as a specific example. Start with some alignment of the earth and Mars (A in Fig. 2). Wait until one sidereal period of Mars has passed so that it returns to the same position in its orbit relative to the stars as seen from the sun. (Remember that you can derive the sidereal period from the observed synodic period in the Copernican model; see Focus 7). The earth has gone around more than one sidereal period (position B in Fig. 2). Triangulate the position of Mars from the two observations by extending your lines of sight for both; where the two lines intersect is the position of Mars (M in Fig. 2).

Suppose that you have drawn an accurate scale diagram; then if the earth–sun distance is 1 AU, you can measure the earth–Mars distance in AU's from the diagram. Or you can solve for the side EM using trigonometry, because you know all the angles in the triangle MSB. A similar approach applies to the other outer planets. The distances found by these methods (Table 3.1) are fixed by the planetary periods and geometry of the heliocentric model.

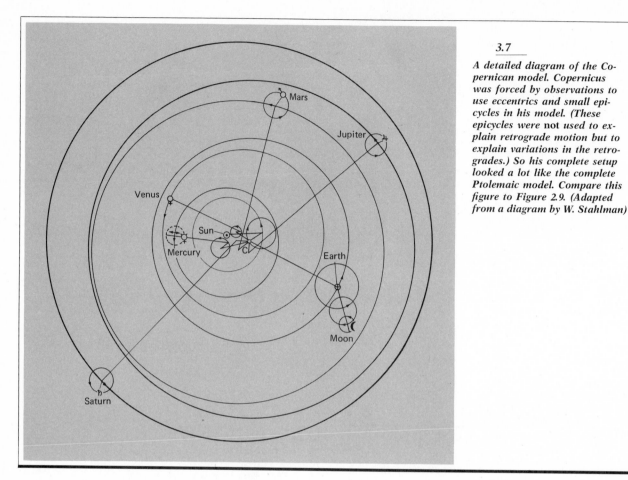

3.7

A detailed diagram of the Co-pernican model. Copernicus was forced by observations to use eccentrics and small epi-cycles in his model. (These epicycles were not used to ex-plain retrograde motion but to explain variations in the retro-grades.) So his complete setup looked a lot like the complete Ptolemaic model. Compare this figure to Figure 2.9. (Adapted from a diagram by W. Stahlman)

Problems with the heliocentric model /
Copernicus eliminated the epicycles as an expla-nation of retrograde motion and at the same time removed equants from the system. How-ever, in practice the heliocentric model pre-dicted planetary positions no better than that of Ptolemy. In fact, the heliocentric model was not even simpler than the Ptolemaic one, judged by a simple count of circles. Although Copernicus eliminated five circles that had been required for retrograde motion, he had to introduce smaller ones to replace the equants. The actual Copernican model came out somewhat more complicated than the original model of Ptolemy (Fig. 3.7).

Copernicus also sidestepped an important issue: that his system violated Aristotelian phys-ics. He did not refute Aristotle's views in detail. A new physics to support his model still needed development. Copernicus had only provided a new geometrical model, not a physical one.

Warning: Do not fall into the trap of think-ing that the Copernican model included a force between the sun and the planets. *It did not.* The planetary motions resulted from the natural motions of the celestial spheres: uniform and circular. As in the Ptolemaic system, they did not require a force.

The impact of the heliocentric model /
Although Copernicus's claims clashed with those of the scholastic scientists and Christian theolo-gians, some astronomers in the middle of the sixteenth century tested the new setup of the planets. Astronomers knew that the *Alfonsine Tables* contained some inaccurate predictions of planetary conjunctions.

Foremost among those willing to try the new techniques was Erasmus Reinhold, the pro-fessor at Wittenberg who had encouraged Rheticus to visit Copernicus. Reinhold quickly calculated planetary position tables based on the Copernican model, which were adopted by almanac makers. These were called the *Prutenic Tables.* However, Reinhold did not swing whole-heartedly to the heliocentric model. Reinhold was not a wholly convinced Copernican; he saw the system as a geometrical model rather than as reality.

As noted earlier, the Copernican model did *not* predict planetary positions any better than an updated Ptolemaic model. Why not? Because Copernicus held to circular, uniform motion. As a result, his model came out similar to the Ptolemaic one, with the change that the sun and not the earth was at the center. What astronomer would switch if the new system offered no obvious advantages?

If astronomers did not rush to accept the sun-centered universe, why did Copernicus bother to develop the idea at all? Certainly, he was strongly motivated by aesthetic reasons; he saw a new harmony in the "design of the universe and fixed symmetry of its parts" that was "pleasing to the mind." The "fixed symmetry" referred to the fact that in the Copernican system the spacing and order of the planets are fixed by observation; in the Ptolemaic system each planet's circles could be treated independently of the others.

In addition, Copernicus may have arrived at a heliocentric model for geometrical reasons. He seems to have believed in the reality of the celestial spheres (Fig. 3.2) and found that a heliocentric rather than a geocentric layout would allow these solid spheres to nest without banging into one another.

3.8

A portrait of Tycho Brahe. He is shown here with the coats of arms of other noble Danish families. Note that two of these are "Rosencrantz" and "Gildenstern." A young playwright in England, William Shakespeare, probably saw this portrait and used these names for characters in **Hamlet.**

3.2

Tycho Brahe: First master of astronomical measurement

Tycho Brahe (1546–1601) rejected the heliocentric model on both physical and observational grounds. He proposed an alternative cosmological model that was a compromise of the classical geocentric universe and the Copernican one. His work is infused with the attitudes of a typical professional astronomer at the time just after the publication of *De revolutionibus;* it emphasizes the fact that the reality of the Copernican cosmology escaped the astronomers of the day, who saw the heliocentric model as merely a geometrical device.

Tycho Brahe (Fig. 3.8) was born in Denmark into a family of noble standing. While Tycho was a child, his uncle, who had no children and wanted an heir, stole him from his parents, supported the boy, and decided that his adopted son should become a lawyer. Young Tycho was sent off with a private tutor to study law in Germany, but he secretly worked on astronomy, spent his allowance on astronomy books, and crept out at night to make observations.

When Tycho returned to Copenhagen he lectured on astrology, a subject in which he had a deep interest. His fame as an astronomer reached the Danish court. Since he seemed destined to be a bright star in the astronomical world, Tycho appeared to deserve royal support.

At about this time a new star, or *nova*, burst into view in November 1572 in the constellation Cassiopeia. (Today we know that a nova is a star normally too faint to be conspicuous that suddenly increases in brightness many times so that it becomes visible to the naked eye. Such an apparently new star is called a *nova* from the Latin *stella nova*, "new star." In the case of Tycho's new star, the event marked an extreme outburst now called a *supernova*.) The nova was so bright that it could be seen in the daytime. Tycho used this rare event in a remarkable way, collecting observations of the nova from all over Europe and showing that the new star occupied the same position in the constellation from all observation points; the nova did not have an observable shift in position and was consequently a great distance from the earth. This observation directly contradicted the Aristotelian cosmos, which required that all changes in the sky take place within the orbit of the moon. Tycho's positioning of the new star beyond the moon collided with the doctrine that the heavens must be immutable.

Tycho's work on the nova of 1572 catapulted him to fame and persuaded King Frederick II of Denmark to make him an offer he could not refuse: his own observatory on an island site over which Tycho would rule as feudal master. The king gave Tycho the use of the island Hveen across the water from Hamlet's castle at Elsinore. With royal funds—estimated by him to be more than a ton of gold—Tycho constructed on Hveen the first modern research observatory (Fig. 3.9): Uraniborg, Castle of the Heavens. Here he worked in grand style; he had the finest observing equipment (much of which he designed himself) and a bevy of assistants, as well as his own paper mill to provide the paper for his own printing press, which published his observations (along with some of his inspired poetry). In the basement Tycho placed an extensive wine cellar for the entertainment of visiting dignitaries.

Convinced that the classical geocentric model was untenable, Tycho devised his own, which retained the earth's central position. Although Tycho viewed the Copernican model simply as a geometrical model to describe planetary motions, he took very seriously Copernicus's dictum that all celestial motions must be

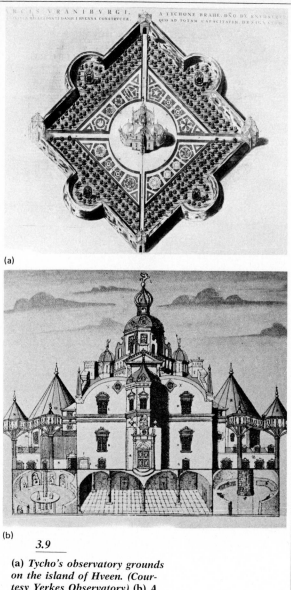

(a)

(b)

3.9

(a) *Tycho's observatory grounds on the island of Hveen. (Courtesy Yerkes Observatory) (b) A close-up of Uraniborg, the first modern astronomical research observatory.*

uniform and circular. Yet Tycho could not accept the revolution of the earth around the sun, for he thought that "the earth, that hulking, lazy body," was "unfit for a motion as quick as that of the ethereal torches." Consequently, Tycho's model was geocentric, but geometrically identical to the Copernican system—all that changed was the center of motion (Fig. 3.10). In Tycho's model the moon and sun revolve around the earth, but all the planets revolve around the sun.

Tycho also had an observational objection to a heliocentric model. With his precision instruments he tried to measure an annual heliocentric parallax (Focus 4) but failed to detect it.

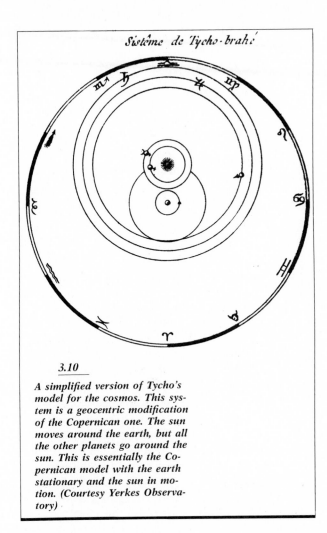

Sistème de Tycho-brahé

3.10

A simplified version of Tycho's model for the cosmos. This system is a geocentric modification of the Copernican one. The sun moves around the earth, but all the other planets go around the sun. This is essentially the Copernican model with the earth stationary and the sun in motion. (Courtesy Yerkes Observatory)

Tycho's equipment could pick up an angular change of as little as 1′ (that's about $\frac{1}{30}$ the angular diameter of the full moon). The lack of a detectable parallax of at least 1′ fortified Tycho's belief that the Copernican model was invalid.

Tycho's main contribution to astronomy was not his planetary model but rather his extensive collection of observations of planetary positions. He made a careful effort to observe planetary positions to the limit of naked-eye ability, at the times of importance—such as during retrograde motion—and also at intermediate times. For the first time in astronomical history a continuous record (1576–1597) was compiled of precise planetary positions.

When Frederick II died, Tycho fell from royal favor because of his despotic ways. He therefore moved with his servants and equip-

ment to Prague, to work for Emperor Rudolph of Bohemia. Here he took on the young Johannes Kepler as an assistant to do theoretical work. When Tycho died in 1601, an era in astronomy ended. A new one began when Kepler created a new astronomy based on Tycho's observations.

3.3

Johannes Kepler and the cosmic harmonies

Despite its heroic shifting of the earth and the sun, the Copernican system was conservative in its intent: to develop a model of planetary motions more in line with classical ideas (uniform, circular motion) than the Ptolemaic model. Copernicus accomplished this goal, but his model ended up no less complicated than Ptolemy's. Also, the Copernican model lacked a basis in physics, which the Ptolemaic model had. The heliocentric model of this time was more geometrical than physical.

Johannes Kepler (1571–1630) forged the new ideas for planetary motion that form the foundations of modern concepts about the nature of the planetary orbits (Fig. 3.11). Kepler made the Copernican world a truly heliocentric one, with the sun cast in a central, *physical* role that is absent from the geometrical plan of *De revolutionibus*. Kepler was the first astronomer to understand that the sun determines the planetary orbits by some physical force. He injected key physics into the heliocentric model and also perfected its usefulness for planetary predictions.

The harmonies of the spheres / Kepler was born about 400 years ago; the date was December 27, 1571, and the place was the small town of Weil der Stadt (near modern Stuttgart, in southwestern Germany). Kepler worked out the time and date of his conception, 4:37 A.M. on May 16, 1571, because he considered it the important date in the casting of his own horoscope. (Remember that in Kepler's day astronomy and astrology were considered one discipline. Much of the duty of a professional astronomer at the time concerned astrological matters.)

In 1589 Kepler entered the University of Tübingen, where his superior mental ability was formally recognized by the school senate. After

3.12

The orbits of Jupiter and Saturn, drawn around a triangle. The ratio of the radii of the circles is almost the same as that for Jupiter and Saturn in the Copernican model.

3.11

Johannes Kepler. "Astronomy has two ends, to save the appearances and to contemplate the true form of the edifice of the world." (Courtesy O. Gingerich)

achieving his B.A. and M.A. degrees, Kepler enrolled in the three-year theological program with the intention of becoming a Lutheran clergyman. In his last year as a theology student he was selected to replace the teacher of mathematics in the Protestant high school in Graz, Austria. Since Kepler was a scholarship student, he was at the bidding of the duke, who in consultation with the Tübingen faculty decided that young Kepler was the suitable man for the job.

His fame as an astronomer began accidentally. One day while teaching, Kepler was struck by the most compelling insight of his life. He had drawn a series of triangles within two circles while explaining to his students the conjunctions of Jupiter and Saturn. As he inscribed the triangles, he noticed that the radius of the inner circles was half that of the outer circle (Fig. 3.12): a ratio that almost equaled the ratio

of the distances of Jupiter and Saturn from the sun. The geometrical ratio is 2 to 1, and the distance ratio is 1.83 to 1. He found this result exciting, for Saturn was the first planet in from the sphere of stars and the triangle is the first (simplest because it has only three sides) plane figure. He thought he had found a geometrical design of the solar system.

Kepler felt he could use this idea to support the Copernican model. While at Tübingen he had been taught astronomy by Michael Maestlin, one of the first people to read *De revolutionibus* carefully. Although Maestlin did not actively promote the Copernican cosmology, he did refer to Copernicus and used some of the tables from *De revolutionibus*. Kepler apparently was excited by the harmonies he found in the new model, which he quickly adopted in his thinking.

One of these harmonies appears in the spacing of the planets and their sidereal periods (Focus sections 7 and 8). Copernicus had not offered an explanation of this relationship. Kepler thought he could: Perhaps a geometrical layout determined the planetary spacings. For three days he worked without solving the problem. Then he realized that the model was actually three-dimensional rather than two-dimensional and so required solid rather than plane figures. From classical geometry Kepler knew that only five regular solids (Fig. 3.13)—solid figures with all faces having the same kind of regular polygons—were possible. The known planets numbered six, separated by five spaces. Kepler thought the five solids might be used to establish the planetary spacings and worked out the details of nesting the solids and spheres (Fig. 3.14). The finished scheme placed the planets in spheres at distances within a few percent of the

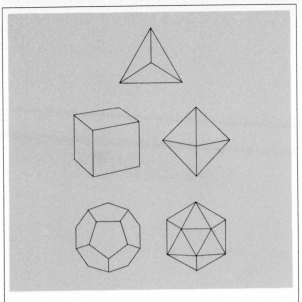

3.13

The five regular solids. These are the only possible solid figures made with faces of regular polygons.

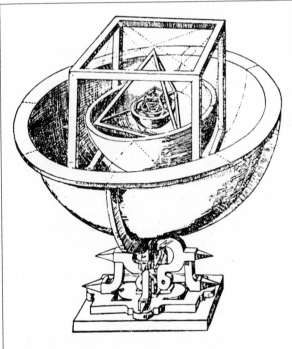

3.14

Kepler's model for the spacing of the planets. During Kepler's time six planets were known, so five spaces existed between them. Kepler knew that only five regular solids exist (Fig. 3.13). He believed that some arrangement of these solids could explain the spacing of the planets in the heliocentric system. (Courtesy O. Gingerich)

accepted ones at the time. Kepler's intuitive—but wrong—insight resulted in a geometrical, heliocentric structure for the solar system. This geometrical framework energized much of Kepler's study of planetary motions and led to lasting results.

Excitedly, Kepler wrote to his former teacher Maestlin, telling him of both the spacing system and another idea: that the sun in the middle of the universe must have some power or force to propel the planets around in their orbits. This view seemed reasonable to him because Mercury, for example, moves faster in its orbit than Venus, and so on. Although Kepler failed to work out the situation mathematically, the idea was firmly implanted in his mind.

In 1594 he published the result of his work in the *Mysterium cosmographicum* (*The Cosmic Mystery*), which announced the details of his geometrical system and asserted his adherence to the Copernican model—the first such printed treatise by any professional astronomer. His intuition that the sun physically directs the planetary motions both justified the Copernican scheme and set the stage for the next development of astronomy in terms of physical laws.

The battle with Mars / In his foreword to the *Mysterium cosmographicum*, Maestlin expressed his appreciation of the new cosmos and his hope that it might soon be tested by comparison with actual observations. Kepler was somewhat insulted by this remark, for he thought that his blueprint explained the observations adequately. However, he did think that he needed better observations to determine the thickness of the spherical shells. To obtain them Kepler turned to the foremost observer of the day: Tycho Brahe.

Tycho had read Kepler's *Mysterium cosmographicum* and although he did not like its mystical approach to astronomy, recognized it as the work of a genius. When he received Kepler's request, Tycho did not honor it, for he felt reluctant to send his hard-earned observations to a believer in the Copernican model. However, he did invite Kepler to discuss the matter personally. Tycho had left Denmark for Prague, and Kepler traveled there to meet him.

Kepler and Tycho met on February 4, 1600, an encounter that was fateful to Kepler and to the history of modern science. During the next ten months the personalities of these two men clashed so strongly that they accomplished little astronomical work.

One night while at a party with a baron, Tycho drank too much. Because it was considered impolite to take leave during the affair, Tycho was not able to relieve himself and suffered a prostate infection, which resulted in his death. In the few days before he died, Tycho urged Kepler to justify his cosmological model from Tycho's observations. Upon Tycho's death, Kepler was promoted to Tycho's position. Kepler was allowed access to the unpublished observational records, but Tycho's heirs believed them to have some financial value and so reserved censorship rights. After some bargaining with the heirs, Kepler attacked the problem of the orbit of Mars.

Kepler worked for four years on the motions of Mars. Starting with a heliocentric scheme that used a circular orbit with an equant and an eccentric, Kepler fitted Tycho's observations within 2′ along the ecliptic. However, the predictions of the planet's position above or below the ecliptic were wide of the mark. This discrepancy struck Kepler as important, for he realized that the planetary orbits must be viewed in three dimensions. He then moved the center of the earth's orbit and found that he correctly predicted the positions above and below the ecliptic, but not along it, where he was off by 8′. Kepler was dissatisfied with the result, for he knew that Tycho's observations were accurate to 1′. He had nevertheless discovered that the plane of the earth's orbit (and eventually of the other planetary orbits as well) passed through the sun. The discovery marked a critical prelude to Kepler's recognition of the other laws of planetary motion, for it gave the sun a special status in the solar system.

Kepler sought a single physical explanation for planetary motion driven by the sun. What force did the sun use to keep the planets in their orbits? Influenced by William Gilbert's work *De magnete*, Kepler envisioned the sun as a fountain of magnetic force that directed the motion of the planets in their orbits. Such an idea required that a planet move fastest in its orbit when it was closest to the sun.

Using the observations of Tycho, Kepler then returned to the Martian orbit and applied

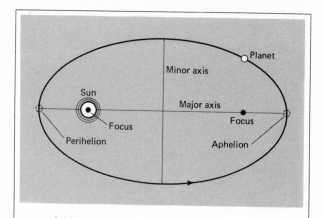

3.15

Kepler's first law. This law states that the shape of the planetary orbits is elliptical (shown here greatly exaggerated), with the sun located at one focus of the ellipse on the major axis. When a planet is farthest from the sun, it is at the aphelion point in its orbit; when closest, at perihelion.

his magnetic-force analysis to find that it worked *if* the true orbit of Mars were *elliptical* (Focus 9) rather than circular. He wrote, "With reasoning derived from physical principles agreeing with experience, there is no figure left for the orbit of the planet except a perfect ellipse." By this process Kepler found the first two of his famous three laws of planetary motion which rested on a physical explanation of the accurate observations of Tycho.

Kepler's laws of planetary motion / Kepler's fame today rests primarily on his three laws of planetary motion, yet these laws were but small fragments in his wider search for harmonies in the physics of celestial motions.

In modern terminology Kepler's laws are:

Law 1. **Law of Ellipses (1609).**   The orbit of each planet is an ellipse, with the sun located at one focus (Fig. 3.15). The other focus is located in space and not centered on any body. Note that the distance from the sun to the planet varies as the planet moves along its elliptical orbit.

Law 2. **Law of Equal Areas (1609).**   The line drawn from the planet to the sun sweeps out equal areas in equal times.

focus 9

PROPERTIES OF ELLIPSES

*Ellipses are geometrically related to circles, so their basic properties are fairly easy to understand. You can make an ellipse by taking a loop of string and holding it down to a board with two tacks. Keeping the string taut with a pencil held against it, draw a curve around the tacks. That curve is an ellipse (Fig. 1). The two tacks mark the two **foci** of the ellipse. Each point on the ellipse has the property that the sum of its distances from the two foci (F_1 to P and F_2 to P in Fig. 1) is the same.*

*The line through the foci to both sides of the ellipse (R_a to R_p) is called the **major axis**. Half this length is the **semimajor axis**, usually designated by a. So the major axis has length 2a. The distance from the center of the ellipse to a focus is designated c; so the distance between the two foci is 2c.*

*How much an ellipse differs from a circle (how "squashed" it looks) is defined as an ellipse's **eccentricity**. Imagine you took the two tacks at the foci and moved them closer together. The ellipse would become more circular. When the two tacks are exactly together, in fact, the ellipse becomes a circle. Its eccentricity then is zero. As the two tacks are moved farther apart, the eccentricity will increase until the tacks sit close to the opposite ends of the major axis. The eccentricity is then nearly one. Note that the eccentricity increases as the distance between the foci does. To define it exactly, the eccentricity, e, is*

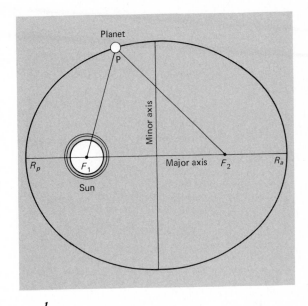

1

An ellipse. Note that the sum of the distances of any point on the ellipse from the two foci (F_1 and F_2) is a constant.

$$e = \frac{c}{a}$$

*If the sun is imagined at one focus (F_1) of a planet's orbit, then R_p, the closest point to the sun, is the **perihelion** point in the orbit. The perihelion distance R_pF_1 is $a - c = a - ae = a(1 - e)$. R_a, the farthest point from the sun, is the **aphelion** point. The aphelion distance R_aF_1 is $a + c = a + ae = a(1 + e)$. Finally, a is also the average distance of a point moving on the ellipse from one of the foci. So when applied to planetary orbits, a is the average distance of a planet from the sun.*

Law 2 notes that the orbital velocities are nonuniform but vary in a regular fashion: The farther a planet is from the sun, the more slowly it moves in its orbit (Fig. 3.16).

Law 3. **Harmonic Law (1618).** The square of the period of a planet is directly proportional to the cube of the planet's average distance from the sun (Fig. 3.17). Law 3 points out that planets move more slowly, in a predictable fashion, the greater their distance from the sun is, a fact implying that any sun–planet force decreases with distance.

The preceding dates are those of publication, not of discovery.

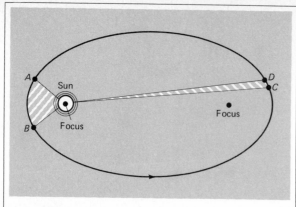

3.16

Kepler's second law. The second law describes the varying orbital speed of a planet in an elliptical orbit around the sun. Consider two equal periods of time: one when the planet is closest to the sun (AB) and one when it is farther away (CD). At AB the planet–sun distance is shorter, so the planet moves faster in its orbit. At CD the planet moves more slowly because it is farther from the sun. In both cases the areas (shaded regions AB to the sun and CD to the sun) covered by a line drawn from the planet to the sun are equal.

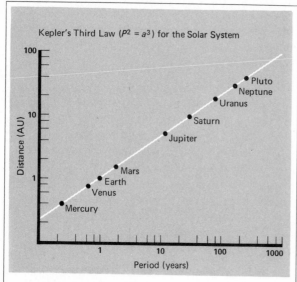

3.17

Kepler's third law. Kepler specifies in his third law a relationship between a planet's orbital period around the sun and its average distance from the sun. This diagram shows for each presently known planet a plot of its orbital period (in years) squared to its distance (in astronomical units) cubed. Note how closely these values fall to the line expected from Kepler's third law.

Kepler discovered Law 2 before Law 1, when he was grappling with the orbit of Mars and the observations of Tycho Brahe. Even before finding Law 2, Kepler had arrived at the crucial conclusion that the planes of all the planetary orbits pass through the sun. This discovery set the stage for Law 1.

Algebraically, the third law may be written

$$P^2 = ka^3$$

If P is the period of the planet's revolution about the sun in years and a is the average distance from the sun in AU's, then the constant k is equal to 1. *An example:* Mars has an average distance of 1.5 AU from the sun. How long does it take Mars to orbit the sun once? *Solution:*

$$P^2 = (1.5)^3 = 3.4$$
$$P = (3.4)^{1/2} = 1.8 \text{ years}$$

Note that the third law applies to *any* body—even a spacecraft—in orbit around the sun.

For orbits of bodies around objects other than the sun, the constant k has a different value that depends on the units chosen for a and P, and also on the central body. (This dependence is discussed in Chapter 4.)

What do these laws mean? They describe all the essential features of planetary motion. The first law points out that the shape of the planetary orbits is elliptical, so a planet's distance from the sun varies (Fig. 3.1). The second law notes that as a planet's distance varies, so does its orbital speed: The closer a planet is to the sun, the faster it goes. You get the sense that the sun pulls a planet toward it, that the planet whips around the sun, and then the sun slows the planet down as it moves away again. The third law says that the farther a planet's orbit is from the sun, the slower its average orbital motion will be. Both the second and third laws imply that the force between the sun and planets is weaker at greater distances, as you'd expect intuitively. Hidden in the third law is an exact description of how the sun–planet force works, how it weakens with distance, but Kepler was not able to figure it out. Not long after Kepler, Isaac Newton (Chapter 4) solved this final puzzle about the ancient problem of the motion of the planets (Section 4.2).

The new astronomy / As he announced in his *Astronomia nova* (*New Astronomy*) in 1609, Kepler had, in his opinion, developed an astron-

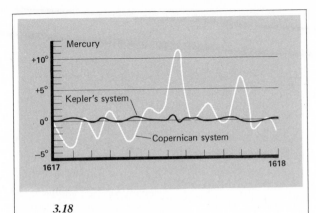

3.18

The accuracy of predictions of planetary positions compared. This diagram shows the difference between the predicted position and the actual position of Mercury in Kepler's model (one of heliocentric, elliptical orbits) and the Copernican model. Note that in the Copernican model the error could be as large as 10°. For Kepler's scheme the error is no more than 1°. (Courtesy O. Gingerich and B. Welther)

omy based not only on geometry but also on physical causes. With the discovery of the ellipse as the shape of the planetary orbits, he satisfied both the observations of Tycho Brahe and his own conviction that the dance of the planets could be conducted by some physical cause. From this approach Kepler calculated the *Rudolphine Tables* (1627), which supplanted both the *Prutenic Tables* based on the Copernican system and the venerable *Alfonsine Tables* calculated from the Ptolemaic system. The *Rudolphine Tables* completely revised the previously shoddy science of theoretical astronomy where a few degrees of error were considered quite accurate. Kepler's predictions were far more accurate than any earlier ones, whether based on the Copernican or the Ptolemaic model (Fig. 3.18).

Kepler broke the ancient spell cast by the idea of perfect circles and uniform motion that had mesmerized astronomers for over 2000 years. Out of Pythagorean and Neoplatonic motivations, Johannes Kepler rewove the fabric of the heavens into a pattern that proclaimed the end of an ancient era and the birth of astronomy as a modern science.

SUMMARY

This chapter covered a crucial episode in the evolution of astronomy. Copernicus, in a return to traditional Greek ideas, attacked the Ptolemaic model and replaced it with a heliocentric one. Copernicus apparently presented his new cosmology on aesthetic grounds, for his model was "pleasing to the mind," because it placed the sun in its appropriate central position in the universe, described celestial motions as uniform without equants, and established a natural order of the planets from the sun based on their increasing sidereal periods, which resulted in a simple explanation of retrograde motion.

But the Copernican model had no direct observational support, for it required a heliocentric parallax that was not observed and predicted planetary positions with no more accuracy than the Ptolemaic model. In addition, the motions of the earth violated the essentials of the physics of the day. Note that from naked-eye observations alone (those described in Chapter 1), you cannot decide between Copernicus's heliocentric and Ptolemy's geocentric model.

*Tycho Brahe's observational legacy formed the basis of Kepler's transformation of the Copernican model into a physical cosmology. Copernicus's model lacked a physical basis and predicted planetary positions no better than Ptolemy's model; so in terms of scientific model making it had two critical weak points. Kepler shored up both: His elliptical orbits led to more accurate positions, and his goal of physical causes invested the sun with an active role in keeping the planets in their places. Although Kepler's use of magnetic forces later proved unworkable, his demand for physical explanations resulted in a cosmological model closely tied to observations. Kepler was driven to find a force whirling the planets around in part because of his discovery that the orbits were, in fact, elliptical. **Such shapes ruled out any model of nesting material spheres to carry around the planets.***

The overt connection of a model with reality as defined by observations lies at the heart of modern scientific explanations. Kepler stands out as the first to require such an interlocking, the first to pull together astronomy and cosmology with the rope of physical laws. (See Table 3.2.)

TABLE 3.2 *A comparison of the Ptolemaic (P), Copernican (C), and Keplerian Models (K)*

Observed "fact"	Explanation
Motion of entire heavens daily from E to W	**P:** Motion of all heavenly spheres E to W **C:** Reflection of rotation of earth W to E **K:** Same
Annual motion of sun W to E through zodiac	**P:** Rotation of sun's sphere W to E in a year **C:** Reflection of annual revolution of earth about sun **K:** Same
Nonuniform motion of sun through zodiac	**P:** Orbit of sun eccentric, speed uniform **C:** Orbit of earth eccentric, speed uniform **K:** Orbit of planet elliptical, speed nonuniform
Retrograde motions of the planets	**P:** Epicycles and deferents **C:** Relative motions of planets, including earth, around sun **K:** Same
Variations in retrograde motions	**P:** Equant, eccentrics **C:** Epicyclets **K:** Nonuniform orbital motion; tilt of planetary orbits with respect to earth's
Distances of planets	**P:** Arbitrary as long as angular relationships correct **C:** Relative distances set by observations **K:** Force relates distances to periods
"Cause" of planetary motions	**P:** Natural motion of celestial spheres; *no force* **C:** Same, *no force* **K:** Magnetic *force* from sun
Accuracy of predictions	**P:** Typically 5° or less; sometimes 10° **C:** Same **K:** Generally about 10'; sometimes as large as 1°.

STUDY EXERCISES

1. What was Copernicus's *primary* objection to the Ptolemaic system? (*Objective 1*)

2. How did Copernicus account for retrograde motion in his system? (*Objective 2*)

3. If you were on Mars, under what astronomical circumstances would you see Jupiter retrograde? the earth? (*Objective 2*)

4. What is the difference between a planet's *synodic* and *sidereal* periods? How can sidereal periods be found from synodic periods? (*Objective 3*)

5. In *your* opinion, what was the major advantage—if any—of the Copernican model over the Ptolemaic one? (*Objectives 1 and 4*)

6. What *force* keeps the planets moving in the Copernican system? (*Objectives 6 and 8*)

7. Give at least two differences between the models of Copernicus and Kepler. (*Objective 8*)

8. What advantages did Kepler's model have over that of Copernicus? (*Objective 8*)

9. Compare the motion of a planet on an elliptical orbit to that on an eccentric circle. Are they very similar or different? (*Objectives 7 and 8*)

BEYOND THIS BOOK . . .

For an excellent analysis of the work of Copernicus and the framework of Western thought in which he developed, read *The Copernican Revolution* (Vintage Books, New York, 1959) by T. Kuhn.

For a modern variety of views about Copernicus and the impact of his work, try *The Nature of Scientific Discovery* (Smithsonian Institution Press, Washington, D.C., 1975), edited by O. Gingerich.

An excellent autobiography of Tycho Brahe is *Tycho Brahe: A Picture of Scientific Life and Work in the Sixteenth Century* (Dover, New York, 1963) by J. L. E. Dreyer.

A fine biography of Kepler is in *Kepler* (Collier Books, New York, 1962) by M. Casper, translated by C. D. Hellman. A technical look at Kepler's work can be found in *An Account of the Astronomical Discoveries of Kepler* (University of Wisconsin Press, Madison, Wisc., 1963) by R. Small.

You can try to tackle a controversial view of Copernicus, Tycho Brahe, Kepler, and Galileo in *The Sleepwalkers* (Grosset & Dunlap, New York, 1963) by A. Koestler; in particular, read part III, "The Timid Canon," and part IV, "The Watershed."

Volume 16 of Great Books of the Western World (Encyclopaedia Britannica, Chicago, 1952) contains a translation of Copernicus's *De revolutionibus.*

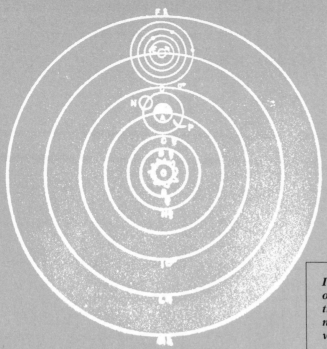

I am much occupied with the investigation of physical causes. My aim in this is to show that the celestial machine is to be likened not to a divine organism, but rather a clockwork . . .

JOHANNES KEPLER

The clockwork universe

4

LEARNING OBJECTIVES

After studying this chapter you should be able to:

1. Describe Galileo's important telescopic discoveries and their impact on the controversy between the Copernican and Ptolemaic systems.

2. Indicate Galileo's purpose in developing a new science of terrestrial motions.

3. Contrast Galileo's astronomy and cosmology to that of Copernicus and Kepler.

4. Describe the difference between accelerated and unaccelerated motion.

5. Cite Newton's three laws of motion and describe each in simple terms using specific examples.

6. Contrast Newton's concept of natural motion to that of Aristotle.

7. With the aid of a graph, describe Newton's law of gravitation.

8. Outline how the moon-apple test confirms Newton's law of gravitation.

9. Contrast Newton's cosmology to that of Copernicus.

10. Use Newton's physical ideas to support a Copernican model.

What makes the world go 'round? For people it may be love. For the planets—according to Isaac Newton—it's inertia and gravitation. Newton achieved the goal that had eluded Kepler: a mechanical model of the cosmos run by a single physical force. Newton saw the force of gravitation as the prime mover in the clockwork universe.

Newton accomplished his great achievement after important groundwork had been laid by Copernicus, Kepler, and Galileo. Copernicus made a crucial move in placing the sun, rather than the earth, at the center of the universe. To displace the earth, Copernicus had to violate the physics of his day and offered no clear substitute. Kepler, motivated by mystical insights, sought to establish a clockwork cosmos driven by a single force. In his choice of a magnetic force he failed. But his demand for a force from the sun to drive the planets in their orbits directly influenced Newton's vision. Galileo recognized that the Copernican model needed a new physics to back it up. He searched for new physical laws by studying the motion of falling bodies near the earth. Galileo did describe the effects of gravity, but he never extended these ideas from the earth to the heavens.

Newton erased the old separation of the earth and heavens. He linked gravity—terrestrial physics—to the orbital motion of the planets—celestial physics. The links he forged were his laws of motion and gravitation.

With Newton's ideas the universe took on a new appearance. No more the closed, finite universe of Ptolemy and Copernicus. In Newton's vision the universe grew to an infinite expanse, driven by a single force: *gravitation.*

4.1

Galileo: Advocate of the heliocentric model

The Italian scientist Galileo Galilei (1565–1642) desired to establish celestial physics on a firm experimental and mathematical basis. In contrast to Kepler, Galileo (Fig. 4.1) was concerned almost exclusively with terrestrial motions, especially those of falling bodies. He felt that to establish the laws of terrestrial motions would do more to cement the structure of the Copernican model than any observations—including those made with a telescope. He failed to achieve this

4.1

Galileo Galilei. "By denying scientific principles, one may maintain any paradox." (Courtesy Yerkes Observatory)

goal, but his discoveries guided Newton's later work.

The amazing telescope / Galileo used his telescope to bolster the Copernican model. He did *not* invent optical lenses or their use in a telescope but he did vastly improve them. And he promoted his astronomical ideas by utilizing the novelty and shock value of telescopic observations. The report of his observations in *Siderius nuncius (The Starry Messenger)* was popularly circulated and brought him a wide public reputation.

By Galileo's time, glass lenses had been known for about 300 years. Their date and place of origin are not clear, but they were used by eyeglass makers to correct defects of vision. The opticians of the day had no physical understanding of how their glasses functioned and had adopted a purely experimental approach to their construction.

In 1609 a messenger returning to Venice brought Galileo the news that a Dutchman had constructed a spyglass that made distant objects appear to be nearby. Although Galileo had little

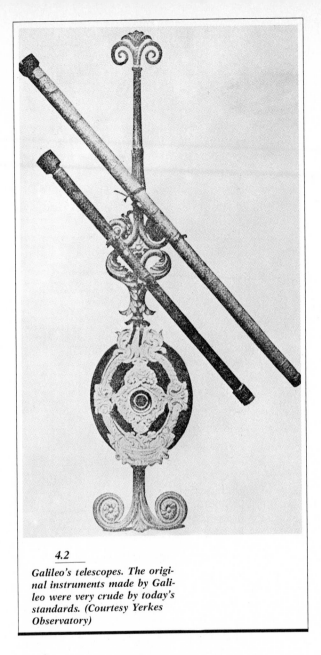

4.2

Galileo's telescopes. The original instruments made by Galileo were very crude by today's standards. (Courtesy Yerkes Observatory)

4.3

Galileo's drawings of the moon as seen through his telescope. (Courtesy Yerkes Observatory)

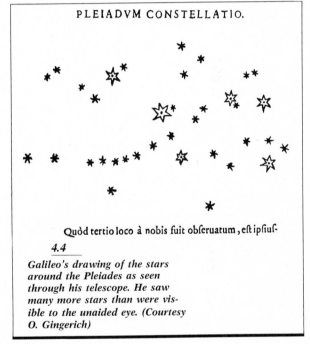

PLEIADVM CONSTELLATIO.

Quòd tertio loco à nobis fuit obſeruatum, eſt ipſiuſ-

4.4

Galileo's drawing of the stars around the Pleiades as seen through his telescope. He saw many more stars than were visible to the unaided eye. (Courtesy O. Gingerich)

experience with optics, he set to work immediately in his workshop to duplicate the instrument (Fig. 4.2). Sparing neither labor nor expense, he succeeded in constructing an optical device that made objects appear thirty times closer than when viewed with the naked eye (Chapter 6). He then put this marvelous tube to astronomical use. Within a few weeks in 1609 and 1610 he made a series of astronomical discoveries that marked a new era in astronomy. Although Galileo was not the first person to build a telescope, he first recognized that the telescope increased our power to perceive reality.

Galileo first observed the moon. He saw that the moon's surface was not smooth and

spherical, as Aristotelian ideas required, but rough, with chains of mountains and valleys and many craters (Fig. 4.3). He determined the height of a lunar mountain from the length of its shadow. This height—about 4 mi—was the correct but astonishing result.

Galileo next peered at the stars. His instrument's power fragmented the faint band of the Milky Way into innumerable stars, more than could be seen individually with the unaided eye (Fig. 4.4). This observation refuted the Aristotelian idea that the sky contained only a certain

4.5

Galileo's observations of the moons of Jupiter. The changing positions indicate that they are revolving around Jupiter. (Courtesy Yerkes Observatory)

number of stars whose number could not change.

Then Galileo found what he considered to be his most important discovery: four new "planets" that no one had seen before. What he found were not actually new planets but, rather, the four brightest moons of Jupiter. To his amazement and joy, Galileo found that these four bodies revolved around Jupiter (Fig. 4.5). From continuous observations he estimated the orbital periods of the Jovian satellites. Here he found another argument against the scholastics, for Jupiter and its satellites resembled a miniature solar system. This fact required a second center of revolution in the cosmos, a notion that collided directly with the Aristotelian doctrine that only the center of the universe could be the center of the revolution—that was the earth. This observation vindicated Copernicus's suspicion that there could be other centers of attraction in the universe.

Galileo wrote up these observations in *Siderius nuncius* (*The Starry Messenger*), which was published on March 12, 1610. His telescopic discoveries, especially that of Jupiter's moons, grabbed the public imagination. The book sold as fast as it could be printed; it brought fame to Galileo and a demand for the telescopes produced in his private workshop. However, he was still cautious in print; although he used his observations to demolish the Aristotelian cosmos, he did not openly advocate the Copernican model or support it with his observations.

Critics quickly scorned Galileo's work by suggesting that he was seeing atmospheric phenomena or that the telescope was an instrument of deception rather than perception. Although such arguments seem strange to us today, they appeared reasonable enough to seventeenth-century people on practical grounds. The art of lens making was not far advanced, so many lenses were flawed by ghost images. (Galileo's telescopes produced images that were far inferior to those in a cheap modern telescope.) His opponents said that although Galileo may have honestly reported what he had seen, his observations might have no direct connection with reality.

Galileo, however, was convinced by the regularity of the telescopic phenomena that he was viewing reality and not illusion. In 1611 Kepler, who was well regarded in scientific circles, backed up Galileo with observations of his own and also developed a theory of optics to support the validity of telescopic observations.

Goaded by the opposition to what he considered indisputable facts, Galileo continued to scan the skies for new marvels. By projecting the image of the sun onto a piece of paper, he observed sunspots (Fig. 4.6). From the motions of the spots along the disk he estimated that the sun rotated about once every 27 days. As defects on the supposedly perfect sun, the sunspots dealt another blow to the tenets of the Aristotelian cosmos. In 1613 Galileo published his results in *The Letters on Sunspots* and made his first direct, printed declaration of his belief in the Copernican model.

The new science of mechanics / Despite his observational triumphs, Galileo still felt that the Copernican model lacked the anchor of a physical understanding of motion such as Aristotle had provided for his own system. Kepler had

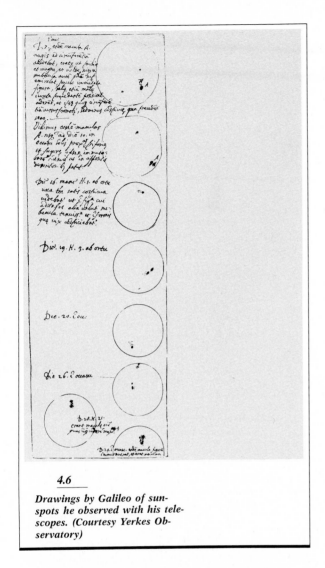

4.6

Drawings by Galileo of sunspots he observed with his telescopes. (Courtesy Yerkes Observatory)

made an important step by his mathematical description of *celestial* motions. Although Galileo ignored most of Kepler's work, he took the next step by devising a mathematical description of *terrestrial* motions, particularly those of bodies falling under the influence of gravity. Galileo aimed to justify the Copernican model by a systematic, experimental search for physical ideas of motion. He unraveled the details of motion produced by applied forces; this study is called *mechanics*. To found the new science of mechanics, Galileo needed an important tool: a description of the motion of falling bodies, that is, the motion of masses under the influence of gravity. But before proceeding with Galileo's contribution to the understanding of motion, let me describe motion more precisely.

Acceleration, velocity, and speed / When you step on a car's accelerator it does just that—accelerates. If you start out at rest, the car goes faster and faster, as you can tell from the speedometer. Or if you are cruising on the highway, you pass a slower car in front of you by stepping on the accelerator. In both instances your velocity changes. That's the essence of acceleration: When your velocity changes you are accelerating.

But what's velocity? It's not simply what you call speed, which tells you how fast you're going. Suppose, for example, that you travel from Albuquerque to Santa Fe, New Mexico; you go from one place to another at some *speed* in some *direction*. Velocity involves direction; you go from one place to another. Speed is how fast you make that trip. For example, if you drive from Albuquerque to Santa Fe, a distance of about 100 km, in one hour, your speed is about 100 km an hour (100 km/h). When you drive back at the same speed, your velocity is different because you're heading in a *different direction*.

Imagine now that you're riding on the outside horse of a merry-go-round. It turns around at a constant speed. Are you accelerating? Yes, because your velocity is constantly changing. How so? The *direction* you're going is constantly changing as you turn around the circle of the merry-go-round. Even though your speed does not change, your direction does. So your velocity is changing, and you must be accelerating.

Of course, you are accelerating if your speed changes while your direction remains the same. And you accelerate if *both* your speed and direction change.

Note that speed and velocity have different technical meanings. *Speed* is the average rate of travel of something and is measured in distance per unit of time—miles per hour (mph), or meters per second (m/sec), for instance. *Velocity* is speed with something added—a direction. *Acceleration* is the rate at which velocity (not speed!) changes. It is measured as a velocity change per unit of time (such as meters per second per second, or m/sec/sec).

Natural motion revisited / One of the nagging problems of Aristotelian physics was that of *inertia*, the tendency of a body forced into motion to retain that motion or of a body at rest to remain at rest; that is, the resistance of a body to changes in its motion. Aristotle had divided motions into two categories: forced and natural (Section 2.3). An example of Aristotelian natural motion is the fall of a rock to the earth—a result of a supposedly natural tendency of earthy material to seek the central point of the cosmos, and it required no force. But the throwing of a rock—a motion at right angles to the natural downward motion—required a continuously acting force to keep up the unnatural, forced motion. However, as you know from playing tennis, baseball, or football, this statement is not strictly true, for after you throw an object, the motion will continue for a while even after the force is removed.

Galileo inverted Aristotle's ideas of natural and forced motion. He concluded that the downward motion of objects resulted from an attractive force—gravity. In addition, he viewed the horizontal motion of objects flying through the air as due to their inertia. This inertial motion, he argued, was a natural one and would continue if no forces, such as air resistance, were applied.

To take this important step, Galileo had to arrive at a description of inertia (Fig. 4.7). He explained his ideas as follows: If a perfectly spherical ball were placed on a hard, flat surface that sloped, the ball would continue to roll down the slope forever if the surface were infinitely large. The greater the slope, the faster the roll. By the same argument, a ball traveling up a slope would eventually stop. If, however, the surface had no slope and the ball were placed on the level with no horizontal velocity, then the ball would remain at rest. A ball on a level surface, if pushed, would continue to move straight ahead at a constant velocity forever, since it is not slowed down by an ascent or speeded up by a descent.

With this concept of inertia, Galileo dealt with the problem of falling bodies. He did not view this motion as natural (as had Aristotle) but as *motion due to a force:* gravity. From a combination of experiments and intuition, Galileo concluded that such motion took place at a constant acceleration, with the object's velocity changing at a constant rate as it fell. (The acceleration due to gravity at the earth's surface has a value of 9.8 m/sec/sec and is usually denoted by *g*. This means that for every second of fall an object gains 9.8 m/sec of velocity.) He also

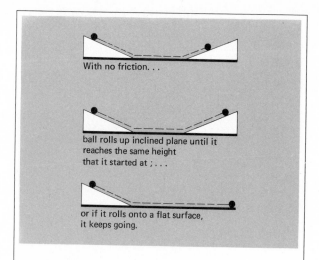

4.7

A demonstration of Galileo's concept of inertia. The trick here is to ignore friction. If you roll a ball down an inclined plane, it will climb up to the same height on another plane with the same slope. Make the angle of the second plane smaller. The ball will have to travel a longer distance to reach the final height. If the ball rolls down the slope onto a flat surface, however, it will just keep rolling along at the same speed. Note that you must ignore the effects of friction, which would slow down the ball's motion.

found that *all* falling masses (not subject to air resistance) have the *same* acceleration. When dropped, they fall the same distance in the same time. This conclusion—that all masses fall with the same acceleration—directly contradicted the scholastic teaching that a heavy body fell faster than a light one and so moved a greater distance in a given time.

You can try the experiment yourself. If you do, use objects of different masses but the same basic shape so that air friction will not confound the results. Apollo astronauts did this experiment on the moon (which has no atmosphere) with a feather and a hammer. Both hit the ground at the same time!

Legend has it that Galileo climbed to the top of the Leaning Tower of Pisa and dropped two different objects, which, to the astonishment of the skeptical professors gathered around the tower's base, hit the ground at the same time. As far as historians can determine, Galileo did *not* actually attempt this experiment, although a friend of his may have. It would have been a risky demonstration, for more likely than not the masses would not have struck the ground simultaneously. The rumored Pisa experiment may not be the only one that Galileo did not do, even though he reported the results in his writings. Some were really mental exercises, but Galileo intuitively reached the correct results most of the time.

The crime of Galileo / Galileo had publicly declared himself a Copernican in 1613. His intellectual vehemence and enthusiasm irritated many of his opponents, some of whom enjoyed substantial power in the Church. In 1616 an official of the Inquisition apparently warned Galileo to stop teaching the Copernican model as truth rather than as a hypothesis (as Osiander had done in his preface to *De revolutionibus*). Galileo's position was held to be contrary to Holy Scripture. At the same time, *De revolutionibus* was placed on the Index of Forbidden Books until "corrections" had been made. (Less than 10 percent of the copies were actually changed.)

These two events, whose implications Galileo did not grasp, initiated a complex chain of events that historians have yet to unravel completely. Galileo, a faithful and obedient Catholic, avoided teaching the Copernican model as true. At the same time, he entered into arguments about scientific truth versus revealed truth. His argumentative spirit promoted his downfall.

In 1623 Cardinal Barberini, a friend of Galileo's and a patron of the sciences, was elected Pope Urban VIII. Galileo thought he saw his chance and had a long audience with the new pope, during which Urban discussed the decree forbidding the heliocentric teachings. Feeling that he had the support of the pope and also of the Jesuit astronomers (many of whom adhered to the Copernican system), Galileo wrote the *Dialogue on the Two Chief World Systems*. With the approval of the Vatican censors, the book was published in 1632, after a few minor corrections had been made. The book supposedly relates an objective debate about the relative merits of the Ptolemaic and Copernican models, with the judgment being rendered in favor of the traditional view. In reality, the text is a thinly veiled polemic supporting the Copernican cosmos, which personally offended Pope Urban VIII.

Immediately Galileo found himself in trouble, for his opponents swiftly countered his claims with theological arguments. The pope himself was incensed because his favorite arguments had been put in the mouth of Simplicio, the supporter of the geocentric viewpoint in the *Dialogue*. (Galileo did not draw Simplicio kindly.) Copies of the book were seized before they left the printers, and the Inquisition summoned Galileo to Rome and forced him publicly to recant his scientific beliefs. His friends were afraid to come to his support. As punishment he was placed under perpetual house arrest and denied the Church sacraments. The *Dialogue* remained forbidden to Catholics until 1835, when the works of Galileo, Copernicus, and Kepler were finally removed from the Index.

Galileo's trial by the Inquisition, although motivated as much by internal Church politics and Galileo's abrasive personality as by conviction that the Copernican system was heretical, frightened intellectuals in regions where the Church exerted power. His confrontation with the Church surprised Galileo, who thought he had divorced theology from science. Despite his public difficulties, Galileo's views on motion became a pivot on which modern physics turned.

Galileo's cosmology / In his *Dialogue* Galileo draws a model of the planetary system. It is essentially a Copernican scheme with no evidence of the ideas of Kepler, such as elliptical orbits. In addition, Galileo makes no attempt to apply his terrestrial mechanics to the motions of the planets.

He views the Copernican model as a simplified one, lacking eccentrics and small epicycles (Fig. 4.8). Here is evidence that Galileo paid little attention to the use of the Copernican model to predict the planetary positions. What struck Galileo was the Copernican cosmology—the order of the universe—rather than the detailed astronomy of planetary motions. He apparently felt, with the same conviction as Copernicus, that the harmony of the planetary order was established from observation. Of course, Galileo relied heavily on his telescopic observations, along with the general arguments of Copernicus (Section 3.1).

Galileo placed the fixed stars in a thick shell far beyond the planets. This stellar shell remained from Greek ideas. However, his spokes-

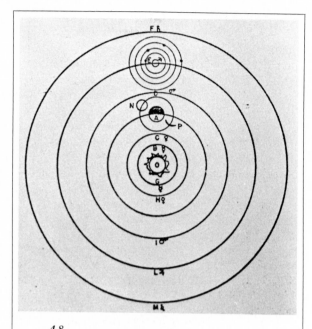

4.8

A drawing of Galileo's heliocentric model. Note that Galileo has added his four moons to Jupiter. Also, he does not show a sphere of stars outside the orbit of Saturn; he leaves open the possibility that the stars extend throughout space. All orbits are circular, despite the discovery by Kepler that they are actually elliptical.

4.9

Isaac Newton. "I have laid down the principles of philosophy; principles not philosophical but mathematical . . ." (Courtesy Yerkes Observatory)

man in the *Dialogue* keeps open the possibility that the universe is not spherical and finite but open and infinite, with the stars sprinkled "through the immense abyss of the universe." Here we find the expansion of the cosmos from a closed space to an infinite universe, a viewpoint that would be supported by Newton.

4.2
Newton: A physical model of the cosmos

Despite his interest in and insight into terrestrial motions, Galileo did not worry about the details of celestial motions. He never bothered to apply his new science of mechanics and understanding of gravity near the earth to the problem of predicting planetary positions. By this omission he failed in his quest for a physical foundation for the Copernican model.

Sir Isaac Newton (1642–1727) emerged as the genius destined to fuse the terrestrial and celestial realms and so to end the long-standing separation initiated by the Greeks. Newton (Fig. 4.9) lived in the era when the role of a "scientist" as we understand the term developed from the new philosophy of experimental science practiced by the scientific societies in Italy, England, and France. One of these—the Royal Society of London for Promoting Natural Knowledge—aided in the maturing of Newton's genius and the promotion of his ideas. With the publication of Newton's *Principia* in 1687, the Royal Society fostered the new physics of motion and the concept of gravitation that has so strongly shaped the modern view of the universe.

The prodigious young Newton / In the small English village of Woolsthorpe (Fig. 4.10), on Christmas Day 1642, Newton's widowed mother gave birth to a sickly child. The fragile baby was so small at birth that it is said he could fit into a quart mug. As a child Newton did not display any outstanding genius. Absentmindedness was one of his more obvious traits; one day he walked home holding a bridle from

4.10
*Newton's house in Woolsthorpe.
An apple tree stands next to the
house. (Courtesy O. Gingerich)*

4.11
*Edmund Halley, a friend of
Newton's. Halley inspired New-
ton to put together the* **Principia.**
*Later he used Newton's laws to
compute the orbit of the comet
that bears his name. (Courtesy
Yerkes Observatory)*

which the horse had escaped, but he never noticed this fact until he arrived at his house.

At eighteen Newton enrolled at Trinity College, Cambridge University. He first intended to
study mathematics as applied to astrology, but a
meeting with Professor Isaac Barrow, who
sensed Newton's abilities, encouraged him to
study physics. In 1665 the bubonic plague overwhelmed England, and the university shut
down. Newton returned to his home and mother
at Woolsthorpe and, in quiet isolation, made discoveries in mathematics, optics, and the science
of mechanics. As he wrote, "In those days I was
in the prime of my invention, and minded
mathematics and philosophy more than at any
other time since."

This fertile period in Woolsthorpe generated
the legend of the falling apple. As is common in
a creative flash of genius, Newton—whether or
not he in fact saw an apple fall—linked two
seemingly unrelated phenomena: the fall of an
apple and the orbit of the moon. He recalled to
his friend and biographer William Stukeley that
he was puzzled by the fall of objects, such as
apples, and wondered about the nature of the
force that attracts masses, such as the moon, to
the earth's center.

On his return to Trinity, Newton showed his
work to Barrow, who soon resigned his position
so that Newton could be elected to it. Because
of his interest in optics, Newton came to invent
the *reflecting telescope* (Chapter 6), which uses a
mirror as the primary light gatherer. His design
was communicated to the Royal Society; after
he constructed a small reflector for them, he
was elected a Fellow of the Society. His election
was not a completely happy one, for his work
on light, which was also communicated to the
Society, brought bitter controversy. Newton resolved never to publish his ideas again.

***The magnificent* Principia** / Newton broke
his vow of nonpublication about ten years later,
when Edmund Halley (1656–1742) requested his
advice on the problem of elliptical orbits described by Kepler's laws. Halley (Fig. 4.11)

queried Newton on the nature of the force between the sun and planets required to produce such orbits and was surprised to hear that Newton had solved the problem in exact detail. Absentminded as ever, Newton had misplaced the solution and could not find it at the moment; he promised Halley that he would send it along later.

Recognizing the importance of Newton's discovery, Halley cajoled his introverted friend to publish the studies and promised to oversee and finance their publication. Newton, stimulated intellectually, labored for two years to complete his *Philosophiae naturalis principia mathematica* (*The Mathematical Principles of Natural Philosophy*). Published in 1687, the *Principia* presented the solution to the problem of planetary motions.

At the beginning of the *Principia* Newton states his intention:

For the whole burden of philosophy seems to consist of this—from the phenomena of motions to investigate the forces of nature, and then from these forces to demonstrate all other phenomena.

After stating his purposes, Newton defines mass, velocity, and acceleration. He then expounds his three "Axioms, or Laws of Motion." In modern terms these famous laws are:

Law I. **The Inertial Law.** A body at rest or in motion at a constant velocity along a straight line remains in that state of rest or motion unless acted upon by a net outside force (Fig. 4.12).

Law II. **The Force Law.** The change in a body's velocity due to an applied net force is in the same direction as the force and proportional to it but is inversely proportional to the body's mass (Fig. 4.13).

Law III. **The Reaction Law.** For every applied force, a force of equal size but opposite direction arises (Fig. 4.14).

These laws of motion are both simple and formidable. They stand in direct opposition to Aristotelian conceptions of force and motion (Section 2.3). Newton's first law takes a logical step beyond Galileo's concept of inertia by postulating that constant, uniform motion is the *natural* state of moving mass anywhere in the universe. The first law gives you a way to judge

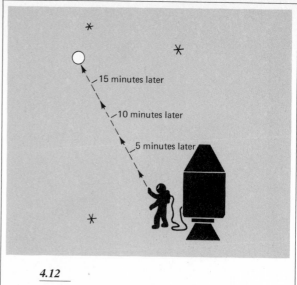

4.12

Newton's first law. The object thrown by the astronaut moves at a constant speed along a straight line. (In space, there is no air to slow down an object's motion.)

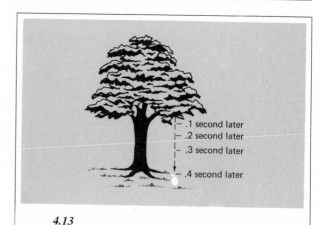

4.13

Newton's second law. A force applied to an object changes its speed, direction of motion, or both. Here, gravity pulls on an apple to accelerate it to the earth, so it falls faster and faster (accelerates) to cover greater distances in the same amount of time.

whether or not a net force is acting on an object: You are told to look for a change either in an object's speed or in the direction of its motion, or in both speed and direction.

The second law extends the recognition from a force to the recognition of its consequences; the direction of the change in motion is in the same direction as the applied force. Furthermore, the amount of acceleration—the change in the object's velocity—depends directly on the size of the force.

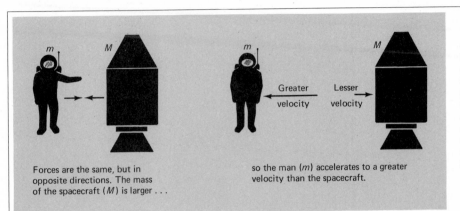

4.14
Newton's third law. Imagine that you are in space next to a spacecraft that has a larger mass than you. Push it. The forces on you and it are equal but opposite, so you and the spacecraft move apart. You have a higher velocity than it because you have less mass, so the same amount of force accelerates you to a higher velocity.

For example, suppose you are floating in space next to a bunch of small objects. You push one. It accelerates and moves away and travels in the direction in which you pushed it. You can also measure its acceleration, its change in velocity. Now push another mass. You measure its acceleration and find that it is half the acceleration of the first. You applied the same force to both objects, so the second must have twice the mass of the first. Newton's second law provides a means to measure mass.

In algebraic form, Newton's second law is

$$F = ma$$

where F is the net applied force, m the object's mass, and a the acceleration resulting from the force. Note that, like velocities, forces have directions—and so do accelerations. An object will accelerate in the *same* direction as an applied force.

The third law recognizes that forces are interactions and must act in simultaneous pairs. If you were still in space and pushed against a large spacecraft, the ship would react to your applied force with an equal but oppositely directed force, pushing you away, as described by Newton's third law. Now the force applied to you and the spacecraft are the same, but the resulting accelerations are different. According to Newton's second law, the acceleration is greater for you than for the spacecraft, because your mass is less. As a result, you would move away from the spacecraft quickly, while it would barely budge. Also, you and the spacecraft would be moving in *opposite* directions.

With these ideas Newton attacked the prob-lem of planetary motion by devising the law of gravitation. Two questions needed to be answered: (1) In what *direction* does the force of gravity act and (2) what is the amount of the force? The first question involves a recognition of the general nature of the force, and the second involves a recognition of the physical properties that determine the force's strength. To answer these questions Newton stood on the shoulders of Kepler: Newton's procedure combined his laws of motion with Kepler's planetary laws to arrive at a law of universal gravitation.

Newton demonstrated that the type of force that causes the elliptical orbits of Kepler's first law is a *central force*—one directed to the center of the motion. Also, he showed that planets moving in orbits under the influence of a central force follow Kepler's second law: the law of areas. Finally, Newton showed from the geometrical properties of ellipses that the force may be described by an inverse-square law and then derived Kepler's third law. In this manner he ensured that his procedure fell in line with the descriptive laws of planetary motion as they were known at his time.

How do the moon and the famous apple enter into this scheme? Newton recognized that gravity causes the apple's fall. Might it not be that the earth's gravity, pulling on the moon, also keeps the moon in its orbit? For simplicity, assume that the moon's orbit is circular. Now, the direction of the moon's orbital motion changes constantly: The moon stays on a circular path rather than moving along a straight line away from the earth (Fig. 4.15). Newton's first law tells you that there is a force acting on

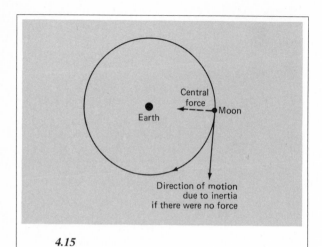

Central force and the moon's orbit. The moon does not move at a constant speed along a straight line. So according to Newton's first law, a force must be acting on it. This force pulls the moon toward the earth, toward the center of its orbit. That force, a central force, is the earth's gravity extended to the moon's orbit. Note that the moon's motion is accelerated motion, because its direction is constantly changing.

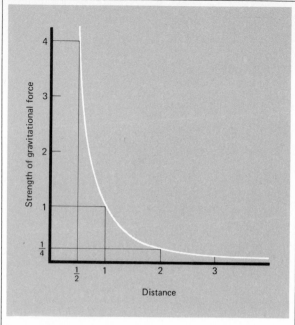

An inverse-square law. This graph shows how the strength of gravitational force changes with distance between masses. At a distance of 1 away, call the force 1 unit. Move twice as far away, to a distance of 2. Then the force is only one-fourth as much. If you move in closer, to a distance of one-half unit, the force is four times as great as that when you are at a distance of 1.

the moon that, according to the second law, results in an acceleration toward the earth's center; such a centrally directed acceleration is called a *centripetal acceleration* (Focus 10). ("Centripetal" means "directed toward the center.") But what causes this centripetal acceleration, and just how can it be described?

Newton generalized from the apple to the moon: "I began to think of gravity extending to the orb of the moon." In this statement he made the creative leap to a bold insight that *every body in the universe attracts every other body with a gravitational force.* This statement became the first *universal* physical law.

In modern algebraic form Newton's law of gravitation is

$$F = \frac{Gm_1m_2}{R^2}$$

where F is the gravitational attraction between two spherical bodies of mass m_1 and m_2, whose centers are separated by a distance R. The symbol G is a universal constant: a number whose value is assumed not to vary with time and lo-

cation in the universe. The value for G in the mks (meter-kilogram-second) system is 6.67×10^{-11}. (See Appendix A.)

What does Newton's law of gravitation mean? First, all masses in the universe attract all other masses. (This force can only attract; it does not repel.) Second, if you consider just two masses for a moment, the amount of the gravitational force depends directly on the amount of material each mass has. So if you doubled the mass of one and kept the distance between the two the same, the force would also double. (Note that what kind of material makes up the masses does not matter.) Third, masses at greater separations have *less* of a gravitational force than those closer together, and this drop-off of force with distance happens in a special way—as the inverse square of the distance. Consider, for example, two masses 1 m apart. A certain amount of gravitational force attracts one to the other. Now move the masses so that they are 2 m apart. The force is less. How much less? By $\frac{1}{2}^2$, or one-fourth as much as when the masses were 1 m apart (Fig. 4.16).

focus 10

CENTRIPETAL ACCELERATION

Circular motion is accelerated motion, even if the speed is constant, because the direction of the motion is constantly changing. This kind of acceleration is called centripetal acceleration, *because it is directed toward the center.*

You have probably felt centripetal acceleration. You experience such acceleration when you turn a corner in a car. It's clear that the faster you are going, the greater the acceleration in turning a corner; if you try turning while going too fast, the friction of the tires on the road cannot produce a strong enough force to make the car change direc-tion and you go into a skid. Now consider the size of the circle. If you are on the free-way making a long gentle curve, even at 90 km/h very little force is needed to change the car's direction. But if you try to turn into your driveway at 90 km/h, that is, on a circle with much smaller radius, the force required to produce that much acceleration would be too great for the tires to handle, and you would probably roll over. So a higher speed or a smaller radius of the circle both mean a larger acceleration. Algebraically,

$$a = \frac{V^2}{R}$$

where a *is the centripetal acceleration;* V, *the circular velocity; and* R, *the radius of the circle.*

Are you sure you grasp this key feature of Newton's law? The gravitational force falls off as the inverse square of the distance between the two masses (Fig. 4.16). So if they were 3 m apart, what would the force be compared to a one-meter separation? Right, $\frac{1}{3}^2$, or $\frac{1}{9}$ as much.

How could Newton test the validity of this law? Here the apple came in handy. He knew that the earth's gravity at its surface (1 earth radius from the center) caused the apple to fall. The earth–moon distance is about 60 earth radii. So if an inverse-square law correctly describes gravitational forces, the acceleration of the moon toward the earth must be $1/(60)^2$ or $\frac{1}{3600}$ less than the acceleration of the apple. (See Focus 11 for details.) Newton then compared his predicted centripetal acceleration with the centripetal acceleration derived from observations of the moon's orbit. As he put it, the predicted and the observed accelerations were "pretty nearly" the same. Newton concluded that the cause of the moon's centripetal acceleration is the same as that of the apple's: the earth's grav-ity. This force, extends out to the distance of the moon, keeping the moon in its orbit, while the moon continually free falls toward the earth.

Confident of his law, Newton launched a massive attack on astronomical problems in the third part of the *Principia* (Section 4.3). One

doubt nagged at the back of his mind: Although he had described gravitational force, what was its cause? His own description required that masses interact over large distances. This action-at-a-distance ran contrary to mechanical views of nature, which explained phenomena in terms of the local collisions of objects. Newton ultimately sidestepped the question of the fun-damental nature of gravitational forces, but his avoidance of the issue was at least consistent with the rest of his philosophy:

I have not yet disclosed the cause of gravity, nor have I undertaken to explain it, since I could not under-stand it from phenomena.

In spite of this evasion, he saw that the cosmos was linked together by eternal, invisible chains.

Warning. Newton's laws of motion, and his law of gravitation, appear quite simple. Indeed, they are and that is their beauty. But be careful that you learn precisely what they do and do not say. For example, is the gravitational force of the moon on the earth bigger or smaller than the gravitational force of the earth on the moon? *Answer:* Neither!—It is exactly the same, for the law of gravity says that the force be-tween objects is proportional to the product of *both* masses.

You should now be able to understand Gali-

focus 11

NEWTON, THE APPLE, AND THE MOON

Next to Woolsthorpe stands an apple tree. I don't think this was the tree whose fruit sparked Newton's creative leap, but it's reassuring to find an apple tree in the vicinity. How did Newton connect the apple's fall to the moon? At that time he was thinking of gravity and wondered if it extended beyond the neighborhood of the earth's surface (Fig. 1). Although they knew about gravity, earlier scientists had made no attempt to allow gravity to work far from the earth. Newton's creative leap came despite traditional opinions that motions on earth and in the heavens were distinctly different.

Newton knew that the distance to the moon was approximately 60 earth radii. He also surmised that if the earth's influence extended to the moon, it grew weaker as the distance increased. How fast did the force grow weaker? Newton guessed that it weakened as the inverse square of the distance. An apple dropping from a tree is 1 earth radius from the center of the earth. So, comparing the accelerations of the moon and the apple, Newton predicted that the moon's acceleration must be (1 earth radius)^2/(60 earth radii)^2 less, or $\frac{1}{3600}$. The acceleration due to gravity at the earth's surface is 9.8 m/sec^2. For the moon, then, the predicted acceleration is 9.8 m/sec^2/3600, or about 2.7×10^{-3} m/sec^2. This acceleration of the moon toward the earth is a centripetal acceleration, for the necessary force—gravity—pulls the moon to the earth's center.

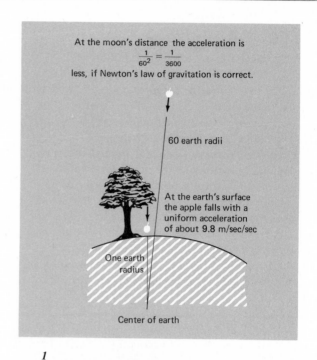

At the moon's distance the acceleration is
$$\frac{1}{60^2} = \frac{1}{3600}$$
less, if Newton's law of gravitation is correct.

60 earth radii

At the earth's surface the apple falls with a uniform acceleration of about 9.8 m/sec/sec

One earth radius

Center of earth

1

The moon and the apple. Newton knew that an apple falling near the earth's surface moves with a uniform acceleration. He imagined what would happen if an apple were placed at the moon's distance (60 earth radii) from the earth. He surmised that the earth's gravity extended out there but that the force was weaker than at the earth's surface. How much less? Less by the inverse square of the distance.

leo's law of free-fall from Newton's viewpoint. Imagine you're going to repeat Galileo's rumored experiment at the Leaning Tower of Pisa by dropping a cannonball and a tennis ball from its uppermost story. The earth exerts a much greater gravitational force on the cannonball than on the tennis ball because of the can-

nonball's much greater mass. However, when the two are dropped, they fall side by side and land at the same time (if you neglect air resistance). So the "effect" of gravity has been in some way the same on both objects, more precisely, the *acceleration* of each is the same, because they speed up at the same rate. Although

Note that Newton did not need to know the mass of the apple or of the moon because their accelerations do not depend on their masses. Galileo (Section 4.1) reached this conclusion from his experiments. Newton made crucial use of this result in the moon-apple test.

How did this predicted value compare with the actual rate of the moon's fall? Newton had found that for a circular orbit the centripetal acceleration has a value (Focus 10)

$$a_c = v^2/R$$

where a_c is the centripetal acceleration, R the radius of the orbit, and v the orbital velocity. For the moon, R equals 3.84×10^8 m. Its velocity is the distance it travels in one orbit divided by the period for one orbit, or

$$v = 2\pi(3.84 \times 10^8 \ m)/(27.3 \ days)$$

One day contains $24 \times 60 \times 60$, or 8.64×10^4 seconds. So the moon's orbital velocity is

$$v = 2.41 \times 10^9 \ m/(27.3 \ days)(8.64 \times 10^4 \ sec/day)$$
$$v = 2.41 \times 10^9 \ m/2.36 \times 10^6 \ sec$$
$$= 1.02 \times 10^3 \ m/sec$$

Then the moon's orbital acceleration is

$$a_c = (1.02 \times 10^3 \ m/sec)^2/3.84 \times 10^8 \ m$$
$$= 2.71 \times 10^{-3} \ m/sec^2$$

This approximates the earlier prediction.

Newton did not have the modern values we just used for the period and size of the moon's orbit and the acceleration due to gravity. He chose a value of the moon's distance that made his results compare closely. Newton felt assured that his approach was correct, although he fudged the figures slightly.

the forces are different, the accelerations turn out to be the same, because gravitational forces are proportional to the masses of the falling objects, but accelerations are inversely proportional to masses (Newton's force law), so the mass cancels out. (Keep this point in mind; it will crop up again in Chapter 7.)

4.3
Cosmic consequences of universal laws

The gravitational force of the earth causes the centripetal acceleration of the moon. This was Newton's central discovery: The earth's gravity keeps the moon swinging around. Newton's discovery resulted in a new understanding of the planetary orbits—the most obvious: The sun's gravity locks the planets in their elliptical orbits. Newton had found the physical interaction between the sun and planets first sought by Kepler. He derived a new form of Kepler's third law that included the gravitational constant G and masses in the constant k (Focus 12). Related to basic physical laws, the revised third law became a potent tool in determining the masses of the planets (if the planet has at least one satellite) and of the sun (Focus 12)—quantities never known before! Newton answered in detail the ancient question of how the planets moved. And he answered it precisely—his predictions of planetary positions were far more accurate than previous ones. Newton's ideas provided the physical support sorely needed for the Copernican model.

The earth's rotation / One objection to the Copernican model was that objects not tied down to the earth should fly off because of the earth's rotation. Newtonian physics explained that objects on the earth had inertia. If thrown upward, they did not lose their inertial motion but continued to move with the ground. So they landed at their starting points. A rotating earth did not leave behind unattached objects.

The earth's revolution / Using the revised third law, you can find that the sun has roughly 3.3×10^5 the mass of the earth (Focus 12). Newton's third law of motion requires equal gravitational forces between the sun and the earth—the force of the sun on the earth equals that of the earth on the sun. However, the second law demands that the earth's acceleration be much greater than the sun's (in fact, 3.3×10^5 times greater!). So the earth orbits the sun rather than the other way around.

The Copernican model now rested on the firm ground of Newton's physics. Newton had created a grand design of motions in the universe that explained, in terms of a physical cause, the ancient problem of the motion of the planets.

focus 12

NEWTON'S REVISION OF KEPLER'S THIRD LAW

Using his laws of motion and gravitation, Newton revised Kepler's third law from the form

$$P^2 = ka^3$$

to

$$P^2 = 4\pi^2 a^3 / G(m + M)$$

where two masses, m and M, orbit each other with separation a and period P. As usual G is the gravitational constant. Note that in Newton's form, $k = 4\pi^2/G(m + M)$; that is, the constant relates to the masses of the bodies involved.

The revised third law allows you to find the masses of celestial bodies. For example, you can use the earth's orbit to find the sun's mass. The earth–sun distance, a, is 1.50×10^{11} m. The earth's period, P, is 365.25 days, or 3.16×10^7 sec. Because the mass of the sun is much larger than the earth's mass, approximate $M_s + m_E$ by M_s. Then

$$M_s = \frac{4\pi^2}{G}\frac{a^3}{P^2}$$

$$= \frac{39.5}{6.67 \times 10^{-11}}\frac{(1.50 \times 10^{11})^3}{(3.16 \times 10^7)^2}$$

$$= 1.99 \times 10^{30} \ kg$$

Note that you need to know the value for G to do this calculation.

If you don't know G, you can still use the third law to find relative masses. Use the earth again, but this time you also need the moon. The moon's distance is 3.84×10^8 m, or roughly 2.6×10^{-3} AU, and the moon's period is 7.5×10^{-2} yr. For the earth and moon,

$$m_E + m_M = \frac{4\pi^2}{G}\frac{a_{EM}^3}{P_{EM}^2}$$

and for the sun and earth,

$$M_s + m_E = \frac{4\pi^2}{G}\frac{a_{ES}^3}{P_{ES}^2}$$

If we don't know G, divide one equation by the other to get

$$(M_s + m_E)/(m_E + m_M) = \left(\frac{4\pi^2}{G}\frac{a_{ES}^3}{P_{ES}^2}\right)\Big/\left(\frac{4\pi^2}{G}\frac{a_{EM}^3}{P_{EM}^2}\right)$$

$$= \left(\frac{a_{ES}}{a_{EM}}\right)^3\left(\frac{P_{EM}}{P_{ES}}\right)^2$$

As before, approximate $M_s + m_E$ by M_s, and $m_E + m_M$ by m_E. Then

$$\frac{M_s}{m_E} = \left(\frac{1 \ AU}{2.6 \times 10^{-3} \ AU}\right)^3\left(\frac{7.5 \times 10^2 \ yr}{1 \ yr}\right)^2$$

$$= (5.7 \times 10^7)(5.6 \times 10^{-3})$$

$$= 3.3 \times 10^5$$

You have found the sun's mass relative to the earth's mass.

Gravity and orbits / To add to its achievements, Newton's physics correctly described the orbits of comets. Through antiquity and the Middle Ages, astronomers believed that comets were objects confined to the earth's atmosphere. Newton and Halley decisively demonstrated that comets orbit the sun in accordance with the law of gravitation (Fig. 4.17). In fact, Halley correctly predicted the return of the comet that bears his name, but he did not live to see it return in 1758. (More on comets can be found in Chapter 12.)

Newton's ideas also led to the discovery of Neptune in 1846, long after the first publication of the *Principia*. Neptune was the first planet to be found by its gravitational effects on another planet. Newton's laws predicted its existence *before* it was observed.

The discovery of Neptune rested upon observed irregularities in the orbit of Uranus. Astronomers had noted small discrepancies between the observed positions of Uranus and those predicted from Newton's laws. Such irregularities occur because all planets attract each other. Jupiter's tug, for instance, influences the orbit of Uranus so that it differs from that ex-

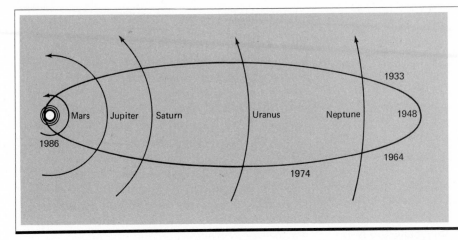

4.17
The orbit of Halley's comet, first worked out by Edmund Halley on the basis of Newton's laws. Note how elliptical it is, with an aphelion beyond the orbit of Neptune.

pected if Uranus and the sun were the only attracting bodies. The undiscovered Neptune revealed itself when Uranus's motion deviated from the path predicted from the effects of the known planets.

Applying Newton's laws to explain the deviations as due to a planet beyond Uranus, the Englishman John C. Adams in 1845 estimated where the unknown planet should be in the sky. About a year later, Urbain J. J. Leverrier in Paris made similar calculations and transmitted them to Johann G. Galle in Berlin, who found the planet on September 23, 1846. Newton's laws triumphed. In the twentieth century, discrepancies in Neptune's orbit stimulated searches for other planets. One search resulted in the discovery of Pluto (see Chapter 11), even though Pluto is actually too small in mass to affect Neptune.

An equally dramatic discovery, which extended the validity of Newton's laws beyond the bounds of the solar system, was the observation of binary star systems in the late eighteenth century. (A binary star system consists of two stars, held together by their mutual gravity, orbiting each other.) William Herschel (1768–1822) and his sister (Fig. 4.18), Caroline Herschel (1750–1848), observed many pairs of stars over a long time, looking for orbital motions. William Herschel suspected that some pairs of stars observed in the sky lay close together not simply because they both happened to be in the line of sight from the earth but because they were actually linked by gravitational forces. The

(a)　　　　　　　　　　　(b)

4.18
(a) *William Herschel, who turned from a career in music to one in astronomy.* **(b)** *Caroline Herschel, William's sister, who worked with William on astronomical observations. (Both courtesy Yerkes Observatory)*

Herschels observed the expected orbital motions. Calculations of the period of binary star system and the separation between the stars confirmed their motions followed Kepler's laws. These laws can be derived from Newton's laws of motion and gravitation. Since binary star systems obey Kepler's laws, they indirectly confirm Newton's laws. (See Chapter 15 for more details on binary star systems.)

Newton's cosmology / The physical ideas that Newton found in the universe resulted in a new conception of the cosmos. For the Greeks, Ptolemy, and Copernicus, the cosmos—enclosed by the sphere of fixed stars—appeared finite and bounded. Galileo had left open the possibility that the universe might be infinite but did not strongly push his case. Newton argued that his laws required that the universe be infinite in extent. His argument went like this: If the universe were finite, gravitation would eventually pull all the matter to the center. As a result, only one cosmic mass would exist. However, we see other masses—stars, for example. In an infinite universe the matter would be pulled into an infinite number of small condensations. Newton believed that this picture was more like the real world, so he concluded that the universe was infinite.

Not all things in heaven and earth sat happily in Newton's infinite universe. The innermost planet, Mercury, posed an annoying problem: The semimajor axis of its orbit rotated in space. This motion could not be completely explained by the attraction of existing planets. Some astronomers thought that the excess rotation was caused by a planet between Mercury and the Sun. Although observations of this hypothetical body—called Vulcan—have been reported, they have so far proved to be mistaken. The supposed Vulcan has never been seen, even when modern observational techniques have attempted to catch its swift flight. (The problem of Mercury's orbit was later solved by Einstein—Chapter 7.)

Newton was also sorely disturbed by the mutual forces among the planets, which he thought must eventually lead to the disintegration of the solar system. To avoid this awful event, Newton envisioned the hand of God occasionally descending to reset the clockwork mechanism of planetary motions, like a conscientious craftsperson making adjustments. The order of the mechanical universe—ordained by the Divine Being—was maintained by His intervention, and the expanses of Newtonian space were benevolently watched by the distant God.

I do not know what I may appear to the world; but to myself I seem to have been only like a boy, playing on the seashore, and diverting myself in now and then finding a smoother pebble or a prettier shell than ordinary, while the great ocean of truth lay all undiscovered before me.

SUMMARY

This chapter presented the revolution in the development of a physical model of the cosmos. Ironically, this transformation was unknowingly ignited by the Copernican model, which lacked unifying physical ideas. Galileo promoted acceptance of the Copernican model with his telescopic observations. He also searched for physical laws to support the system and found laws for motion under gravity, but he did not apply them to the heavens. Motivated more by the design of the Copernican model than by the details of planetary motion, Galileo ignored the discoveries of Kepler and saw the planets as swinging in circular orbits.

*With the publication of Newton's **Principia** the Copernican model finally acquired its physical foundation. But to build this support Newton (and Galileo) had to challenge Aristotle's ideas about motion—especially his concept of natural motion. To Aristotle a falling rock followed its natural motion, so no force was needed. By developing a clear concept of inertia—natural motion—Newton turned around Aristotle's idea and saw a falling rock as **forced** motion and that force was gravity. Coaxed by the apple and moon he then strung together motions in the heavens and on the earth with the ties of gravitation—a unified model of the cosmos.*

Note how the idea of natural motion lies at the heart of fundamental physical ideas and also, finally, at the conception of the cosmos that evolves from it.

*One more point: From observations such as those described in Chapter 1, you cannot tell the difference between a heliocentric and a geocentric model. Physics, however, can help you decide. Newton did not have direct observational support for a heliocentric system. But such a system fell in line with his physical ideas. His comprehensive picture of the world so persuaded people that they accepted its heliocentric framework **before** they had direct observational evidence of its validity.*

Newton's universe was infinite but as carefully crafted as a clock. His laws of motion and gravitation describe what makes the world go 'round. Newton even anticipated the launching of satellites into orbit (Focus 13). These univer-

focus 13

ORBITS AND ESCAPE VELOCITY

Newton was the first to work on the problems of putting objects into orbit. From his analysis, which was based on his laws of motion and gravitation, arises the concept of escape velocity, the minimum velocity an object needs to escape the gravitational bonds of another.

Imagine, as Newton did, a giant cannon placed on the top of a very high mountain and aimed parallel to the ground (Fig. 1). Fire a cannonball. It travels some distance, then falls to the ground. If you use more powder in the cannon, the ball travels farther along the earth before it hits the ground. If you put a large enough charge in the cannon, the ball goes completely around the earth in a circular orbit, returning to the cannon. The inertial motion of the ball just compensates for the falling due to gravity. Now dump in a larger charge. With a starting velocity greater than that needed for a circular orbit, the cannonball travels around the earth in an elliptical orbit. Increasing the starting velocity makes the orbit more elliptical. Eventually, the orbit becomes so elliptical that the semimajor axis is infinitely long, and it would take the ball an infinite time to return. So it never returns. This velocity is called the escape velocity. Any velocity larger than it produces the same effect: The object leaves the gravitational grip of another, never to return.

What determines how large an escape velocity any object has? Consider the earth. Its escape velocity is about 11 km/sec. Suppose that you kept the earth at its present size but increased its mass. Then its escape velocity would increase. Now suppose that you kept its mass the same but decreased its radius. The escape velocity again increases because the earth's surface is closer to it's center. Basically, an object's mass and size determine its escape velocity.

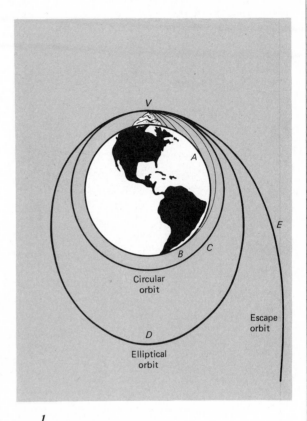

1

Launching satellites, according to Newton. He reasoned that a cannonball had to be fired with some minimum velocity in order to go into a circular orbit around the earth rather than return to it (C). Higher velocities resulted in elliptical orbits (D). Eventually, a certain velocity—called the escape velocity— is reached where the projectile does not return to the earth or stay in orbit about it (E). (Adapted from a diagram in the Principia)

In algebraic form, the escape velocity equation is:

$$v_{es} = \left(\frac{2GM}{R}\right)^{\frac{1}{2}}$$

where M is the object's mass, R its radius, and v_{es} its escape velocity.

sal laws worked so well that his viewpoint went unchallenged until the twentieth century, when Albert Einstein created a new theory of gravitation (Chapter 7).

STUDY EXERCISES

1 Use one of Galileo's telescopic discoveries to support the Copernican model and refute the Aristotelian–Ptolemaic one. (*Objective 1*)

2 What important discovery of Kepler's was ignored by Galileo? (*Objective 3*)

3 Describe Galileo's concept of inertia. (*Objective 2*)

4 You have two balls of the same size and shape. One is made of lead, the other, of wood. You drop them together. What happens? (*Objectives 2, 5, and 6*)

5 Suppose you're out in space and push away from you an object that has the same mass as you. What happens? (*Objective 5*)

6 Argue that an inverse law for gravitation, $1/R$, fails the moon-apple test. (*Objective 8*)

7 Describe two ways in which Newton's model differed from that of Copernicus. (*Objective 9*)

8 Use Newtonian physics to argue that the earth rotates on its axis and revolves around the sun, and so answer the main physical objections to the Copernican model. (*Objective 10*)

BEYOND THIS BOOK . . .

Galileo's conflict with the Church and his vibrant personality make him perhaps the most famous of the astronomers in the popular eye. For a look into Galileo the man, read *Galileo* by B. Brecht (better yet, see a production of the play) or *The Star-Gazer* (Putnam, New York, 1939) by Z. de Harsanyi, translated by P. Tabor.

For a detective-style analysis of Galileo's problems with religious authority, try *The Crime of Galileo* (University of Chicago Press, Chicago, Ill., 1959) by G. de Santillana.

For a view of Newton's work, nothing beats the *Principia: Mott's Translation Revised* (University of California Press, Berkeley, Calif., 1966), translated by F. Cajori.

You can get to know Galileo by reading *Dialogue Concerning the Two World Systems* (University of California Press, Berkeley, Calif., 1967) translated by S. Drake. *Discoveries and Opinions of Galileo*, also by Drake, contains a translation of *The Starry Messenger.*

For insight into how Galileo actually arrived at the correct analysis of the motion of falling bodies, read "Galileo's Discovery of the Law of Free Fall" by S. Drake in *Scientific American*, May 1973, p. 84.

A short bibliography of Newton is "Isaac Newton" by I. B. Cohen, *Scientific American*, December 1955, p. 73; see also "Newton's Discovery of Gravity," March 1981, p. 166.

For details about how Neptune was found, look at *The Discovery of Neptune* by M. Grosser (Harvard University Press, Cambridge, Mass., 1962). Now available as a Dover paperback.

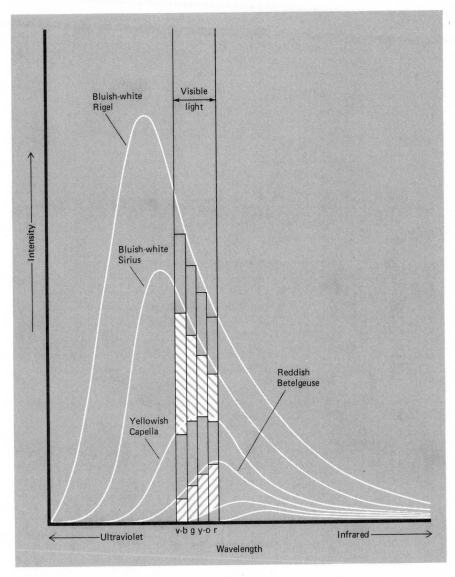

Bluish-white
Rigel

Visible
light

Bluish-white
Sirius

Reddish
Betelgeuse

Yellowish
Capella

Intensity

Ultraviolet

v-b g y-o r

Infrared

Wavelength

1

The continuous spectra of stars with different surface temperatures. The colors in the visible range are indicated by v-b for violet to blue, g for green, y-o for yellow to orange, and r for red. Note how the peak of the emission shifts to shorter wavelengths with higher temperatures. As a result, the colors of stars of different temperatures viewed over the visible range of the spectrum, differs. Hotter stars are bluer than cooler ones. Also note that the visible range samples only a small part of the entire spectrum emitted by stars.

3   The spectra of most stars look like that of the sun—absorption spectra. In terms of Kirchhoff's model for the formation of the sun's dark lines, what does this similarity tell us about the physical conditions in other stars? (*Objective 3*)

4   Suppose you had a box of hydrogen ions. What kind of line spectrum would they produce? (*Objective 8*)

5   What observational clue tipped off astronomers that the spectral sequence, as determined by spectral lines, was a temperature sequence? (*Objectives 7, 8, and 9*)

6   A *B*-star is much hotter than an *A*-star. So you expect that hydrogen atoms, on the average, move around faster in a *B*-star and collide more frequently. Yet the Balmer lines from a *B*-star are *weaker* than those from an *A*-star. Explain the discrepancy in terms of the energy-level model for atoms. (*Objective 9*)

7   Arrange the following kinds of electromagnetic radiation in order from the *least* to the *most* energetic:

a X-rays
b radio
c ultraviolet
d infrared
(*Objective 6*)

8   When you look at the spectrum of the moon, it resembles that of the sun. Explain. (*Objective 3*)

BEYOND THIS BOOK . . .

For a more technical but very readable description of spectroscopy and stars read *Atoms, Stars, and Nebulae* (Harvard University Press, Cambridge, Mass., 1971) by L. Aller.

The Nature of Light and Color in the Open Air (Dover, New York, 1954) by M. Minnaert investigates the nature of light through natural phenomena you've probably seen. Also relevant reading for Chapter 6.

Otto Struve and Velta Zebergs trace the development of ideas about stellar spectra in Chapters X and XI of *Astronomy in the 20th Century* (Macmillan, New York, 1962).

LEARNING OBJECTIVES

After studying this chapter you should be able to:

1. Describe the impact of observations on scientific models.

2. Present at least one example of an observation in astronomy that led to a new model and one that confirmed or refuted an existing model.

3. Outline the main functions of a telescope—light-gathering, resolving, and magnifying power—and relate each to specific optical characteristics of a telescope's design.

4. Compare and contrast reflecting and refracting telescopes; include a sketch of the optical layout of each in your comparison.

5. Compare a radio telescope to an optical telescope in function, design, and use.

6. Cite a key drawback of a radio telescope compared to an optical telescope and describe how radio astronomers cope with this problem.

7. Describe what is meant by the term "invisible astronomy."

8. Contrast an infrared telescope to an optical one in terms of its functions, design, and use.

9. Discuss at least two advantages a space telescope has over a ground-based telescope.

. . . All astronomical research must in the end be reducible to a visual observation . . .

AUGUST COMTE: Cours de Philosophe Positive

Telescopes and our insight to the cosmos

6

This chapter turns from astronomical concepts (the focus of previous chapters) to astronomical tools. Telescopes (and other equipment, such as spectroscopes) spring from advances in technology. The technological development of astronomical tools affects *what* we observe and *how* we observe. It expands, deepens, and sharpens our perceptions of the cosmos. What and how we observe act as a prelude to and confirmation of our models of astronomical objects—and the universe itself.

The image you may have of an astronomer is someone sitting out all night in the cold peering through a telescope. That was accurate in the past, but today it is rare for an astronomer actually to *look* through a telescope, other than to confirm that it is set on the desired object of study. Instead, he or she uses many kinds of instruments to study the radiation from the stars—instruments that can provide much more accurate and detailed information than the naked eye.

In the course of this century the technical advances have been so great that the labor of observing and explaining has been divided somewhat, between the observational astronomers, who work with telescopes, and the theoreticians, who work with pencil and paper and computers and may never use a telescope in their lifetime. The technology has even become too complex for any one observer to master, and he or she often now works with teams of engineers and technicians. This chapter will not discuss all the recent technological advances but will look at some of the developments providing new ways of observing the universe, and the influence these have had on our astronomical models.

Observations accelerate the evolution of astronomical ideas. By them, the effectiveness of models are judged. From this judgment some models are discarded; new ones, proposed, and a few, finally adopted. Not all new observations have dramatic effects. In many instances the change brought on by the change of vision is slow and subtle. Slowly or swiftly, new observations compel new conceptions of the cosmos.

6.1

Observations and models

How do observations and models interact? The process usually goes like this (Section 2.1): Mod-els spring from observations, whether straightforward or subtle. Basic astronomical observations naturally drove people to create models of the cosmos. The earliest of these were mythical (Section 2.2). The Ptolemaic model marked the first detailed attempt at a scientific explanation of the observations (Section 2.4). This model had two key functions: (1) It used geometrical, physical, and aesthetic ideas to *explain* what was seen and (2) it *predicted* planetary positions. A key aspect of the prediction is that it must be quantitative, that is, have definite numbers attached to it. Then how well a model corresponds to actual observations becomes crucial to its acceptability.

Not until Tycho Brahe (Section 3.2) did nontelescopic observations (Fig. 6.1) reach the limits imposed by the human eye. Brahe's technical achievement compelled Kepler (Section 3.3) to take a discrepancy of 8' seriously. The failure of the Copernican model with *circular* orbits to fit the data resulted in Kepler's devising a model with *elliptical* orbits. Their success formed a critical link in the evolutionary chain to Newton's idea of gravitation and a model of a cosmos tied by a force (Section 4.3).

But prior to Brahe's observations and the astronomical use of the telescope by Galileo, both the Ptolemaic and Copernican models explained the motions of the planets. And both made predictions just about as badly. Since both models were equally well confirmed observationally, astronomers had to rely on aesthetic and philosophical beliefs to make a choice between the two. In fact, the crucial observation to distinguish the simple heliocentric and geocentric models—heliocentric parallax—was not made until the 1830s, about two and a quarter centuries after the introduction of the Copernican model! Only by then had the techniques of measuring stellar positions become accurate enough to detect heliocentric parallax, which amounts to less than 1″ for even the nearest star. Copernicus guessed correctly that the stars were very far from the earth compared with the earth–sun distance.

To sum up: Observations form the building blocks for model making and can also act as the driving force that causes models to be discarded. Their destructive effect often comes from new observations that don't fit the scheme of accepted models.

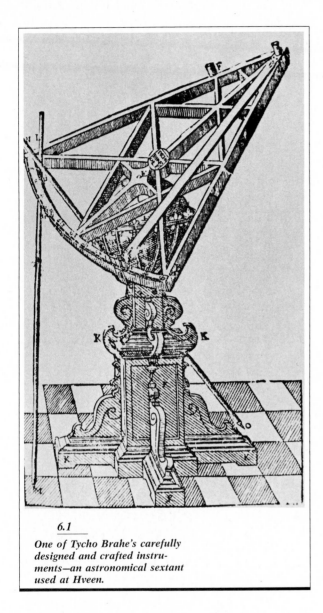

One of Tycho Brahe's carefully designed and crafted instruments—an astronomical sextant used at Hveen.

with theoretical models in light of whatever observations we have. Theoretical model making may also be tied to technology; for example, electronic computers make it possible to manipulate quickly very detailed models of astronomical objects. Such play usually leads back to observations—again.

6.2
Visible astronomy: Optical telescopes

Comte had good reason to believe that all astronomy must rest on *"visual* observation" (emphasis mine). In the nineteenth century large telescopes began to peer beyond the solar system and local stars. Meteorites were not yet believed to be objects from space. No moon rocks had been ferried to the earth. Surely astronomers looked but did not (because they could not) touch or feel.

As extensions of the human eye, telescopes amplified the power of detection without extending the spectral range of our vision. Today we can sense much more than the visual part of the electromagnetic spectrum (Section 5.3), as you find in the next section. This section restricts itself to optical telescopes—those that manipulate light detectable by the eye. Before dealing with telescopes, let me tell you a little about *optics*—how light is controlled. You need to understand some basic optics to understand how telescopes work.

Refraction, reflection, and images / When traveling through space of a uniform medium, light moves along straight lines. These paths are called *light rays.* Using lenses, mirrors, and prisms, we can change the direction of light rays or even break up white light into its component colors (light of different wavelengths). How light rays are affected by bouncing off or passing through materials is the essence of optics.

When light crosses the boundary from one transparent material to another (from air to glass, for example), its direction generally changes (Fig. 6.2). This bending of light rays is termed *refraction.* Refraction occurs because light travels at different speeds in different substances. Consider what happens as a consequence when a beam of light—a bunch of rays—hits glass from air at some angle. The first part of the beam to strike the glass enters it and

One other point: Astronomy, in comparison with physics or chemistry, is not an *experimental* science but is an *observational* one. Astronomers cannot bring a star or planet into a terrestrial lab to investigate its physical characteristics. We can only work with what we are given—for the most part, the light from celestial objects.

You should not, however, get the impression that astronomy is totally devoid of experimentation. Astronomers experiment in two basic ways. First, we can make different kinds of observations of the same object. That's the importance of technological innovation, for it provides new tools for new experiments. Second, we can play

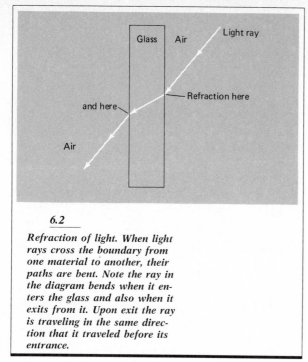

6.2

Refraction of light. When light rays cross the boundary from one material to another, their paths are bent. Note the ray in the diagram bends when it enters the glass and also when it exits from it. Upon exit the ray is traveling in the same direction that it traveled before its entrance.

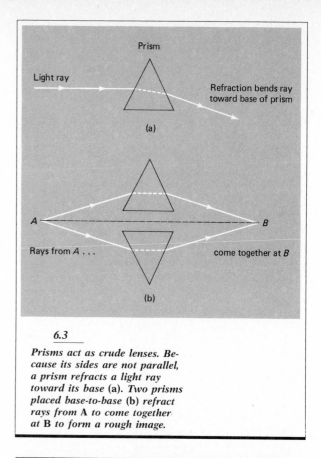

6.3

Prisms act as crude lenses. Because its sides are not parallel, a prism refracts a light ray toward its base (a). Two prisms placed base-to-base (b) refract rays from A to come together at B to form a rough image.

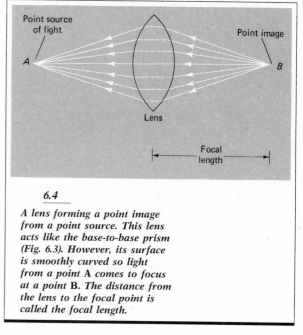

6.4

A lens forming a point image from a point source. This lens acts like the base-to-base prism (Fig. 6.3). However, its surface is smoothly curved so light from a point A comes to focus at a point B. The distance from the lens to the focal point is called the focal length.

slows down. The rest of the beam continues to move at a faster speed and so gains on the light already in the glass. This catch-up results in the front of the beam turning toward the glass.

Here's an analogy: Imagine the line of a marching band turning a corner. To do this and to keep a straight line, the people on the inside have to march more slowly than those on the outside. The line turns around some angle and remains straight.

One key point: The amount of refraction depends on the wavelength of light, with blue light bent more than yellow, and yellow more than red. The shorter the wavelength, the greater the amount of refraction.

You have all seen yourselves in a mirror, so you know that smooth surfaces return light by bouncing back the rays. This process is *reflection*. A light ray bounces off a polished surface the same way a ball bounces off a smooth wall: The ball rebounds at the same angle at which it hits. Reflection like this does not depend on the wavelength of the light; red and blue light are reflected the same way at the same angle.

The point of optics is to make *images* by refraction or reflection. An image occurs when light rays are gathered together in the same relative alignment as when they left an object.

How can refraction form an image? Suppose light travels through a glass prism (Fig. 6.3(a)). Because the sides of a prism are not parallel, a light ray does not come out along its original path but is bent toward the prism's base. Now place two prisms base to base (Fig. 6.3(b)). Then two light rays from a point source converge at a point. However, rays entering the prisms at different angles converge at different points. To get all rays to come to the same point requires a smoothly curved surface. Such a piece of glass is a *lens* (Fig. 6.4).

A lens brings rays from a point source to

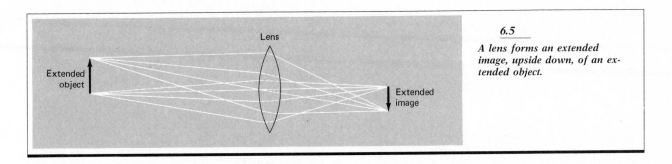

6.5

A lens forms an extended image, upside down, of an extended object.

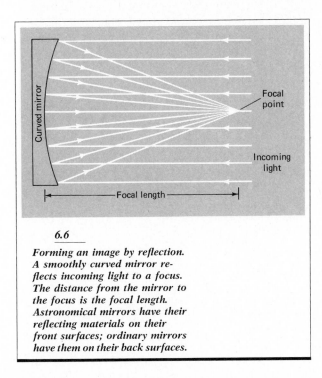

6.6

Forming an image by reflection. A smoothly curved mirror reflects incoming light to a focus. The distance from the mirror to the focus is the focal length. Astronomical mirrors have their reflecting materials on their front surfaces; ordinary mirrors have them on their back surfaces.

an image at its focus that is a point. From an object of finite size, the lens makes an image of the object by focusing rays from each point of the source onto a separate point in the image. This image is generally smaller than the object and upside down (Fig. 6.5). For objects at large distances, the distance from lens to the image is approximately the same for all objects. This distance is termed the *focal length*.

How can a mirror make an image? You know that an image from a flat mirror is undistorted (but reversed right to left). An irregularly curved mirror, such as one in a funhouse, creates a distorted image. A smoothly curved mirror—whose surface, for instance, curves like the inside surface of a sphere—brings all the light to a focus (Fig. 6.6).

Telescopes / Basically, a telescope is an instrument that gathers up light and allows you to examine an image at a focus. To make a telescope you need a lens or mirror, called the *objective*, to bring light to a focus. Then a magnifying lens called an *eyepiece* allows visual examination of the image.

Essentially, there are two types of telescopes, distinguished by their objectives: *refracting telescopes* (or *refractors*) that use a lens (Fig. 6.7), and *reflecting telescopes* (or *reflectors*) that use a mirror (Fig. 6.8). Galileo's telescope was a refractor, Newton's, a reflector. A telescope's size is denoted by the size of its objective; for instance, a 10-cm reflector has a mirror with a 10-cm diameter.

Newton designed the reflector because of a critical drawback of the refractors of his day. Since simple lenses act essentially as prisms, light of different colors has different focuses because the amount of bending depends on color. So images viewed through a refractor have color halos (when one color is in focus and other colors are out of focus and fuzzy). Newton noted that reflection, in contrast to refraction, did not make light break up into colors. (Later lenses were designed to eliminate most of their color problems.)

How can you view the image of a reflector? Newton put a small mirror tilted at 45° to the path of light to direct the focus out the side of the telescope tube (Fig. 6.8), where an eyepiece is placed. Telescopes today typically use a different optical design called a *Cassegrain* (Fig. 6.8). All large telescopes built now are reflectors (Fig. 6.9).

Functions of a telescope / Whether a reflector or refractor, a telescope has one primary function—to gather light. A telescope is basically a light bucket, collecting photons. How much light a telescope can collect depends on the

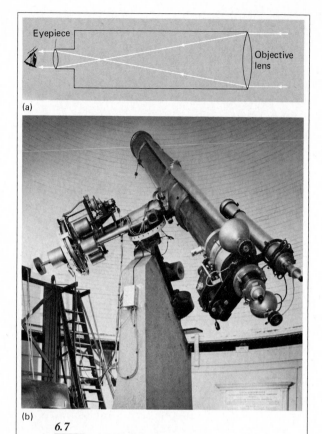

(a)

(b)

6.7

(a) *The design of a simple refracting telescope. An objective lens gathers the incoming light and brings it to a focus. An eyepiece lens allows you to view a magnified image of that made by the objective. (b) The "Great Refractor" of Harvard College Observatory. Built in the middle of the nineteenth century, this refracting telescope has a 15-in objective lens. In its day it was one of the largest telescopes in the world. (By permission of Harvard College Observatory)*

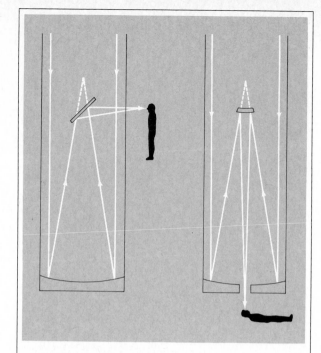

6.8

The design of reflecting telescopes. The main problem is the placement of the eyepiece to view the image made by the objective mirror. Newton placed a small, flat mirror in the telescope's tube to reflect the light out to one side, where the eyepiece is positioned (left). This is called a Newtonian reflector. A more common modern design uses a small convex mirror to reflect the light back down through a hole in the objective mirror (right). Here an eyepiece can be placed for viewing. This is called a Cassegrain reflector.

area of its objective. So a mirror with *twice* the diameter of another can gather *four* times as much light. That's one reason astronomers want large telescopes—big mirrors that have plenty of light-gathering ability.

The second function of a telescope is to separate, or *resolve*, objects that are close together in the sky. This ability is called *resolving power*. It depends on the diameter of the objective and also on the wavelength of the light. For the same wavelength the resolving power in-

creases directly as the objective's diameter. So a mirror *twice* the size of another has *double* the resolving power.

The resolving power of big telescopes is limited by the telescopes themselves and by the earth's atmosphere as well. You have probably noticed that stars twinkle. The twinkling comes from turbulence in the air that makes the atmosphere act like a huge, nonuniform lens. The motion of blobs of air, like the shimmering above a hot road, distort and blur images through a telescope. Even on the best of nights, the 200-in Hale telescope does not resolve better than a 4-in telescope.

The limit the earth's atmosphere sets on the resolving power of big telescopes makes a strong case for placing a large telescope in space.

Finally, the least important of a telescope's functions is its *magnifying power*, the apparent

6.9

The Cerro Tololo 4-m telescope. Located in Chile, this is typical design of a contemporary, large telescope. A 4-m mirror is pretty large—about the size of a small car. (Courtesy Cerro Tololo Inter-American Observatory)

increase in the size of an object compared with visual observation. Magnifying power depends on the focal length of the objective and the focal length of the eyepiece. Changing the eyepiece on a telescope changes its magnifying power as follows: The *shorter* the focal length of the eyepiece, the *greater* the magnifying power. For example, if you put in an eyepiece with *half* the focal length of a previous one, you *double* the magnifying power.

Don't develop the impression that the astronomers observe with their eyes. They seldom do. Some light-sensing device, called a *detector,* is usually placed at the focus. The detector may be a photographic plate (light-sensitive materials

on glass rather than on film); that's how many of the photos in this book were made. Or it may be an electronic detector similar, for example, to a television camera. These days astronomers rarely—if ever—use their eyes for observations.

To sum up: The three principal functions of a telescope are (1) to gather light, (2) to resolve fine detail, and (3) to magnify the image. Of these, I cannot overemphasize the importance of light-gathering power. Most astronomical objects are extremely faint. Without a telescope you can see about 6000 stars. Even a small 6-in telescope allows you to see some *half a million* stars. That is the real power of a telescope—to enable us to see objects that we would otherwise not know existed.

Your own telescope? / This book, or the course you're taking, may spark or develop your interest in observing. If so, you're probably wondering what telescope you should buy.

I won't recommend specific brands here, but I can give you a little general advice. First, decide how much money you can spend. Then recognize that, because light-gathering power is paramount, you want to select the *largest aperture* telescope with decent mechanical parts that you can find within your budget. On a cost basis, this requirement pretty much forces you to consider only reflecting telescopes.

You might be surprised to learn that I don't own a telescope. Instead, I use the telescope at the University of New Mexico's Capilla Peak Observatory (Fig. 6.10) or apply for access to telescopes at observatories such as Kitt Peak National Observatory (Fig. 6.11), where I carry out my research projects.

New telescopes, big surprises / Observing is filled with surprises, for the universe is filled with objects stranger than we can imagine. In my opinion, astronomy is a science driven primarily by observations rather than by theory. Observers come upon strange objects in space and turn to their theoretical colleagues to devise clever models to cope with the new information.

It's impossible for me here to list just all the discoveries of telescopes that transformed astronomy. Instead, I will briefly present a few representative cases and their locations in this book.

1. Galileo's telescopic discoveries (*Section 4.1*). Here, for the first time, was *direct observational evidence* that could be used to refute the

6.10

A student setting up the 61-cm telescope of the University of New Mexico's Capilla Peak Observatory.

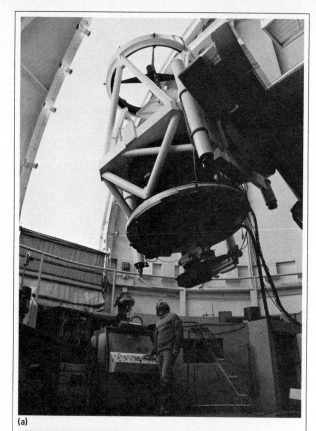

(a)

(b)

6.11

(a) *Mike Zeilik getting the 1.3-meter telescope at Kitt Peak National Observatory set up for daytime operation. Daytime? Yes, because I'm observing in the infrared part of the spectrum, and the sky is just as dark in the infrared during the day as at night. (Photo by G. Henson)* **(b)** *Operating the 1.3-meter telescope. As with almost all large optical telescopes, this one is controlled by a computer commanded by the observer. (Photo by G. Henson)*

cosmological model of Aristotle and Ptolemy held in the seventeenth century. Prior to Galileo's work, the available observations could be fit into either a geocentric or a heliocentric scheme.

One observation of Galileo's lay strangely dormant for years: the recognition that the Milky Way consisted of a multitude of stars. Much later and very slowly, astronomers probed the Milky Way to discover that we live in a *galaxy*, a vast pinwheel of stars (Chapter 14).

2. The discoveries of Uranus, Neptune, and Pluto (*Sections 4.3, 11.4, and 11.5*). William Herschel came upon Uranus by accident in 1781—his observations did not aim directly at the discovery of new planets. This discovery shook up those who believed that the number of planets was ordained in some mystical way.

Work on the orbit of Uranus lead to the discovery of Neptune in a triumphal application of

Newton's laws of motion and gravitation. In its turn, Neptune prompted the search that culminated in the discovery of Pluto in 1930.

3. The discovery of double stars (*Sections 4.3 and 15.2*). Another discovery of Herschel's in the nineteenth century, binary stars—two stars bound in an orbit by mutual gravity—demonstrated that Newton's laws applied *beyond* the solar system. This confirmation demolished once and for all the concept of separate physical laws for the local and distant realms of space.

Observations of binary stars permit us to determine the masses of the companion stars that, in turn, lead to the discovery that the masses and luminosities of stars are related (Section 15.2). This is crucial information for ideas about the evolution of stars (Chapter 19).

4. The discovery of galaxies (*Section 14.6 and Chapter 17*). Large telescopes allow astronomers to peer deep into space. Beyond our galaxy they encountered other galaxies—vast billions of systems of stars and other material bound together by gravity. Using spectroscopy (Chapter 5), astronomers found that galaxies had spectra that resembled what is expected from adding together the individual spectra of huge numbers of stars, much like the sun.

The discovery of galaxies in the twentieth century expanded our view of the universe in two ways: first, that just as there are billions of stars in our galaxy, there are probably billions of galaxies with billions of stars; and second, that the study of galaxies leads directly to the study of the universe as a whole—the subject of the next chapter. This study found that the *universe itself evolves* (Chapter 7).

These few examples show how probing space expands our understanding of the universe. Telescopes transformed the cosmos from a small dull realm in which the planets moved against a static background of stars to a vast, restless universe beyond our reach but within our comprehension.

6.3
Invisible astronomy

Your eye senses only a tiny sliver of the electromagnetic spectrum (Section 5.2). When you have your teeth X-rayed at the dentist, the X-ray machine does not glow brightly when it's on. But the film placed in your mouth senses the X-rays and gives an internal picture of your teeth. When you stand next to an almost dead fire, the coals look black. But your skin senses heat—infrared radiation—on it.

These examples focus on one aspect of invisible astronomy—the need for equipment that can detect the radiation you'd like to observe. The development of detectors is a technological enterprise, often with no direct drive from astronomy. (For instance, sensitive infrared detectors basically evolved for military purposes.)

There's also a less obvious aspect to invisible astronomy: whether or not the radiation from space can make it to the earth's surface. Our atmosphere effectively absorbs large blocks of the electromagnetic spectrum, especially ultraviolet, X-rays, some infrared, and short-wavelength (millimeter) radio waves. The radiation that is absorbed may have journeyed for millions or billions of years, only to be snuffed out in the last 0.001 second of its trip, never making it to the earth's surface.

The obvious way to get around atmospheric absorption is to go above it. This is space astronomy. (In this book, space astronomy includes rockets, balloons, and airplanes.) So invisible astronomy has two natural divisions—that which can be done from the ground and that which must be accomplished in space.

Ground-based radio / Radio astronomy was born in 1930 when Karl Jansky (Fig. 6.12) undertook a study for the Bell Telephone Company of sources of static affecting transoceanic radiotelephone communications. Jansky identified one source of noise as a celestial object: the Milky Way in Sagittarius. Jansky's discovery was published in 1932 but had little impact on the astronomers of the day.

However, a radio engineer, Grote Reber, read Jansky's work and decided in his spare time to search for cosmic radio static. By the 1940s Reber had made detailed maps of the radio sky. He sensed that a new astronomy was in the making and took an astrophysics course at the University of Chicago to learn more about astronomy and discuss his discoveries with astronomers—only a few of whom were impressed.

World War II forced technical developments in radio and radar work. Accidentally, John S. Hey in Britain discovered that the sun strongly emitted radio waves. After the war Hey continued his astronomical pursuits at radio wavelengths, as did other groups in Britain, Holland,

6.12
Karl Jansky with the radio antenna in Holmdel, New Jersey, that he used to discover extraterrestrial radio emission. (Courtesy Bell Labs)

and Australia. Radio astronomy was reborn as a technological fallout from research scientists forced to deal with practical problems.

A common type of radio telescope, a radio dish (Fig. 6.13), functions like a reflecting telescope. Essentially, it's a radio wave bucket with a detector (a radio receiver) at the focus of the dish, which reflects and concentrates radio waves the same way a mirror does in a reflecting telescope (Fig. 6.14).

Radio astronomers cannot see radio sources like an optical astronomer can. The radio receiver that detects the incoming radio waves translates the signal into a voltage that can then be measured and recorded (see Fig. 6.15).

Our atmosphere allows some millimeter, centimeter, and longer wavelengths to reach the ground. These can be observed both day and night. Radio telescopes can even observe on cloudy days at the longer wavelengths. Because large radio dishes are easier to construct than large mirrors, radio telescopes are typically much larger than optical telescopes and more sensitive because they can catch more radiation. These are a few of the advantages of radio compared to optical astronomy.

But radio telescopes have one major drawback: low resolving power. How so? Resolving power depends on both the size of the objective and the wavelength of the gathered light. Radio

6.13
The back of the dish of a radio telescope, one of the antennas of the VLA (Very Large Array). The surface of the dish acts like a mirror to reflect radio waves to a focus. It is about 25 m in diameter.

6.14

Surface of a radio dish, the antenna of Fig. 6.13. The dish reflects the radio waves to a small convex dish (at top center) that reflects the radio waves down through a hole in the main dish (left side of bottom center platform) to a radio receiver below.

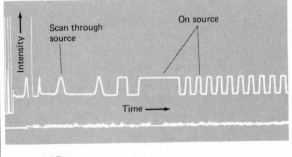

6.15

A radio observation. The intensity of the signal is measured by a strip-chart recorder. Observation by M. Zeilik at Haystack Observatory.

waves are much longer than visible light, typically 100,000 times as long. So if an optical and a radio telescope had the same size, the radio one would have 100,000 times *less* resolving power. An example: For a radio telescope to have the same resolving power as the 200-in Hale telescope not limited by the atmosphere, it would have to have a diameter of about 500 km! Obviously, a single dish of this size cannot be built on the earth.

But there's a method for making a small radio telescope function as if it were a large one. Imagine two radio telescopes placed, say, 10 km apart. By synchronizing the signals received by both, they act like a single dish with a diameter of 10 km—but only for a strip across the sky. (That's because they act like two small pieces at the opposite ends of a larger dish.) To get good resolving power in a small, more or less circular region of the sky requires an array of coordinatd radio telescopes. The largest such telescope, called the Very Large Array (or VLA), is in New Mexico (Fig. 6.16). The VLA has a resolving power at centimeter wavelengths equivalent to that of a moderate-size optical telescope.

Ground-based infrared / Carbon dioxide and water in the earth's atmosphere absorb much of the incoming infrared radiation. The infrared astronomer can peer through only a few restricted wavelength ranges: 2–25, 30–40, and 350–450 microns. (A micron is 10^{-6} meter.) Such observations are best made from high sites in dry climates, where the least amount of water vapor is in the atmosphere above the telescope.

How does an infrared telescope differ from an optical one? Essentially, it differs in the detector at the telescope's focus. Because our eyes and photographic film sense infrared radiation poorly, special infrared detectors are required; sensitive ones suitable for astronomical work have been around for only about 10 years. A common infrared detector is a *bolometer;* it is a tiny chip of germanium (about the size of the head of a very small nail) cooled to very low temperatures—about 2 K. When infrared radiation strikes a bolometer, its resistance to an electric current changes. Such changes can be measured electronically, and the amount of variation indicates how much infrared energy a bolometer is absorbing.

(a)

(b)

6.16

(a) *A part of two arms of the VLA and the central control building. (Courtesy NRAO)* (b) *The view down one arm of the VLA.*

Infrared observing has at least three distinct advantages over optical observing. First, infrared radiation is hindered less by interstellar dust (Section 15.4) than visible light, so you can see through dust more readily. Second, cool celestial objects (3000 K and cooler) give off most of their radiation in the infrared. Typically, such cool objects cannot be seen in visible light but are bright in the infrared. Infrared astronomy brings the cold universe into view. Third, infrared observing can be done during the day, when crowded telescopes are not wanted by optical astronomers. Very little infrared sunlight is scattered by the air, so the infrared sky is just as dark during the day as at night.

Space astronomy / What about the parts of the infrared spectrum that do not penetrate to the ground? Also, what about the ultraviolet light and X-rays? Such radiation can only be detected above the earth's atmosphere from airplanes, balloons, rockets, or satellites.

For example, most of the far infrared (wavelengths longer than about 40 microns) does not make it to the ground. But at altitudes of 20 km or so, very little of the earth's atmosphere remains. Far-infrared observations can be made at these altitudes from balloon-borne telescopes (Fig. 6.17). The equipment is a reflecting telescope equipped with a bolometer.

For ultraviolet astronomy, methods of light

A JOINT PROJECT OF
SMITHSONIAN ASTROPHYSICAL OBSERVATORY
HARVARD COLLEGE OBSERVATORY
UNIVERSITY OF ARIZONA

(a)

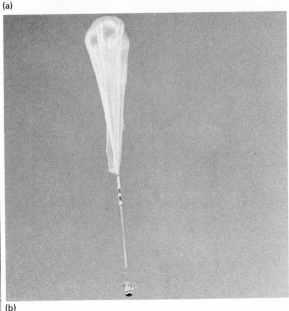

(b)

6.17

(a) *The 40-inch far-infrared telescope of the Center for Astrophysics and the University of Arizona. This telescope is lifted by balloon to an altitude of about 90,000 feet. (b) The 40-inch telescope at launch, carried aloft by a 9 million cubic foot helium balloon.*

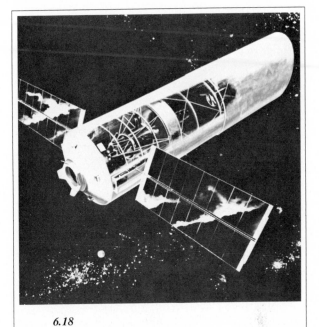

6.18

An artist's conception of the optical space telescope in orbit around the earth. The space telescope will be a reflector with a 2.4-m mirror. The shuttle will place it in an orbit 400 km above the earth's surface.

gathering and detection remain similar to optical astronomy. Photographic plates and some television tubes respond well to ultraviolet light, so detection presents no serious problem. Because glass absorbs ultraviolet light, refracting telescopes cannot be used, but reflectors work perfectly well.

For the high-energy realm of X-ray and gamma-ray astronomy, the problems of light gathering and focus demand that those telescopes have little resemblance to optical ones. X-rays pass through most ordinary matter and so are almost impossible to reflect. In recent years X-ray telescopes have used the fact that X-rays can be reflected from certain surfaces if they strike at very small angles, almost parallel to the reflecting surface. Such reflections produce reasonable images.

Gamma rays are so energetic that to focus them is almost an impossible task. Gamma-ray telescopes don't produce images as such, but they do indicate from what general direction in the sky the gamma rays originate.

Finally, the space astronomy to come will involve large telescopes (Fig. 6.18). The main advantage here (besides the lack of bad weather) is that a space telescope can be used to the practical limit of resolving power rather than as limited by the atmosphere. NASA plans to put a space telescope into earth orbit using the space shuttle.

SUMMARY

New technology produces new telescopes. These in turn provide new views of the universe: first, by gathering and detecting light too faint to be sensed by the eye; second, by resolving details in the structure of astronomical objects; and third, by providing magnified views of what's in the sky.

These new observations influence astronomical models in at least two ways: (1) They provide the grand vision that sets the birth of models. (2) They confirm or refute the predictions of models. So observations have a pull-push function in astronomy; they pull along new ideas and push them to confirmation—or over the edge to oblivion.

Contemporary astronomy—that of this century—has revealed a new face of the universe quite different from that perceived by optical astronomy. It's a restless, complex universe. Both low-energy (radio and infrared) and high-energy (ultraviolet, X-ray, and gamma-ray) astronomy provide complementary views of the newly sensed objects and familiar friends—a rich, sparkling cosmos.

STUDY EXERCISES

1   How did Galileo's telescopic observations support the Copernican model and refute the Ptolemaic/Aristotelean one? (*Objective 1*)

2   What telescopic observations were *critical* to the confirmation of the Copernican model? (*Objectives 1 and 2*)

3   What is the most important function of a telescope? (*Objective 3*) How do refracting telescopes accomplish this function? Reflecting telescopes? (*Objective 4*)

4   How do radio telescopes differ from optical telescopes? How are they similar? What advantages do they have? (*Objectives 3 and 5*)

5   Suppose you were presented with optical, infrared, and radio telescopes, all with the same objective size. List them in order of *increasing* resolving power. (*Objectives 3, 4, and 5*)

6   Imagine that you are going before a congressional hearing to justify the expense of putting a telescope in space. What arguments would you use to persuade the committee? (*Objective 9*)

7   Name one advantage of an infrared telescope over an optical one. (*Objective 8*)

BEYOND THIS BOOK . . .

For an intriguing analysis of the development of radio astronomy in Great Britain, read *Astronomy Transformed* by David Edge and Michael Mulkay (Wiley, New York, 1976).

For a more American view on radio astronomy, try *The Invisible Universe* by Gerrit Verschuur (Springer-Verlag, New York, 1974).

An insight into astronomy as an experimental science can be found in *Experimental Astronomy* by Jean-Claude Pecker (Springer-Verlag, New York, 1970.)

Colin Ronan in *Invisible Astronomy* (Lippincott, Philadelphia, 1972) makes a good case for how new techniques in astronomy lead to new views of the universe.

In *Scientific American* you can read about "Infrared Astronomy" by G. Murray and J. Westphal, August 1965, p. 20; "Intercontinental Radio Astronomy" by K. Kellerman, February 1972, p. 72; "Ultraviolet Astronomy" by L. Goldberg, June 1969, p. 92; "X-Ray Astronomy" by H. Friedman, June 1964, p. 36; "The X-Ray Sky" by H. Schnopper and J. Delvaille, July 1972, p. 26; and "Gamma-Ray Astronomy" by W. Krauschaar and G. Clark, May 1962, p. 52.

Sky and Telescope and *Astronomy* magazines contain ads by telescope manufacturers; also consult classified ads by individuals selling used telescopes (generally good buys because they don't wear out much).

focus 18

SOME EXPERIMENTAL TESTS OF GENERAL RELATIVITY

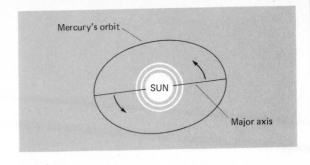

Precession of Mercury's orbit. The major axis of the orbit rotates in space with respect to the stars.

Einstein's model for gravitation would be no more than a fascinating idea if it did not make numerical predictions that could be tested experimentally—predictions of effects unknown or unexplained by Newton's model for gravitation. Here are two essential solar system tests: the deflection of light in curved spacetime and the precession of Mercury's orbit.

Deflection of light / *The sun's mass strongly distorts spacetime in the solar system. As described in Section 7.3, light paths are bent, and this bending is greatest for light that just skirts the edge of the sun. So a solar eclipse is a natural event in which to try to measure the deflection of light from stars. General relativity predicts that the deflection should amount to 1.75 arcsec.*

These are hard observations to make, for careful photographs must be made of the sun and stars during eclipse and also of the stars without the sun in the vicinity. Also, total solar eclipses (Section 1.5) don't usually conveniently fall at established observatories, so astronomers must lug their telescopes to distant locations.

Results have ranged from 1.43 to 2.7 arcsec. The prediction is 1.75 arcsec. Errors may be as large as 20 percent. The scatter in the observed values reflects the difficulty of doing this observation.

Modern technology permits a similar experiment to be done more precisely by radio astronomers. Radio waves and light are essentially the same, so these deflections should also occur for radio signals from distant objects. Some quasars (Chapter 18) are intense radio sources, and each October the sun eclipses quasar 3C279. By monitoring the position of 3C279 relative to a nearby quasar (3C273), radio astronomers, using a technique called interferometry, can accurately (to about 0.1 arcsec) measure the angular separation (Focus 1) between the two quasars. This experiment has been done a number of times, and the observed separation has been within 10 percent of the value predicted by general relativity.

Precession of Mercury's orbit / *Astronomers have known for a long time that the major axis of Mercury's orbit does not remain fixed in space with respect to the stars (Fig. 1). The axis rotates around, or* **precesses,** *in the plane of the orbit. Most of this shifting arises from the gravitational attraction of the other planets on Mercury. But when this effect and others are taken into account, there remains a residual shift of 41 arcsec a century (which means the orbit turns through an extra 360° in about three million years).*

What causes this precession? Newtonians had dreamt of an undiscovered planet—called Vulcan (no, not Mr. Spock's planet)—orbiting within the orbit of Mercury. But no such planet has been found. General relativity predicts a precession because of the strong curvature of spacetime close to the sun. (Precession due to curvature also happens for Venus, the earth, Mars, and so on, but it is much smaller for these planets than for Mercury.) The predicted value for Mercury is 43 arcsec per century—if the sun is perfectly spherical. So the observed and predicted results agree to within 4 percent.

The hooker here is the "if" previously stated. If the sun is slightly oblate, the nonspherical distribution of mass will also cause Mercury's orbit to precess. Because the sun is so bright, it's quite difficult to find out if it is oblate. Early experiments done at Princeton by Robert Dicke and M. Goldenberg indicated a mild solar oblateness. Later work by Henry Hill and colleagues, however, found no measurable oblateness. So it appears that general relativity accurately accounts for the precession of Mercury's orbit.

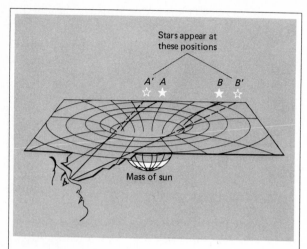

Stars appear at
these positions

A′ A   B B′

Mass of sun

7.10

Einstein's model explaining the change in the observed angular separation of the stars. In Einstein's view the mass-energy of the sun curves spacetime around it. The light from the stars follows this curved spacetime when the sun lies between them as seen from the earth. When the sun is not there, their light does not pass through a strongly warped region of spacetime, and so they appear closer together. (Adapted from a diagram by C. Misner, K. Thorne, and J. Wheeler)

warped, not flat. The amount of warping decreases as the distance from the sun increases. That's why earth, for example, follows an orbit more strongly curved than that of Jupiter.

To sum up the difference in Newton's and Einstein's models for gravity: Newton concentrates on *forces*, Einstein on *courses*. Newton sees gravity as a force acting between all matter, a force whose strength depends on the amount of matter. Einstein focuses on the paths of objects in spacetime; such paths, for free-falling objects, don't depend on the amount of matter. (Proof is Galileo's experiment—two objects of different mass fall with the same acceleration.) So the paths that free-falling objects take—their natural motion—are guided by the local geometry of spacetime.

Warning and Notice: Einstein's geometrical ideas about gravity and spacetime will *not* be used, in general, in the rest of this book. For most purposes, Newton's model of gravitation is a perfectly good one, because in most cases the curvature of spacetime is very small. So you do not need to master Einstein's ideas to the same depth and competency as you do Newton's. Einstein's general theory crops up when we deal with the universe as a whole (the rest of this chapter and Chapter 21) and with black holes (Chapter 20).

7.4

Geometry and the universe

So far you've seen Einstein's picture of gravity in a small region of spacetime, such as near the sun. But his general theory applies also to the universe. It allows you to picture the geometry of the cosmos as it relates to the motion of the whole universe. Keep in mind that three basic geometries are possible: hyperbolic, closed, and flat. Remember also that Einstein does not state which geometry must apply; he leaves this open to experimental confirmation.

Imagine again living in two dimensions on the surface of a sphere. Start at any point and walk on a straight line away from it. Eventually, you'll return to your starting point, because a sphere has so much curvature that it comes back on itself. Suppose the universe has the same geometrical properties (in spacetime) as a sphere's surface. Then if you send out light signals, they could eventually return to you. Why? Because *if* the universe contains enough matter

moves along a straight line. When it crosses a depression, the ball follows a path that bends, compared to the path on the flat. The amount of bending depends on the depth of the depression and how fast the ball travels. In Einstein's general theory of relativity, mass and energy create local warps in spacetime. The amount and density of mass-energy determine how steep the depression is. As an object moves through a warped region of spacetime it follows a straight-line, natural motion path. In warped spacetime this path appears curved to us. But no force acts on the object. This is essentially how Einstein understood the nature of the gravitational force locally. Experimental tests (Focus 18) indicate that this understanding is correct.

Einstein considered the orbits of the planets in the same way. All the planets move on straight-line paths in spacetime. These paths appear as elliptical orbits in three dimensions. The paths appear curved because spacetime is

and energy, its spacetime will close back on it-self. (*Warning:* If the universe is closed, it does *not* have an edge. Consider again a sphere's surface; you can go around it many times and never find an edge.)

We don't know for sure yet that our universe *is* closed—that depends on whether it contains enough matter and energy to curve it sufficiently. But if it does contain enough, then it will be finite (and unbounded), just like the surface of a sphere is finite (and unbounded), and light could go all the way around.

Obviously, this method of finding out if the universe is closed is impractical—the universe is large and the speed of light finite. Let's turn this idea around. The density of mass (and energy, since $E = mc^2$) determines the curvature of spacetime. If this density is a certain critical amount (or greater), then the universe curves back on itself and is closed. Einstein's general theory gives this critical density: It is roughly 5×10^{-30} g/cc. (That's about one hydrogen atom for every cubic meter of space.)

In 1917 Einstein constructed a model of the universe with a closed geometry. How different from Newton's model, which had to be infinite (Section 4.3)! In a geometrical sense Einstein's model was akin to the finite, closed picture of Aristotle (Section 2.3). In fact, Einstein's model was also static.

A few years after Einstein proposed his model, astronomers discovered it was *wrong*. They found that the universe is not static but *expanding!* Einstein's theory was right, but his specific model was wrong. Later, he and others proposed other models that naturally incorporated the expansion of the universe.

A quick tour of the universe / Before investigating general relativity's impact on cosmological ideas, let's look at the content and scale of the universe. (The rest of this book will describe the contents of the astronomical universe in detail.)

Because the universe is a big place, you need a long measuring stick. I'll use what I consider the most natural one: light travel time. You're probably familiar with the term *light year* (abbreviated *ly*)—the distance light covers in a year (at a speed of about 3×10^5 km/sec) which amounts to about 9.5×10^{15} m or 63,000 AU. Other useful light units are: a light second, 3×10^8 m; light minute, 1.8×10^{10} m; light hour,

1.1×10^{12} m; light day, 2.4×10^{13} m; and a light month, 7.8×10^{14} m.

Let's start the trip out with a familiar astronomical body—the earth (Fig. 7.11(a)). Light can speed across the earth's diameter in roughly 10^{-2} sec. Our sun (Fig. 7.11(b)) has a much larger size than the earth—a few light seconds. The sun is a hot ball of gas, heated by fusion reactions in its center (Chapter 13)—those are the sources of its light. Sunlight zips to the earth from the sun in roughly 8 min. It reaches Pluto, the outpost of the solar system in about 5 light hours.

Stars are bodies like the sun. The nearest—Alpha Centauri—lies some 4 light years away. The stars near the sun and all those you can see in the night sky (Fig. 7.11(c)) make up a disk of stars called the *Milky Way Galaxy*. The gravity of its contents—mostly stars, some 10^{11} of them—holds the Galaxy gracefully together. The Galaxy has a diameter of approximately 120,000 ly.

The nearest galaxy to the earth that resembles our Milky Way is the Andromeda galaxy (Fig. 7.11(d))—so named because it appears in the constellation of Andromeda as seen from the earth. The Andromeda galaxy is about 2 million ly distant.

The Andromeda galaxy and the Milky Way Galaxy are parts of a local group of galaxies, bound by gravity. This neighborhood cluster of galaxies has a diameter of some 3 million ly. In this century astronomers have found that the universe contains many clusters of galaxies (Fig. 7.11(e)). The largest are tens of millions of light years in diameter. Clusters of galaxies are spaced apart, on the average, by hundreds of millions of light years.

A key concept: Light travels at a fast but finite speed. Cosmic distances are huge. So when looking out into space, you are looking back in time. The further out you peer, the deeper into the past you see. The light received now from galaxies left them many millions or billions of years ago.

Astronomers have found that these clusters of galaxies are not stationary. They are all moving away from each other. This cosmic motion implies that the universe is expanding.

The expanding universe / At the beginning of this century the development of large telescopes allowed astronomers to record the spectra of galaxies. Because most galaxies are made

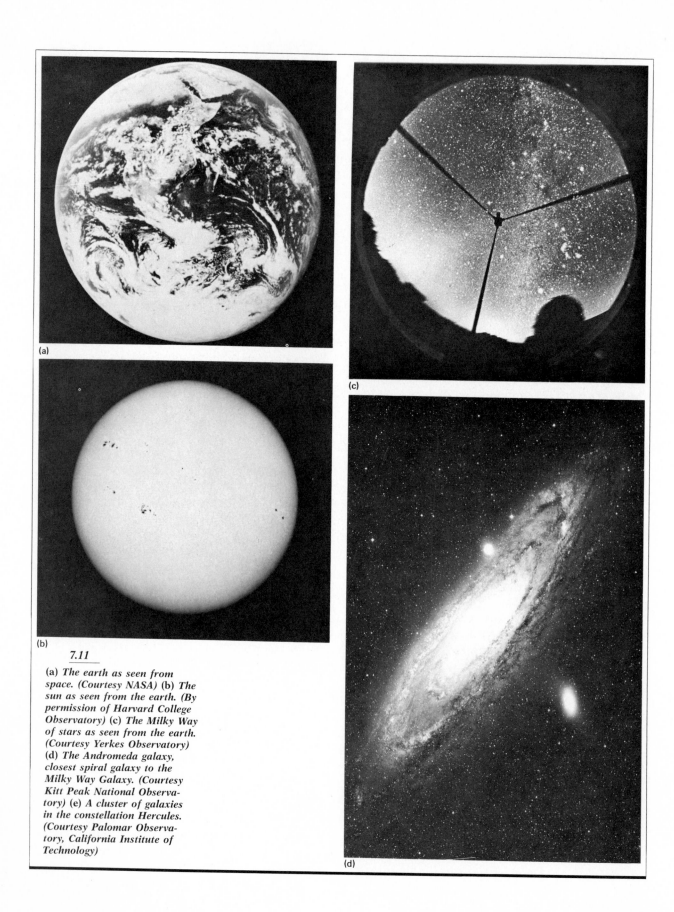

7.11

(a) *The earth as seen from space. (Courtesy NASA)* (b) *The sun as seen from the earth. (By permission of Harvard College Observatory)* (c) *The Milky Way of stars as seen from the earth. (Courtesy Yerkes Observatory)* (d) *The Andromeda galaxy, closest spiral galaxy to the Milky Way Galaxy. (Courtesy Kitt Peak National Observatory)* (e) *A cluster of galaxies in the constellation Hercules. (Courtesy Palomar Observatory, California Institute of Technology)*

(e)

primarily of stars, they have spectra like stars (Section 5.2); their spectra consist of dark lines against a continuous background. However, for most galaxies, the identifiable dark lines did not appear at their correct places in the spectra. ("Correct" means at the same wavelengths measured for a stationary source on the earth.) The wavelengths of the dark lines are typically shifted toward the red end of the spectra. This red shift implies that the galaxies are moving away.

How does this shift occur? It results from the wave properties of light (Section 5.3) and is called the *Doppler effect* (see Focus 19 for details). Here's a brief description of the Doppler effect: Suppose you have a light at rest that emits one wavelength. You can measure the

wavelength of emission with a spectroscope. Now imagine the light source moving *away* from you at a constant velocity (Fig. 7.12). When you measure the line's wavelength again, it will be *longer* than you found previously. The line has shifted toward the red end of the spectrum; it is *red shifted*. Now suppose the source moves toward you. Then you will find the line to have a shorter wavelength; it has shifted toward the blue end of the spectrum. The line is *blue shifted*. So you see a blue shift if you and the source approach and a red shift if you and it draw apart. The amount of the shift depends on the relative velocity of you and the source along your line of sight to the source. The greater the relative velocity is, the greater will be the observed shift in the wavelength.

focus 19

THE DOPPLER SHIFT

The beauty of the Doppler shift is that astronomers can use it to find the line-of-sight velocities of luminous objects without having to know their distance and with just one observation. The Doppler shift is named after Christian J. Doppler (1803–1853), who first noticed the effect in sound waves. Later the French physicist Armand Hippolyte Fizeau (1819–1896) applied the Doppler shift to light waves and recognized its importance in astronomical applications. In honor of these two men it should be called the Doppler–Fizeau shift. Most people call it the Doppler shift.

The Doppler shift occurs with all kinds of waves—light, sound, and even water waves. Let me give you an example with water waves. Imagine you are out in a small motorboat to fish (Fig. 1). You have been sitting in one spot for a while with little luck, and the rhythm of the waves, generated by a gentle wind, has lulled you almost to sleep. You decide to move for better fishing. First you go into the wind (the wave source). You notice that you bob up and down more frequently than when you were at rest; the wavelength appears to have gotten shorter. Just for fun you drive the boat with the wind. You discover that your bobbing is less frequent; the waves seem to you to have a longer wavelength. The explanation is simple: When you moved in the direction of the waves, you had to catch up with each; when you went into them, they caught up to you.

That's the Doppler shift. When you are moving toward a wave source, the waves appear more frequent and shorter in wavelength; in contrast, when you move away from a wave source, the waves appear less frequent and the wavelength longer. It's the relative velocity along the line of the sight—called the radial velocity—that causes the Doppler shift.

Now consider light waves, which you can't see directly. You can, however, see col-

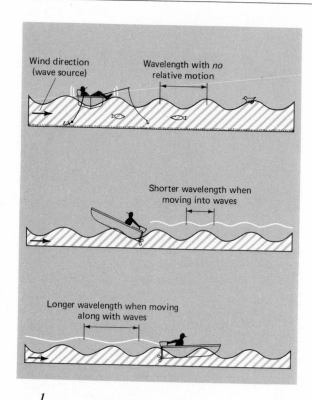

1

Wavelength and relative motion—an example using water waves.

ors of light, which relate directly to wavelength. Keep in mind that red light has a longer wavelength than blue.

Imagine a stationary light source giving off just one particular wavelength every second (Fig. 2). Each wave travels outward with velocity c, the speed of light. When the source is not moving, all the waves are concentric and separated by the wavelength of emission.

Now imagine that the source moves from point S_1 to point S_2 in one second, and so on. At each point (S_1, S_2, S_3, S_4,) it emits a wave (1,2,3,4) that travels out at c. In the direction of its motion the source catches up a bit with the wave it has just emitted, so for an observer at A the wavelength appears shorter. This observer sees the distance between the waves as compressed and so observes a Doppler shift to the short-wavelength end of

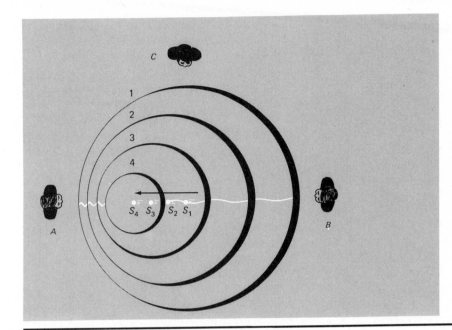

2

The Doppler shift in detail. Imagine a source giving off just one wavelength of light and moving from right to left (arrow). In one second it goes from S_1 to S_2, and so on. In the direction of its motion the source catches up to the waves it emitted, so the wavelength appears shorter to an observer in this direction. Opposite the direction of motion the source moves away from the waves it has emitted, so the wavelength appears longer in this direction. So a blue shift results in the direction of motion, a red shift, in the opposite direction.

the spectrum. In contrast, an observer B sees the waves as spread apart, a Doppler shift to the long-wavelength end of the spectrum. An observer at C, at right angles to the direction of the source's motion, measures no change in the wavelength and consequently no Doppler shift. Note that only the velocity along the line of sight contributes to the Doppler shift. *It is also important to remember that the Doppler shift does* not *depend on the distance between the observer and the source but only on their relative velocities.*

The astronomer uses the Doppler shift to determine the line-of-sight velocities of celestial objects (such as stars) relative to the earth by using spectral lines to measure wavelength shifts. He or she takes a spectrogram of the object and at the same time superimposes a comparison spectrum from a stationary source. The comparison is at rest with respect to the telescope and provides the normal (zero relative velocity) placement of the lines with respect to which the astronomer measures the shift for certain lines. With the measured shift and the value of c, the astronomer calculates the relative velocity between the source and earth by

relative velocity
= *(shift in wavelength/original wavelength)* $\times c$

or,

$$v_r = (\Delta\lambda/\lambda_0) \times c$$

where λ_0 is the original wavelength of the spectral line (the rest wavelength), $\Delta\lambda$ is the shift in wavelength, and v_r is the relative radial velocity of approach (blue shift) or recession (red shift), and c is the speed of light.

Here's an example: A strong dark line from absorption by calcium has a rest wavelength of 3933 Å. (Å stands for the wavelength unit of Angstroms, with $1\,Å = 10^{-10}$ m.) Suppose you measure this line in the spectrum of a moving object and find it shifted to 3972 Å. Is the object moving away or toward you? —away, since the wavelength is longer. How fast?

$$\Delta\lambda = 3972 - 3933 = 39\,Å$$

$$v_r = \frac{39}{3933}\,(3 \times 10^8\,m/sec)$$

$$= 3 \times 10^6\,m/sec$$

$$= 3000\,km/sec$$

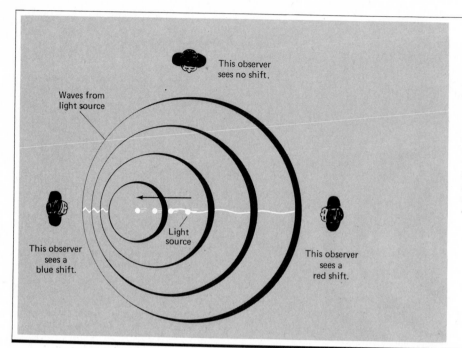

Waves from light source

This observer sees no shift.

This observer sees a blue shift.

Light source

This observer sees a red shift.

7.12

The Doppler effect for light. Imagine a light source moving (arrow) from right to left. If you stood in the path of its approach, you would see its light blue shifted compared to how it appeared when stationary. If you stood behind it and watched it move away, you would find that its light was red shifted. In contrast, if you stood at right angles to the motion, you would see no shift at all.

Note: For speeds much less than light, which is the usual case, it's only the part of the velocity *along the line of sight* that contributes to the Doppler shift. An object may, for example, move at some angle relative to your line of sight. Only the part of its velocity directly toward or away from you results in a Doppler shift. This line-of-sight part is called the *radial velocity.*

The Hubble law / By 1917 Vesto M. Slipher (1875–1969) had measured the velocities of 15 galaxies, and all but two had red shifts, which implied they were receding from our Galaxy. By 1928 Slipher had obtained spectra for over 40 galaxies, and the trend was becoming clear: Most galaxies were apparently moving away from our Galaxy. (Fig. 7.13).

At about the same time, Edwin P. Hubble (1899–1953) had determined the distances to some galaxies and noted an unexpected direct relationship between radial velocity and distance: For every million light years farther out, the galaxies had 170 km/sec more velocity. Modern astronomers use the unit *parsec* (abbreviated pc) more often than light year (see Appendix A). The conversion is: one pc = 3.26 ly = 3.09×10^{13} km. In these units, for every million parsecs, or megaparsec (Mpc), far-

ther out, the galaxies had 550 km/sec more velocity. (Modern measurements give a much smaller value.) In later collaborative work Hubble and Milton L. Humason (1891–1972), using the 100-inch telescope, added more data to support the trend. This relationship, now known as *Hubble's law*, states that the distance to a galaxy and its recessional velocity are directly related.

The number connecting the distance and velocity is called *Hubble's constant* and is usually indicated as *H*. It's the slope of the line on a radial velocity–distance plot such as Fig. 7.14. The steeper the slope is, the larger will be the value of *H*.

Hubble and Humason thought the *H* was 550 km/sec/Mpc. Today astronomers believe that *H* lies between 50 and 100 km/sec/Mpc. (The exact value is disputed. Chapter 17 deals with the controversy.) This book uses 50 km/sec/Mpc. This value means that for every megaparsec from our Galaxy, the radial velocity of other galaxies is 50 km/sec higher. For example, a galaxy at 5 Mpc travels at 5×50, or 250 km/sec radial velocity, whereas one at 10 Mpc moves at 10×50, or 500 km/sec.

Here's a concrete analogy. Picture an astronomy class in a large lecture hall. Suppose that at the end of the class the instructor lets

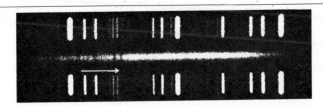

7.13

The red shift in the spectrum of a galaxy. On the left is a picture of a galaxy, on the right its spectrum. In the spectrum (at the head of the white arrow) are two dark lines. These lines are from calcium in the stars that make up the galaxy. The bright-line spectrum above and below the galaxy's spectrum was made at the telescope when the galaxy's spectrum was taken; it marks the wavelengths at rest. The length of the arrow indicates how much the calcium lines are shifted in the galaxy's spectrum compared with the positions of the same lines in the comparison spectrum. The red shift (length of arrow) results from a line-of-sight speed of 15,000 km/sec. (Courtesy Palomar Observatory, California Institute of Technology)

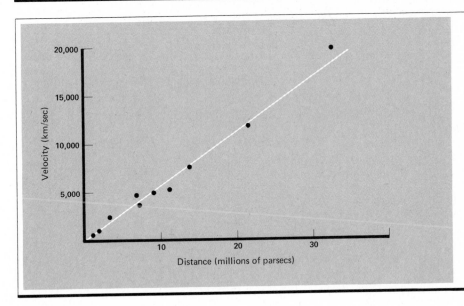

7.14

Hubble and Humason's distance–velocity relationship for galaxies. Plotted here is a galaxy's recessional velocity (in kilometers per second), as determined from its red shift, against its distance (in millions of parsecs, or megaparsecs). The straight line indicates the trend of the data (points). It shows that for every megaparsec farther away from our galaxy other galaxies show a recessional velocity of 550 km/sec. This is a graphical representation of the Hubble law with a Hubble constant, H, of 550 km/sec/Mpc.

people leave in the following special manner: Those in the back row go out with a higher velocity than those in front, and the speed with which people leave depends directly on how far away they are from the instructor. So if the people in the back row are 10 times as far away as the people in the front, they leave with 10 times the speed. Now suppose the instructor tells everyone to walk directly away from the lecture hall for some period of time (say 10 min) and then stop. If the instructor at the end of that time runs around the campus looking for the class, he or she would find the back-row people 10 times farther away from the lecture hall than those in the front row. This is an example of uniform expansion obeying a Hubble law.

The discovery of this trend, that more dis-

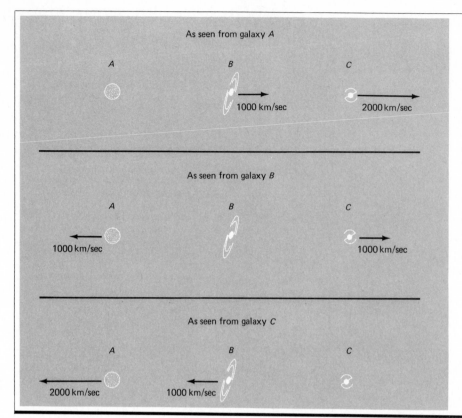

As seen from galaxy A

A   B   C

1000 km/sec   2000 km/sec

As seen from galaxy B

A   B   C

1000 km/sec   1000 km/sec

As seen from galaxy C

A   B   C

2000 km/sec   1000 km/sec

7.15

Uniform expansion explained. Imagine three galaxies (A, B, and C) equal distances apart. Picture yourself at galaxy A. If these galaxies expand uniformly, then B appears to be moving away from you at 1000 km/sec and C at 2000 km/ sec. Now move yourself to B. From there, A appears to be moving away at 1000 km/sec, and so does C. Now jump to galaxy C. From here, B appears to move away at 1000 km/sec and A at 2000 km/sec. Note that none of these locations is a "center" of expansion, yet each one seems to be.

tant galaxies move away faster, caused a radical revision of Einstein's static model for the universe. It appeared that the entire universe was expanding. As Hubble quipped, "The history of astronomy is the history of receding horizons." And Einstein later admitted that his 1917 static model was the "biggest mistake of my life"—a mistake which he and others quickly corrected to allow an evolving universe.

The meaning of Hubble's law / Hubble and Humason were careful to term the galaxies' rush away as "apparent." Taken at face value the measured red shifts fixed us in the center of the universe. Having been rudely thrust away from the center by Copernicus, astronomers felt somewhat uncomfortable at being repositioned there. Was the Milky Way, our own Galaxy, now enthroned again with the universe centered on it?

A simple argument demonstrates that our Galaxy does not really have a privileged status. From our viewpoint the rest of the universe appears to be retreating from our Galaxy. But if the expansion is *uniform,* then the view from any other galaxy will be the same (Fig. 7.15). Transported to another galaxy with the usual bundle of tools, an astronomer would plot the same Hubble law as he or she does from our Galaxy. Another galaxy appears, to those in it, as the "center" of the expansion, so no privileged position actually exists.

As a concrete analogy, imagine a jungle gym with a person located at each intersection of the bars (Fig. 7.16). Suppose the bars expanded at the same constant rate. Each observer would see all other observers moving away from him or her. How fast they moved would depend on their distance. One twice as far away as another would move twice as fast. Since the expansion is uniform, all the observers would describe the expansion in the same way, and each would think that he or she was in the center. If everyone plotted a graph of distance versus velocity, all the graphs would look the same and resemble the Hubble law for galaxies. And everyone would obtain the same value for H.

Now imagine the jungle gym *contracting* at

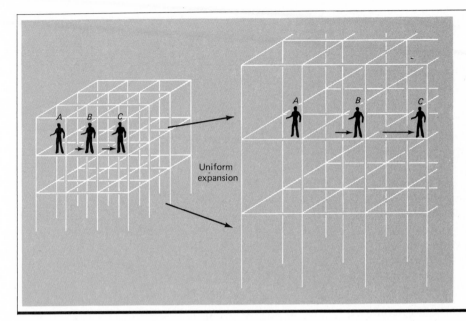

Uniform expansion

7.16

Uniform expansion in three dimensions. Imagine three people (A, B, and C) lined up at the intersections of a huge jungle gym. If it expands uniformly, then person A sees person C moving away twice as fast as the one at B. Person C sees the same: A moves away twice as fast as B. All these people infer the same distance-velocity relationship. And each would observe the same value for the rate of expansion, as in Fig. 7.15.

a uniform rate. After a finite time everyone will arrive together. This is uniform contraction—analogous to the universe contracting. This analogy implies that the expansion of the universe we see now must have begun a finite time in the past. Having a value of the Hubble constant of roughly 50 km/sec/Mpc, you can estimate about when the expansion began (Focus 20): 13 billion years ago.

Astronomers call this beginning of the universe's expansion the Big Bang.

7.5

Relativity and the cosmos

With the discovery of the expanding universe, cosmologists began devising models that would account for the expansion. These models must be consistent with Einstein's general theory and the Hubble law.

Warning: When first confronted by the expansion of the universe, people commonly have the misconception that the universe expands "into empty space." That's wrong; don't think of it! It is *space itself* that is expanding. And it does not expand into "something" or even "nothing," because the phrase "expand into" is meaningless in this context.

In these models the average cosmological density, the Hubble constant, and the geometry of spacetime (whether flat, hyperbolic, or spher-

ical) are physically and mathematically interrelated. Let me show you how, using the concept of escape velocity (Focus 13).

Escape velocity and cosmology / Imagine throwing an object off the earth. You have to throw it upward with a velocity of at least 11 km/sec (the earth's escape velocity) in order for it to fly into space, never to return. If the object is thrown with less than escape velocity, it goes upward more and more slowly until it stops and falls back to the earth.

With the idea of escape velocity in mind, consider the universe and the galaxies in it. Any one galaxy in the universe is analogous to the ball. The galaxies were once all "thrown away" from one another, for we now see an expansion. Imagine a galaxy at a distance R from us. Newton showed that there is no net gravitational force produced by any matter farther away than R and that the net effect of all matter within the distance R is as if this total mass were concentrated at the center (as long as the matter is distributed uniformly). If there is enough mass within the distance R, the escape velocity will be larger than the expansion velocity. Note that "enough mass within the distance R" means a high enough density. So if the density is large enough, the galaxies will not have escape velocity; the expansion velocities will decrease with time and eventually reverse as gravity herds all

focus 20

HUBBLE'S CONSTANT AND THE AGE OF THE UNIVERSE

*You can infer from the measured value of H the time since the expansion of the universe began. To do this simply you need to make the assumption that the expansion rate is uniform. So in the past or future the value of H remains the same. (***Warning: This assumption does*** not ***apply to the universe as we know it. For any realistic model H must decrease with time. However, this assumption allows a simple calculation of the oldest possible age of the universe from the present value of H.)***

At a constant velocity you know that the distance, d, traveled is equal to the velocity, v, multiplied by the time, t. In algebraic form,

distance = velocity × time

or

$$d = vt$$

For example, if you travel in a car from Boston to New York (a distance of 400 km) at a constant speed of 80 km/h, the trip takes 5 hours. You reach this conclusion because

$$t = \frac{d}{v}$$

Hubble's law written as an equation (rather than presented on a graph) is

$$v = HD$$

Here v is the recessional velocity of a galaxy, D the distance to the galaxy, and H the Hubble constant. If H has the units km/sec/Mpc and D is given in Mpc, then v comes out in km/sec. For example, H is about 50 km/sec/Mpc, and suppose you find a galaxy 10 Mpc from our galaxy. Then its recessional velocity is

$$v = (50 \, km/sec/Mpc)(10 \, Mpc)$$
$$= 500 \, km/sec$$

Now compare the Hubble law written as

$$\frac{1}{H} = \frac{D}{v}$$

to the trip formula

$$t = \frac{d}{v}$$

You see that the travel time equals 1/H. If H is 50 km/sec/Mpc, then 1/H equals 2×10^{10} years. So the expansion of the universe started about 2×10^{10} years ago.

This conclusion is valid **only** *if the assumption of uniform expansion is correct. In fact, it's not, for matter's self-attraction slows the expansion down, so the universe is actually* **younger** *than calculated for uniform expansion. For the flat case, the age is 13 billion years.*

---

the galaxies together. If the average density is too low, the galaxies will have more than escape velocity; gravity will never bring the galaxies all together, and the expansion will continue indefinitely.

Consider these two cases—expansion forever and eventual collapse. In the first, the explosion of the Big Bang gave matter just escape velocity, so after a very long time (infinity), the expansion stops and the galaxies stay the same distance apart (infinite!). This case corresponds to a flat geometry. In the second, where matter has less than escape velocity, at some time all

galaxies reach a maximum separation. Then they draw together until they collide. This case corresponds to a closed geometry.

In the third case, the Big Bang imparted matter a speed greater than the escape velocity. The expansion slows down, but after an infinite time the galaxies still move away from each other and do so forever. This case corresponds to a hyperbolic geometry.

So cosmic spherical, flat, and hyperbolic geometries relate physically to cases of less than, equal to, and greater than escape velocity for the matter in the Big Bang. Now, from Einstein's general relativity *and* the observed value of the Hubble constant (50 km/sec/Mpc), a flat universe requires a density of about 5×10^{-30} g/cc. If the universe has a density less than this value, it is hyperbolic; greater, it is closed. So if we can find out the average density of matter and energy in the universe, we have an experimental basis for determining the geometry of spacetime! Observations of the Hubble constant combined with general relativity provide a way to find out if the universe is open or closed.

Making such an observation is not easy. First, astronomers can see out to about 10 billion light years. Second, we can see only those masses that radiate or absorb radiation at detectable wavelengths, intense enough to register on our instruments. Third, we need some method to determine the mass of observed objects. Current methods of observation cannot detect "invisible" objects. The most recent density derived from estimating the mass in galaxies, about 4×10^{-31} g/cc, neglects the contribution of such undetected objects and all other unnoticed masses. We get this value by estimating the mass with the largest volume of space possible, then dividing the mass by the volume to get the density. The observed density amounts to about 12 times less than is needed to close the universe, but it falls near the necessary value. For cosmologists who prefer a closed universe, the close-but-not-quite results have spurred a search for the missing matter needed to close the universe. (The matter is not missing at all if the universe has an open geometry.)

Geometry and Hubble's constant / Whether or not the Hubble constant has the same value at all locations and times also depends on the geometry of the universe. Perhaps the expansion rate has been faster or slower in the past than it is now. As you peer deep into space, the value of *H* changes, and the Hubble diagram (Fig. 7.17) is not a straight line but bends up (if the expansion has been faster in the past) or down (if the expansion has been slower in the past). If the Hubble line curves up enough, the universe is closed and spherical; if it curves down, the universe is open. (The situation is complicated because the evolution of galaxies also affects the Hubble relation.)

Examine the Hubble diagram in Figure 7.17. Those galaxies that are the farthest away (in the

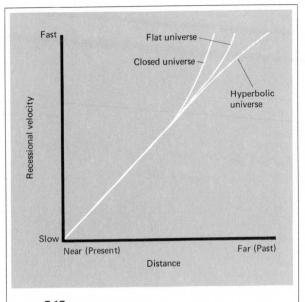

7.17

The geometry of the universe and the Hubble diagram. If we look far enough out in space (and so back in time), the Hubble diagram can be used to infer the geometry of the cosmos. If the universe is closed, the graph will bend up *compared with the plot expected for a flat universe. This tells us that the expansion was much greater in the past than now. Where the observed distance-velocity plot for galaxies falls on this theoretical diagram indicates the overall geometry of the universe.*

upper right-hand part) are also those whose light comes to us from the farthest time in the past when the expansion rate (and so the Hubble constant) must have been much larger than it is now. The far away galaxies tell about the expansion rate in the past; if it were much larger then, the slope of the Hubble graph must have been greater than it is now. (Remember, the slope of the graph is *H*.) The Hubble constant now is given by nearby galaxies (the lower left-hand part of the Hubble diagram). So you expect the Hubble plot to bend upward for the distant galaxies compared to nearby ones. (So you see that *H* isn't really a constant; it's constant only in the sense that the ratio of velocity to distance is the same for all galaxies at any

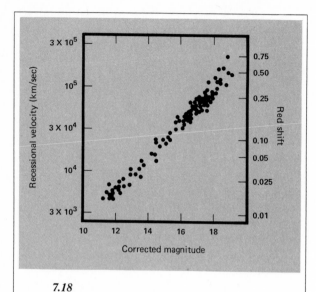

7.18

A Hubble diagram for galaxies out to a red shift of 75 percent. The horizontal axis, labeled "corrected magnitude," is an indirect measure of a galaxy's distance; the vertical axis is the recessional velocity in km/sec (left) and red shift ($\Delta\lambda/\lambda_0$). (From Kristian, J. et al., the Astrophysical Journal, vol. 221, p. 383, copyright 1978 by the American Astronomical Society)

rush together (astronomers would see spectral shifts to the blue) into a dense conglomeration with (theoretically) zero size. The universe would then crush everything into high-energy light (Chapter 21).

Which fate does the Hubble diagram display? Unfortunately, the observations have not yet settled the issue. Here's one problem: As far out as galaxies can be observed, the observational errors are as large as the effect being sought. So deviations from a straight-line Hubble plot are hard to see (Fig. 7.17). Another problem: As previously mentioned, it's difficult to separate the evolution of galaxies from the evolution of the universe.

Results to date have been a mixed bag, some supporting an open universe, others closed. Jerome Kristian, Allan Sandage, and James Westphal have extended the Hubble diagram out to red shifts of 75 percent the speed of light (Fig. 7.18). At face value the observations indicate the universe is closed. But if galaxies evolve rapidly with time, the results are consistent with a flat model. These astronomers state that "the case is not yet settled."

particular time; at different times that ratio may be different.)

What's the future for the universe in these various cases? In all three there is some moment when the expansion begins. In a closed universe the rate of expansion slows down and eventually stops; then the universe contracts. In a hyperbolic universe, the rate of expansion doesn't slow down as rapidly, and it never stops. Even after infinite time the galaxies are still moving apart at a finite velocity. In the borderline case of a flat universe the expansion slows down just enough so that it comes to a stop after infinite time.

The future of the universe / There seem to be two possible cosmic destinies: In one the expansion grinds on like the wheel of karma forever, and the universe gradually thins out. In the other the expansion slows down, stops, and reverses, and then the universe collapses. During the time of diminishing size, the galaxies

SUMMARY

To model the universe properly requires consideration of the geometry of spacetime. Mathematics by itself provides a wide range of choices. Only experiments and observations can confirm the geometry suitable for the universe. The choices can be boiled down to three: flat, hyperbolic, or closed (Table 7.1). Present observations don't tell for certain which is correct.

Newtonian physics assumes that the geometry of the universe is flat. This assumption implicitly underlies Newton's first law of motion and concept of inertia. Einstein, in contrast, demanded that the geometry of the universe be put to an experimental test. His general theory of relativity allows the cosmos to have any geometrical properties; it is not limited to only one choice.

Einstein arrived at this view from a reconsideration of space, time, and gravitation. In the process he revised the Newtonian view that gravity is a force. Instead, he pictured gravity as a manifestation of the local geometry of space-

TABLE 7.1 *Geometry of the universe and observations*

	Hyperbolic	*Closed*	*Flat*
Extent in space	Infinite	Finite	Infinite
Extent in time	Infinite	Finite	Infinite
Bounded?	No	Yes	No
Average density ($H = 50$ km/sec/Mpc)	Less than 5×10^{-30} g/cc	More than 5×10^{-30} g/cc	Equals 5×10^{-30} g/cc
	(Observed average density is about 4×10^{-31} g/cc.)		
Hubble plot	Bends downward	Bends strongly upward	Bends slightly upward
Age to date ($H = 50$ km/sec/Mpc)	More than 13 billion years	Less than 13 billion years	Equals 13 billion years
Future	Expansion forever	Expansion stops; collapse	Expansion forever

time. From where does mass get its moving orders? Newton would have answered: from other masses, acting at a distance. Einstein says instead: from the local geometry of spacetime.

This transformation of the concept of gravitation led to new models of the universe. What observations relate to these models? The most important one was the discovery of red shifts in the spectra of galaxies. Interpreted in terms of a Doppler effect, these red shifts indicate that other galaxies are moving away from us. This recessional motion follows a trend: The farther away a galaxy is, the faster it recedes. This trend is known as Hubble's law. It implies that the universe is expanding. When combined with the general theory of relativity, Hubble's law demands that the universe itself evolves. So space and time also evolve.

Contemporary cosmological models have evolved a long way from the conceptions of the Greeks. No more are the earth and sky separated. No more are the heavens static for eternity. We now perceive the universe as an evolving entity, understandable because of universal physical laws. Such is the power of scientific models that we can hold even the universe in our heads.

STUDY EXERCISES

1 Suppose you hear on the radio that astronomers have discovered a galaxy 500 Mpc from us. Use the Hubble law to estimate how fast that galaxy is receding from us. (*Objective 6*)

2 Assume that H equals 50 km/sec/Mpc. At what distance would the recessional velocity equal half the speed of light (150,000 km/sec)? (*Objective 6*)

3 Describe standing on the earth in Newton's terms and in Einstein's. (*Objectives 1, 2, and 3*)

4 Describe orbiting the earth in Newton's terms, and contrast this to Einstein's description. (*Objectives 1, 2, and 3*)

5 In Einstein's model, how is the geometry of the universe related to the average density of the universe? (*Objective 8*)

6 Suppose you were an astronomer in the Andromeda galaxy with the same tools as an earth-bound astronomer. You measure the distances and Doppler shifts from galaxies. What would you see? (*Objectives 6 and 7*)

BEYOND THIS BOOK . . .

You are probably all excited and tremendously confused by Einstein's theory of relativity. My advice: Go slowly and don't be frustrated. Think on it and the basics will come to you, but it may take a while. Try *Relativity* (Crown, New York, 1961) by A. Einstein, *The Meaning of Relativity* (Princeton University Press, Princeton, N.J. 1956), *Relativity and Common Sense* (Doubleday, Garden City, N.Y., 1964) by H. Bondi, and *Albert*

Einstein: Creator and Rebel (Viking, New York, 1972) by B. Hoffman in collaboration with H. Dukas.

The best book I've found on the nonscientific side of Einstein is R. Clark's *Einstein: The Life and Times* (World, New York, 1971).

I bet you find it hard to picture four dimensions. For a satirical analogy in fewer dimensions read *Flatland* (Dover, New York, 1952) by E. A. Abbott.

After you've read the preceding references, try "The Curvature of Space in a Finite Universe" by J. J. Callahan in *Scientific American*, August 1976, p. 90.

The Cosmic Frontiers of General Relativity (Little Brown, Boston, 1977) by W. Kaufman deals in more depth with Einstein's ideas.

The Red Limit (Bantam Books, New York, 1977) by T. Ferris gives good insights into the development of modern cosmology.

An excellent book on *special* relativity is *Space and Time in Special Relativity* by N. David Mermin (McGraw-Hill, New York, 1968).

A good recent exposition of relativity and cosmology is *The Big Bang* by Joseph Silk (Freeman, San Francisco, 1980).

I have led you on a long trip through space and time. I hope that you have found at least some of it fascinating. I do. I have always been intrigued by the cosmological ideas of ancient people, such as the Babylonians. It is amazing to see these ideas start from simple astronomical observations and evolve into explanations of the workings of the universe.

Modern cosmological ideas have similar goals. With their telescopes, astronomers find that the universe contains innumerable galaxies. Each of these contains some billions of stars. The galaxies appear to be moving away from us. We can understand this expansion by applying physical laws we believe to be true—in this case Einstein's general theory of relativity. The theory tells us how the universe is expanding. And that we can think about the past and possible future of the universe. Our universe may keep expanding forever. Or it may collapse on itself. Observations, when combined with Einstein's theory, will actually be able to tell which will happen.

What distinguishes our present conception of the cosmos from those of the past? Basically I think it is the demand that conceptual models both explain and predict what we observe. Such was not the case for Babylonian cosmology. Some prediction was involved, but no explanation in terms of natural phenomena was attempted. The idea of making models to understand the world originated with the Greeks. Ptolemy's geocentric picture represents the first complete scheme of the cosmos, intended to explain and predict planetary motions. But Ptolemy apparently did not believe that his model corresponded to the real world, for example, that the planets actually moved on epicycles.

Starting with Copernicus, astronomers

began to devise models that corresponded closely to reality, as given by observations. Kepler, for example, believed that the magnetic force from the sun actually pushed the planets around in their orbits. Newton later described correctly the nature of the force between the sun and planets. But he would not discuss what gravitational forces really were; he dealt only with their effects. Einstein moved one step deeper. He attempted, in the general theory of relativity, to explain the nature of gravity. He saw gravity not as a force but as a manifestation of the geometry of spacetime. In doing so he rediscovered the importance of geometry in the physical scheme of things—an attitude first taken by the Greeks.

This part has emphasized cosmological models, especially their aesthetic aspects. Astronomy does, however, deal with other kinds of scientific models. For instance, Chapter 5 introduced the Bohr model of the atom to explain how matter emits and absorbs light. This model, when applied to the sun's spectrum and stellar spectra, directly implied that the stars are other suns.

Scientific models will be discussed throughout this book. Whenever one appears, be sure to try to understand it so you can state (1) the aesthetic, geometrical, and physical bases of the model, (2) the assumptions behind the model and their reasonableness, (3) what key observations the model attempts to explain and how well it does so, and (4) how to make predictions from the model.

Finally, remember that no scientific model is ever final; it is always subject to revision—or complete replacement. This fact underlies the evolution of models, as you've seen from our conceptions of the cosmos in this part.

The Planets:
Past and Present
PART 2

Not long after I had built myself a larger telescope, the space programs of the United States and the Soviet Union began to send home their first results. I watched in amazement as the first spacecraft to the moon plunged into its pitted surface, sending back—in a dying gasp—somewhat fuzzy photos. With less amazement I remember myself and some friends, beer in hand, watching on the TV those ghostlike images of Astronaut Armstrong stepping onto the moon. Those moments did not attract me as much as when flyby missions to the planets sent their detailed close-ups to earth. Then we gained a new vision of our planetary neighbors.

Part 2 focuses on the members of the solar system. I emphasize the revised pictures of these bodies that recent space probes have provided. I start off with the earth, the planet we know the best. That investigation provides the model and methods to investigate the other planets, including our companion, the moon. I'll compare what we know about the planets in an evolutionary context; then take a brief look at the debris that float among the planets: comets, asteroids, and meteoroids. Finally, this part closes with an examination of models for the formation of the solar system.

All the objects we see *now* in the solar system have evolved since their formation. By investigating their present physical properties, we can infer what they might have been like in the past. Some solar system objects—like the earth—have evolved dramatically. Others—like the moon—have changed relatively little.

Don't let details here detract you from the main theme: some insight into how the solar system formed (Chapter 12). I have highlighted the information that has importance, and brought some of it together in Chapter 12, which presents an updated—but still unfinished—scenario for the formation of the solar system. You will see that this picture implies that many other solar systems probably exist in the Galaxy as a natural consequence of the birth of stars—another main theme in cosmic evolution.

Spaceship earth:
A restless world

LEARNING OBJECTIVES

After studying this chapter you should be able to:

1. Describe one method for determining the earth's mass.

2. Sketch the interior structure of the earth, indicating the composition of each general region.

3. Argue simply that the earth's core must be denser than its crust, and also that the core probably has a nickel-iron composition.

4. Argue that the earth's interior structure implies that it must have been molten at some time.

5. Give the estimated age of the earth, and explain the method by which this estimate is arrived at. (Be sure to give the assumptions and observations.)

6. Describe at least two ways in which the earth's atmosphere affects astronomical observations and two ways it affects the earth's surface environment.

7. Explain how the earth's atmosphere acts like a blanket that keeps the earth's surface relatively warm.

8. Describe the possible evolution of the earth's oceans.

9. Outline a possible model for the evolution of the earth's crust and interior.

10. Outline a possible model for the evolution of the earth's atmosphere, pointing out the interactions of air, oceans, crust, and life.

We travel together, passengers on a frail spaceship, dependent on its vulnerable reserve of air and soil; all committed for our safety to its security and peace; preserved from annihilation only by the work and love we give our fragile craft.

ADLAI STEVENSON

CHAPTER 8

CENTRAL QUESTION *What are the physical characteristics of the earth, and how have they changed since our planet's formation?*

How small the earth is! Really a little planet, whirling around one ordinary star; and no longer the center of the universe, as people believed for over 4000 years. But that change in cosmic position does not mean we should value the earth any less. For the earth is our delicate ship, protecting us on our dark passage through space.

With the aid of a modest telescope, astronomers on Mars would see terrestrial clouds as the most distinct features (Fig. 8.1). Typically, the clouds cover about 50 percent of the surface and reflect back sunlight, so the earth appears bright. However, the swirls of cloud cover also obscure features such as oceans and continents and make it hard for extraterrestrial astronomers to see directly any evidence of human civilization.

This chapter looks at the physical makeup of the earth, the only planet known for certain to be inhabited. Because we live here, we study this planet in more detail than any other. Our present understanding of the earth indicates that it is the most evolved of the terrestrial planets—it has changed dramatically in physical structure since its formation. We will use our home planet as the basis of comparison for understanding the makeup and evolution of the other earthlike objects—Mercury, Venus, Mars, and the moon.

8.1

The earth from space, taken from Apollo 11. Note how extensive the cloud cover is. (Courtesy NASA)

8.1

The mass and density of the solid earth

How can you find out the earth's mass? Recall (Section 4.1) the discovery by Galileo that all masses at the earth's surface have the same acceleration due to gravity, *g*. Newton's law of gravitation (Section 4.2) relates this acceleration to the earth's mass and radius and to the gravitational constant, *G*. So if you know *G* (from lab experiments), the earth's radius, and *g*, you can figure out the earth's mass from Newton's law. The mass comes out to about 6×10^{24} kg.

Knowing both the earth's mass and its volume (from its radius), you can compute its average density. Density is the mass per unit volume (Focus 21); if you divide the earth's mass by its volume, you obtain a density of 5.5 g/cc, or 5.5 times the density of water. This average density indicates that the earth, in bulk, consists of a combination of rocky and metallic materials.

(Most rocks have a density of about 3 g/cc; iron, a density of 8 g/cc.)

Rocks at the earth's surface have an average density about half the average density of the whole earth. This difference implies that the core of the earth must be denser than the average. Present estimates indicate that the earth's core is perhaps 12 g/cc. The weight of the overlying layers compresses the core and creates the high central density.

8.2

The interior of the earth

Geologists generally divide the interior of the earth into three distinct layers: the core, the mantle, and the crust (Fig. 8.2). The *core* is the central zone and extends almost halfway to the surface. The core's high density implies that it is probably composed of iron and nickel. (Some of the iron is probably combined with sulfur.)

focus 21

DENSITY

Imagine that you have two suitcases, the same size, so they contain the same amount of space. Fill one with small rocks and the other with peanuts, both packed as tightly as possible with the least amount of air space. Close the suitcases. Lift them. What do you expect? One suitcase—the one filled with rocks—will weigh more than the other. That means that it has more mass in the same amount of space, or volume. The suitcase filled with rocks is denser *than the one filled with peanuts.*

Density is a measure of how well material is packed into a given space. Different densities are characteristic of different materials. For example, water has a density of about 1 gram per cubic centimeter (1 g/cc); rocks about 3 g/cc; iron about 8 g/cc; and wood about 0.7 g/cc. You can test which of these materials is more dense or less dense than water: Rock and iron sink when placed in water, but wood floats.

Warning: *Don't confuse density with mass or size alone. For example, the sun is much more massive and larger than the earth, yet it has a much lower average density. Why? The sun is a gas, whereas the earth is made of rocks and metals.*

In simple equation form,

$$density = \frac{mass}{volume}$$

Apply this to the earth, whose mass is roughly 6×10^{24} kg and radius 6400 km (Table 8.2). Note that 6×10^{24} kg $= 6 \times 10^{27}$ g and 6400 km $= 6.4 \times 10^8$ cm. Then

$$density = \frac{6 \times 10^{27} \, g}{\frac{4}{3}\pi(6.4 \times 10^8 \, cm)^3}$$

where the earth is taken to be spherical, so its volume is $\frac{4}{3}\pi R^3$. And

$$density = \frac{6 \times 10^{27}}{\frac{4}{3}\pi(2.6 \times 10^{26})} = \frac{6 \times 10^{27}}{1.1 \times 10^{27}}$$
$$= 5.5 \, g/cc.$$

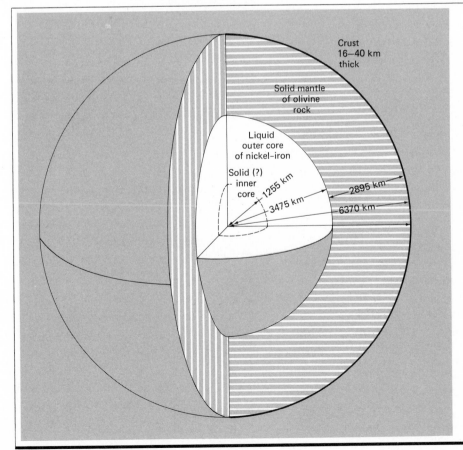

8.2

A model of the earth's interior. It consists of three main parts: crust, mantle, and core. The thin crust of granite and basalt is the earth's skin. Below it lies the mantle, which is probably made of olivine—a silicate of iron and magnesium. The core likely consists of iron and nickel in combination with sulfer. (Adapted from A. N. Strahler, **The Earth Sciences,** *Harper & Row, 1971)*

Crust 16–40 km thick

Solid mantle of olivine rock

Liquid outer core of nickel-iron

Solid (?) inner core

1255 km

3475 km

2895 km

6370 km

focus 22

SOUNDING OUT THE EARTH'S INTERIOR

Because none of our devices can plumb the earth's inner sanctum, geologists rely on natural earthquakes to map the lower depths. An earthquake occurs when two adjoining or overlying rock layers slip against one another because of built-up internal pressures. As the rocks move they generate vibrations, called seismic waves, *in the adjacent rock material. These seismic waves travel through the globe in two basic forms:* transverse *and* longitudinal *waves.*

Transverse waves move up and down as they travel in a material. You can generate your own transverse waves by tying down a rope at one end and shaking the other end up and down. Transverse waves can travel through solids but not through liquids. When they run into a liquid they gradually dissipate. Longitudinal waves are push–pull waves; the most common example is sound waves. From your experience with sound waves, you know that longitudinal waves can travel through solids, liquids, and gases.

The speed of a wave depends on the medium through which it passes. For example, the denser the material is, the faster the waves will go. When the medium suddenly changes, both the speed and the direction of the wave abruptly change. When geologists record seismic waves, the changes in the wave speed and direction allow them to infer the physical properties of the earth's interior. For this technique the geologists look at the arrival of P (longitudinal) and S (transverse) waves from the earthquake. The P-waves are the first recorded by a seismograph; the S-waves arrive next. The S-waves do not penetrate the core, and the P-waves travel slowly through the core. Hence the core must be liquid rather than solid, as the mantle is (Fig. 1).

The reception of earthquake waves provides information about the size of the core. The core shields out the S-waves from reception on the side of the earth opposite the earthquake's origin. It can also cause the P-waves to change direction sharply at the interface of the core and mantle. As a consequence, some areas of the earth receive both P- and S-waves, some only P-waves, and some no waves at all. From this information

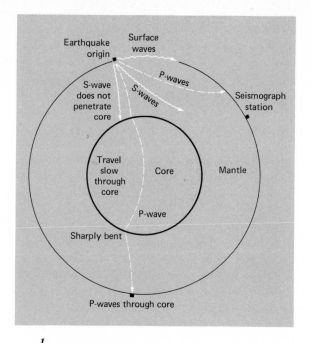

1

The paths of seismic waves in the earth's interior. To a seismograph station on the same side of the earth as an earthquake, S-waves and P-waves travel the same path. On the other side of the earth, only P-waves arrive because S-waves do not pass through the liquid core. (Adapted from A. N. Strahler, The Earth Sciences, *Harper & Row, 1971)*

we determine the size of the core compared with that of the mantle.

Put together, this information gives a sketch of the earth's interior properties (Fig. 2). The P-wave velocity exhibits two abrupt changes, which mark the outer and inner core. The S-waves suddenly vanish at the outer core's boundary. The density of the material must rise rapidly in the core (c) but must not be much different in the inner core. The temperature (b), after a rapid increase in the crust and mantle, does not change much in the core, but it is high enough (about 2600 K) to melt the outer core.

The seismograph is important to the astronomer, for it is being used to determine the interior structure of the moon and will be used on the other planets. Such information is valuable for any theories of the origin of the solar system and the formation of its planets.

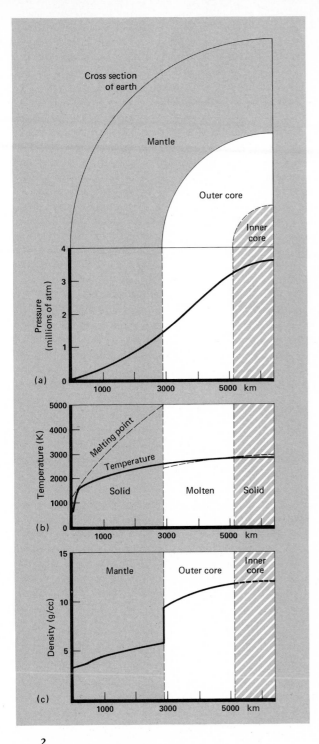

2

A model of the earth's interior inferred from seismic waves. Note that the pressure increases continually with depth (a) and the temperature (b) at first rises quickly, then levels off. A sharp increase in density (c) marks the transition between the mantle and the core. (Adapted from A. N. Strahler, **The Earth Sciences,** *Harper & Row, 1971)*

TABLE 8.1 *The ten most abundant terrestrial elements*

Element	Symbol	*Terrestrial average* (percent by mass)*
Iron	Fe	34.6
Oxygen	O	29.5
Silicon	Si	15.2
Magnesium	Mg	12.7
Nickel	Ni	2.4
Sulfur	S	1.9
Calcium	Ca	1.1
Aluminum	Al	1.1
Sodium	Na	0.57
Chromium	Cr	0.26

Source Adapted from *Principles of Geochemistry*, 3rd ed., by Brian Mason (Wiley, New York, 1966).
* The averages listed include both the crust and the interior. The very high concentrations of iron and nickel in the core contribute the largest amount to the averages of these elements. The crust itself is about 75 percent silicon and oxygen.

Extending above the core is the *mantle*, roughly 2900 km thick. The mantle material is rock made of iron and magnesium combined with silicate (a silicate mineral called olivine). The mantle is plastic. Under slow, steady pressure such material flows like a liquid, but sudden changes in pressure cause it to snap and fragment like glass.

Encasing the mantle is a thin *crust*, the solid surface layer, which varies in depth from 16 to 40 km. Most of the crustal material (Table 8.1) consists of rocks that have solidified from molten lava (so they are called igneous rocks). These rocks are basalt: a combination of oxygen, silicon, aluminum, magnesium, and iron. They comprise the ocean basins and the subcontinental sections of the crust. The continental masses are mostly granite made of oxygen, silicon, aluminum, sodium, and potassium. Because the granite is less dense than the basalt (granites contain less iron and magnesium), the continental plates float on the basalt. Also, because the mantle is denser than the basalt and granite, the entire crust floats on the mantle. (See Focus 22 to find out how geologists can "see" into the earth's interior.)

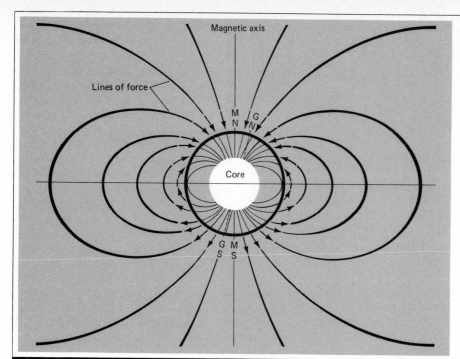

8.3

A model of the earth's magnetic field. The shape of the magnetic field resembles that of a giant bar magnet stuck in the earth. The magnetic axis (MN to MS) is not aligned with the spin axis (GN to GS) but is tilted about 20°.

To sum up: The earth's interior is *differentiated*. This means that it consists of layers with the least dense materials at the surface and the most dense at the center. How did the earth get this way? Present theories (Chapter 12) see the earth as formed such that its material was well mixed up. Imagine the interior then heating up enough so that it is mostly molten (or at least plastic). Then the dense materials (iron, nickel) would settle at the core, and the less dense materials (quartz, aluminum silicates) would form a froth on top.

What heated the interior?—probably radioactive decay (Focus 23). In the past the earth had more radioactive material than now—about six times as much. The heating from the decay of so much radioactive material could melt the interior.

8.3

The earth's age

Geologists now estimate the earth's age at 4.6 billion years (with a range of error of 0.1 billion years) on the basis of radioactive dating (Focus 23), although the oldest known rocks on the earth's surface are not actually this old. The most ancient known rocks, found in West Greenland, have been dated by rubidium-strontium decay at 4.0 billion years. (Rubidium has a half-life of 5×10^{10} years.) These rocks are *igneous rocks*, meaning that the material was first molten and then cooled to form the present rocks. Geologists estimate that the time required for the crust's initial melting and cooling, to form the first rocks, was about 0.5 billion years.

So by this estimate (they vary) the solid earth's age is approximately 4.5 billion years, the age of the rock plus the estimated time to form them. The estimate for the earth's age falls close to that for meteorite material (4.55 billion years) and lunar material (4.6 billion years), determined by the same radioactive dating techniques. The near coincidence of these ages implies that the solar system formed in a short time about 4.6 billion years ago (Chapter 12).

Warning: Two assumptions have been made in this estimate: (1) the rocks have not been globally heated since they first formed; (2) about 0.5 billion years is a reasonable guess for the time between the earth's formation and the solidification of its crust. The ages given in this section are still being refined.

8.4

The earth's magnetic field

You can visualize the earth's magnetic properties by imagining a giant bar magnet located in the core (Focus 24). The magnetic lines of force protrude from the *south magnetic pole* in the Southern Hemisphere and return to the *north magnetic pole* in the Northern Hemisphere. The magnetic axis, which connects the magnetic poles, is inclined about 20° from the spin axis and does not quite pass through the earth's center (Fig. 8.3). The part of this magnetic field that is parallel to the earth's surface orients a compass needle along the lines of force so that the needle points to the north and south magnetic poles.

focus 23

RADIOACTIVE DATING OF ROCKS

The radioactive dating technique depends on the natural instability of the nuclei of radioactive elements, such as uranium. When these nuclei decay, they break apart into simpler nuclei. Given just one atom, you cannot estimate when it will decay because the process is random; but given a large number of atoms, you can determine a gross rate of disintegration. (An analogous process is the popping of popcorn. It is impossible for you to predict which kernel will pop next, but you can estimate when the entire batch will be finished.) Half a piece of uranium-238, (see Appendix G for an explanation of this notation), decays to lead in 4.5 billion years, and so on, even though the decay time for one uranium atom cannot be specified.

The length of time required for half the material to disintegrate is called the half-life of the element (Fig. 1). Given a rock sample containing uranium-238 and nonradiogenic lead, and knowing the half-life of the uranium, you can calculate the age of the sample.

Uranium is not the only element that can be used in radioactive dating: rubidium (^{87}Rb), which decays to strontium (^{87}Sr), with a half-life of 47 billion years; and potassium (^{40}K), which decays to the inert gas argon (^{40}Ar), with a half-life of 1.3 billion years, can also serve as radioactive clocks. Whatever elements are used, the derived date is the time elapsed since the rocks last solidified.

How do you get from knowing the half-life of radioactive elements to the age of a rock sample? You must assume that you know the original composition of the sample when it solidified. Suppose, for example, that your sample is potassium-40. In 1.3 billion years, half of the potassium decays to argon-40. In 2.6 billion years, only a quarter of the potassium remains, and so on. Now if the argon is trapped in the sample and doesn't escape, the amount of argon relative to the amount of potassium changes with time—less

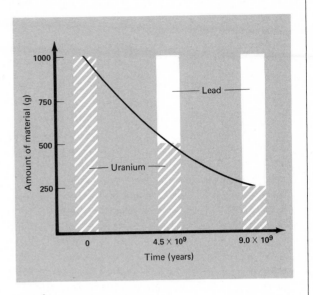

1

Radioactive decay of uranium 238, illustrating the concept of half-life. Uranium 238 has a half-life of 4.5 billion years. This means that during one half-life, half of the original uranium 238 decays into lead. In the next half-life time, half the remaining uranium 238 turns into lead, and so on.

potassium, more argon. So if you can estimate the percentage of various elements, especially the radioactive ones, that the sample had at the outset, the amount of change from the original percentages tells you the age of the sample.

For example, suppose a rock sample now contains equal numbers of potassium-40 and argon-40 atoms. If there were no argon atoms in the rock originally, they must all have come from decay of potassium-40. Exactly half have decayed (and half remain), so the rock must be one half-life old, 1.3 billion years. How old is a rock that contains 7 times as many argon-40 atoms as potassium-40 atoms? If all the argon came from decay of potassium, the remaining potassium-40 is one-eighth of the original. So three half-lives must have elapsed ($\frac{1}{8} = \frac{1}{2} \times \frac{1}{2} \times \frac{1}{2}$), and the rock must be $3 \times 1.3 = 3.9$ billion years old.

focus 24

MAGNETIC FIELDS AND FORCES

A field is another scientific model; it is a way of describing space that is somehow modified by the presence of matter. All magnetic fields come from electrical charges in motion. A bar magnet (Fig. 1) has no outward sign of motion, but the circulation of electrons around iron nuclei sets up its magnetic field. You have probably seen an electromagnet in operation. Here an electric current—a flow of charged particles—passing through a loop of

wire creates a magnetic field. The earth's magnetic field is probably generated by the internal circulation of charged particles. The magnetic fields around the earth and the sun have two poles; this characteristic allows us to think of these fields as if arising from giant bar magnets buried in the earth and sun (Fig. 2).

To help visualize a magnetic field, take a very small compass and move it around a magnet (Fig. 1). The changing direction of the compass needle shows the direction of the magnetic lines of force. The spacing of the magnetic lines of force indicates the relative

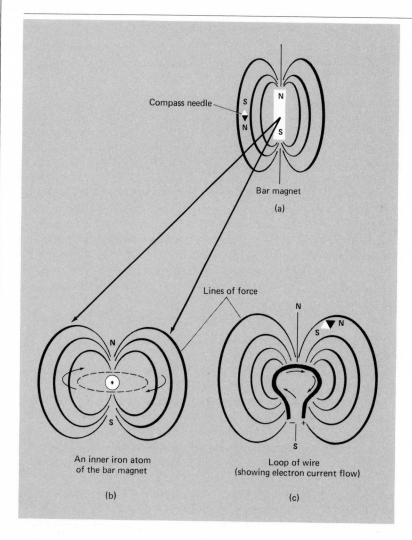

Compass needle

N S S N

Bar magnet

(a)

Lines of force

N N S

An inner iron atom of the bar magnet

(b)

Loop of wire (showing electron current flow)

(c)

1

The similarities of magnetic behavior. At top (a) the direction of a small compass needle follows along the magnetic field lines of a small bar magnet. Its field comes from the flow of electrons around the nuclei of iron atoms (b). The flow of electrons (an electric current) through wire makes an electromagnet (c).

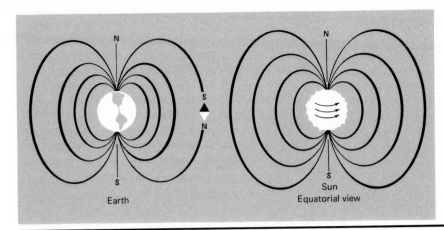

Magnetic fields of the earth and sun. Note that the shapes of these fields are similar to that of a bar magnet.

strength of the magnetic field: The closer the spacing is, the stronger the field will be.

Charged particles and magnetic fields interact in such a way that the particles find it difficult to cross the field lines. Instead, the charged particles tend to spiral along the field lines, the direction of the spiral twist depending on whether the particle is positively or negatively charged (Fig. 3). As a concrete analogy, imagine the magnetic field lines as elastic bands. If a charged particle attempts to plow across the bands, it encounters a resistance and stretches the field lines. So charged particles and magnetic fields are linked together by their interactions. (This is how the earth's magnetic field traps charged particles from the sun.)

This linking is important for understanding what happens to a magnetic field that is immersed in an ionized gas (such as the sun). If the ionized gas moves, it carries the magnetic field lines with it. For example, if the gas is moving turbulently, it tangles and jumbles up the direction of the magnetic field lines.

To sum up: Moving charged particles produce magnetic fields. In turn, magnetic fields affect the motions of charged particles. The linking of magnetic fields and charged particles has important astrophysical consequences.

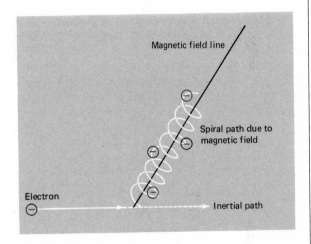

3

The path of a charged particle (an electron) in a magnetic field. When the electron tries to move across a field line, a force acts on it, causing its path to move around the line. When the electron moves parallel to a field line, it does not have any force act on it. The combination of these two effects produces a spiraling motion of the electron.

The earth's magnetic field changes in both direction and intensity. Over long periods the magnetic poles have actually switched north and south at least nine times during the past 3.5 million years and probably many more times in earlier ages (Section 8.7).

The source of the earth's magnetic field and the mechanisms for its changes are buried deep in the earth. They relate to the liquid nature of the iron-nickel core. The metal can conduct electrical currents, so it acts like a giant dynamo and electromagnet, generating electricity and creating a magnetic field. The earth's rotation supposedly helps to stir the currents in the core. This *dynamo model* for the earth's magnetic field—if correct—has a major implication for other planets: Any planet that exhibits a strong magnetic field must have a substantial liquid conducting core and must rotate rapidly.

Warning: The dynamo model has yet to be worked out in detail. For instance, little agreement has developed to date on how the fluid core flows, what drives these motions, and how these flows generate the complex field we measure at the surface. Recent work indicates that the flow may be driven by gravitational energy liberated as heat as dense materials migrate to the center of the core and less dense materials flow outward.

In 1958 early U.S. space satellites detected a region encircling the earth that contained a large number of protons and electrons. Later satellites revealed a similar but larger region farther from the earth's surface. These two doughnut-shaped belts of energetic particles trapped by the terrestrial magnetic fields are called the *Van Allen radiation belts* (Fig. 8.4), after their discoverer, James A. Van Allen. The solar wind and solar flares (Section 13.5) provide the particles trapped in the Van Allen belts.

The Van Allen belts are only one aspect of the interaction of the earth's magnetic field with the charged particles that continually stream from the sun. In fact, the earth's magnetic field affects the flow of interplanetary charged particles for many tens of earth radii out into space. This region is called the earth's *magnetosphere* (Fig. 8.5). As the particles from the sun run into the earth's field, they cannot flow across the field lines but are forced along them (Focus 24). Like the blunt prow of a boat in water, the earth's field deflects particles around it and

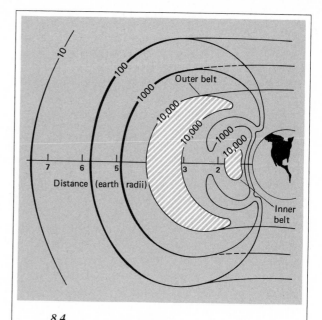

8.4

The Van Allen radiation belts. These zones of trapped charged particles encircle the earth in a doughnut shape. The outer belt extends about 4 earth radii (26,000 km) from the earth's center. The charged particles in the belt are protons and electrons from the sun. The numbers on the contour lines indicate the average density (it changes) of such particles.

leaves a wake in the direction opposite the sun. Most charged particles flow around the earth, but a few are caught in the field to make the Van Allen belts.

8.5
The blanket of the atmosphere

To us the atmosphere is a blessing: It provides oxygen for breathing, shields out the ultraviolet radiation of the sun, and furnishes a thermal blanket to keep the surface warm. Astronomers sometimes feel that the atmosphere is a curse, for it absorbs ultraviolet light, X-rays, and some infrared and radio radiation from space. However, an understanding of its composition and structure provides information useful for the study of other planetary atmospheres.

Our atmosphere contains, relative to the total amount available, approximately 78 percent

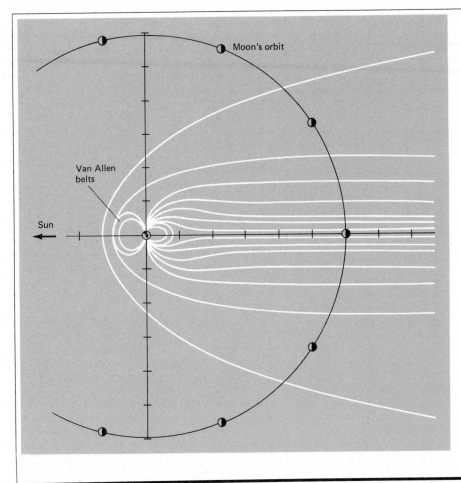

8.5

The earth's magnetosphere. This zone of magnetic influence is created by the interaction of the earth's magnetic field with charged particles flowing out from the sun. Note the scale is much larger here than in Fig. 8.4.

nitrogen (N_2), 21 percent oxygen (O_2), 0.9 percent argon (Ar), 0.03 percent carbon dioxide (CO_2), and traces of other elements, of which compounds with water vapor are the most important (Fig. 8.6). (The water vapor content varies.) Among the minor constituents are carbon monoxide (CO), sulfur dioxide (SO_2), and nitrogen dioxide (NO_2).

The weight of the upper atmospheric layers makes the lower portion denser than the upper, just as a sandwich at the bottom of a pile is squashed by the weight of the sandwiches on top of it. The gas pressure at sea level on the earth's surface, where the entire atmosphere is piled above it, is called *one atmosphere.* The atmospheric pressure and density decrease with height—rapidly at first, then more slowly, but they never reach zero.

Although the atmosphere is a continuous gas, with no definite boundaries, it is often con-venient to discuss it in terms of various regions, or "spheres." The division between the regions is somewhat arbitrary, and can be chosen in different ways, depending on the physical or chemical properties of interest. Considering how temperature changes with height in the atmosphere (Fig. 8.7), we get four basic divisions: troposphere, stratosphere, mesosphere, and thermosphere. In the *troposphere* the temperature decreases upwards from the solar-heated surface. In the *stratosphere* the temperature stops decreasing, and even rises somewhat, because of heating by absorption of ultraviolet light in an ozone layer. The temperature falls again in the *mesosphere,* due to a decrease in heating from ultraviolet absorption. Finally, heating by absorption of X-rays and far ultraviolet radiation raises the temperature again in the *thermosphere.*

Within the stratosphere is an *ozone layer,* at

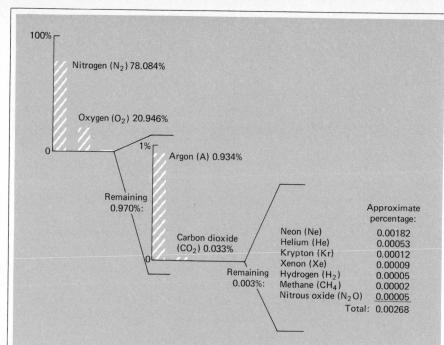

8.6

*The composition of the earth's lower atmosphere. Gases whose amounts vary, such as water vapor, are not shown. (Adapted from A. N. Strahler, **The Earth Sciences**, Harper & Row, 1971)*

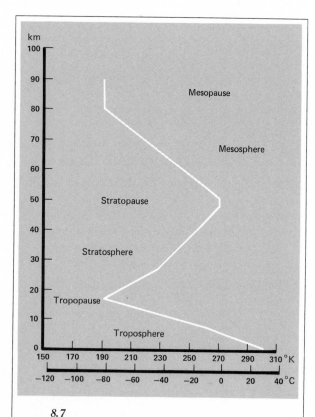

8.7

The earth's atmospheric temperature profile in the first 100 km of the atmosphere. The profile changes with both season and latitude; shown here are average values. (Adapted from a NASA diagram)

a height of about 20 to 30 km. It plays a critical role for the existence of life on the earth. Ozone is a combination of three oxygen atoms to form the molecule O_3. To create ozone from normal molecular oxygen requires energy. Ultraviolet light from the sun provides the energy; normal molecular oxygen absorbs this radiation and dissociates into two oxygen atoms. This atomic oxygen then combines with another oxygen molecule to make ozone. The ozone is destroyed by both dissociation caused by more ultraviolet photons and combination with atomic oxygen.

The ozone layer of the stratosphere blocks out ultraviolet radiation. Some life forms, such as humans, have developed on the earth in an environment sheltered from the ultraviolet light; they are so suspectible to this fairly lethal radiation that even a mild exposure results in a painful case of sunburn. A large dose can kill you. Even relatively mild doses over a long time promote skin cancer in fair-skinned people. For example, New Mexico, which has relatively clear skies and a high elevation, has one of the highest per capita skin cancer rates in the world among its Anglo residents.

Within the thermosphere, from a height of about 100–500 km, lies the *ionosphere*. Here oxygen and nitrogen soak up X-rays from the sun and become ionized during the day. The ions and electrons make up layers that reflect shortwave radio waves, and so allow surface shortwave radio contact over the visible horizon.

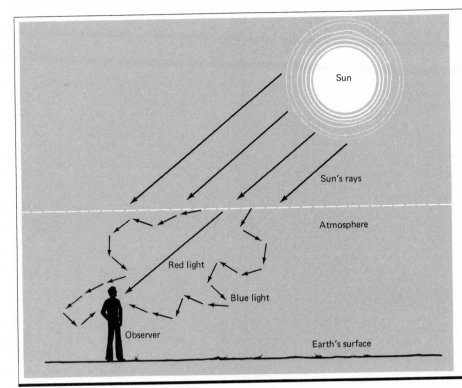

8.8

Why the sky is blue. Air molecules allow long-wavelength (red) light to pass through relatively unhindered. But short-wavelength (blue) light is scattered in all directions by the air. Looking at the sun you see long-wavelength light directly. The blue light, however, scatters around, so in every direction you look you can see blue light—and a blue sky.

Because any free gas lacks a distinct boundary, the atmosphere has no sudden end. It gradually peters out to the interplanetary medium. However, as the atmosphere becomes thinner, collisions between atoms become less likely, and the distance between collisions increases. At a low enough density the chances for an atom to escape into space become fairly large if it is traveling faster than the escape velocity (Focus 13). The region at about 500–700 km above the earth's surface, where atoms can escape, is called the *exosphere*. This layer effectively defines the top of the atmosphere.

8.6
The atmosphere and incoming radiation

The earth's atmosphere endlessly frustrates the ground-based astronomer. (I've experienced cloudy observing runs *weeks* long!) Also, because of the ozone layer, the astronomer cannot view the ultraviolet radiation from celestial bodies.

Even on the clearest nights, atmospheric turbulence causes telescopic images to flicker and so imposes the fundamental limitation on a telescope's ability to see clearly two objects close together in the sky. The extent to which the atmospheric turbulence affects the image is termed *seeing*. When the seeing is good, stellar images are sharp, steady pinpoints about 1″ in diameter. At times of poor seeing, the images waver like candle flames in a gentle breeze. Occasionally star images blow up to sizes of 10″–20″, about 10 times larger than those seen in the best conditions.

Atmospheric extinction and reddening / The atmospheric layers also absorb some of the light that penetrates them. This absorption of light is called *atmospheric extinction*. The closer an object appears to the horizon, the greater is the atmospheric thickness through which the object's light must pass, and so the dimmer it becomes. Because of atmospheric extinction, the rising full moon has about half the brightness of the same moon overhead.

Air molecules absorb sunlight as well as preferentially scatter blue light more than red light. The atmosphere depletes a beam of light of its shorter (bluer) wavelengths, which scatter uniformly through the sky, and so make the sky look blue. In any direction you look you see blue light, and so the entire sky is blue (Fig. 8.8).

8.9

The general cloudiness of the earth's atmosphere. These clouds and the oceans' surfaces reflect back into space about 35 percent of the incoming visible light. (Courtesy NASA)

Light of longer wavelengths reaches you directly along the line of sight. The sinking sun appears a burning red because its radiation passes through a lot of atmosphere to you. Along this path most of the blue light is scattered out, leaving mostly red light.

Albedo / All the planets and their moons shine by reflected sunlight, as does the earth when viewed from space. A celestial body's reflecting ability in the visible range of the spectrum is called its *albedo*, the ratio of the light reflected to the incoming light. If an object reflected all the light that struck its surface, its albedo would be 1.0. The clouds in the earth's atmosphere help to reflect visible light (Fig. 8.9), and about 35 percent of the incident light reflects back into space; the earth's albedo equals 0.35. The atmosphere and surface absorb the other 65 percent. The exact amount varies somewhat because it depends on the extent of the cloud cover.

Greenhouse effect / Of the incoming light not reflected, 15 percent is absorbed into the troposphere, and the remaining 50 percent of the original strikes the ground and heats it and the air in contact with the surface. However, if this direct solar radiation were the only source

of heat, the temperature at the ground would be a frigid 253 K (or −20°C). Water would always be frozen! The average temperature at the surface is actually much higher, about 293 K (20°C.)

How does this happen? Visible radiation from the sun gets through to the surface and heats the earth. In turn the earth emits infrared radiation (which we commonly call heat). *If* this infrared radiation simply escaped into space, the earth would be too cold for life. But this infrared radiation *doesn't* escape completely. The infrared is absorbed by the earth's atmosphere (mostly by water vapor and carbon dioxide). The atmosphere heats up by absorbing this radiation. Some goes off into space (about 8 percent); the rest radiates back to the ground and so heats it. Both direct sunlight and infrared radiation from the atmosphere heat the earth's surface. The atmosphere acts like a blanket, insulating the ground from space and so helping to warm the earth.

If you have ever visited a high, arid climate, such as New Mexico, you know what a dramatic effect water vapor in the atmosphere has on the ground temperature. Water vapor absorbs infrared radiation, so the more humid the atmosphere, the more opaque it is to infrared and the better it insulates. For instance, in Albuquerque on a clear winter's day the high temperature can typically reach 15°C and, if the night is also clear, drop to −10°C at night. But if it's cloudy at night, the low may be only 0°C or so. Why the difference? At night the ground radiates away, in the infrared, the energy it absorbed during the day. On a cloudy, high-humidity night, the additional water vapor in the air traps the outgoing infrared radiation from the ground more than on a clear night. So the air temperature stays higher because not as much heat escapes to space.

This warming of the ground by the atmospheric trapping of infrared radiation is often called the *greenhouse effect* by analogy to one process that keeps a greenhouse warm. Glass is transparent to visible light but opaque to infrared. So sunlight enters the greenhouse and warms the interior, which emits infrared. This heat can't radiate through the glass, so it stays to help warm up the interior.

To sum up: Any planetary atmosphere that is more or less transparent to sunlight but opaque to infrared will act to keep the planet's surface warmer than if the planet had no atmosphere. Typically, carbon dioxide and water vapor act to trap the infrared. This trapping causes the temperature to rise until the net energy flow outward equals that coming in.

Note: The greenhouse effect is probably misnamed. Experiments have shown that the absorption of infrared radiation is not the main factor that keeps the greenhouse warm. When the glass is replaced by a rock-salt window (which transmits infrared), the greenhouse gets almost as hot. How? The air, heated by contact with the hot inside of the greenhouse, cannot escape. This inhibition of airflow occurs with *any* roof. However, the phrase "greenhouse effect" is so ingrained in the astronomers' vocabulary, I'll continue to use it in this book.

8.7
The restless earth: Evolution of the crust

What is the origin of the continents, the oceans, and the ocean basins between the continents? The earth's surface is divided roughly into two levels: the continents and the ocean basins, with an average height difference of about 5 km. Ero-

sion and water transport of materials should gradually erase the difference in height between the oceanic and continental plains. Given the great age of the earth (Section 8.3), the fact that these levels still stand apart implies that somehow the mountain heights and ocean depths are regularly replenished.

Earthquakes and mountains / In the nineteenth century geologists pointed out that the zones of active volcanoes and frequent earthquakes are concentrated along the chains of young mountain ranges and submarine ridges. They argued that earthquake and volcanic activity must be associated with mountain and island building. Modern research on the locations of earthquakes backs up this idea.

Another clue to this activity shows up in the ocean basins, especially in the Atlantic. Modern sonar measurements have revealed a *midoceanic ridge*, an almost continuous submarine mountain chain that extends through the ocean basins (Fig. 8.10). The midoceanic ridge indicates that important geologic processes take place in the ocean basins.

Continental drift / These facts fell together as a coherent picture during the 1960s with the revival of the model of *continental drift*, the idea that the present continents were at one time a unified landmass that fragmented and drifted apart. In 1910 Alfred L. Wegener (1880–1930) of Germany suggested that displacements of the earth's crust could shift the position of the continents. In Wegener's picture the continents were originally joined in one vast land area, which broke up about 200 million years ago (Fig. 8.11). Today's evidence points to two primordial landmasses: one called Gondwanaland, in the Southern Hemisphere; the other called Laurasia, in the Northern Hemisphere. These may have broken from a single landmass called Pangaea.

The modern development of the continental drift model centers on the idea that the crust and upper mantle of the earth consist of brittle plates. These plates move horizontally over the plastic part of the mantle, and contain both the continental and oceanic parts of the crust. Overall, the evolution of the earth's surface is viewed as the result of the meanderings of six enormous plates.

Evidence from the magnetic characteristics of the ocean floors near ridges argues for the

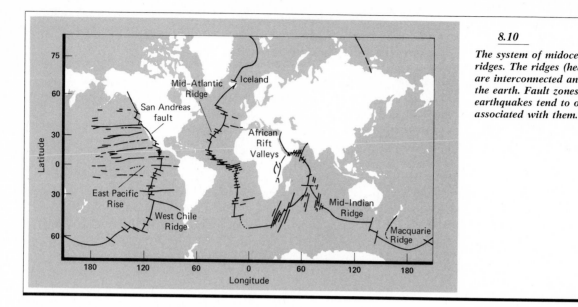

8.10

The system of midoceanic ridges. The ridges (heavy lines) are interconnected and circle the earth. Fault zones where earthquakes tend to occur are associated with them.

continental drift model of crustal evolution. If the continents do move apart, the seafloor between them must be spreading. Oceanographic cruises across the Atlantic have found that the seafloor material contained remnants of ancient magnetism. When lava solidifies to form igneous rock, the iron minerals in the rock align with the earth's magnetic field. The reversals of the direction of the earth's magnetic field in the past are preserved in the rock. They have a startling pattern. On both sides of the mid-Atlantic ridge the reversal patterns appear identical— each side is a mirror reflection of the other. How does this happen? If the seafloor spreads, it needs a continuous supply of new material to add additional area. Lava flowing out pushes older material aside in both directions. When the lava solidifies, the rock on either side freezes in the magnetic field alignment.

The alignment of magnetic field reversals indicates both that new material emerges from a rift in the center of the ridge and what the rate of expansion of the seafloor is. The movement is about 2–4 cm per year at its fastest speed across the mid-Atlantic ridge. The rate amounts (if constant) to more than 8,000 km in 200 million years, enough to push apart the Old and the New World.

Plate tectonics / What accounts for the renewal of the ocean plains? Lava that oozes out from the earth's mantle. Crustal plates float like large rafts on the mantle. Where one plate crashes into another, the impact raises up mountains. In some regions one plate may force another to fold under and descend into the mantle (Fig. 8.12). A plate's descent eliminates surface material essentially at the same rate it is created, so the earth's radius does not expand to accommodate the swelling plates. Because the plates' creation and destruction zones make natural fault areas, earthquakes and volcanoes predominate along the lines of plate collision (Fig. 8.10). (A *fault* occurs where two rock masses have fractured and slipped apart.)

This model of the earth's crustal activity and evolution—seafloor spreading and the creation and destruction of crustal plates—is called *plate tectonics*. It pictures the earth as having a restless crust, with plates growing, sliding, and colliding.

What moves the plates? One model pictures the upper part of the mantle as divided into large convection cells (Fig. 8.13). The mantle's plasticity allows a slow flow upward, horizontally, and downward. At the region of horizontal flow, friction between the plate and the mantle drags the plate along with the mantle's flow. The upwelling magma supplies new materials to the plate. The energy source for such convection is still unknown. It may come from radioactive decay or from internal heat persisting from the time when the earth formed.

Although many details are uncertain, the main point is clear: The earth's crust has

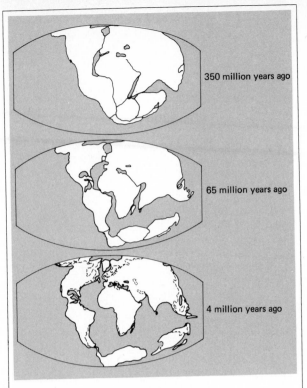

8.11

Wegener's original model for the separation of the continents from one large landmass (sometimes called Pangaea). Evidence now suggests that the present continents came from two super continents, once very close together: Laurasia, made up of what is now North America, Greenland, and Eurasia; and Gondwanaland, made up of South America, Africa, India, Australia, and Antarctica.

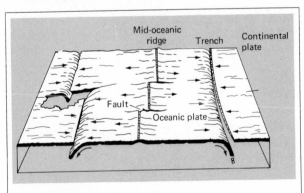

8.12

Interactions of oceanic and continental plates. The oceanic plates gain new material from the flow out of the oceanic ridges. As the oceanic plates expand, they crash into continental plates. Here mountain building and earthquakes occur. Also, where plates collide one can be forced down below the other into the mantle, returning material to it.

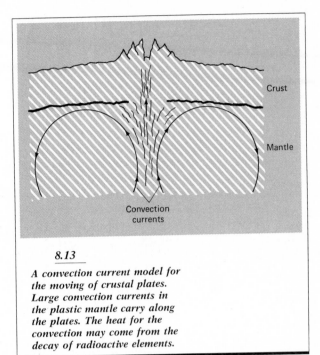

8.13

A convection current model for the moving of crustal plates. Large convection currents in the plastic mantle carry along the plates. The heat for the convection may come from the decay of radioactive elements.

evolved since its formation and is changing right now. In the investigation of other terrestrial planets, we will look for evidence of their crustal evolution. (Note that the earth's ocean basins, because they have been recently formed, are the youngest parts of the earth's crust.)

8.8
Evolution of the atmosphere and oceans

No other planet in the solar system has the earth's combination of an extensive atmosphere plus oceans of liquid water. The earth's favorable environment for the origin, evolution, and persistence of life can be attributed to the atmospheric and oceanic fluids that transfer solar heat around the globe. This fine thermostat has been working for hundreds of millions of years. However, the atmosphere and oceans have changed throughout geologic time, influenced by and influencing the earth's biological evolution. The future of life on the earth depends critically on the future of its fluid system.

Origin and evolution of the oceans / If our model for the origin of the solar system is any good (Chapter 12), the earth had no oceans when it formed 4.6 billion years ago. The primeval surface may have been very hot, about a few thousand degrees Kelvin. When the surface had cooled to about 373 K (100°C), maybe one or two continents existed on the surface, and the rest of the surface comprised the initial ocean basin. This large tub contained very little water then, only a few percent of the present volume.

The rest of the oceanic water came from the earth's interior. When magma breaks through the crust, it carries a variety of gases, such as carbon dioxide, and also a large amount of water vapor (such as in the Mt. Saint Helens eruption). The steam arises from water trapped in the solid earth when the planet formed—water that has never before seen the light of day. The present rate of water production gassing out from the interior, if it has been constant for 4.6 billion years, accounts for the water in the oceans today. Slowly that volume increases.

When the new water steams up from the mantle it is fresh; it does not contain the salts that make up 3.5 percent of seawater. (The other 96.5 percent is pure water.) The solids that produce the saltiness come from two sources: (1) substances such as chlorine and sulfate from volcanoes and (2) minerals from the land, carried by runoff waters to the sea. Because both new salts and new water are added to the oceans, the saltiness remains fairly constant.

The earth's oceans now cover 71 percent of its surface with an average depth of 4 km. These figures have been roughly the same over the past billion years. But the configuration of the oceans must have been much different because of plate tectonics (Fig. 8.11).

The evolution of the atmosphere / The outgassing from the earth's interior that created the oceans also influenced the development of the earth's atmosphere. In fact, the earth's atmosphere evolved from the chemical interplay of the solid and fluid earth (Fig. 8.14).

It's important to understand that the earth's atmosphere does not exist in isolation from the other parts of the earth with which it has contact. Take its interaction with the oceans with carbon dioxide (CO_2) as an illustrative example.

The carbon dioxide now in the atmosphere is removed by plant photosynthesis and returned by respiration (we breathe out carbon dioxide, for example), organic decay, and the burning of fuels. On the average, a carbon dioxide molecule spends only 6 years in the atmos-

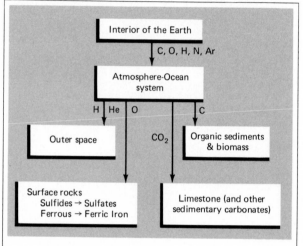

8.14

The interaction of the earth's interior, oceans, and atmosphere. Our atmosphere does not exist by itself; rather, it is in a delicate balance with the interior, crust, oceans, and all living things (the biomass). Gases, such as carbon dioxide and water vapor, flow out of the interior into the atmosphere. But the atmosphere loses material to outer space (very light gases such as hydrogen and helium), to surface rocks (where oxygen combines with sulfides and ferrous iron to make sulfates and ferric iron), to limestone and other rocks with carbonates (carbon dioxide in water solution eventually ends up in these rocks), and to living creatures (such as we, who breathe in oxygen and give off carbon dioxide).

phere before it returns to the biomass—the surface reservoir of organic (living and dead) material. More carbon dioxide resides in the top well-mixed 70 m of the oceans, dissolved in the form of bicarbonate ions (HCO_3^-), and even more is stored in the deep oceans. The bicarbonate ions flow into the oceans from rivers, coming from the weathering of surface rocks. In oceans, organisms convert the bicarbonate into carbonate for shells. Part of this ends up as sediment on the ocean bottoms.

The point of the preceding discussion is not to describe the earth's carbon dioxide budget (it doesn't!) but to show you the complicated interactions of atmosphere, oceans, and biomass on

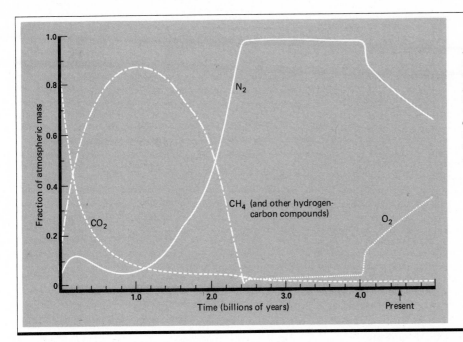

8.15

A model for the evolution of the earth's atmosphere. Shown here over 5 billion years is the fraction of the atmosphere's mass in the form of carbon dioxide (CO_2), nitrogen molecules (N_2), oxygen molecules (O_2), and methane (CH_4). The model is based on theoretical calculations by M. H. Hart.

the earth. These interactions must be understood in order to work out the evolution of the atmosphere. We do *not* yet clearly understand all the details. So any discussion of the evolution of the earth's atmosphere (or any other planet) must be taken as a working model.

With this word of warning, let me present one reasonable model of atmospheric evolution. If present ideas of planetary formation are correct, the earth's first atmosphere did not at all resemble the present one; it may have contained hydrogen and helium. But these gases, because they are so light, escaped from the earth into space. The second atmosphere arose mostly from outgassing from the solid earth. Active volcanoes, for instance, now spew out carbon dioxide, sulfur dioxide, hydrogen, nitrogen, water, methane, and ammonia—gases that were trapped in the earth when it formed. (In addition, some gases—such as helium and argon—come from the decay of radioactive materials.) The outgassed materials (which are still entering the atmosphere) interact with the oceans, surface materials, and biomass in complex ways. For example, carbon dioxide is now added to the atmosphere by volcanoes, organic decay, and combustion of fossil fuels. Carbon dioxide is taken out by plants and is being dissolved in the oceans, where much of it eventually ends up in limestone rocks. The balance,

however, has changed with time, so the atmospheric composition has evolved.

Michael H. Hart has made a computer simulation of how this evolution might have happened (Fig. 8.15). His calculations indicate that the earth's second atmosphere started out with a large amount of carbon dioxide. (The water vapor had quickly rained to end up in oceans.) The carbon dioxide ended up in the oceans and rocks, so 3 billion years ago the atmosphere consisted mostly of methane (CH_4) and other hydrogen-carbon compounds.

At this time the atmosphere contained little free oxygen, so the earth had no ozone layer. Ultraviolet light readily penetrated and broke up methane, ammonia, and water. The hydrogen from these molecules fled into space. Some of the oxygen freed from the water combined with some of the methane and gradually eliminated it. The rest of the oxygen eventually created an ozone layer, cutting out the ultraviolet from interacting with most of the atmosphere. Nitrogen became the dominant constituent of the atmosphere.

The high abundance of atmospheric oxygen was produced (and is now maintained) by biological activity. Geologic evidence indicates that the transformation to an oxygen-rich atmosphere occurred about 2 billion years ago, when plant activity and photosynthesis bloomed. (See

Chapter 22.) The increase in oxygen was probably a gradual, continuous one. About 1 billion years ago the atmosphere may have contained only 10 percent of the present amount of free oxygen. A large increase occurred about 600 million years ago. The oxygen content suddenly increased to present levels, along with a sudden proliferation of life.

The evolution of the earth's surface temperature / How hot it gets at the earth's surface depends on how much energy it receives from the sun and how well the greenhouse effect operates. Less solar energy results in lower temperature. A better greenhouse effect (more carbon dioxide and water vapor in the atmosphere) delivers higher temperatures.

People have disturbed the natural carbon dioxide balance by extracting fossil fuels from the earth, burning them for energy, and so adding to the carbon dioxide in the atmosphere. In addition, our destruction of forests has eliminated a substantial part of the green plants that take in atmospheric carbon dioxide and add some of their carbon to the atmosphere. The ocean can absorb only part of the excess.

Our activities have a net result of increasing the percentage of carbon dioxide in the earth's atmosphere. This increase is big enough to have been observed; it amounts to an increase of 5 percent over the past 30 years. Although there is still much controversy over what the impact of this increase will be, it may result in a temperature increase of about 2°C by 2020 A.D., if the overall water vapor and cloudiness do not change. This could have serious effects on climate and atmospheric circulation.

The distant future of the earth's climate may not be pleasant for our descendants. Models of stellar evolution (Chapter 19) predict that the sun's luminosity will slowly increase with time. As the sun grows brighter, the earth's surface temperature will increase. More water will evaporate and increase the atmospheric trapping of infrared radiation, which, in turn, will increase the temperature. About 4 billion years from now, according to some theoretical calculations, the increased temperature will completely evaporate the oceans and produce a hot, steamy atmosphere. If people have not vacated the earth by then, and if technology cannot reduce the steambath, the survivors, if any, will be forced to leave their superheated home.

SUMMARY

This chapter has scanned the earth's structure from its dense core to the tenuous top of the atmosphere. Three of the four elemental divisions made by the ancients fit the earth's structure well: earth, water, and air. Although the solid earth constitutes the bulk of our planetary environment, the atmosphere and oceans are more fundamental to our survival. The two fluid systems transport energy around the earth and continually erode the surface. The evolution of the atmosphere and oceans has directly shaped the geological and biological evolution of our home planet (Table 8.2).

TABLE 8.2	*Vital statistics of the planet Earth*
Average radius	6371 km
Mass	5.967×10^{24} kg
Average density	5.518 g/cc
Escape velocity	11.2 km/sec
Age	4.6 billion years

Source   Astrophysical Quantities, 3rd ed. by C. W. Allen (London, Athlone Press, 1973).

The rise of mountains yields finally to the onslaught of wind and rain. Mountains are scrubbed away, but the collisions of continental plates push up new peaks to replace the worn ones. The restless earth moves with the tremor of earthquakes and also with the slow drift of continental masses. Viewed over a long enough time, the mountain ranges move like waves of rocks across the earth's surface. The energy for this motion derives from currents in the mantle, apparently generated from the heat of radioactive decay. In contrast, solar heating drives wind and water currents and waves. The fourth ancient element—fire—fuels our planet in two forms: solar energy and radioactive decay. These two forms of fire energize the evolution of the earth.

Our planet is old, about 4.6 billion years in age, a span of time incomprehensible to creatures as limited in life span as we. Although old, the earth is not static. Rather, the planet dynamically—but slowly—evolves. The earth's structure and evolution, which we know in more detail and depth than that of any other planet, serves as a model for the investigation of similar bodies within the solar system. No longer at the physical center of the astronomical universe, the blue-white earth still occupies a special place in relation to humanity: It is our tiny, fruitful home, our ship journeying through space.

STUDY EXERCISES

1 Explain how you could determine the earth's mass by jumping off a building. (Explain it; don't do it!) (*Objective 1*)

2 Contrast the composition of the earth's core to its crust. (*Objectives 2 and 3*)

3 Discuss uncertainties in the statement "The earth's age is 4.6 billion years." (*Objective 5*)

4 Make a simple argument to demonstrate that the earth's core must be denser than its crust. (*Objective 3*)

5 Describe two effects that the earth's atmosphere has on sunlight passing through it. (*Objective 6*)

6 Suppose the amount of water vapor in the atmosphere suddenly increased by a large amount. What would happen to the earth's surface temperature? (*Objective 7*)

7 How can volcanoes affect the evolution of the earth's oceans and atmosphere? (*Objectives 8 and 10*)

8 Where did the oceans come from? (*Objective 8*)

9 What parts of the earth's surface are the *youngest*, that is, the most recently formed? (*Objective 9*)

BEYOND THIS BOOK . . .

R. Seiver compares the earth with the other planets in the solar system in "The Earth," *Scientific American*, September 1975, p. 82.

There are many geology books available. I have found *The Earth Sciences* (Harper & Row, New York, 1971) by A. N. Strahler a useful reference.

Planetary Geology (Prentice-Hall, New Jersey, 1975) by N. M. Short contains comparative information about the earth's evolution in Chapter 13.

An excellent article on the fate and role of carbon dioxide in the atmosphere is "The Carbon Dioxide Question," by G. Woodwell, *Scientific American*, January 1978, p. 34.

For more on the dynamo model, see "The Source of the Earth's Magnetic Field" by C. Carrigan and D. Gubbins, *Scientific American*, February 1979, p. 118.

Read the details about "Plate Tectonics" by J. F. Dewey, *Scientific American*, May 1972, p. 56.

LEARNING OBJECTIVES

After studying this chapter, you should be able to:

1. Compare the moon and Mercury in size, mass, and density.

2. Describe the moon's surface features and indicate a possible formation process for each.

3. Describe Mercury's surface features and indicate a possible formation process for each.

4. Compare and contrast the surface environments (temperature, atmosphere, surface features) of the moon and Mercury to each other and to the earth.

5. Sketch the lunar interior, as surmised from Apollo experiments.

6. Sketch a model of Mercury's interior, and contrast it to the interior of the earth and the moon.

7. Compare and contrast the evolution of the moon and Mercury to each other and to the earth.

8. Outline a possible history for the moon's evolution in light of Apollo results; present evidence for each of the major stages.

9. Compare and contrast two models of the moon's origin using Apollo results to support or refute the models.

The moon and Mercury: Dead worlds

9

Every one is a moon and has a dark side which he never shows to anyone.

MARK TWAIN: Pudd'nhead Wilson's Calendar

9.1

A composite picture of the first and last quarter moons to show the full face with surface details. At a real full moon the straight-down sunlight leaves no shadows and so washes out surface features. (Courtesy Lick Observatory)

9.2

The cratered surface of Mercury. (Courtesy NASA)

Through a small telescope—such as Galileo's—the moon strikes you as a stark world, tantalizingly close (Fig. 9.1). Fascination with this neighbor bred tales of traveling to the moon. The stories range from men borne aloft by birds to the cannon-powered voyage described by Jules Verne. His astronauts, after their launch from Florida, circled the moon and returned home by plunging into the sea. Verne had the right idea! NASA carried out his vision with additions. In July 1969 Neil Armstrong's one small step imprinted an indelible mark in history (and on the moon's surface). The event fulfilled many earlier dreams: the first visit to an alien planet.

Another body in the solar system has a similar look—Mercury (Fig. 9.2). Like the moon, Mercury is a small, airless world, pockmarked with many craters.

Both the moon and Mercury are now dead worlds. Their interiors are cooler than the earth; no heat drives the motions of crustal plates. No mountains rise, no volcanoes fume and without atmospheres, no wind or water wears down their landscapes. Their heyday of activity has passed!

This chapter compares the tiny worlds of the moon and Mercury to each other and to the earth to provide an insight into their evolution. The emphasis will fall on our moon because of the Apollo mission returns, which give us solid clues to reconstruct the moon's history and so infer that of Mercury's in comparison.

9.1
The moon's orbit, rotation, size, and mass

Greek astronomers knew that the moon circles the earth. But they did not have an accurate determination of the moon's distance. Aristarchus (Section 2.3) estimated that the moon was 10 earth diameters away. He was wrong; the

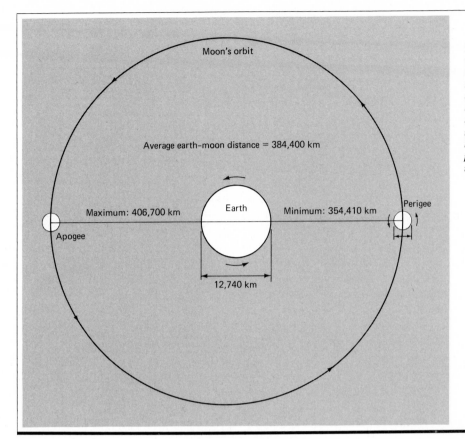

9.3

The orbit of the moon relative to the earth. Shown here are the minimum perigee and maximum apogee distances. The earth and the moon are not drawn to the same scale as the distances but do have their correct relative sizes. The view is looking down on the orbital plane from above the earth's north pole.

actual figure is close to 30 earth diameters (Fig. 9.3), or about 384,400 km.

In 1969 the Apollo 11 astronauts deposited special reflectors on the moon's surface. Later Apollo missions put down other such reflectors. These devices reflect laser light, which travels between the earth and the moon. The bouncing of light off the moon permits measurements of the moon's distance from the earth to an accuracy of about 0.3 m!

The moon revolves relative to the earth in an elliptical orbit. During a month the earth–moon distance varies (Fig. 9.3). When the moon is closest to the earth it is at *perigee*. The most distant point is called *apogee*. The difference between apogee and perigee is just over 50,000 km.

***History of the moon's orbit* /** The orbit of the moon has not always been as it is now. Gravity ties the earth and moon together. Tides are one consequence of this coupling. Tidal friction slows down the earth's rotation rate by one second every 50,000 years. This decrease results

in an increase of the earth–moon distance (Focus 25). The moon spirals away from the earth at about 4 cm a year (Fig. 9.4). Billions of years from now, the moon will be so far from the earth that the length of the month (longer than now) will equal the length of the day (also longer). Then the day will be 55 present earth days long.

The moon must once have been much closer to the earth. American physicist Gordon MacDonald believes that the closest approach of the moon took place about 1.2 billion years ago. At that time—if his calculations are correct—the month was about 6.5 h long, the day 5 h long, and the moon only 18,000 km from the earth. The moon would have looked like an enormous defaced balloon in the sky! It would have covered 11°, which is 22 times its present angular size.

***The one-faced moon* /** If you have looked at the moon—even occasionally—you have grown used to the sight of its same face toward the

focus 25

TIDES

The detailed behavior of tides at specific locations on the earth is extremely complicated, but the general ebb and flow is apparent. Generally, coastal points experience two high tides (and two low tides) a day separated by 12 h and 25 min on the average. So the complete cycle of tides takes about 24 h and 50 min, approximately the same as the daily motion of the moon.

Newton's law of gravitation provides a general explanation of the overall features of the tides, which arise from the moon's gravity. This explanation idealizes the earth as a smooth ball covered with water. The moon pulls gravitationally on both the earth and the water. The solid earth body is attracted to the moon as if all of its mass were concentrated at a point in the center. However, the water on the surface is free to move around, and the difference between the moon's gravitational forces on the earth and the ocean waters results in tides.

Let's look at the details. Imagine that the earth's surface is level and covered completely with a layer of water. Consider for a moment the moon's gravitational attraction at three points lined up with the moon (Fig. 1). Recall that the force of gravity decreases as the inverse square of the distance between masses. So the moon's gravitational force must be greater at A than at B, and greater at B than at C. The greater the force acting on the same mass is, the greater its acceleration will be. So a mass at A has a greater acceleration than a mass at C, and a mass at B has a greater acceleration than a mass at C. The difference between these accelerations is crucial. Because of the difference, the water at A bulges ahead of the earth (point B), and the water at C lags behind the earth and forms a bulge on the earth's side opposite the moon. So we have two high tides: one on the side of the earth toward the moon, and one on the opposite side. These two high tides take place about a half-day apart.

Note that it is the differences in gravitational forces that account for the tides. These differences are known as tidal gravitational forces. In contrast to normal gravity, they tend to pull objects apart.

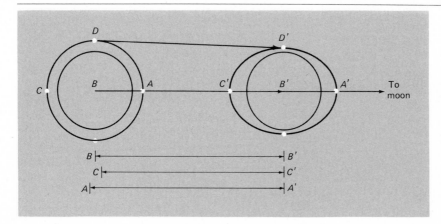

1

Tides. Imagine a perfectly smooth earth covered with water (B). Compare what happens to water at A, C, and D pulled by the moon's gravity. How far the water falls in a given time depends on its distance from the moon; water at A falls farther than that at B because A is closer to the moon and attracted with a greater force. Water at D and the earth's center fall the same distance because their acceleration is the same. So as the earth falls toward the moon (from B to B'), water on one side falls a bit more (from A to A'), and on the other side, a bit less (from C to C'). Water moves down from D to help supply the tidal bulges; so the water depth at D is less than at A' or C'.

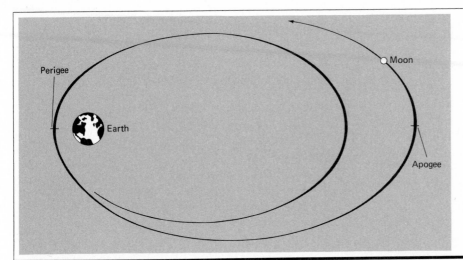

The moon slowly spiraling away from the earth. As the earth's spin slows down because of tidal friction, the moon moves away from the earth, so the earth–moon system has constant angular momentum. The effect is highly exaggerated in this figure. This increase now amounts to about 4 cm a year. The moon's elliptical orbit becomes larger and more eccentric. (The view of this diagram is directly down on the orbital plane.)

earth. The moon must rotate on its axis in order to keep the same side facing the earth (Fig. 9.5). In fact, the moon rotates on its axis with a period of 27.3 days—the same as its period of revolution about the earth with respect to the stars. Until satellites were placed in orbit around the moon, we had only faint ideas about the appearance of the back side, the side turned away from the earth.

If you stood on the moon's near side, you would see the earth suspended—never rising or setting—against the stars. With the earth always in sight, astronauts on the near side can communicate directly here by radio.

Lunar orbiters have allowed us to see the moon's once mysterious far side (Fig. 9.6). Their photos show that the far side looks different from the near side (Fig. 9.1). It is almost completely cratered, with little of the dark, smoother areas that cover much of the near side's surface.

The lunar day / The moon keeps the same face to the earth but not to the sun. It rotates one time with respect to the sun in 29.5 days; so the moon's solar day is 29.5 (earth) days long. Everytime you see a full moon in the sky, it is noon on the near side.

The moon's size / If you know the distance from the earth to the moon, you can find its physical diameter from an observation of its angular size (Focus 1). The result is 3476 km, about one-fourth the earth's diameter. If the earth were the size of your head, the moon would be about the size of a tennis ball. On the

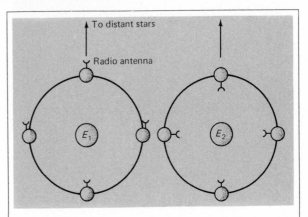

9.5

The moon's rotation. The moon keeps the same face toward the earth because its rotation period (with respect to the stars) is the same as its revolution period (also with respect to the stars). To see this, imagine an Apollo astronaut on the moon pointing a radio antenna at the earth. Suppose the moon always kept the same side pointing toward the same direction in space. Then the astronaut, who had originally set the antenna straight at the earth, would find the earth slowly moving out of the line of sight (E_1). In this case people on the earth would see the moon's entire surface during a month. But this is not the case. Instead, the moon rotates at the same rate it revolves, with respect to the stars. So an antenna aimed at the earth (E_2) remains fixed on it.

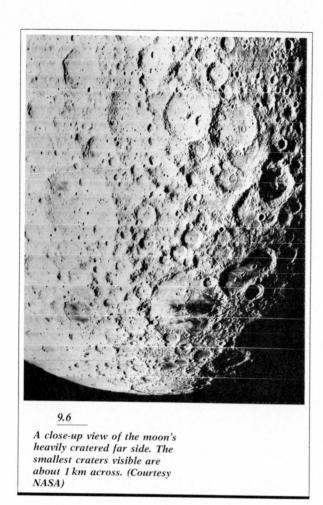

9.6

A close-up view of the moon's heavily cratered far side. The smallest craters visible are about 1 km across. (Courtesy NASA)

same scale, the moon's orbit would have a diameter of about 12 m.

The moon's mass and density / You can't get the moon's mass by simply using Kepler's third law (Focus 12), for that will give you the *combined* mass of the earth and moon from the moon's distance and orbital period. Along with the third law, you need to make use of the *center of mass* of the earth–moon system.

What is the center of mass? If you have ever ridden on a seesaw, you have experienced what is meant by center of mass: It is the balance point of the system. Suppose you and a friend with the same mass swing on the ends of the seesaw. To balance it, the turning point must be placed on the seesaw's center. Now suppose a heavier friend gets on. To balance, you must move the seesaw so that you have more length than your friend (Fig. 9.7). Note that where the balance point lies gives you an

idea of the ratio of the two masses involved. For instance, if your friend has *twice* the mass, he or she will have *half* the length you have to balance.

The earth and the moon also balance, as a consequence of Newton's third law (Section 4.2). Each moves in an ellipse around the center of mass (Fig. 9.8). The motion around the center of mass can be measured by observing monthly shifts in the positions of the other planets. The earth–moon center of mass lies 4645 km from the earth's center in the direction of the moon (Fig. 9.8). The moon does *not* revolve around the center of the earth! From the location of the center of mass, we find the mass of the moon to be $1/81.3$ that of the earth, or 7.4×10^{22} kg.

From the mass and radius, the average density is 3.3 g/cc, about the same density as rocks in the earth's mantle.

9.2

The moon's surface environment

A telescope shows the moon as a rugged world (Fig. 9.9). Craters abound and mountains leap up, challenging the edge of space.

Because the moon has a smaller mass and radius than the earth, its surface gravity is one-sixth that of the earth. So objects weigh one-sixth as much on the moon as they do on the earth (Focus 17). An easy way to lose weight is to travel to the moon! The astronaut who must lug around a 180-pound life-support system on the earth carries the equivalent of only 30 pounds on the moon. But the astronaut must be careful. Although the weight of the life-support system is much less, its mass is the same on the moon or earth (or anywhere). So to stop running, for example, requires the same effort. That's why the astronauts looked so clumsy on the moon in the television pictures.

The moon has no atmosphere to speak of. This fact was known before the Apollo missions, because if you watch the moon move in front of a star, the star will suddenly vanish without warning. Any substantial atmosphere would dim the star gradually before it disappeared behind the moon's disk.

Why does the moon have essentially no atmosphere? Gravity holds down the atmosphere of any celestial body. An atmosphere consists of a gas of molecules and atoms, moving at

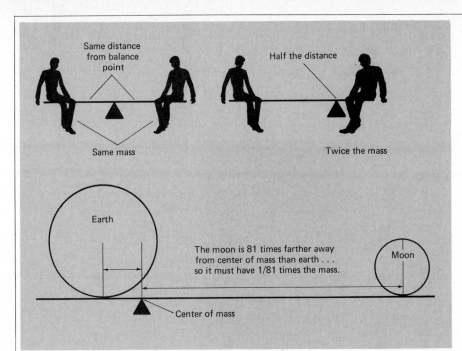

Same distance from balance point

Same mass

Half the distance

Twice the mass

Earth

The moon is 81 times farther away from center of mass than earth . . . so it must have 1/81 times the mass.

Moon

Center of mass

9.7

Center of mass. Suppose you and a friend are swinging on a seesaw. If you both have the same mass, the balance point of the seesaw is at the center. But if you have twice the mass of your friend, the balance point is twice as far from your friend as you. The same analysis applies to the earth–moon system.

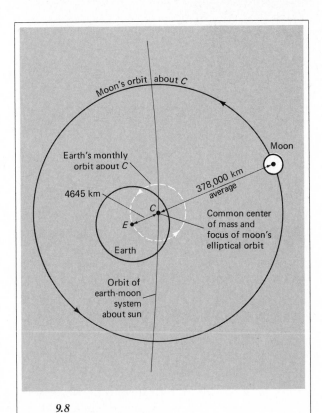

Moon's orbit about C

Earth's monthly orbit about C

4645 km

378,000 km average

C

E

Earth

Common center of mass and focus of moon's elliptical orbit

Orbit of earth-moon system about sun

Moon

9.8

The center of mass of the earth–moon system. Both the earth and the moon revolve around their center of mass once a month. Note that the system's center of mass is located about 4645 km away from the center of the earth. The view here is down on the earth's north pole.

various velocities. The temperature of the gas is a measure of the average velocity of the particles in it (Focus 30). Typically, gas particles collide frequently. But in the thin upper layers of an atmosphere, far fewer collisions occur. If a gas particle has escape velocity (Focus 13) here, it speeds off into outer space. For the moon the escape velocity is 2.4 km/sec. At typical lunar temperatures, gas particles at the surface have escape velocity. Most gases have escaped from the moon's gravitational grasp since its formation. Some heavy gases and material from the solar wind might make up a lunar atmosphere. But the surface density must be extremely low. The exhaust from the Apollo 11 landing dumped more gases into the atmosphere than had existed there before the landing. These gases will not stay around long: for instance, oxygen dumped at the moon's surface escapes the moon in about 100 years.

The earth's atmosphere acts like an insulating blanket. During the night it retains much of the heat received in the previous day. Lacking such atmospheric insulation, the moon experiences a greater temperature range during a lunar "day" (which lasts a month of earth time). Under direct sunlight the moon's surface temperature exceeds 370 K, and at midnight it drops to 125 K.

Here's how to estimate an airless planet's surface temperature from its energy budget. (An atmosphere makes the situation more complicated.) Suppose only sunlight heats the planet's surface (Fig. 9.10). But the surface does not ab-

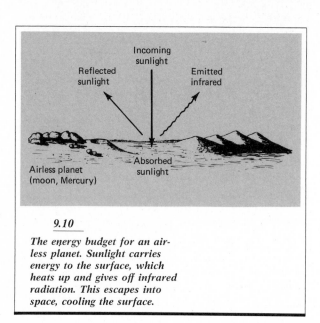

9.10

The energy budget for an airless planet. Sunlight carries energy to the surface, which heats up and gives off infrared radiation. This escapes into space, cooling the surface.

sorb all the incoming sunlight. Some is reflected back into space. The albedo of the surface indicates how much light is absorbed and how much is reflected. The moon's albedo is about 7 percent, which means that it reflects 7 percent of the light that hits it and absorbs the remain-

ing 93 percent. (Even though a full moon seems to shine brightly in the sky, the moon's surface is really quite black.) The absorbed sunlight heats the surface; it radiates mostly infrared radiation because of the low temperature. The balance between the incoming sunlight and outgoing infrared determines the surface temperature of the sunlit side. At night, there is no energy input from the sunlight, and the infrared—because no atmosphere exists to trap it—radiates away into space. Because the lunar night is so long (about 15 earth days), the surface has a long time to cool and the temperature plummets to 125 K. The large noon-to-midnight temperature difference, some 250 K, occurs because the moon rotates slowly and has no atmosphere. You would expect the same situation for any airless, slowly rotating planet.

Without a significant atmosphere the moon has no shield from lethal X-rays and ultraviolet radiation from the sun, or from small, solid particles from space. The moon's cratered surface presents a fierce, unfriendly place for people. The Apollo astronauts, protected in their bulky life-support systems (Fig. 9.11), found the moon bleakly beautiful but uninviting.

Astronaut Buzz Aldrin on the moon. The astronauts must carry along bulky life-support systems because the moon has no atmosphere. Note the gold-coated visor that keeps out harmful radiation from the sun. This is my favorite moon picture. Because the visor acts like a mirror, you cannot see the face of Aldrin, but you can view the surrounding scene in reflection. (Courtesy NASA)

9.3
The moon's surface:
Pre-Apollo

Until the Apollo astronauts walked upon the lunar surface and sampled it, the study of the moon was confined to viewing it from the earth, orbiting satellites, or lunar landers. These investigations provoked many questions: How did the craters form? When did they form? This section briefly surveys the moon's surface as a preview to the results of the Apollo landings.

The consistent study of the lunar surface commenced in 1609, when Galileo turned his telescope to the moon (Section 4.1). Although none of his drawings showed any features that can be positively identified today, his pioneer work sparked an explosion of careful observa-

tions. Galileo unfortunately named the dark areas *maria* (Latin for "seas"; the singular form is *mare*) because he thought these regions were water beds. (No water exists on the moon's surface.) I will use "maria" rather than "seas," because the English word implies water more forcefully than the Latin one.

The moon viewed through a small telescope or binoculars is always fascinating. Lunar craters give the moon a pock-marked face. Mountains and craters irregularly rim the moon's edge. Some mountains stand alone in the maria, whereas others link in long ranges. Splashes of bright rays flower from some craters. The moon appears as a rough, old world that has suffered significant violence, carving its splotched surface.

Maria and basins / Photographs from satellites orbiting the moon show that most of the maria lie in the northern half of the moon's hemisphere that is fixed toward the earth. The maria appear dark compared with the rest of the surface. (Their albedo is lower.) Their stretches form the face of the "man in the moon."

Along with their darker appearance, the maria have other general features that are clues to their formation. The maria look circular in shape, are interconnected, and have smooth surfaces compared with the brighter, cratered regions. Also, the maria have lower elevations, by about 3 km, than the rest of the surface. The maria are called the lunar *lowlands* and the other lighter-colored areas the *highlands*.

The vast flat extents of the maria appear to be a solidified lava flow. If you look carefully at the regions around the maria, you can find craters flooded in by the dark material from the mare (Fig. 9.12). This indicates that the lava flow that formed the maria occurred *after* the lunar crust formed and after the formation of some craters. In other words, the lunar maria fill up large, shallow *basins* on the moon's surface. For example, you can easily see the Mare Imbrium basin (Fig. 9.13) on the moon's near side. It's roughly circular in outline and has a diameter of about 1200 km. The moon's most striking basin lies on its far side: Mare Orientale (Fig. 9.14). Note how the concentric rings of mountains make it look like a bull's-eye! The outer rim of mountains (the Cordillera Mountains) has a diameter of about 970 km and rises to a height of 7 km. Surrounding this basin for about 1000 km out lies a blanket of lighter material covering the older lunar surface. Mare Imbrium would resemble Mare Orientale if most of its filling material were removed.

Astronomers have found concentrations of mass in the basins beneath most of the maria. These are called *mascons*. One mascon, for example, under Mare Imbrium has a mass of 1.6×10^{19} kg and an average density of 3.7 g/cc. (Note that this density is *greater* than the average density of the moon.) If this mascon were spread out to cover California, it would be 12 km thick! The fact that almost all maria have associated mascons requires some process to produce large amounts of a dense material under the maria.

9.12

A close-up of a mare's surface (the Ocean of Storms). Note how much smoother, darker, and lower in elevation the mare appears in contrast to the background highlands. Also note the baylike area near the center where the mare meets the highlands. It appears that a lava flow has filled in a crater here. (Courtesy NASA)

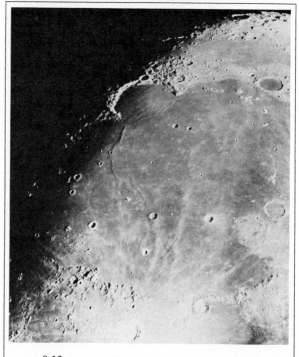

9.13

Mare Imbrium in the moon's northern hemisphere. (Courtesy Yerkes Observatory)

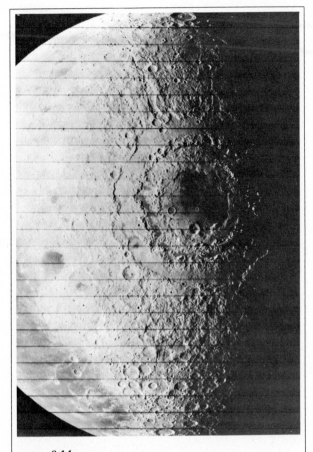

9.14

Mare Orientale on the moon's far side. The Cordillera Mountains ring the basin like a bull's-eye. (Courtesy NASA)

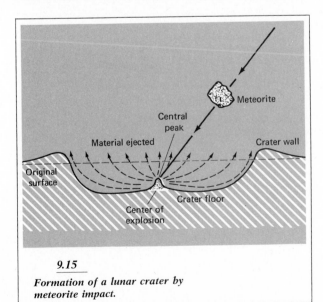

9.15

Formation of a lunar crater by meteorite impact.

Craters / Craters (from the Greek word meaning "cup" or "bowl") litter the moon almost everywhere. They range widely in size, from many smaller than a coin to five with diameters greater than 200 km. (That's about the size of Connecticut.)

Some characteristics of lunar craters seem fairly universal. Craters are generally round and come in many different sizes. The heights of the rims of lunar craters are small, compared with the diameters, and the floors are depressed, compared with the surrounding landscape. The terrain just outside large craters has a wavy look as if shocked by an explosion.

What formed the craters? One idea is the *impact model* of crater formation: objects from space slamming into the moon to punch out the craters (Fig. 9.15). Another view is the *volcanic model*. The craters were the cones left over from a lava eruption. The volcanic model requires that the moon's interior be hot enough to provide lava.

Earth has a few craters made by the impact of solid bodies from space and also some made by volcanoes. Significant differences exist between the two. No volcanic crater on the earth is larger than 5 km, whereas some impact craters are larger. The outer slopes of a volcanic crater are smooth. An impact produces a crater with undulating slopes, usually covered by debris. If the debris and crater wall were put back into an impact crater, they would fill it up. Volcanic craters are smaller. Material blasted out by an impact falls in streaks, leaving a raylike pattern. Volcanoes eject material in a more uniform pattern. Large chunks of thrown-out material can create small secondary craters around impact craters. Volcanoes have no secondary craters.

Almost all lunar craters display impact characteristics (Fig. 9.16). For example, rays emanating from some craters indicate an impact origin. The conclusion: Impacts sculpted almost all the lunar craters.

What projectiles made these impacts? Small, solid bodies now orbit the sun, which are called meteorites (Section 12.1) when they strike the earth. If they pass close enough to the moon, they will collide with it. But no evidence exists for large craters. So the era of heavy impact craters took place in the past. The Apollo missions hoped to find out when.

(a)

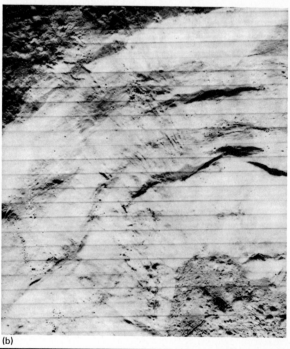

(b)

9.16

(a) *The crater Aristarchus, about 60 km wide, with its ray system. The light-colored rays appear to center on the crater. Note the wavy contours of the surface just outside the crater. This arose from the shock of impact that formed the crater. (Courtesy NASA) (b) A close-up of the southern wall of Aristarchus, showing evidence of impact and erosion by impacts of particles from space. (Courtesy NASA)*

9.17
An Apollo lunar module going down for a landing. (Courtesy NASA)

9.4

The moon close up:
Apollo mission results

Complex computers helped pilot the Apollo 11 spacecraft to the moon (Fig. 9.17). The craft returned with a cargo of 22 kg of the moon. Those lunar samples, collected by astronauts Neil Armstrong and Edwin Aldrin in slightly less than three hours, were probably the most expensive scientific specimens ever gathered. They were also the most fascinating: the first pieces of another world brought back to the earth.

The Apollo program, now ended, conveyed almost 400 kg of lunar material from six different sites. Scientists have examined only about 10 percent in detail. Already these samples and other experiments in the Apollo program have provided the first deep understanding of a planet other than the earth. We can now sketch out physical details of the moon and outline its history.

The lunar surface / The Apollo samples reveal the physical and chemical nature of the lunar surface. The very top layer is a porous, somewhat adhesive layer of debris (Fig. 9.18). It consists of fine particles (called lunar *soil*) and larger rock fragments. All soil samples contained a large amount of mostly round pieces of glass (Fig. 9.19), making the surface slippery.

The rocks returned from the moon fall into three general categories: (1) dark, fine-grained rocks similar to terrestrial basalts (magnesium/iron silicates), (2) light-colored igneous rocks with visible grains called *anorthosites* (aluminium/calcium silicates), and (3) *breccias*, rock and mineral fragments cemented together (Fig. 9.20). A fourth type of rock was less common; it is like terrestrial basalts but contains high amounts of potassium (K), rare-earth elements (REE), and phosphorus (P). This material has been dubbed KREEP. The anorthosites and KREEP make up the rugged lunar highlands.

9.18

The moon's surface, which consists of fine particles—called soil—and larger rock fragments. Note how well the imprints of the tire treads stand out, emphasizing that the surface's consistency is like that of wet sand. (Courtesy NASA)

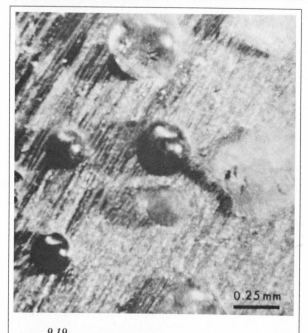

0.25 mm

9.19

Small glass spheres, typically found in the moon's soil. (Courtesy NASA)

5 mm

9.20

A breccia from the moon's surface (Apollo 11 sample). This rock is formed from the fusing together of smaller rock fragments. The surface pits arise from bombardment by small meteorites. (Courtesy NASA)

What do these characteristics imply? First, because the moon rocks are igneous rocks, they formed from the solidification of lava. Now, the rate at which lava cools determines the grain size of igneous rocks: Fast-cooling results in small grains, slow-cooling, in large grains. So the dark rocks (found in the lowlands) cooled faster than the light-colored ones (found in the highlands). In addition, the light-colored rocks are less dense than the dark ones. This difference arises from the fact that the anorthosites contain calcium and aluminum silicates rather than the iron-magnesium silicates of the mare basalts.

Second, we can infer how the breccias formed. Imagine newly made igneous rocks on the moon's surface. Bodies from space pound into these rocks, fragmenting and heating them. The heat cements some fragment together to make breccias. The loose, left over material makes up the lunar soil.

In a few important ways, moon rocks are quite different from the earth's igneous rocks. First, they contain more titanium, uranium, iron, and magnesium. Second, compared with earth rocks or meteorites, they are depleted of elements that would condense at relatively low temperatures (1300 K). The elements are called *volatiles* and include sodium, potassium, copper, argon, and chlorine. Third, a few lunar samples contain minute amounts of complex carbon (organic) compounds. This discovery does not mean that life existed on the moon; organic compounds can be formed in nonbiological processes. Some meteorites (Chapter 12) also contain carbon compounds. So the carbon compounds in the lunar soil may have been carried there by infalling bodies. Fourth, the moon rocks contain *no* water. Earth rocks always have some water locked up in their minerals. The moon rocks were found to be bone dry.

In one critical way, on a nuclear level, the moon and the earth are similar. The isotopic composition of oxygen (relative abundances of oxygen-16, -17, and -18) in the lunar samples is the same as that for the earth. Studies of the oxygen isotopic compositions of meteorites show a distinct variation among samples. Some meteorites are thought to be primitive materials from the condensation of the solar nebula. Indirect evidence suggests that the variation in oxygen isotopes corresponds to condensation in different parts of the cloud out of which the solar system formed. The identity for the earth and moon establishes that these bodies formed in the same general region of space.

Finally, compare the bulk densities of the moon and the earth: 3.3 g/cc versus 5.5 g/cc. This difference implies that the moon contains less metals than the earth and probably does not have as large a nickel-iron core (if any!) as the earth.

Ages of lunar samples / Moon rocks are dated by the same radioactive-decay techniques used to date earth rocks (Focus 23). One caution: These methods give the time since the rock last solidified. If a rock was heated sufficiently since its original formation, radioactive dating gives a younger age than is correct.

Only a few fragments from the lunar soil have ages as great as 4.5–4.6 billion years. The light-colored rocks from the highlands generally are the oldest: 3.8–4 billion years. The KREEP basalts are younger, from 3.4 to 3.6 billion years old. The dark-colored rocks from the maria are the youngest, some only 3.2–3.3 billion years old and a few as old as 3.8 billion years.

What do these ages reveal about the history of the moon's surface? The moon formed a little more than 4.6 billion years ago. After formation, the present highlands solidified, about 4 billion years ago. Then the lava flows that made the maria took place.

The moon's interior / The Apollo missions probed the moon's interior with the same seismic-wave methods used to look into the earth (Focus 22). The astronauts placed seismometers on the moon to measure moonquakes (Fig. 9.21). These instruments found the moon to be an inactive world (compared with the earth). Few moonquakes occur, and those take place about 800 km below the surface. Such shocks release only about 10^2 to 10^5 J (joules), barely a tremble by earth standards. If you stood directly over the strongest moonquake so far recorded, you would not even feel your feet shake. Geologically the moon is now a quiet world.

This low seismic activity indicates that the moon is cold and solid down to a depth of about 800–1000 km (Fig. 9.22). This region makes up the moon's mantle, which very likely consists of pyroxene-rich silicates that are a little more dense than the surface. Encasing the mantle is the crust, which is layered. On the very surface lie the rocks found in the Apollo missions: highland anorthorsites, lowland basalts, and KREEP. At a depth of about 25 km the crust consists of anorthosite-rich silicates.

It is not completely certain if the moon has a well-defined core. If it does, the core probably makes up the inner 500 km of the moon. It may be hot—about 1500 K—and molten in whole or in part. Evidence for a hot core comes from the measurement of heat flowing up through the lunar surface. The amount of heat flow is three times as great as that for the earth—a larger, hotter body. So some part of the moon's interior must be relatively hot. The mantle is solid and cool, so the core must be the source of the heat outflow.

Although the moon's core is hot, it cannot be molten metals like the earth's. Note that the moon's bulk density is too low for a large fraction of the core to be iron and nickel. Now, the moon's magnetic field is *very* weak, only 10^{-4} as strong as the earth's. Applying the dynamo model for a planet's magnetic field (Section 8.4), we expect that, because the moon rotates more slowly than the earth, the moon's field would be weaker. And, because the core is probably not molten (and so doesn't flow easily) and probably does not contain a large fraction of metals, we also expect the moon's field to be weaker still. And it is, in line with the dynamo model.

9.21

Neil Armstrong deploying seismic detectors on the moon's surface (Apollo 11). (Courtesy NASA)

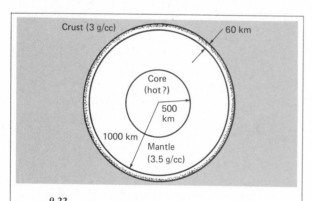

9.22

A model of the moon's interior, inferred from seismic measurements. The moon probably has a crust, mantle, and core. The core may be hot enough to be molten—perhaps with a temperature as high as 1500 K. It is denser than the mantle but not nickel-iron like the earth's core. The moon's mantle probably is made of much the same material as the earth's—silicates such as olivine.

Curiously enough, some of the surface rocks returned to earth are magnetized much more than expected from the strength of the moon's field now. Iron minerals in a rock preserve the magnetic field present at the time of a rock's solidification. So in the past the moon's magnetic field must have been stronger than now; how is a puzzle not yet solved.

Conjectured lunar evolution / The Apollo results provide a basis for a scenario of the moon's history since it formed. The inferred sequence of events (Table 9.1) relies heavily on the dating of the lunar rocks.

About 4.6 billion years ago the moon formed. Whether or not the moon came together in the vicinity of the earth, it probably formed by the gathering together of chunks of material. These pieces continued to plunge into the moon after most of its mass gathered. During the first 500 million years after formation, projectiles from space bombarded the surface and heated it enough so that it melted. Less dense materials floated to the surface of the melted shell; volatile materials were lost to space. Then the crust began to solidify from this melted shell about 4.4 billion years ago. From 4.1 to 4.4 billion years ago, the crust slowly cooled while the bombardment from space tapered off. This debris made many of the craters now found in the highland areas.

Below the surface, the moon's material remained molten. About 3.9–4.1 billion years ago a few huge chunks smashed the crust to produce basins that later became maria. For example, the Mare Orientale basin formed some 4 billion years ago when an object about 25 km across smashed into the moon. Only later did the basins fill with lava. As the crust lost its original heat, short-lived radioactive elements (which decay rapidly) reheated sections of it. From 3.0 to 3.9 billion years ago, lava from the radioactive reheating punctured the thin crust beneath the basins, flowing into them to make the maria.

For the past 3 billion years the crust has been inactive. However, small particles from space have incessantly plowed into the surface since it solidified. The sand-sized grains scoured the surface, smoothed it down, and pulverized it. Continued bombardment churned the fragmented surface. Impacts melted the soil, which swifty cooled to form breccias and glass spheres. The moon's surface today resembles a heavily bombarded battlefield—constantly fragmented, stirred up, and melted.

It is difficult to fit a stronger past magnetic field into the preceding picture. One possibility (not conclusive!) goes like this: Whatever the moon formed out of had a weak magnetic field, so its core originally had a field. The crust melted, then cooled. As it solidified, the weak field of the core magnetized the crust. Then somehow the core heated up and lost its magnetic field, just as a bar magnet loses its field when heated up to a high enough temperature. The moon's core now has a very weak magnetic field, and only the alignment of iron minerals in the crustal rocks attests to the earlier existence of a stronger field.

To recap (Fig. 9.23): We suppose the moon to have formed at least 4.6 billion years ago. But no whole rock samples are this old, only a few fragments. The rocks fall into two age groups: highland rocks about 4 billion years old and lowland rocks about 3.5 billion years old. The highland rocks are the oldest and must have

TABLE 9.1   Evolution of the moon: A contemporary model

Event(s)	Time (billion years ago)	Process(es)
Formation	4.6	Accretion of small chunks of material
Melted shell	4.4–4.6	Infall of material and/or radioactive decay melts outer layer; volatile elements lost
Cratered highlands	4.1–4.4	Crust solidifies while debris still falls in to crater it
Large basins	3.9–4.1	Less debris hits surface, but a few large pieces smash crust to produce basins; KREEP basalts flow out from magma below solid crust
Maria	3.0–3.9	Flooding of basins by magma produced by radioactive decay
Quiet crust	3.0–now	Surface bombarded by small particles to pulverize and erode it.

Source "Evolution of the Moon: The 1974 Model" by H. H. Schmitt, *Space Science Reviews,* 1975, vol. 18, p. 259.

(a)   (b)

melted and solidified before the lowland rocks of the maria. What could have melted these rocks? Possibilities are: (1) the heat from radioactive decay and (2) the energy from the impact of many bodies falling in from space. A mighty bombardment could melt the crust. Meanwhile the region below the crust heated and then melted from radioactive decay. The crust solidified. A few last large objects broke the crust, releasing the lava to form the maria and the mascons beneath. Everything cooled, and now the moon appears as a desolate, quiet planet.

9.5
The origin of the moon

The moon is thought to have formed 4.6 billion years ago. Its origin, however, still presents major problems. The implications of the Apollo cargo so far have clarified a few aspects of the moon's origin, but none of the rival models have completely claimed supremacy in explaining the moon's origin. These models fall into three broad categories:

1 fission model
2 binary accretion model
3 capture model

The *fission model*, the earliest of these probable ideas, was developed in 1898 by Sir George H. Darwin (1845–1912) and recently revived and revised. Darwin surmised that the earth must have been spinning more rapidly in the past than at present (an idea now substantiated). A faster rotation rate would have created a greater equatorial bulge than now exists. If the earth were molten, its equatorial speed may have become so great that friction and gravitational attraction would no longer have been able to hold the bulge to the earth. A chunk of mantle detached. It then spiraled out from the earth, cooled, and formed the moon (Fig. 9.24).

The fact that the average density of the moon and the average density of the earth's mantle rock are roughly the same lends support to the fission model. In 1889 O. Fisher speculated that the moon had split off from the Pacific Ocean basin and so it would consist of mantle material.

Fisher's fission model was widely accepted for about 30 years. Then it ran into major difficulties. First, the angular momentum of the earth–moon system must be conserved (Focus 26). If you joined the moon to the earth now, the combined mass would spin much faster than the earth does now—about four times faster (once every 8 h). But that rate is *not* fast enough to separate the lunar mass from the earth. Second, such a separation would take place at the earth's equator, where its rotation

(c)

9.23

A model for the moon's surface evolution. (a) The moon 3.9–4 billion years ago. The surface has solidified and is marked by the infall of fragments left over from its formation. Most of the lunar surface was saturated with craters. (b) The moon 3.0–3.1 billion years ago. The shattered surface allows magma from the interior to flow out and fill lowland basins. The maria are dark because the magma filling them contains more iron and magnesium than the highland rocks. (c) The moon now. Many of the large rayed craters formed on the surface after the formation of the maria. Parts of the maria have lightened from the material blown out in the formation of new craters. (Paintings by D. Davis and D. Wilhelm, U.S. Geological Survey)

speed is the fastest. If angular momentum is conserved (Focus 26), the orbital plane of the broken-off mass must remain in the earth's equatorial plane. In fact, the moon's orbit is tilted with respect to the earth's equator (Fig. 9.25); the tilt varies, but the smallest angle it makes is 18.5°. Third, the evolution of crustal plates requires that the configuration of the ocean basins changes constantly and rapidly. So existing basin features cannot be used to argue that the moon left the earth in the distant past. Fourth, the present rate of tidal friction would indicate that the moon separated from the earth only 1.2 billion years ago; but the earth was certainly solidified long before that.

Besides these problems, the Apollo results dealt the fission model a knockdown blow: The lunar basalts differ critically in chemical composition and water content from the terrestrial basalts that line the ocean basins. So the fission model, though once intriguing, is no longer a promising idea.

The *binary accretion model* views the moon as created out of the same primitive cloud as the earth, rather than as born from our planet (Fig. 9.26). Solid particles grew from a gradual condensation of gas. These eventually accreted into the moon and earth. The moon formed so close to the earth that earth's gravity held the

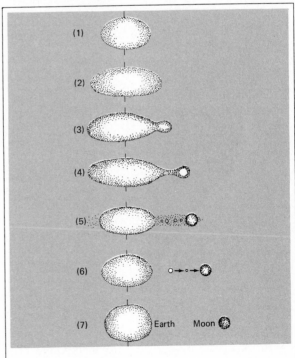

(1)

(2)

(3)

(4)

(5)

(6)

(7) Earth   Moon

9.24

Formation of the moon by fission from the earth. A piece of mantle detaches from the young, rapidly spinning earth to form the moon. Debris from the breakoff rain down on the moon (and earth) to form many of the present craters.

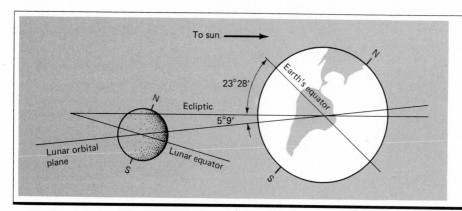

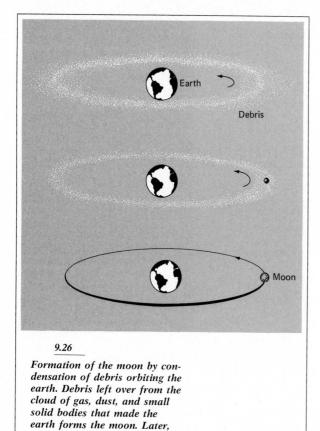

9.26

Formation of the moon by condensation of debris orbiting the earth. Debris left over from the cloud of gas, dust, and small solid bodies that made the earth forms the moon. Later, pieces falling in crater the moon's surface.

moon in a close orbit. The leftover bits and pieces from the formation of the two planets fell onto the moon (and earth) and heated its primitive surface.

Some lunar scientists argue that the composition of lunar minerals discredits this idea. The moon and the earth are somewhat *different* in composition. And the moon has no water. In addition, the moon has no dense iron core and a smaller percentage of iron, overall, than the earth. If the embryonic environment and materials of the two bodies were the same, it is difficult to see how the earth accumulated iron and the moon did not. On the other hand, the oxygen isotopic composition of the earth and the moon are the same; this fact supports the condensation-accretion models. This model has the same difficulty as the fission model in accounting for the short evolution time of the lunar orbit.

Around 1955 the *capture model* (Fig. 9.27) was developed. In it a vagabond moon did not form with the earth or from it, but rather, in some other part of the solar system. By chance, the moon traveled close enough to the earth to be captured gravitationally. The earth caught the moon in a highly eccentric and retrograde orbit; that is, the moon orbited the earth *opposite* the direction of the earth's rotation. In this circumstance the earth's tidal bulge acts to slow down the moon at its closest approach, so its orbit decreases in size (Focus 25). The tidal bulge also acts to change the inclination of the moon's orbit, tipping it over toward the same direction the earth rotates. Eventually, tidal forces flip the orbit, and now the tidal bulge works to speed up the moon on its closest approach and so make the orbit larger—as happens now at a rate of about 4 cm a year.

The capture model agrees in part with the inferred evolution of the earth–moon system (Fig. 9.28). If the moon is now moving away from the earth, it must have been closer in the past. The capture model requires a moon that

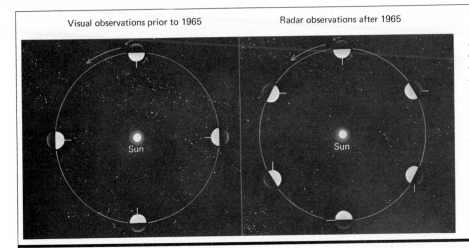

Visual observations prior to 1965 — Radar observations after 1965

Sun

Sun

59 days (Fig. 9.30). This new result astounded many astronomers, for all maps drawn since Schiaparelli's time had supported the 88-day rotation period.

How did this happen? The trick is this: Mercury's rotation period is two-thirds its orbital period. An exact 2–3 ratio (rotation 58.65 days, revolution 88 days) implies that Mercury's spin and orbit are coupled. How? Most likely by tidal interaction (Focus 25) with the sun so that Mercury has lost spin angular momentum (Focus 26).

Mercury's size / Once you know Mercury's orbit, you can find its physical size from its angular diameter. Mercury turns out to be a tiny world, only 2440 km in radius. That's only about 40 percent larger than our moon.

Mercury's mass and density / Mercury has no known natural satellite. So it's hard to determine its mass accurately. During the Mariner 10 mission the spacecraft sped past Mercury three times. Its acceleration due to Mercury's gravity was accurately measured, so we now have a good value for Mercury's mass: 0.055 that of the earth, or about 3.3×10^{23} kg.

For such a small radius, Mercury has a fairly large mass, indicating its bulk density must be high. It is: 5.42 g/cc, almost the same as the earth's. Comparing Mercury's interior with that of the earth, you expect a large nickel-iron core (Fig. 9.31) and a rocky mantle. Although no seismic information exists to confirm this interior model in detail, it's probably correct.

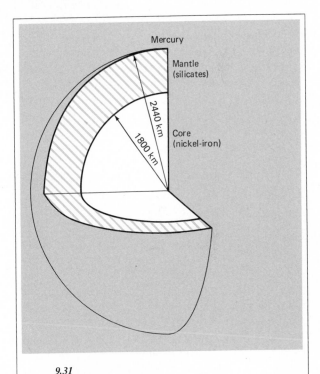

Mercury

Mantle (silicates)

2440 km

1800 km

Core (nickel-iron)

9.31

A model for the structure of Mercury's interior. Although Mercury is smaller than the earth, its average density is about the same. So Mercury must have a nickel-iron core that is large compared to the size of its mantle.

9.8

Mercury's surface environment

Suppose that, at perihelion at noon, you stood on the equator of Mercury. To do this, you would need to be made of sturdy stuff, because the surface temperature would be about 700 K! The surface temperature drops to 425 K at sunset and reaches about 100 K at midnight. This range of temperatures is the widest known in the solar system.

The long solar day (176 earth days) and low escape velocity (4.2 km/sec) make it unlikely that Mercury has an extensive atmosphere. Gas molecules, even the more massive ones, would easily be heated to escape velocity. So any atmosphere could not be expected to last long.

The Mariner 10 space probe that winged its way past Mercury had on board an ultraviolet spectrometer to search for an atmosphere. This device detected an atmosphere (of sorts) of helium and hydrogen. But the surface atmospheric pressure was very small, less than 10^{-15} that of the earth.

The following may give you some idea how incredibly thin Mercury's atmosphere is. Imagine taking one cubic centimeter of earth's air and spreading it out over the whole state of Ohio. That's how dilute the atmosphere of Mercury is: only about *10,000* particles in a cubic centimeter!

No atmosphere means no insulation from space. That's why the range of noon-to-midnight temperatures on Mercury is so severe. Night on our moon and Mercury are almost the same: no insulating blanket, so infrared radiation from the sunless side escapes directly into space during the long night. Some heat is supplied from the interior by conduction. So both bodies have about the same midnight temperatures: about 100 K. What happens at noon? The surface temperature then depends on the surface albedo and distance from the sun. The moon and Mercury have about the same albedo. But Mercury is 2.5 times closer to the sun than the moon. So you'd expect it would be hotter at noon, in the vicinity of 600 K. That's just about what is measured.

With the day so hot and the escape velocity so low, how does it happen that Mercury has any atmosphere at all? Especially of helium, a very low-mass gas? You'd expect helium by itself to last only about a month before it is lost

to space. One answer is the solar wind. Mercury's atmosphere does fly out into space, but the influx of material from the solar wind, which contains 2–20 percent helium, could possibly replenish the loss. A problem here is Mercury's magnetic field, which deflects much of the solar wind, except when it is very strong. Another source, at least for helium, is decay of radioactive elements in Mercury's interior. This balance between loss and gain results in a thin, but detectable atmosphere.

9.9

The surface of Mercury close up

Television cameras on board Mariner 10 scanned Mercury's surface as the spacecraft passed close by three times. The images sent back increased our resolution of planetary detail by 5000 times. And what a view: A surface like our moon (Fig. 9.32)! There are differences, though: fewer craters 20–50 km in size; no mountains; many shallow, scalloped cliffs, called *scarps* (Fig. 9.33), reaching lengths of hundreds of kilometers and rising to 1 km heights; fewer basins and larger lava flows; and more relatively uncratered plains amid the heavily cratered regions. These differences are important, yet the general similarity jumps out at you. Mercury's highlands are riddled with craters like the moon's bleak highlands. Light-colored rays (Fig. 9.34) spring from some of the craters, an indication that these were formed by violent impacts during Mercury's stormy past. Some craters are over 200 km in size, comparable to the biggest lunar craters.

One key difference between the moon and Mercury results from the fact that Mercury has twice the surface gravity of our moon. Material ejected from an impact will cover a smaller area than from an impact with the same energy on the moon. So secondary impact craters cluster more tightly around their primary craters, and ejected material that forms rays does not spew out as far.

What of large maria basins, such as those found on the moon's near side? Mariner 10 found but one: the Caloris ("hot") basin on the northwest part of the planet (Fig. 9.35). Since the Caloris basin sat on the sunrise line, only about half of it was photographed. It probably has an overall diameter of some 1300 km. The

9.32

Mercury's surface. The north pole is at the top and the equator extends from left to right about two-thirds down from the top. A large (1300 km across) circular basin is at left center just coming out of the shadow. Note the bright-rayed craters. (Courtesy NASA)

9.33

A scarp more than 300 km long extends diagonally from upper left to lower right. (Courtesy NASA)

9.34

Close-up of rayed craters on Mercury. The crater near the center with the rays extending from it is about 30 km across. Note the central peak, such as found in impact, rayed craters on the moon. (Courtesy NASA)

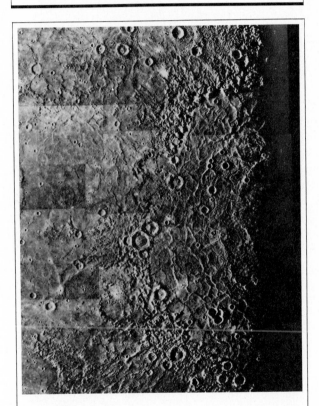

9.35

A flooded basin on Mercury. Here you can see about half the largest region (the Caloris basin) that looks like lunar maria. The interior of the Caloris basin (partially hidden in the shadow) has been flooded in by molten material. This photo spans about 1600 km from top to bottom. (Courtesy NASA)

9.36

Weird terrain on Mercury's surface on the side opposite the Caloris basin. This opposition suggests that this rugged region may have resulted from shock waves from the Caloris impact. (Courtesy NASA)

basin is bounded by rings of mountains about 2 km high. In size and structure the Caloris basin resembles the moon's Orientale basin: the blasted area from the impact of a large celestial chunk (some tens of kilometers in size) pushed up mountains, ejected material that fell over a large area, and sculpted the older surface.

The Caloris basin has a crinkled floor, perhaps fractures from rapid cooling of lava. Here you can also see older craters flooded by the lava outpouring from the Caloris impact. The Caloris impact may have been so strong that shock waves actually traveled through Mercury to the other side of the planet, disturbing the surface there. In fact, opposite Caloris lies a jumbled region, unique on Mercury's surface (Fig. 9.36). Hills and ridges cut across craters and the intercrater plains. This region of weird terrain may be the cross-planet disruption powered by the Caloris impact.

All these similarities do not mean that the moon and Mercury are identical. Their surfaces differ in at least three ways: (1) Mercury's surface has scarps hundreds of kilometers long, (2) even the most heavily cratered regions are not completely saturated with craters, and (3) Mercury has fewer small craters, compared to the number expected if the craters had

formed at the same rate as on the moon. From the last two, you can infer that either the cratering material had a different range of sizes for Mercury than for the moon or some process modified the surface after the cratering.

Mercury's scarps are unique so far in the solar system. They vary in length from 20 to over 500 km and have heights from a few hundred meters up to 1–2 km. Individual scarps often transect different types of terrain. If the regions photographed by Mariner 10 represent Mercury's overall surface, the characteristics of the scarps imply that Mercury's radius has shrunk some 1–3 km. How? Probably from the cooling of its core, or crust, or both.

9.10
The evolution of the moon and Mercury compared

What forces have shaped the surfaces of Mercury and the moon? The evidence is clear: impacts of projectiles from space that pitted the surfaces with craters. Both the moon and Mercury lack substantial atmospheres, so there is no erosion from weathering. And both are tiny worlds with interiors relatively cool, compared to the earth's interior. So neither one has much if any volcanic activity nor has undergone the continual surface evolution such as that the earth experiences from the shifting of crustal plates.

The lack of atmospheres and crustal evolution probably relates to the small masses of Mercury and the moon. Their surface gravities are so low that most gases exceed escape velocity, and atmospheres are not retained. The small masses also imply that internal heating from radioactive decay would be less, compared with that for the earth, and the flow of heat outward would be so fast that both bodies would cool off quickly. The earth is hot at its interior, and the outward flow of heat sets up currents in the plastic mantle; these power the evolution of the earth's crust. Both Mercury and the moon lack this combination of a hot interior and plastic mantle.

Without wind and water erosion and crustal evolution, the moon and Mercury retain the evidence of their early years. The similarities of surface features suggest similar histories. For example, the Caloris basin on Mercury resembles maria on the moon. The lunar maria were probably formed by the impacts of large bodies creating large basins; then the inflow of lava filled them to make the maria. Such processes most likely also formed the Caloris basin.

Lunar analogies imply a working model for the evolution of Mercury. (But keep in mind that we know less about Mercury than about the moon, so the details of the model are less certain. In particular, nothing is known about Mercurian rocks.) Mercury probably went through the following general stages: (1) heating of the surface (by impacts or radioactive decay) and formation of a solid crust, (2) heavy cratering, (3) formation of impact basins, (4) filling in of basins by lava flows, and (5) low-intensity cratering. We can't date this sequence as for the moon because there are no rock samples from Mercury's surface for radioactive dating. But a lunar comparison suggests that the intense sculpting of Mercury's surface took place about 4 billion years ago, not long after the planet formed.

The earliest phase of cratering (stage 2) must have been wiped out by later volcanism. This conclusion comes because the intercrater plains seem to have covered up any scars from the earliest accretion. At about the same time, the scarps developed from global shrinking of the crust, interior, or both.

Basin formation (stage 3) must have come at the end of the heavy bombardment of the surface. A few large pieces crashed into the surface; one made the Caloris basin. Not long after this time, widespread lava flows (similar to that which made the lunar maria) created the broad, smooth planes such as those adjacent to the Caloris basin (stage 4).

Since then, a few impacts (stage 5) punched out the rayed craters. But basically, Mercury has evolved little since its formative times. It is now a dead world.

9.11
The mystery of Mercury's magnetic field

As Mariner 10 winged past Mercury, it detected, much to everyone's surprise, a weak planetary magnetic field—about 10^{-2} times the strength of the earth's magnetic field at its surface. Small as this sounds, it's sufficient to carve out a magnetosphere in the solar wind (Fig. 9.37). Here the magnetic field deflects the charged particles

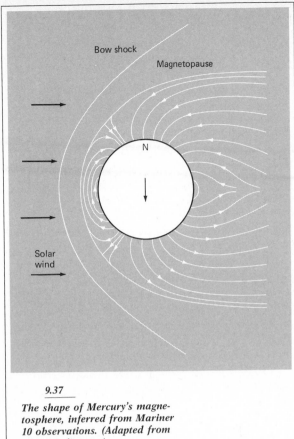

9.37
The shape of Mercury's magnetosphere, inferred from Mariner 10 observations. (Adapted from a NASA diagram)

(mostly protons) of the solar wind around the planet.

Mercury's field appears to be a dipole, more or less aligned with its spin axis. So, in general, Mercury's magnetic field is similar to the earth's, only weaker. And that's a problem. Mercury must, like the earth, have a nickel-iron core. But it's presumed to be relatively cold and solid now because a small planet loses heat quickly. Now recall (Section 8.4) that the earth's magnetic field supposedly arises from swirling motions in its hot, liquid nickel-iron core. The churning is thought to be driven by the earth's spinning. Because Mercury rotates much more slowly than the earth and is expected to have a cool core, no one really expected it to have a planetwide magnetic field.

What's the explanation? No one knows for sure. It may be that the dynamo model is incorrect; after all, Venus, which has a much larger and presumably hotter core than Mercury, has no detectable magnetic field. (But Venus rotates even more slowly.) Or perhaps the field is left over from an older time. Or maybe it originates from the planet's interaction with the solar wind. Or perhaps small planets with cool nickel-iron cores produce magnetic fields by a mechanism not yet imagined.

SUMMARY

The moon and Mercury are worn-out, inhospitable worlds. Essentially, no atmosphere clings to their surfaces. Without a protective atmospheric blanket, temperatures range widely from noon to midnight. In addition, bodies from space have incessantly bombarded the surfaces. This bombardment has pulverized the surface layers, eroding them to a smooth finish.

The American and Russian space programs have brought back samples from our moon's surface. From them, we can reasonably infer the moon's history. Moon rocks fall into two broad categories based on age and composition. The samples from the maria are the younger, averaging 3.6 billion years in age. The lighter aluminum-rich samples from the highlands are older, generally about 4 billion years old. Both types of rock show evidence of previous melting and rapid cooling. The first melting of the primeval surface took place about 4 billion years ago; it may have been caused by the infall of objects that also made many of the craters. Later, a few larger objects formed the mascons and maria, which then filled with lava. Since that time, some 3 billion years ago, the moon has been an inactive planet, a silent companion to the earth.

We do not yet have samples from the surface of Mercury. But from a direct comparison of Mercury and the moon's surface, we infer that Mercury's history was very similar. Also, we expect the timing of events was roughly the same, too.

The moon and Mercury are dead worlds, their dramatic evolution ended. Compared with the earth, they are fossil planets rather than living ones.

STUDY EXERCISES

1 Suppose you stepped out of TWA flight 101 onto the moon's surface. You look slowly around, at both the ground and the sky. How does what you see differ from what you would see on the earth? (*Objectives 2 and 4*)

2 Suppose you stepped out of TWA flight 102 onto the surface of Mercury. How would the scene differ from that on the earth? (*Objectives 3 and 4*)

3 Argue from a comparison of average density that the moon *cannot* have a nickel-iron core like the earth's; that Mercury *must* have a nickel-iron core. (*Objectives 1 and 7*)

4 How were most of the craters on the moon formed? On Mercury? Back up your statement with specific evidence. (*Objectives 2 and 3*)

5 What specific evidence do we have that the moon's lowland regions (maria) formed *after* the highlands? (*Objective 8*)

6 You are writing a grant proposal to NASA to do research on the origin of the moon. Describe the theory you plan to support in the best light possible. (*Objective 10*)

7 Compare the characteristics of the Orientale basin on the moon to the Caloris basin on Mercury. (*Objectives 4 and 7*)

8 In *one* sentence, describe how the surfaces of the moon and Mercury *differ*. (*Objectives 2, 3, and 4*)

9 Neither the moon nor Mercury has a substantial atmosphere. Why? (*Objective 4*)

10 In *one* sentence, describe the difference between the interiors of the moon and Mercury. (*Objectives 5, 6, and 7*)

BEYOND THIS BOOK . . .

The Apollo missions have produced a flood of data on the moon. You can find a short summary in "The Moon" by J. A. Wood, *Scientific American,* September 1975, p. 92.

For data about the moon as planet, see *Planetary Geology* (Prentice-Hall, Englewood Cliffs, N.J., 1975) by N. M. Short. Another book with the same approach is *Geology of the Moon* (Princeton University Press, Princeton, N.J., 1970) by T. A. Mutch.

For a personal story about Apollo 11, read *Carrying the Fire* (Farrar, Straus and Giroux, New York, 1974) by M. Collins.

Voyages to the Moon (Macmillan, New York, 1960) by M. H. Nicolson is an amusing contrast to modern voyages to the moon.

C. Chapman writes about the evolution of Mercury in *The Inner Planets* (Scribner's, New York, 1977).

For a pictorial tour of Mercury, look at *The Atlas of Mercury* (Crown, New York, 1977) by C. Cross and P. Moore.

B. Murray discusses the results of Mariner 10 about Mercury in "Mercury," *Scientific American,* September 1975, p. 58.

LEARNING OBJECTIVES

After studying this chapter, you should be able to:

1. Compare Venus, and Mars in size, mass, and density to each other and to the earth.

2. Compare and contrast the surface environments (temperature, atmosphere, general surface features) of Venus and Mars to each other and to the earth.

3. List the three main constituents of the atmospheres of Venus and Mars and compare these to the earth.

4. Sketch a model for the interiors of Venus and Mars and compare them to the earth's interior.

5. List the major surface features of geologic importance on Venus and Mars and compare them to those on the earth.

6. Contrast the planetary magnetic fields of Venus and Mars to the earth's.

7. Evaluate your chances of survival on Venus and Mars.

8. Discuss the role of cratering in the shaping of the surfaces of Venus and Mars.

9. Discuss the implications of the volcanoes of Mars for the evolution of the Martian surface and atmosphere.

10. Compare and contrast the inferred geologic histories of Venus, Mars, and the earth; justify an ordering of these planets from the least to the most evolved.

Venus invited me in the evening whispers
Unto a fragrant field with roses crowned, . . .
JOHN CLEVELAND

Venus and Mars: Evolved worlds

10

CHAPTER 10

CENTRAL QUESTION *What forces have shaped the evolution of Venus and Mars, planets with hot interiors and substantial atmospheres?*

Venus, the brilliant light of love (Fig. 10.1); Mars, the red sign of war (Fig. 10.2)—these two worlds come the closest to the earth in space. And these planets resemble the earth more closely than any other planets in the solar system. They are truly terrestrial planets.

Yet in many ways the similarities are superficial. The differences go much deeper. Venus is blistering hot at its surface—hotter even than Mercury at noon! A thick, dense atmosphere of carbon dioxide presses heavily on the barren ground. On Mars the atmosphere also consists of carbon dioxide, but it's thin, offering no protection from the incoming solar ultraviolet and no hindrance to the outgoing infrared. Mars is mostly a cold desert, where the water ceased to flow at least tens of millions of years ago.

How did Venus and Mars end up so different from the earth? What forces shaped their evolution? This chapter deals with the comparative evolution of these worlds.

10.1
Venus: Orbital and physical characteristics

Viewed from the earth, Venus can outshine every celestial body except the sun and the moon. If you know where to look, you can even spot Venus during the day. Venus shines so brilliantly because its unbroken swirl of clouds reflects 77 percent of the incoming sunlight back into space (Fig. 10.1). This cloud cover completely frustrates any attempt to view its surface features by optical telescopes.

But we are now piercing Venus's cloudy veil to uncover the mysteries of this world. Radar beams, bouncing off the surface, tell what the topography is like. Spacecraft have passed by the planet, gone into orbit around it, and plunged through the atmosphere to its forbidding surface. What a difference from the earth! Surface temperatures hit 750 K. The atmospheric pressure is an unrelenting 100 atm, and the atmosphere contains mostly carbon dioxide.

Venus has gained the reputation of being the earth's twin sister. In terms of size (the diameter of Venus is 12,104 km; earth, 12,756 km), average density (Venus, 5.2 g/cc earth, 5.5 g/cc), and mass (Venus, 0.82; earth, 1.00), the sisterhood is appropriate. In most other ways Venus has a personality tremendously different from the earth. No oceans, streams, or lakes; no

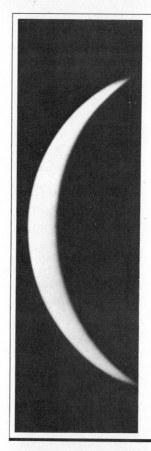

10.1

Venus photographed in blue light. (Courtesy Palomar Observatory, California Institute of Technology)

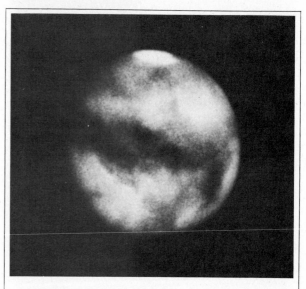

10.2

Mars photographed in red light, August 1956. Note the white pole cap and irregular, dark surface features. (Courtesy Mt. Wilson Observatory, Carnegie Institute of Washington)

plants or animals; no gentle, cool breezes. Instead, a veritable hell!

Revolution and rotation / Second planet from the sun at an average distance of 0.72 AU, Venus completes one orbit in only 225 days. Venus's orbit is the most circular of all the planets—so Venus's distance from the sun varies by only 1.4 percent perihelion to aphelion.

Thwarted by the lack of a surface view because of the unyielding cloud cover, astronomers before 1961 had no real idea of Venus's rotation rate. Some proposed 24 h (arguing that Venus is the earth's twin), and others decided that the rotation period must equal the revolution period, 225 days. (These people were misled by the incorrect rotation rate agreed upon for Mercury.) Since 1961, radar echoes have been bounced off the surface of Venus. Measuring the Doppler shift (Focus 19) in the returning signals, radar astronomers have found that Venus rotates once every 243.01 days—retrograde. Retrograde rotation means that it spins from east to west, rather than west to east as does the earth. So on Venus, the sun (if you could see it through the clouds) rises in the west and sets in the east.

This long retrograde rotation results in a solar day on Venus 117 terrestrial days long. But because of the clouds, an inhabitant of Venus could never see the sun's disk directly. Like an overcast day on earth, it would be light during the day, but the sun's intensity on Venus is only about 1/100 that at the earth's surface—10 W for every square meter.

One curious fact about Venus's rotation—if Venus spun once every 243.16 days, it would rotate exactly four times between the interval when Venus and the earth are aligned on the same side of the sun. (This alignment is called *inferior conjunction.*) Note that value is very close to, but not exactly, the 243.01-day rotation period. So Venus almost presents the same face to the earth at successive inferior conjunctions—almost, but not quite! Right now, it's not completely clear why Venus's rotation period is so close to being in resonance with the earth and its orbital period. It may arise from tidal forces or, perhaps, be only coincidence.

Size, mass, and density / The earth–Venus distance is measured directly by radar. Then from the planet's angular diameter, you can calculate its physical diameter and radius. Venus

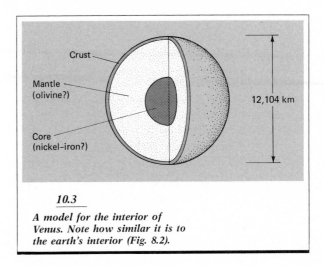

10.3

A model for the interior of Venus. Note how similar it is to the earth's interior (Fig. 8.2).

turns out to have a radius of 6052 km—only 5 percent smaller than the earth.

Like Mercury, Venus has no known natural satellite. So we can accurately find the mass of Venus only by sending spacecraft to it. Venus's mass comes out to be 0.815 times that of the earth, or 4.86×10^{24} kg.

With the mass and size in hand, you can find out Venus's bulk density: 5.20 g/cc—almost the same as that of the earth. We guess (because we do not yet have seismic data for Venus), that the interior of Venus should closely resemble the earth's interior (Fig. 10.3). We expect a rocky crust (which the Venus landers confirmed), a mantle, and a nickel-iron core. Because Venus has a lower density than the earth, it probably has a somewhat smaller core.

Where's the magnetic field? / But this model has a severe problem. A nickel-iron core, liquid in part, implies by comparison with the earth that Venus should have a planetary magnetic field. Because Venus rotates 243 times more slowly than the earth, you expect its internal dynamo to be weaker and so the magnetic field should be less intense than the earth's. No probe to date has detected *any* magnetic field. If one exists, it must be at least 10^4 times weaker than the earth's magnetic field! That's *much* weaker than expected from a simple dynamo model. What a magnetic mess—Mercury has a planetary field, and Venus does not. Mars has a barely detectable magnetic field (discussed a little later in this chapter). Clearly the simple dynamo model is not the whole story.

10.2

The atmosphere of Venus

If you read only the last section, you might think Venus and the earth were essentially the same. Not true! The atmosphere of Venus differs remarkably from the earth—a key piece in understanding the planet's evolution.

Clouds / The clouds of Venus, yellow-white in color, enshroud the planet completely (Color Plate 5). That's why so little was known of Venus for so long.

Recent efforts have gathered much new information about the clouds of Venus. The cloud tops (which you see in a telescope) reach about 63–67 km above the surface. (The highest clouds on the earth go up to about 16 km.) Ultraviolet photography by Mariner 10 revealed that these cloud tops flow with the upper atmosphere (Fig. 10.4)—patterns similar to jet streams of the earth. Ringing the equator, the clouds whiz around at roughly 360 km/h—fast enough to orbit the planet in only four days in a direction opposite its rotation (Fig. 10.5). At the poles, they blow at 160 km/h. In addition to this planetwide circulation, winds also blow from the equator to the poles in large cyclonic cells 100–500 km in diameter. They culminate in two giant cloud vortices capping the polar regions.

What drives such fierce winds in the upper atmosphere of Venus? We don't know for certain. It's generally believed that solar heating does the trick, as on the earth, but details have yet to be worked out. Although it is windy in

10.4

Venus photographed in ultraviolet light by Mariner 10. Note the streamlike flow of the clouds at both poles. The dusky markings seen in photos taken from the earth are the darker regions easily visible here. These are places where we are looking deeper into the clouds. (Courtesy NASA)

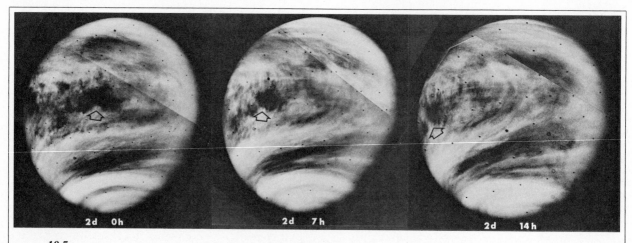

2d 0h   2d 7h   2d 14h

10.5

Rapid motions of the cloud features (arrow) in the upper atmosphere of Venus. They circle the planet in about four days. (Courtesy NASA)

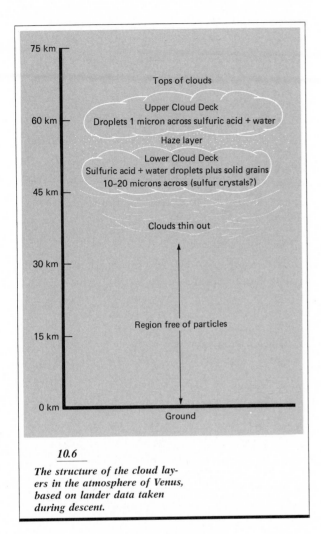

75 km

Tops of clouds

Upper Cloud Deck
Droplets 1 micron across sulfuric acid + water

60 km

Haze layer

Lower Cloud Deck
Sulfuric acid + water droplets plus solid grains
10–20 microns across (sulfur crystals?)

45 km

Clouds thin out

30 km

Region free of particles

15 km

0 km

Ground

10.6

The structure of the cloud layers in the atmosphere of Venus, based on lander data taken during descent.

through but still not a pea-soup fog. The clouds of Venus aren't particularly murky, just very extensive.

What are the clouds made of? The best proposal to date, by Andrew Young, sees the upper level clouds as concentrated solutions of sulfuric acid. Models of the clouds designed to match their observed infrared spectrum imply that they contain a solution of sulfuric acid and water.

Clouds of sulfuric acid and water do *not* mean that Venus has a lot of water. Although the atmosphere and clouds of Venus do contain some water vapor, it doesn't amount to very much, compared with the total amount of water on the earth. If all the earth's water (in the atmosphere and oceans) were spread in a uniform layer over its surface, that sheet of liquid would be 3 km thick. All the water in the atmosphere of Venus (none exists on the surface because it's so hot) would amount to a layer only 30 cm thick. So our earth has about 10,000 times as much water as Venus does.

Atmosphere and surface temperature / What kind of atmosphere does Venus have? Since 1932 we have known that the atmosphere contains carbon dioxide, but we did not know how much. Interplanetary probes launched by both the United States and the Soviet Union indicate that the atmosphere contains about 97 percent carbon dioxide, 3.3 percent nitrogen, and traces of argon, water vapor (0.1–0.4 percent), oxygen, hydrogen chloride, hydrogen fluoride, hydrogen sulfide, sulfur dioxide, helium, and carbon monoxide.

The Soviet Venera descents found the surface pressure to be 90–100 atm, and the sunlit surface temperature about 730–750 K (Fig. 10.7). The U.S. Pioneer–Venus probes recorded 755 K. This high temperature probably results from the effective trapping of surface heat (Section 8.6) because carbon dioxide absorbs infrared radiation well. Venus is so hot due to an extreme greenhouse effect.

Stop for a second and think how hot it is on Venus: 700 K is about 430°C, or 800°F! That's about two times the temperature your oven broiler operates at. You'd certainly be well-roasted on Venus.

Upper atmospheric winds on Venus blow from the day to the night sides and from equatorial to polar regions. The wind flow carries

the upper atmosphere of Venus, it's very calm at the surface. In fact, the winds below an altitude of 10 km blow at a gentle 3–18 km/h.

Back to the clouds themselves. The Pioneer-Venus probes found that the clouds float in two broad layers (Fig. 10.6). Above the cloud tops is a 30-km-thick haze layer. The upper cloud deck tops at roughly 65 km and has a thickness of some 5 km. Here the liquid drops in the clouds have diameters of about 2 microns. Below the upper deck sits a thin haze layer. Below that, at 49–52 km height, exists the lower cloud deck, by far the densest layer. The cloud particles here are both liquid and solid. Below 49 km the clouds gradually thin out; below 33 km the atmosphere is clear of any particles down to the surface.

In the densest part of the clouds the visibility is less than a kilometer, dangerous to fly

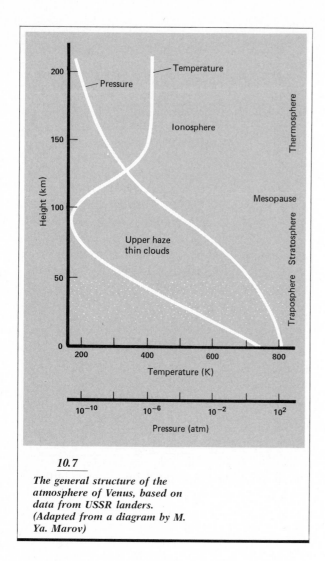

10.7

The general structure of the atmosphere of Venus, based on data from USSR landers. (Adapted from a diagram by M. Ya. Marov)

the extreme pressure and temperature. Two landers—Venera 9 and 10 in 1975—sent back close-up photos of the surface before failing (Fig. 10.8). These pictures show slabby rocks about 50–70 cm long and 15–20 cm wide. A few rocks have small holes that look like they were once filled with gas, implying a volcanic origin. Some rocks show jagged edges, indicating little erosion, and others show blunted, rounded edges, indicating considerable erosion. The rocks rest on loose, coarse-grained dirt. A fine material fills the nooks and crannies of the rocks.

What kind of rocks are these? Measurements by the landers of radioactive potassium, uranium, and thorium in the rocks indicate that at one lander site they are basaltic, like those lining the earth's ocean basins (Section 8.2), but at the other site they are granitic, like the earth's mountains. Both types are igneous rocks formed from lava.

Radar mapping / The Venera pictures gave a worm's-eye view of the surface. But what is the more general lay of the land? We now have a pretty good, overall idea from ground-based radar maps and radar mapping by the Pioneer-Venus orbiter. These maps reveal a varied terrain: mountains, high plateaus, canyons, volcanoes, ridges, and impact craters. Overall, Venus looks fairly flat. Elevation differences are small, only 2–3 km, with the exception of a few highland regions. Here the land reaches up to 10–12 km, compared with 4 km highland–lowland differences on the moon and Mercury, 25 km differences on Mars, and 19–20 km on the earth (Mt. Everest is 8.85 km high, and the Japanese trench, 11.03 km deep).

The southern half and the northern half of the mapped face of Venus differ remarkably. The northern region is mountainous with uncratered *upland plateaus*. In contrast, the southern part consists of relatively flat *cratered terrain*.

What hints do the radar maps provide about the evolution of Venus? Be forewarned that these interpretations are preliminary and subject to revision.

The early radar images (Fig. 10.9) picked up two highland regions some 1000 km across—about the size of continental masses on the earth. A third was discovered later in a new map of the planet's northern regions (Fig. 10.10).

heat. Along with the very effective atmospheric insulation, this helps to keep the temperatures fairly constant over Venus's surface. They vary about 10 K or less. So it doesn't cool off much at night.

10.3
The surface of Venus

How to investigate Venus's surface? By two methods: (1) landing probes on the surface to examine it close up and (2) bouncing radar (which can penetrate the clouds) off the surface and analyzing the reflections.

Surface photographs / From 1972 to 1978, the Russians landed six probes by parachute on Venus's surface. These landers stopped working within an hour or two after landing because of

10.8

A close-up of the surface of Venus, taken by Venera 9. The skyline is visible in the corner, indicating that at the time this picture was taken, little dust was in the atmosphere. The rocks are a few tens of centimeters in size. Note that some are angular (indicating little erosion) and some are rounded. A few of the rocks appear filled with small holes, an indication of volcanic origin.

10.9

An early radar map of Venus. Bright areas tend to be regions of higher elevation. (Courtesy D. Campbell, R. Dyce, R. Ingals, G. Pettengill, and I. Shapiro; observations at Arecibo Observatory)

range, called Maxwell Montes (Fig. 10.12), contains the highest elevations on Venus seen to date: some 12 km. Radar shows that this range is rough, as expected from a lava flow. And some radar views indicate a volcanic cone near Maxwell's center. The northern mountain range rises about 3 km above Ishtar; the western one reaches only 2 km above the plateau.

These three mountain ranges may have folded and risen in response to moving plates in Venus's crust, and so may be analogous to mountains built from plate tectonics on the earth.

Cratered terrain / The southern half of Venus's face consists of low, rolling plains apparently punctuated by craters (Fig. 10.13), both large craters (up to 800 km in diameter) and smaller ones, less than 1 kilometer in size. These are probably impact craters. (Craters smaller than this size do not form on Venus because the dense atmosphere completely burns up small-sized incoming debris before it reaches the ground.) The craters of Venus resemble those on the moon, Mercury, and Mars: They have high peaks in their centers—a direct clue to their impact origin. In general, the craters are shallow from erosion (probably by wind)—only about 500 m deep.

One Soviet lander came down in the midst of the southern terrain. Its instruments indicated that the rock was more granitic than basaltic. This fact is one clue that at least some of the surface here is ancient. Later lava flows could have poured out basaltic rock. Also, the fact that craters are still seen here also implies the surface must be old; otherwise volcanoes and mountain building would have obliterated all the craters.

Two have now been named: The great northern plateau is called *Ishtar Terra,* and the southern one is *Aphrodite Terra.* The Beta-Delta region is now called *Beta Region.*

Upland plateaus / Ishtar is huge (Fig. 10.11)—some 1000 by 1500 km. (That's larger than the biggest upland plateau on the earth, the Himalayan plateau.) Three mountain ranges border Ishtar on the west, north, and east. The eastern

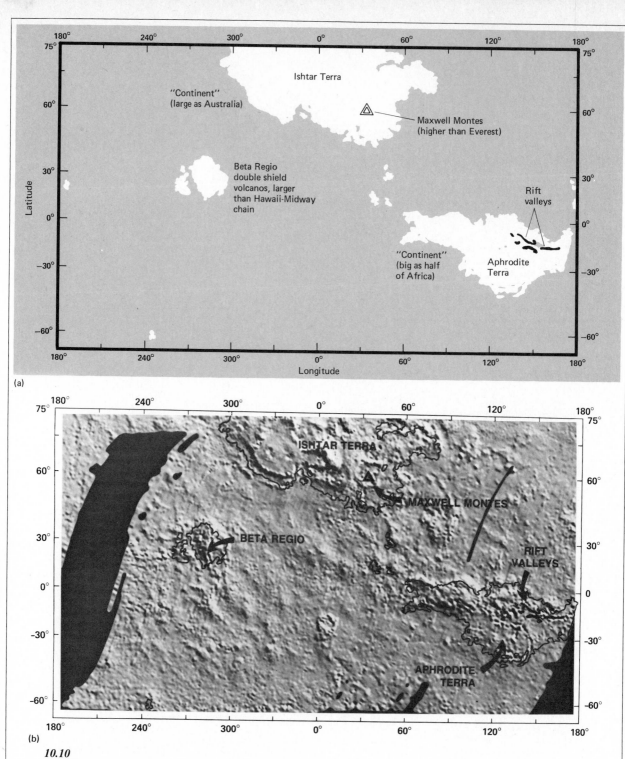

10.10

(a) *A map of the highland regions on Venus's surface. Because of the distortion of a spherical surface drawn as a flat map, Ishtar looks larger than Aphrodite, but it isn't. (b) A radar map of part of Venus's surface, done by the Pioneer–Venus orbiter. This map has been computer processed to enhance regions where there are changes in the elevation of the land. Black areas are regions that were not mapped. The most prominent features are: Ishtar Terra, an upland mass about as large as Australia; Beta Regio, a double shield volcano, larger than the Hawaii-Midway volcanic chain; Maxwell Montes, a mountain higher than Mt. Everest; and Aphrodite Terra, an upland mass about half as large as Africa. (Courtesy NASA)*

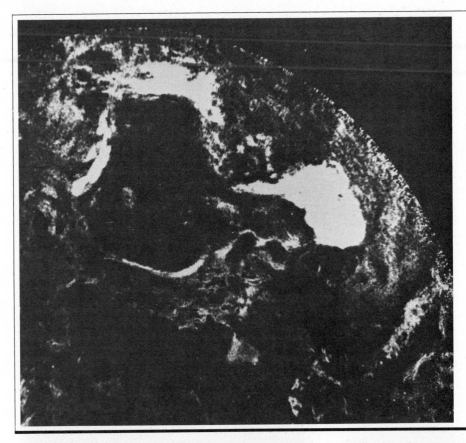

10.11

Radar map of the Ishtar region. The brightness indicates the degree of roughness of the surface; the brightest regions are the roughest. The Ishtar plateau, in the upper center, is ringed by mountains. The bright area to the right is Maxwell. (Courtesy D. Campbell, R. Dyce, and G. Pettengill; observations at Arecibo Observatory)

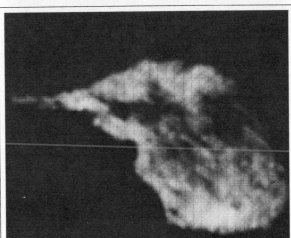

10.12

Maxwell at a resolution of about 100 km. Here is the highest elevation on Venus: 11 km. The dark area to the right may be a crater partially filled with lava. (Courtesy D. Campbell, R. Dyce, and G. Pettengill; observations at Arecibo Observatory)

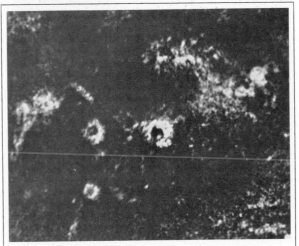

10.13

Ring-shaped features 1500 km west of the Alpha region. The largest is 100 km. These may be impact craters. (Courtesy D. Campbell, B. Burns, V. Boriakoff; observations at Arecibo Observatory)

One high region reaches up from the cratered terrain: Aphrodite. Aphrodite is huge—almost 3000 km across, about half the size of Africa. It also has a rough surface that hits 7–10 km in height.

Volcanoes on Venus / The Beta Region, which seems to contain at least two separate volcanoes, appears to be an enormous volcanic complex that forms from a great north–south fracture zone (Fig. 10.14). The volcanoes here have gentle slopes; they are called *shield volcanoes*. (Instead of a sharply uplifted cone, shield volcanoes are relatively flat, like an armor shield.) Often shield volcanoes have a collapsed central crater at their summits.

One volcano in the Beta region has a diameter of 820 km, a height of 5 km, and a summit crater 60 by 90 km. In contrast, the island of Hawaii on the earth (a volcanic island) is 200 km across and 9 km high. (The largest volcano on Mars, Olympus Mons, is 550 km in diameter and 20 km high—Section 10.8.) So Venus may have the largest diameter volcanoes in the solar system! It is not known if they are active; probably not.

If the size and mass of a planet are known, geologists are able to relate the height of a volcano to the thickness of the crust below it. On the earth the Hawaiian volcano Mauna Loa is 9 km high and the crust below it is 57 km thick. Because the earth and Venus are so similar in mass and size, the 10-km volcano on Venus should have an underlying crust of about the same thickness, some 60–65 km. (In contrast, the largest volcano on Mars requires a much thicker crust—some 130 km.)

Rift valleys / Venus has large mountains and also sports enormous canyons. On the near side of Venus (the one facing the earth at inferior conjunctions), a huge canyon extends for more than 1300 km. It is about 150 km wide and 2 km deep. On the other side of Venus an even larger canyon scars the landscape: it is 5 km deep, 320 km wide, and at least 1400 km long. (Its length has not yet been completely mapped.)

The canyons of Venus appear to be *rift valleys* (Fig. 10.15), which form along fault zones rather than by water erosion. (A rift valley splits New Mexico; the Rio Grande flows down its length.) Rift valleys appear on the earth where the crust is spreading apart.

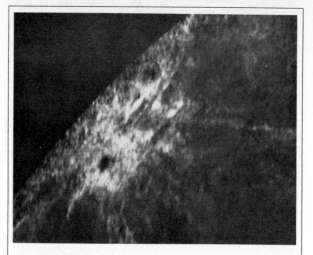

10.14

Radar map of the Beta region. This section appears to contain a large volcanic peak, called Theia Mons, a shield volcano some 5 km high. The streaks radiating outward are possible lava flows, and the central dark region is the volcano's crater. (Courtesy D. Campbell, B. Burns, and V. Boriakoff; observations at Arecibo Observatory)

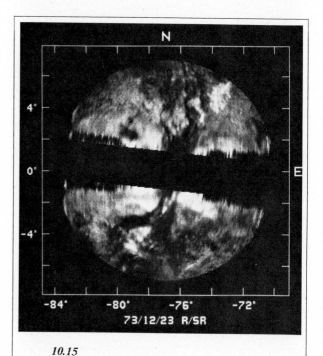

10.15

Radar map of a large canyon system on Venus (dark strip from top to bottom across the center). The area in this map is about the size of Alaska; the dark central bar is an artifact of the mapping technique. (Courtesy R. Goldstein; observations made at Goldstone station of the Jet Propulsion Lab under contract with NASA)

To sum up: The surface of Venus has mountains, plateaus, volcanoes, impact craters, lava flows, and rift valleys. For all this variety, the surface is remarkably flat: Only 18 percent of the mapped surface extends above 7 km, 11 percent above 10 km. In contrast, about 30 percent of the earth's surface reaches above 10 km. An even greater contrast pops up when comparing the lowland basin areas of the earth (the ocean basins) and Venus: The earth's surface is about 70 percent basins, whereas Venus's surface is only 15–20 percent. Venus does not appear to have lunar-type basins, lowlands filled by lava flows.

As indicated by the presence of craters, the lowlands of Venus must be older than the rest of the crust. The highlands are more evolved. That's just the opposite of the earth, where the lowlands (the ocean basins) make up the youngest part of the crust. The earth's continents are older. On Venus the highlands are younger than the lowlands.

Venus and earth compared / Overall, the surface of Venus resembles Mars now more than the earth. How did the differences develop, even though Venus has about the same size, density, mass, interior composition and structure? Probably from the lack of liquid surface water; Venus has no oceans or rivers. On earth, rainwater reacts with atmospheric carbon dioxide to produce carbonic acid; this, in turn, combines with calcium to produce limestone. On Venus the carbon dioxide cannot be trapped this way. It stays in the atmosphere, keeping up the severe greenhouse effect.

On earth, water helps the continents float and drift on the mantle. It acts as a lubricant and lowers the melting point of the rock. The crust of Venus has experienced some crustal plate movement. The evidence: its rift valleys, where the plates have pulled apart, and its mountain plateaus, where plates have collided. But the widespread cratered terrain indicates that plate movement has not been an extensive planetwide process, as it has been on the earth.

10.4
The evolution of Venus

What implications do these observations have for the evolution of Venus? Right now we can really only speculate. It does seem, though, that the early history of Venus (earlier than 4 billion years) must have followed the earth's early history, because both planets have similar mass, density, and size. The later history more closely resembled that of Mars.

By inference, Venus formed about 4.6 billion years ago with the other terrestrial planets (Chapter 12). As happened to the earth, Venus's interior differentiated from internal heating. During the first 500 million years, a crust—part basalt and part granite—formed and solidified. About 4 billion years ago, large masses bombarded the surface, and fractured the crust. Volcanoes erupted. Bombardment by smaller bodies from space cratered the surface. About 3 billion years ago, intensive bombardment ended, and erosion has somewhat altered the ancient surface of Venus.

Since then, limited plate movement helped to push up some highland regions. Rift valleys appeared. Huge volcanoes vented through cracks in the surface; their cones formed the shield volcanoes of today. Venus seems to have evolved in a sequence similar to the earth but more slowly and not as greatly.

10.5
Mars: General characteristics

The ruddy spectacle of Mars has sparked interest since recorded time. Its unique, bloody color and swift motions in the sky marked Mars as a special planet (Fig. 10.16). Telescopes revealed polar caps, dust storms, and permanent dark features. In this century Mars appeared to be the most likely home of extraterrestrial life in the solar system, as portrayed in the fantasies of H. G. Wells and other science fiction writers.

Unfortunately, the Viking landers have dampened this optimistic attitude—Mars seems barren of life as we know it (more in Chapter 22). These and other spacecraft have presented a new Mars (Fig. 10.17): a planet that is a cross between the earth and the moon, with plentiful, ancient craters, giant canyons, and huge, extinct volcanoes (Color Plate 3).

Martian orbit, day, and seasons / Mars orbits the sun at an average distance of 1.52 AU. But Mars's distance from the sun varies considerably (9 percent) because its orbit is fairly eccentric. Consequently, the distance between Mars and the earth at opposition—when both planets lie on the same side of the sun—ranges from less than 56 to more than 101 million km.

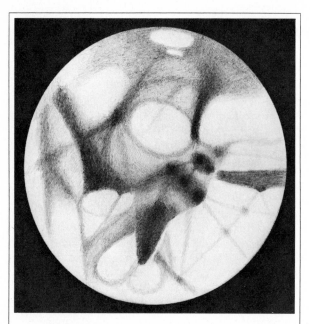

10.16

Mars. A drawing made of sur-face features seen through a telescope in 1926. (Courtesy Lick Observatory)

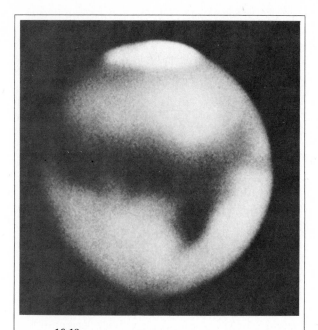

10.18

Surface markings on Mars visi-ble from the earth. A white pole cap tops the planet. The light regions are yellow-brown. Both the light and dark regions are red in the sense that they reflect more red light than blue. (Courtesy Lick Observatory)

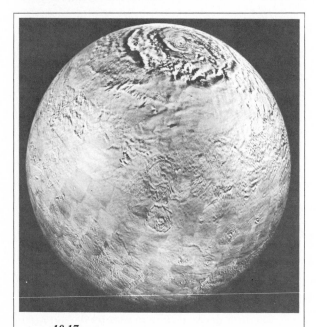

10.17

Mars. A mosaic of the surface of Mars compiled from Mariner 9 photos. At the top is the re-sidual north pole ice cap. Just below the center is the giant volcano Olympus Mons. (Cour-tesy NASA)

Surface markings visible through telescopes make the Martian rotation rate easy to measure (Fig. 10.18). In 1659 the Dutch physicist Chris-tian Huygens (1629–1695) observed the rotation rate to be close to 24 h. Modern measurements place the value at 24 h, 37 min; a day on Mars lasts only a bit longer than on the earth.

How do the Martian seasons compare with the earth's? The equator of Mars inclines about 25° to its orbital plane. This angle is about the same as the earth's ($23\frac{1}{2}°$), so the Martian sea-sons vary like those of the earth, although Mars's spin axis points to a different direction in space. (Standing on the Martian north pole, you would find Deneb—the brightest star in Cygnus the Swan—almost directly overhead.) Because Mars takes longer to orbit the sun than the earth, Martian seasons last about twice as long as ours. Also, the eccentricity of the orbit gives the seasons different lengths.

Size, mass, and density / With a known dis-tance and measured angular diameter, you can

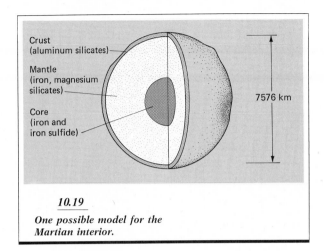

Crust
(aluminum silicates)

Mantle
(iron, magnesium
silicates)

Core
(iron and
iron sulfide)

7576 km

10.19

One possible model for the Martian interior.

get Mars's size: 3394 km in radius. That's only 53 percent the earth's radius. So Mars is about half the earth's size, but larger than Mercury (by about 40 percent).

Mars has two satellites, so Kepler's law gives (Focus 12) its mass from their orbits: It is only 6.4×10^{23} kg, about 11 percent the earth's mass. Then the mass and size give Mars's density: 3.9 g/cc, only a bit higher than the moon's (3.3 g/cc) and much less than the earth's (5.5 g/cc).

This comparatively low density implies that Mars's interior (Fig. 10.19) must be different from the earth's. In particular, its core must be smaller and probably consists of a mixture of iron and iron sulfide (FeS), which has a lower density than the materials in the earth's core. The Martian mantle probably has the same density as the earth's. The exact composition of the mantle is not known and many different models have been developed. One by John Lewis has a mantle with olivine (an iron-magnesium silicate), iron oxide (FeO), and some water (0.3 percent).

Planetary magnetic field / Mars has an extremely weak planetwide magnetic field—only 2×10^{-3} the strength of the earth's. Such a small value presents a puzzle if the dynamo model correctly describes the origin of planetary magnetic fields. Mars rotates as fast as the earth. Although the core is smaller, it should contain a substantial amount of iron or nickel-iron. There is no seismic evidence that the core is liquid, but the evidence for past volcanic activity implies a hot mantle and so a hot, somewhat liquid, core. So Mars should have a moderately strong field—but it doesn't.

10.6

The Martian atmosphere and surface temperature

Astronomers have known for a long time that Mars has an atmosphere. From observations made from 1777 to 1784, William Herschel concluded that apparent changes in the surface features were actually due to "clouds and vapors floating in the atmosphere of the planet." Many astronomers afterward believed that the Martian atmosphere was like the earth's but thinner.

Well, thin it is, but nothing like the earth's! The Viking landers found average surface pressures of roughly 0.005 atm—$\frac{1}{200}$ the earth's surface pressure. (You'd have to travel 40 km up in the earth's atmosphere before the pressure falls that low.) This thin atmosphere consists of 95 percent carbon dioxide, 0.1 percent molecular oxygen, 2.7 percent molecular nitrogen, and 1.6 percent argon—not really very different in relative composition from the atmosphere of Venus.

The Viking orbiters measured the water vapor in the atmosphere and found the greatest amounts in the high northern latitudes. Peak concentrations were about 0.01 mm of precipitable water—meaning that if all the water above that location rained to the surface, it would form a layer only 0.01 mm thick. On earth, the atmospheric water vapor is typically several centimeters of precipitable water, and of course, the oceans are several kilometers thick. Mars is a very dry planet compared with the earth.

Water cannot flow on Mars today because of the low surface pressure. Only in the deepest canyons, where the atmospheric pressure is higher, could water be liquid on the surface. However, it is common to have water ice on Mars, either on the surface or in the clouds (Fig. 10.20). There is also some evidence for water in a permafrost layer beneath the surface.

Although the atmosphere contains mostly carbon dioxide, its low density does not provide much protection against temperature extremes. At the Martian equator, when Mars is closest to the sun, the difference between noon and midnight amounts to almost 100 K. The summer tropical high of 310 K (37°C) is exceptional. For a period of two Martian months the surface temperature remains below the freezing point of water both day and night across the entire planet. Basically, Mars is a very cold, very dry desert.

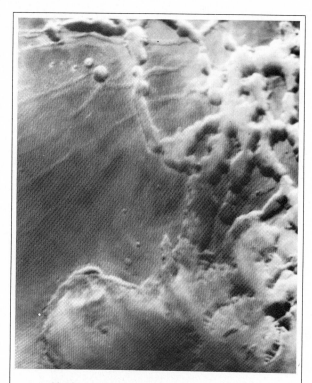

10.20

Canyons on Mars in the morning, filled with clouds. (Courtesy NASA)

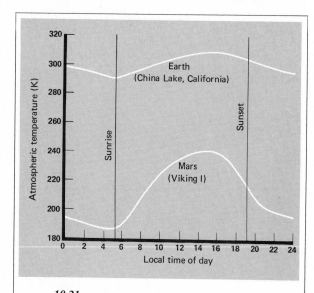

10.21

The daily variation of the surface temperature of Mars compared to a desert site on the earth. The lower solid curve is based on actual measurements by Viking 1.

At the Viking 1 site, 23°N latitude, the air temperature near the ground ranges (Fig. 10.21) from −85°C to −29°C. (That's −121°F to −20°F!) At the Viking 2 site, which is farther north, the temperature falls even lower and water condenses on the surface. The layer of water ice observed coating the rocks and soil is extremely thin—less than a millimeter. The frost remained for about 100 days. One model for the development of the frost layer pictures solid water and carbon dioxide adhering to dust in the atmosphere. The icy dust settles to the surface, where the sun evaporates the carbon dioxide. The dust and water ice make up the thin frost layer.

As the Viking landers plunged through the Martian atmosphere, they measured the air temperature at different elevations. From these and other data, we can now compare the temperature profile of the atmosphere of Mars with that of the earth (Fig. 10.22). Note that both atmospheres have a steady drop in temperature up to an altitude of about 10 km; in this lowest region, the sunlit ground heats the air. Because of its thinness, the atmosphere of Mars is expected to be cooler than it is; a small amount of suspended dust absorbing infrared from the ground makes the difference. The temperature peak at 50 km on earth is caused by the absorption of solar ultraviolet in the ozone layer. Mars has no corresponding peak, so it probably lacks a definite layer of ozone above the ground. In the earth's atmosphere above 100 km, the temperatures rise again because of absorption of solar ultraviolet and X-rays. No such heating takes place in the Martian atmosphere, simply because it's so thin.

10.7

The Martian surface viewed from the earth

Because we must look through two atmospheres, the view of Mars is usually poor in clarity and detail. A small telescope shows the main surface features: the white polar caps, light reddish-orange regions, and dark areas. It took spacecraft visits to Mars to improve dramatically the resolution of our vision.

Sands of Mars / The definite surface features of Mars are dark, apparently greenish-gray areas, in contrast to the orange-reddish color of the rest of the surface. Some early observers thought that these features were oceans. This

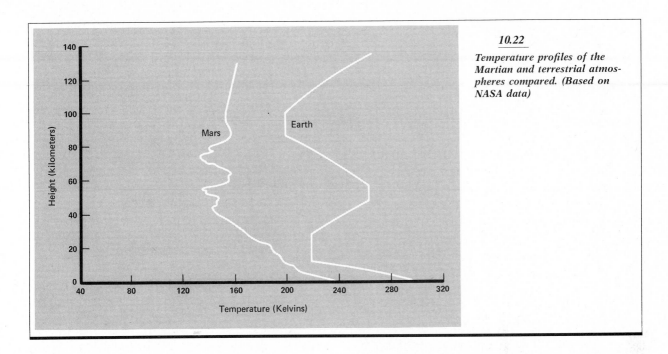

10.22

Temperature profiles of the Martian and terrestrial atmospheres compared. (Based on NASA data)

idea was discarded when the surface pressure was found to be too low for liquid water. Other observers contended that the dark regions were green and so indicated vegetation. This greenness turns out to be an illusion caused by the contrast of the light and dark areas—the dark regions are *not* really green. They are actually red, but not so red as the light regions.

The light orange and yellow-brown regions make up almost 70 percent of the Martian surface. They give Mars its striking reddish appearance. In 1934 the American astronomer Rupert Wildt suggested that these areas contain ferric oxide—rusted iron! Iron oxides come in many forms on the earth; all are characteristically brown, yellow, and orange. Infrared observations have added support to the idea that the surface contains substantial rusted iron combined with water—perhaps as much as 1 percent of the surface is water bound up with minerals.

The Viking landers' measurements were compatible with a surface composition of about 19 percent ferric oxide (Fe_2O_3). In addition, they measured about 44 percent silica (SiO_2), which leads to the conclusion that silicate minerals make up a major part of the surface. The Martian surface is covered with rusty sand (Color Plate 4).

Planetwide dust storms / The red sand, some of which is much smaller-grained than

that on earth's beaches, is blown up by fierce winds—greater than 100 km/h—to create planetwide dust storms. These dust storms occur most violently when Mars is closest to the sun. Then the dust clouds, whipped up to heights of 50 km, shroud the entire planet. They cover Mars in a yellow haze for about a month. It takes many months for the fine dust to settle back completely to the surface. These global storms sandblast the surface and mix it up so much that the surface composition over the planet becomes essentially the same.

This wind-driven dust causes most of the changes in Martian surface features seen in the past. For example, the wind storms blow dust into dunes or deposit it in streaks around mountains and craters.

The Martian canals and polar caps / In 1877 Schiaparelli recorded Martian surface features in great detail. He charted a number of dark, almost straight features, which he called *canali*, Italian for "channels." This word was translated into English as "canals," which implied to some people that they were artificial structures.

Some observers could not see any canals. But others, especially those who regarded them as natural waterways, continued to find more. These so-called canals ignited the curiosity of the American astronomer Percival Lowell (1855–

10.23

Percival Lowell. ". . . the soli-darity of the Martian land sys-tem points to an efficient gov-ernment. . ." (Courtesy Yerkes Observatory)

1915). To pursue his interest in Mars, Lowell (Fig. 10.23) in 1894 founded an observatory near Flagstaff, Arizona, to take advantage of the excellent observing conditions there. Shortly afterward he published Martian maps showing a mosaic of over 500 canals (Fig. 10.24). In a series of popular books Lowell argued that the canals were artificial waterways, constructed by Martians to carry water from the polar caps to irrigate arid regions for farming.

Lowell believed that the polar caps were water ice and that the dark regions were areas of vegetation that displayed seasonal growth, prompted by water from the polar caps. The polar caps are indeed largest in winter and smallest in summer.

The polar caps *do* consist mostly of water ice, especially the residual cap left in the summer, which ranges in thickness from year to year from 1 m to 1 km (Fig. 10.25). The outer reaches of the caps, prominent in winter, consist of carbon dioxide ice, which condenses at a lower temperature than water ice. (At Martian surface pressures, water ice condenses at about 190 K, carbon dioxide ice at 150 K). Lowell was right—water does exist on Mars—but it's not freely flowing on the surface, because the temperature is too cold and the pressure too low. (If all the water in the polar caps could cover the surface as a liquid, it would form a layer only about 10 m deep.)

But Lowell was wrong about the vegetation

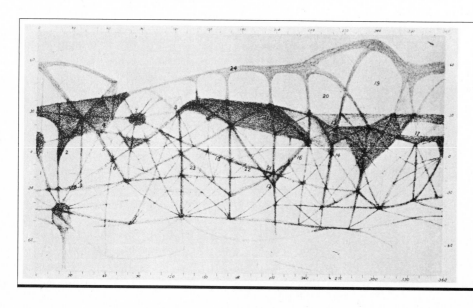

10.24

Surface features of Mars, including "canals," as drawn by Percival Lowell in 1896–1897. (Courtesy Lowell Observatory)

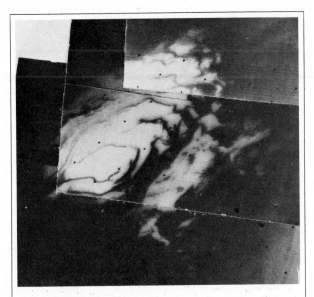

10.25

The residual pole cap on Mars in the summer. The ice is water ice (mixed with the Martian soil). Note the layered appearance. (Courtesy NASA)

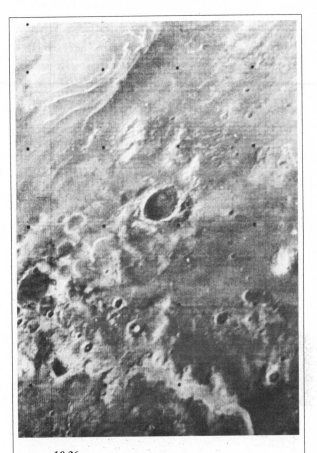

10.26

The south pole cap of Mars (Mariner 7). Craters and bare spots are plainly visible through the icy material of the cap, an indication that the part of the pole cap here cannot be more than a few meters thick. (Courtesy NASA)

and the canals. Some astronomers now believe that wind-blown dust deposits might have created temporary features that were seen as the largest and fuzziest of the canals. The smallest ones were likely an illusion, guided by wishful thinking.

10.8

The invasion of Mars by the earth

Mars is now a desert world. It never had a chance to invade the earth—Martians don't exist! But we've invaded Mars—not to conquer, but to learn; not to destroy, but to detect. We have found out that Mars was once an active world but is now a quiet cold desert.

The surface of Mars / Overshadowed by the glamor of Apollo 11, Mariners 6 and 7 reinforced the view (first developed from the Mariner 4 pictures of 1965) that the surface of Mars resembles that of the moon. They photographed abundant Martian craters visible even under the thinner regions of the polar caps (Fig. 10.26). The Martian craters did resemble impact craters but tended to be shallower than their lunar counterparts. Their flat floors and low rims indicated that they had been strongly eroded.

Was Mars, like the moon, a dead world? No, for the photographs taken by Mariner 9 also showed spectacular features of a geologically active planet. (See Color Plate 3 for a color view of Mars from space.) The extensive photographic survey by Mariner 9 showed that the two Martian hemispheres have different topological characteristics: The southern is relatively flat, older, and heavily cratered; the northern is younger, with extensive lava flows, collapsed depressions, and huge volcanoes. Near the equator, separating the two distinct hemispheres, lies a huge canyon, called Valles Marineris (Fig. 10.27). This chasm is 5000 km long (about the length of the United States), some 500 km wide

10.27

A close-up of part of Valles Marineris, taken by the Viking 1 orbiter from 4200 km. One wall of the canyon shows remains of a number of large landslides. (Courtesy NASA)

in places, and bordered by branching tributaries that look as if they have been carved by water.

On July 20, 1976, exactly seven years to the day after Neil Armstrong stepped out on the moon, Viking 1 touched down on Mars on the plains of Chryse (Fig. 10.28(a)). Not long after, Viking 2 dropped to the Martian surface on the plains of Utopia (Fig. 10.28(b)). Seen close up, the Martian surface is bleak and dry. Large rock boulders are strewn about, amid gravel, sand, and silt. The boulders are basaltic. Some contain small holes (Fig. 10.29) from which gas has apparently escaped; the holes make the rock look spongy. On earth, such basalts originate in frothy, gas-filled lava; the Martian rocks probably had a similar origin.

Both landers presented indirect evidence for once flowing Martian surface water. The Chryse region seems to be a flood plain where water sorted the smaller rocks into gravel, sand, and silt. The ground there also resembles the hardened soil of the earth's deserts. Such soil forms when underground water percolates upward and evaporates at the surface. Upon evaporating, the water leaves behind minerals that harden the soil. Mineral analyses by Vikings 1 and 2 indicated that the soil does contain evaporated minerals, such as epsom salts.

The arroyos of Mars / The Mariner 9 mission discovered and the Viking orbiters confirmed a number of sinuous channels that appear to have been cut in the surface by running water (Fig. 10.30(a)). The largest ones have lengths up to 1500 km and widths as great as 100 km. (These channels are *not* the canals seen by Lowell and others; they are not straight and are too small to be visible from the earth.)

These channels resemble the arroyos commonly found in the southwestern United States. An *arroyo* is a channel in which water flows only occasionally. During the rainy season (the summer months) in New Mexico violent thunderstorms will suddenly dump torrents of rain. The deluge of water, which is not soaked up by the hard soil, flows downhill—into the Rio Grande River rift valley, for example. The rush of water erodes the land into arroyos (Fig. 10.30(b)), some of which are quite large.

What characteristics of the Martian channels make us think that they were actually formed by flowing water? The evidence is pretty

(a)

(b)

10.28

(a) *A Viking 1 panoramic view, showing sand dunes and large rocks. On the horizon in the picture's center are two low hills that may be the rim of a distant crater. Small rocks are about 10 cm in size. The boulder closest to the lander is 3 m in diameter; the farthest one, 8 m across.* (b) *A wide-angle view of the Viking 2 surroundings. Note that many of the rocks are porous, indicating a volcanic origin. (Both courtesy NASA)*

10.29

Close-up of the Martian surface near Viking 2. The rocks here are 10–25 cm in size. (Courtesy NASA)

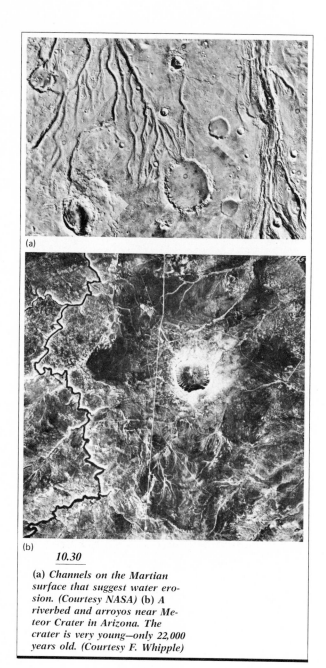

(a)

(b)

_10.30_

(a) _Channels on the Martian surface that suggest water erosion. (Courtesy NASA)_ **(b)** _A riverbed and arroyos near Meteor Crater in Arizona. The crater is very young—only 22,000 years old. (Courtesy F. Whipple)_

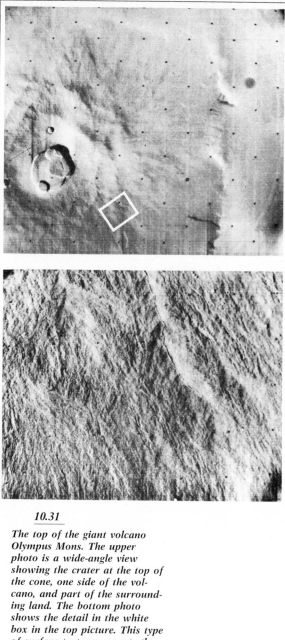

_10.31_

The top of the giant volcano Olympus Mons. The upper photo is a wide-angle view showing the crater at the top of the cone, one side of the volcano, and part of the surrounding land. The bottom photo shows the detail in the white box in the top picture. This type of surface texture suggests the flow of material from the volcano's top. (Courtesy NASA)

strong: (1) The flow direction is downhill. (2) The flow patterns meander (compare the channels in Fig. 10.30(a) with that in Fig. 10.30(b)). (3) Tributary structures indicate where several flows merged to form a larger one. (4) Sandbars are cut by smaller flow channels, as is commonly found in arroyos on the earth.

The presence of Martian arroyos requires extensive running water for at least a short period of time. Because Mars cannot have liquid surface water now, conditions for it must have occurred in the past.

The Martian volcanoes / By far the most awesome Martian features are the shield volcanoes clustered on and near the Tharsis ridge. The largest is Olympus Mons, some 550–600 km across at its base (Fig. 10.31). Telephoto close-ups show a wavy texture of the cone's surface that is the result of lava flows (Fig. 10.31). The cone reaches 25 km above the surrounding plain, and its base would span the bases of the islands of Hawaii, which are made of several

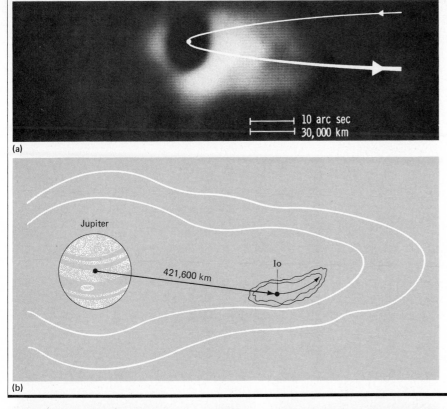

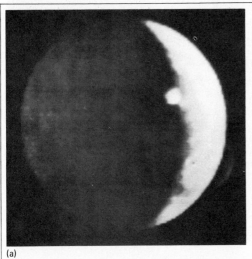

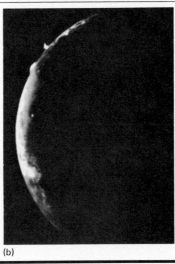

11.13

(a) *Sodium cloud around Io. The size and position of Io have been drawn in. (Courtesy of Bruce Goldberg and the Jet Propulsion Laboratory)* (b) *Extent of Io's sodium cloud. Although the cloud is most dense right around Io, it extends around Jupiter along Io's orbit and a less dense part of the cloud extends over Jupiter's poles. (Based on data by R. Brown, L. Trafton, P. Wehinger, S. Wyckoff, and A. Frohlich)*

11.14

(a) *Volcanic eruptions in Io— discovery photograph. One eruption is lower right at the moon's edge; the other is the bright patch at the night–day line. Voyager 1 photo.* (b) *Voyager 2 photo shows continuing eruptions. (Both courtesy NASA)*

Because volcanic activity continually alters Io's surface, it must be very young. No impact craters appear on Io; volcanic flows have covered them up. Io's surface seems to be the youngest in the solar system—probably less than one million years old.

Why is Io so actively volcanic? One possible model, proposed by Stanton Peale, Patrick Cassen, and Ray Reynolds, views Io's interior as melted from tidal forces produced by the other three Galilean satellites. The model calculations indicate that the tidal heating of Io now amounts to about three times more than the current radio-active heating rate estimated for our moon. Peale, Cassen, and Reynolds in fact predicted "widespread and recurrent volcanism" on Io before the Voyager 1 photos were obtained.

Europa / The surface features of Europa consist of bright areas of water ice among darker, orange-brown areas. Europa's surface is crisscrossed by stripes and bands that may be filled fractures in the moon's icy crust (Fig. 11.16).

Europa appears much less active than Io—no volcanoes are seen here. Yet Europa's surface too is almost devoid of impact craters.

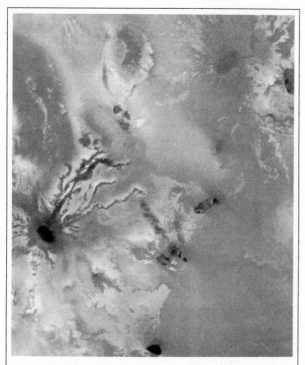

11.15

Io close up. The dark spot with the irregular radiating pattern near the bottom is a volcanic crater with lava flows. (Courtesy NASA)

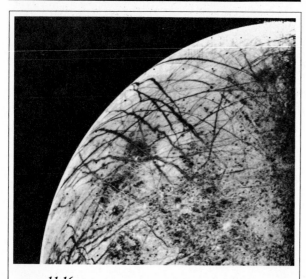

11.16

A close-up of Europa with a resolution of about 4 km. Note the dark cracks streaking across the surface. (Courtesy NASA)

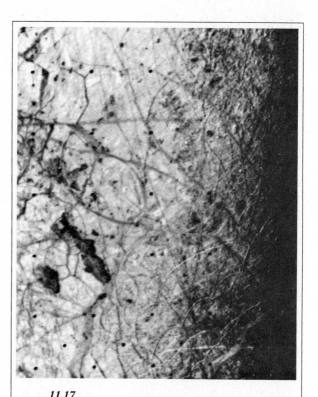

11.17

A closer view of Europa by Voyager 2 from 225,000 km. The area of the photo is about 600 by 800 km along the day–night line, which highlights the surface features. Visible are complex, narrow ridges seen as curved bright streaks, 5–10 km wide and about 100 km in length. Also visible are dark bands, 20–40 km wide and thousands of kilometers long. (Courtesy NASA)

Only three possible ones have been identified. So Europa's surface cannot be a primitive one; it must have evolved since its formation. The crust must have been warm and soft sometime after formation to wipe out evidence of the early, intense bombardment.

On first glance, the most impressive features on Europa are dark markings that crisscross its face, making it look like a cracked eggshell (Fig. 11.17). Some of these cracks extend for thousands of kilometers, split to widths of 50–200 km, but reaching depths of only 100 m or so. Europa's surface is really incredibly smooth—compared to its size, its dark markings are no deeper than the thickness of ink drawn on a ping-pong ball.

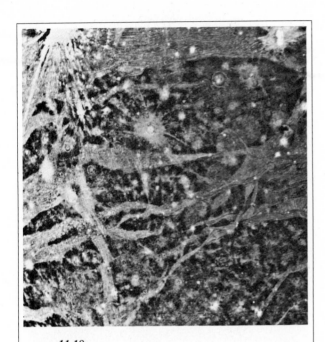

11.18

The surface of Ganymede; the smallest features are about 2.5 km across. Numerous impact craters are visible; those with bright rays are probably younger than those without. The brighter banded regions may arise from faulting of the icy surface. (Courtesy NASA)

Europa's cracked surface indicates that its solid, icy crust is thin and its interior hot and primarily molten. How did Europa get this way? One tentative model proposes that its crust long ago may have been a slush kept partially melted by a molten interior—hot, perhaps, because of tidal stresses. As Europa cooled, its crust turned to smooth, glassy ice. Tidal stresses may then have cracked the icy surface into patterns that resemble pack ice on a frozen sea on the earth. Darker material from the interior welled up to fill in the cracks.

Ganymede / Largest moon of Jupiter, Ganymede ranks overall as the largest moon in the solar system. Its surface looks strangely like our moon's, with dark, marialike regions. Yet, it also has huge faults along its surface, like Europa.

Ganymede has two basic types of terrain (Fig. 11.18): *cratered* and *grooved*. Craters up to 150 km in size densely mark the cratered terrain. Their abundance indicates that the cra-

tered terrain is old, some 4 billion years. Compared with those on the moon and Mercury, the craters are shallow for their size and some have convex rather than concave floors. The craters of Ganymede also differ from those of the moon and Mercury in that they have central pits rather than central peaks. There are no large-scale mountainous regions or large basins on Ganymede either; in fact, nowhere on the satellite is there any relief greater than about 1 km. In some regions there are small bright patches with just a hint of surrounding walls, which look as if a crater has sunk into a soft surface. All these features suggest that the crust of Ganymede is somewhat plastic. Crater rims and mountains slowly sink back into the surface; crater floors gradually fill in. This plastic flow probably is due to the large amount of water ice in Ganymede's crust.

Many craters on Ganymede have very bright rays extending from them (Fig. 11.18), attesting to their formation by impacts on an icy surface.

In contrast, the grooved terrain separates the cratered terrain into polygon-shaped segments. From a distance Ganymede's grooved terrain looks like a sand desert crossed by dune buggy tracks. The grooved terrain consists of a mosaic of light ridges and darker grooves where the ground has slid, sheared, and torn apart. The ridges have widths of 10–100 km, lengths of 100–1000 km, and heights of about 200–300 km.

Ganymede's surface is covered with cracks called *transverse faults*, where the ground has moved sideways for hundreds of kilometers (Fig. 11.19(a)). Earth has many transverse faults; for example, in the ocean basins along midoceanic ridges where upwelling new rock forces the crustal plates apart.

Ganymede's bulk density is low, so it must contain about half water and half rock. Occasional stresses on the water–rock crust have created the fracture patterns. Some ridges and grooves overlie others, an indication that many episodes of crustal deformation have happened in the past.

Some craters cover the grooved terrain; in some places, the ridges and grooves lie on top of craters. Near the south pole, a large basin covers the land—in its general structure it resembles basins on the moon. So it probably

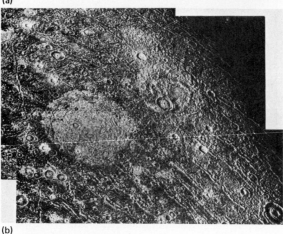

(a)

(b)

11.19

(a) *Ganymede—grooved and ridged terrain. (Courtesy NASA)*
(b) *Voyager 2 photo of Ganymede, taken from a distance of 85,000 km. Visible here are impact craters of different ages overlaying curved troughs and ridges that mark a huge impact basin. The brightest craters are the youngest (most recent), the darker ones older because the ejected material darkens with age. At the bottom, the younger grooved terrain flows over the older ridges of the impact basin. (Courtesy NASA)*

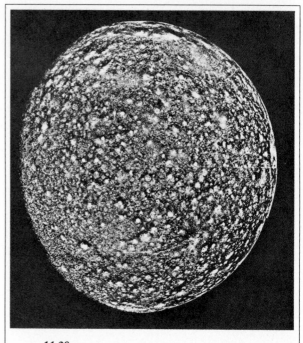

11.20

Voyager 2 photo from 390,000 km of the cratered surface of Callisto. (Courtesy NASA)

formed the same way: by the violent impact of a large object from space. Craters on top of this basin (Fig. 11.19(b)) imply it formed early in the satellite's history, perhaps within a billion years after Ganymede's accretion.

From studying the earth's moon, we believe that the era of intense cratering ended some 3–4 billion years ago. So Ganymede's surface is 3–4 billion years old; that is, Ganymede has been geologically inactive for over 3 billion years.

Callisto / Farthest out of the Galilean moons, Callisto (Fig. 11.20) has a surface that most resembles the moon and Mercury. It is riddled with craters of a wide range of sizes. Many have pitted centers, some have bright ice rays; others are filled with ice. Callisto's craters are shallow—less than several hundred meters deep. Why? Because the surface is a mixture of ice and rock; the surface slowly flows, flattening out the ups and downs of the land.

Callisto has one huge and beautiful multi-ringed feature (Fig. 11.21). Its central floor is 600 km in diameter; 20 to 30 mountainous rings that have diameters of up to 3000 km surround

11.21

The giant ringed basin of Callisto. (Smallest features are about 7 km in size.) The bright circular spot in the basin's center is about 600 km across; the outer rings, 2600 km. Note the lack of high ridges, ring mountains, or a large central depression. (Courtesy NASA)

it like a bull's-eye. The rings look like a series of frozen waves. They might have been formed in a stupendous collision that melted subsurface ice, caused the water to spread in waves that quickly froze in the −180°C surface temperature. The ripple marks are preserved as rings—frozen blast waves.

The central floor of this ringed feature has fewer craters than the rest of the terrain. This difference indicates that the impact forming the rings occurred after much of the cratering—probably 3.5–4 billion years ago.

Asteroidal moons / Orbiting closer to Jupiter than the Galilean satellites is Amalthea. It whizzes around once every 12 h only 150,000 km above the cloud tops. Voyager 1 got a photo of this small, cold world (Fig. 11.22). About 10 times larger than Phobos, it is also elongated, 270 by 155 km along its major and minor axis. The surface is cratered and has a dark red color. Amalthea keeps its long axis pointed at Jupiter; like the Galilean satellites, its rotation period equals its orbital period. The temperature on the surface is about −120°C. This moon's irregular shape, small size, and dark, cratered surface imply it is asteroidlike in character (more about asteroids in Chapter 12).

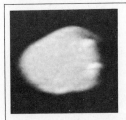

11.22

Amalthea, Jupiter's innermost moon. The indentations near the bottom and upper right may be craters. Amalthea keeps its long axis pointed toward Jupiter and so rotates once every 12 h. (Courtesy NASA)

The surfaces of Jupiter's other moons were not photographed by the voyager missions. These satellites are smaller than Amalthea. They also seem to be asteroidlike bodies, and perhaps they are indeed captured asteroids. (This is possible, for, after all, Jupiter lies just outside the asteroid belt.)

The rings of Jupiter / Jupiter actually has millions of moons—tiny ones that make up its recently discovered ring system.

Voyager 1 took the first direct photo of Jupiter's rings (Fig. 11.23). They are so thin (less than 30 km thick) that they are essentially transparent. The rings are best viewed when edge-on; then the particles scatter light effectively.

Because Voyager 2 knew where to look, it took a dramatic picture of the backlit rings (Fig.

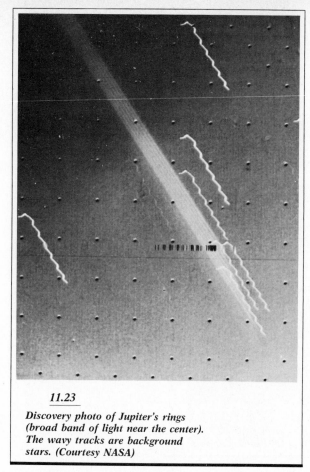

11.23

*Discovery photo of Jupiter's rings
(broad band of light near the center).
The wavy tracks are background
stars. (Courtesy NASA)*

11.25

*A close-up of Jupiter's rings.
Note the bright edge and diffuse, broad inner region. (Courtesy NASA)*

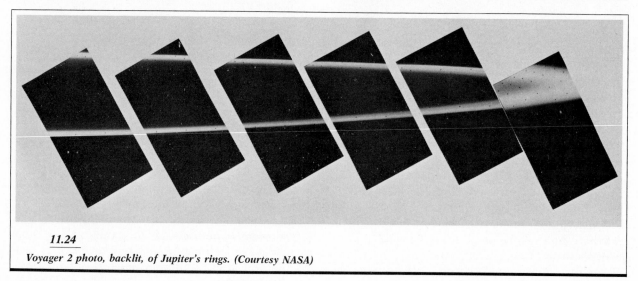

11.24

Voyager 2 photo, backlit, of Jupiter's rings. (Courtesy NASA)

11.24). A close-up view (Fig. 11.25) shows the rings have a definite structure. The outer, brightest part is 800 km wide and lies about 128,500 km from Jupiter's center. Within it is a broader ring some 6000 km wide. And within that ring lies a faint sheet of material that extends from 119,000 km out from Jupiter's center down to the cloud tops.

Compared with Saturn's rings (Section 11.3) and those of Uranus (Section 11.4), the Jovian rings are closer to their parent planet (outer edge at 1.8 Jupiter radii) and between Uranus's and Saturn's rings in width.

What makes up the rings? They must consist of small particles. Voyager 2 photographs imply an average particle diameter of some 10 microns. They reflect blue light poorly, a characteristic of asteroids, meteorites, and the surfaces of the largest Jovian moons. But the particles' composition is not yet known.

11.3

Saturn:
Jewel of the solar system

Outpost of the five ancient wandering stars, Saturn bears a marked resemblance to Jupiter, but its ring system outranks in splendor that of the larger planet. Saturn has a slightly smaller size and less mass than Jupiter. It has the lowest density of any of the planets—only 0.68 g/cc, even less than that of water.

Physical properties / The atmospheric structure of Saturn (Color Plate 16) is similar to that of Jupiter. Although not so conspicuous because of a thick haze layer, it also has belts running parallel to the circles of latitude (Fig. 11.1). Disturbances in the belts rarely occur (only ten spots have been observed to date from the earth), compared with their frequency on Jupiter. Voyager 1 discovered a reddish spot, but much smaller than the Great Red Spot on Jupiter; clouds only a few hundred kilometers across were detected at high latitudes.

The atmosphere of Saturn probably has much the same composition as that of Jupiter. So far methane, ammonia, ethane (C_2H_2), and hydrogen have been detected. The ammonia is less than that found on Jupiter; probably just as much exists, but at the lower temperature of Saturn ($-180°C$) it has frozen and fallen out of the upper atmosphere. Infrared spectroscopy has detected abundant molecular hydrogen, and a substantial percentage of helium is expected. Pioneer 11 observations, confirmed by Voyager, give abundances (by mass) of 73 percent hydrogen and 26 percent helium, about the same as for Jupiter (and for the sun).

Saturn's clouds appear far less colorful than those of Jupiter. The predominant colors are a faint yellow and orange. Because of the low temperatures on Saturn—86–92 K—the clouds lie lower in the atmosphere and a high-altitude haze subdues our view. However, the pictures obtained by Voyager showed much of the same complexity (Fig. 11.26) of cloud patterns seen on Jupiter, with wind speeds 5 times higher, up to 500 m/sec near the equator.

Saturn's interior (Fig. 11.27) probably reflects Jupiter's composition; theoretical estimates are about 74 percent hydrogen, 24 percent helium, and 2 percent heavier elements. Again, this composition is roughly the same as that of the sun, but with more heavy elements.

11.26

Turbulence and jet stream flows in the upper atmosphere of Saturn. Compare with Jupiter (Fig. 11.6). (Courtesy NASA)

Saturn may have a small, rocky core some 20,000 km in diameter and a mass of about 20 earth masses. Other models have the metallic hydrogen region extending right to the center.

Saturn is now known to resemble Jupiter in two other important respects: (1) Infrared observations show that Saturn emits more energy, as infrared radiation, than it receives from the sun at all wavelengths. The excess amount is about twice the energy Saturn receives from the sun. As for Jupiter, this excess heat may be left over from the planet's formation (Chapter 12). (2) Observations of radio bursts from Saturn imply that it, too, has a magnetic field—but only $\frac{1}{20}$ as strong as that of Jupiter and so the magnetosphere is only one-third as big. Pioneer 11 and Voyager measured this field in some detail and found the magnetic axis aligned with Saturn's rotation axis, and the field pattern much more regular than for Jupiter. The magnetic field is probably produced by a dynamo effect in the liquid metallic hydrogen zone of Saturn, in the

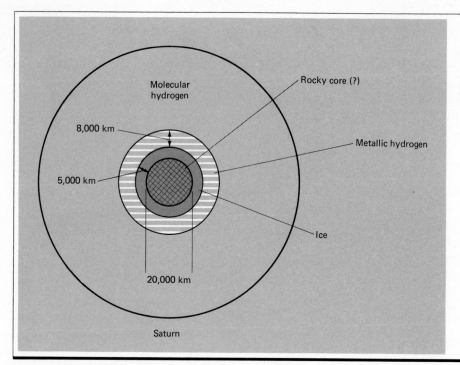

11.27

A model for the interior structure of Saturn. Note how much smaller the zone of metallic hydrogen is compared to that for Jupiter (Fig. 11.9).

same way it is presumably produced in Jupiter. But because the metallic hydrogen region lies deeper in Saturn, the irregularities in the field lie buried beneath the surface, inaccessible to spacecraft measurement.

Satellites / Saturn's band of moons totals at least 17 (Table 11.2). The largest one, Titan, has a mass of 1.37×10^{23} kg and a diameter of 5120 km. Its density is more than 1.95 g/cc. Christian Huygens first noticed Titan, in March 1655, as a tiny star close to the planet. During an interval of about 20 years, no other satellites were discovered. Then Giovanni Cassini observed Iapetus and Rhea, and some years later he also found Tethys and Dione. More than a century passed before four smaller satellites (Mimas, Hyperion, Phoebe, and Enceladus) were spotted. Another small satellite, named Janus, was detected in 1966, but its existence was in doubt for many years. Then in 1980 *two* satellites were found in about the same orbit ascribed to Janus. Voyager confirmed these, and discovered three more, one just outside the A-ring, and two which straddle the new F-ring. Another recent discovery lies between Enceladus and Tethys, and another co-orbits with Dione.

TABLE 11.2 Saturnian satellites

Object	Radius (km)	Density (g/cc)	Distance from Saturn's center (km)
Outer edge of A-ring			137,400
S-15	50	?	138,200
S-13	100 ± 50	?	139,400
F-ring			140,600
S-14	125 ± 50	?	141,700
G-ring			150,000
S-10	100	?	151,400
S-11	70 × 35	?	151,450
Mimas	195 ± 5	1.2 ± 0.1	185,500
Enceladus	250 ± 10	1.1 ± 0.6	238,000
S-16		?	289,600
Tethys	525 ± 10	1.0 ± 0.1	294,700
Dione	560 ± 10	1.4 ± 0.1	377,400
S-12	40 ± 20	?	377,400
Rhea	765 ± 10	1.2 ± 0.3	527,000
Titan	2,560 ± 10	≥ 1.95	1,222,000
Hyperion	155 ± 20	?	1,481,000
Iapetus	720 ± 20	1.2 ± 0.5	3,560,000
Phoebe	70 ± 40	?	12,930,000

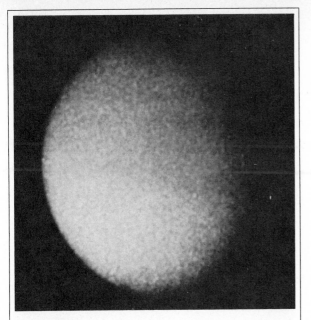

11.28

The clouds of Titan in a Voyager 1 photo taken from 4.5 million km. Titan's southern hemisphere is the lighter region at the bottom half; note the well-defined boundary at the equator. The clouds in the northern hemisphere appear darker in contrast. The overall color of the clouds is a reddish-orange. (Courtesy NASA)

11.29

The surface of Dione (Voyager 1 photo from 240,000 km). Note the many impact craters. The bright radiating patterns visible are probably rays from impact cratering. Also visible are irregular valleys that are old surface faults eroded by impacts. (Courtesy NASA)

Except for outermost Phoebe and Iapetus, all the satellites stick close to Saturn's equatorial plane. They are all much smaller than Titan, less than 800 km in radius. Masses for some of the satellites were determined from their gravitational attraction on Pioneer 11 and Voyager. The corresponding densities range from 1.00 g/cc for Tethys to 1.40 for Dione, all similar to the densities of the outer Galilean satellites of Jupiter.

Titan has given astronomers many surprises. It was the first satellite found to have an atmosphere. The ultraviolet spectrometer on Voyager showed that the atmosphere consists mostly of nitrogen (99 percent) with about 1 percent methane. Several kinds of hydrocarbons have also been detected, including ethane, acetylene, ethylene, and hydrogen cyanide. The atmosphere's surface pressure, determined from the weakening of Voyager's radio transmissions when it went behind Titan, is about $1\frac{1}{2}$ atm. The corresponding surface temperature is 92 K.

Close-up pictures of Titan (Fig. 11.28) show a fuzzy ball with more color variation than expected. A stratospheric layer of orange smog at least 280 km thick was directly visible, and also a blue color along Titan's edge (Color Plate 18).

This variation indicates that the atmosphere varies in composition. The Pioneer flyby also found the light reflected by the atmosphere to be highly polarized—a direct indication that it contains smoglike particles. No surface features were seen. The surface was completely obscured from Voyager's view also, but the pressure and temperature data, along with the spectroscopic detections of nitrogen and hydrocarbons, have led some to speculate that the surface is covered with organic tars along with pools of liquid nitrogen.

Although much smaller than Titan, Saturn's other satellites are just as interesting. The four largest, next to Titan, are Iapetus, Rhea, Dione, and Tethys, with diameters ranging from 1050 to 1530 km. They appear heavily cratered (Fig. 11.29) and covered with wispy white streaks (Fig. 11.30). In a few cases the streaks form rayed patterns around impact craters, but mostly they do not. They are probably deposits of frozen ice, but whether from material emanating from the interior or from debris deposited by colliding cometary bodies is unknown.

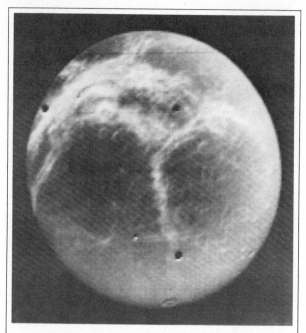

11.30

Dione, showing bright, wispy markings that are probably deposits of surface ice. (Courtesy NASA)

11.31

The surface of Mimas, showing its large impact feature. This crater is more than 130 km in diameter—about one-quarter the diameter of Mimas. Note the raised rim and central peak, typical of impact features found on the terrestrial planets. Note the other impact craters, some 15–45 km in diameter. (Courtesy NASA)

Although all the satellites show brightness variations over their surface, Iapetus is the most extreme. Like the rest of Saturn's satellites, it is locked into orbit with the same face toward Saturn at all times. The hemisphere leading in its orbit is only one-sixth as bright as that following (like the difference between a blackboard and a field of snow), suggesting that the leading surface is covered with dark debris picked up during its journey around the planet.

With one exception, the smaller of the nine named satellites are also cratered. On Mimas, for example, Voyager found a huge crater (Fig. 11.31) 130 km across (about one-fourth the moon's diameter), with walls 9 km high, perhaps the deepest in the solar system. A slightly larger impact probably would have shattered Mimas completely; cracks and troughs on the side opposite the crater were produced by the shock of the impact. The one exception to the general roughness is Enceladus, which appears remarkably smooth. One possible explanation: Because the orbital period is almost exactly half that of Dione, tidal forces might have provided internal heating, keeping the surface soft, until after the crater-making bombardment was finished.

The new satellites of Saturn are all small bodies, 100 km or less in radius. Their interesting characteristics are not their surfaces so much as their orbits. At 151,000 km from Saturn lie moons 11 and 12 (Fig. 11.32(a) and (b)) in almost exactly the same orbits, differing by only 50 km in semimajor axis. Because the orbits aren't *exactly* the same, neither are the periods, and the satellites must from time to time pass each other. However, their sizes are bigger than the separation of their orbits, so they *cannot* pass, unless they deviate from their average orbit. The dynamics of this collision avoidance maneuver has yet to be worked out. (The co-orbiting satellite following Dione is locked into a position 120° away along the orbit, and never catches up.)

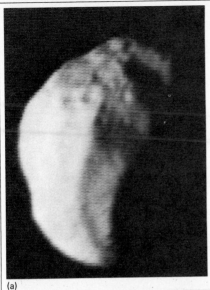 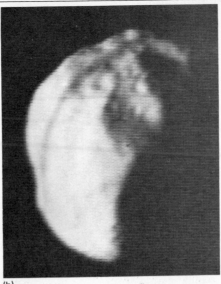

(a) (b)

11.32

Photos of Saturn's eleventh moon, showing its south polar region. Note the impact craters on this moon, which is only 135 by 70 km in size. The photo on the left (a) and the one on the right (b) were taken 13 min apart. Note the narrow shadow in (b), which was probably cast by a narrow ring of Saturn a few thousand kilometers from the moon. (Courtesy NASA) (c) A schematic diagram of Saturn's rings and the orbits of some of its moons. The view is from above Saturn's north pole. Note that the scales of the two halves of the figure differ. (Adapted from a NASA diagram)

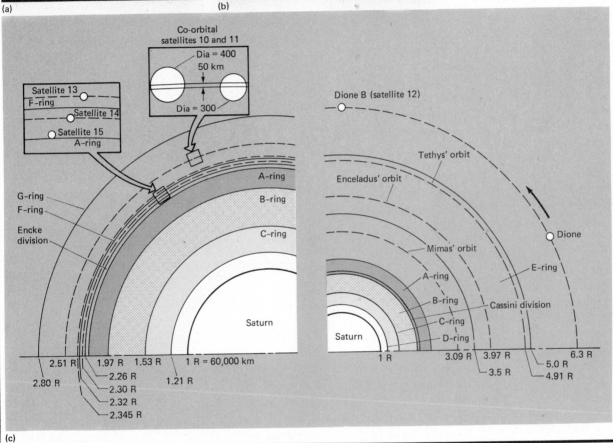

(c)

Two satellites lie close in to Saturn, just inside and outside the narrow F-ring (Fig. 11.32(c)). Nicknamed the "sheepdog" satellites, their combined gravitational influence keeps the F-ring particles from wandering outside a narrow range of orbits. How so? The faster moving inside satellite accelerates the inner ring particles as it passes, causing them to spiral out to larger orbits (just as the tidal force of the earth on the moon causes it to spiral outward); conversely, the slower moving outer satellite accelerates the outer ring particles as they pass by, causing them to spiral inward. A similar mechanism is thought to operate with the satellite just outside the A-ring, accounting for its very sharp outer boundary.

Ring system / In 1659 Huygens observed that Saturn "is surrounded by a thin, flat ring" that does not touch the body of the planet. Further observations by Cassini uncovered a gap in

Huygens's single ring; this gap is known as *Cassini's division*. The rings lie in Saturn's equatorial plane tipped about 26° to the orbital plane, and because of their tilt, they change their appearance as viewed from the earth during the course of Saturn's revolution about the sun.

The near disappearances of the edge-on rings indicate that they are very thin, no more than 5 km thick. Observations by A. Dollfus indicate a thickness of 2.4 km. Although thin, the rings are wide; the three main rings visible from the earth reach from 71,000 to 140,000 km from Saturn's center (1.2–2.3 Saturn radii).

The high-resolution photographs obtained by the Voyager spacecraft revealed spectacular detail (Color Plate 17) in the ring system. Although the A-ring is relatively smooth, the B- and C-rings break up into numerous small ringlets (Fig. 11.33), like grooves on a phonograph record. Many hundreds, perhaps a thousand, light and dark ringlets surround the planet, with widths as small as 2 km, the best resolution of the Voyager cameras. Some (in the C-ring) appear elliptical in shape, rather than circular. Even the Cassini division, apparently empty as seen from earth, was revealed to be filled with at least 20 ringlets (several of the brightest are visible in Fig. 11.33). The true cause of all this complexity is as yet unknown.

Even more unexpected was the discovery of dark, spokelike features in the B-ring (Fig. 11.34). The spokes rotate with the rings, but with constant angular velocity (like the spokes of a wheel), rather than like orbiting bodies following Kepler's laws. A clue to their origin came with the realization that the angular velocity of the spokes is the same as that of Saturn itself. One tentative explanation is that small particles acquire a charge, are lifted out of the ring plane, and rotate with Saturn's magnetic field.

Pioneer 11 discovered a new ring out beyond the previously known ones. Called Ring F, it lies 3500 km outside the edge of the rings visible from the earth. Ring F is some 320 km wide and a mere 3–4 km thick. Voyager resolved this ring into a complex system of knots and a braided structure of at least three strands (Fig. 11.35). What produces such a noncircular, asymmetric structure is not yet understood. Evidence for another such very narrow ring (the G-ring), 10,000 km farther out, was obtained unexpect-

11.33

A computer-processed picture of Saturn's rings, taken by Voyager 1 from a distance of 8 million km, shows abut 95 individual rings. (Courtesy NASA)

edly from the Voyager photograph of one of the co-orbiting satellites. A narrow shadow is visible, which is not present on other photos.

Two other extremely faint rings are known. The E-ring, discovered photographically from earth and confirmed by Voyager, extends out beyond the F-ring to at least 6.5 Saturn radii (400,000 km). A ring inside the C-ring was photographed by Voyager 1 (Fig. 11.36). Called the D-ring, it extends at least halfway to the surface of Saturn. Such a ring had been reported earlier, but the ring seen by Voyager is much too faint to have been detected with ground-based telescopes.

The rotation rate of the rings is measured by their Doppler shift (Focus 19). The velocities range from 16 km/sec at the outer boundary of ring A to 20 km/sec at the inner boundary of ring B. The measured velocities agree with the theoretical velocities calculated from Kepler's third law for individual masses placed at the ring distances from Saturn; this agreement indi-

12.6

A comet far from the sun (Comet Cunningham, 1940); note the lack of a visible tail. (Courtesy Harvard College Observatory)

12.7

The parts of a comet. The diffuse coma—which, if bright enough, can be seen by the naked eye—encases a bright, starlike nucleus, assumed to be no more than a few hundred kilometers in size. The gas tail, made of atoms and ions given off by the nucleus, streams out opposite the sun. The dust tail follows along the orbital path of the nucleus when the comet is close to the sun.

12.5). But not all comets have tails, and those that do display them only when close to the sun. Far from the sun, a comet has no visible tail (Fig. 12.6). When first sighted through a telescope, a comet typically looks like a hazy dot. This bright head of a comet is called the *coma* (Fig. 12.7). Sometimes a coma contains a starlike point called a *nucleus*. Cometary nuclei must be very small—much less than 50 km across, perhaps only 1 or 2; none has ever been seen as more than a point of light. As a comet dives toward the sun, it brightens and usually sprouts a tail, which may stretch for millions of kilometers (Color Plates 6 and 7).

Comets may have two types of tails: gas and dust (Fig. 12.8). The gas tail has an emission-line spectrum with conspicuous lines from carbon monoxide, carbon dioxide, nitrogen, and free radicals of ammonia and methane. The light from the dust tail is simply reflected sunlight.

A comet's coma, when far from the sun, shows a spectrum of reflected sunlight, which indicates solid particles. At about 1 AU from the sun the coma shows emission lines from molecules of carbon, cyanogen (CN), oxygen, hydroxyl, and hydrides of nitrogen (NH and NH_2). Still closer to the sun, emission lines of silicon, calcium, sodium, potassium, and nickel appear.

How can we explain this change in the coma's spectrum and the growth of gas and dust tails? In the 1950s Fred L. Whipple devised a plausible picture—the *dirty-iceberg model* of a comet. Whipple proposed that a comet nucleus is a compact, solid body made of frozen gases (ices) of water, carbon dioxide, ammonia, and methane embedded with rocky material (Fig. 12.9). Beyond Jupiter, low temperatures keep the ice-rock conglomerate together. As the nucleus nears the sun the ices vaporize, releasing gases and dust, which form the coma and tail. After many solar passages the nucleus runs out of ices, and only the rocky material remains. The comet is dead—it can no longer make its beautiful tail.

Meteoroids, meteors, and meteorites / What happens to the solid material that marks a dead comet? It orbits the sun as small bodies called *meteoroids*. (Other meteoroids may be pieces of asteroids.) Occasionally the earth runs into these meteoroids, and they dive through our atmosphere to make a *meteor*, a flash of light associ-

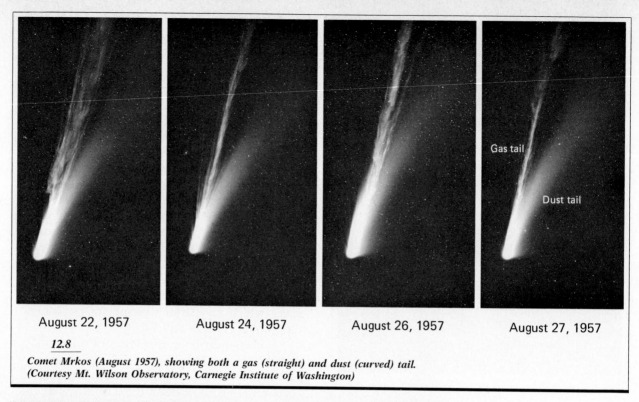

August 22, 1957   August 24, 1957   August 26, 1957   August 27, 1957

12.8
*Comet Mrkos (August 1957), showing both a gas (straight) and dust (curved) tail.
(Courtesy Mt. Wilson Observatory, Carnegie Institute of Washington)*

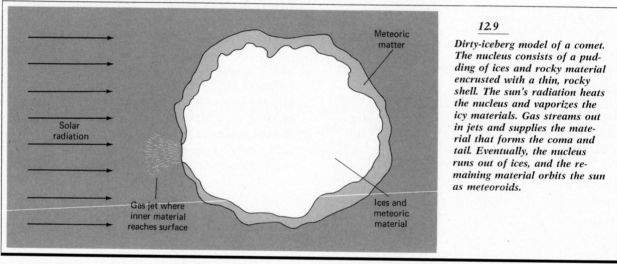

12.9
Dirty-iceberg model of a comet. The nucleus consists of a pudding of ices and rocky material encrusted with a thin, rocky shell. The sun's radiation heats the nucleus and vaporizes the icy materials. Gas streams out in jets and supplies the material that forms the coma and tail. Eventually, the nucleus runs out of ices, and the remaining material orbits the sun as meteoroids.

ated with the burning of a solid particle in the atmosphere (Fig. 12.10).

If a meteoroid survives its plunge and strikes the earth's surface, it is then called a *meteorite*. Astronomers classify meteorites in one of three broad categories: irons, stones, and stony-irons. The irons, which are the most common ones found, consist of about 90 percent iron and 9 percent nickel. You can easily identify an iron meteorite because it has a high density and looks like a piece of melted metal (Fig. 12.11). Stones are made of light silicate materials similar to earth rocks, so they are difficult to tell apart from an ordinary stone (Fig. 12.12). When magnified, some stones are seen to contain small silicate spheres, called *chondrules*

(Fig. 12.13). Such stone meteorites are known as *chondrites*. Stony-iron meteorites represent a crossbreed between irons and stones and typically contain small stone pieces set in iron.

As you may expect, irons are the most dense meteorites, with densities ranging from 7.5 to 8 g/cc. Stones are the least dense, averaging from 3 to 3.5 g/cc. Stony-iron meteorites, because they are a mixture of stones and iron, have an intermediate density of about 5.5–6 g/cc.

One of the most curious kinds of chondrites are the *carbonaceous chondrites* (Fig. 12.14). The chondrules in these meteorites are embedded in material that contains a large amount of carbon compared with that in other stony chondrites—

12.10

A meteor. This was an unusually bright one, known as a fireball. (Courtesy F. L. Whipple)

12.11

Widmanstätten figures (the crystal patterns) in a nickel-iron meteorite from Glorietta, New Mexico. (Courtesy Institute of Meteoritics, the University of New Mexico)

12.13

Chondrules, round silicate spheres found in meteorites known as chondrites. Note that they are not uniform. They consist of different minerals packed together. (Courtesy F. L. Whipple and the Smithsonian Astrophysical Observatory)

12.12

A piece of a stony meteorite from Canyon Diablo, Arizona. (Courtesy Institute of Meteoritics, the University of New Mexico)

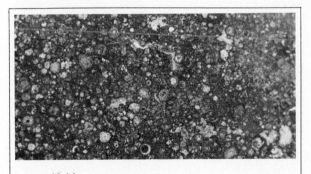

12.14

A carbonaceous chondrite meteorite from Allende, Mexico. This close-up view shows the chondrules. (Courtesy Institute of Meteoritics, the University of New Mexico)

typically from about 1 to 4 percent carbon by mass. Their carbon content gives these meteorites a dark appearance.

Carbonaceous chondrites also contain significant fractions of water (ranging from about 3 to 20 percent) and volatile materials. In addition, the relative abundances of metals in carbonaceous chondrites more closely resemble those found in the sun's photosphere than those in the crust of the earth. We know that the earth is a highly evolved body now, as its differences from the sun demonstrate. So carbonaceous chondrites must be rather primitive bodies whose composition reflects fairly well the abundances of materials in the primeval cloud out of which the sun and planets formed.

What about iron meteorites? What is their origin? An important clue comes from etching with acid a polished surface of an iron meteorite. Large crystalline patterns—called *Widmanstätten figures*—become visible (Fig. 12.11). Terrestrial iron does not show such patterns when etched. Widmanstätten figures clearly distinguish meteorite from terrestrial iron and also give a clue to the history of the meteorite material. A nickel-iron mixture, when cooled *slowly* under low pressures from a melting temperature of about 1600 K, forms large crystals. The key point here is that the cooling must be very gradual (about 1 K every million years). But metals conduct heat well, and in the cold of space, a molten mass of nickel and iron would cool rapidly and not form large crystals. So how could nickel-iron meteorites grow Widmanstätten figures? They need protection from the cold. So it's likely that nickel-iron meteorite material solidified *inside* small bodies, termed *parent meteor bodies*. To allow a cooling of only 1 K every million years these must be at least 100 km in radius.

How do such bodies form? Probably with the formation of the solar system. Parent meteor bodies are envisioned to have been only a few hundred kilometers across. Once formed, they could be heated by the radioactive decay of short-lived isotopes, such as aluminum-26. When heated to melting, a parent meteor body differentiates—the densest material falls to the core and the least dense froths to the surface. So the object ends up with a core of metals and a cover of rocky material, which cools to form a crust. This insulates the molten metals and al-lows them to cool slowly—about 1 K every million years—and form Widmanstätten figures. Much later, parent meteor bodies collide and fragment. Pieces from the outer crust make stony meteorites, pieces from farther down become stony-iron meteorites, and the core produces the iron meteorites.

Are any parent meteor bodies around now? Possibly yes—as asteroids.

Notice that the view of meteorites outlined here implies that their parent bodies were among the first solid objects to form in the origin of the solar system. So the ages of meteorites should provide a direct indication of the age of the solar system. Meteorites can be dated by using radioactive-decay techniques (Focus 23); such methods give ages very close to 4.6 billion years. It is from meteorites that astronomers have a direct, reliable estimate of when the solar system formed.

12.2

Pieces and puzzles

The dynamical and chemical properties of the solar system impose crucial limitations on any theory of its formation. These features serve as broad templates for shaping more specific questions.

Chemically, the solar system is comprised of three broad categories of material: solar, terrestrial, and icy (Table 12.1). Each group is distin-

---

TABLE 12.1   Generalized classes of solar system materials

Class	Elements	Melting point
Terrestrial	Silicon, magnesium, aluminum, iron, etc., plus oxygen in chemical composition	2000 K
Icy	Carbon, nitrogen, oxygen, plus hydrogen in chemical composition	273 K
Solar	Hydrogen, helium, neon, argon, etc.	14 K

Note In 1950 Harrison Brown pointed out that the material of the solar system falls into three natural categories delineated by melting points. The materials in the solar group are the most abundant because they are representative of the solar composition.

TABLE 12.2 General composition of the major bodies in the solar system

Bodies	Materials in composition (%)		
	Terrestrial	Icy	Solar
Terrestrial planets	70	30	0
Asteroids	70	30	0
Jupiter	1	10	90
Saturn	1	30	70
Uranus	10	80	10
Neptune	20	70	10
Comets	15	85	0

SOURCE Adapted from *Earth, Moon and Planets,* by Fred L. Whipple (Harvard University Press, Cambridge, Mass., 1968).

TABLE 12.3 Distribution of mass and angular momentum in the solar system

Object	Mass (% of total)	Angular momentum (% of total)
Sun	99.86	0.5
Jovian planets	0.132	99.0
Terrestrial planets	0.003	0.2
Asteroids	0.00003 (?)	0.1 (?)
Comets	0.0000003 (?)	0.2 (?)

guished primarily by its melting point. The solar and icy materials together are sometimes called *volatiles.* These are generally not solid under the conditions expected during the solar system's formation. The bodies of the solar system, including the comets and asteroids, are composed of various combinations of the three groups. In Table 12.2 you see the kinship of Uranus and Neptune with the comets, of Jupiter and Saturn with the sun, and of the terrestrial planets with asteroids.

Warning: These three gross divisions do not mean that the materials cannot exist in a non-solid form. For example, the sun contains terrestrial materials—but as gases (because the sun is hotter than 2000 K), not as solids. In fact, the sun contains, in terms of total mass, more terrestrial materials than all the terrestrial planets put together. Likewise, the sun also contains the icy group as gases.

Note: By now you should recognize the importance of an object's density in giving a key clue about its composition. (That's why astronomers are so eager to determine the densities of bodies in the solar system.) As a general rule, you can consider objects with densities of about 1 to be made of icy materials; with densities of about 3 to be made of rocky materials; and with densities of about 7 to be made of metals, mostly iron. Bodies with densities between these are mixtures. For example, a density of about 2 implies a combination of icy and rocky materials, and that of about 5, a mix of rocky and metallic stuff.

Dynamically, the solar system exhibits a surprisingly regular structure. Viewed from above the earth's North Pole, the solar system displays the following orbital-rotational characteristics:

1 All the planets revolve counterclockwise around the sun.
2 With the exception of Pluto, the major planets have orbital planes that are only very slightly inclined with respect to the plane of the ecliptic (that is, they are essentially *coplanar*).
3 Most of the natural satellites revolve in the same direction that their primaries rotate and lie very close to their primaries' equatorial planes.
4 With the exception of Mercury and Pluto, the planets move in orbits that are almost circular.
5 With the exception of Venus and Uranus, the planets rotate counterclockwise (in the same direction as their orbital motion).
6 The planets together contain more angular momentum than the sun (Table 12.3).
7 Three of the Jovian planets have rings.

A successful model must explain as many of these dynamical properties as possible. A good model is not simply the one that accounts for the greatest number of the preceding characteristics. It must explain these in some internally consistent, simple fashion (Section 2.1). (That is what is meant by a model being "aesthetically pleasing.")

The sun contains most of the mass in the solar system. The rest lies mostly in or close to the plane of the solar system, which is also the plane of the sun's equator. In terms of mass distribution, the solar system appears very thin. If it were the size of an average pancake, the solar system would be only 1 cm thick (about the thickness of a pancake), disregarding Pluto's orbital inclination.

Although the sun holds 99 percent of the system's mass, it contains less than 1 percent of the angular momentum (Focus 26). The outer planets have the most, 99 percent of the total (Table 12.3). If all the planets with their present angular momenta were dumped into the sun, it would spin once every few hours rather than once a month. Any model of the solar system's origin must account for this distribution of angular momentum.

Finally, a successful model must deal with the dynamical and chemical regularities of the system, as well as with the interplanetary debris: comets, asteroids, and meteoroids (Section 12.1). Contemporary models consider these bodies to be important relics of the solar system's formation.

Most models of the system's genesis take one of two basic forms: (1) *nebular models,* in which the sun condenses from an interstellar cloud of gas and dust that also forms a disk (a solar *nebula*—"nebula" is Latin for "cloud"), out of which the planets condense or (2) *catastrophic models,* in which the occurrence of a catastrophic event involving the sun leads to the injection of gaseous material (which condenses to the planets) into solar orbit. Nebular and catastrophic models have battled for about 200 years, with fluctuating success, for the dominating intellectual position among astronomers. (Nebular models are now on top and likely to remain so.)

12.3
Early ideas of the origin of the solar system

Nebular models interpret the existence of the solar system as a natural consequence of the sun's formation and, perhaps, of any star's formation. If nebular models are correct, planetary systems may be very common in our Galaxy and in other galaxies. The opposing catastrophic models require a rare, one-of-a-kind event. So if

12.15
Marquis de Laplace (1749–1827).
(Courtesy Yerkes Observatory)

they are the right approach, planetary systems among the stars could be rare. Here's a brief look at the origins of such contrasting pictures of the solar system's formation.

Nebular models / Immanuel Kant (1724–1804) first developed a detailed picture of the dynamical evolution of the solar system consistent with the law of gravitation. Arguing by analogy with Saturn's rings, he depicted the solar system as forming from a disk-shaped nebula containing a large percentage of dust.

Later, in 1796, the French mathematician Pierre Simon (Fig. 12.15), Marquis de Laplace (1749–1827), presented in *The System of the World* an elaborate Newtonian treatment of the history of the solar system. The dynamical structure of the solar system was the springboard of Laplace's approach. Laplace imagined that the sun in its primitive state condensed from a cloud of gas and dust. As the sun condensed, it would have been surrounded by a hot, tenuous atmosphere, which also condensed but left behind rings of material. Collisions and

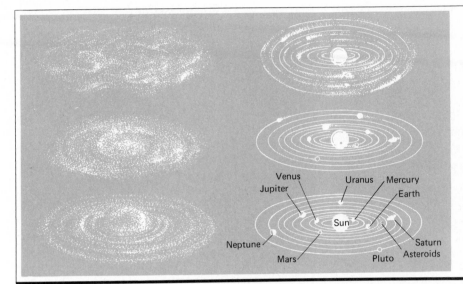

Laplace's nebular model for the formation of the solar system. Here the solar system originated from a vast cloud of gas and dust. The cloud contracts because of its own gravity and breaks up into concentric rings about a dense nucleus (similar to Saturn and its rings). Material in these rings formed the planets, and a similar process resulted in the formation of satellites around the planets. The central part of the nebula became the sun.

mutual gravitational attraction of the particles in these rings would have lumped the material into a single body, a planet. Later the planetary bodies would have contracted and in the process would have shed material to form the satellites (Fig. 12.16). Like Kant, Laplace pointed to Saturn as a concrete example of this process.

The essential features of the Kant–Laplace nebular models—that the sun and then the planets form from a nebula—are the foundations of the modern approach. The formation of the sun takes place in a flattened nebula. The planets grow from this nebula.

How does this growth happen? There are three possible methods: (1) gravitational collapse, (2) accretion, and (3) condensation. *Gravitational collapse* works only if regions in the nebula have enough mass so that they contract by their own gravity to form a planet. (This was Kant's view.) *Accretion* occurs when small particles collide and stick together to form larger masses that eventually grow into planets. An example: As snowflakes fall through the air, they can collide and stick to form clusters of snowflakes. (Laplace thought that accretion was important in forming planets.) *Condensation* involves the growth of small particles by the sticking together of atoms and molecules. An example: Water molecules combine to form raindrops. Note that each of the processes involves objects of different sizes.

The most compelling objection to the

Kant–Laplace picture comes from the present distribution of angular momentum (Table 12.3). Imagine that the nebula out of which the sun and planets form is rotating slowly. As the nebula collapses, it spins faster. It also flattens out from an originally spherical shape. (Here again is the conservation of angular momentum; Focus 26). The sun forms from the central part of the nebula. When the sun has finally formed, it should be spinning very rapidly—once every few hours. Actually, the sun spins 400 times more slowly than this rate, predicted from the conservation of angular momentum. But as mentioned before, the sun would spin once every few hours *if* the present angular momentum in the planets were added to it. The angular momentum is there, but not in the right place! To adopt the Kant–Laplace nebular model requires a process to account for the angular momentum distribution, a mechanism not developed until this century (Section 12.4).

Note that the conservation of angular momentum reinforces the most compelling feature of a nebular model: The sun and planets form out of a rotating cloud, so naturally the sun rotates and the planets revolve in the same direction. Also, the cloud finishes its collapse as a disk, and the planets' orbits do align in a thin disk.

Catastrophic models / Early in this century the American scientists (Fig. 12.17) Thomas C. Chamberlain (1843–1928) and Forest R. Moulton

12.17

(a) *Thomas C. Chamberlain.* (b) *Forest R. Moulton. (Both courtesy of Yerkes Observatory)*

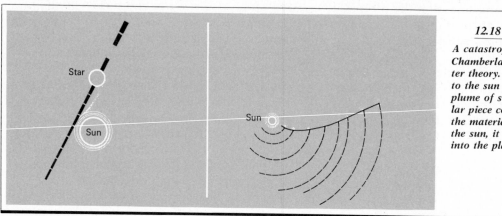

12.18

A catastrophic model: the Chamberlain–Moulton encounter theory. A star passes close to the sun and draws out a plume of solar material. A similar piece comes off the star. As the material moves away from the sun, it cools and condenses into the planets.

(1872–1952) adopted a version of a catastrophic model that avoided the angular momentum problems of the nebular models. These astronomers envisioned a star skirting the sun and raising giant tides in the solar atmosphere, tides produced by gravitational forces. The tongues of material from the sun and star eventually condensed to form *planetesimals* (small bodies a few hundred meters across), which accreted to planetary-sized bodies (Fig. 12.18). Excess material either fell into the sun or left the solar system entirely. Because the planets obtained all their angular momentum from the passing star,

they could easily pick up more angular momentum than the sun has.

All variations of catastrophic models run into four basic difficulties. First, the probability of an encounter or collision between the sun and another body is extremely low. The separation between stars and the small relative velocities of stars near the sun make even a close encounter unlikely. For example, the frequency of a sun–star encounter is about once in 10^{21} years, a period much longer than the age of the universe, which is estimated to be roughly 10^{10} years. A catastrophic model implies that the solar system must be unique, since it formed in a freak event.

Second, the expansion of hot material from the sun must be rapid, so it would be difficult to form planets. Astronomer Lyman Spitzer calculated in 1938 that a filament of solar material massive enough to form planets must come from deep in the sun, where it is quite hot (about 1 million K). Such hot gases suddenly expelled into space would expand and dissipate rather than condense.

Third, the total amount of matter ejected from the sun is insufficient to form the planets. More than 99 percent of such material would fall back to the sun, even if the encounter were close enough to raise a sufficient mass. To create the planetary masses requires a filament mass equal to the present mass of the sun.

Fourth, the detailed composition of the terrestrial planets differs greatly from that of the sun in some important respects. For example, the deuterium-hydrogen ratio on the earth is about 10^{-4}. In the sun the thermonuclear fusion reactions quickly consume deuterium at low temperatures, so the deuterium-hydrogen ratio is small (about 10^{-7}). If the earth condensed from solar material, it should have the same relative abundance of deuterium to hydrogen. It does not. Observations have found the deuterium-hydrogen ratio in the atmosphere of Jupiter to be about 10^{-5}. This value is much larger than expected if Jupiter were made of material torn from the sun. So even though Jupiter has a composition like that of the sun, it cannot have been formed directly out of solar material.

To summarize: Catastrophic models were designed primarily to account for the angular momentum distribution in the solar system. They suffer from the rarity of close encounters between stars and from the difficulty of forming planets from hot gases in space. Nebular models naturally accounted for most of the dynamical properties of the solar system but failed to predict correctly the angular momentum distribution. One strong feature of the nebular model is its natural link to the formation and evolution of stars.

12.4
An overview of nebular models
The main objection to a nebular model was the present distribution of angular momentum in

the solar system. How do contemporary theories cope with this problem? One idea has been worked on in detail. It involves the interaction of magnetic fields and charged particles to rearrange the distribution of angular momentum. The basic solution requires that the spin of the central part of the nebula be decreased and transferred to the outer regions.

Charged particles and magnetic fields interact so that the particles spiral along the magnetic lines of force (Focus 24). Such interactions provide a way to transfer spin from the young sun (in the center of the nebula) to the outer parts of the nebula. As the sun forms, it heats up the interior regions of the nebula. Here the gas is ionized, so charged particles are abundant. The magnetic field lines trap these particles. As the sun rotates, it carries its magnetic field lines with it; these drag along the charged particles (Fig. 12.19), which in turn unite with and drag along the rest of the gas and dust. So the magnetic field spins the material around in the nebula near the sun. At the same time, the mass of the nebula resists the rotation. This drag on the magnetic field lines stretches them into a spiral shape (Fig. 12.20). The magnetic field links the material in the nebula to the sun's rotation. So the nebular material gains rotation (and angular momentum) at the sun's expense.

Whatever process transferred the angular momentum, the transfer must have taken place *before* large solid objects formed in the nebula. The transfer mechanism just described will work effectively only on gases. With this in mind, here is a skeletal sketch of a modern nebular model. The main problem is how to get a lumpy solar system out of a smooth, diffuse cloud—that is, how to form the planets.

Prior to the formation of the planets, the solar nebula must condense from an interstellar cloud of gas and dust. This cloud may have had a mass more than a thousand times that of the sun. A small blob with perhaps twice the mass of the sun broke off and collapsed quickly. As it did, it formed into a disk (Fig. 12.21) and heated up as the gravitational energy converted to kinetic energy (Focus 28). The temperature at the center rose to at least 2000 K but dropped off rapidly at the edges. Such temperatures resulted in pressures that balanced the inward pull of gravity. The collapse halted. To

focus 28

GRAVITATIONAL CONTRACTION AND HEATING

Whenever a mass pulls itself in by its own gravity, it heats up. This natural process is so important astronomically that you must understand the basic physics. It involves the conversion of gravitational potential energy into kinetic energy (heat) and radiative energy (light).

To understand this process of energy conversion, consider a ball held above the earth's surface (Fig. 1). Its velocity is zero; it has no kinetic energy. But it does have potential energy. Release the ball. As it falls, its velocity increases. So its kinetic energy increases. In fact, the more it falls, the more its velocity increases and the greater its kinetic energy.

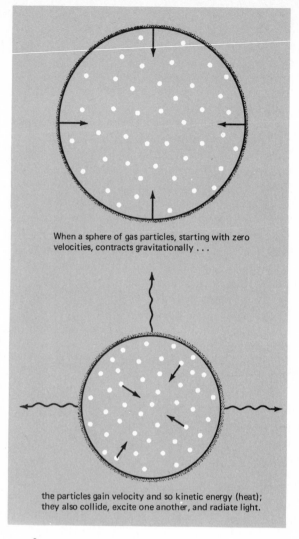

When a sphere of gas particles, starting with zero velocities, contracts gravitationally . . .

the particles gain velocity and so kinetic energy (heat); they also collide, excite one another, and radiate light.

2

Gravitational collapse converting gravitational energy into heat (kinetic energy) and light.

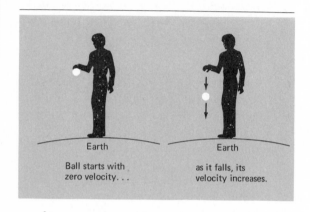

Earth — Ball starts with zero velocity . . .

Earth — as it falls, its velocity increases.

1

Conversion of gravitational energy into kinetic energy (energy of motion) by the fall of a mass.

Instead of a single ball, picture a cloud of gas that contains a large number of atoms (Fig. 2). Each can be thought of as the preceding ball. Imagine the cloud contracting gravitationally, from the combined forces of all the atoms in it. As the cloud contracts, the atoms gain velocity. Though the velocities might initially all be directed generally inward, collisions among the atoms will soon distribute the velocities in random directions. So the atoms' kinetic energy of random motion increases. Because temperature is a measure of the average kinetic energy of random motion of the atoms (Focus 30), the tem-

perature of the gas also increases. Meanwhile the density is also increasing as the atoms come together. With this increase in the velocity of the particles and the density of the gas, the number of atomic collisions increases. These collisions excite some atoms. When the excited electrons drop to the lower energy, radiation is emitted. Net result of gravitational contraction: Some of the initial gravitational potential energy is converted to thermal energy, and some is emitted as radiation. In fact, exactly one-half goes into thermal energy (heat) and the other half ends up as radiative energy (light).

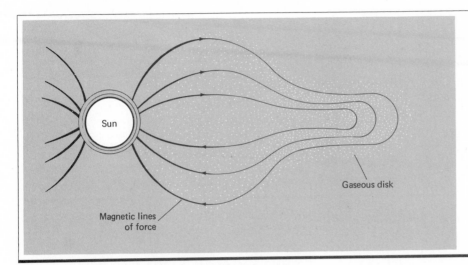

12.19

The primeval solar magnetic field (side view looking at the sun's equator). The field lines go out from the sun into the ionized gas in the primeval nebula.

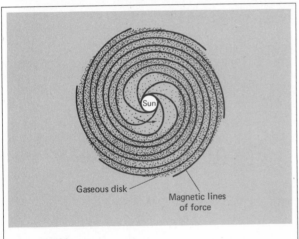

12.20

Top view of the primeval solar magnetic field. The field lines are locked into the ionized gas close to the sun. One end of the field rotates with the sun, and the other end is dragged by the material in the disk. So the field lines curl up on themselves and also push along the disk material in the same direction as the sun rotates. Some of the sun's spin is transferred out to the nebula.

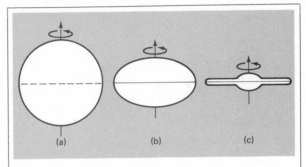

12.21

The collapse of the primeval nebula. When the collapse begins (a) the interstellar cloud has a diameter of about 1 ly. The cloud's material falls mostly parallel to its spin axis to form a disk (b). At the end of the collapse (c), the disk has a diameter of about 60 AU and a thickness of about 1 AU.

agree with the present orbital inclinations of the planets, the disk must have spread out at the edges, where gravity was the weakest (Fig. 12.22). At the center, the thickness of the nebula was about 0.5 AU; at the edges, 20–30 AU from the center, the thickness was about 1 AU. Here the temperature was only about 100–200 K.

The high temperatures at the center vaporized any dust there. As the nebula cooled, new dust grains condensed from the gas. The composition of the new grains depended on the temperature where they formed. Metallic grains formed close to the center. So the hot interior of the nebula filled with grains of terrestrial materials (Table 12.1); farther out, where the temperatures were lower, icy grains formed along with terrestrial and metallic ones. This condensation at different temperatures explains the terrestrial–Jovian compositional split. These condensed grains were small. By accretion they could form pebble-sized objects. These heavy

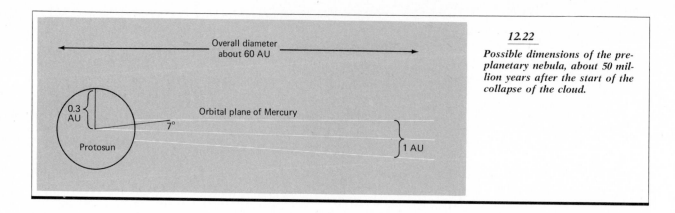

12.22

Possible dimensions of the pre-planetary nebula, about 50 million years after the start of the collapse of the cloud.

particles quickly fell into the plane of the nebula to form a very thin disk of solids in a thicker disk of gases.

Somehow these particles accreted into planetesimals. These bodies—perhaps as large as a kilometer in size—combined to form larger bodies, called the *protoplanets*. Meanwhile the sun ignited its fusion fires. The young sun blew off material that swept away large amounts of leftover gas and dust. This sweeping out requires that the nebula must have contained at least 0.1 solar mass, and maybe as much as 1 solar mass.

Is there any observational evidence for the formation of dusty nebulas around stars? Yes, a little. Infrared observations of young stars (Section 19.5) indicate that dust surrounds them. From the conservation of angular momentum (Focus 26), you expect that the dust forms a disk. Recent infrared polarization observations of suspected massive protostars, some done by Paul Heckert, myself, and other infrared astronomers also imply that the dust grains orbit the youngest of these in disks rather than in spherical shells.

The rest of this chapter focuses on the details of the processes that formed the planets. But be forewarned! Many competing models exist, and no one to date is completely satisfactory, which leads to a lot of confusion. To quote William K. Hartmann, a worker in the field: ". . . there is not yet a unified, well-accepted modern theory of planet formation . . ."

12.5

The formation of the planets

Much research work in the 1970s has focused on the complex problem of how to get planet-sized objects out of dust grains. That's no easy task!

How do the planets grow? A protoplanet model includes at least three stages for planetary growth. In the first stage, turbulence in the nebula helps the growth of planetesimals. Second, the protoplanets then grow by direct collision and accretion of planetesimals. Third, when they gain enough mass, they gravitationally pull in passing material. In a few million years to hundreds of millions of years a protoplanet's formation is completed.

The chemical condensation sequence / The original protoplanet picture left a crucial detail unanswered: How did the protoplanets acquire differences in chemical composition? Recent research has developed the concept of a *condensation sequence* (Focus 29), an idea first suggested by chemist Harold Urey and worked out in detail by John Lewis and others. Urey noted that the nebula's center must have been hot, a few thousand degrees Kelvin. Here, solid grains, even iron compounds and silicates, could not condense. Elsewhere, what materials would condense as new grains depended on the temperature. Below 2000 K, grains made of terrestrial materials would condense (Table 12.1); below 273 K grains of *both* terrestrial and icy materials could form.

Note that the temperatures reached in the nebula also affect dust grains already in it. Icy grains vaporize wherever (and whenever) the temperature rises above 273 K; terrestrial grains (iron and silicates) evaporate at temperatures of roughly 2000 K. Wherever in the nebula temperatures never hit those of vaporization, the appropriate grains remained.

Recent research has reached even more

focus 29

THE CHEMICAL CONDENSATION SEQUENCE

The condensation sequence (Table 12.4) is an important element in the contemporary picture of the solar system's formation. It explains to a reasonable degree the differences in composition of the planets.

The most obvious fact of this difference is the two general classes of planets, Jovian and terrestrial. Overall, as you move out from the sun, the amount of volatile substances increases with respect to nonvolatile ones. This general trend is evidence that the Jovian planets formed farther out in the nebula, where the temperatures were lower.

But that's not the only chemical differences among the planets. For example, all of the terrestrial planets have different compositions. Can this also be tied in to their distances from the sun and so to the temperatures at which they are formed? Yes, according to the condensation sequence idea. (Actually, there are two basic condensation sequence theories. I'll present only one of them, the one that assumes there were no substantial changes in the temperature of the nebula while the planets were accreting. In other words, planetary accretion took place faster than the nebula cooled.)

Start out with a temperature of about 2000 K in the solar nebula. (This is about the lowest temperature at which all the materials will be vaporized.) The first compounds to condense out in this model would be compounds of calcium oxide (CaO), aluminum oxide (AlO_3) and rare earth oxides (Table 12.4). Next, starting at about 1500 K, an iron-nickel material similar to that found in iron meteorites would condense. In the next step, silicates, such as those found in stony meteorites and the rocks on the earth's surface, would form. In particular, various kinds of feldspars, a mineral commonly found in rocks, would be made. When the temperature dropped to 680 K, hydrogen sulfide gas (H_2S) would act on iron to form the mineral triolite (FeS). Any leftover iron would combine with oxygen and silicon to make minerals such as olivine (Fe_2SiO_4), a dark mineral common in the rocks that make up the lunar maria. Below 170 K, argon gas freezes. At 10 K, neon and helium condense. It is unlikely that temperatures in the solar nebula were any lower than this.

The composition of carbonaceous chondrites supports this model. The chondrites are probably samples of the primordial solid stuff in the solar nebula, and can be examined in the lab. The mineral triolite (FeS) is found in almost all chondrites. The mineral olivine is also common. In addition, some chondrites contain large amounts of volatiles, especially water. These characteristics of chondrites are just those expected from the condensation sequence model.

specific conclusions about the sequence in which compounds could condense from a heated nebula (Table 12.4). At different temperatures the gases available and the solids previously formed react chemically to produce a variety of compounds. Here's the key result of the condensation sequence: The densities and compositions of the planets can be well explained with the condensation sequence *if* the temperature in the nebula fell off *sharply* from the center outward. Then at different distances from the sun, the different temperatures allowed different chemical compounds to condense and form grains that eventually made up the protoplanets. If a material could not condense because the temperature was too high, it would not end up in the protoplanet. For instance, the terrestrial planets lack the icy and gaseous materials common in the Jovian planets because at their close distances to the sun, the temperatures were too high for the condensation of icy and gaseous materials. In contrast, the Jovian planets pretty much reflect the original composition of the nebula (and cosmic abundances in general).

Some recent calculations by A. G. W. Came-

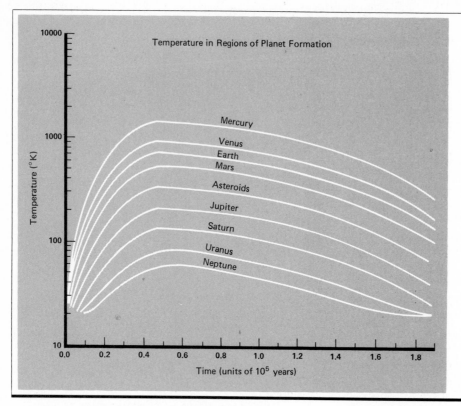

12.23

Possible temperatures in the preplanetary nebula. As the nebula collapses, the temperatures within it rise, level off, and then fall. Each curve gives the temperature with time for the distance from the sun where we expect each planet to form. (Adapted from a diagram and calculations by A. G. W. Cameron)

ron show how temperatures might differ in the solar nebula at different places and times (Fig. 12.23). His models indicate that the nebula starts out cool (less than 100 K), increases in temperature until a maximum is hit in about 50,000 years, then declines. The key point to note here is how the maximum temperatures decrease with increasing distance from the sun: For the region of the formation of Mercury, the temperature reaches about 1500 K; for Mars, about 500 K; and for Uranus, about 70 K. This drop off with time and distance from the sun is necessary for the condensation sequence to work out. Note that this evolution of the nebula's temperature implies that the grains of terrestrial materials survive except within the orbit of Mercury. Grains of the ices survive outside the orbit of Mars.

This condensation sequence predicts in detail chemical differences among the terrestrial and Jovian planets. Let me take Mercury, the earth, and Mars for comparison. At Mercury's distance, the temperature would be low enough for nickel-iron and silicates of magnesium to con-

dense, along with oxides of uranium, potassium, and thorium. The condensates of the radioactive elements provide one source of heating; accretion provides another. These heating sources drive the differentiation of the protoplanet. The resulting protoplanet would have a large nickel-iron core and a mantle of such silicates; Mercury does have such an interior structure (Section 9.7).

At the earth's distance the temperature is considerably lower, about 600 K. Here, silicates of both iron and magnesium could condense, along with iron oxide and iron sulfide. Water would be bound up with minerals, perhaps as much as 5 percent of the total. So the model predicts a planet with a smaller nickel-iron core than Mercury's containing sulfur (in the form of iron sulfide) and a larger mantle, rich in silicates and oxides of iron and magnesium. The earth does appear to have such an interior (Section 8.2).

What about Mars? Here the temperature was lower still. The resulting core would consist mostly of iron sulfide, not nickel-iron, and the

TABLE 12.4 *Equilibrium condensation sequence in the solar nebula*

Temperature (K)	Reactions
1600	Condensation of metals combined with oxygen (oxides)
1300	Condensation of iron-nickel
1200	Condensation of silicates
1000	Reaction of sodium with silicates and aluminum oxide to form common minerals such as feldspar
450–1200	Combination of iron and oxygen to form iron oxide, becoming olivine
680	Combination of iron with sulfur to form triolite (FeS)
425–550	Combination of water vapor with minerals such as olivine
175	Condensation of water ice
150	Reaction of ammonia (NH_3) with water ice
120	Reaction of methane (CH_4) with water ice
20–65	Condensation of inert elements such as argon and neon
1	Condensation of helium

mantle would be olivine, rich in iron oxide and water. We don't know the interior of Mars very well, but the prediction from the condensation sequence agrees with our general inferences about the Martian interior (Section 10.5).

Note that it is how *low* the temperature falls that determines the reactions to produce the condensates. For example, at the earth's position in the nebula, all the reactions in Table 12.4 down to 600 K can take place. The reactions at temperatures lower than 600 K do not happen.

In general, the condensation sequence requires a certain minimum temperature to be reached in order to account for the known chemical composition of the planets. Roughly, these temperatures are 1400 K for Mercury, 900 K for Venus, 600 K for the earth, 400 K for Mars, and 200 K for Jupiter.

The condensation sequence correctly predicts that Mercury has a larger, denser core than the earth and that Mars has a smaller, less dense one. Such successes imply that the compositions of the planets did arise from simple chemical reactions between the gas and dust in the nebula—reactions whose results depended on the local temperature.

The aggregation of the planets / How do you get from small dust grains to large protoplanets? If grains collide, they stick together and so accrete to form larger, perhaps pebble-sized, objects. These quickly fall into the plane of the nebula. These pebbles then accumulate into planetesimals.

Peter Goldreich and William Ward have proposed a model that gets the pebbles together into planetesimals. They have found that a thin disk of pebbles quickly fragments so that pebbles accumulate gravitationally into planetesimals a few kilometers in size. Whatever materials happen to be available at a certain distance from the center of the nebula make up a planetesimal. So the planetesimals reflect the compositions established by the condensation sequence.

Once the planetesimals have formed, they might gather into larger bodies, perhaps almost as large as the moon. Somehow (details as yet unknown!) these objects finally end up in a few protoplanets. Here gravity would help. Once the planetesimals have gathered (in a few tens of thousands of years) into a few somewhat larger bodies (500 km in size), their masses would be enough to help pull in other smaller masses from a distance. So a growing planet will sweep clear a zone of the nebula in order to feed its mass. For the terrestrial planets to grow to their present sizes, calculations indicate an aggregation time of roughly 10^8 years.

When the central regions of the nebula finally form the sun, an intense solar radiation pressure and a strong solar wind (a solar gale!) push leftover gases out of the solar system.

The leftover planetesimals bombard the planetary surfaces, leaving remnant craters on the terrestrial planets. This bombardment heats the surfaces of the planets. Radioactive decay heats the interiors and melts them. Dense elements, such as iron and nickel, sink down to form a core. Less dense materials, such as silicates, float to form surface froth that cools to become the crust. So the planets become differentiated in their interiors.

Jupiter and Saturn—A different story? To make matters somewhat confusing, Jupiter and Saturn may have formed in a different way from the planetesimal accretion model just described. In analogy with starbirth (Chapter 19), Jupiter and Saturn may have condensed gravitationally from single large blobs of material in the nebula, rather than by accretion of planetesimals. In fact, the chemical compositions of Jupiter and Saturn match those of stars fairly closely. The main difference arises from the fact that Jupiter and Saturn don't have enough mass to get hot enough to ignite fusion reactions. The heat they do gain comes from the conversion of gravitational potential energy into heat during gravitational contraction (Focus 28).

Harold Graposke and colleagues have made theoretical calculations of the evolution of Jupiter from a hot beginning, after the proto-Jupiter had come together gravitationally. They assume a solar mixture of material (74 percent hydrogen, 24 percent helium, and 2 percent everything else) and start the calculations with a proto-Jupiter 16 times Jupiter's present size, a central temperature of 16,000 K, a surface temperature of about 1000 K, and a luminosity of almost 10^{-2} the sun's present luminosity. Gravity quickly pulls in the proto-Jupiter. In only a million years the planet shrinks to just about twice its present size, its central temperature is about 40,000 K (the interior is heated by the gravitational contraction), and its luminosity drops to about 10^{-5} the sun's luminosity. The shrinking then slows down because the planet's interior is liquid, and liquids are difficult to compress. In the next 4.5 billion years Jupiter contracts to its present size and its central temperature drops to 16,000 K as it loses some of its heat of formation to space at a rate of 1.8×10^{-9} times the solar luminosity.

Saturn followed a similar evolutionary sequence. Now it emits only 8×10^{-11} the sun's luminosity, and its central temperature has dropped to 7000 K. This is enough to show up as an excess of infrared energy emitted by Saturn of at least 45 percent more than the total energy it receives from the sun.

The early high luminosity of Jupiter may explain, in the context of a condensation sequence, why the Galilean satellites decrease in density going outward from Jupiter (Section 11.2). This density decrease implies, for example, that Callisto contains proportionally more icy materials than Io. At Io's closer distance, less ice condensed than at Callisto's distance. If Jupiter were hot at the time of the satellites' formation, the inner ones would not have accreted as much icy materials as the outer ones. So the Galilean moons may mimic the condensation and accretion of the terrestrial planets.

In fact, the evolution of Jupiter and Saturn may follow that of the solar system generally. Their rings may be unaccreted material.

The asteroids: A planet that didn't make it? Contemporary research on asteroids has provided new clues about their origin. It seems likely that asteroids are planetesimals that just didn't get together to make a planet—rather than the popular idea that they are remnants of a planet that exploded.

What are these clues? First, we have an idea of the surface compositions of the larger asteroids. Some reflect light in a way characteristic of basaltic rocks (such as those that cover the lunar maria and the earth's ocean basins), and others are much darker, indicating that they contain a substantial percentage of carbon compounds. (In fact, the darkest of these reflect about the same amount as a lump of coal.) These asteroids resemble a class of carbonaceous meteorites that are dark because they contain carbon compounds (roughly 1–5 percent carbon).

Second, the lighter-colored, rocky asteroids tend to be found in the inner part of the asteroid belt and the darker ones, in the outer regions. At the belt's outer edge about 80 percent of the asteroids are dark ones. It's reasonable to believe that these compositional differences across the belt reflect differences in the primitive material that condensed to form the asteroids. Since their creation, the asteroids' orbits have not changed very much.

These reflectivity differences fit in nicely with the condensation sequence (Focus 29). At the inside of the belt the temperatures were low enough for rocky materials to condense but too high for carbon-bearing materials to do so. Farther out, both types of materials condensed to end up in planetesimals.

Why didn't they form a planet? Probably

12.24

Chondrules. These are probably the most primitive solid objects made in the formation of the solar system. (Courtesy F. L. Whipple and the Smithsonian Astrophysical Observatory)

because of the gravitational effects from the proto-Jupiter. Recent theoretical calculations indicate that the proto-Jupiter (and the proto-Saturn) formed quickly—in a time as short as perhaps a few months. Their formation happened fast simply because a lot of material gathered together, which drew in more material, and so on. Once the proto-Jupiter had formed, it would tug on the planetesimals just within its orbit. Meanwhile the Sun would pull these planetesimals toward it. In this tug-of-war, the orbits of the planetesimals changed from circular to elliptical. Some crashed into others, shattering them into smaller pieces. Some of these pieces caromed into the inner part of the solar system and eventually rained onto the surfaces of Mercury, Venus, the moon, Earth, and Mars—you can see some of these bombarded regions today. The remainder of the broken planetesimals stayed in the region about 3 AU from the sun—these remnants are today's asteroids.

Meteorites and planetesimals / The characteristics of chondritic meteorites (Section 12.1) support the condensation picture. Their chemical composition (similar to the sun) and un-mixed structure suggest that they are the original condensed material of the nebula—either as solids or droplets. They accumulated in planetesimals less than 1000 km in diameter. The chemical composition of chondrules suggest that the bulk of their condensation took place at temperatures around 500–700 K. (According to the condensation sequence, this range produces materials like those that make up the earth.) About a million years after formation, radioactive decay reheated some planetesimals, melting them partially and allowing them to differentiate into iron cores and stony mantles. Other planetesimals did not melt and differentiate and so preserved their droplet structure (Fig. 12.24). The planetesimals that were not gathered into a protoplanet became the parent meteorite bodies. These bodies collided and fragmented to make the pieces that are picked up as meteorites after they fall to the earth.

What happened to other planetesimals? Some may have collided at high speeds with others and disintegrated into small pieces. A few may have passed close enough to a protoplanet to be captured in an orbit as a satellite. Others may have experienced near misses. Their orbits might have changed enough to throw them out of the solar system. Beyond Jupiter, planetesimals would be mostly icy materials; these may have formed comets.

The nebular model and observations / How well does this amalgam of contemporary models match up with the chemical and dynamical properties of the solar system?

On the chemical side, it does pretty well. The condensation sequence tied into the nebular model explains how the planets fall into two compositional classes (terrestrial and Jovian), and how planets in the same class differ in detailed chemical composition.

On the dynamical side, the model has some successes and a few failures. Compare the model's results to the features listed in Section 12.2:

1   The planets' revolution and sun's rotation: well explained as the original rotation of the nebula and conservation of angular momentum.

2   Coplanar orbits: well explained by the conservation of angular momentum applied to the nebula's rotation, which requires that it flatten into a disk as it collapses.

3   Satellite systems: well-explained if formed as miniature solar systems.

4   Circular orbits: explained fairly well by the interactions and sweeping up of planetesimals.

5   Planets' rotation: expected from spin of the nebula but not clearly worked out.

6   Angular momentum distribution: decent attempts but weak detailed solution.

7   Planetary ring systems: explained vaguely, like the asteroids, as unaccumulated debris.

SUMMARY

A Possible Scenario of the Solar System's Early History

I say "possible" to emphasize that the story outlined here amalgamates a few, but not all, contemporary ideas. Unmanned exploration of the solar system will provide new information for a more complete model. Also, the calculations needed to back up the details of the models are very difficult to make. Results so far have been only approximate, and some may be just plain wrong. For now, the scenario outlined in this chapter remains tentative and incomplete.

1. Process of Nebular Collapse. *Time: about 4.6 billion years ago. Duration: 10–50 million years. A slowly rotating interstellar cloud of gas and dust collapses gravitationally from a diameter of about 50,000 AU. Mass: maybe as much as a few thousand solar masses. The cloud fragments, and one piece with at least 1.1 solar masses (maybe 2 solar masses), continues to collapse. Pressure and density increase. Rotation rate increases. Cloud forms a disk about 60 AU across and 1 AU thick. Disk heats up more at center (about 2000 K) than at edges (about 100 K). Dust vaporizes near center.*

2. Transfer of Angular Momentum. *Duration: maybe as short as a few thousand years. The sun's magnetic field transfers spin from sun to disk.*

3. Evaporation and Reformation of Grains; Formation of Planetesimals. *Duration: 10^5 years. Grains condense in disk, composition being dependent on temperature. Generally, denser terrestrial materials are near center, icy materials farther out. Grains hit and stick together, forming pebbles a few centimeters across. In a few years pebbles fall into plane. Gravity brings them together as planetesimals, a few kilometers across (Fig. 12.25).*

4. Formation of Protoplanets. *Duration: as much as a few hundred million years. Planetesimals accrete to form protoplanets. Sun forms and heats disk (Fig. 12.25).*

5. Dissipation of the Nebula. *Duration: at most, a few million years. Solar gales and radiation sweep out leftover gaseous material from nebular disk. Violent flares on sun may contribute to the process.*

6. Evolution of Protoplanets. *Time: about 4.5 billion years ago. Duration: a few million years. Inner protoplanets heat up and differentiate. Jupiter and Saturn slow down in their contraction and sharply decline in luminosity.*

7. Formation of the Earth–moon System. *Time: 4.6 billion years ago. Duration: perhaps a few hundred million years. Debris in space near earth accumulates to form moon at a distance of about half the moon's present distance. Leftover chunks of nebular material fall into earth and moon.*

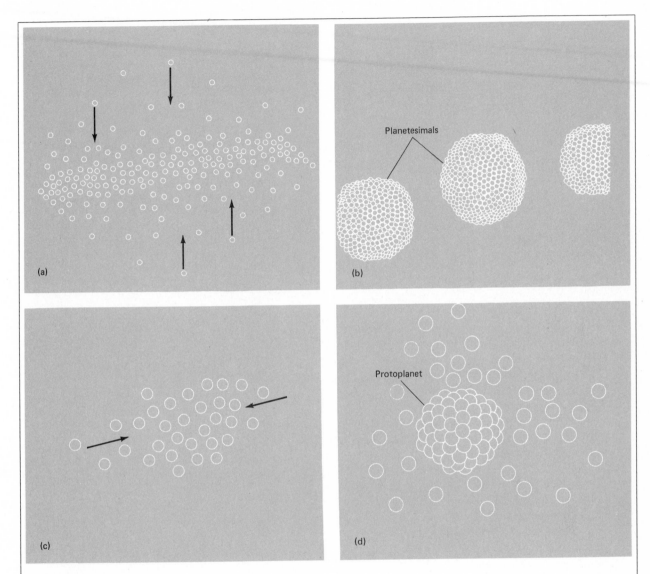

12.25

The formation of the planets: a contemporary model. Dust grains in the nebula collide and stick to form small clumps. These fall into the midplane of the nebula to form a thin disk (a). Gravity pulls these into asteroid-size bodies—the planetesimals (b). These collect by gravity in clusters (c) to make up the cores of the protoplanets (d). (After work by A. G. W. Cameron, adapted from a diagram in Scientific American, *September 1975, copyright 1975 by W. H. Freeman Co.)*

STUDY EXERCISES

1   What was the almost fatal flaw in the original Kant–Laplace nebular theory? (*Objective 4*)

2   What one planet fits least well into the general chemical and dynamical properties of the solar system? Why? (*Objective 1*)

3   What strikes you as the most important objection to any catastrophic theory? (*Objective 3 and 6*)

4   Use the condensation sequence to explain the general chemical differences between the earth and Jupiter. (*Objectives 7 and 8*)

5   Outline the currently accepted sequence of planetary formation. (*Objectives 3, 7, and 10*)

BEYOND THIS BOOK . . .

Up-to-date nontechnical material on the origin of the solar system is hard to come by. I suggest you try, after reading this chapter, "The Origin and Evolution of the Solar System," by A. G. W. Cameron, in *Scientific American*, September 1975, p. 32. An explanation of the condensation sequence is "The Chemistry of the Solar System," by J. Lewis, in *Scientific American*, March 1974, p. 50.

If you'd like to tackle some technical articles, read *On the Origin of the Solar System*, a book of the Centre National de la Recherche Scientifique de France, 1974 (ISBN 2-222-01512-X).

W. Hartmann has a relatively nontechnical review of "The Planet-Forming State: Toward a Modern Theory," in *Protostars and Planets* (University of Arizona Press, Tucson, 1978), edited by T. Gehrels Articles in Part V are also pertinent but more technical; some of their introductions are good.

You have run into many details about the solar system in the previous six chapters. Don't let this wealth of information detour you from the main point: What do the present characteristics of the solar system tell us about its origin and evolution? By now you realize that the details of the "how" have not yet been worked out. But the general scheme does emerge from the information at hand. It shows the formation and evolution of the sun. The closeness in age of the sun, moon, earth, and meteorites implies that the system's formation took place over a short span of time compared with ages of about 4.6 billion years. Planets—on which we expect life—apparently form with a star (or stars). Here we find a crucial connection between the origin of stars and planets, and planets and life—one of the important themes of this book.

The modern view for the formation of the solar system involves a nebular model. The start of the process requires the collapse of a huge interstellar cloud of gas and dust. What starts such a collapse? We really don't know yet. We have evidence for enormous clouds of gas and dust existing between the stars. We can also see young stars that have formed from such clouds. But we don't know what provokes the collapse, or the details of how the material ends up as stars. One point

is clear: Such a formation process ends up with a group of stars or a star with a planetary system. So the fact that stars are common implies that planets are common, too. But we know of only one such solar system—our own.

Since their birth, the planets have evolved—some more than others. The Jovian planets have undergone few significant changes since their formation—essentially they have retained their youthful appearances. In contrast, the terrestrial planets have reshaped their interiors and surfaces and transformed their original atmospheres—those of small mass less so than those of greater mass. And the earth, a restless planet, has changed the most since its formation—its appearance now is radically different from its face and interior at the time of its birth. A large measure of that transformation occurred because life arose on our planet—and no other planet in the solar system, as far as we can tell.

I can't help wondering how many other planetary systems circle other stars in the sky. How many near-stars, such as Jupiter? How many jeweled Saturns? How many barren, dead places such as Mercury? And how many planets like the earth exist—where perhaps my counterpart also dreams of other inhabited worlds?

The Universe of Stars and Galaxies

PART 3

How are the stars arranged in space? Astronomers have only recently been able to answer this question; in fact, no big breakthrough was made until the 1920s. They found that the sun resides in a vast pinwheel of stars that has a diameter of about 120,000 light years. This system of stars—called the Milky Way Galaxy—contains perhaps as many as 100 *billion* other stars, many like the sun. Chapters 14, 15, and 16 deal with the discovery and exploration of the Galaxy. This exploration hinges on an understanding of the physical natures of stars. This knowledge comes from an examination of the nearest star, our sun, so Chapter 13, about the sun, introduces this part.

The universe does not end at the boundary of the Galaxy. Go out some September night and locate the constellation Andromeda—the thin lady in the sky. Now if you are observing from a very dark place, you can see a faint smudge, like a dim cloud, in Andromeda. That light is from another galaxy, a lot like our own. The radiation reaching your eye has been speeding through space for over 2 *million* years! Yet the galaxy in Andromeda is one of the closest galaxies to us.

To look deeper into space you need a telescope. With a telescope you find more galaxies than individual stars. The universe is truly a universe of galaxies. Their general characteristics are described in Chapter 17, along with their importance in marking the expansion of the universe.

When you look at a galaxy, it appears quiet and serene, as if not much is happening. New telescopes (Chapter 6), however, have permitted astronomers to investigate galaxies at many wavelengths (along with the visible). They have found that most galaxies—especially in their centers—violently generate energy (Chapter 18). Some galaxies appear to have suffered cosmic explosions, blasting jets of material outward at almost the speed of light. This other aspect of the universe of stars and galaxies—its violent face—is an important subtheme of cosmic evolution.

Thou disk of the Sun, thou living God! . . .
Thou goest up on the Eastern horizon to
dispense life
To all which thou has created

Ancient Egyptian hymn to the Sun-god

LEARNING OBJECTIVES

After studying this chapter, you should be able to:

1. Outline a contemporary method used to find the sun's distance.

2. Show in detail how to find the sun's size, mass, and density.

3. Describe step by step how astronomers measure the sun's luminosity.

4. Describe at least one method for finding the sun's surface temperature.

5. Describe the appearance of the sun's spectrum when viewed through a spectroscope and what atomic processes make the spectrum.

6. List the sun's two most abundant elements, and tell how these and others have been found.

7. State the type of thermonuclear reactions that are supposed to produce the sun's energy, the conditions required for such reactions to take place, and the input materials and output products of those reactions.

8. Apply Einstein's mass–energy relation to the production of solar energy.

9. Trace the flow of the sun's energy from its core to the earth, and in this sequence describe how the features of the quiet sun result from this energy flow.

10. Present the results of the solar neutrino experiment, and discuss the impact of these results on our understanding of the sun's energy generation.

11. Select one feature of the active sun, describe its characteristics, and explain it in terms of energy flow and magnetic fields.

The sun: Local star

13

CHAPTER 13

CENTRAL QUESTION *How does the sun produce its energy, and how does the flow of this energy outward from its core affect the sun's physical structure?*

Sunlight gives life. All creatures on the earth are children of the sun, for the sun provides essentially all the life-sustaining energy for this planet. The sun now warms the earth and drives the weather cycle. In the past it raised the vegetation that produced our present fossil fuels. When these give out, we will likely turn to the sun directly for our usable energy.

What is the sun? Basically, a hot, huge ball of gas with fierce reactions firing its core. There deep in the heart of the sun, the energy bound up in matter is released. Slowly, over tens of millions of years, that energy (as light) erratically flows to the sun's surface. Free of the sun's material, it flies into space. And 8.3 min later, a very small part of that light strikes the earth, and miracles occur.

For astronomers, the sun is important for reasons in addition to these. Our sun is a star. It has the same basic construction as the other stars in the sky, which are seen directly only as pinpoints of light. How to find out the physical characteristics of these distant lights? By using our sun as a guide. The sun serves as the local laboratory for testing our ideas about stars in general; our understanding of stars hinges on our understanding of the sun.

13.1

A solar physical check-up

How large is the sun (Fig. 13.1)? How massive is it? Before you can tackle such questions, you need an essential fact: How far is the earth from the sun? (You will find throughout the book that a critical question—perhaps *the* critical question in all of astronomy—is finding out the distance to celestial objects.) Other facts can be inferred from an analysis of sunlight without having to know its distance. Here's what can be learned more or less directly about the sun.

How far? The earth's orbit about the sun is elliptical. Its semimajor axis, which is an average earth–sun distance, has a length called one *Astronomical Unit* (abbreviated *AU*). So the earth is one AU from the sun. How large is the AU in some basic physical units, such as kilometers?

Recall that simple angular measurements establish the scale of the solar system in terms of the AU (Section 3.1) and that Kepler's laws (Section 3.3) completely describe the orbital motions of the planets, with AUs as the measur-

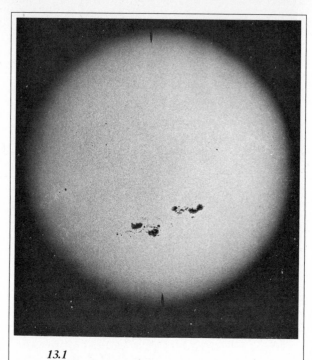

13.1

The sun's photosphere. Note that the photosphere has a granular look. The dark regions are sunspots. (Courtesy Mt. Wilson Observatory, Carnegie Institution of Washington)

ing unit. So at any time, you can draw up a scale map of the solar system, with the planets' positions all neatly laid out in AUs.

To work out the distance scale in kilometers requires that only one segment, known in AUs, be measured in kilometers. An analogy: Suppose you're given a map of your region of the United States with no distance scale in kilometers but laid out in correct relative distances. Hop in your car and drive between two points on the map while keeping a close track of the distance in kilometers between these two points, which are separated on the map by so many centimeters. Then you've found the distance scale in kilometers for the entire map.

To do the same for the solar system, astronomers use the fact that the speed of light is accurately measured in the lab. Then radar signals, which travel at light speed, are bounced off Venus, and the time between transmission and reception is accurately measured. The earth-Venus distance in kilometers at that time of observation is

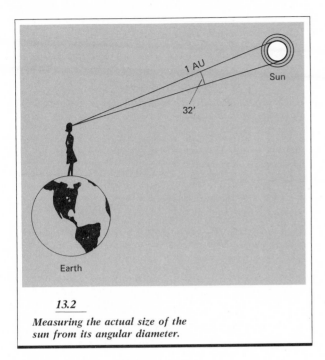

13.2

Measuring the actual size of the sun from its angular diameter.

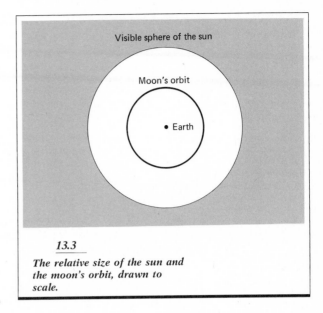

13.3

The relative size of the sun and the moon's orbit, drawn to scale.

$$d = \left(\frac{t}{2}\right)c$$

where d is the distance, c the speed of light (in km/sec), and t the *round trip* travel time of the sign. (We need to divide by 2 to get the one-way travel time.) Kepler's laws give the earth–Venus distance at the measurement time in AUs. So you have a known fraction of an AU in kilometers, and hence the AU in kilometers— 1.496×10^8 km, in fact. (Remember it by rounding off to 150 million km.)

Why bother with bouncing radar off a planet? Why not bounce it off the sun, and measure the AU directly? For two reasons: The sun is itself a powerful radio *source*, and it does not reflect radar signals very well.

How big? Viewed from the earth, the average angular size of the sun is 32'. (That's about $\frac{1}{2}°$, or half the tip of your finger at arm's length.) Because you know the AU in kilometers, you can calculate the sun's actual size from its angular size (Focus 1; Fig. 13.2). The sun's diameter is roughly 1.4 million km, or 109 times the earth's diameter (Fig. 13.3). Imagine the earth the size of a dime. Then the sun would be about 2 m in size and 200 m from the coin-sized earth.

How massive? To find the sun's mass, you use Newton's second law and law of gravitation (Section 4.2 and 4.3), along with the earth's orbital period and distance (which gives the orbital velocity). The sun's mass comes out to about 2×10^{30} kg (Focus 12).

How dense? Density (Focus 21) is a measure of how compressed material is. Because the sun is a sphere, you can easily compute its volume from its size and then divide its mass by its volume to get its average density: 1.4 g/cc. That's only 40 percent denser than water.

Warning: Don't confuse density with mass (or size) alone. For example, the sun is more massive and larger than the earth, yet it has a much lower average density. Why? The sun is a gas whereas the earth is made of solid rocks and metals. In fact, most stars are made of gases (Focus 30).

13.2

Messages from sunlight

Most of what is known about the sun and other stars is information carried by light (Chapter 5). To decode the message of sunlight and starlight takes up much of the ingenuity of astronomers. With the basics about atoms and spectroscopy in mind (Sections 5.2 and 5.3), here's a look at the sun.

Solar energy / The sun's *luminosity* is its total output in radiative energy each second. By the time the radiation reaches the earth, it has

focus 30

ORDINARY GASES

To understand what happens inside the sun and other stars, you must have some idea of how gases behave, because stars are huge balls of gas. Let me describe a simple model for ordinary gases.

A gas consists of particles—atoms, molecules, or ions, or perhaps all of these. Simplify the situation in a real gas by imagining all the particles to be the same—tiny hard spheres. Picture these spheres trapped in a small box. Once set into motion the spheres keep moving, bounding off the walls of the box and colliding with each other (Fig. 1).

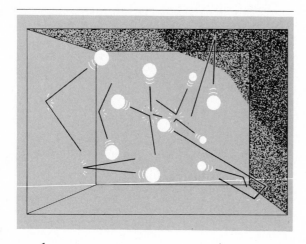

1

Hard-ball model of an ordinary
gas in a box.

Because of all these collisons, any one sphere will at times move faster or slower; but over some time the sphere has a definite average speed. Also because of collisions, all the spheres in the box have the same average speed. Physicists use this average speed of the particles in a gas as a measure of its **temperature.** *If all the particles were motionless, a gas's temperature would be zero. At room*

temperature, *about 300 K, the average speed is about 3 km/sec. Higher temperatures mean higher average speeds of the particles.*

Suppose you put a partition into the gas container. The spheres ram and bounce off both sides of this partition; each collision exerts a small force on it. The combined force of all collisions is the **pressure** *of the gas. Imagine you increased the temperature of the gas. The average speed of the particles increases, so they collide with each other and into the partition more frequently and with greater force. The pressure increases. How, in relation to the increase in temperature? For ordinary gases the increase is a direct one. So if you double the temperature, the pressure doubles.*

What happens to the pressure if you increase the number of particles in the box? (You've done this if you've pumped up a bicycle tube, for then you forced more air particles into it.) Adding more particles to the same space increases the density of particles; that is, on the average, each cubic centimeter contains more particles. For a gas, the number of particles in a cubic centimeter is called the **number density.** *Suppose you increased the number density four times without changing the temperature. Each cubic centimeter now contains four times as many particles. So four times as many collisions occur, on the average, against the partition, and each collision has the same average force as before. The pressure increases—it is four times greater. Increasing the number density directly increases the pressure of an ordinary gas.*

This hard-sphere model shows us that gas pressure depends directly on both the number density and the temperature.

In algebraic form this relationship is

$$P = 1.38 \times 10^{-22} nT$$

where T is the temperature in Kelvins, n is the number density in a cubic centimeter, and P is the pressure in atmospheres (sea level pressure on the earth).

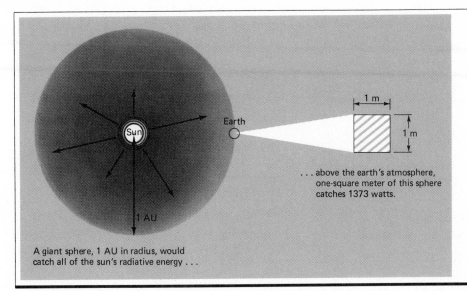

13.4
Measuring the sun's luminosity from the earth.

1 m

1 m

. . . above the earth's atmosphere, one-square meter of this sphere catches 1373 watts.

A giant sphere, 1 AU in radius, would catch all of the sun's radiative energy . . .

Sun

Earth

1 AU

spread out across an enormous area in space—the area of a sphere with a radius of 1 AU. So you cannot measure directly the sun's luminosity.

So how can the sun's luminosity be found? Take a special detector in a satellite orbiting the earth. (Why? Because the earth's atmosphere absorbs some sunlight.) Point the detector directly at the sun. Measure the radiant energy absorbed by the detector: It amounts to 1373 W for each square meter of the detector's area. So on a surface 1 AU in radius (an imaginary sphere surrounding the sun), every square meter catches this amount of energy (Figure 13.4). Totaled up over the entire surface, the energy amounts roughly to 3.8×10^{26} W. That's enough power to light 3.8×10^{24} hundred-watt light bulbs.

The earth intercepts only a small part of this energy. At most 1 kW falls (on a clear day in New Mexico) on a square meter of the earth's surface. In one year the earth's surface actually receives about 10^{18} kilowatt-hours (kWh). At the rate of 5¢ per kilowatt-hour, the solar energy hitting the earth each year would cost 5×10^{16}.

Geological evidence indicates that the sun's luminosity has not varied more than 30 percent over the past 3.5 billion years. Satellite measurements show that it does not vary now more than a tenth of a percent (but even this small change may still affect the earth's climate).

Long-term observations imply a variation of only 0.25 percent during the past 50 years.

The sun's surface temperature / The sun's color (basically white) provides a handle for finding its surface temperature. That is, you can assign a temperature to the sun's surface by examining its continuous spectrum (Focus 16).

To see how, consider heating a piece of metal in a very hot flame. At first the metal emits a dull red light. Then, as it gets hotter, it glows more brightly red, then orange, yellow, yellow-green, white—until it finally glares blue-white hot. So the overall color change in the visible region of the spectrum relates to the temperature of the metal. Which is another way of saying that a metal's continuous spectrum changes with temperature.

How do color and continuous spectra relate? Consider the metal's emission in some detail (Fig. 13.5). Measure the brightness at a range of wavelengths (from ultraviolet to infrared) for the metal at different temperatures. That is, plot the metal's spectrum. Note three features in these spectra: (1) the emission *peaks* at some wavelength, (2) the peak shifts to *shorter* wavelengths as the metal gets hotter, and (3) the metal emits *more* intensely at *all* wavelengths at *higher* temperatures.

Notice that your eye, because it responds only to the visible region of the spectrum (violet to red), sees only a small portion of the complete spectrum. (For example, your eye doesn't

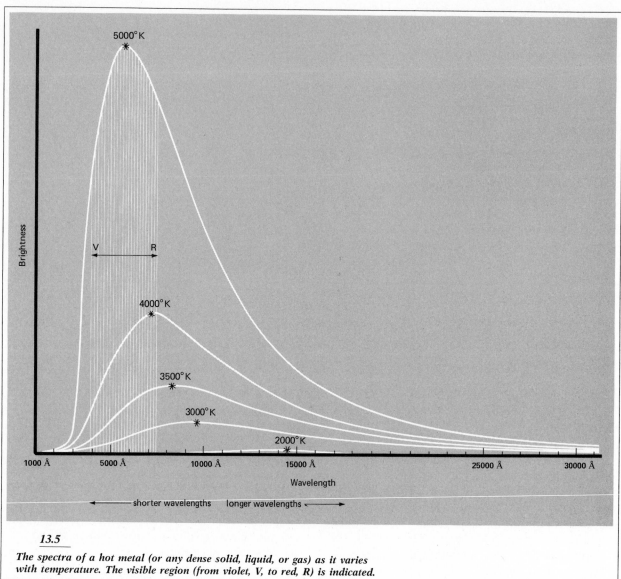

13.5

The spectra of a hot metal (or any dense solid, liquid, or gas) as it varies with temperature. The visible region (from violet, V, to red, R) is indicated.

sense any of the infrared emission.) Yet, for the temperature range considered here, your eye does reasonably discern the shift in the balance of colors at the peak emission.

An object whose spectrum has the shape shown in Figure 13.5 and the variation with the temperature previously described is called a *blackbody radiator* or simply a blackbody (Focus 31). The radiative output and spectrum of a blackbody depend only on its temperature and not on other properties (such as composition). Perfect blackbodies do not actually exist, but the sun (and other stars) emit radiation some-

what like an ideal blackbody. The wavelength at which a star's continuous spectrum peaks relates to its temperature (Focus 31): The *higher* the temperature is, the *shorter* the wavelength of the peak will be.

One often confusing point about blackbodies: How come they are called "black" when they give off light? Blackbodies are so named from their light-absorbing abilities; they absorb light at any wavelength completely and reflect none. (If you beam light at the sun, none would reflect back.) When a blackbody absorbs radiative energy, it heats up and emits at all wave-

focus 31

RADIATION FROM BLACKBODIES

A blackbody is an object that absorbs completely any radiation that falls on it. Because it absorbs energy, a blackbody must heat up and give off radiation. The radiation from a blackbody has a characteristic shape (Fig. 1) that depends only on the temperature of the body and not on anything else, such as its composition. You can think of a blackbody as an energy homogenizer. For example, suppose that it absorbs the energy from many bright spectral lines. The blackbody heats up and emits radiation that has a characteristic shape with no trace of lines.

A blackbody has a number of special characteristics. First, a blackbody with a temperature greater than absolute zero emits some *radiation at* all *wavelengths. Second, a hotter blackbody emits* more *energy at* all *wavelengths than does a cooler one. Third, a hotter blackbody emits a* greater proportion *of its radiation at* shorter *wavelengths than a cooler one. And fourth, the total amount of radiation emitted by a blackbody depends on the* fourth power *of its temperature. So if one blackbody is twice as hot as another of the same size, it emits $2^4 = 2 \times 2 \times 2 \times 2$, or 16 times as much energy.*

It is very difficult to make a perfect blackbody. However, the sun and the stars emit radiation almost like a blackbody does, so the above characteristics can be applied to their continuous spectra.

Two of the properties of blackbodies are described by simple equations. One, the amount of energy emitted each second for every square meter of a blackbody at temperature T Kelvins is

$$E = 5.67 \times 10^{-8} \, T^4 \text{ watts (W)}$$

For example, every square meter of the sun's photosphere (5780 K) emits about 6.3×10^7 W.

Second, the wavelength at which the energy output from a blackbody peaks is

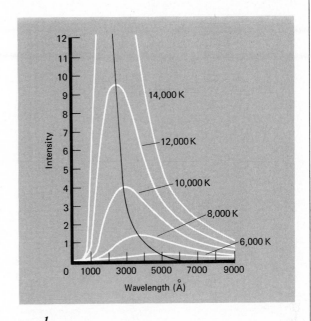

1

The spectrum of a blackbody emitter. Shown here are spectra from blackbodies with temperatures of 6000, 8000, 10,000, 12,000, and 14,000 K. Note the following: (1) The hotter the blackbody is, the shorter will be the wavelength of peak intensity (black line); (2) all blackbodies above absolute zero emit at all wavelengths; and (3) hotter blackbodies radiate more intensely at all wavelengths.

$$\lambda_{max} = 2.9 \times 10^{-3}/T$$

where T is the temperature in Kelvins and λ_{max} is the wavelength, in meters, at which the peak output occurs. For the sun the peak for a temperature of 5780 K is about 4.9×10^{-7} m, or 4900 Å.

Note that both these equations can be used to infer the sun's surface temperature. To use the first you need to find out how much energy each square meter of the surface puts out. For the second you have to determine at what wavelength the sun's spectrum peaks. These methods of determining temperature can be applied to other stars.

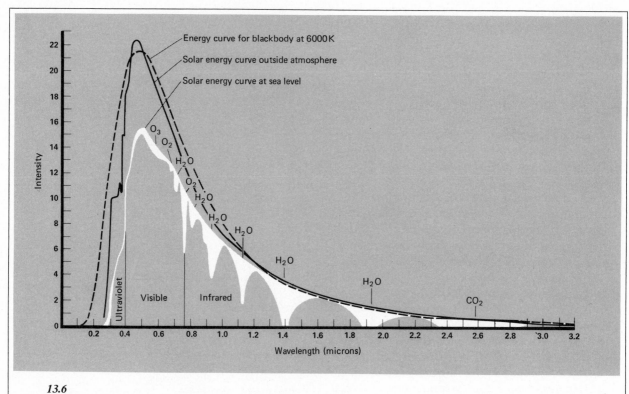

13.6

The absorption of the sun's radiation by the earth's atmosphere. The sun's radiation measured above the earth's atmosphere is indicated by the solid line. (Note how close this curve comes to a blackbody at 6000 K; this shows that the actual energy output closely resembles that of a theoretical blackbody.) The shaded curve shows the actual measured spectrum at sea level. It is indicated whether carbon dioxide (CO_2), water (H_2O), or ozone (O_3) is responsible for the absorption.

lengths, even though the peak of emission may not be visible to our eyes. Physically, a good absorber, when heated, is a good radiator.

Examine the sun's continuous spectrum (Fig. 13.6), as measured at the earth's surface. Note that when the spectrum is measured at sea level, the earth's atmosphere absorbs parts of it—especially the ultraviolet (absorbed by ozone, O_3) and the infrared (absorbed by water vapor and carbon dioxide). However, because very little of the visible light is absorbed, you can determine that the spectrum peaks at about 0.5 microns (5000Å). Without the atmospheric absorption (Fig. 13.6), the sun's spectrum follows a more or less continuous curve with this one peak in the yellow-green part of the spectrum. To produce this peak requires a surface temperature of about 5800 K.

Opacity / If the sun's continuous spectrum has a blackbody shape, then the region emitting must be a good absorber of light. What does the absorbing?

To see this point, you need to understand the concept of *opacity*. On a clear day you can see to far distances (many kilometers) through the air. The air is transparent to light; its opacity is low. On a very foggy day you can't see far at all. The air is opaque to light.

What makes a gas opaque? Interactions of light with atoms and electrons. When a photon is absorbed, it no longer exists and so can't carry energy any farther. The photon's energy is not destroyed—it has just been transferred to an electron. When the electron loses the energy, it emits a photon. But—and this is the key point—that photon can be emitted in *any* direction, in-

cluding back in the direction from which it originated. It heads off and moves only a short distance before it is absorbed. When another
photon is reemitted, it probably zips off in a different direction. So photons in an opaque gas
travel very short distances before they are absorbed. In a gas of lower opacity they travel
greater distances.

The opacity of a gas relates to how far photons can travel, on the average, between absorptions. It depends on how much of the absorber
is there (its density) and how effectively it absorbs.

Back to the sun. If the sun emits like a
blackbody, its outer layers of material must be
opaque to light. What produces this opacity? It
turns out to be a very strange type of hydrogen
ion: a *negative hydrogen ion.* (Recall, Section
5.3, that ions typically have *positive* charges because of the loss of one or more electrons.) At a
temperature of about 6000 K a hydrogen atom
can pick up a *second* electron and so have a net
negative charge. However, this extra electron is
not tightly bound to the nucleus. It can absorb
light efficiently in the visible and infrared regions of the spectrum.

If the layer where the gases become opaque
in the visible region of the spectrum defines the
visible surface of the sun, that layer is only
100–200 km thick and has a temperature of
5800 K. It is the sun's photosphere ("sphere of
light"), that part of the sun you see when you
look at it directly.

The solar absorption-line spectrum / Recall
(Section 5.3) that a spectroscope shows the solar
spectrum to consist of a continuous spectrum
crossed with dark lines. How, in detail, is this
spectrum produced?

To see how, you must use the concept of
opacity again. Consider the transition that produces the 4383 Å line of iron (Fig. 13.7). The
absorption or emission of this line is not infinitely narrow. It has a finite width, centered on
4383 Å, where the iron atom absorbs very well.
At somewhat shorter or longer wavelengths—say,
4379 Å or 4387 Å—the iron atom can still absorb
light, but not as well. In other words, a gas containing iron has a much higher opacity for 4383 Å
photons (at line center) than for those with
wavelengths a few Ångstroms shorter or longer.

In the photosphere the opacity at the centers of lines traps the photons. They travel very

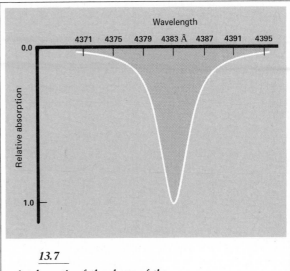

13.7

*A schematic of the shape of the
4383 Å iron absorption line in
the sun's spectrum. The line is
darkest at its central wavelength and less dark (less able
to absorb) at wavelengths away
from the central one.*

short distances and so have little chance of escaping into space. The density of the photosphere drops rapidly from bottom to top. So the
opacity decreases, as fewer atoms are available
to do the absorbing. Eventually, it falls enough
for photons, even at the wavelengths of line
centers, to escape.

As a result, the absorption lines form at *different levels* in the photosphere. At line center,
where the opacity is high, the light emerges
from higher up in the photosphere, where the
gas is cooler and emits less intensely. Off the
line center, where the gas is more transparent,
the light emerges from lower, hotter layers,
which emit more intensity. So a line is
brighter—less dark—away from its center.

Note again that absorption lines are *not*
perfectly black, containing *no* energy. They are
only dark relative to continuous emission at
neighboring wavelengths.

In the photosphere, the temperature rises
quickly as you go down in the photosphere: a
few thousand Kelvins in a few hundred kilometers. It is this sharp temperature change that
results in the sun's dark-line spectrum. Also
note that the photosphere's pressure amounts to
about 10^{-2} that at the earth's surface, and its

density is only 10^{-3} that of the earth's atmospheric density.

Astronomers have analyzed more than 20,000 lines in the solar spectrum to find the chemical composition of the atmosphere. The intensity of the dark lines from a particular chemical element relates to how much of that element is found in the atmosphere. The line's intensity also depends on the temperature and density in the photosphere. Iron produces many of the absorption lines; others come from hydrogen, calcium, and sodium.

Identifying particular elements is a straightforward job. But it's a harder task to find out an element's actual abundance. To determine the abundance you need to know how atoms of a particular element absorb and emit light. Then you must make up a model of the sun's photosphere. You can construct this model from theoretical calculations and basic physical concepts; it consists of a list of different temperatures, densities, and pressures at different depths in the photosphere. Then add some amount of the element, and calculate how intense its absorption lines must be. Try to match the calculated intensity to the observed intensity by playing with different values of the abundance. A match between observed and calculated intensities gives the correct abundance.

Warning: This procedure gives you only the abundance in the *photosphere;* it does not tell you directly the abundance in the *interior.*

Most of the 92 naturally occurring elements have been definitely identified in the solar spectrum. Most of the atmosphere's mass is hydrogen (68 percent) and helium (31 percent). All other elements (loosely called "metals" or "heavy elements" by astronomers) make up a mere 1 percent of the sun's mass.

The absence of an element's absorption lines in the visible spectrum is *not* a sure sign that it does not exist in the sun. Perhaps so little of the element is present that it does not produce detectable absorption lines. Or the strongest absorption lines may be in a region of the sun's spectrum unobservable through the earth's atmosphere. Or the temperature of the sun's atmosphere may inhibit the formation of the element's spectral lines. If the conditions are too hot or too cool, the lines do not form.

Helium is a good example. The sun's visible spectrum does not show any absorption lines of helium. Why not? In the photosphere the temperature is too low to excite helium to levels that can absorb photons of visible wavelengths. Above the photosphere the temperature rises to 40,000 K. Here the temperature is high enough to excite helium atoms, and you can find bright lines from helium. In fact, helium (from the Greek word *helios,* "sun") was discovered in the sun's spectrum before it was found on earth. However, there are too few excited helium atoms in this hot region to produce emission lines strong enough to be seen directly in contrast to the bright continuous spectrum, except during a solar eclipse.

13.3
The quiet sun
The designation "quiet" relates to seemingly placid regions on the face of the sun. This word describes those solar phenomena characteristic of large regions for long periods of time; for instance, the steady flow of energy out of the sun. This energy flow, from core to surface and beyond the atmosphere, controls the environment of the quiet sun.

The quiet sun that can be seen directly consists of the sun's outer layers—together known as the atmosphere. Because the sun's atmosphere is a gas, it does not have distinct layers with sharp boundaries. But the atmosphere splits into three substantially different zones based on abrupt changes in temperature: the photosphere, chromosphere, and corona.

Photosphere / The sun's photosphere has a granular structure (Fig. 13.8). The surface has a cobbled appearance, an individual "cobblestone" having an irregular shape about 2000 km across. (This is half the size of the United States!) Each granule has a lifetime of about 10 min. In a time-lapse motion picture sequence the granulation looks like the top of a bubbling pot of oatmeal. You can visualize the photospheric granulation as the top layer of a seething zone where hot blobs of gas spurt to the surface, radiate energy, cool, and flow downward. The boiling photosphere has a region of convection (Focus 32) just below it. Here the outward flow of energy heats the gas and makes it boil. The base of the convection zone is thought to lie at about 0.9 solar radius.

One curious and newly discovered fact about the photosphere: It pulsates in waves

focus 32

ENERGY TRANSPORT: CONDUCTION, CONVECTION, RADIATION

Thermonuclear fires blaze in the sun's center, creating energy. Eventually that energy makes it to the earth. How does the energy get transported from deep in the sun to us?

In general, energy is carried by the processes of conduction, convection, or radiation. If you've ever relaxed in front of a roaring fire, you've experienced all of these. You are directly warmed by the fire's heat, infrared radiation that travels directly from the fire to you to be absorbed by your skin. That's energy transported by radiation. Much of the energy from the fire, however, is wasted up the chimney. The fire heats the air just around it. Air is gas (Focus 30), and the air expands and becomes less dense. Cooler, denser air flows in and pushes the hotter air up—up and out of the house, where it cools off. This transport of energy by mass motions of a gas (or liquid) is convection. Finally, you may have by mistake left the poker in the fire. If you grab the handle without thinking, you yell upon finding it very hot. It got that way from conduction: The poker's atoms that were actually in the fire were heated and so moved around at high speeds. They banged into their neighbors, agitating them. These collided with their neighbors, and so on throughout the poker from one end to the other. The kinetic energy (temperature) was transferred by direct collisions along the poker.

In ordinary stars like the sun, radiation or convection can carry energy along. (Conduction does not play an important role because the sun's material is a gas.) Which process is at work? That depends on the local conditions in the gas. The general rule is this: The transport process that can work most efficiently is the one that does operate. For most of the sun's interior—about 0.9 of the radius—energy flows most efficiently by radiation. Only in the outer 0.1 of the radius does convection come into play. We see the top of this convective zone as the turmoil of the photosphere (Fig. 1). The hot gas bubbling up here radiates, and it is these photons that leap out and through space.

Note that for a large part of the sun's radius, energy is carried by radiation. Why does the situation change? How well radiation transports energy through a material depends on a property of that material known as its opacity. Basically, opacity measures how efficiently a material absorbs photons. In the sun's core, photons travel about 1 mm between absorptions. The gas here is fairly opaque, but radiation is still more efficient than convection for transporting the energy. As photons journey toward the surface, they run into a region where the temperature is low enough so hydrogen atoms form. These suddenly make the gas extremely opaque and dams up the radiation flow—so much so that convection can transport energy more efficiently, and a convection zone forms.

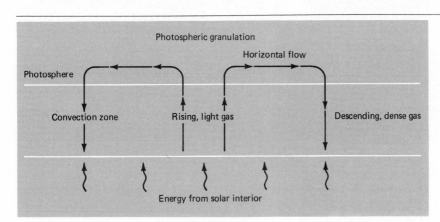

1

Flow of gas in the convective zone of the sun, just below the photosphere. Hotter gas, which is less dense than cooler material, rises to the top of the photosphere. It radiates energy, cools off, and descends.

with a period of about 5 min. In this time the photospheric gases rhythmically rise and fall some hundreds of kilometers over areas 2000 to 3000 km in diameter. These pulsations, like a solar heartbeat, are thought to be caused by low-frequency sound waves generated in the convection zone.

Chromosphere / Just before and after totality in a solar eclipse, a bright, pink flash appears above the edge of the photosphere. This is the chromosphere ("sphere of color"), the solar atmosphere just above the photosphere. The pink color comes from the emission of the first line of the Balmer series (Section 5.3), called H-alpha, in the red region of the spectrum.

A spectroscope directed at the chromosphere during its fleeting appearance shows a bright-line spectrum (Fig. 13.9). The temperature, density, and pressure in the chromosphere determine the intensities of its emission lines. So the line intensities provide clues to the physical conditions there (Color Plate 11).

The chromosphere begins a few hundred kilometers above the photosphere and extends only about two thousand kilometers higher, where it merges into the corona. It is about 1000 times less dense than the photosphere but, surprisingly, gets much hotter. The temperature rises from 4300 K to 10^6 K in the 2500 km of the chromosphere that extends above the photosphere. This rise to high temperatures produces the emission lines from this region.

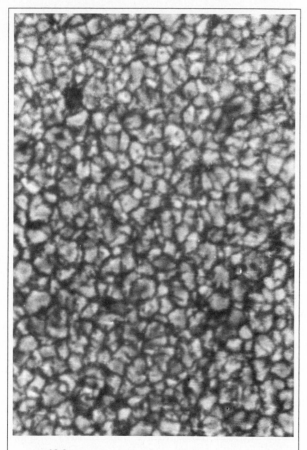

13.8

The granular structure of the sun's photosphere. (Courtesy of the Pic du Midi Observatory, France)

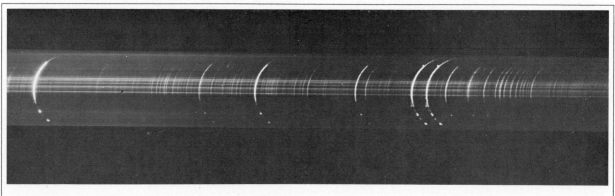

13.9

The bright-line spectrum of the chromosphere, visible just before a total eclipse. Note that the bright spectral lines here are curved. This happens because the curved sliver of the light of the chromosphere acts like a curved slit. (Courtesy Mt. Wilson Observatory, Carnegie Institution of Washington)

13.10

Jets of hot gas along the edge of the sun. These jets, called spicules, transport material and energy from the photosphere to the chromosphere. (Courtesy Mt. Wilson Observatory, Carnegie Institution of Washington)

Their temperatures are about 8000 K. Because of the fountains of spicules, the chromosphere is not a uniform layer. The chromosphere ends—jaggedly—at the tops of the spicules.

Back to why the chromosphere is hotter than the photosphere. The key here may be energy carried by sound waves—regions where the gas is compressed, alternating with where it is rarefied. These sound waves can be generated by turbulence in the sun's convective zone (Focus 32), as it pumps material up through the photosphere. The spicules mark this pumping process. The sound waves give up their energy to the chromosphere when they crash into it. The energy they lose heats up the chromosphere so that most of the chromosphere is hotter than the photosphere. (*Note:* Not all solar astronomers accept this explanation.)

Corona / You can see the sun's splendid corona directly during a total solar eclipse (Fig. 13.11 and the cover photo). Although almost as bright as the full moon, the corona is normally obscured by the sunlight scattered in the earth's atmosphere. During a total eclipse, when the photosphere is blocked out, the sky becomes dark enough for the corona to be visible. Stars and the bright planets can be seen through it.

Spectroscopes show that the corona emits bright lines. These were a mystery for many years. Some astronomers attributed these lines to an element—called coronium—not found on the earth. This was quite upsetting! However, in 1940 the Swedish scientist Bengt Edlén demonstrated that highly ionized atoms of iron, nickel, neon, and calcium, rather than a strange element, produced the emission lines. (Recall, Section 5.3, that when an atom loses an electron, its energy levels change.) Because it takes large amounts of energy to rip many electrons off an atom, the corona must be very hot. For example, to strip iron of 16 of its normal 26 electrons requires a temperature greater than 2 million K. Although Edlén solved the problem of coronium, his solution presented another question: What makes the corona so hot?

Satellites such as Skylab that have observed the sun have provided some evidence for an understanding of the coronal heating. Most of the corona's emission lines arise in the ultraviolet region of the spectrum and so are not visible from the earth's surface. Recall that it takes a certain amount of energy and so a certain tem-

You may be wondering why you don't see emission lines from the chromosphere when you look through it down to the photosphere. The answer: The chromosphere has such a low density that it is essentially transparent to the light passing through it. The photospheric spectrum (continuous and absorption lines) makes it through the chromosphere, which adds only a little emission.

Why is the chromosphere so hot compared with the photosphere? A clue comes from observing it over the edge of the moon just before totality. Large spears of gas called *spicules* (Fig. 13.10) constantly pierce the chromosphere. These jets of hot gas can spurt up to heights of 10,000 km and fade away again in several minutes. They have diameters of about 1000 km.

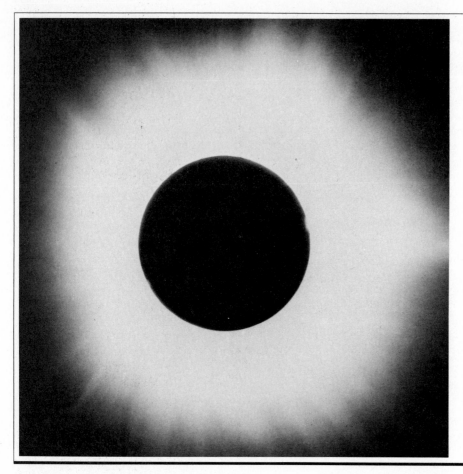

13.11
*The corona during a total
eclipse, Mexico, March 7, 1970.
(Courtesy NASA)*

perature to form ions of various elements. Each
ion of an element can serve as a thermometer
to indicate the temperature in the region from
which emission lines of that ion arise. These
thermometers indicate that at the zone between
the chromosphere and the corona, the temperature jumps sharply—roughly 500,000 K in just
300 km (Fig. 13.12). This abrupt temperature increase resembles the increase in the zone between the photosphere and chromosphere. So it
may result from the same physical process:
transport of energy by sound waves from the
chromosphere to the corona.

This model of sound waves generated by
the convection zone heating the sun's chromosphere and corona has recently hit a snag. The
model predicts that stars with substantial convection zones should have coronas; those without, should not. Because the sun's corona is so
hot, it emits X-rays; other stars with coronas
should also emit X-rays intensely. Those without

will not. Observations by the Einstein Observatory, an X-ray telescope (Chapter 6), show that
all types of stars emit X-rays strongly, and so
have hot coronas—even those stars that were
not thought to have substantial convective
zones.

Solar wind / The corona does not end suddenly but extends into space to distances
greater than indicated by its visual appearance.
The corona moves; it continually flows out from
the sun. How? Because of its high temperature,
the coronal gas exerts a large outward pressure—a greater force than the inward pull of
gravity. As a result, the gas from the corona
streams away from the sun. The gas stream becomes the *solar wind*, so named because of its
high velocity. At the earth's orbit the solar wind
whips by at up to 700 km/sec. The particles in
the solar wind (mostly protons and electrons,
with a number density of a few particles/cc)
travel from the sun to the earth in about five

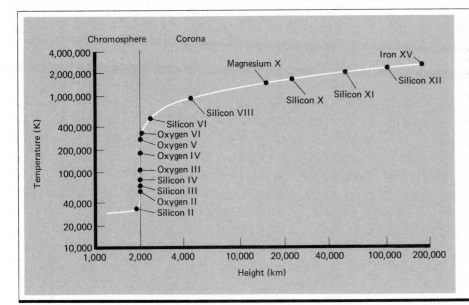

13.12

Ions used to flag temperatures in the corona. Because the corona is very hot, atoms in it are highly ionized. For a given element it takes higher temperatures to ionize it more. So how much a certain element is ionized indicates the temperature at which it is found. Stages of ionization are marked by a Roman numeral next to the element's name; the numeral II, for example, denotes that the atom has lost one electron. Note that the corona's temperature increases rapidly above the chromosphere and then levels out to about 2 million K.

days. (In contrast, light takes 8.3 min.) The earth swims through the solar spray and catches some of the particles in its magnetic field. The solar wind blows out about 10^{-14} solar mass per year; that's only 10^{-8} an earth mass in a year.

13.4
Energy from the solar interior

The interior of the sun contains the bulk of the sun's mass and the furnace that generates its energy. All the features of the quiet sun, from photosphere to solar wind, result from the energy flow from the interior regions where they are produced. How does the sun generate so much energy?

Energy sources / The source of the sun's energy had been a disturbing question for astronomers for about a century. The crux of the problem is not just the rate of energy production but its longevity. The sun has been producing energy for at least 3.5 billion years, according to present geological evidence.

During the nineteenth century, when the earth was found to be very old, the source of the sun's power became an embarrassingly difficult puzzle for physicists to explain. Energy from ordinary chemical reactions, such as burning, could not provide the amount necessary. If the sun were composed entirely of oxygen and coal, it would have burned to a dark cinder in a

few tens of thousands of years. In the middle of the nineteenth century Hermann von Helmholtz (1821–1890) and William Thomson, Lord Kelvin (1842–1907), proposed that the sun shone because it was releasing gravitational energy (Focus 28).

Because of the sun's substantial mass, a contraction rate of only 40 meters a year would liberate the required energy. The gravitational energy stored in the sun would last for about 50 million years, far longer than the earth's age as determined by the nineteenth-century geologists. However, under the impact of Darwin's theory of biological evolution (Chapter 22), later geological investigators pushed the earth's age further and further back, so the resources of gravitational energy were no longer sufficient to account for the sun's shining.

Albert Einstein provided a key idea about the sun's energy at the beginning of this century. Grappling with the fundamental nature of electromagnetic waves, he demonstrated in the special theory of relativity that mass and energy are related by the equation (Section 7.2)

$$E = mc^2$$

where E is the energy (in joules) released in the conversion of mass m (in kilograms), and c is the speed of light (in m/sec). One joule of energy per second is one *watt* of power. Because c^2 is a large number (about 9×10^{16}), a minute

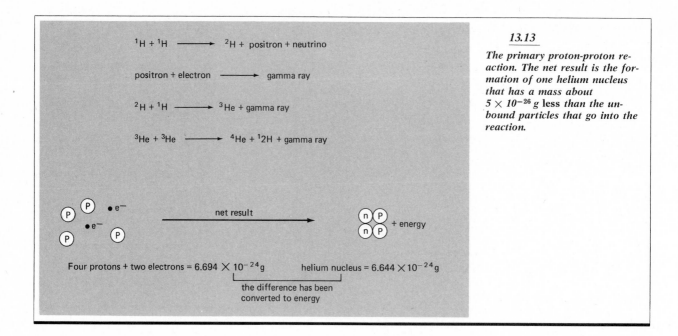

13.13

The primary proton-proton re-action. The net result is the formation of one helium nucleus that has a mass about 5×10^{-26} g less than the unbound particles that go into the reaction.

mass stores enormous energy. For example, the conversion of 1000 kg of matter into energy unleashes roughly the total energy consumption of the United States in one year!

Nuclear transformations / How can matter be changed into energy? Two operations in nature unleash the energy frozen in the nucleus of an atom: *nuclear fission* and *nuclear fusion*. In the process of nuclear fission a nucleus of a heavy element (such as uranium or plutonium) splits into two lighter nuclei. The mass of the remnants adds up to less than that of the original nucleus. The deficit in mass is released as energy. In nuclear fusion the nuclei of lighter elements are fused together to create a nucleus with more protons and neutrons. However, the product has less mass than the original particles that have been put in. This mass has been converted to energy.

It is unlikely that nuclear fission contributes to the solar luminosity because the sun has relatively few heavy elements. In fusion reactions, what atomic nuclei are involved? The natural candidates must meet stringent requirements: (1) Because like electric charges repel, and the greater the charge is, the greater the repulsive force will be, nuclei with small charges are more apt to combine. (2) An adequate supply of the nuclei that serve as fuel must be available. Hydrogen is the most abundant element with

the smallest nuclear charge (one proton). The fusion of hydrogen nuclei results in the production of helium. To make a helium nucleus from hydrogen nuclei releases 4.5×10^{-12} J of energy. That's not much energy; but so many hydrogen nuclei react each second that they easily supply the sun's luminosity.

Two sets of reactions are possible processes for the transmutation of hydrogen to helium: the *proton-proton chain* (*PP chain* for short) and the *carbon-nitrogen-oxygen cycle* (*CNO cycle*). The latter is a minor contributor to the energy of the sun, but it is an important source in more massive stars (Chapter 19). A collision between two protons initiates the PP chain (Fig. 13.13); if these nuclei collide with enough energy (a temperature of at least 8 million K), the protons stick together. A heavy hydrogen (^{2}H) forms, consisting of a proton and a neutron. The other positive charge breaks away as a positron. (A *positron* is the antiparticle of the electron and carries a positive instead of a negative charge.) Almost lost in the shuffle is a neutral, massless particle called a *neutrino*, which zips away at the velocity of light. The dense solar interior offers no barrier to the neutrino's escape, and, in about two seconds, the neutrino breaks into space, carrying away some energy.

In the solar interior the positron quickly collides with an electron, and the two antiparti-

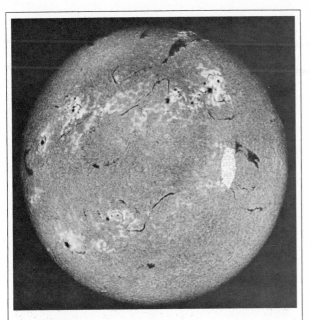

13.24

Prominences, visible in these photos taken in H-alpha light, appear as dark, cloudlike objects against the photosphere. (Courtesy Sacramento Peak Observatory, operated by AURA, Inc.)

material raining down into the photosphere from it while, simultaneously, an infall of gases from the corona replenishes the prominence.

Flares / Sunspots are floating islands of electromagnetic storms. In analogy to terrestrial thunderstorms, these solar storms generate short-lived, violent discharges of energy called *solar flares*. These energetic bursts are usually associated with sunspots and sometimes bridge the gap between two close spots. Near large sunspots about 100 small flares occur each day. The elapsed time between the birth of a flare and its rise to peak intensity is only a few minutes—even for a large flare—and the decay time is about an hour. Emitting myriad forms of energy—X-rays, ultraviolet and visible radiation, high-speed protons, and electrons—a large flare blows off about 10^{25} J, the equivalent of the energy released by a bomb of 2 billion megatons (Fig. 13.25).

Because closely packed sunspot groups are the most likely places for large solar flares, the concentration of flare energy is probably due to local kinks in the magnetic fields. Flares often recur in the same location in active regions and may act as escape valves that release unstable accumulations of energy.

13.25

Material shot off the sun by a solar flare. Along with high-energy radiation and visible light, a solar flare ejects charged particles (mostly protons) into space. (Courtesy NASA)

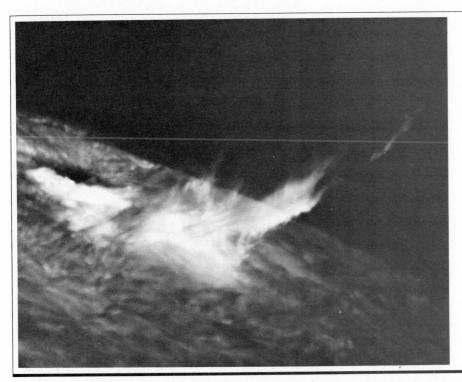

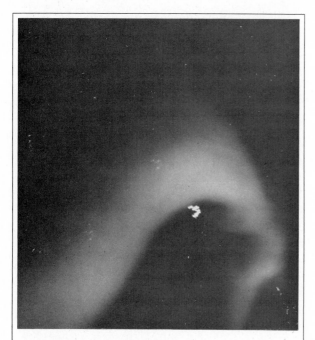

13.26

Aurora in the earth's atmosphere, taken from a NASA aircraft at 40,000 ft. An aurora occurs when charged, energetic particles from the sun excite the earth's upper atmosphere. (Courtesy NASA)

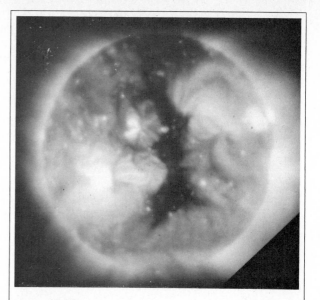

13.27

The sun seen in X-ray light. Very hot regions (a million Kelvins or so) appear bright in this picture, so most of these regions are hot gas in the sun's corona. The looped appearance of streamers in the corona arises from strong magnetic fields. The dark region of the corona at the top pole and running down the middle of the sun's disk is a coronal hole. (Courtesy G. Vaiana, American Science and Engineering, and Harvard College Observatory)

Flares blast energy into the corona and also shoot out energetic particles, mostly protons and electrons, into space. A majority of the flare's energy, however, escapes as X-ray and ultraviolet radiation. Arriving at the earth about 8.3 min later, the flare's radiation rips through the upper atmosphere and tears electrons from neutral atoms. The increase in local ionization in the atmosphere disrupts shortwave, long-distance radio communication. A few days later the lagging protons and electrons ominously approach the earth, but they are usually trapped by the earth's magnetic field.

Occasionally, the magnetic reservoirs overflow with charged particles, particularly at times of sunspot maxima when flare activity is at its peak. As the particles spill into the earth's upper atmosphere, the swift electrons bump into atmospheric atoms and excite them. When the atoms deexcite, they emit visible radiation, which produces the aurora borealis in the Northern Hemisphere (Fig. 13.26).

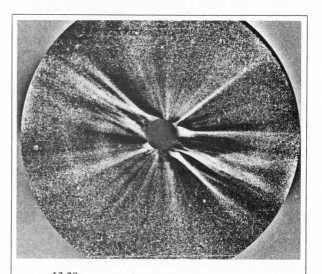

13.28

Streamers in the sun's corona, taken during a total eclipse in June 1973. The streamers are visible out to a distance of about 12 solar radii. They show the magnetic field configuration and solar wind flow out beyond the region near the photosphere. (Photo courtesy C. Keller and the Los Alamos Scientific Laboratory)

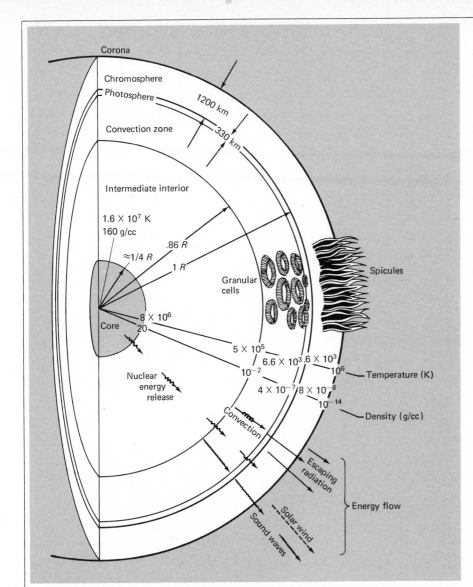

13.29

The outward flow of energy from the sun's core. The features of the quiet sun arise from the continuous flow of energy produced in the core out to space. Photons carry the energy most of the way out—to the inner edge of the convective zone. Here the rising and falling motion of bubbles of gas carries energy to the sun's surface, where most of it zips off as photons. Some of the outward energy flow takes the form of sound and shock waves that heat the chromosphere and the corona and generate the solar wind.

Coronal holes / Because the coronal gas is so hot, it emits low-energy X-rays and shows up in X-ray photos of the sun (Fig. 13.27). These pictures reveal that the coronal gas has an irregular distribution above and around the sun. Notice the large loop structures; these show where the ionized gas flows along magnetic fields that arch high above the sun's surface and return to it. The hot gas is trapped in these magnetic loops.

Note also in Figure 13.27 that some regions of the corona appear dark—especially at the top pole and down the middle part of the sun. Here the coronal gas must be much less dense and hot than usual; these regions are called *coronal holes*. The coronal holes at the poles do not appear to change very much, but those above other regions seem somehow related to solar activity.

What makes a coronal hole? Solar astrono-mers believe that coronal holes mark areas where magnetic fields from the sun continue outward into space rather than flow back to the sun in loops. So the coronal gas, not tied down in these regions, can flow away from the sun out of the coronal holes; this is the source of the solar wind (Fig. 13.28).

SUMMARY

The sun is a star: a huge, gaseous, thermonuclear reactor. In its core, hydrogen fuses to helium. All general solar features result from the interaction of matter with the energy generated in the core, flowing outward (Fig. 13.29). The energy-producing core occupies a quarter of the sun's radius. Here the awful crush of gravity packs the material to a density of 160 g/cc—ten times denser than the densest materials in the earth. The fury of the release of thermonuclear energy by the PP chain keeps the core at about 16 million Kelvins. Gamma-ray photons created in the fusion reactions journey to the surface and lose energy. At about 0.86 of the sun's radius the outgoing photons heat the gas rapidly enough to create a convection zone. This region produces the granular structure of the photosphere. The photons flee into space at the photosphere, creating the continuous and absorption spectrum of the sun. Most of the escaping photons are in the wavelength range of visible light, but some X-ray ultraviolet, and radio waves emerge in the radiative scramble.

Supersonic waves generated in the convection zone carry energy out from the photosphere to heat the upper chromosphere and corona to high temperatures. As a result of the high temperatures, the gas in the corona pushes itself out from the sun to form the solar wind.

After all the twists and tangles, the solar radiation eventually reaches the earth. The atmosphere filters out a large part of it. What gets through sustains the earth. The light also provides astronomers with clues to the physical conditions of the local star.

STUDY EXERCISES

1   Why do astronomers need to send instruments above the earth's atmosphere in order to measure the sun's luminosity? (*Objective 3*)

2   Suppose you looked at sunlight with a spectroscope. Describe in general what you would see. (*Objective 5*)

3   For what reason do you not see helium lines in the sun's dark-line spectrum, even though helium is the sun's second-most abundant element? (*Objective 5*)

4   What is happening to the chemical composition of the sun's core because of nuclear fusion? (*Objective 7*)

5   How long does it take photons produced in the sun's core to get to the surface? How long for neutrinos? (*Objective 9*)

6   Describe how you can estimate the sun's surface temperature from its color. (*Objective 4*)

7   Why do astronomers bounce radar signals off *Venus* in order to get the distance to the *sun?* (*Objective 1*)

8   What is the problem in considering gravitational contraction as the source of the sun's energy? (*Objectives 7 and 8*)

BEYOND THIS BOOK . . .

E. N. Parker paints a contemporary picture of the nearest star in "The Sun," *Scientific American,* September 1975, p. 42.

Some aspects of the active sun are treated in Part V of *The New Astronomy and Space Science Reader* (Freeman, San Francisco, 1977), edited by J. C. Brandt and S. P. Maran.

A technical description of the sun is *The Quiet Sun* by E. G. Gibson, NASA special publication S-271, 1970.

For some popular articles on the sun, look at "The Fiery Sun" in *Natural History,* May 1972, p. 48; "The Sun: Still at the Center of Our Thoughts," *Popular Astronomy,* 1975, vol. 1, no 1, p. 36; and "Our Sun," *Astronomy,* 1978, vol. 6, no. 1, all by J. Pasachoff.

For more details on the sun's outer atmosphere, read "The Solar Corona" by J. Pasachoff, *Scientific American,* October 1973, vol. 233, p. 68.

Surveying the Milky Way Galaxy

14

LEARNING OBJECTIVES

After studying this chapter you should be able to:

1. Make a rough sketch of the Milky Way, including the sun and its distance from the galactic center.

2. Explain the difference between apparent and absolute magnitude; define flux and relate it to apparent magnitude.

3. Outline how you can use a star's absolute magnitude to find its distance.

4. Show with a simple diagram how to find a star's distance from its heliocentric parallax.

5. Outline the methods used by astronomers to find a star's surface temperature and size.

6. Sketch a Hertzsprung–Russell diagram for stars, using luminosity (or absolute magnitude) and spectral class (or temperature) as the axes (being sure to label the positions of the sun, main sequence, giants, supergiants, and white dwarfs).

7. Use the Hertzsprung–Russell diagram to infer the luminosities, surface temperatures, and sizes of stars represented on it.

8. Relate a star's color to its surface temperature.

9. Outline the method by which the distance to a cepheid variable can be determined.

10. Argue, as Shapley did, that the observed distribution of globular clusters in the sky leads to the conclusion that the sun is *not* located at the center of the Galaxy.

How are the stars arranged in space? The appearance of the Milky Way prompted the search for the extent and distribution of stars. On a moonless night you can trace out the soft, luminous band of the Milky Way wrapped like a fine scarf around the celestial sphere. Ever since Galileo discovered that the Milky Way consisted of a multitude of faint stars, astronomers have tried to determine the arrangement of these stars in space.

This chapter deals with the quest for a detailed map of the nearby regions of space. I look at this question historically to see how astronomers have attacked this puzzle and to show the key importance of distance measurements and the properties of stars in solving it.

The search culminates with the discovery of the Galaxy: a vast, flat pinwheel of stars, gas, and dust. Only one out of billions of stars, the sun sits about half way out from the Galaxy's center.

The discovery of the Galaxy marks the second shock to humanity's ideas about its place in the cosmos. The first came from Copernicus (Section 3.1): The earth was not the center of the universe. After Copernicus, astronomers believed that the universe was sun-centered, and early ideas of the Galaxy pictured the sun in its center. In the twentieth century, however, astronomers found that the sun lies nowhere near the galactic center but rather is close to its edge. Humanity lives in a suburb of stars.

14.1

The Milky Way in the constellation Aquila. South of Cygnus, the Milky Way splits into two bands. The star Altair is in the lower left corner. (Courtesy Harvard College Observatory)

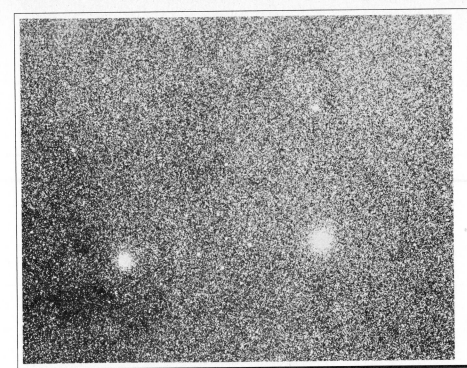

14.2
A large telescope reveals the incredible number of stars in the Milky Way. (Courtesy Kitt Peak National Observatory)

14.3

An open cluster of stars (Messier 67). (Courtesy Palomar Observatory, California Institute of Technology)

14.1
A tour of the Milky Way

Let me take you on a quick tour through the Milky Way as visible from the earth. Imagine that you are on the top of a mountain in the desert of southern New Mexico. The warm September day slowly cools as the sun vanishes behind the purple hills to the west. The silver of the crescent moon has set with the sun.

The brightest stars appear. Overhead you see the Northern Cross in the constellation Cygnus. As the darkness gathers, you pick out the wispy glow of the Milky Way. Scan down the Milky Way to the south. Before you reach Scorpius, you find that the Milky Way splits into two distinct bands (Fig. 14.1). This dark blot between the bands is called the Great Rift. Near it lie the brightest regions of the Milky Way visible from the Northern Hemisphere.

Now view this region with binoculars. What do you see? Stars, in countless numbers (Fig. 14.2). The more intently you look, the more you see. Slowly scan around the constellations Scorpius, Scutum, and Sagittarius. You get the impression that in any location where you see more or fainter stars, you are looking deeper into space. Occasional areas appear swept clean of the stars. Are there no stars here? Or does something block out the starlight?

If you scan a large enough area, you will come across small clusters of stars (Fig. 14.3). These groups are called *open* or *galactic clusters*.

14.4

A bright nebula (Messier 16) surrounding a cluster of young stars. (Courtesy Kitt Peak National Observatory)

14.5

A globular cluster. Note how densely the stars are packed in the center. Two globulars also appear in Fig. 14.2. (Courtesy Kitt Peak National Observatory)

A few you see immersed in a faint, glowing cloud (Fig. 14.4). Such a cloud is called a *nebula* (See Color Plates 19 and 20 for pictures of nebulas). One other object you can pick out with your binoculars: very dense star clusters (Fig. 14.5). These appear more tightly packed than the galactic clusters and more symmetrical in shape; they are called *globular clusters.*

Stars in loose and tight clusters, irregular clouds of glowing material, dark blotches, individual stars everywhere: These are the contents of the Milky Way viewed with binoculars or a small telescope. How far out are you seeing stars? Which are the closest, and which the farthest? What is their layout in three dimensions? Seeing the Milky Way encircling the sky (Fig. 14.6), you have the impression that the sun is situated in a cluster of stars that is thick in the center and then thins out.

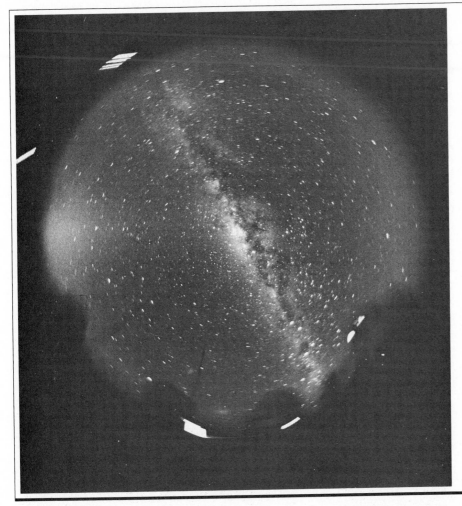

14.6

A wide-angle view of the southern Milky Way. Taken by Art Hoag at Cerro Tololo with a Nikon 225° lens, this photo shows the band of the Milky Way, the two Magellanic Clouds (on both sides of the flagpole at bottom), and the zodiacal light (bright areas stretching up from the horizon at left). (Courtesy A. Hoag)

Earlier astronomers had similar impressions. Before I present the story of their detective work, let me give away the story's end by sketching our present model of the Milky Way Galaxy (Fig. 14.7). Astronomers now picture the Galaxy as a vast disk of stars with a bulge in the middle. It has an overall diameter of about 120,000 light years (ly) and a thickness of 20,000 ly. The sun lies in the Galaxy's suburbs, about 30,000 ly from the center but almost directly in the Galaxy's plane. The sun and other stars whirl around the Galaxy at speeds of hundreds of kilometers per second. Such rapid motion accounts for the flatness of this system of stars.

How did astronomers discover this enormous island of stars? How did they probe the sky in three dimensions to find out the structure of the Galaxy?

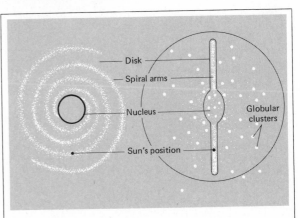

14.7

A contemporary model of the Milky Way Galaxy, a huge disk of stars about 120,000 ly in diameter. The nucleus contains a denser concentration of stars than the disk. Globular clusters encircle the disk and nucleus.

focus 33

THE ASTRONOMER'S MAGNITUDE SCALE

*Astronomers talk about two different kinds of magnitudes: apparent and absolute. The ap-*parent magnitude, m, *of a star expresses how bright it appears, as seen from the earth, ranked on the magnitude scale. Two factors affect the apparent magnitude: (1) how luminous the star is and (2) how far away it is from the earth.* Absolute magnitude, M, *expresses the brightness of a star as it would be ranked on the magnitude scale if it were placed 10 pc (32.6 ly) from the earth. Since all the stars would be placed at the same distance, absolute magnitudes reflect differences in actual luminosities.*

The magnitude scale on which stars are rated has evolved from a convention first established by Hipparchus and now traditional. In his catalog of stars he classified their apparent magnitudes by rating the brightest star he could see as magnitude 1 and the faintest as magnitude 6. As this system evolved, some stars were found to be brighter than magnitude 1; for example, Vega is magnitude 0, and Sirius is magnitude −1.4. The first peculiarity to note about the magnitude scale is that the larger negative *magnitude a star (or any celestial object) has, the* brighter *it is; but the larger the* positive *magnitude is, the* fainter *will be the star (Fig. 1).*

How the human eye judges light affects the magnitude scale. Suppose you tried to es-timate the relative brightness of a 100-W and a 200-W light bulb. The second bulb does not appear twice as bright as the first. And a 400-Watt light bulb will not appear four times as bright. But the difference *in brightness between the 100 and 200-W bulbs will appear the same as the difference between 200 and 400-W bulbs. The eye senses equal* ratios *of brightness as equal* differences.

Stars of first magnitude are 100 times brighter than stars of sixth magnitude; a difference of 5 magnitudes corresponds to a brightness ratio of 100. A difference of 1 magnitude then amounts to a brightness ratio of 2.512. This strange number pops up because $2.512 \times 2.512 \times 2.512 \times 2.512 \times 2.512 = 2.512^5 = 100$, another way of stating that a difference of five magnitudes equals a ratio of 100 in brightness. Table 14.1 will help you keep straight the magnitude differences and brightness ratios.

Both the absolute and the apparent magnitudes are given on the same scale. For example, the apparent magnitude of the sun is about −26. The brightest star in the sky, Sirius, has an apparent magnitude of −1.4. The difference in magnitude is 25; for every five magnitudes the brightness ratio is 100. So Sirius is $10^2 \times 10^2 \times 10^2 \times 10^2 \times 10^2 = 10^{10}$ times less bright than the sun in apparent magnitude. This result tells you nothing about the luminosities of the sun and Sirius, only how bright they appear in the sky. In contrast, the absolute magnitude of the sun is approximately +4.8; of Sirius, +1.5. The dif-

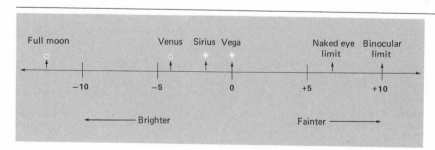

1

The astronomical magnitude scale. Key point: The larger the negative *magnitude is, the* brighter *the object will be; the larger the* positive *magnitude is, the* fainter *it is.*

TABLE 14.1	*Conversion of magnitude differences to brightness ratios*
A magnitude difference of:	*Equals a brightness ratio of:*
0.0	1.0
0.2	1.2
1.0	2.5
1.5	4.0
2.0	6.3
2.5	10.0
4.0	40.0
5.0	100.0
7.5	1000.0
10.0	10,000.0

ference in absolute magnitudes is 3.3, corresponding to a brightness ratio of approximately 20 (Table 14.1). This comparison of absolute magnitudes tells you that Sirius is roughly 20 times as luminous as the sun. A similar comparison can be made to find the luminosities of other stars.

You can convert from magnitude differences to brightness ratios quickly by using the formula

$$\frac{b_1}{b_2} = (2.512)^{m_2 - m_1}$$

where b_1 and m_1 are the brightness and magnitude of star 1 and b_2 and m_2 are the brightness and magnitude of star 2. Let me do the preceding example with Sirius (star 1) and the sun (star 2) more carefully here.

$$\frac{b_{Sirius}}{b_{Sun}} = (2.512)^{m_{Sun} - m_{Sirius}}$$
$$= (2.512)^{4.8 - 1.5}$$
$$= (2.512)^{3.3}$$
$$= 21$$

This result gives the luminosity of Sirius compared to the sun at visual wavelengths.

14.2
Herschel maps the Milky Way

In the latter part of the eighteenth century the astronomer William Herschel (who discovered Uranus—Section 11.4) utilized systematic observational techniques to attack the problem of the Milky Way's structure. Herschel had constructed telescopes that dwarfed other instruments of the day. With these powerful tools he set out to establish the extent of the Milky Way by counting stars in selected regions of the sky. Herschel thought that directions where he found large numbers of faint stars were places in which the Milky Way extended the farthest.

This procedure required a number of assumptions to make it workable. One assumption can be stated as: *Brightness means nearness* (or *faintness means farness*.) In other words, you assume that all stars are essentially the same and give off the same amount of light. So if they were all placed the same distance from the earth, they would all have the same brightness. The brightness a star has when viewed from the earth is termed its *apparent magnitude*. Astronomers use a historically derived magnitude scale on which apparent magnitudes are measured (details in Focus 33). For now all you need to keep in mind is this: Fainter stars have higher numbers on the magnitude scale (a star of apparent magnitude +3 is fainter than one with apparent magnitude +2), and the very brightest stars have apparent magnitudes less than zero, with the larger negative numbers indicating the brighter stars (see Fig. 1 of Focus 33). For example, Sirius with apparent magnitude −1.4 appears brighter than Vega with apparent magnitude 0.0.

If you have looked even casually at the night sky, you have seen that stars do *not* have the same apparent magnitudes. If you assume that all stars have the same luminosity, then the differences in apparent magnitudes reflect differences in distances from the earth. The brightest stars are the closest, fainter ones are more distant.

You make this kind of distance judgment every day. If you view a city at night from a high vantage point, you can estimate distances by the brightness of visible lights. You judge that the brightest lights are the closest ones. (Note that your estimates are inaccurate if smog enshrouds a city. You then judge that lights

focus 34

THE INVERSE-SQUARE LAW FOR LIGHT

The farther away you move from a light source, the dimmer it appears. How much the intensity decreases relates in a very specific way to how far you are from the source.

Imagine the following experiment (which you can do if you have the equipment). Put a bare light bulb (any wattage) in a socket and turn it on. Take a light meter—a device used to measure the intensity of light, commonly found with automatic cameras—and place it 1 m from the bulb (Fig. 1). Note the reading on the light meter, and call that one unit. Now move the light meter 2 m from the bulb; its reading will be one-fourth that at the 1-m position. Move the light meter to a distance of 3 m; the reading will now be one-ninth that at 1 m. Note that the light intensity decreases as the **inverse square** *of the distance. (What would the reading be at 4 m? Right— one-sixteenth that at 1 m.)*

Why does this inverse-square relation happen? Imagine a light source placed in the center of two spherical shells, one having twice the radius of the second (Fig. 2). The radiation from the source spreads out more by the time it hits the second shell than does that in the smaller sphere. Both have the same total amount of radiation because the

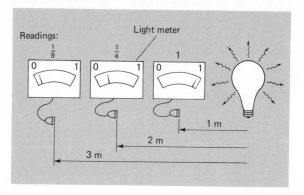

1

Light intensity and distance. Take a sensitive light meter, place it 1 m from any light bulb, and note the reading. Then place the light meter at a distance of 2 m. The reading will be one-fourth the first. At a distance of 3 m, it will be one-ninth the first. This experiment shows you that light intensity decreases inversely as the square of the distance: $(\frac{1}{2})^2 = \frac{1}{4}$, $(\frac{1}{3})^2 = \frac{1}{9}$.

light source is the same, but this radiation is spread over a larger area in the larger sphere. How much larger? The area of a sphere is directly related to the radius squared; so the larger sphere has four times the area of the

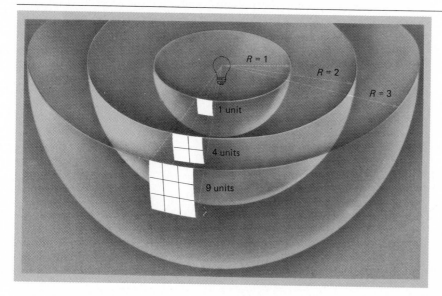

2

The geometry of the inverse-square law for light intensity. Imagine a light source in the center of three transparent spheres. Consider one unit of area on the inner sphere. The light passing through this one unit spreads out as it travels away from the source, so when it hits the second sphere it covers 4 units. And when it strikes the third sphere it covers 9 units of area. So the same amount of light has been spread over larger and larger areas. Therefore the amount of light in one unit of area of the second and third spheres is decreased by just the amount that the light has spread out. (Adapted from a diagram in **Contemporary Astronomy** *by J. Pasachoff, Saunders, 1981)*

smaller one, and the light spreads out four times as much. Now pick any square centimeter of surface for both spheres. Because of the radiation's dilution over a larger area, the small patch you select on the larger sphere has only one-fourth as much light striking it as the patch on the smaller sphere. If the ratio of radii were increased to 3 (third shell), the decrease in brightness would be by 9; if increased to 4, the decrease would be by 16. In equation form,

$$\frac{\text{new brightness}}{\text{old brightness}} = \left(\frac{\text{old distance}}{\text{new distance}}\right)^2$$

or

$$\frac{b_2}{b_1} = \left(\frac{d_1}{d_2}\right)^2$$

where b_1 and d_1 are the old brightness and distance and b_2 and d_2 are the new brightness and distance.

Suppose you observe that the apparent brightness of one star is 100 times that of another. If you assume that both stars have the same luminosity, how do their distances compare? The brighter one must be ten times as close than the fainter one, that is, with $b_2 = 100 b_1$.

$$100 = \left(\frac{d_1}{d_2}\right)^2$$

$$10 = \frac{d_1}{d_2}$$

where d_1 is the distance to the fainter star, and d_2 is the distance to the brighter star.

The inverse-square law relates absolute and apparent magnitudes. The relation is

$$m - M = 5 \log d - 5$$

where d is the distance to a star in parsecs, m is its apparent magnitude, and M is its absolute magnitude. If you know two of these three quantities, you can find the third.

Here's an example with Sirius, whose apparent magnitude is about −1.4 and whose distance is 2.67 pc. Then the absolute magnitude of Sirius is

$$-1.4 - M = 5 \log 2.67 - 5$$
$$-M = 5(0.426) - 3.6$$
$$-M = 2.1 - 3.6$$
$$M = +1.5$$

dimmed by smog are farther away than they actually are.)

With this and other assumptions, Herschel devised a program of counting stars in selected regions of the sky (Fig. 14.8). From the number counted he estimated the distance to the edge of the Galaxy. He could do this in relative terms: how far the stars were from the earth compared with the distance of a standard star. Herschel chose Sirius as his standard. He could calculate a star's distance compared with that of Sirius because he knew that the light from a star decreased in a special way with the distance (Focus 34). Because he did not know the distance to Sirius in kilometers, he could not establish the scale of the Milky Way. He could—and did—estimate its relative proportions as far out as he could see (Fig. 14.9).

Herschel concluded that the stars were arranged in a thin slab, with the sun not far from the center. The contours of the edge of the stars' distribution were irregular to account for the differences he discovered from his star counting.

From this picture of the Milky Way Herschel made a bold mental leap beyond it. His telescopes had helped him to find nebulous objects in the sky. He was able to resolve many of these into clusters of stars. These observations led him to conclude in the 1780s that all spiral-shaped nebulosities were distant stellar systems that could ultimately be resolved into stars by large enough telescopes. So he inferred that these clouds were other milky ways and that our Galaxy would appear like them, if viewed from a distance. Herschel's leap is a good example of how our picture of local space directly affects our vision of the rest of the universe.

14.3
Direct measurement of stellar distances

Herschel's plan was thwarted in part because he did not know the actual distances to stars. Not until the nineteenth century did astronomers develop a direct method to find the distances to nearby stars: triangulation, similar to that done by surveyors on the earth. Stellar triangulation, which involves distances of light years, is called *heliocentric parallax* (Focus 35).

You actually observe parallaxes every day, although you are usually not aware of it. Hold

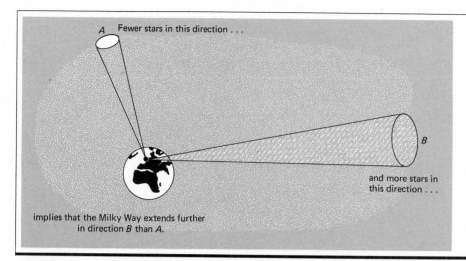

A   Fewer stars in this direction . . .

B

and more stars in
this direction . . .

implies that the Milky Way extends further
in direction B than A.

14.8

Herschel's star-counting technique to infer the shape of the Galaxy. In certain areas of the sky Herschel counted the number of stars that could be seen with his telescope. With his assumptions he could conclude that in directions where he counted more stars (B compared to A) the Milky Way extended farther.

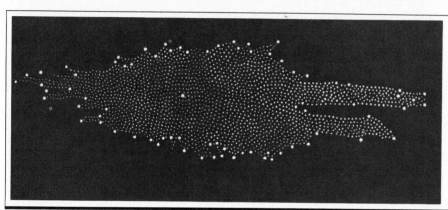

14.9

Herschel's picture of a cross section of the Milky Way, as inferred from star counting. Herschel assumed that he could see to the edges of the Milky Way with his telescope. He concluded that the Milky Way is "a very extensive, branching, compound congeries of millions of stars." (Courtesy Yerkes Observatory)

your hand with one finger extended at arm's length. Now alternately open and close each eye. Your finger will appear to jump back and forth relative to the distant background. This angular shift in your finger's position is the parallax of your finger. Now if you measure the amount of shift (in angular measure) and the distance between your eyes, you can calculate how far your finger is from your head.

Imagine that your finger is a nearby star, the background more distant stars, and your eyes the sighting positions of the earth in orbit around the sun, separated by a time of six months. From these two positions in the earth's orbit (separated by 2 AU), the nearby star appears to shift in position (this angular shift is its parallax), compared with the more distant stars (Fig. 14.10). Measure the angular size of that shift. Because you know the diameter of the earth's orbit, you can calculate the distance to

the star. Note that the *farther* away a star is, the *smaller* its parallax will be.

In algebraic form, the parallax relation is simply

$$\text{distance (in parsecs)} = \frac{1}{\text{parallax (in arcsec)}}$$

The unit of distance here, a *parsec* (abbreviated pc), is equal to 206,265 AU, 3.085×10^{16} m, or 3.26 light years (ly). Here is an example. The parallax of Sirius is 0.37 arcsec, so the distance to Sirius is

$$\text{distance} = \frac{1}{0.37}$$
$$= 2.67 \text{ pc}$$
$$= 8.8 \text{ ly.}$$

Heliocentric parallax works accurately only for close stars. The parallax of Sirius, a very

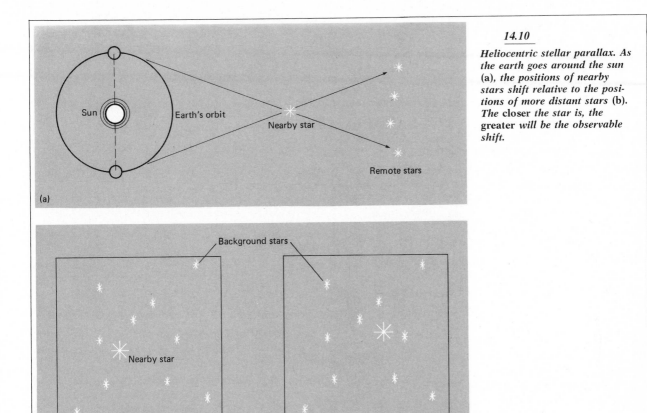

14.10

Heliocentric stellar parallax. As the earth goes around the sun (a), *the positions of nearby stars shift relative to the positions of more distant stars* (b). *The closer the star is, the greater will be the observable shift.*

close star, is less than one second of arc, which is about 1/2000 the angular diameter of the moon. Parallax techniques have an accuracy of about 0.01 arcsec, so parallaxes out to about 300 ly can be measured accurately.

Most stars in the Milky Way are more distant than 300 ly. How are their distances measured? By ingenious, indirect methods. One, called spectroscopic parallax, comes later in this chapter. Another relies on a fact not yet discussed: that stars move in space.

14.4
Stars traveling through space

Early in 1718 Edmund Halley (Section 4.2) compared the positions he had found for Arcturus and Sirius with those given by Ptolemy. Halley found that these stars had moved a considerable amount in 1500 years; the "fixed" stars were not in fact fixed but moved about in space. In

one year the change in a star's position, as seen from the earth, amounts to a very small angular movement. Over many years—such as the time between Ptolemy and Halley—the changes add up and so are easier to observe (Fig. 14.11).

Proper motion / The change in position in the sky of a star due to its motion in space with respect to other stars is called its *proper motion*. Observing the proper motions of stars tells us something about their distances. Suppose you observed the proper motions of a few stars. Some, you found, move faster than others. Your natural inclination would be to think that those moving the fastest were the closest. Here's another rule of thumb to estimate stellar distances: *Swiftness means nearness (or slowness means farness).* (*Note:* This is the *angular speed*, not the actual speed in space. The rule assumes that the actual speeds of stars are roughly the same.)

focus 35

HELIOCENTRIC STELLAR PARALLAX

Parallax occurs when you view a relatively close object from each of two ends of a baseline. As the earth moves from one place in its orbit to another, the nearby stars' position seems to change relative to the more distant stars. The maximum shift occurs when you view the star six months apart, so you are sighting from opposite sides of the earth's orbit. The angular shift (actually half the shift) is the star's parallax. Measure the amount of that shift. Then, because you know the diameter of the earth's orbit, you can calculate the distance to the star. This method of determining the star's distance is called heliocentric parallax.

Now suppose you travel out into space and look back at the earth–sun separation (1 AU). You keep going until the angular size of the AU is 1 second of arc. Suppose you station a star at this point and hurry back to the earth. You observe this star for one year and measure its shift. One-half of the total shift for one year would equal 1 second of arc. We say the star is 1 parsec from the sun, that is, the distance at which the parallax is one second of arc, a distance roughly equal to 3.26 ly. Suppose the star were twice as far away; it would have half the parallax, $\frac{1}{2}''$. If at half the distance, its parallax would double and be 2''. Note this simple inverse relationship of parallax and distance. Algebraically,

$$d = \frac{1}{p}$$

where d is the distance in parsecs and p is the parallax in seconds of arc.

An example: the star 40 Eridani has a parallax of 0.2 arcsec. How far is the star from the sun? Since the star's parallax is one-fifth that for a star 1 parsec away, 40 Eridani must be 5 pc distance. Explicitly,

$$d = \frac{1}{0.2}$$
$$= 5\,pc.$$

Here's a simple geometrical explanation for the parallax formula. Travel out in space to some star. Then draw an imaginary circle

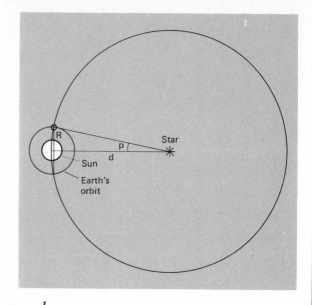

$\underline{\quad 1 \quad}$

Geometry for heliocentric parallax.

(Fig. 1) centered on the star and through the sun (S) so the circle's radius is d. Note that the parallax angle, p (in degrees), is some fraction of the total circle (360°). Also, R, the earth–sun distance (one AU), corresponds closely to an arc on the circumference of the circle; its fraction of the circumference is the same as the fraction p is of 360°. So

$$\frac{R}{2\pi d} = \frac{p}{360°}$$

and

$$d = \frac{360° R}{2\pi p}$$

Convert 360° to seconds of arc:

$$d = \frac{360 \times 60 \times 60}{2\pi} \frac{R}{p}$$

$$= 206{,}265 \frac{R}{p}.$$

Now R is one AU; define one parsec as 206,265 AU. Then

$$d\ (pc) = \frac{1}{p\ (arcsec)}$$

or

$$d\ (light\ years) = \frac{3.26}{p\ (arcsec)}$$

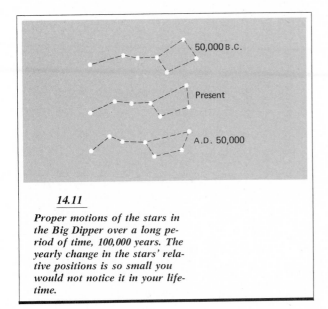

14.11
Proper motions of the stars in the Big Dipper over a long period of time, 100,000 years. The yearly change in the stars' relative positions is so small you would not notice it in your lifetime.

With this assumption, the proper motions of stars reflect their relative distances. Suppose, for example, that you are watching a crowd of Christmas shoppers. Everyone is hustling about as quickly as possible. In their common rush the people end up moving at about the same speed relative to one another. They tend to travel in groups heading for the same store. Those closest to you move across your line of sight more quickly than the ones farther away. The closer groups appear to have larger proper motions.

This example points out a complication in the swiftness means nearness rule. The shoppers rushing by in the Christmas crowd move not only *across* your line of sight; some move *along* your line of sight. Or a shopper may be moving

at an angle with respect to your line of sight. So the shopper's motion consists of two parts: motion across your line of sight and motion along it (Fig. 14.12). The same situation occurs for stars. Seen from the earth, their motion in space has two parts: *proper motion* across the line of sight and *radial velocity* along the line of sight.

We luckily possess a powerful tool to determine radial velocities: the Doppler effect (Focus 19). Combined with its observed proper motion, the measured radial velocity allows us to separate the star's line-of-sight velocity from its motion across the line of sight if we know the distance to the star. Then we can translate the star's proper motion into a velocity in kilometers per second. From the velocities along and across the line of sight we can find the star's motion through space.

The sun's motion / The proper motions of stars provide valuable information on the sun's motion in space, relative to the nearest stars. In 1783 Herschel noted that the sun's motion should show up as a part of the proper motions of stars, varying in a regular way with position on the sky. He called the direction in which the sun moves in space the *apex* of its motion. From the proper motions of only 13 stars, Herschel deduced that the apex of the sun's motion lies in the constellation Hercules, next to Lyra. How? He noted that the direction of the proper motions of his dozen stars radiated outward from a point in that direction. They converged on a point in the opposite part of the sky, the *antapex*, in the constellation of Columba, south of Orion. He guessed that this effect was caused by the motion of the sun through space.

Imagine this situation with the following

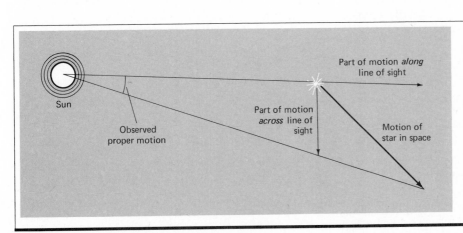

14.12
*The motion of stars in space. Relative to the sun, stars can move in space at any angle relative to our line of sight. Proper motion is that part of a star's motion that is **across our line of sight**. The radial part of the motion **along our line of sight** can be measured by the Doppler shift. These two parts can be added together to give the actual motion of the star in space only if its distance is known.*

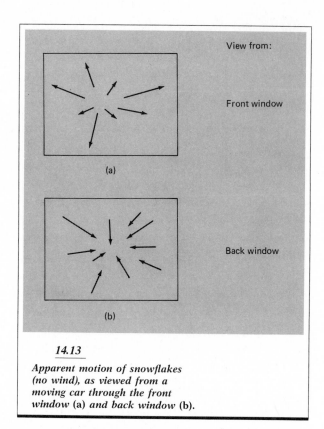

14.13

Apparent motion of snowflakes (no wind), as viewed from a moving car through the front window (a) and back window (b).

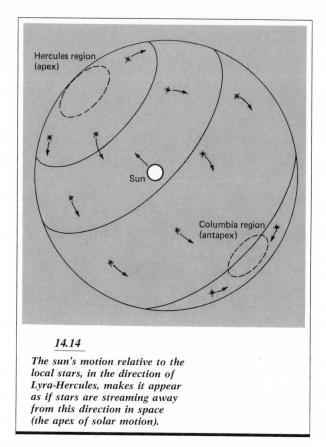

14.14

The sun's motion relative to the local stars, in the direction of Lyra-Hercules, makes it appear as if stars are streaming away from this direction in space (the apex of solar motion).

analogy. Consider standing in a snowfall with no wind blowing. Then the snowflakes fall in their usual shifting patterns. Drive a car through the snowstorm. Peering through the front windshield you note that the snowflakes appear to fan out from a point directly in front of the car (Fig. 14.13(a)). If you use the rearview mirror to look out the back window, the snowflakes appear to converge at a point behind it (Fig. 14.13(b)). Their apparent motions only reflect the car's motion through the swarm of falling snowflakes.

Similarly, the sun's motion at about 20 km/sec through the local stars creates the effect of an apex and antapex of solar motion (Fig. 14.14). How to find out how fast the sun is moving? By using the Doppler shift (Focus 19). In general, stars in Hercules have blue-shifted spectra; those in Columba show red shifts. If you measure the blue shifts for a number of stars in the Hercules region and find an average, it comes out to about 20 km/sec.

Statistical parallaxes / Now the main point—using stellar motion to determine distances. Astronomers can only measure directly (by heliocentric parallax) distances to local stars.

To plot the structure of the Galaxy requires a reach beyond the local stars. How? One way involves observing the average proper motions of selected groups of stars.

Consider this analogy. Suppose you are riding along a highway past a skyscraper-studded city with a mountainous backdrop on your right. If you open and close your eyes successively (try this only when you're riding, not driving), one at a time, no building shifts position relative to the background mountains: The city is too far away from you to show a parallax using your eyes to set the baseline. The parallax method fails because the baseline is too small. However, as your car speeds along past the city, you notice that the buildings slowly move, relative to the mountains, and in the direction opposite your direction of motion. You can measure the amount of angular displacement they go through in a certain length of time (say a minute). The longer you drive, the larger the angular displacements become, and the farther away you can see measurable shifts.

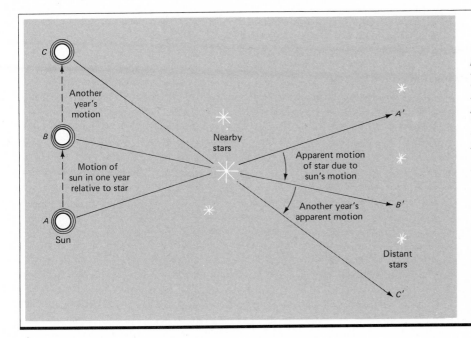

14.15

The sun's motion and statistical parallaxes. Suppose that all stars are stationary relative to each other and that only the sun moves (A to B to C). Compared with background stars, a nearby star—because of the sun's motion A to B—will appear to move a certain angular distance in a year (A' to B'). Let another year go by and the sun will move farther (B to C), so the star's apparent motion is greater (B' to C'). Wait for many years and you acquire a large baseline to measure far distances, since the sun moves about 4 AU a year. Note: This illustration singles out one star. Actually, the method applied to groups of stars whose motions relative to each other average out to zero.

Because you know your speed, you know how far you traveled to see a certain angular shift. This information would allow you to compute the distance to the buildings, using the parallax relation.

Replace the car with the sun and earth (Fig. 14.15), the city with a group of stars, and the mountains with background stars, farther away than the selected group. The nearby stars will appear to move with respect to the background stars, in a direction opposite to the solar motion. (Note that you neglect the motion of the earth around the sun now—to talk of the solar motion means the motion of the entire solar system, earth included, through space.) The trick is this: You must choose a group of stars whose *average* motions are zero so that their *average* proper motion reflects the sun's motion relative to them; they must also be at about the same distance. (The buildings in the city are at the same distance and do not move relative to each other.) If you took a single star, you wouldn't know whether its proper motion was due to its own velocity through space or to the sun's velocity.

An example: Choose from all over the sky stars of spectral class *A* having apparent magnitude of +5. (As you will find in the next section, these stars have about the same luminosity, so this group of the same apparent magnitude

must all lie at about the same distance from the sun.) Subdivide the sky into small groups of these stars, and measure the proper motion of each group. You will find that these groups seem to reflect the sun's motion: They stream away from the apex of the sun's motion. Their average angular speed is 0.04 arcsec a year. Now, in a year, the sun moves about 4.2 AU toward the apex. A shift of 0.04 with a baseline of 4.2 AU gives a distance of 340 ly (105 pc). So the *average* distance to *A*-stars of fifth magnitude is 340 ly.

This technique is called *mean* or *statistical parallaxes* to emphasize that it permits estimates of *average* distances to groups of stars. But it greatly extends the range of distance determinations—out to about 1500 ly. This information provides a crucial leap beyond the direct measure of distances to the nearest stars. This leap leads to the discovery of the observational foundation to stellar astrophysics: the Hertzsprung–Russell diagram.

14.5
The Hertzsprung–Russell diagram: Key to the stars

In order to deduce the general physical properties of stars, astronomers had to discover that two of these fell into a pattern: luminosities and temperatures.

How luminous? When you have looked carefully at the night sky, you've probably noticed that stars do not have the same brightness. Some, like Sirius, shine brilliantly. Others, such as faint Polaris, the North Star, barely stand out to our vision. In astronomical terms, stars have different apparent magnitudes (Focus 33).

What does such a statement imply about the stars' luminosities? Not much in any direct way. A star's apparent magnitude relates directly only to how much energy from that star is striking the earth. The sun—the nearest star—provides ample energy at the earth's surface. In fact, you can measure sunlight with a thermometer. But light from the brightest star in the night sky, Sirius, is far too feeble to affect a thermometer.

The rate at which energy from a star (or any celestial object) arrives each second over a square meter at the earth is called its *flux*. For instance, the flux from the sun is 1373 W/m^2 (Section 13.2). Measurements with telescopes show that Sirius delivers to the earth about 1.1×10^{-7} W for every square meter of the earth's surface; that's the flux of Sirius. So the flux from Sirius is 10^{-10} less than that from the sun. That's why Sirius appears fainter than the sun. Or, in astronomical terms, Sirius has a greater (more positive) apparent magnitude than the sun.

To find Sirius's luminosity, you essentially use the same procedure followed for finding the sun's luminosity (Section 13.2). Recall the method: You measured the sun's flux, found its distance in kilometers, constructed an imaginary sphere with the earth–sun distance as its radius, and then totaled up all the energy hitting that sphere. In essence, you used the inverse square law for light (Focus 34). To find a star's luminosity by analogy: measure the star's flux (apparent magnitude), find its distance, determine the area of a sphere around the star with a radius equal to the star–earth distance, and add up the flux over the total area. The problem, of course, is getting the distance.

Heliocentric parallax observations show that Sirius is 8.8 ly away. Or the distance to Sirius is 551,000 times the distance to the sun. Now imagine that you moved Sirius up to the sun. It would appear much brighter than it is now—in fact, 25 times brighter than the sun appears. So

Sirius is actually 25 times more luminous than the sun, since, at 1 AU, you would receive 25 times more flux from it than from the sun over all wavelengths.

The point is: You cannot determine how luminous a star is unless you know its distance. Any star's flux (apparent magnitude) depends on *both* its luminosity and distance. When you see a faint star, you do not know whether it is very luminous and far away or not very luminous and close by.

If you can find a star's distance (by heliocentric parallax, for example), you can find its luminosity from its flux. You measure how much light from the star strikes a square meter at the earth's distance from the star. Then imagine the star pulled into the sun's distance. The inverse-square law, with the star's distance known, gives the flux that would be received from the star. Compare that flux to the flux from the sun. So from the comparison we know how luminous the star is compared with the sun and how much power it puts out.

Absolute magnitude and luminosity / You should have noticed that the trick to finding luminosities is to compare the brightness of a star with that of the sun, with both stars at the same distance. Astronomers do this imaginary comparison by a system called *absolute magnitude*. Imagine that you could place all stars the *same* distance from the earth. Then differing distances would not play a role in how bright stars appeared. Any differences in magnitudes among them would arise only from differences in luminosities.

Astronomers do set stars, in an imaginary way, at a standard distance in order to compare their luminosities directly. However, they do not use the earth–sun distance as the standard distance; rather, they use a distance of 10 parsecs (pc), which is the same as 32.6 light years (ly).

Imagine that you could transport the stars in the sky, including the sun, to 10 pc from the earth. Stars closer than this distance would grow fainter; those farther would increase in brightness, as expected from the inverse-square law. How bright a star would appear at 10 pc from us is termed its *absolute magnitude*.

Here are a few examples to help you with this concept. The sun, at 1 AU, has an apparent magnitude of −27. Move it out to 10 pc; it would look dimmer, and at 10 pc it would have an apparent magnitude of about 4.8; that becomes the sun's absolute magnitude. Now do the same with Sirius, whose distance from us now is 2.7 pc and whose apparent magnitude is −1.4; move it farther away to 10 pc and it would look dimmer, until its magnitude appears to be 1.5. That's the absolute magnitude of Sirius. Now try Polaris, which is 240 pc (780 ly) from the sun. Its apparent magnitude is 2.3. Moving it to 10 pc by bringing it closer, so it would appear brighter, with an absolute magnitude of −4.6

Compare the absolute magnitudes of these stars: the sun, 4.8; Sirius, 1.5; Polaris, −4.6. Note that Polaris is actually the most luminous, followed by Sirius, with the sun last.

This example should show you that apparent magnitude, absolute magnitude, and distance are related to one another. If you know a star's distance and apparent magnitude, you can work out its absolute magnitude. In fact, if you know any two of the three properties, you can find the third. For instance, if you knew a star's apparent and absolute magnitude, you could determine its distance. But there's a catch to this neat method: You must be able to find a star's absolute magnitude (or luminosity) *independent* of a knowledge of its distance. Can you do this? Yes! The secret lies in the spectral classes of the stars, which relates to their surface temperatures. (This is a good place to review Chapter 5, especially Sections 5.3 and 5.4.)

Colors, temperatures, and sizes / Recall (Focus 16) that the colors of stars relate to their surface temperatures. Basically, the coolest stars appear reddish, and the hottest, blue-white. The spectral classification of stars (Section 5.4) relates to surface temperatures and to colors. Stars of the same spectral type all have the same surface temperatures. For example, the sun is a spectral type G2 with a temperature of 5800 K; all G2 stars have photospheric temperatures of 5800 K.

Curiously enough, stars of the same spectral type do *not* necessarily have the same luminosity. For instance, Betelgeuse, the bright star in Orion's shoulder, and Proxima Centauri (the faint star in the triple-star system Alpha Centauri) both have a surface temperature of about 3000 K. But Betelgeuse is about 120,000 times more luminous than the sun (its luminosity actually varies), and Proxima Centauri has about 5×10^{-5} the sun's luminosity.

How can these stars differ so much in luminosity? Recall that stars radiate like blackbodies (Focus 31) and that blackbodies with the same temperature emit the same amount of energy from each square meter. That's the case for Betelgeuse and Proxima Centauri. But Belelgeuse is about 10^8 times more luminous. The difference must be one of size: Betelgeuse is much larger than Proxima Centauri and has a greater surface area. So even though both stars pour out equal amounts of energy from each square meter of surface, Betelgeuse has much more surface area and, in total, emits more energy each second.

A star's luminosity depends on *both* its surface temperature and its size. If two stars have the same surface temperature, the larger one will be the more luminous. If two stars have the same size, the hotter will be the more luminous. This complication (Focus 36) actually helps in sorting out the properties of stars, because size and temperature differences show up in stellar spectra.

The Hertzsprung–Russell, or luminosity–temperature, diagram / In 1905 Ejnar Hertzsprung (1873–1972) discovered that the widths of dark lines in a star's spectrum are related to its luminosity. Hertzsprung indirectly found distances to groups of stars of the same spectral class using statistical parallaxes (Section 14.4). He found that, in general, stars of the same spectral type with narrow dark lines are *more* luminous than those with broad lines. This discovery led to a way of distinguishing between large and small stars by using their spectra.

Independently of Hertzsprung, Henry N. Russell (1879–1957) arrived at a similar interpretation from different data. Russell determined stellar parallaxes from photographs. From the distances and apparent magnitudes of the stars, he calculated their absolute magnitudes and plotted them with respect to spectral class. Russell found that the absolute magnitude—hence the luminosity—generally correlated with spectral class. However, he noted that stars of the same spectral class with narrow spectral lines were more luminous than those with broad lines, so they must be larger.

focus 36

STARS AS BLACKBODY RADIATORS

The sun's spectrum closely resembles that of a blackbody. In fact, all normal stars have the same property—the deviation from a blackbody is small.

For a spherical blackbody you find a simple relation among its luminosity, L, radius, R, and temperature, T:

$$L = 4\pi R^2 \sigma T^4 (watts)$$

Here σ is a constant with the value of 5.67×10^{-8} if R is in meters and T in Kelvins. You can apply this relation to stars since they radiate like blackbodies. You then see that a star's luminosity is directly related to its surface area ($4\pi R^2$) and how much energy is emitted by each square meter of surface (σT^4), where T is the star's surface temperature (in Kelvins).

Now you can see one way you can infer the radius of a star from its luminosity and surface temperature. Determine its luminosity and temperature, then plug these values into the preceding relation, and you have an idea of the radius.

This relation also tells you that a giant and a main-sequence star of the same spectral type have different sizes—a giant is a giant! Stars of the same spectral type have the same surface temperatures. But giants are more luminous than main-sequence stars. So they must have greater surface area and so a larger radius. (If σT^4 is the same, $4\pi R^2$ must be greater.)

The key point: *A star's luminosity depends on **both** its surface temperature and its radius. If you know the luminosity, you need to be able to estimate the surface temperature in order to estimate the radius.*

Russell published a diagram of such a relation, plotting absolute magnitude versus spectral class for the Pleiades and Hyades clusters. Such a plot for any group of stars is known as the Hertzsprung–Russell (or H-R) diagram. In its modern variation *the H-R diagram guides astronomers to the physical properties of stars.*

How to make an H-R diagram? First, find stars close enough to the sun to measure their distances reliably by parallax. Then calculate their absolute magnitudes from the distances and apparent magnitudes. The absolute magnitudes tell you how luminous the stars are compared with the sun. Next step: Take spectra of the stars to find out their spectral class. From the spectra you determine how hot the stars are. Then plot the absolute magnitude of each star against its spectral type, that is, its luminosity against temperature.

That's the basic method. Look at the results. First an H-R diagram for all the stars within 20 ly (6 pc) of the sun (Fig. 14.16). Notice that most of the stars are less luminous and cooler than the sun. (In fact, you see them mainly because they are so close.) The star Alpha Centauri A has almost the same luminosity and temperature as the sun. This star is the sun's twin and is also the star nearest to us. (Alpha Centauri A is one member of a triple-star system with Alpha Centauri B and Proxima Centauri, and in this sense is unlike the sun.) Finally, note that the stars' properties do not fall in a random scatter. Rather, there is a trend; if you draw a line through the points from luminous, hot Sirius to the coolest, faintest star in the lower right-hand corner, you have identified the *main sequence.* Most stars fall on the narrow strip of the main sequence in the H-R diagram.

Consider another H-R diagram (Fig. 14.17): the brightest stars you can see. Compare it with the previous plot. What a difference! Almost all these stars have a much higher luminosity than the sun. And many of them are also much hotter (spectral class *A-* and *B-*stars). The main sequence no longer appears so obvious.

What are the physical differences among these stars? Take the star Betelgeuse, whose

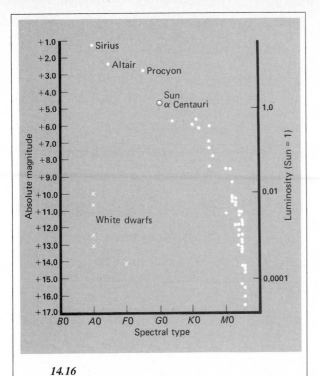

14.16

A Hertzsprung–Russell diagram for stars within 20 ly of the sun. Note that the vertical axis can be plotted either in absolute magnitude or luminosity (where, roughly, an absolute magnitude of +5 corresponds to the sun's luminosity) and the horizontal axis, in surface temperature or spectral type.

properties put it in the upper right-hand corner of the H-R diagram in Fig. 14.17. Here is a star whose surface is much cooler than the sun's. (If you look at Betelgeuse in Orion, you can see that the star appears reddish.) So if Betelgeuse were the same size as the sun, it would be much less luminous. But Betelgeuse has a luminosity 120,000 times that of the sun. To be so much cooler and more luminous than the sun, Betelgeuse must be much larger (Focus 36). In fact, astronomers have measured Betelgeuse and found it to have a diameter about 1200 times that of the sun—a star so big that it could swallow up Mars if it were placed in our solar system! Astronomers call Betelgeuse a red *supergiant* star.

Here is the reason that the H-R diagram for the nearest stars (Fig. 14.16) differs from that for the brightest stars (Fig. 14.17): The first diagram contains ordinary stars with sizes like that of the sun; no giants are among the nearest stars, for they are very rare. The sun is a main sequence star. Most of the stars in the sun's vicinity are also main sequence stars, of spectral class *M*. So they are cool and not very lumi-

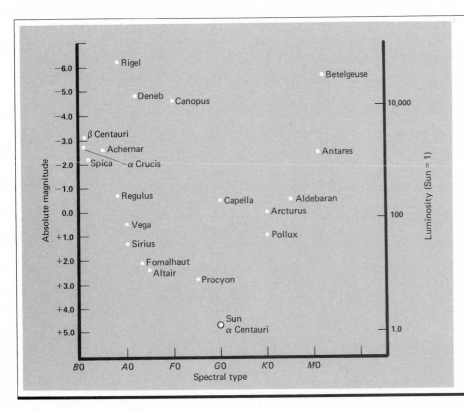

14.17

A Hertzsprung–Russell diagram for the brightest stars in the sky. Axes are the same as in Fig. 14.16. Note that the sun and Alpha Centauri have almost the same luminosity and surface temperature. Also note, compared to Fig. 14.16, the addition of many stars more luminous than the sun.

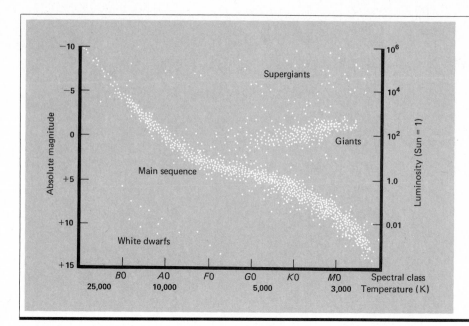

14.18

A Hertzsprung–Russell diagram for a large number of stars. Each star is represented by a point that denotes its absolute magnitude (luminosity) and spectral class (surface temperature). The stars fall into four general regions. Most lie along the main sequence. Many others fall into the giant region of luminous yellow to red stars. A small number make up the very luminous supergiants and the low luminosity white dwarfs. Note, compared with Figs. 14.16 and 14.17, the scale of the vertical axis has been changed to include a wider range of luminosities.

nous. The second diagram contains many giant and supergiant stars, still visible among the brighter stars because of their high luminosity, even though they are scattered widely through space.

Now piece these two diagrams together and add more stars (Fig. 14.18 and Color Plate 9). Most stars fall on the shallow "S" of the main sequence. A scattering of stars cuts across the tip of the diagram; these are the very luminous supergiants. A group of relatively cool but luminous stars extends off the main sequence: These are the giants. Finally, note a bunch of stars in the lower left-hand corner of the diagram. These stars have very high temperatures but low luminosities, so they must be very small. These peculiar stars are called *white dwarf stars* or *white dwarfs*.

Spectroscopic parallaxes / Once you have an H-R diagram for many stars, you can use it to infer approximate distances to stars. How? First, find out the spectral type of a star. Suppose it's an *M*-star. Then look at the H-R diagram to find the luminosity (or absolute magnitude) of an *M*-star. Here a problem arises: *M*-stars have a range of luminosities, from 1.6×10^{-5} the sun's luminosity for main-sequence *M*-stars to about 10^5 solar luminosities for supergiant ones. How to decide what luminosity an *M*-star is?

Fortunately, a star's spectrum indirectly indicates a star's luminosity. Recall that the strengths of Balmer lines relate to a star's temperature. To absorb Balmer lines, the hydrogen atoms must be excited by collisions—collisions with sufficient energy to raise the electrons one energy level. How energetic the collisions are depends on the temperature in a star's atmosphere. But for gases at the same temperature, the *rate* of collisions in a second depends on the density of the gases. So in a denser gas, collisions are more frequent than in a less dense gas at the same temperature (and so having the same energies in the collisions). Now giant stars, because they are so huge, typically have lower density atmospheres than main-sequence stars. The more frequent collisions in main-sequence stars make certain absorption lines in their spectra appear broader than the same lines in spectra of giant or supergiant stars (Fig. 14.19). So a star's size, and hence its luminosity, is given indirectly by the widths of certain absorption lines when comparing the spectra of stars of the same spectral type.

Such an analysis reveals that stars fall into *luminosity classes*. The recognized luminosity classes are (Fig. 14.20): Ia, most luminous supergiants; Ib, less luminous supergiants; II, luminous giants; III, normal giants; IV, subgiants,

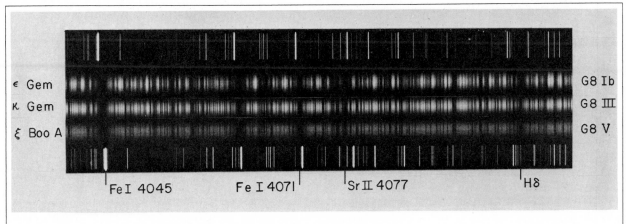

14.19

Determining a star's luminosity class from its spectrum. Here are the spectra of three stars all with the same surface temperature (spectral class G8). The top spectrum is for a supergiant star, the middle for a giant star, the bottom for a main-sequence star. The different intensities of certain dark lines permit astronomers to infer the luminosity class of the stars. (Courtesy Lick Observatory)

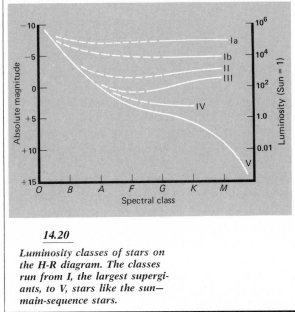

14.20

Luminosity classes of stars on the H-R diagram. The classes run from I, the largest supergiants, to V, stars like the sun—main-sequence stars.

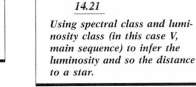

14.21

Using spectral class and luminosity class (in this case V, main sequence) to infer the luminosity and so the distance to a star.

and V, main-sequence stars. The sun falls into luminosity class V.

So a star's spectrum allows it to be classified by both spectral type *and* luminosity class. For a given spectral type, you can estimate, within a range of probable error (the width of a luminosity class on the H-R diagram), the luminosity (or absolute magnitude; Fig. 14.21). If you

know a star's luminosity and its flux, you can calculate its distance. Or, equivalently, if you know its apparent and absolute magnitude, you can also find the distance. The procedure for working out distances from spectra is called the *spectroscopic distance method* or *spectroscopic parallaxes.*

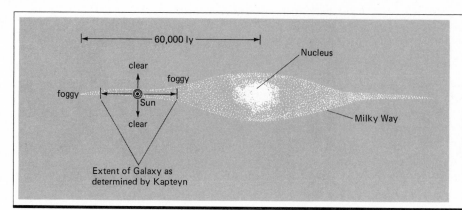

Why people thought the Milky Way to be heliocentric from star counts. The earth is located in the midplane of the Galaxy's disk, where a large amount of interstellar dust resides. This dust cuts out the light of distant stars, especially in the direction toward the Galaxy's center. This fogginess misled people to infer that the Galaxy was heliocentric and a lot smaller than it actually is.

The H-R diagram allows astronomers to infer the physical properties of stars from their spectra. This leads to unraveling the structure of the Milky Way Galaxy.

14.6

The discovery of the Galaxy

At the turn of this century a surge of observational data generated new tactics for unmasking the layout of the Milky Way Galaxy. Astronomers photographed a large part of the sky. Such photographs provided a valuable resource for improving upon Herschel's star-count method to map out the shape of the Galaxy.

Prelude: The Kapteyn universe / In 1901 Jacobus C. Kapteyn (1851–1922) employed statistical parallaxes to find the average distances of stars in the Milky Way. Kapteyn's study provided the distance scale for an outline of the Galaxy given by the star counts—essentially Herschel's technique. Consequently, the Galaxy attained the grand dimensions of 26,000 ly in diameter and 6500 ly in thickness, with the sun within 8000 ly of the center. This is smaller than the actual dimensions but much larger than anyone had previously imagined.

Kapteyn did have one worry that later turned out to be important: the absorption of starlight in space. If absorption did occur, distant stars would be so faint that they would not be seen. Kapteyn was correct; interstellar dust does absorb starlight. The evidence for interstellar absorption by dust came later than Kapteyn's work and served to reset the boundaries of the Galaxy. In particular, the cutting off of the starlight caused Kapteyn to ascribe a small, almost heliocentric character to our Galaxy (Fig. 14.22),

which astronomers now know is neither heliocentric nor small.

Variables: A new distance indicator / Another technique of surveying the stars came from an unexpected quarter in 1908. While studying variable stars in the Magellanic Clouds—two small galaxies in the southern sky now thought to be physically connected with our Galaxy—Henrietta S. Leavitt (1868–1921; see Fig. 5.10) discovered that when the apparent magnitudes of a certain type of variable star were plotted against their periods, a definite relationship appeared (Fig. 14.23). Since all the stars in the Small or Large Cloud are essentially at the same distance from the sun, the plot of apparent magnitude against period could be translated into a plot of absolute magnitude against period, if the distance to the Clouds is known. Somehow the periods of these variables were related to their luminosities: The longer the period is, the greater the luminosity will be.

The next year Hertzsprung pointed out that the variables Leavitt had discovered had light curves similar to that of the star Delta Cephei. A star whose light varies in a regular fashion is known as a *periodic variable;* Delta Cephei sets the standard for one such class of variables— called *cepheid variables* or *cepheids*—by the unique shape of its light curve.

What's a *light curve?* Suppose you measured the brightness of a star (or any celestial object) over a period of time. A plot of the star's brightness with time is the star's light curve (Fig. 14.24). Cepheid light curves show a cyclical, wavelike pattern of brightness variation.

Hertzsprung deduced from Leavitt's data that a unique relationship exists between the

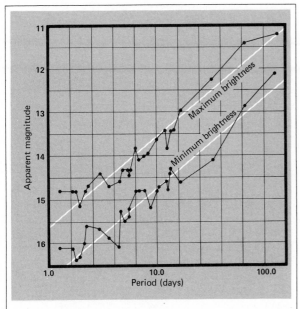

14.23

Leavitt's original period-luminosity relation (plotted here as apparent magnitude against the period in days) for cepheids in the Magellanic clouds. The upper line is the average for the points when the cepheids are at maximum brightness; the lower one for times of minimum brightness. (Based on data in the Harvard Circular, *No. 173, 1912)*

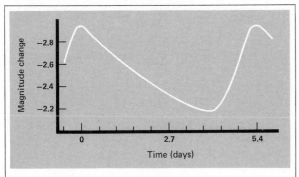

14.24

A light curve for a typical cepheid variable star (Delta Cephei—the prototype of the class). It shows how the observed brightness of the stars varies with time. Note that the rise in brightness is steep, but the decline, less shown. This shape of the light curve is characteristic of cepheids as a class. The period of one cycle of brightness variation is 5.4 days.

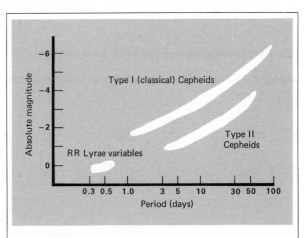

14.25

A simplified period-luminosity relation for cepheids. The cepheids are now known to fall into two groups (Type I and Type II). RR Lyrae stars are very short-period variables that are found in globular clusters. Each of these variables has its own period-luminosity relation. In general, for these stars, you see that the **more luminous** *the variable star, the* **longer** *its period.*

luminosity of a cepheid variable and its period. This connection is called the *period-luminosity relationship* (Fig. 14.25). We can find distances to cepheids by the following method: (1) Find a cepheid; (2) measure its period (a relatively easy task that does not depend on any knowledge of the star's distance or spectral class); (3) find the star's absolute magnitude from the period-luminosity relationship; and (4) knowing the star's apparent magnitude, calculate its distance (Focus 37). The period-luminosity relationship played a vital and versatile role in surveying the Galaxy. With only one cepheid you can find the distance to some object with which the cepheid is associated, such as a cluster of stars. (More about cepheids in Chapter 19.)

Shapley dethrones the sun / In the second decade of this century Harlow Shapley (Fig. 14.26) proposed a radical idea about the size of the Milky Way Galaxy and the sun's position in this island of stars. The observational foundation of his model rested on using the period-luminosity relation of cepheids. His model evicted the sun from its central status in the Galaxy, the second significant move of humankind away from special status in the universe.

focus 37

DISTANCES TO CEPHEID VARIABLES

The key to this technique is the period-luminosity relationship (Fig. 14.25) calibrated in absolute magnitude. With this plot available, finding the distance to a cepheid is a straightforward process. Only two measurements are required: (1) the star's apparent magnitude and (2) its period of light variation.

Suppose we measure the variable's period and find it to be 10 days. Turn to Fig. 14.25. For classical cepheids the absolute magnitude corresponding to a 10-day period is −3. Now suppose that the apparent magnitude is +7. The difference between the apparent and absolute magnitudes is +7 − (−3), or +10. Hence the star is so far away that it is 10 magnitudes fainter than it would appear if it were 10 pc away. (Recall the definition of absolute magnitude, Focus 33). Ten magnitudes equals a brightness ratio of 10^4, so the star is as much farther away from 10 pc as the amount needed to dim its brightness by 10^4.

Recall (Focus 34) that light diminishes in intensity by the inverse-square law. To get a decrease by 10^4 requires a distance increase of $\sqrt{10^4}$, or 10^2. So the star is 100 times farther away than 10 pc, or 1000 pc.

To work this problem out algebraically:

$$M - M = 5 \log d - 5$$
$$7 - (-3) = 5 \log d - 5$$
$$15 = 5 \log d$$
$$3 = \log d$$

So

$$d = 10^3 \, pc$$
$$= 3.3 \times 10^3 \, ly$$

Note: *This technique assumes that dust does* **not** *cut out the light from the cepheid. If it did, the apparent magnitude would be fainter than it actually is, and you would estimate the star to be farther away than its actual distance.*

14.26
Harlow Shapley (1885–1972). "We are all brothers of the boulders, cousins of the clouds." (Courtesy of Harvard College Observatory)

Shapley worked for his doctorate at Princeton University under Russell. In his research Shapley became familiar with techniques for observing variable stars. With this new Ph.D., he was offered and accepted a position at Mt. Wilson Observatory. During 1914 Shapley published two papers that foreshadowed his work on the size of the Galaxy. One paper dealt with variable stars in the globular cluster M13 (M13 is the abbreviation of Messier 13, which stands for the thirteenth object in a catalog of nonstellar objects put together by Charles Messier in 1781), the other, with the nature of variable stars. When he recognized that the variables he observed in globular clusters had the characteristics of cepheids, he adopted the technique of deriving the distance to the cluster by using a calibrated period-luminosity relation. "Calibrated" means that the luminosities of some cepheids had been measured to provide a plot

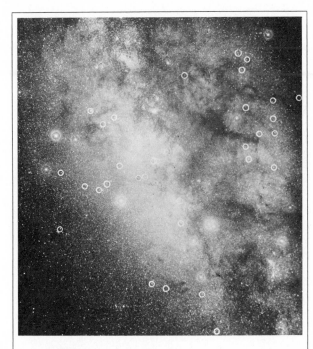

14.27

The concentration of globular clusters in the sky in the direction of the galactic center. Each white circle marks a globular cluster. About one-third of all known globulars lie in this region of the sky, which is only 2 percent of the entire sky. (Courtesy Harvard College Observatory)

bration was off, so he underestimated the luminosities of nearby cepheids by about 4. By coincidence, the first mistake—which overestimated the variables luminosities by 4—just about canceled out the second error. But he also was unaware of another problem that caused him to overestimate the distance to globulars—he ignored light absorption by interstellar dust.

In 1915 Shapley noted that globular clusters did not follow the distribution of stars along the Milky Way by sticking along the plane. Rather, they tended to be widely distributed, with an odd concentration in the direction of Sagittarius (Fig. 14.27). No other objects were so strangely arranged relative to the Milky Way. In the closer globular clusters he could distinguish what he thought were cepheid variables. With his own calibration of the period-luminosity curve, Shapley found these closer clusters to be at a distance about 39,000 ly from the sun. Later he estimated M13 to be 100,000 ly distant. This number was staggering, for it placed the globular clusters outside the boundaries of the Galaxy as mapped by Kapteyn.

The nonuniform distribution of globulars in the sky remained a nagging problem. Shapley thought that the globulars were gravitationally allied with the Galaxy in a uniform distribution. Then the observed nonuniformity indicated that the sun was not placed in the Milky Way's center. After some hesitation Shapley accepted this idea: The globular clusters orbited the Galaxy's center and outlined its extent. Then Shapley concluded that the sun must be on the outskirts of the Galaxy.

Here's Shapley's argument in detail. It rests on the simple observation of the distribution of globular clusters in the sky.

Globular clusters concentrate in the southern sky (Fig. 14.27). From what vantage point do we, whirling around the sun, view these groups of stars? The key lies in a valid assumption about the distribution of the globulars in and around our Galaxy. Shapley knew that our Galaxy had the shape of a flattened disk. He could have assumed that the globular clusters followed the same distribution in space as ordinary stars. However, you would then expect that the apparent globular cluster distribution in the Milky Way would more or less coincide with the distribution of stars. Such a coincidence does

of luminosity (rather than apparent magnitude) against period.

Here Shapley faced a difficult and crucial problem: How to get the calibration when no cepheid is close enough to the sun to have its parallax measured! To overcome this lack, Shapley examined the proper motions of a number of nearby cepheids. He then applied the statistical parallax method to estimate the distance to the cepheids. With this estimate, he then could translate apparent magnitude into absolute ones, and so calibrate the period-luminosity relation (as has been done for Fig. 14.25).

It turns out that Shapley made two mistakes in his procedure. First, he was wrong in assuming that the variables in globulars were the same as those in the disk of the Galaxy. (They are not; the variables in globulars actually are RR Lyrae stars, which have a *different* period-luminosity relationship.) Second, his cali-

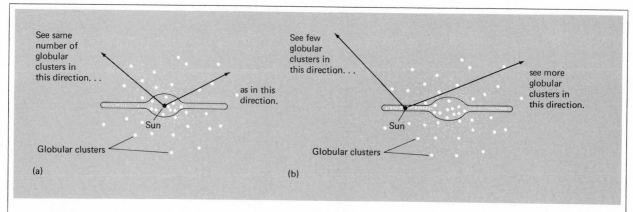

14.28

The position of the sun in the Galaxy inferred from the observed distribution of globular clusters in the sky. Assume that globular clusters are uniformly distributed around the center of the Galaxy. Suppose the sun were located at the center (a). Then you would see roughly the same number of globular clusters in every direction you looked in the sky. But this is not so; globulars are concentrated in one direction in the sky. Consider instead that the sun is off to one side of the Galaxy (b). Then looking toward the center, you see more globular clusters than in any other direction. This is the observed situation.

not exist. So Shapley assumed that the globular clusters had a uniform spherical distribution around the Milky Way's center.

To illustrate the observational consequences of this assumption, suppose the sun were located in the center of the Galaxy (Fig. 14.28). Trace lines of sight in a number of different directions. Because you have assumed a central vantage point in a uniform distribution of objects, every line of sight you choose should intercept the same number of globular clusters. Hence the expected distribution would be uniform over the sky, but this uniformity does not in fact occur. Shapley therefore had the choice between dropping his assumption and explaining the observed distribution by some lopsided, nonuniform distribution in space. Such an assumption would have run counter to his aesthetic grain. An alternative was to move the sun away from the center (Fig. 14.28). Now some lines of sight cut longer distances than others through the globular clusters, so more clusters are seen in these directions than along shorter lines of sight. The expected distribution is not symmetric but is most concentrated in the direction of the galactic center. So when the sun was moved from the center, the predicted result matched the observational one.

When Shapley used what he thought were cepheid variables to determine the distances to globular clusters, he was able to estimate the dimensions of the Milky Way. The figure he finally arrived at for the galactic diameter—300,000 ly—was too large in the light of modern measurements. Although the size of the Milky Way was incorrect, Shapley's repositioning of the sun resulted in a new place for mankind in the universe.

The spiral nebulas / What about Herschel's spiral nebulas (Fig. 14.29)? Were they, like globulars, part of the Milky Way? The question of their status—whether or not they were connected to our Galaxy—remained unsettled, primarily because no distances had been found for them. If they were other galaxies and if they were the same size Shapley proposed for the Galaxy, then their distances, as implied by their small angular diameters, must be immense—*millions* of light years.

In 1917 George W. Ritchey of Mt. Wilson accidentally discovered one of the strongest pieces of evidence for the distances and nature of the spiral nebulas. While photographing spiral nebulas to determine their motion in space, Ritchey caught the flash of a nova in NGC 6946 on July 19, 1917. (A *nova* is a star whose bright-

14.29

A typical spiral galaxy, Messier 33 (M33) in Triangulum. (Courtesy Lick Observatory)

ness suddenly increases and then slowly fades.) Astronomers recognized the significance of this event: Since a nova could occur in a cluster of stars but not in a cloud of gas, NGC 6946 could not be just a nebula. Other plates at Mt. Wilson were searched, and more novas were discovered.

Heber D. Curtis (1872–1942) of Lick Observatory took part in the nova search. He regarded the novas as proof that the spiral nebulas were misnamed, that they were actually systems of stars rather than disks of gas. To support this contention, he devised a clever method by using novas as distance indicators. From the observed apparent magnitude of novas in spirals, Curtis could estimate the distances (Focus 38). Utilizing the novas to confirm that some spirals were distant galaxies, he argued that Shapley's measurements of the size of the Galaxy were incorrect and that Kapteyn's smaller value was the proper one.

The Shapley-Curtis debate / The opinions of Shapley and Curtis represented the views of two different schools of thought among astronomers around 1920 concerning the spiral nebulas. The older view, upheld by Curtis, pictured the spiral nebulas as galaxies of approximately the same size and shape as the Galaxy (roughly 30,000 ly in diameter). The opposing view, espoused by Shapley, pictured the Galaxy as outlined by globular clusters and about 300,000 ly in diameter. This size ruled out the spiral nebulas as galaxies, because their relatively close distances, as estimated by Shapley, were not consistent with the large diameters required if the spirals were the same size as the Galaxy. Shapley relegated the spirals to a place as minor members at the fringe of the Galaxy. His view was simultaneously radical and conservative, for his large Milky Way excluded similar systems, whereas Curtis envisioned a universe filled with spiral galaxies.

focus 38

DISTANCES TO NOVAS

In 1918 a bright nova appeared in the constellation of Aquila and was closely studied by astronomers. The next year Edward E. Barnard found a small nebula around the fading nova. A study of the Doppler shift in its spectrum of emission lines showed that the nebula was expanding. The radial velocity of expansion was 1700 km/sec, a rate that corresponded to an increase of angular size of roughly 1 arcsec per year. Because the actual expansion rate was known from the Doppler shift, it became possible to compute the nova's distance so that the rate in kilometers per second matched the angular expansion. With the distance determined, the absolute magnitude was found to be a little greater than −8 at maximum.

Nova Aquilae was the first galactic nova to have its absolute magnitude found. With the discovery of novas in other galaxies—notably M31 in Andromeda—Heber D. Curtis devised a simple method to use novas to determine distances. Curtis first assumed—using simplicity and the uniformity of nature as his philosophical foundations—that novas in another galaxy were the same as novas in our Galaxy. In particular, he believed that both galactic and extragalactic novas have about the same absolute magnitudes at maximum.

(Some support for this idea came from the fact that most novas in the same galaxy have the same apparent magnitudes at maximum.) Using −8 as the absolute magnitude at maximum, Curtis compared this value with the apparent magnitude at maximum to find the distance to the nova and the galaxy.

An example. Suppose a nova in M31 shines at apparent magnitude +16 at maximum light. The difference between the apparent and absolute magnitudes is 24 magnitudes. Hence the star is fainter than it would be at 10 pc by 24 magnitudes. A difference of 24 magnitudes corresponds (Table 14.1) to a ratio of $10^2 \times 10^2 \times 10^2 \times 10^2 \times 40 = 40 \times 10^8$ in brightness. To be this much fainter than the same star at 10 pc, the nova must be $(40 \times 10^8)^{1/2} = 6.3 \times 10^4$ times more distant, that is, at 6.3×10^5 pc, or 6.3×10^2 kpc. (The accepted distance to M31 is 6.8×10^2 kpc.)

Algebraically,

$$M - M = 5 \log d - 5$$

$$16 - (-8) = 5 \log d - 5$$

$$24 = 5 \log d - 5$$

$$29 = 5 \log d$$

$$\frac{29}{5} = \log d$$

$$d = 6.3 \times 10^5 \ pc$$

or

$$= 2.1 \times 10^6 \ ly$$

Shapley and Curtis debated their respective positions at the April 1920 meeting of the National Academy of Sciences in Washington, D.C. The kernel of the conflict between Shapley and Curtis was not the general shape of the Milky Way, the sun's position within it, or the fundamentals of any of the astronomical surveying methods. It was philosophical: Did other galaxies exist in the universe?

Both men were right in their general scheme of the Galaxy, but neither had arrived at the correct size; Shapley's was three times too large, and Curtis's was too small by the same amount. (In the present view, the Galaxy is about 120,000 ly across; the sun is half of the Galaxy's radius from the center.) Curtis did score some points for the other-galaxy theory, which Shapley later accepted after considering additional evidence. (One piece came when M31, the nearest spiral, was resolved into stars by the 100-inch telescope.)

However, Shapley had shaken one of our cosmic foundations, and people could no longer imagine themselves proudly in the center of the Galaxy, but must rather humbly accept their place in the outskirts.

SUMMARY

I have narrated astronomers' efforts, in the span of two centuries, to piece together the construction of the Milky Way. You have seen that fitting together the celestial architecture depended on the measurement of distances, which in turn is based on the fundamental properties of stars and electromagnetic radiation. Star counting—like that of Herschel, von Seeliger, and Kapteyn—gives only the relative shape of the Galaxy. Parallaxes were first used to set the distance. Later the H-R diagram was used to get distances. But the big breakthrough came with Leavitt's discovery of the period-luminosity relationship for cepheids. Once known in terms of absolute magnitude, this relationship could be used to find the distances to globular clusters and that the Galaxy was large, with the sun far from the center.

The astronomical outlook on the Galaxy was wedded to the attitude of whether other galaxies populated the universe. In particular, the spiral nebulas, which astronomers had observed for a century, acted like a cosmic mirror whose image influenced the picture of the Milky Way. Were the spiral nebulas—as Shapley believed in 1920—simply clouds of gas that were small parts of the Milky Way? Or, as Curtis argued, were these really other galaxies, island universes of stars? Curtis proved right in this respect. Today, astronomers recognize that many of the so-called spiral nebulas are actually galaxies. Then the spiral structure of these objects raised another question: Does the Milky Way Galaxy also have a spiral structure? The answer, as you will see in Chapter 16, is yes.

STUDY EXERCISES

1   Why doesn't a star's apparent magnitude directly tell you its luminosity? (*Objective 2*)

2   You observe a star to have apparent magnitude 10. I tell you its absolute magnitude is 5. How far is the star in parsecs? (*Objective 3*)

3   Suppose you measure the heliocentric parallaxes of two stars and find that one is half the other. What are the *relative* distances of the two stars from the sun? (*Objective 4*)

4   Capella and the sun are almost the same spectral type, so both stars have about the same surface temperature. Yet Capella has a luminosity about five times as large as that of the sun. How can you explain this difference? (*Objective 5*)

5   Suppose you are trying to find the distance to a star by spectroscopic parallax. Imagine that, unknown to you, dust between you and the star significantly dims and reddens the star's light. Would you overestimate or underestimate the star's distance, compared with its actual distance? What clue would tip you off that dust has botched your distance determination? (*Objectives 2, 3, and 5*)

6   Suppose you identify a cepheid variable with a period of 30 days. What is its approximate absolute magnitude? You observe its apparent magnitude to be 10. What is its approximate distance in parsecs? In light years? (*Objective 6*)

7   Imagine that the sun *were* located in the center of the Galaxy. How would globular clusters be distributed in the sky? (*Objective 7*)

8   Rigel, in Orion, has an apparent magnitude of 0.11; Betelgeuse, 0.8. From which star do we receive *more* flux at the earth? (*Objective 2*)

9   Consider three stars with the following spectral types: MI, GIII, and AV. Which is hottest? Which is largest? Which is most luminous? (*Objectives 6 and 7*)

BEYOND THIS BOOK . . .

Two excellent books about the evolution of ideas about our Galaxy and other galaxies are *The Discovery of Our Galaxy* by C. A. Whitney (Knopf, New York, 1971), and *Man Discovers the Galaxies* by R. Berendzen, R. Hart, and D. Seeley (Science History Publications, New York, 1976).

For more on cepheids read "Pulsating Stars and Cosmic Distances" by R. Kraft, *Scientific American*, July 1959, p. 48 and "Pulsating Stars" by J. Percy, June 1975, p. 66.

O. Struve and V. Zebergs trace the development of ideas about stars and the Galaxy in *Astronomy of the 20th Century* (Macmillan, New York, 1962).

LEARNING OBJECTIVES

After studying this chapter you should be able to:

1. Summarize the physical differences between old and young Population I and Population II stars, and indicate on a drawing of the Milky Way the regions where you find them.

2. Cite what observational evidence indicates that you are looking at a physical binary star system rather than at two unconnected stars that appear close together.

3. Outline how binary star systems are used to find the masses of stars and state clearly the assumptions made and observations needed.

4. Describe how astronomers establish the mass-luminosity relation for main-sequence stars, sketch such a relation (or write it down in equation form), and use it to estimate masses of stars from their luminosities (or vice versa).

5. Indicate at least three differences between galactic and globular clusters.

6. Present observational evidence for the existence of gas and dust among the stars.

7. Describe the different forms in which the interstellar gas is found, and how each form is observed.

8. Describe the general physical characteristics of reflection nebulas, emission nebulas, and giant molecular clouds.

9. Describe the effects of interstellar dust on starlight.

10. Indicate the possible physical properties of interstellar dust.

11. Outline the general contents of the disk, nucleus, and halo of the Galaxy.

12. Describe what optical, infrared, and radio observations tell astronomers about the nucleus of the Milky Way.

As twixt the poles, with lesser lights and great
Patterned, the Galaxy so whitely glows
That thereof sages question and debate.
DANTE: Paradisio

The contents of the Milky Way Galaxy

15

The Galaxy has a fascinating complexity in both content and structure. You met some of the galactic contents in the previous chapter: supergiant, giant, and dwarf stars; globular clusters; open clusters; and cepheid variables. Each of these objects helped to reveal some aspect of the Galaxy's overall structure that was discovered in the beginning of this century.

This chapter takes a closer look at the contents of the Galaxy. You will find that the stars, classified on the basis of their physical characteristics, tend to fall into two broad categories called *stellar populations*. These populations are found to mark three distinct regions of the Galaxy: the flat disk, the bulging nucleus, and the enormous halo.

A census of the stars in the disk closest to the sun shows that many—if not most—come in gravitationally bound groups. Two stars in orbit around one another make up a binary star system. Binaries provide the only means to measure directly the masses of stars. Many stars are bound in larger groups called *clusters*, such as galactic clusters (found in the disk) and globular clusters (found in the halo).

Is the space among the stars empty? No, not at all! Radio and optical astronomers have uncovered an interstellar medium that consists of gas and dust. Hydrogen makes up most of the gas, but there are some surprises: molecules such as water and carbon monoxide. The gas particles outnumber the dust particles about 10^{12} to 1. However, the dust particles contain at least 1 percent of the mass of the interstellar medium and play important roles in the formation of planets (Chapter 12) and stars (Chapter 19) that are born out of the interstellar medium. It is an active place, whipped by the violence of the explosions of massive stars.

A brief look at the nucleus, in which lurks a mysterious energy source, and the encompassing, massive halo rounds out the tour of the contents of the Milky Way Galaxy.

15.1
Stellar populations

With the general outline of the Galaxy developed, astronomers turned to working out its structure in detail. One new insight came by accident, helped by World War II. In 1944 Walter Baade was working at the 100-inch telescope

at Mt. Wilson, and as it was wartime, the German-born Baade was restricted to staying in the Mt. Wilson–Pasadena area. While his colleagues were off working for the government, Baade had considerable access to the 100-inch telescope. In addition, Los Angeles and neighboring towns were blacked out, resulting in an unusually dark sky.

Baade used film sensitized to red light. He photographed the *Andromeda galaxy*, M31 (Fig. 15.1), and resolved the central region into stars. (See Plate 21 for a color photo of M31.) Making an H-R diagram of the stars in the central bulge, he found that most of the brighter stars were red giants, and few were main-sequence stars. He was impressed by the similarity of these stars to those in the globular clusters studied by Shapley. He also noted the differences between these stars and those found in the solar neighborhood or in galactic clusters. From those observations Baade noticed that the stars in a galaxy—like ours or M31—fall into two groups, which he called *Population I* and *Population II* (Fig. 15.2).

Baade also observed that the two populations were found in different regions of the Andromeda galaxy and inferred the same situation in our Galaxy. Astronomers had found the Galaxy to be shaped like a thin *disk*. Viewing some other galaxies, such as Andromeda, they noted a bright *nuclear bulge* in the central region; its core is the *nucleus*. Globular clusters mark out the third general region of the Galaxy: a *halo* that is spherically distributed around the nucleus. The halo consists of globular clusters, some stars, a little hot gas, and so far invisible material.

What kinds of stars populate these three regions of the Galaxy? Baade concluded that the stars in the disk outside the nuclear bulge are mostly Population I. The nuclear bulge he labeled as primarily Population II. And the halo stars, which are mostly in globular clusters, he also assigned to Population II.

Astronomers now recognize that Baade's division of stars into two and only two populations was too simple. They have since learned that the stars in globular clusters are *not* the same as those in the nuclear bulge. Although both groups contain numerous red giants, the globular cluster stars contain a much smaller

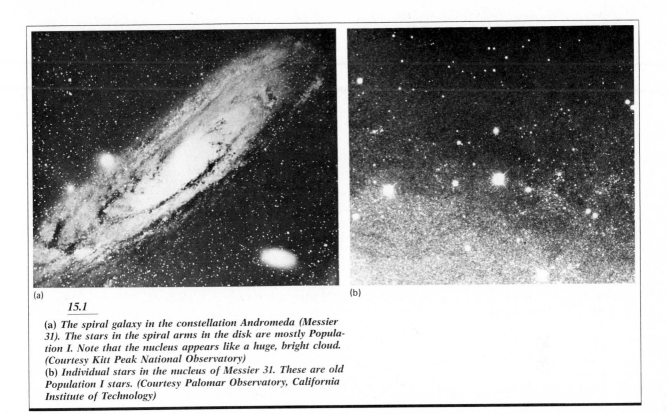

15.1

(a) *The spiral galaxy in the constellation Andromeda (Messier 31). The stars in the spiral arms in the disk are mostly Population I. Note that the nucleus appears like a huge, bright cloud. (Courtesy Kitt Peak National Observatory)*
(b) *Individual stars in the nucleus of Messier 31. These are old Population I stars. (Courtesy Palomar Observatory, California Institute of Technology)*

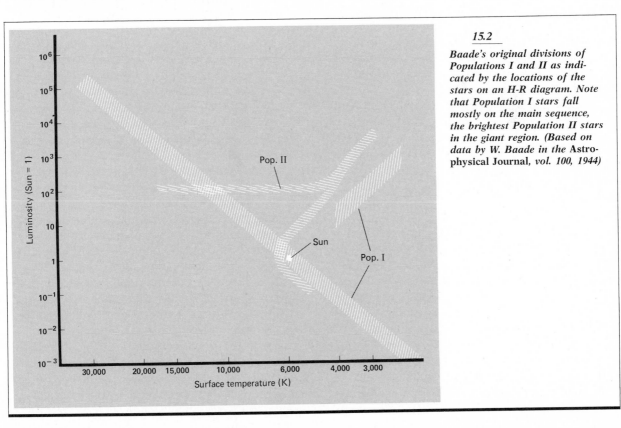

15.2

Baade's original divisions of Populations I and II as indicated by the locations of the stars on an H-R diagram. Note that Population I stars fall mostly on the main sequence, the brightest Population II stars in the giant region. (Based on data by W. Baade in the Astrophysical Journal, *vol. 100, 1944)*

abundance of heavy elements, whereas the stars in the nucleus have about the same abundance as in the sun. Astronomers today, therefore, refer to stars in the nuclear bulge as *old Population I*, those in the disk as *young Population I*, and only those in the halo as Population II. Some astronomers make even more divisions, for there is no strict boundary between groups, but for simplicity, I'll stick with these three. (For further discussion of populations, in the context of stellar evolution, see Chapter 19.)

In summary: Young Population I stars are found in the Galaxy's disk. The most luminous are hot, blue stars—the youngest are only a few million years old. About 2 percent of their mass is heavy elements. Astronomers call these stars *metal-rich*. ("Metals" refers to all elements except for hydrogen and helium.) Old Population I stars are found in the nuclear bulge. They are also metal-rich, but the most luminous are red giant stars. They are old, more than 10 billion years in age. Population II stars are found in the halo, especially in globular clusters. The most luminous are red giant stars. Typically, they have only about 1 percent of the heavy elements found in Population I, that is, 0.02 percent of the total. These stars are called *metal-poor*. They are also old, the oldest stars in the Galaxy. (Chapter 19 describes how to determine the ages of stars; remember that the sun is about 4.6 billion years old.)

With these stellar populations giving a general view of stars in the Galaxy, here's a look in detail at its contents.

15.2
The disk of the Galaxy, I: Stars

The Galaxy's disk contains stars, gas, and dust. The gas and dust together make up the interstellar medium. The sun lies almost in the midplane of the disk. Here, about half the mass is trapped in stars and half in gas and dust. The stars are examined first (this section) and then the interstellar medium (next two sections).

The common stars / Recall from Section 14.5 the H-R diagrams for the brightest stars (Fig. 14.16) and for the stars within 20 ly of the sun (Fig. 14.17). Both groups complemented each other—the brightest stars contained many that were very luminous and the nearest stars, many of very low luminosity.

One goal of studying the Galaxy is to find out, on the average, the properties of stars in a typical volume of space. For example, if you looked at a cube 1000 ly on each side, how many stars would you find with the sun's luminosity? How many 100 times more luminous? In other words, what would a star census of the Galaxy look like?

To take such a census requires a combination of methods to get the distances and luminosities of many stars. Heliocentric parallaxes provide the distances for nearby stars. Both spectroscopic and statistical parallaxes gives distances for the distant stars (which turn out to be the most luminous ones). The final census, for stars of all spectral types, is called the *luminosity function* (Fig. 15.3). It is a compilation of how many stars of a given luminosity can be found in a typical volume of space in the disk of the Galaxy.

What does this census reveal? First, the bulk of stars are ones of very low luminosity—main-sequence M-stars. Even the sun has a greater luminosity than most of the stars in the disk. Second, although very luminous stars are rare, they contribute the most to the background starlight in the disk. For example, to match one star of 100 solar luminosities takes one *million* stars of 10^{-4} solar luminosity.

In a typical region of the Galaxy near the Sun, there is about 0.0014 solar mass of stars in a cubic light year, emitting 0.0017 solar luminosity of visible light. The stars are spaced about 7 ly apart. The Galaxy's disk is empty in terms of stars!

How thick is the disk? Because there is no sharp boundary to the Galaxy, the answer depends on the meaning of thickness and which objects are chosen to measure it. For example, use stars and define the thickness as the distance from the plane where the density of stars falls to half its midplane value. Using G-, K-, and M-stars to define the thickness gives a result of about 2300 ly. The Galaxy's disk is thin compared with its diameter of about 120,000 ly.

Stars in groups / The stars closest to the sun tend to cluster in multiple star systems held together by gravity. Within 16 ly of the sun there are 60 individual stars, of which 28 occur in multiple star systems and 32 are by themselves. This roughly 50–50 division of the local stars reflects the more general clustering of stars

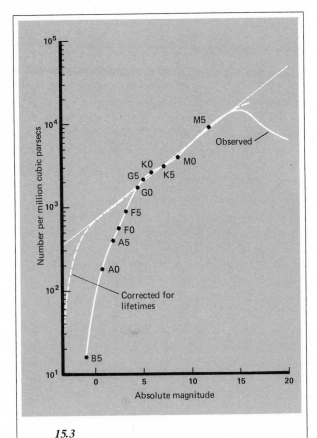

15.3

A luminosity function for stars in a typical volume of space in the Galaxy. The solid line indicates the observed numbers of stars of different spectral type; the dashed line is what we should see of the high-mass stars but don't because of their relatively short lifetimes.

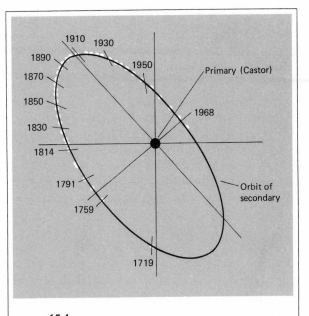

15.4

Motion of a visual binary star, Castor and companion. The orbit of the companion is drawn as if Castor were motionless. In fact, both stars revolve around a common center of mass with an orbital period of about 380 years. The orientation is that of a tilted elliptical orbit against the sky. (Orbit determined by K. A. Strand)

in the Galaxy. A recent survey of 123 sunlike stars found 57 two-star (binary) systems, eleven triple-star systems, and three quadruple-star systems. So of their sample, more than half—57 percent—of the stars had at least one gravity-linked companion. This sample probably reflects the frequency of multiple-star systems for sunlike stars in the Galaxy.

Binary stars / Two stars bound together by their mutual gravity in orbit around each other are called *binary stars* or a *binary star system*. Binary pairs are a common way of life for stars in the Galaxy. More important for astronomers, binary star systems provide the only direct way to determine the masses of stars—a key astrophysical quantity.

All binary systems are physically the same. But they are observed in different ways. So binary stars are put into one of three classes according to how they were discovered: visual, spectroscopic, and eclipsing.

In a *visual binary*, a telescope clearly shows both stars. With enough observations, you can trace the orbital path of the fainter star (called the *secondary*) around the brighter one (called the *primary*). Because a supposed pair may be only an accidental line-of-sight juxtaposition of two physically separate stars, astronomers must sometimes wait for many years to confirm that the two stars are really bound by gravity (Fig. 15.4). As you expect from Kepler's third law, binary stars with large separations will have large periods. For instance, Castor and its companion have an orbital period of 380 years. Application of Kepler's third law (in Newton's revised form—Focus 12), with a knowledge of the orbital period and the semimajor axis, provides

focus 39

SIRIUS: A BINARY SYSTEM

Recall (Focus 12) that Newton rewrote Kepler's third law in a form that included the gravitational constant, G, and the masses of the bodies involved. Let M_1 and M_2 be the masses of two stars in a binary system. Then the relationship between the period, P, and the average distance between the two stars, a, is

$$\frac{a^3}{P^2} = \frac{G(M_1 + M_2)}{4\pi^2}$$

Suppose the system is aligned so that from the earth we look face down on the orbit. If you know the distance to the system in AU's and measure the angular separation between the two stars, you can find a in AU's. You get the period by watching the stars revolve for a long time. So you know everything necessary to find

$$M_1 + M_2 = \left(\frac{4\pi^2}{G}\right)\left(\frac{a^3}{P^2}\right)$$

the sum of the masses of the two stars.

If you want this sum to come out in **solar masses,** *you use*

$$M_1 + M_2 = \frac{a^3}{P^2}$$

with years the units for P and AU's the units for a.

Use Sirius as a specific example. It is a binary system whose primary star, Sirius A, is the one you see in the sky. Its companion, Sirius B, is much fainter. From the orbital motion of Sirius B relative to A, the orbital period is observed to be 50 years. The dis-

tance to the stars is 8.64 ly; from this and the angular separation you find the actual separation (semimajor axis) to be about 20 AU.

Applying Kepler's third law to the Sirius system,

$$M_A + M_B = \frac{20^3}{50^2}$$

$$= \frac{8000}{2500} = 3.2 \text{ solar masses}$$

Now Sirius A is about twice as close to the center of mass as Sirius B. So from the center of mass relation

$$\frac{M_A}{M_B} = \frac{a_B}{a_A}$$

with $2a_A = a_B$, you get

$$\frac{M_A}{M_B} = \frac{2a_A}{a_A} = 2$$

and

$$M_A = 2M_B$$

You now know the sum and ratio of the masses. So

$$2M_B + M_B = 3.2 \text{ solar masses}$$
$$3M_B = 3.2 \text{ solar masses}$$
$$M_B = 1.07 \text{ solar masses}$$

and

$$M_A = 2.13 \text{ solar masses}$$

A careful study of Sirius A and B finds that the system has a period of 50.09 years and a total mass of 3.196 solar masses. Sirius A has a mass of 2.143 solar masses, a radius of 1.678 solar radii, and a surface temperature of 9970 K. In contrast, Sirius B has a mass of 1.053 solar masses, a radius of 0.0073 solar radius, and a surface temperature of 29,500 K.

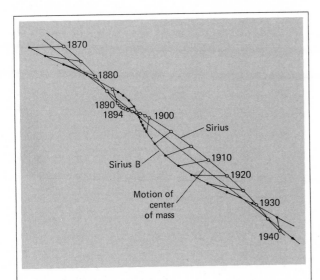

15.5

Motions of the binary star system Sirius and its companion, Sirius B. This figure shows two motions: that of Sirius and its companion about their center of mass and that of the center of mass with the stars relative to background stars seen from the earth, as the center of mass moves through space. So the two stars make a corkscrew motion against the sky. If, as in this case, only the primary star is easily visible, the wiggle in its motion is the tip-off that it has a companion.

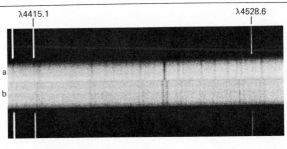

15.6

Spectra of a spectroscopic binary system (Mizar). The spectrum at the top and the one below it were taken at different times. In the upper spectrum (a) only single dark lines are visible. In the lower one (b) the lines are double because the secondary has come out from behind the primary with a line-of-sight velocity different from that of the primary star. So its lines are Doppler shifted relative to those of the primary. The bright-line spectra above and below the dark-line spectra serve to mark the reference wavelengths of the spectral lines. (Courtesy Mt. Wilson Observatory, Carnegie Institution of Washington)

the *sum* of the masses of the revolving stars (Focus 39).

To deduce the *individual* stellar masses requires one additional piece of information: the location of the center of mass of the system. Each star swings around the center of mass at a distance inversely proportional to its mass; so the more massive of the two stars is closer to the center of mass (Section 9.2). Because of the system's motion in space, the center of mass traces a straight line through space, while the two stars spiral around it (Fig. 15.5). This signature identifies the binary and the center of mass so that the individual masses can be computed.

Three comments. First, you must know the *distance* to the binary in order to find the stars' masses. Why? Because you need the stars' separation in AU to apply Kepler's third law. Second, you do not need to see the faint companion in order to detect a binary system. Even if

the companion shines so faintly as to be invisible, the primary star still traces a cyclical wiggle in the sky due to its motion about the center of mass. Astronomers diagnose a star with a wavy proper motion as a primary with a massive but invisible companion. (More about such invisible companions in Chapter 22.) Third, after a binary is found, astronomers sometimes discover later that the system has more stars. The star Castor, in Gemini, is a good example. A small telescope resolves two stars, while larger telescopes reveal that each of the two is itself double. In addition, a remote companion to this system revolves in a huge orbit about the other four, and it also is double. Castor's celestial ballet is composed of a total of six stars!

Spectroscopic binaries / Suppose two stars are so close together that you cannot resolve them with a telescope. Their orbital periods will be short, so the stars move around quickly. This binary system can be identified by looking for two sets of lines in the spectrum (one set from each star—Fig. 15.6) and measuring the Doppler

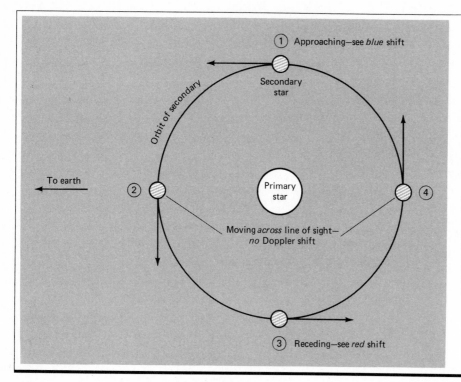

① Approaching—see *blue* shift

Secondary
star

Orbit of secondary

To earth

②

Primary
star

④

Moving *across* line of sight—
no Doppler shift

③ Receding—see *red* shift

15.7

The cycle of Doppler shifts from an eclipsing binary system. For simplicity, assume that the primary star is fixed (not revolving around the center of mass). When the secondary is at position 1, it is moving toward the earth, so its spectral lines appear blue-shifted. At 2, the secondary moves across our line of sight, so we see no shift. The same is true at 4. Finally, at position 3, the secondary moves away from us, so we see a red shift. So from 1 to 2 we find a decreasing blue shift, from 2 to 3 and increasing red shift, from 3 to 4 a decreasing red shift, and so on. The view here is looking straight down on the orbital plane.

shifts (Focus 19) produced by the orbital motion. This is a *spectroscopic binary*.

To see how to use the Doppler shift, imagine the more massive star to be stationary, with the secondary revolving about it. As the secondary recedes from the earth, you see its spectral lines red-shifted compared with those of the primary; as the secondary approaches, you see its lines blue-shifted (Fig. 15.7). At the intermediate points, when the secondary travels across the line of sight, you see no shift. If the two stars do not differ greatly in luminosity, both spectra can be observed, especially the cycle of shifts of the secondary with respect to the primary. (The smaller mass star will have the higher velocity, because it is farther from the center of mass.) Sometimes the spectrum of the secondary is too faint to be seen. You then use the Doppler shift in the primary's spectrum alone.

These relative wavelength shifts can be turned directly into relative velocity shifts by using the Doppler shift (Focus 19). Now, from the orbital period of the system, you use the velocities and the period to get the radius of the orbit. Then if you know the tilt of the orbit (easy for eclipsing binaries; next subsection),

you use Newton's form of Kepler's third law to obtain the sum of the masses.

Note: In this method, because you can measure the actual velocity of the stars in kilometers/second, you get the actual radius of the orbit, in kilometers, not just the angular radius. So unlike the case for a visual binary, you do *not* need to know the distance of a spectroscopic binary in order to find the stars' masses.

Eclipsing binary stars / If a binary orbit lies nearly or exactly on our line of sight, one star periodically eclipses the other as seen from the earth. Such an arrangement is called an *eclipsing binary system*. (An eclipsing pair is usually also spectroscopic.)

Algol, the "demon star" in the constellation of Perseus, is the prototype of eclipsing binaries. It has a period of 2.87 days and, in mideclipse, plummets 1.2 magnitudes in brightness (Fig. 15.8)—easy to see by eye. Observations of Algol's brightness variations give a crucial piece of information: the tilt of the orbit is about 82°. A 90° inclination would put both orbits edge-on to our view. Algol A, the brighter star (260 solar luminosities) is a B8 V (surface temperature 13,000 K); its companion, Algol B, is a fainter (5

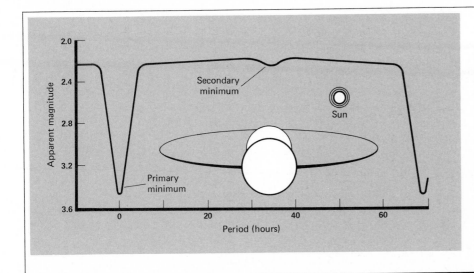

15.8

Algol, an eclipsing binary system. The two main stars lie almost edge on as seen from the earth. Algol, the primary, is a B-star with a diameter about three times that of the sun. Its dimmer companion is cooler—a G-star with a surface temperature similar to the sun's. The eclipse of Algol by its cool companion produces the largest dip (primary minimum) in the light curve, a plot of how the observed brightness changes with time. When the companion circles around Algol, the loss of light is less, so a smaller dip (secondary minimum) occurs in the light curve.

solar luminosities) *G*-type star (surface temperature 4600 K).

Recent spectroscopic observations of Algol B find that Algol B orbits at 201 km/sec, Algol A, at 44 km/sec, if the orbit is inclined 82°.4. The velocities and the period indicate that Algol A orbits 1.71×10^6 km from the center of mass, Algol B, at 7.9×10^6 km. So Algol A has a mass 4.6 times that of Algol B. The total separation is 9.6×10^6 km. Kepler's third law gives the total mass of the system as 4.51 solar masses. Combining this total mass with the spectroscopic mass ratio, Algol A turns out to be 3.7 solar masses, Algol B, 0.81 solar masses.

Eclipsing binaries give directly one other property of the stars: their diameters. Here's how. When Algol B passes in front of Algol A, the duration of the eclipse depends on the diameter of B relative to A and the relative orbital speeds. The Doppler shift provides those speeds. So the duration of the eclipse provides the sizes of each star, with the inclination known. For Algol the radius of each star is 3.08 solar radii for A, and 3.23 solar radii for B.

The mass-luminosity relation for the main sequence / Binary systems provide us with a direct measure of stellar masses. In most cases the luminosities of the two stars can be determined. When plotted against the stars' masses found from the orbits, the luminosities fall in a definite pattern (Fig. 15.9). A star's mass determines its luminosity, and the resulting correla-

tion is called the *mass-luminosity relation*. Basically, the mass-luminosity relation shows that a star's luminosity is *roughly* proportional to the third power of its mass. For example, a star with a mass ten times that of the sun has about $10^3 = 1000$ times the sun's luminosity.

Main-sequence stars follow the mass-luminosity relation fairly well; hence *the upward swing in luminosity of the main sequence from M- to O-stars reflects an increase in the stars' masses* (Fig. 15.10). So main-sequence *O*-stars are more massive than main-sequence *M*-stars. Astrophysicists had predicted the mass-luminosity relation theoretically, and its confirmation came from investigations of binary stars. (In Chapter 19 you will see the key role of the mass-luminosity relation for stellar evolution.)

Note from the mass-luminosity diagram that the masses of other stars do not differ widely from the sun's mass. Stars differ less in mass than in any other physical characteristic. According to theoretical considerations, stars with masses greater than about 100 solar masses are unstable, and bodies with masses less than roughly 0.01 solar mass cannot become stars. The narrow range of stellar masses is borne out by the H-R diagram and the mass-luminosity relation.

Galactic clusters / Astronomers have many star clusters in the Galaxy, for example, the Hyades and Pleiades (Fig. 15.11). Their motion across the sky confirms that the stars in each

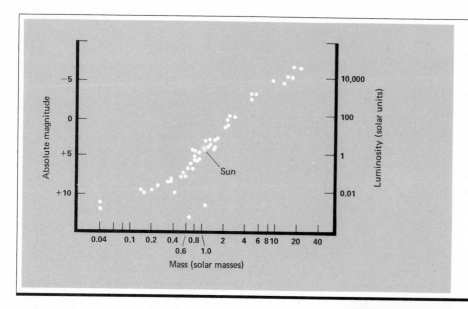

15.9

The mass-luminosity relation for main-sequence stars, as determined from binary systems, in which the individual masses can be determined. These stars are also those whose distances can be measured, so their luminosities can be calculated. Note that stars that have 10 times the mass of the sun shine with about a 1,000 times the luminosity.

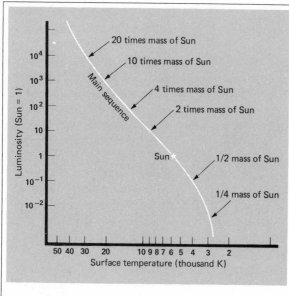

15.10

The mass for stars on the main sequence of the Hertzsprung–Russell diagram. Note that the stars with the highest surface temperatures are the most massive.

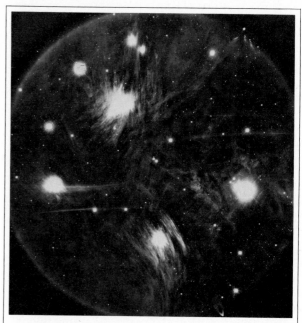

15.11

The Pleiades, an open cluster of young stars. They are still immersed in a cloud of dust, a remnant from the interstellar cloud from which the stars were born. (Courtesy Kitt Peak National Observatory)

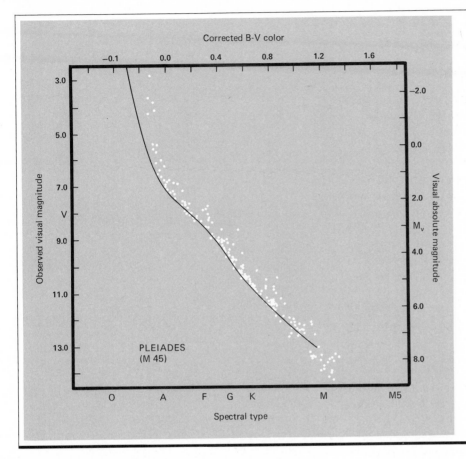

Corrected B-V color

Observed visual magnitude

Visual absolute magnitude

Spectral type

PLEIADES
(M 45)

15.12

A Hertzsprung–Russell diagram for the Pleiades. (From "An Atlas of Open Cluster Colour-Magnitude Diagrams" by G. L. Hagen, the David Dunlop Observatory, 1970)

group are physically associated by gravity and move together through space. Clusters such as the Hyades and Pleiades, which contain fewer than 100 to several hundred stars, are usually found in or near the Milky Way; hence they are called *galactic clusters* or, sometimes, *open clusters* because their density of stars is low (a few stars per cubic light year) compared with that of globular clusters (Section 15.6). Astronomers assume that because the members of a galactic cluster are bound by gravity, they must have had a common origin and so have similar ages and compositions.

One important characteristic of open clusters is their similar H-R diagrams. The one for the Pleiades is pretty typical (Fig. 15.12). Note that the stars below spectral type *A0* fall squarely on the main sequence. Above *A0*, the stars lie above and to the right of the main sequence. Clusters whose distances can be measured directly show the same properties: The lower-mass stars fall on the main sequence, but

at some point, the higher-mass stars turn off it (Fig. 15.13).

From such H-R diagrams, astronomers can estimate the distance to faraway open clusters (Focus 40). Another method uses the observed proper motions, and the criterion *swiftness means nearness*. Generally, the farther away a cluster is, the smaller is its proper motion. So a comparison of the motions in the sky of two galactic clusters gives a rough estimate of their relative distances. If the distance to one is measured, then the distance to the other can be found out.

The H-R diagram for galactic clusters displays an important general fact about the kinds of stars in galactic clusters: They are young, metal-rich Population I. This is expected, because most galactic clusters are within 10,000 ly of the sun and less than 50 ly from the galactic plane. So they hug the Galaxy's disk. Later, you will see that the fact these stars come in groups implies that they are born in groups.

focus 40

DISTANCES TO OPEN CLUSTERS

By assuming that the stars in the lower part of the main sequence of all open clusters are essentially the same, you can find the distances to clusters. This procedure involves two steps: (1) construct an H-R diagram of apparent magnitude plotted against spectral class for the open cluster in question; it will show a main sequence; (2) match this cluster's main sequence to that for open clusters whose distances are known. This match-up gives the difference between the apparent magnitudes along the main sequence of the cluster whose distance is not known and the absolute magnitudes along the main sequence of the cluster whose distance is known. The difference between the apparent and absolute magnitudes provides the distance to the cluster.

This method works because all the stars in a given open cluster are the same distance from the sun, even if that distance is unknown. So the differences in the apparent magnitudes of a cluster's stars directly reflect their differences in luminosities.

Suppose you have the H-R diagram for a cluster whose distance is found by independent means. (The Hyades is used as the standard cluster.) So you know its H-R diagram in terms of luminosity (or absolute magnitude) versus spectral type. Now select an open cluster whose distance you don't know and determine the fluxes (apparent magnitudes) of its stars and their spectral types. From these data plot an H-R diagram. Then line up the main sequence of the standard calibrated cluster with that of the distant cluster (Fig. 1). The apparent magnitudes of the cluster at an unknown distance correspond to absolute magnitudes of the cluster at a known distance. So you can find the difference between

the apparent and absolute magnitudes and so the distance.

In the figure $m - M$ *is 5.5. So*

$$m - M = 5 \log d - 5$$
$$5.5 = 5 \log d - 5$$
$$10.5 = 5 \log d$$
$$2.1 = \log d$$
$$d = 126 \text{ pc or } 410 \text{ ly}$$

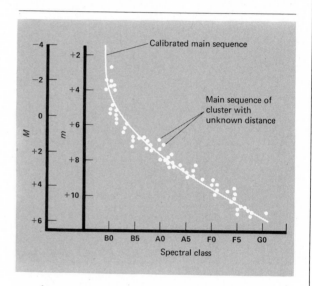

1

Finding distances to open clusters using the H-R diagram. From clusters whose distances we can measure, we have an H-R diagram calibrated in absolute magnitude and therefore luminosity. Suppose we have an H-R diagram for a cluster whose distance we don't know; it is a plot of apparent magnitude versus spectral type. Line up the main sequences of the two diagrams. Then read off the difference between the apparent magnitudes and the absolute ones. This difference gives the distance. Here the difference is about 5.5, so the distance is 125 parsecs, or about 400 ly.

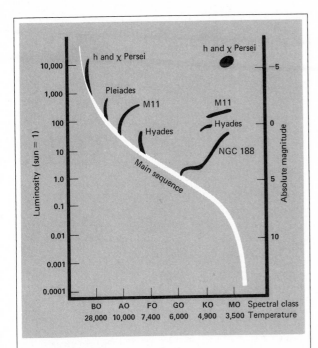

15.13

Schematic H-R diagram for some open clusters whose distances are known. For these, at least the lower part of the main sequence (light region) is intact. Each cluster turns off the main sequence at a different point; above this turnoff point the cluster's stars do not lie on the main sequence. Note that almost all the stars are Population I (refer to Fig. 15.2).

15.3

The disk of the Galaxy, II: Interstellar gas

Interstellar space contains both gas and dust; this material makes up the *interstellar medium.* The gas comes in three basic states: molecules, atoms, and ions. The dust is usually mixed in with the gas but is greatly outnumbered by the gas particles. This section examines the interstellar gas; the next one, the dust.

What in general is known about the interstellar gas? First, it is made mostly of hydrogen. Second, it tends to clump in clouds. Third, a hot, dilute gas exists between the clouds. Fourth, the gas in different locations contains neutral atoms, ionized atoms, free electrons, and

molecules. Fifth, on the average, the interstellar gas is very tenuous—roughly one hydrogen atom in a cubic centimeter: a vacuum by earthly standards! The average distance between interstellar atoms is roughly 10^8 times larger than the size of the atoms themselves. If two people were separated by a proportional distance relative to their size, they would be about 10^8 m apart—roughly the distance between the earth and moon. Sparse as it is, the interstellar gas occasionally clumps and forms stars.

Bright nebulas / On a winter's night you can easily spot the constellation Orion (see Fig. 1.1 and the January star chart in the endpapers). Dangling from Orion's belt is a short sword; if you look closely, the middle star appears fuzzy. A small telescope pointed at this fuzzy patch shows you a diffuse, convoluted cloud surrounding a small cluster of stars. This bright cloud is called the *Orion Nebula.* ("Nebula" is the Latin word for "cloud," and the use of nebula is an astronomical holdover from the last century.) Only 1500 ly from the earth, the Orion Nebula (Fig. 15.14) is roughly 16 ly in diameter.

At the end of the nineteenth century, spectroscopic analysis demonstrated that these bright nebulas consist of gas. How? The bright nebulas showed spectra with *emission* lines. Recall from Kirchhoff's rules for spectra (Section 5.2) that an emission-line spectrum indicates a hot, diffuse gas. The Orion Nebula, for example, has emission lines of hydrogen, helium, and oxygen dominating its spectrum.

In the 1930s Edwin Hubble demonstrated that nebulas such as that in Orion do not originate their own energy but, rather, absorb the energy from hot *O*- or *B*-stars located in or near the nebula. The essential physical process is: The gas absorbs high-energy ultraviolet photons given off by the central star (or stars) and gives off photons in emission lines at lower energies. This process of splitting high-energy photons into ones of lower energy is called *fluorescence*—a similar process occurs in a fluorescent light, which, like a bright nebula, also has an emission spectrum.

The star in a bright nebula is quite hot—about 30,000 K—and emits many photons with enough energy to ionize hydrogen. Most of these photons are absorbed by the gas surrounding the star so that, out to a considerable

15.14

A typical emission nebula, the Orion Nebula, which is the closest one to the earth—only 1500 ly away. (Courtesy Lick Observatory)

distance (a few tens of light years), the gas is almost totally ionized and at a temperature of about 10,000 K. This zone of ionized hydrogen around a hot star is known as an *H II region* (Fig. 15.15) because the hydrogen is in its second (ionized) state. (H I stands for neutral hydrogen and H II for ionized hydrogen.) Astronomers use the terms H II region, emission nebula, and bright nebula interchangeably.

The light from bright nebulas arises primarily from the process of the recapture of electrons by the protons (hydrogen nuclei). The electrons can be captured in any of the available energy levels and then drop down until they finally reach the ground state. As the electrons lose energy, they emit light, mostly the Balmar-alpha line at 6563 Å. (Details in Focus 41.) The lines are called *optical recombination* lines.

Optical astronomers don't have a monopoly on viewing bright nebulas: Radio astronomers can also see them, in two ways—first, by photons of radio emission, in what are called *radio recombination lines*. The process resembles that for optical recombination lines (Focus 41). Such

lines can be picked up by a radio telescope operating at the right wavelength (usually a few centimeters—Fig. 15.16). Second, H II regions are visible by means of their continuous radio emission mostly at millimeter and centimeter wavelengths. This continuous radio emission can be mapped by a radio telescope (Fig. 15.17). From such maps, astronomers can infer how much ionized gas is contained in an H II region (the Orion Nebula, for example, contains about 300 solar masses).

Interstellar atoms / Investigations of bright nebulas show that they are composed almost entirely of ionized hydrogen. So a neutral, mostly hydrogen gas was ionized to form them.

Until the 1950s, astronomers surmised that hydrogen atoms (designated H I) populated interstellar space, but they had not observed the H I gas. In fact, the Dutch astronomer Hendrick C. van de Hulst had suggested in 1944 that interstellar hydrogen atoms might be so abundant as to be detectable by radio telescopes at a wavelength of 21 cm (Focus 42). This gas was finally detected in the 1950s.

Surveys of interstellar hydrogen atoms with radio telescopes at 21 cm find that most H I is concentrated in the plane of the Milky Way Galaxy. On the average, the hydrogen atoms have a temperature of 70 K and a density of 0.33 atom in a cubic centimeter. So in a volume of space equivalent to the volume of your body, you'd find only 3×10^4 hydrogen atoms, whereas in fact your body contains some 10^{27} atoms.

The hydrogen atoms tend to clump in small clouds. A typical H I cloud has a density of some 20 atoms/cc, a diameter of roughly 16 ly, and a distance of approximately 1000 ly from the next nearest cloud. These clouds move at about 6 km/sec relative to each other.

As you might expect, other gases are in interstellar space. Even before atomic hydrogen was observed with radio telescopes, optical observations had revealed the presence of several other kinds of atoms. Superimposed on the spectra of some stars, astronomers found sharp, dark lines of elements such as sodium (Fig. 15.18). These narrow absorptions are produced when starlight passes through cool regions of the interstellar gas. Recall Kirchhoff's rules (Section 5.2): An absorption spectrum results when light from a continuous source passes through a cooler gas. But what indicates that

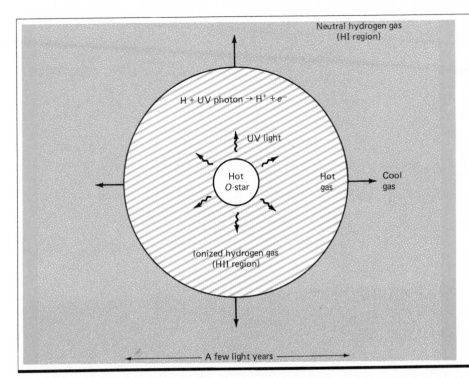

A schematic diagram of an H II region. The hot O-star (or stars) in the center emits ultraviolet light that can ionize the hydrogen gas for a few light years around. The absorption of the ultraviolet light heats up the hydrogen to a temperature of about 10,000 K. The hot, ionized gas expands into the cool, neutral gas that surrounds it.

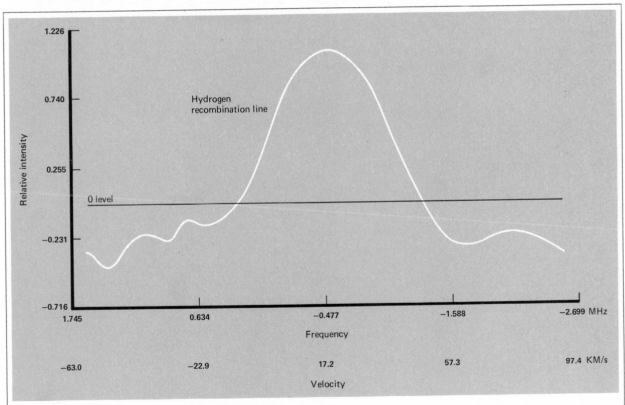

15.16

Observation of a hydrogen recombination line from the emission nebula Messier 17. (Data taken by N. L. Cohen at Haystack Observatory)

focus 41

THE LIGHT FROM EMISSION NEBULAS

Almost all the atoms in an emission nebula (H II region) are ionized. Most of these atoms are hydrogen. When a bare hydrogen nucleus captures an electron, it gives off light. The details of this process are complicated by all the energy levels of the atom (Section 5.3).

To simplify matters, consider the lowest four energy levels in hydrogen (Fig. 1). Imagine a hydrogen atom with an electron in the lowest level. The atom absorbs a high-energy ultraviolet photon. This additional energy kicks the electron out of the nucleus's grip entirely and ionizes the atom. The electron zips around by itself with any one of a large possible range of energies. Ions and free electrons flying around are the typical state of the gas in an H II region. The ions travel around seeking an electron to combine with. This does not happen often because the gas in the nebula is sparse, only about 10^3 atoms/cc.

Suppose the ion does pick up an electron.

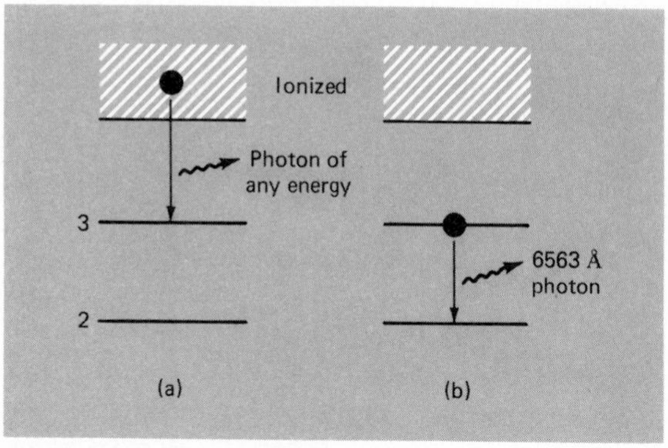

1

The recombination emission process for hydrogen. When a hydrogen nucleus—a proton—captures a free electron (a process called recombination), a photon of any energy can be emitted (a) because the electron could have had any energy over a wide range. Once the electron is bound to the atom (b), it gives off photons with specific energies as it drops down the energy levels. For example, if the electron falls from level 3 to level 2, it emits a 6563 Å photon, the hydrogen-alpha line. Note: only a few of the actual energy levels are shown here.

This process is called recombination. The electron does not necessarily end up in level 1. If it does, it emits an ultraviolet photon that can ionize another atom. Quite quickly, another ultraviolet photon zaps the atom and ionizes it again.

Imagine that the electron is caught in the highest level (4). It emits a low-energy photon. Does the electron stay in level 4 for long? No, because the electron seeks the lowest energy state (level 1). It can get there by dropping through the levels one by one or by skipping over some, just as you could go down stairs one at a time or by skipping a few. However, as the electron drops down to the lowest level, it must emit a photon with each drop.

Suppose the atom catches the electron in level 3. Then if the electron drops to level 2, it gives off a photon with a wavelength of 6563.2 Å, the emission line that results is called the H-alpha line. It is the most common emission line from a nebula and makes them appear red.

You may wonder why the next drop, from level 2 to level 1, is not the brightest line. This drop produces an ultraviolet photon at a wavelength of 1216 Å. Few of these photons make it out of the nebula, because they are constantly absorbed by hydrogen atoms. Even if they did get out, you would never see them because the ultraviolet light does not penetrate the earth's atmosphere.

Because all these photons are produced from the capture of an electron by an ion, they are called recombination lines. So far I've discussed optical photons; the same process can also produce radio ones. Hydrogen atoms have some energy levels, spaced very close together, near the ionization limit. The differences between levels here correspond to radio energies. Imagine a proton capturing an electron in one of these levels; when the electron drops to the next lower level, it emits a radio-energy photon. These result in radio recombination lines.

Finally, an H II region can produce radio emission simply from the electrons whizzing past protons. As the opposite charges attract, the electrons' paths are bent. So the electrons are accelerated but remain free; their energy changes and they emit electromagnetic radiation, mostly at millimeter and centimeter wavelengths. Because many different electrons undergo different energy changes at the same time, a continuous spectrum results rather than a single emission line.

TABLE 15.1 *Some interstellar molecules observed to date*

Complexity	Inorganic		Organic	
Diatomic	H_2	Hydrogen	CH	Methylidyne radical
	HD	Deuterized hydrogen	CH^+	Methylidyne ion
	OH	Hydroxyl radical	CN	Cyanogen radical
	SiO	Silicon monoxide	CO	Carbon monoxide
	SiS	Silicon monosulfide	CS	Carbon monosulfide
	NS	Nitrogen sulfide		
	SO	Sulfur monoxide		
Triatomic	H_2O	Water	CCH	Ethynyl radical
	HDO	Heavy water	HCN	Hydrogen cyanide
	N_2H^+	Protonated nitrogen	DCN	Deuterium cyanide
	H_2S	Hydrogen sulfide	DNC	Deuterium isocyanide
	SO_2	Sulfur dioxide	HCO^+	Formyl ion
4-atomic	NH_3	Ammonia	H_2CO	Formaldehyde
			HNCO	Isocyanic acid
			H_2CS	Thioformaldehyde
			HC_2H	Acetylene
			C_3N	Cyanoethynyl radical
5-atomic			H_2CNH	Methanimine
			H_2NCN	Cyanamide
			HCOOH	Formic acid
			HC_3N	Cyanoacetylene
			H_2C_2O	Ketene
6-atomic			CH_3OH	Methyl alcohol
			CH_3CN	Methyl cyanide
			$HCONH_2$	Formamide
7-atomic			CH_3NH_2	Methylamine
			CH_3C_2H	Methylacetylene
			$HCOCH_3$	Acetaldehyde
			H_2CCHCN	Vinyl cyanide
			HC_5N	Cyanodiacetylene
8-atomic			$HCOOCH_3$	Methyl formate
			CH_3C_3N	Methyl cyanoacetylene
9-atomic			$(CH_3)_2O$	Dimethyl ether
			CH_3CH_2OH	Ethyl alcohol
			HC_3N	Cyanotriacetylene
			CH_3CH_2CN	Ethyl cyanide

The cores of these clouds are unusual places compared with the average interstellar medium. Here the temperatures are a frigid 10 K and the densities get as high as a *million* molecules in a cubic centimeter. That's an immense concentration by interstellar standards, yet it is only 10^{-13} the density of molecules in the air at the earth's surface. Giant molecular clouds are so huge, though, that they contain an enormous number of molecules in total.

One important property of the location of these clouds in space: H II regions, which surround young, massive stars, are always found next to molecular cloud complexes. This proximity suggests that giant molecular clouds play a key role in the process of star formation.

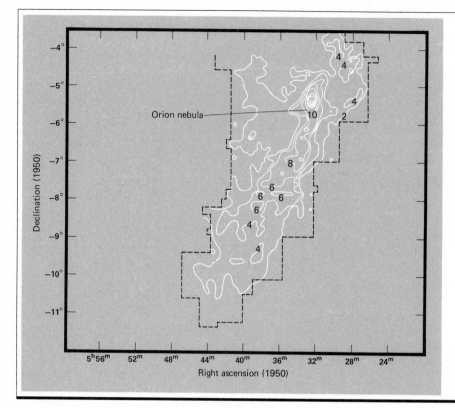

Orion nebula

Declination (1950)

Right ascension (1950)

15.20

A carbon monoxide map of the giant molecular cloud associated with the Orion Nebula. The hottest, densest part of the cloud lies just above the contour marked "10." The visible Orion Nebula and the Trapezium lie just below and to the right of this peak of the molecular emission. This map was made with the Columbia University 4-ft-mm wave antenna. (Adapted from a figure by M. Kutner, K. Tucker, G. Chin, and P. Thaddeus in the Astrophysical Journal, *vol. 215, p. 521, copyright © 1977 by the American Astronomical Society)*

Molecular masers / The normal emission from interstellar molecules usually comes from excitation by collisions with other particles (typically H_2) nearby. Take the hydroxyl radical, OH, for example, which has four closely spaced energy levels sit near its ground state. Collisions can excite these levels. When OH deexcites, it can emit four lines in the radio part of the spectrum. The most intense of these lines usually is that at 1667 MHz, then 1665, 1612, and 1720 MHz.

In 1965 a radio astronomy group at the University of California discovered hydroxyl while observing the Orion Nebula. But the emission was not that expected from a hot H II gas at 10^4 K. Rather, the temperature of the gas would have to be 10^{12}–10^{13} K to explain the observed features! This high temperature was physically impossible, for the hydroxyl molecule couldn't exist under such conditions—it would be dissociated into H and O.

What was happening in Orion? Clearly, the emission was somehow amplified over its normal intensity. How? By the same process that operates in a laser, but working at microwave frequencies.

Laser is an acronym for *l*ight *a*mplification by *s*timulated *e*mission of *r*adiation. *Maser* is the same, with "*m*icrowave" substituted for "light." The main idea in either case is the same: Atoms or molecules in a gas are excited to some particular energy state and then stimulated to fall to a lower energy state at a more rapid rate than normal. (Details in Focus 43.)

Hydroxyl is not the only cosmic maser. Water has maser emission at one frequency—22,235 MHz or 1.35 cm. Silicon monoxide, SiO, can be a maser at 43,122 MHz (6.95 mm) and 86,243 MHz (3.47 mm).

Despite the lack of understanding of how such masers work, astronomers do know that many hydroxyl and water interstellar masers tend to be found near giant molecular clouds. The regions of maser emission are extremely small, only a few tens of AUs across, and very dense, at least 10^8 atoms/cc. They turn out to be signposts of incipient starbirth (Chapter 19).

Let me sum up what is known generally of the interstellar gas (see also Table 15.2):

1 *H II regions.* Zones of glowing, ionized hydrogen surrounding young, hot stars (spectral types *O* and *B*); contain a minor

SUMMARY

Three general regions make up the Galaxy; the nuclear bulge, the disk, and the halo. Most of the material in each region is in the form of stars that are classified in three general groups: old and young Population I and Population II. Population I stars are typically metal-rich, and associated with regions of gas and dust. Population II stars are usually metal-poor, old, and in regions relatively free of interstellar material.

The halo consists of Population II stars, almost all in globular clusters. The galactic nucleus cannot be observed directly, but from observations of other galaxies, astronomers infer that most of the stars situated there are old Population I. In the disk away from the nucleus—such as in the neighborhood of the sun—young Population I stars abound.

Along with the Population I stars in the disk is an interstellar medium that consists of gas and dust. The gas is mostly hydrogen atoms and molecules. The molecules are concentrated in huge clouds. The dust particles are small—about 1 micron or so—and may be composed of iron, graphite, silicates, ice, or some mixture of all these. The dust cuts out the light from distant stars—the blue more than the red.

One of those regions hidden from our optical view is the Galaxy's nucleus. Radio and infrared observations have penetrated the dust veil here to find a place very different from the part of the Galaxy where the sun is located. The nucleus contains old Population I stars, singly and in clusters. It also contains molecular clouds, dust, ionized gas, and surprisingly young O- and B-stars, all concentrated in a region of space only hundreds of light years in size.

Remarkably, stars tend to cluster, a fact that suggests that many stars are born in groups. The motions of two stars in the marriage of a binary star system enable us to measure the masses of stars and to find that massive stars are more luminous than those with lower masses. So the main sequence turns out to be a sequence of mass, luminous O-stars having more mass than the fainter M-stars. The O-stars burn out very quickly, so wherever O-stars are seen, they must be relatively young. These young, hot stars play a crucial role in delineating the detailed structure of the Galaxy—the topic of the next chapter.

STUDY EXERCISES

1 Are the stars in the Pleiades cluster Population I or II? Give your reasons! (*Objectives 1 and 5*)

2 Suppose you find a main-sequence star with a luminosity about 1000 times that of the sun. What is the star's approximate mass? (Just determine the correct power of 10.) What if the star were 100 times the sun's luminosity? (*Objective 4*)

3 A bright nebula, such as the Orion Nebula, has a bright-line spectrum. Use Kirchhoff's rules to guess the physical conditions in the nebula. (*Objective 6*)

4 What three effects does dust have on starlight? (*Objective 8*)

5 Radio observations show that some of the radio emission from the galactic center has characteristics of radio emission from H II regions. What can you guess about the physical characteristics (such as size and temperature) of these areas? (*Objective 8*)

6 How do you know that two stars close together in the sky actually make up a binary system? (*Objective 2*)

7 In general, how do the contents of the nuclear bulge of the Galaxy compare to that in the disk? (*Objective 11*)

8 Describe *one* way to observe each of the following in the interstellar medium: H I gas, H II gas, coronal gas, and molecules. (*Objectives 7, 8, and 9*)

9 What are the most likely materials to make up interstellar dust? (*Objective 10*)

10 How can you tell the difference between a reflection nebula and an emission (H II) one? (*Objective 8*)

BEYOND THIS BOOK . . .

The Discovery of the Galaxy (Knopf, New York, 1971) by Charles A. Whitney gives an exciting presentation of the evolution of ideas about the Galaxy.

The Milky Way (Harvard University Press, Cambridge, Mass., 1974) by P. and B. Bok presents an up-to-date astronomical summary of our Milky Way.

"Molecules in Space" by B. E. Turner in *Scientific American*, p. 51, March 1973, has details about the study of molecular clouds.

"Globular Clusters" by I. Iben in *Scientific American*, p. 26, July 1970, looks closely at stars in globulars.

"The Milky Way Galaxy" by B. Bok, *Scientific American*, May 1981, p. 92, gives a comprehensive look at the Galaxy's contents.

Our spiral Galaxy

16

LEARNING OBJECTIVES

After studying this chapter you should be able to:

1. Explain at least one astronomical difficulty in trying to figure out the structure of the Galaxy from our location in it.

2. Sketch the spiral arm structure of the Galaxy near the sun, naming the nearby arms and their positions and distances from us.

3. Describe *spiral arm tracers* and how they're used.

4. Present the observational evidence for this spiral structure; that is, describe what methods astronomers use to work out the positions of spiral arms.

5. Sketch the speed at which the Galaxy rotates at different distances from the center (the *rotation curve*) and, from it, outline how to find the approximate mass of the Galaxy.

6. Describe the sun's orbit around the galactic center.

7. Explain how radio astronomers use 21-cm observations to trace spiral arms, indicate the limitations of their method, and explain its advantage over optical observations.

8. Compare the optical and radio spiral-arm maps.

9. Describe the contents of a typical spiral arm.

10. Describe the evolution of spiral arms in terms of the density-wave model for spiral structure.

A broad and ample road, whose dust is gold,
And pavement stars, as stars to thee appear
Seen in the galaxy, that milky way . . .

JOHN MILTON: Paradise Lost

Like a majestic cosmic pinwheel, the Milky Way Galaxy spins slowly in space. The main body of the Galaxy is a flat disk, so it must rotate rapidly about an axis at a right angle to the plane through the nucleus. Our sun, along with most of the stars in its neighborhood, orbits the center of the Galaxy at speeds of about 250 km/sec. Since the sun is about 33,000 ly from the nucleus, it completes one revolution roughly every 250 million years. The sun orbits the Galaxy with more than 200 *billion* other stars.

What is the structure of this enormous system of stars? Optical astronomers can probe the structure near the sun, and radio astronomers can study regions farther away. These optical and radio probes show that the Galaxy does have a spiral structure—a pattern inferred from spiral designs observed in other galaxies (Fig. 16.1). The maps of the Galaxy's spiral structure, drawn to date, are incomplete and subject to revision. The details are not yet in, but astronomers have been able to establish the broad outlines of the Galaxy's structure, a remarkable achievement, considering that the sun is buried *within* the dusty disk of the Galaxy.

The dynamics of the Galaxy provide hints about the origin, persistence, and evolution of the spiral arm structure. Recent theoretical work, aided by the development of electronic computers, has developed new ideas about the physical cause of the Galaxy's spiral structure. One model links many of the galactic entities described in the previous chapter into the process of galactic evolution. The Galaxy's structure evolves—but at a rate so slow that neither you nor I will see any changes in our lifetimes.

16.1
An overview
of the Galaxy's structure

As discussed in the previous chapter, the Galaxy has three main parts: a nucleus (nuclear bulge plus core), a disk, and a halo. The disk, the main body of the Galaxy, has a diameter of some 120,000 ly and a thickness of about 2000 ly. Population I stars and interstellar clouds of gas and dust inhabit the disk, the gas extending out farther than the stars. The sun resides a little above the central plane at a distance of approximately 33,000 ly from the Galaxy's center. (Some recent studies suggest a lower value for the dis-

16.1

A typical spiral galaxy, Messier 101. Our Milky Way has a general structure similar to this. (Courtesy Kitt Peak National Observatory.)

tance to the center, perhaps as low as 28,000 ly, but I will use the still standard value of 33,000 ly in this book. If the value does turn out to be smaller, it will *not* have any great impact on any conclusions presented here.)

The sun is in a bad position to observe the Galaxy's structure. Imagine, for example, that you are watching a half-time show at a football game. The band has set up some elaborate formation. Up in the stands you can easily observe what the formation looks like. But suppose you were down on the field instead, at the edge of the formation. It would at first appear to be a jumble! You could eventually figure out the shape if you could find the distances to all the band players. Then you could plot their positions from you as you looked around in a circle. But suppose you had to do this mapping in a smog so dense that only the closest people were visible. Then you would need some other method of estimating distances—perhaps by the intensity of the sound of the instruments that comes through the smog.

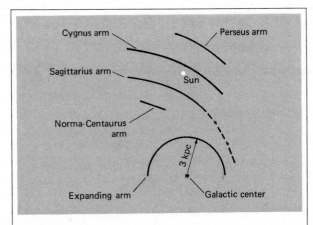

16.2

Segments of spiral arms near the sun. Our solar system lies on the inner edge of the Cygnus arm, in a small branch sometimes called the Orion spur. Outward lies the Perseus arm. Inward are at least two arms: the Sagittarius and Norma-Centaurus arms. Very close to the galactic center is the ill-defined expanding arm. The arms are named after the constellations in whose directions they lie as seen from the earth.

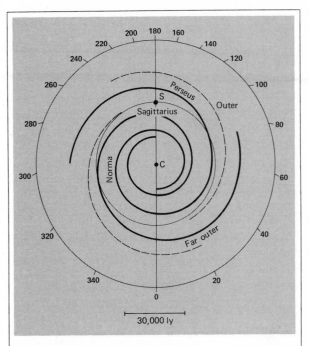

16.3

One model for the overall spiral structure of the Galaxy. The sun is located at S, about 33,000 ly from the center (C). The numbers around the outer circle indicate the galactic latitude as viewed from the sun; the direction toward the center marks zero galactic longitude. In this model the Galaxy has a two-armed pattern near the center (solid lines) that becomes a four-armed spiral (solid plus dashed lines) farther out. All astronomers would not agree with this picture.

Optical astronomers, who try to find the distances to features that mark spiral arms, run into interstellar dust. Radio waves are not so easily stopped by the dust. So radio astronomers can hear the radio emission from clouds of gas that probably mark spiral arms. But they have difficulty in finding the distances to those clouds. The results from the two techniques do not agree in all details but have uncovered the following structure.

The sun lies on the inner edge (Fig. 16.2) of a poorly defined structure called the *Cygnus arm*. (*Note:* Astronomers use the word "arm" to indicate a well-defined *segment* of a larger, overall spiral-arm structure. I'll use it the same way, but you should be aware it refers to pieces of larger structures.) Outward, about 10,000 ly from the sun, lies an arm parallel to the Cygnus arm; since it is in the direction of the constellation Perseus, it is called the *Perseus arm*. At about 6,000 ly interior to the sun curves the *Sagittarius arm*. Some evidence indicates that another arm may lie 13,000 ly from the sun toward the galac-

tic center; it is often called the *Norma arm*. Finally, encircling the galactic center at a distance of about 10,000 ly (3 kpc) is the *3-kpc arm*, or *expanding arm*, so called because this innermost arm is moving toward us at roughly 50 km/sec, expanding away from the center.

Astronomers cannot yet see the whole scheme. But many other spiral galaxies have two arms that wind around the nucleus. They guess that our Galaxy also has four major arms tightly wound around the nucleus (Fig. 16.3). The arms previously mentioned probably are parts of the major arms.

What defines a spiral arm? You find many

O- and *B*-stars in a spiral arm. Also, the overall density of material—gas, dust, and stars—inside a spiral arm is about ten times that in the region between arms. The spiral arms contain most of the gas, dust, and young stars in the Galaxy. Near the sun, stars contain about 50 percent of the spiral-arm material; the other half forms the clouds of gas and dust in the interstellar medium. In contrast, for the Galaxy as a whole, only a few percent of the material is gas and dust. A typical segment of a spiral arm has a width of 1500 ly and a thickness of 500 ly, within which lie the stars, gas, and dust.

Our Galaxy rotates. All its material revolves around the nucleus. At the sun's position, material circuits the Galaxy at about 250 km/sec. If you imagine zooming out into space up above the north pole of the Galaxy, you could watch the sun revolving *clockwise* around the Galaxy once every 250 million years. You would also notice—if you observed for a long enough time—that regions farther out than the sun revolve more slowly. You might suppose that this difference in speeds eventually would cause the spiral arms to wind up and disappear: The ends of the arms trail the inward sections in the direction of rotation. So eventually, the arm would spread out around the Galaxy. But the spiral arms persist! What maintains the spiral arms? This is a central question in the evolution of our Galaxy and others like it.

16.2

Galactic rotation

The sun and its nearest neighboring stars are only a drop in the galactic bucket. Located in the galactic disk, far from the center of the Galaxy, the local stars appear to be moving in a variety of directions at different speeds. In relation to the other local stars, the sun moves at a speed of about 20 km/sec. But how to find out what motion the sun and nearby stars share in relation to the center of the Galaxy?

During the nineteenth century, astronomers grew aware of the sun's motion in space as reflected in the motions of nearby stars. One pioneer astronomer, Bertil Lindblad (1895–1965), proposed that these motions occur partly because of the orbital motion of the stars about the Galaxy. So from those motions you can infer the character of the Galaxy's rotation.

This inference was done by measuring the radial velocities (using the Doppler shift) of the brightest *O*- and *B*-stars in the sky. The results can be explained if stars nearer to the center of the Galaxy revolve faster, and those farther out, slower. Does this make sense? Most stars are concentrated in the galactic disk, which surrounds the dense central nucleus. The stars exert a gravitational attraction on one another. Out in the disk where the sun dwells, the great mass of the nucleus attracts a star more strongly than does any other part of the Galaxy. So here stars are attracted essentially toward the center.

You can see that the set up resembles the flattened system of planets forming the solar system. Although the planets attract each other, each orbits about the sun. Each one responds to the overwhelming gravitational attraction of the central sun. It can be argued that the stars in the galactic disk revolve about the nucleus of the Galaxy much as the planets revolve around the sun. The forces are similar, so the motions should be similar. In other words, the stellar motions should follow Kepler's laws (Section 3.3), and the orbital velocities of the stars should decrease with increasing distance from the Galaxy's center—just as, for example, the orbital velocity of Mars is less than that of the earth.

In fact, the velocities *don't* follow Kepler's law exactly, and that reveals an important fact about the Galaxy—the major part of the mass is *not* concentrated at the center, which is quite different from the case of the solar system. This idea was first demonstrated in 1927 by Dutch astronomer Jan Oort.

Near the center of the Galaxy (inner 1000 ly) the orbital motion is a bit different, because the Galaxy's mass is not all concentrated in a central body. Stars near the center do not feel so large an attraction as would be expected if the mass were concentrated in the nucleus. So they travel more slowly in their orbits than expected from Kepler's laws (Fig. 16.4).

The sun's orbit and the mass of the Galaxy / How fast does the sun move around the Galaxy? Astronomers use a variety of indirect approaches to find this out. One method uses the motions of globular clusters. The globulars orbit the Galaxy in random orbits with

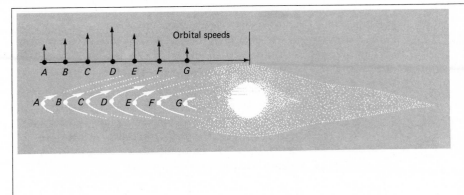

16.4

Galactic orbital speeds. Imagine stars at orbits A–G. From A to D the orbital speeds increase inward, as expected from the way the planets orbit the sun. But inward of D the orbital speeds decrease. This happens because as you move toward the central hub of the Galaxy, you leave more and more material behind. This material exerts a force, say, on the star at F, partly counteracting the pull toward the nucleus. A star at F has more matter pulling outward on it than a star at E. So star F orbits more slowly than E. The changeover (star D) is about 20,000 ly from the nucleus.

a roughly spherical distribution around the nucleus. With respect to the nucleus, the average motion of all the globular clusters is roughly zero. In other words, the system of globulars has no overall rotation about the galactic center (although individual clusters move rapidly, some in one direction, some in another). A study of the radial velocities of the globular clusters shows the sun's motion with respect to the system of globulars. Because the system of globulars has no rotational motion with respect to the nucleus, the sun's motion found in this way is its motion with respect to the Galaxy's center. Such an analysis shows that the sun moves at 250 km/sec. (Recent work, using other methods, finds values in the range of 220–225 km/sec. But the adopted international standard is still 250 km/sec, which I'll use in this book.)

The sun's distance from the galactic center is much harder to determine than its orbital velocity, in part because you cannot see the center optically. But you can look above and below the galactic plane, where obscuration is less, to observe objects thought to be symmetrical about the galactic center. Then if you can find the distances to these objects, we can infer our distance from the center. That's the essence of Shapley's technique, which used globular clusters (Section 14.6). Modern measurements follow the same basic method and come up with distances that range from 24,000 to 33,000 ly, with

an average of 28,000 ly. (This book will stick with the international standard of 33,000 ly.)

Knowing the sun's velocity and distance, you apply Kepler's third law to deduce the mass of the Galaxy (Focus 44). The result, about 10^{11} solar masses, refers only to the mass interior to the sun's orbit.

With the sun's orbital distance and velocity known, you can use these values to find the *galactic rotation curve*—how fast an object some distance from the galactic center revolves around it. As previously stated, in the simplest case you'd expect Keplerian motion in the outer regions (Fig. 16.5a). In fact, the observed rotation curve (Fig. 16.5b) does not follow this simple pattern, according to radio data. From close to the center out to 1000 ly, the curve rises steeply, then drops, bottoming out at about 10,000 ly. It then rises slowly out to the position of the sun. CO observations show the rotation curve in the outer parts of the Galaxy. They find that the curve rises more steeply beyond the sun, reaching almost 300 km/sec at 59,000 ly.

What does this curve reveal? Even the outer parts of the Galaxy do not revolve in a Keplerian fashion, so much of the Galaxy's material must lie out beyond the sun's orbit. From the rotation curve out to 59,000 ly, the Galaxy's mass is 3.4×10^{11} solar masses. So at least as much mass lies exterior to the sun as interior to it! The Galaxy must have a massive halo.

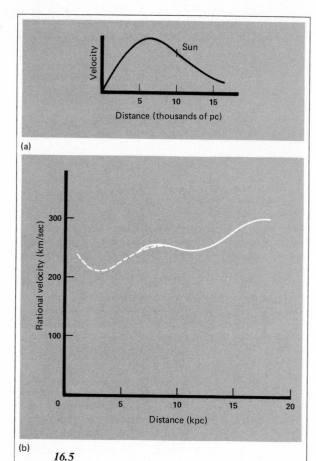

(a)

(b)

16.5

(a) *A simplified rotation curve for the Galaxy. The line-of-sight motions of stars relative to the sun provide a means to find their orbital speeds. Note that the curve has the characteristics described in Fig. 16.4, which assumes a mass concentration at the Galaxy's center.* **(b)** *The actual, observed rotation curve of the Galaxy (compare to previous figure). The dashed part of the curve is based on atomic hydrogen (H I) data; the solid line fits data from carbon monoxide measurements of molecular clouds made out to 59,000 ly from the galactic center. (Adapted from a diagram by L. Blitz, M. Fich, and A. Stark)*

16.3
Galactic structure from optical observations

In 1951 Walter Baade and N. U. Mayall studied the structure of the spiral galaxy nearest to the Milky Way: M31 (Fig. 16.6). They found that the spiral arms stood out most strongly in blue-sensitive photographs. When examined in detail, the photographs showed that *O*- and *B*-supergiants, *O*- and *B*-associations, H II regions, and Population I cepheids traced out the spiral structure remarkably well. So these objects are called *spiral tracers.*

The next natural step was to apply these spiral tracers to our Galaxy to determine the location and extent of its spiral arms. This operation is not simple. First, it requires an accurate technique for measuring the distance to each of the tracers. Second, optical observations are restricted by the blotting out of starlight by dust. Most of the interstellar dust lies concentrated in the galactic plane, so the sun sits in the thick of the interstellar smog. Third, the sun's location in the plane gives a poor vantage point for seeing the Galaxy's spiral structure, because we are forced to observe it edge on rather than face on.

H II regions and supergiant *O*- and *B*-stars trace the arms best because their high luminosities make them visible over large distances (Fig. 16.7). In addition, cepheids have been used effectively to delineate spiral features (Fig. 16.7). The cepheids have the advantage that their distances are easy to determine by the period-luminosity relation (Focus 37).

You must take these optical maps with a bit of caution. The data extend only to about 16,000 ly, and a larger range is needed to outline the spiral arms definitely. In addition, although the outline of spiral structure is assuredly correct, observations of other galaxies show that irregularities also commonly occur. It's futile to draw a master diagram from optical data alone.

Although disagreements have arisen about the details, most optical astronomers concur that their investigations have found at least three major arm segments spaced about 7000 ly apart. The Galaxy appears to have a spiral structure with much irregularity in the general pattern.

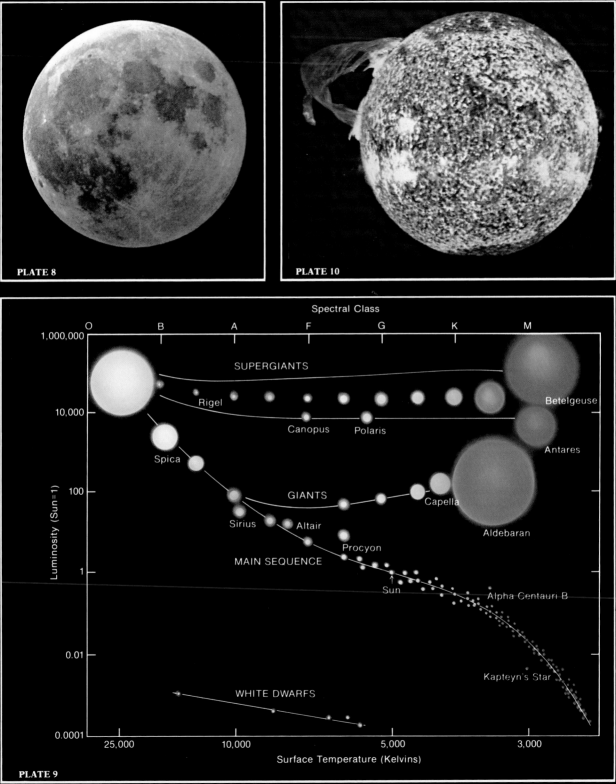

PLATE 8

PLATE 10

Spectral Class

O   B   A   F   G   K   M

SUPERGIANTS

Rigel

Betelgeuse

Canopus   Polaris

Antares

Spica

GIANTS

Capella

Sirius   Altair

Aldebaran

Procyon

MAIN SEQUENCE

Sun

Alpha Centauri B

WHITE DWARFS

Kapteyn's Star

Luminosity (Sun=1)

1,000,000

10,000

100

1

0.01

0.0001

Surface Temperature (Kelvins)

25,000   10,000   5,000   3,000

PLATE 9

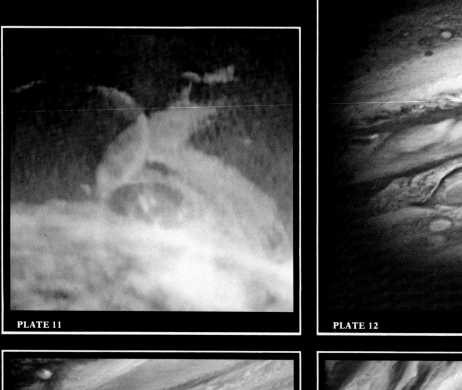

PLATE 11

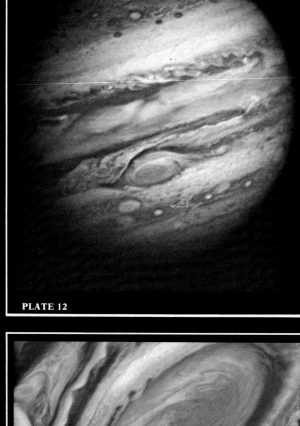

PLATE 12

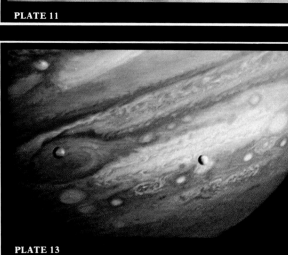

PLATE 13

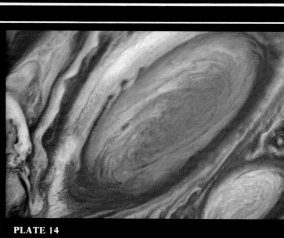

PLATE 14

PLATE 15

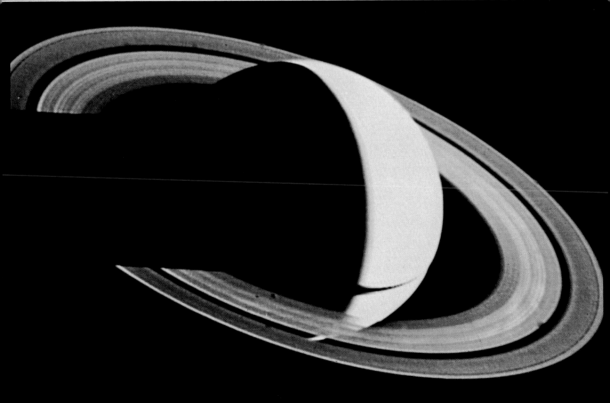

PLATE 16

PLATE 17

PLATE 18

PLATE 19

PLATE 20

PLATE 21

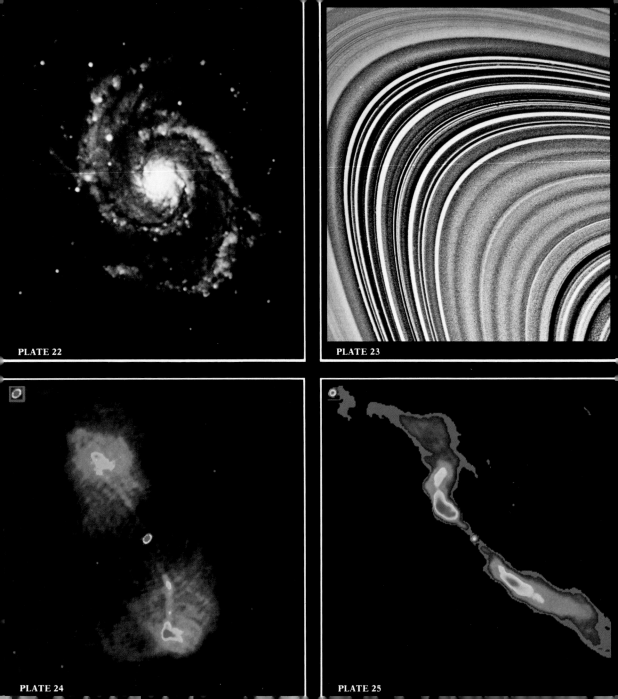

PLATE 22

PLATE 23

PLATE 24

PLATE 25

LEARNING OBJECTIVES

After studying this chapter you should be able to:

1. Describe the general physical characteristics of spiral, elliptical, and irregular galaxies: for instance, their differences in size, shape, mass, color, types of stars, and amount of gas and dust.

2. Describe how the criteria "brightness means nearness" and "smallness means farness" can be used to estimate the relative distances to galaxies.

3. Indicate what *observations* clinched the idea that the "spiral nebulas" were actually other galaxies.

4. Describe what "standards" are used to find distances to galaxies.

5. Outline the contemporary method of finding distances to distant galaxies, starting with the Astronomical Unit and ending with the Hubble constant.

6. Evaluate the weaknesses in the procedure you outlined so you can estimate the possible errors in distances to galaxies.

7. Indicate how getting distances and radial velocities for galaxies results in a value for the Hubble constant.

8. Discuss the uncertainty in the value of the Hubble constant.

9. Define a cluster of galaxies and describe contents of the local group of galaxies.

10. Evaluate the evidence for intergalactic material between and/or within clusters of galaxies.

Look, friend, at this universe
with its spiral clusters of stars
flying out all over space
like bedsprings suddenly bursting free . . .
EDWARD FIELD: Prologue

Beyond the Milky Way: Galaxies

17

I don't know of any celestial object quite as grand as a galaxy. One moonless night on Mt. Hopkins I had a few spare moments on the 1.5-m telescope. I pointed it at a bright spiral galaxy. What a stunning sight through the eyepiece! I could see the star-bright nucleus and misty swirl of its spiral shape. Billions of stars caught in a whirlpool spanning hundreds of thousands of light years!

The galaxies form the basic elements of our modern cosmological vista. Their sheer numbers are beyond our comprehension (Fig. 17.1). The world's largest telescopes reveal a universe of galaxies whose numbers are as impossible to count as the number of grains of sand on all the beaches of the earth. The diversity of structure in these galaxies is also astounding; even more surprising is the fundamental unity found in spite of their wide variety. The fact that galaxies can be divided into broad divisions hints at a common evolutionary process.

The galaxies form the skeleton of the universe. The crucial problem is the measurement of their distances. Many conclusions of modern cosmology hinge on the correct establishment of extragalactic distances. This chapter notes that the notorious difficulties of surveying our Galaxy are amplified when we try to appraise the

vastness of the universe. In spite of present errors and problems, our vision of the universe, underpinned by the theory of general relativity, has a coherence that allows us to draw conclusions about how the universe began.

17.1
The resolution of the Shapley-Curtis debate

Recall (Section 14.6) that Curtis opposed Shapley on the question whether the "spiral nebulas" were simply outer members of the Milky Way, as Shapley claimed, or galaxies in their own right. Shapley addressed the extragalactic "nebulas" question only in passing; Curtis spent most of his time on the issue.

Curtis felt that the observations of novas in the spirals gave a clue to their nature. Only groups of stars—not clouds of gas—could display nova explosions.

Curtis also argued that the wide range of apparent angular sizes of spirals—approximately 2° for M31, the nearest, to 10′ and less for the smallest—required a large range of distances and so could not be part of the Galaxy. Starting from the principle of the uniformity of nature, Curtis assumed that all spirals have roughly the same diameter. The range in observed sizes

17.1

Galaxies. Look carefully at this picture. Almost every object in it is a galaxy. This is the central region of a cluster of galaxies in Coma Berenices. (The object near the upper central region with four points is a star.) (Courtesy Kitt Peak National Observatory)

TABLE 17.1 *General properties of different types of galaxies*

	Spirals	*Irregulars*	*Dwarf ellipticals*	*Giant ellipticals*
Diameter (ly)	60,000	23,000	10,000	150,000
Mass (Solar Masses)	10^{11}	10^9	10^6	10^{13}
Luminosity (Sun = 1)	10^{10}	10^9	10^8	10^{11}
Color	Blue (disk) Red (halo)	Blue	Red	Red
Neutral gas and dust	5%	15%	Less than 1%	Less than 1%
Types of stars	Young (disk) Old (halo and nucleus)	Young	Old	Old

SOURCE Adapted from a table by H. L. Shipman.

17.14

Rotation curves for seven spiral galaxies. Note that the curves flatten out at large distances from the nucleus, implying a significant amount of mass lies in the outer regions of the galaxy. (Adapted from a figure and data by V. Rubin, W. K. Ford, Jr., and N. Thonnard, Astrophysical Journal (Letters), vol. 225, p. L107, copyright 1978 by the American Astronomical Society)

For binary galaxies, you again use the versatile Doppler shift. Imagine two galaxies orbiting about the center of mass of the binary. Then, just like with visual binary stars (Section 15.2), apply Newton's form of Kepler's third law to find the masses, if you knew the distance, the angular size of the orbit, the period, and the position of the center of mass. However, galaxies revolve too slowly to see their actual orbits, periods, and relative centers of mass. So you cannot find the individual masses of binary galaxies. All you can measure are the present radial velocities and the separation; you don't know what part of the orbit the galaxies are on or what the inclination is, and therefore you don't know what the true orbital velocities are. But if you examine a large sample of galaxies and assume their orbits are nearly circular and randomly oriented to the line of sight, you can estimate from these data the *average* masses of the galaxies sampled.

A recent investigation of 279 binary systems, mostly spirals, used the Doppler shift of the 21-cm line to get their velocities. The results: an average mass of 1.0×10^{12} solar masses for these spirals.

The study of our Galaxy shows that some of the material in the disk of a spiral resides in the form of H I. We detect H I in the Galaxy by the 21-cm line. We can observe H I in other galaxies the same way and, by adopting simple models for the distribution and temperature of the H I gas, we can estimate a galaxy's H I content.

An analysis of these data for a sample of spiral and irregular galaxies finds that the H I mass makes up a small fraction of the total mass—only 0.03 for lenticulars and 0.22 for irregulars. The Hubble sequence from *S0* to *Irr*, the different galaxy types contain increasing fractions of H I relative to their total mass. For example, *Irr* galaxies have more H I gas, relative to their total mass, than *Sa* galaxies.

Luminosities / If you know their distances and apparent magnitudes, you can work out the absolute magnitudes of galaxies and also their luminosities. The problem is: It's not easy to measure a galaxy's apparent magnitude. Why not? Because a galaxy thins out gradually at its edge. It's hard to be sure that you're catching all the light from the galaxy. In addition, corrections have to be applied for light absorption: first, for that due to dust in our Galaxy, and second, for that due to dust in the other galaxy itself (especially for spirals). Finally, you must correct for the fact that most galaxies are tilted to our line of sight, so you measure only some fraction of their total light output.

The absolute magnitudes of galaxies range from -8 (2×10^5 solar luminosities) for dwarf ellipticals to -25 (10^{12} solar luminosities) for supergiant (cD) ellipticals. These latter types are very rare, however. The Galaxy, if you could see it all from space, has an absolute magnitude somewhere near -21 (2.5×10^{10} solar luminosities).

Mass-luminosity ratios / Divide the total mass of a galaxy by its luminosity. You then have its *mass-luminosity ratio* (abbreviated M/L), an indication of the average energy output per unit solar mass from the Galaxy. (It is usually expressed in units of solar masses and solar luminosities.)

Modern determinations by Edwin Turner using binary galaxy masses give 35 for the average mass-to-light ratio for spiral galaxies and about twice as much for giant ellipticals and lenticulars. (For comparison, the M/L ratio for stars in the sun's neighborhood is about 1.)

Why do ellipticals have a larger M/L? The simplest way is to assume elliptical galaxies contain a greater percentage of low-mass stars with low-light output—main-sequence stars of class *M*. If true, this extra abundance of *M*-stars would mean that ellipticals should be redder in overall color than spirals (see subsequent discussion). Other possibilities are: neutron stars, black holes (including perhaps a giant one in the nucleus), and dark interstellar matter, which contribute to *M* but not to *L*.

Colors / As for stars, you can measure the colors of galaxies. The color of a galaxy depends on the predominate stellar type in its mixture of stars; it relates directly to the kind of stars in the galaxy. For example, a galaxy with many *O*- and *B*-stars is bluer than a galaxy with many red *M*-stars.

In fact, a direct correlation exists between galaxy type and its color. Ellipticals tend to be much redder than spirals, and spirals, redder than irregular galaxies. Within the spiral group, the galaxies are redder as their nuclear bulges grow larger and their spiral arms, less extensive.

Another way to describe a galaxy's color is to specify the stellar spectral class whose color resembles that of the whole galaxy. The ellipticals have the same colors as *K*-stars, as do *Sa* galaxies, whereas *Sb* galaxies resemble stars of class *F* to *K*, and *Sc* galaxies show the color of class *A* to *F*, as do irregulars.

The progression of color from the bluer irregulars to the redder ellipticals reflects a trend in the composition of the galaxy's population. It used to be thought that their red color meant that the ellipticals and nuclei of spirals contained Population II stars, like those in the globular clusters. But later work discovered that these stars, though old, nevertheless have a high metal abundance. Therefore it is more appropriate to call them old, metal-rich Population I. In general, an old Population I predominates in ellipticals, whereas a much younger Population I stands out in the irregulars. The mixture in the spirals is determined by the size of the nucleus (old Population I) compared with that of the spiral arms (young Population I). (Metal-poor Population II probably plays a minor role in all *large* galaxies, existing mainly in the globular clusters and halo.)

Here is a way to remember the primary difference among galaxy types: Recall that our Galaxy has a halo and nucleus of reddish stars and spiral arms of bluish stars. Imagine our Galaxy without the halo and nucleus. What remains (the arms) is like the stars, gas, and dust found in irregular galaxies. Now imagine our Galaxy stripped of its spiral arms. The remains (nucleus and halo) are typical of the composition of elliptical galaxies.

To sum up: Galaxies contain stars, gas, and dust. The mixture of gas, dust, and stars, as well as the stellar types, relates closely to a galaxy's type and structure. Colors and spectra show

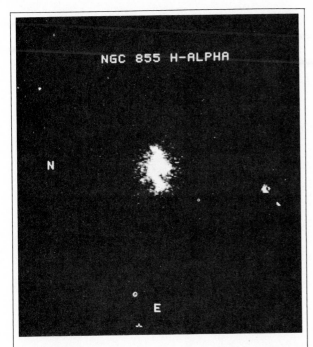

17.15

A photo of the H-alpha emission from the nucleus of the elliptical galaxy New General Catalog (NGC) 855. This emission indicates that ionized hydrogen exists in the nucleus. (Photo by H. Butcher and G. Gisler with the 4-m telescope at Kitt Peak National Observatory; courtesy of G. Gisler)

that the nuclei of spirals contain an old metal-rich Population I; the arms, much younger stars. Most elliptical galaxies have colors similar to those of spirals' nuclei, and irregular galaxies appear most akin in color and spectra to spiral arms. Ellipticals contain very little gas and dust. In contrast, spirals and irregulars embrace extensive quantities of interstellar material. In spirals, the gas appears as H I clouds, or as H II regions cloaking O- and B-stars. Although the masses of galaxies are difficult to measure for distant systems, in general, giant ellipticals are the most massive and irregulars, the least massive.

Warning: Don't think that elliptical galaxies are *completely* devoid of gas and dust. Roughly 10 percent of ellipticals have detectable emission from gas—usually ionized and confined to the nuclear region (Fig. 17.15).

17.5
Clusters of galaxies

If you ever get the chance, take a close look at a photographic survey of the sky (such as the Palomar Sky Survey). On some photos you'll see extensive swirls of gas and many stars. But on the photos of regions where the stars thin out—away from the Milky Way—you can see the tiny forms of galaxies. If you look at enough photos, you will notice that if you find one galaxy, you're likely to see others nearby. You have found that galaxies tend to come in clusters (Fig. 17.16). George Abell comments that, on the Palomar Sky survey, "tens of thousands" of clusters of galaxies are "easily identified." In fact, it may be that *all* galaxies belong to clusters—though many of these clusters may be a simple marriage of two galaxies. The universe is one of clusters of galaxies!

The local group / The nearest cluster of galaxies is the one to which the Galaxy belongs. It is called the *local group of galaxies*, or simply the *local group*. This aggregation takes up a volume of space nearly 10 million ly across in its long dimension (Fig. 17.17). Our Galaxy is located near one end of the local group, and M31 is near the other.

As the most massive objects in the cluster, the Galaxy and M31 dominate its motions and secure the other members gravitationally. In fact, the Galaxy and M31 orbit each other. The other members of the local group come along with us and M31 for the ride. The local group contains at least 28 galaxies; they consist of some three spirals, 11 irregulars, and 14 ellipticals (Table 17.2). Some of these ellipticals are quite faint and are called dwarf ellipticals to distinguish them from the giant ellipticals found in other clusters. The obscuring matter in the Milky Way may cloud our sight of other members, especially faint dwarf ellipticals.

Let me turn to some of the more important members of the local group.

The Large and Small Magellanic Clouds (Fig. 17.18) are closest to the Milky Way. They are, in fact, connected to our Galaxy by a bridge of hydrogen gas. The two Clouds are physically connected to each other by a large but thin envelope of neutral hydrogen. Both are distorted by tidal forces from our Galaxy.

The Large Magellanic Cloud (abbreviated

Cluster of galaxies in Virgo. (Courtesy Kitt Peak National Observatory)

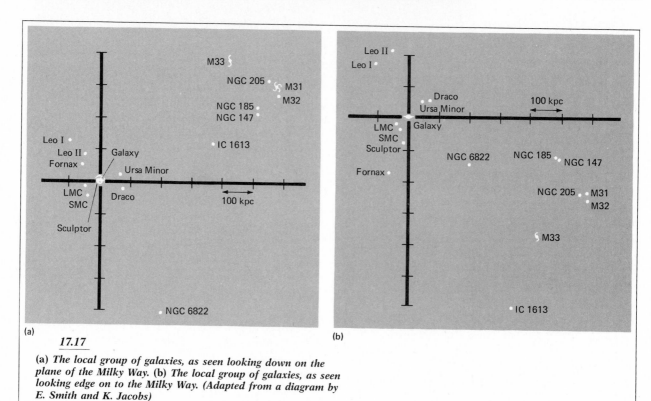

(a)

(b)

17.17

(a) *The local group of galaxies, as seen looking down on the plane of the Milky Way.* (b) *The local group of galaxies, as seen looking edge on to the Milky Way. (Adapted from a diagram by E. Smith and K. Jacobs)*

TABLE 17.2 *Physical properties of some galaxies in the local group*

Name	Type	Diameter (kpc)	Distance (kpc)	Mass (solar masses)
Milky Way	Spiral	4	. . .	3.4×10^{11}
NGC147	Dwarf Elliptical	2.4	680	?
NCG185	Dwarf Elliptical	2.9	680	?
NGC205	Elliptical	4.2	680	?
M31	Spiral	52	680	4×10^{11}
M32	Elliptical	2.1	680	2×10^{9}
SMC	Irregular	5	60	?
Sculptor	Dwarf Elliptical	2.4	86	3×10^{6}
IC1613	Irregular	4	680	?
M33	Spiral	18	700	2×10^{10}
Fornax	Dwarf Elliptical	6.2	188	2×10^{7}
LMC	Irregular	8	53	?
Leo I	Dwarf Elliptical	1.8	230	3×10^{6}
Leo II	Dwarf Elliptical	1.3	230	10^{6}
Ursa Minor	Dwarf Elliptical	2.4	68	10^{5}
Draco	Dwarf Elliptical	1.0	77	10^{5}
NGC6822	Irregular	1.7	660	?

Note NGC stands for a listing in the *New General Catalog;* M for the Messier Catalog.

17.18

The Large and Small Magellanic Clouds. These two irregular galaxies are the closest galaxies to the Milky Way. They are connected to us by a bridge of hydrogen gas. (Courtesy of Harvard College Observatory)

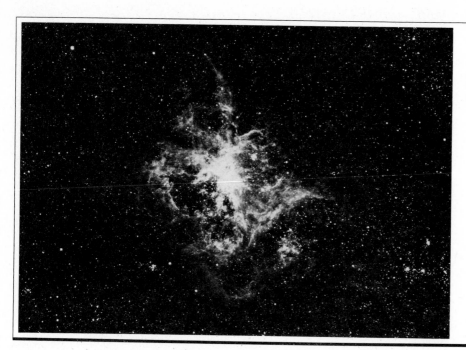

17.19

The giant emission nebula 30 Doradus in the Large Magellanic Cloud. (Courtesy Kitt Peak National Observatory)

LMC) contains stars totaling about 20 billion solar masses and orbits 170,000 ly from the Milky Way. Spectra of a large number of stars in the LMC show that most stars are similar to those in the solar neighborhood, with more *O*- and *B*-stars. Over 2000 variables have been discovered in the LMC; about 600 of these are the famous cepheids, which established the period–luminosity relation. Radio studies demonstrate that the LMC has large amounts of neutral hydrogen gas, a total of approximately 3 billion solar masses. The gas is also evident from the more than 400 emission nebulas found in it so far. One of these nebulas, called 30 Doradus, illuminated by a cluster of *O*- and *B*-stars, extends over 1,600 ly in diameter and contains roughly 5 million solar masses of material (Fig. 17.19).

The Small Magellanic Cloud (SMC) has a stellar population similar to the LMC although it is much smaller—a mass of only 2 billion solar masses, one-tenth that of the LMC. Its distance is about 205,000 ly; its distance from the LMC is roughly 26,000 ly.

The Magellanic Clouds are not the only galaxies close by. A swarm of six dwarf galaxies accompanies the Galaxy in space. These dwarf galaxies have masses of only about a million solar masses and range from 160–980 kly in distance from the Galaxy.

M31, a large spiral, is visible to the unaided eye on a moonless night. With binoculars you find an elliptical, hazy patch of light. M31 tilts 15° to the line of sight. Because of the tilt, dark lanes of obscuring material are plainly visible along with the spiral arms marked by *O*- and *B*-stars. A halo of globular clusters surrounds M31 like bees around a hive, in a distribution like that around the Galaxy.

M33 is the only other large spiral in the local group (Fig. 17.20). It is the closest *Sc II* galaxy to us, only 2.7 million ly away. M33 has wide, open spiral arms, which are resolved into stars; most of these are blue supergiants. Because M33 is so close, astronomers have been able to investigate in detail its dark dust lanes, H II regions, open star clusters, novas, and cepheid variables. M33 has an overall diameter of about 60,000 ly—only about half the size of the Galaxy.

Other clusters of galaxies / Other clusters range from compact distributions (Fig. 17.21) to rather loose arrays of galaxies. The Fornax cluster, one relatively close by, displays a wide variety of types of galaxies, even though the total number is only 16. The huge Coma cluster (Fig. 17.22) spreads over about 23 million ly of space and contains thousands of galaxies. From these observations, astronomers find that a typical cluster contains about 100 galaxies and is sepa-

17.20

The spiral galaxy Messier 33 (M 33) in the constellation Triangulum. It is a Hubble-type Sc galaxy; note the small nucleus and spread-out spiral arms. (Courtesy Lick Observatory)

17.21

A small cluster of galaxies, Stephan's quintet. (Courtesy Lick Observatory)

17.22

A large cluster of galaxies, the Coma cluster, which contains thousands of galaxies. Only some are visible in this wide-angle photo. But look carefully—almost every image is a galaxy. Fig. 17.1 shows the central region of this cluster. (Courtesy Lick Observatory)

rated by some tens of millions of light years from its neighboring clusters.

George Abell has cataloged and studied 2712 rich clusters of galaxies that contain a number of bright galaxies. ("Rich" means having more than 50 galaxies within a radius of 6.6 million ly). Abell finds that the clusters tend to fall into two groups, which he calls simply *regular* and *irregular*. Regular groups have (1) a marked spherical symmetry, (2) a high concentration of galaxies at the center, (3) many bright *E* and *S0* galaxies, (4) 1000 or more bright galaxies, (5) masses on the order of 10^{15} solar mass, and (6) no subclustering. In contrast, irregular groups have (1) little symmetry, (2) no concentrated, single center, (3) mostly spiral and irregular galaxies, (4) 10–1000 bright galaxies, (5) masses from 10^{12}–10^{14} solar masses, and (6) subclustering into two or more groups.

An example of a regular cluster is the *Coma cluster* (Fig. 17.1); note the large, bright elliptical galaxy near the center about which the others seem to concentrate; it is a supergiant *E* galaxy. Examples of irregular clusters are the local group and the *Virgo cluster*. Of the 205 brightest galaxies in the Virgo cluster, the four brightest are giant ellipticals; but, in all, ellipticals make up only 19 percent compared with the spirals 68 percent. The Virgo cluster covers about 7° in the sky (14 times the diameter of the moon!), which implies that its physical diameter is some 10 million ly at a distance of 62 million ly.

Clusters and the luminosity function of galaxies / In Section 15.2 you learned that the local stars have a luminosity function; that is, a certain number of stars can be found in a given range of luminosity. The basic trend is that very few extremely luminous (*OB*) stars exist, compared with the large numbers of low-luminosity *M*-stars.

From the description of the local group, you might suspect a similar hierarchy for galaxies. Recall that only three local galaxies are very luminous (the Milky Way Galaxy, M31, and M33), whereas most galaxies in the local group are dwarf, low-luminosity galaxies. So galaxies have a luminosity function somewhat like that of stars: There are many faint galaxies and few bright ones in a cluster.

Much of a cluster's mass, then, must reside in small, very faint galaxies. However, the total mass of a cluster is very difficult to estimate—in part because not all the material in them can be seen at visual wavelengths. So adding up the masses of all the visible galaxies gives a lower limit to a cluster's mass. On the other hand, if a cluster is assumed to be gravitationally bound, then the motions of its galaxies places a higher limit on the mass. The actual value is greater. Masses range from 10^9 to 10^{15} solar masses. However, astronomers have not yet been able to tell if clusters are bound and stable or unstable and expanding.

Superclusters / Are there clusters of clusters of galaxies? That is, do superclusters exist? Abell notes that in his catalog of 2712 clusters, he sees evidence of roughly 50 superclusters, each containing about 11 clusters and having diameters of about 250 million ly.

Much work on superclustering has been done by Gerard de Vaucouleurs. He finds evidence for a *local supercluster* that has a diameter of some 100 million ly. It contains the local group, Virgo cluster, and Coma cluster among others, for a total mass of some 10^{15} solar masses. The center of mass lies in or near the Virgo cluster; our Galaxy moves at about 500 km/sec about it.

Now to return to the difference Aaronson, Huchra, and Mould found for the Hubble constant using the Virgo cluster only (65 km/sec/Mpc) and other clusters of galaxies (95 km/sec/Mpc). One explanation of the difference of 30 km/sec/Mpc is that the local group has a motion *toward* the Virgo cluster, resulting in a smaller Hubble constant in that direction. If so, the velocity would amount to some 480 km/sec. The local supercluster may have a large enough overall density to produce this motion, resulting in an apparent slowdown in the expansion of the universe in this direction.

The cosmic tapestry / What does the universe of galaxies look like on the grand scale? James E. Peebles and co-workers have investigated in detail a survey of a million galaxies (Fig. 17.23) performed by Donald Shane and Carl Wirtanen of Lick Observatory. (This survey took 12 years to complete!) They find that galaxies cluster in knots and filaments. These are chains of galaxies and clusters (looking like a chain-linked fence). Nearly all galaxies are within these clusters, with huge holes between

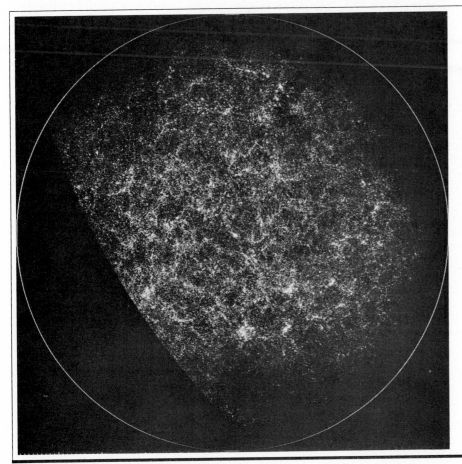

17.23

The universe of galaxies. More than a million galaxies, brighter than apparent magnitude +19, are plotted here. The lighter a region, the more galaxies it contains. Note the clumpy, chainlike structure. (Courtesy P. J. E. Peebles; based on the Lick galaxy catalog by C. Shane and C. Wirtanen)

them devoid of luminous matter. Here you see the explosive imprint of the big bang—a filamentary texture similar to that of supernova remnants.

17.6
Intergalactic matter

Is intergalactic space empty? Or does an intergalactic medium exist like the interstellar medium? If an intergalactic medium is present, it may contain both gas and dust. The gas (probably hydrogen) may be in neutral form, or it may be ionized.

We can look for the intergalactic medium in two locations: (1) *between* the clusters of galaxies and (2) *within* clusters of galaxies.

Matter between clusters / To get some idea of how much material might be in an intergalactic medium, imagine the following: Take the matter from all the galaxies you can see and spread it out over the entire volume of space you can observe. This spread-out material would have a density of about 4×10^{-31} g/cc. (That's about two hydrogen atoms every 10 cubic meters.) Recall that this density is about 10 times less than that needed to close the universe (Section 7.5). For the intergalactic medium to be significant, its density would need to be about this large. What is the evidence for such a density of dust, neutral hydrogen, or ionized hydrogen?

Consider the possibility of intergalactic dust. Such dust, if it resembled the interstellar dust in our Galaxy (Section 15.4), would extinguish and redden the light from distant galaxies. This extinction and reddening has been searched for but not found. So intergalactic space cannot contain very much dust.

How might we detect neutral hydrogen? Hydrogen atoms are very good absorbers of ultraviolet, especially at 1,216 Å, the absorption produced when the electron is excited from its ground state to its first excited state (Section

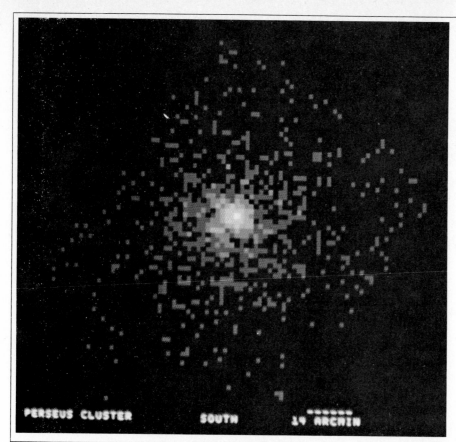

PERSEUS CLUSTER   SOUTH   14 ARCMIN

17.24

A map of the X-ray emission from a cluster of galaxies in the constellation Perseus. The light parts of the image indicate X-ray emission (dark areas indicate no detected X-rays); the lighter a region, the stronger the detected X-ray emission. (From observations by P. Gorenstein, D. Fabricant, K. Topka, F. Harnden, Jr., and W. Tucker; courtesy of P. Gorenstein)

5.3). Such ultraviolet absorption has been sought in the spectra of distant objects with both small and large red shifts. It has not been detected. This lack of ultraviolet absorption implies that neutral hydrogen cannot have a density greater than about 1.7×10^{-36} g/cc. Because these observations probe the universe's past, they also imply that any intergalactic gas must have remained highly ionized for most of the history of the universe.

These arguments leave ionized hydrogen (H II) as the most likely candidate for the intergalactic medium. Because intergalactic material would not have a high density, ionized hydrogen would take a very long time to find an electron and recombine. Unfortunately, detecting a low-density ionized gas is a tough job. If the gas is cool (a few thousand Kelvins), you can hunt for radio emission. Results to date have been negative. If hot (a few tens of millions of Kelvins), you can hunt for X-ray or ultraviolet emission.

X-rays do come from superclusters. Edwin Kellogg has reported that in a survey of X-ray observations made to date 15 X-ray sources are probably clustered in seven nearby superclusters. He notes that the sources consist of X-ray bright spots centered on rich clusters of galaxies—an observational fact implying that any hot gas in these superclusters is strongly clumped,

with little in between the clumps. So there doesn't appear to be much hot gas *between* clusters.

Matter within clusters / For over 40 years astronomers have known about a puzzling characteristic of clusters of galaxies: Their masses estimated from the motions of the galaxies (if the cluster is gravitationally bound) come out about ten times greater than those calculated by adding up the estimated masses of visible galaxies. In what form could this unseen material exist?

One possibility is that spiral galaxies have much larger and more massive halos than normally believed. These halos would be dark, need to be about a million light years in size, and contain about 10 times the mass of the disk. The flat rotation curve of our Galaxy and other spirals supports this idea.

Another good candidate is ionized hydrogen gas. Recent X-ray observations back up this idea. At least 40 clusters of galaxies are known to emit X-rays (Fig. 17.24). Their X-ray luminosities range from 10^{36} to 10^{38} W. The sizes of the X-ray cores range from 160,000 ly to 5 million ly. The richer clusters tend to be more powerful X-ray emitters.

One reasonably confirmed model for this X-ray emission is that it comes from hot, ionized gas. This model requires typical temperatures of 10 to 100 million K and densities of about 10^{-3} ion/cc to explain the X-ray observations. So astronomers have reasonable evidence of intergalactic gas in clusters, about equal in mass to the galaxies. But its density neither appears sufficient to bind the cluster gravitationally nor appears sufficient to close the universe.

SUMMARY

This chapter has jumped out beyond the Milky Way to describe some of the objects found in the rest of the universe. The answers, all crucial questions about the physical properties of galaxies, hinge on a knowledge of their distance. Beyond the limited range of present objects of known luminosity, we must rely on the calibration of the Hubble constant and on the assumptions of cosmology to estimate the distances to galaxies that are only dimly viewed even by the largest telescopes.

The distances to other galaxies seem enormous. Suppose our Galaxy were shrunk down to the size of a dime—about 1.5 cm. Then the nearest galaxies—the Magellanic Clouds—would be almost two dimes away. The Andromeda galaxy would be about 45 cm away, at the other end of the local group. But the nearest cluster of galaxies—the Virgo cluster—would be almost 4 m away! The limits of the distance-measuring techniques would reach to a distance of over 1 km.

The fact that galaxies similar in form exist throughout the observable universe reaffirms the assumption of the uniformity of nature. So as you delve into the structure and evolution of the Milky Way, you are also investigating ideas about the rest of the universe. Finally, you run into the largest bound structures you can see in the universe: superclusters of galaxies. These vast swarms of stellar systems mark the peak of the pyramid of gravitational groupings in the universe and are linked to the processes in which the universe was created.

STUDY EXERCISES

1 Which galaxies appear redder, ellipticals or spirals? (*Objective 1*)

2 Which galaxies contain more gas and dust, spirals or irregulars? (*Objective 1*)

3 At the same distance from us, would irregular galaxies appear larger than spiral ones? (*Objectives 1 and 2*)

4 How do astronomers know that other galaxies are made of stars? (*Objective 3*)

5 Suppose the value of the Hubble constant was 100 km/sec/Mpc rather than 50 km/sec/Mpc. How does this change affect the distances to galaxies inferred from red shifts and the Hubble constant? (*Objectives 5 and 7*)

6 Describe how supergiant *O*- and *B*-stars can be used to estimate distances to nearby galaxies. State the assumptions and limits of this method. (*Objective 6*)

7 Why must intergalactic gas be both ionized and hot? (*Objective 10*)

8 Which type of galaxies is the most massive? (*Objective 1*)

9 About how large is the local group? Are most of the galaxies in it large spirals and ellipticals or dwarf galaxies? (*Objective 9*)

10 What observational evidence is there that spiral galaxies have massive halos? (*Objective 1*)

BEYOND THIS BOOK . . .

Galaxies (Harvard University Press, Cambridge, Mass., 1972), by H. Shapley, recently revised by P. Hodge, gives a comprehensive view of galaxies.

The Realm of the Nebulae (Dover, New York, 1958) by E. Hubble was first published in 1936. Compare it with *Galaxies* by Hodge.

Galaxies and Cosmology (McGraw-Hill, New York, 1966) by P. Hodge deals with the observed and physical properties of galaxies and their relationship to the universe.

"The Content of Galaxies" by W. Baade in *Scientific American*, vol. 195, p. 93, 1956, is a dated article but still useful for basic ideas.

For a gorgeous tour of the galaxies, examine *The Hubble Atlas of Galaxies* (Carnegie Institution, Washington, 1961) by A. Sandage.

"The Clustering of Galaxies" by E. Groth, P. J. E. Peebles, M. Seldner, and R. Soneira, *Scientific American*, November 1977, p. 76, examines the cosmic tapestry in detail.

Cosmic explosions: Violent evolution

18

LEARNING OBJECTIVES

After studying this chapter you should be able to:

1. Contrast synchrotron (nonthermal) to thermal radiation with special emphasis on how synchrotron radiation is produced.

2. Outline the observational evidence for violent activity in our Galaxy and others, with special emphasis on synchrotron radiation.

3. List the observational characteristics of quasars.

4. Sketch a possible model that accounts for the observed properties of quasars.

5. Describe the observed properties of active galaxies, with special emphasis on radio observations.

6. Discuss the possible energy sources for quasars and active galaxies.

7. Compare and contrast the Milky Way, active galaxies, and quasars.

8. Outline the method used to estimate distances to quasars, and discuss its uncertainties.

9. Evaluate the theoretical difficulties that arise if quasars are placed very far away.

10. Discuss possible alternatives to quasars as distant objects.

How calm the universe appears, caught up in the well-controlled generation of energy in stars and the strict Newtonian dance of matter—until the middle of the twentieth century a gentle cosmos. Rare outbursts such as novas only occasionally shattered the stillness of the cosmos.

The advent of radio astronomy ripped off the veil covering a violent universe. Radio astronomers found the nucleus of our Galaxy to be a stupendous radio emitter. They also detected intense radio sources beyond the Galaxy. Such sources at enormous distances required a tremendous outpouring of energy at radio wavelengths. Later work by infrared astronomers revealed that some extragalactic radio sources emitted even more energy at infrared than at radio wavelengths. By the 1970s so much observational evidence had accumulated that violent events in the cosmos, especially associated with the nuclei of all kinds of galaxies, were recognized as common. The opening of the high-energy end of the electromagnetic spectrum in X-ray and gamma-ray astronomy has enhanced our awareness of the violent aspects of the universe. This awareness has reached maturity recently with the observational exploration of active galaxies—galaxies whose power in the radio, infrared, and X-rays amounts to many times their optical output.

Quasars—starlike objects with large Doppler shifts—are one new and puzzling element in the range of cosmic violence. Originally discovered as radio sources, quasars have the largest known red shifts of any extragalactic objects. If the red shifts of quasars result from the general expansion of the universe, then the quasars must be the most energetic bodies in the universe. In one hour some quasars spew energy equal to the amount generated during the sun's entire lifetime! At the fringes of the cosmos, quasars represent some of the first-made objects in the visible universe—and the most powerful. The mystery still remains of how the quasars produce their energy—and the answer may relate them to the evolution of active galaxies.

18.1

Violence in the nuclei of galaxies

Galaxies appear as the most splendid and serene bodies in the universe. As astronomers have gained access to more regions of the electromagnetic spectrum (Chapter 6), some galaxies—and the nuclei of most—have acquired the aspect of a compact arena of violent events. The kernel of the nucleus is too small to investigate in galaxies, except M31 in Andromeda, and too obscured to observe optically in our Galaxy. The processes at work in the heart of a galaxy are as yet unknown.

Evidence of violence in the Galaxy / Chapters 15 and 16 presented the structure and contents of our home Galaxy. Here are these recent results about the nucleus in the context of cosmic violence.

The galactic nucleus lies at the center of the radio source Sgr A, which is two sources—Sgr A East and Sgr A West. The central core of Sgr A West, which has a radio size of less than 20 AU, marks the actual heart of the Galaxy. Infrared observations show that the galactic nucleus shines brightly at infrared wavelengths between 2 and 350 microns (Fig. 18.1). The peak of the infrared emission comes from a region only 3 ly across. Detailed maps show that the nucleus holds a cluster of infrared sources. The infrared luminosity of the nucleus is more than 10^8 solar luminosities at long wavelengths for a region some 2° around Sgr A.

The region near the galactic nucleus also puts out high-energy photons: X-rays and gamma rays. The X-ray emission from an extended region around the galactic center, roughly coinciding with the source of the far-infrared emission. The X-ray intensity varies; it averages about 10^{30} W (10^4 solar luminosities). The energy emitted in gamma rays from one degree around the galactic center is 10^{27}–10^{28} W (about 10 solar luminosities).

Emission at such a wide range of wavelengths indicates that the spectrum of the nucleus is in part nonthermal (Focus 47). That is, some of the emission must be by the *synchrotron* process. So high-energy electrons, perhaps from some explosion, spiraling in intense magnetic fields, must exist in the nucleus.

The process of synchrotron emission is so important to this chapter and to astrophysics in general that you must have the basic concept clearly in mind. That is, whenever *charged* particles accelerate, they give off electromagnetic radiation, which is basically how a radio trans-

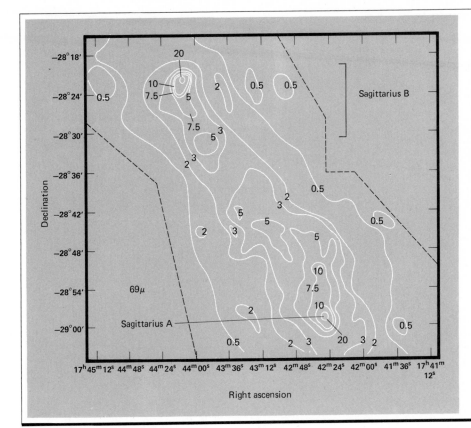

18.1

Infrared emission (at a wavelength of 69 microns) in the region of the galactic center is shown in this intensity contour map. (See Appendix F for how to read such a map.) Note that there are two strong peaks: one at the position of Sgr A, the other at Sgr B. This infrared emission comes from dust heated by the light from young, hot stars. (Courtesy G. Fazio and the Center for Astrophysics)

mitter works; electronically, the transmitter forces electrons to accelerate back and forth in the antenna at the frequency of operation. These moving charges emit a radio wave at the frequency of their antenna oscillation. Now recall (Focus 24) that magnetic fields can bend the paths of charged particles—electrons more easily than protons because electrons have much less mass and so a lower inertia. So if electrons move through magnetic fields, their paths will be bent and the particles accelerated. (Remember that curved motion is accelerated motion according to Newton's laws.) As a result, the electrons emit electromagnetic radiation. In general, the faster the electrons are traveling, the more energetic the radiation they emit. And the stronger the magnetic fields are, the more energetic will be the emission. Of course, as the electrons emit, they lose energy and so slow down. (Details in Focus 47.)

In summary, the nucleus of the Galaxy appears to harbor violent activity. The support for the model of violence in the nucleus includes (1) the presence of ionized gas, (2) energy emitted from a very small region, (3) nonthermal radiation at a wide range of wavelengths, and (4) a densely packed concentration of rapidly rotating gas within 3–4 ly of the galactic center.

You'll see in what follows that most large galaxies have similar characteristics and galaxies more active than the Galaxy display such energy output at a much higher scale of violence.

18.2
Active galaxies

Radio astronomers have found that many radio sources lie beyond our Galaxy and have nonthermal spectra. Many have turned out to be some kind of galaxy. Those galaxies with nonthermal spectra have been lumped into the category of *active galaxies.*

But how active is "active"? I'll use the term here in contrast to "normal," which applies to galaxies like ours. Basically, an active galaxy's spectrum does not look like that emitted by a collection of stars. It has infrared, radio, ultravi-

focus 47

THERMAL AND NONTHERMAL RADIATION

Focus 31 introduced the concept of a blackbody by the properties of absorption and emission. You saw that the spectrum of blackbody radiation has a characteristic shape. The energy output increased from longer to shorter wavelengths, peaked at a wavelength that depended on the blackbody's temperature, and then decreased at shorter wavelengths until it approached zero.

The spectrum of blackbody radiation is the archetype of thermal radiation, *which arises basically from the motions of the particles involved. The greater the motions are, the higher will be the output of radiation (and the hotter the source).*

Nonthermal radiation does not have the characteristic spectrum of blackbody radiation. In general, the nonthermal spectrum increases in intensity at longer wavelengths (Fig. 1). Synchrotron radiation *is a frequently found source of nonthermal radiation that arises from the acceleration of charged particles (usually electrons) in a magnetic field. As described in Focus 24, moving charged particles interact with magnetic fields so that they spiral around the magnetic field lines rather than traveling across them (Fig. 2). Because it is always changing direction, the particle is continually accelerated and thus emits electromagnetic radiation. The frequency of the radiation is directly related to how fast the particle spirals; the faster the spiral is, the higher is the frequency. Increasing the magnetic field strength tightens the spiral and so increases the frequency. The velocity of the charged particle also affects the frequency directly, so more energetic particles can produce higher frequency radiation, but they also require strong fields to keep them in a tight spiral. As the particle radiates, it loses energy and generates lower energy radiation. So a synchrotron source needs a continually replenished supply of electrons in order to keep emitting at relatively short wavelengths.*

One important point about synchrotron radiation: It is polarized. *What does it mean for electromagnetic radiation to be polarized? Recall (Section 5.3) that light has wave properties. Such waves are polarized if the planes of their up-down motion are preferentially oriented in some direction. Thermal radiation, such as from the sun, has no preferred*

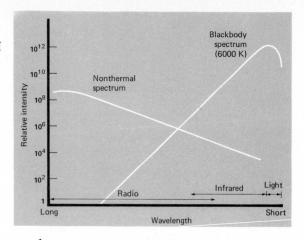

1

A comparison between a blackbody (thermal) spectrum of 6000 K and a nonthermal synchrotron spectrum.

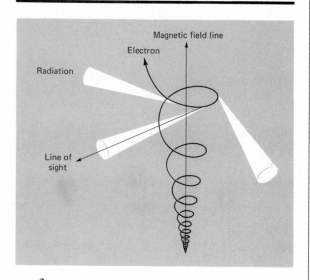

2

Synchrotron radiation from an electron spiraling in a magnetic field.

alignment: The planes of wave vibration are found in all directions in equal numbers. Synchrotron-emitting electrons, when viewed side on in their spiral motion, appear to be moving back and forth along almost straight lines. Their synchrotron emission has its waves more or less aligned in the same up-down plane. So synchrotron radiation is polarized and, at visible wavelengths, can be observed as such with polaroid filters.

The term synchrotron emission *derives from the fact that such radiation was first observed from the General Electric synchrotron, which used magnetic fields to contain electrons accelerated to high energies.*

olet, and X-ray outputs greater than that in the optical and a nonthermal spectrum. Table 18.1 lists some of the typical properties of active galaxies. Figure 18.2 compares the spectra of some active galaxies to that of a normal galaxy. Note that the Galaxy emits over the same wavelength range as an active galaxy but not so strongly or with the same spectral shape.

There are a lot of observations of active galaxies but little understanding of them right now in terms of successful models. For this reason, I'll limit the discussion to the major classes of active galaxies.

Radio galaxies / You find radio galaxies by searching for their radio emission. Two principal types have cropped up: *compact* and *extended*. "Extended" means that the radio emission is larger than a photographic image of the galaxy; "compact," the same size or smaller. Compact radio galaxies often display very small radio sources—typically no more than a few light years in size. Extended radio sources, in contrast to the compact ones, sometimes show a double structure—two giant lobes, up to millions of light years in extent, symmetrically balanced on opposite sides of the nucleus.

Messier 87 (M87) is a fine example of a compact radio galaxy. A giant elliptical galaxy, M87 dominates the Virgo cluster of galaxies. It lies about 65 million ly away and is the nearest elliptical galaxy that presents direct evidence for violent activity. A radio source only 1.5 light *months* in diameter appears in M87's core, along with a group of other compact radio sources. Poking out from the core, a remarkable, optically visible jet (Fig. 18.3) fires out into space over a length of some 6000 ly. The jet has a luminosity of roughly 10^{34} W (10^7 solar luminosities); its emission is polarized.

A beautiful photograph taken by Halton Arp shows that the jet contains at least six blobs of material, each no more than a few tens of light years in size (Fig. 18.4). And Arp and colleagues have found that, over 22 years, the blobs have changed slightly but significantly in intensity and polarization. Arp has also found a fainter jet is visible on the opposite side of the galaxy from the brighter one—in other words, a counterjet.

M87 also emits X-rays with about 50 times more energy than its optical emission—about 5×10^{35} W (10^9 solar luminosities) in X-rays

---

TABLE 18.1 *Properties of active galaxies*

1. High luminosity, greater than 10^{37} W

2. Nonthermal emission, with excess ultraviolet, infrared, radio, and X-ray flux (compared with normal galaxies)

3. Rapid variability and/or small size (few light years at most)

4. Peculiar photographic appearance: high contrast in brightness of nucleus and large-scale structure

5. Explosive appearance or jetlike protuberances

6. Broad emission lines (sometimes) and nonstellar spectrum

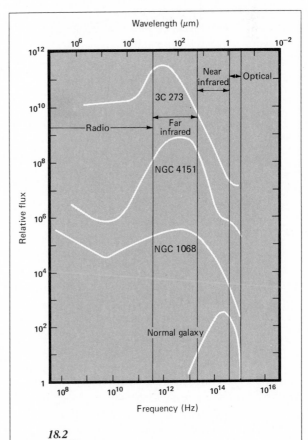

18.2

A comparison of the spectra in the radio, infrared, and optical for three active galaxies and a normal galaxy. (Adapted from a diagram by R. Weymann)

18.3

A short-exposure photo of the active galaxy Messier 87 (M87). Note the jet in the lower right extending from the nucleus. (Courtesy Kitt Peak National Observatory)

as the electrons spiral in the magnetic fields (intensity about 10^{-5}–10^{-6} G), they emit photons and so lose energy. Traveling slower, they then emit lower frequency photons, and so on. The rate of loss of energy by the electrons is greatest at the highest energies and less at lower energies, if the magnetic fields are constant in strength. The fact that the jet's knots from radio to X-ray are coincident implies that the same electrons power all emission within a knot.

But what keeps the emission going? How do the electrons get replenished? There are many models but none are completely satisfactory. For example, the jet may be a continuous stream of material with the knots produced by instabilities in the flow.

Other elliptical galaxies possess nuclear jets. For example, radio observations have detected a jet in the nucleus of the elliptical galaxy NGC 6251 (Fig. 18.6). The nuclear jet has a length of only 5.5 ly, its material exceeds a temperature of 10^8 K, and it starts only 7 ly from the nuclear core. In fact, radio jets are common. Almost all radio galaxies of the lowest luminosities have jets (see Color Plates 24 and 25).

At first glance, extended radio galaxies are a completely different beast from compact radio galaxies. Cygnus A, one of the strongest radio sources in the sky and one of the first discovered, provides an excellent example of the typical double structure of an extended radio galaxy. Its radio output, some 1.2×10^{38} W (10^{11} solar luminosities), comes from two giant lobes set on opposite sides of the optical galaxy (Fig. 18.7). Each lobe has a diameter of 55 thousand ly—about half the size of the Galaxy! They hang roughly 160 thousand ly away from the central galaxy. Each lobe contains a cloud of energetic electrons and strong magnetic fields that store incredible amounts of energy. Some 10^{53} J is needed to account for the radio luminosity lasting 10^7–10^9 years. This is more energy than produced by all the stars in the Galaxy in 10^8 years!

The central galaxy of Cygnus A (Fig. 18.8) is a giant elliptical galaxy with a dust lane across its middle. It has an active nuclear region, with a spectrum showing emission lines and synchrotron emission. But beyond 24,000 ly from the center, the spectrum is just that of a mix of stars. This galaxy appears to have blasted out the two clouds now visible as radio lobes some 10^7–10^9 years ago.

from the whole galaxy. The jet itself is now also known to emit X-rays. High resolution observations show that the jet contains X-ray knots.

A recent VLA map of M87's jet confirmed that its radio emission (Fig. 18.5) coincides with the optical and X-ray emission. The radio knots correspond to the optical ones. So the jet overall emits over a wide range of frequencies—from radio to X-rays—and the knots of the jet each generate this spectrum of energies.

Observed at a wide range of wavelengths, the radio spectrum looks nonthermal. This fact led Russian astronomer Josif Shklovsky to propose that much of the emission comes from the synchrotron process, including the optical emission from the jet. The polarization of the jet's light (about 25 percent) supports this model. This synchrotron emission presents a problem, however. The electrons emitting light lose energy quickly—in only a few hundred years for the radio emission, a few tens of years for the optical, and a few days for the X-rays. That is,

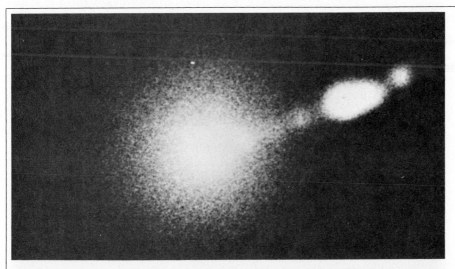

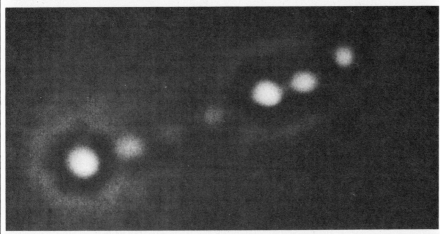

18.4

A close-up of the optical jet in M87. The upper view is a conventional photo. In the lower view, the photo has been computer processed to suppress the rest of the galaxy and to bring out the structure in the jet. Note that six blobs are clearly visible. (Courtesy H. Arp)

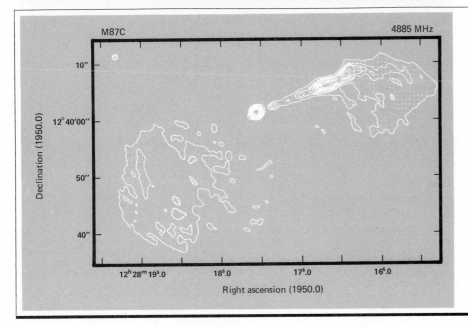

18.5

A high-resolution radio map of the central region of M87, made with the VLA at a frequency of 5 GHz. Note the radio jet—which coincides with the optical one—extending to the right from the nucleus. (Courtesy F. Owen; observations by F. Owen and P. Hardee)

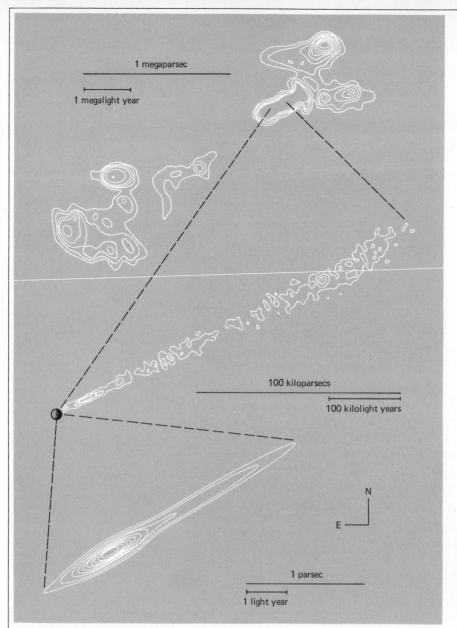

1 megaparsec

1 megalight year

100 kiloparsecs

100 kilolight years

N

E

1 parsec

1 light year

18.6

*A radio jet in the elliptical gal-
axy NGC 6521. The upper map
shows the central region of the
galaxy; the middle one, an enlarged view of the radio jet; the
lower one, of the jet alone—
note the very small-size scale.
(Adapted from a diagram by
A. Readhead, M. Cohen, and
R. Blanford)*

18.7

*A radio map of Cygnus A, and
extended, twin-lobed radio galaxy. The patch in the center
represents the optically visible
galaxy (next figure). On each
side of the nucleus lie immense
lobes of radio emission. (Based
on observations by S. Mitton
and M. Ryle with the Cam-
bridge Radio Telescope)*

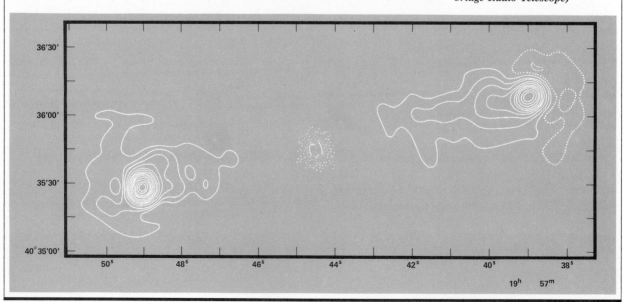

36'30'

36'00'

35'30'

40° 35'00'

50ˢ   48ˢ   46ˢ   44ˢ   42ˢ   40ˢ   38ˢ

19ʰ   57ᵐ

18.8

An optical photo of Cygnus A. Only the bright nucleus is visible, with a dust lane cutting through its middle. Compare with the next figure of a much closer elliptical galaxy, Centaurus A. (Courtesy Lick Observatory)

18.9

Centaurus A (NGC 5128), a radio galaxy. Note the dust lane across the galaxy's middle, like that in Cygnus A. (Courtesy Kitt Peak National Observatory)

Centaurus A (NGC 5128) is another strong radio source similar to Cygnus A: a supergiant (*cD*) elliptical (*E2*) galaxy bisected by an irregular dust lane (Fig. 18.9). At a distance of 13 million ly, Centaurus A is the closest active galaxy; it almost outshines M32 visually. Viewed with a radio telescope (Fig. 18.10), Centaurus A has two huge outer lobes, 650,000 and 1,350,000 ly in size. Closer in, another pair of radio lobes sit on the edges of the optical galaxy; these are some 33,000 ly in size. The inner and outer lobes are not in perfect alignment.

Centaurus A also emits X-rays intensely; the source is very small and coincides with the nucleus. Remarkably, the X-ray emission varies. For instance, during July–August 1975 the X-ray luminosity was 1.3×10^{36} W; during July–August 1976 it was 6.9×10^{35} W. During the same time the radio flux also varied, but only about half as much. The nucleus of Centaurus A also emits infrared and radio strongly. These observations, with those taken at X-ray energies, show that the nuclear emission is nonthermal.

The nucleus of Centaurus A is now known to have a direct connection to the inner radio lobes. Recently, the Einstein X-ray Observatory has detected an X-ray jet streaming northeast from the nucleus and consisting of at least seven distinct blobs (Fig. 18.11(a)). This discovery prompted Jack Burns, E. Schreier, and E. Feigelson to observe Centaurus A with the VLA—a very difficult observation, because Centaurus A is so far south that it's above the horizon only a few hours a day as viewed from New Mexico. The VLA map at a 20-cm wavelength (Fig. 18.11(b)) shows radio emission along a jet that extends to one of the nuclear radio lobes. The jet has a bloblike structure that coincides with the X-ray blobs. So Centaurus A and M87 look similar in that both have nuclear jets.

M87 and Centaurus A are examples of minority groups of radio galaxies. *Narrow-tailed sources* make up the majority, of which *head-tail* galaxies are one subgroup. As implied by the name, head-tail radio galaxies have a radio head (around the visible galaxy) and an ex-

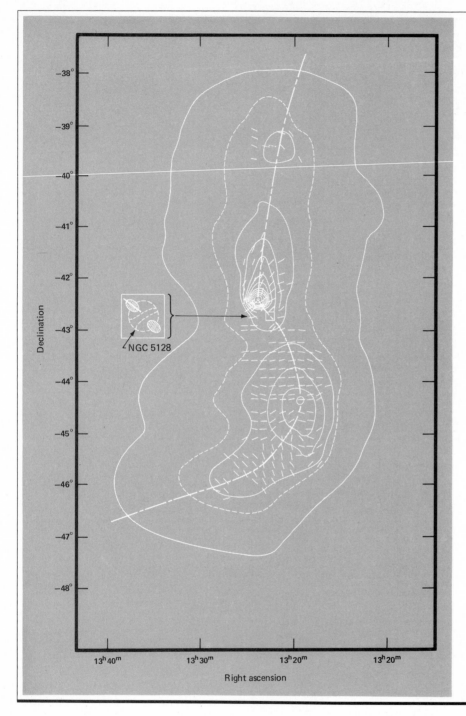

18.10
Radio emission from Centaurus A. This map shows the enormous extent of the two radio lobes. The short lines in the contours indicate the direction of the local magnetic fields. The optical Galaxy is the size of the small square in the center. The insert of it—enlarged—outlines the Galaxy, dust lane, and inner radio lobes. (Courtesy R. M. Price; based on observations by B. Cooper, R. M. Price, and D. Cole)

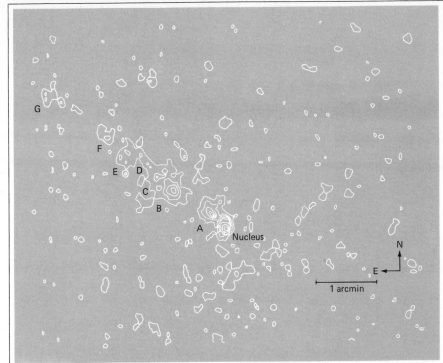

(a)

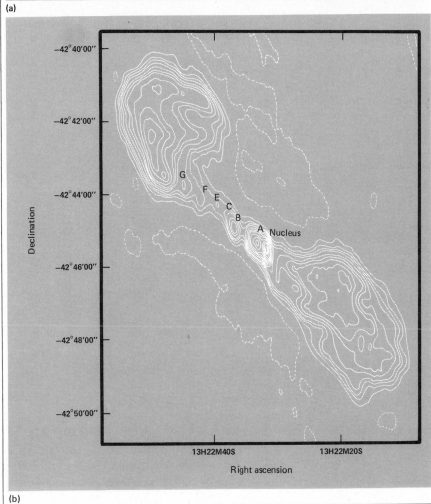

(b)

18.11
(a) *An X-ray map of the nuclear region of Centaurus A, taken with the Einstein X-Ray Observatory. Note the X-ray knots (A, B, C, D, E, F, and G) extending from the nucleus. These make up an X-ray jet. (Courtesy P. Gorenstein, E. Schreier, and E. Feigelson.)*
(b) *A radio map made with the VLA of the nuclear region of Centaurus A. Note the two inner radio lobes and the radio jet extending from the nucleus to the lobe at the upper left. The jet consists of a series of blobs that correspond well to the ones in the X-ray map. (Courtesy J. Burns; observations by J. Burns, E. Schreier, and E. Feigelson)*

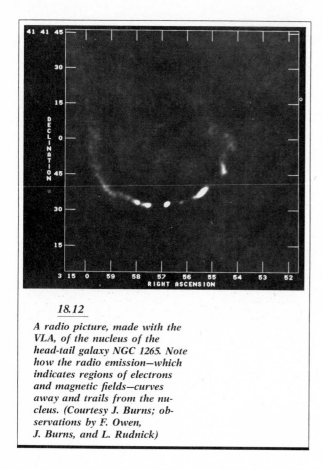

18.12

A radio picture, made with the VLA, of the nucleus of the head-tail galaxy NGC 1265. Note how the radio emission—which indicates regions of electrons and magnetic fields—curves away and trails from the nucleus. (Courtesy J. Burns; observations by F. Owen, J. Burns, and L. Rudnick)

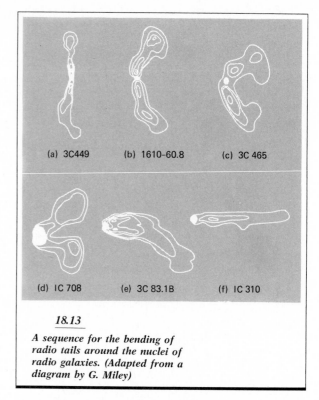

18.13

A sequence for the bending of radio tails around the nuclei of radio galaxies. (Adapted from a diagram by G. Miley)

tended tail. NGC 1265 (Fig. 18.12) in the Perseus cluster of galaxies is a good example. All galaxies with tails do not have them trailing. Instead, you find a sequence in the amount of bending shown by the tails (Fig. 18.13), which ranges from 180° apart (double source—Figure 18.13(a)) to 0° (head-tail source—Fig. 18.13(f)). At high resolution the heads often contain radio jets (Fig. 18.12).

How to explain this structural sequence? Recall that clusters of galaxies contain a hot, ionized medium. Imagine that a galaxy, moving rapidly through this medium, shoots out material (high-speed electrons, for instance) in a jet. As the galaxy travels along, it leaves behind a radio-visible trail—a fossil record of where it's been. Here's an analogy: Imagine driving a car slowly and blowing smoke out of an open window. The air stops the motion of the smoke and it leaves a trail behind the car. Similarly, material flowing out of a galaxy is slowed down by the surrounding medium and the moving galaxy leaves it behind (Fig. 18.12).

So head-tail galaxies interact with nearby gas and show that a significantly dense gas exists in clusters. In fact, the discovery of head-tail galaxies prompted the acceptance of intracluster gas *before* X-ray observations (Section 17.6) confirmed its existence and showed it to be very hot (about 10^7 K).

What powers M87, Centaurus A, and other radio galaxies? The clues are: nonthermal emission, usually polarized, with nuclear jets that have a bloblike structure and often point to twin lobes of extended emission beyond the nucleus. Occasionally, X-rays, radio, and optical emission come from the same blobs in the jets. This evidence suggests that the synchrotron process provides the emission. The nucleus provides the high-energy electrons. These are expelled as either a fairly constant beam of particles or a sequence of ionized blobs that are thrown out along a magnetic field, so half the particles fly in one direction; the other half, in the opposite direction. If the nuclear machine is active and stable, extended lobes of ionized material build up at the end of the jets. Repeated bursts

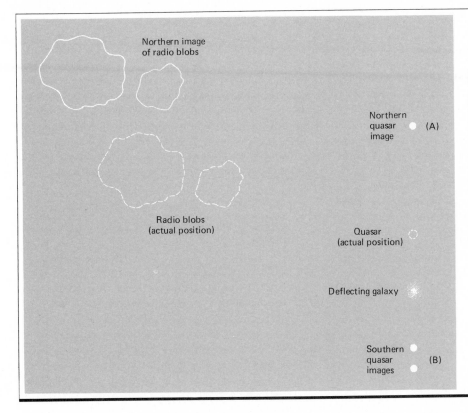

Northern image
of radio blobs

Radio blobs
(actual position)

Northern
quasar
image   ● (A)

Quasar
(actual position)

Deflecting galaxy

Southern   ●
quasar   (B)
images   ●

18.29

A schematic drawing of the optical illusion of the double quasar. The actual quasar and its radio emission (broken outlines) are invisible. An elliptical galaxy just below the actual quasar acts as the gravitational lens. It forms three images of the quasar: one above and two below the quasar's actual position. Only one image of the radio blobs is made—above and to the left of the actual position of the radio emission. The two lower images of the quasar lie almost on top of each other and so are not separately visible. (Adapted from a diagram by F. Chaffee)

galaxies share some observed characteristics. Let me make a few specific comparisons here.

First, radio galaxies. Most have only absorption lines in their spectra. Those that have emission lines come in two types. One type has *narrow* emission lines, with emission line Doppler widths of 400–800 km/sec. Narrow-lined radio galaxies make up about 2/3 of the total. The other 1/3 have broad lines of hydrogen and helium, some as wide as 10^4 km/sec. Other emission lines for these galaxies tend to be narrow.

Low-red-shift (close by in space and time) quasars have optical spectra that resemble the broad-line radio galaxies in terms of the emission lines present, their widths, and also the shape of the optical continuous spectrum. For instance, the hydrogen and helium lines of such quasars have widths of 3000–6000 km/sec.

Quasars also resemble Seyferts in their emission-line spectra. Recall that Seyferts come in two types on this basis: the Seyfert 1 class that have broad hydrogen lines and narrow lines of other elements and the Seyfert 2 class that have all broad emission lines. The Seyfert 1 galaxies, just like the broad-line radio galaxies,

resemble low-red-shift quasars in terms of their emission spectra. So the physical conditions in the regions producing the spectra must be basically the same in Seyfert 1 galaxies and in low-red-shift quasars.

In addition, Seyferts look like quasars: the nuclei of both are starlike; a few nearby quasars have been shown to have galaxylike disks surrounding them. The colors of Seyferts with the largest nuclei resemble the colors of quasars. And the nuclei of Seyfert 1 galaxies vary in light over periods of months—which implies, by the light-travel time argument, that the emitting region cannot be larger than a few light months in size.

Finally, compare quasars and BL Lac objects. First, there is a pronounced difference: BL Lac objects do *not* have strong emission lines. So now compare the continuous spectra of quasars and BL Lac objects. In both BL Lacs and quasars the nonthermal nature of the continuous emission stands out most clearly compared with other active galaxies. Assuming the nonthermal emission is synchrotron, BL Lac and the quasar 3C 279 need about the same magnetic field intensity (roughly 3×10^{-6} G) to account for their synchrotron spectra in the radio range.

BL Lac objects and about 15 percent of radio-bright quasars show wide variations in optical output over periods of days, weeks, and months. These swings in brightness often occur very abruptly.

To sum up: Active galaxies and quasars share some of the same *observed* properties and so, by inference, some of the same *physical* properties. The general aspect that's the most striking is the nonthermal emission from a region only a few light years in size.

Are active galaxies and quasars related? / The observations suggest, but do not prove, that quasars have some connection with active galaxies. One popular idea views them as similar objects at different stages of evolution. That is, the quasar phenomenon signals very violent activity in the nucleus of a galaxy at a very early stage in its life. Other active galaxies are older quasars, and so are less active: The sequence would be roughly quasar, BL Lac, Seyfert, then radio galaxy stages, ending up with a normal galaxy. This sequence seems likely because, in general, quasars have the greatest red shifts; Seyferts, less; and radio galaxies, the smallest. So if the red shifts are cosmological (see next subsection), then quasars are younger (less evolved) than Seyferts, which are younger than radio galaxies. (Remember, high red shift means you are looking far back in time.)

One other possible connection relates to radio structure. Quasars have high luminosities and tend to exhibit symmetrical double structures. The higher luminosity active galaxies have similar radio shapes. So the physical processes responsible for both may be the same. The nuclear jets imply that this structure is somehow tied to violent activity in the nuclei of luminous active galaxies and quasars.

This comparison suggests that quasars are linked to active galaxies in an evolutionary fashion: Quasars may be young, hyperactive galaxies. And most (or all galaxies) may go through evolutionary stages that resemble quasars, then active galaxies, and finally, normal galaxies—which have some of the properties of active galaxies but display them less violently.

A composite Hubble diagram (Fig. 18.30) suggests that this evolutionary sequence may be

the case. When the red shifts and apparent magnitudes are plotted for normal galaxies, radio galaxies, and quasars, the three groups appear to merge together. Quasar luminosities average 10^{38} W; radio galaxies, 10^{37} W; and normal galaxies, 10^{36} W. This decrease in luminosity and the merging of positions in the Hubble plot may indicate an evolutionary connection among the groups.

This evolutionary connection is a nice idea but has one severe drawback: It implies that the energy source in quasars relates directly to that in active galaxies. Astronomers simply don't know the nature of that energy source—yet. If it is a black hole, then all (or most) galaxies need to have a supermassive black hole in their nucleus (Section 21.7).

Alternative views about quasars and their red shifts / Some of the problems of quasar energy production ease if quasars are relatively close by rather than at cosmological distances. ("Close" means millions of light years rather than hundreds of millions.) For example, if 3C 273 were 100 times closer than it is, it would emit only 10^{10} solar luminosities (4×10^{36} W)— about the luminosity of an ordinary galaxy— from a region about a light year in diameter.

What part of our thinking would have to change if quasars were not really far away? Well, we'd have to pull back from the interpretation of their large red shifts as cosmological. Instead, all or part of their red shift would result from another cause. This is not an easy step to take, for then you have abandoned the simplest explanation for quasars' red shifts. Perhaps the queasiness with quasars is strong enough to warrant it; at least a few astronomers think so. This dissent has fueled the red-shift controversy about quasars.

Frankly, most astronomers believe that quasars' red shifts *are* cosmological—some further evidence follows. I will treat the opposition's views here very briefly.

What are possible causes of noncosmological red shifts? (1) Doppler shifts from radial velocities that are not cosmological, (2) gravitational red shifts (Focus 49), and/or (3) new physical laws. Because there's no way to deal with (3) and Focus 49 discusses (2), only (1) will be dealt with here.

Quasars might acquire large, noncosmological velocities if they were small objects shot

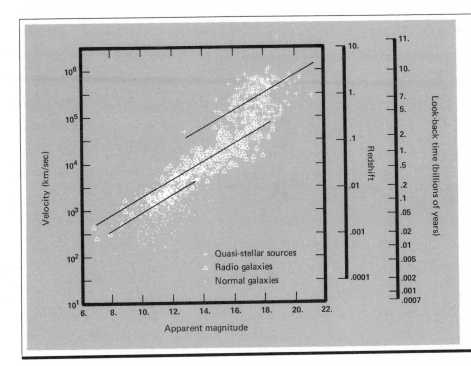

18.30

A composite Hubble diagram for quasars (crosses), radio galaxies (triangles) and normal galaxies (dots). Note how the three groups seem to merge together. (Courtesy of K. Lang; from K. Lang, S. Lord, J. Johanson, and P. Savage, **Astrophysical Journal,** *vol. 202, p. 583, copyright © 1975 by the American Astronomical Society)*

from galaxies by gigantic explosions. (Recall that we have evidence of explosions in our Galaxy and in active galaxies.) Then, if the quasar is shot away, the red shift of the quasar would be the Doppler shift from its expulsion plus the Doppler shift of its parent galaxy. You would see a very large red shift from the combination of the two. If shot toward the earth, subtract the radial velocity of the quasar from its parent galaxy; if the quasar moves fast enough, you see a blue shift. At least, it will be *less* of a red shift than the galaxy.

Put aside for a moment the problem of what physical mechanism could shoot quasars from galaxies. What do you expect from this model? That you would find galaxies and quasars close together in the sky more often than you'd ever expect by chance. But remember, when you look at the sky you see both near and distant objects. Just because you see a galaxy and quasar close together does not mean that they are the same distance away or physically associated.

The proponents of alternative models of quasars' red shifts believe that observational evidence supports the association of some quasars with galaxies. For example, Halton Arp and co-workers have investigated quasars near the *S0*

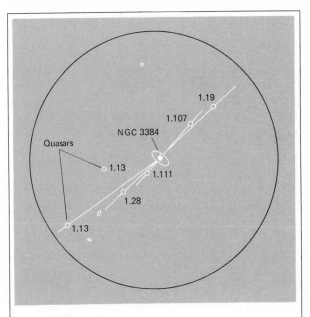

18.31

Orientation of the galaxy NGC 3384 and nearby quasars. The numbers indicate the red shifts. (Adapted from a diagram by H. Arp, J. Sulentic, and G. di Tullio, **Astrophysical Journal,** *vol. 229, p. 489, copyright © 1979 by the American Astronomical Society)*

focus 49

THE GRAVITATIONAL RED SHIFT

The most important observational fact about quasars is their large red shifts. If these red shifts are produced by expansion of the universe, then quasars must be very far away. How far can be estimated from the red shift and the Hubble constant, as done in Chapter 17 for ordinary galaxies.

What else might produce large red shifts from quasars? One suggestion makes use of the gravitational red shift, an effect predicted by Einstein's theory of relativity. Imagine what happens when you throw some object up in the air, against the pull of the earth's gravity. As if flies upward, it slows down until it turns downward (if you did not throw it with escape velocity) and falls to earth. Recall that kinetic energy depends on how fast an object moves. So as the object goes up and slows down, it loses kinetic energy.

Consider what happens to a photon in the same situation. A photon has an equivalent mass ($m = E/c^2$), so the earth's gravity pulls on it like any other mass. You'd expect the photon to lose kinetic energy. But photons can travel only at the speed of light, no slower or faster. So if the photon loses energy, it can't slow down like an ordinary mass. What happens? It does lose energy, not by slowing down but by increasing its wavelength. So gravity red-shifts the light escaping from some object. The amount of the shift depends on how massive the object is and its size. The more mass there is, the greater is the red shift, and the smaller the diameter is (for the same mass), the greater is the red shift.

In equation form,

$$\frac{\Delta\lambda}{\lambda_0} = \frac{GM}{c^2 R}$$

where $\Delta\lambda = \lambda - \lambda_0$, λ_0 is the rest (laboratory) wavelength, M the mass, and R the radius of the object, c the speed of light, and G the gravitational constant.

Now quasars must be fairly small in size—no more than a light year or so. Their enormous production of energy implies that they must also be fairly massive. A large mass and small size mean that the gravitational red shift of photons leaving quasars may be significant, compared with the red shift due to the expansion of the universe.

galaxy NGC 3384. They find eight quasars within 30 arcminutes of the galaxy; six have similar red shifts (from 1.11 to 1.28), much different from the galaxy's red shift of 0.003. Of these, five are on straight lines drawn through the nucleus of NGC 3384 (Fig. 18.31). Arp and colleagues argue that this association in space is not chance but indicates a physical association of the galaxy and the quasars, as if the quasars had been ejected from the galaxy. (Recall how radio galaxies tend to eject material symmetrically.)

Note that alignment arguments don't conclusively *prove* physical association. There are about 300 bright galaxies and 60 bright quasars in the sky. Suppose you scattered 300 corn kernels and 60 tomato seeds over a huge map of the sky, and then asked yourself what were the chances of a corn kernel and a tomato seed being as close to or closer than a certain distance. You would calculate the chances of these occurrences, and if they were actually more frequent, you could argue for a physical connection that makes the associations more frequent than expected. But it is still possible for the associations to be simply chance.

A more compelling case occurs if evidence were found of an actual physical connection between a quasar and a galaxy—such as bridges of gas and dust. Arp thinks that he has found one strong case: the galaxy NGC 4319 and the quasar Markarian 205 (Fig. 18.32). The galaxy has a red shift of 0.006, corresponding to radial velocity of 1800 km/sec, and the quasar a red shift of 0.07, corresponding to a radial velocity of 21,000 km/sec. Arp contends that a bridge of luminous material, visible in the photograph,

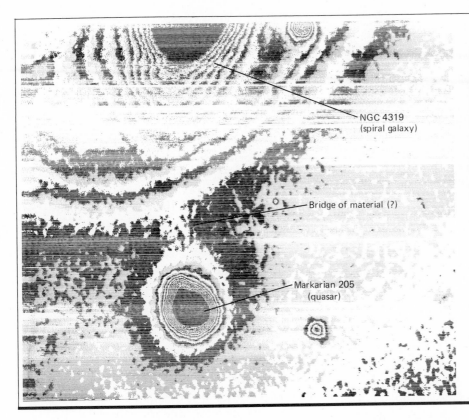

NGC 4319
(spiral galaxy)

Bridge of material (?)

Markarian 205
(quasar)

18.32
Possible evidence for a physical link between a galaxy and a quasar. This figure is a computer-generated contour map of a photo. The object at the top is the spiral galaxy NGC 4319. Below it appears the quasar Markarian 205. A bridge of material (?) seems to link the two images, but the supposed bridge may result from a bending of the images, a result of the photographic process. (Courtesy R. Lynds and Kitt Peak National Observatory)

connects the galaxy and quasar—certainly a strong argument if true! However, not all astronomers who have photographed these objects have picked up the possible bridge.

One strong argument against quasars as objects shot from galaxies is: A few quasars should have *blue* shifts, because some should be aimed at us. But no blue-shifted quasars have been found to date.

Support for cosmological red shifts comes from a study by Alan Stockton. He chose an *unbiased* sample of 27 quasars; that is, he did not intentionally choose quasars known to be close to galaxies. In this sample he finds 29 galaxies within 45 arcseconds of the quasars; of these, 13 have red shifts within 1000 km/sec of the quasar in the vicinity. (Why an allowable spread of 1000 km/sec? Because in a cluster of galaxies, 1000 km/sec is the typical spread in velocities. So two galaxies or a galaxy/quasar pair could belong to the same group, and so be the same distance away, and have a 1000 km/sec difference in radial velocities.) The chances of eight such red-shift agreements is less than one in a million for random associations, based on

the red-shift distribution of galaxies. So the cosmological nature of these red shifts is strong, and the study supports the concept that quasars' red shifts do not arise in other ways.

In a few cases, quasars appear in the same direction as clusters of galaxies. It's hard to prove that they actually are members of the cluster, rather than just in the foreground or background, because it is difficult to obtain spectra of the cluster galaxies, which are much fainter than the quasar. One good example is the quasar 3C 206, which seems to be surrounded by about 200 faint galaxies (Fig. 18.33). The red shift of the quasar, from its emission lines, is 0.206. A faint envelope surrounding the quasar has the color and luminosity of an elliptical galaxy, with absorption lines showing a red shift of 0.200. A nearby pair of galaxies has a red shift of 0.203. These observations support the idea of cosmological red shifts for quasars and also the notion that they are related (in an evolutionary way) to active galaxies.

The red-shift controversy still rages. It will take a tremendous amount of strong evidence to shake the simple cosmological view.

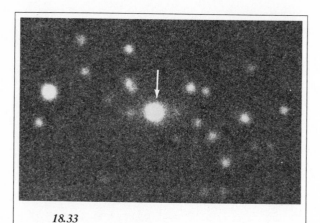

18.33

The quasar 3C 206 (arrow) surrounded by galaxies, which probably all lie in the same cluster. (Courtesy H. Spinrad; observations by S. Wyckoff, P. Wehinger, H. Spinrad, and A. Boksenberg)

SUMMARY

This chapter has investigated the enormous range of cosmic violence in the spectacular outbursts from quasars and the nuclei of galaxies.

You have seen that the nuclei of galaxies are active. Such nuclei and quasars eject matter in the form of massive clouds, high-energy particles, and perhaps discrete objects (such as quasars themselves). Both active nuclei and quasars appear to have extremely small regions (less than a few light years in diameter) where the violent processes originate. In addition, the range of objects examined—from ordinary galaxies to Seyferts to quasars—may represent an evolutionary sequence typical of all so-called normal galaxies.

A key point: Although astronomers have many observations of quasars and active galaxies, they still have no good idea of their energy source—the demon in their cores.

This investigation has also revealed the pervasiveness of nonthermal sources of radiation. This type of emission requires the input of high-energy electrons in a small volume of space with an intense magnetic field. The universe has two aspects, like the Roman god Janus: a slowly evolving one detectable by its thermal emission and an explosive one—a violent universe—marked by the rapid release of a wide range of radiation.

STUDY EXERCISES

1   What observational evidence is there that the synchrotron process produces some radiation from active galaxies and quasars? (*Objectives 1 and 2*)

2   Contrast the evidence for violence in the Milky Way with that for any active galaxy. (*Objectives 2 and 4*)

3   What evidence is there that quasars are far away? (*Objective 8*)

4   What *observational* evidence indicates that, for many quasars, their light must pass through clouds of thin, cool gases? (*Objective 4*)

5   What powers a quasar? (*Objectives 4 and 6*)

6   Evaluate the strengths and weaknesses of the model of quasars as objects shot from galaxies. (*Objectives 9 and 10*)

7   If synchrotron emission is the source of most of the output from active galaxies and quasars, what is the main problem for keeping the emission going for a long time? (*Objective 1*)

8   What is the most outstanding observational characteristic of quasars? (*Objective 3*)

9   Describe at least two similarities between active galaxies and quasars. (*Objective 7*)

10   How does the discovery of radio jets in some active galaxies help us to explain their radio lobe structure? (*Objective 5*)

BEYOND THIS BOOK . . .

Black Holes, Quasars, and the Universe (2d edition) by H. Shipman (Houghton Mifflin, Boston, 1980) has an excellent presentation of the controversy over quasars.

Mercury, November/December 1974, contains "The Quasar Controversy—An Interview with Caltech Astronomer Halton Arp."

"The Evolution of Quasars" by M. Schmidt and F. Bello in *Scientific American*, vol. 224, p. 54, 1971, argues for fast evolution of quasars in the early universe.

William Kaufmann has a good section on quasars and their red shifts in *Astronomy: The Structure of the Universe* (Macmillan, New York, 1977).

R. Weymann discusses "Seyfert Galaxies" in *Scientific American*, January 1969, p. 28, and M. Disney and P. Veron look at "BL Lacertae Objects" in *Scientific American*, August 1977, p. 32.

For a detailed look at the double quasar, read "The Discovery of a Gravitational Lens" by F. Chaffee, *Scientific American*, November 1980, p. 70.

I have presented an aspect of the universe that is probably not so familiar to you as the solar system. You may be staggered by the size and number of galaxies that have been observed. The galaxy that is the most difficult to see is our own Milky Way because we are embedded in it. But by using complementary observational techniques, astronomers have found that the Milky Way is a rotating, flat system of billions of stars. It has a size of about 120,000 ly and a spiral structure, the details of which have not yet been mapped out. The Galaxy is one of the largest in the local group of about 20 galaxies, all bound together by gravity. Most other galaxies are also found in clusters. These clusters may actually form enormous superclusters in space. The only known larger grouping is the universe itself.

Looking back, you can see the hierarchy of things in the universe. Atoms are clustered in planets and stars, which gravity holds together in planetary and stellar systems. These are clustered in galaxies. Usually galaxies are found in clusters of galaxies, and maybe the clusters form superclusters. So you see that gravity plays a prime role in the structure of the universe.

This universe of galaxies is immensely spread out. Consider the distances in terms of light-travel time. The light from the Andromeda galaxy that we see now left there about the time that the first humans appeared on the earth. The light from the Coma cluster left when reptiles first developed on the earth. The light from the most remote clusters of galaxies visible to the 48″ Schmidt telescope departed when one-celled organisms began to populate the earth.

Despite these vast distances, galaxies are actually close together, in a relative sense, when compared with planets and stars. In the solar system, planets are spaced out about 100,000 times their sizes. In the Galaxy, stars are spaced out about a million times their sizes. But, in a cluster of galaxies, the spacing is only about 100 times a galaxy's size. The universe of galaxies is vast but somewhat crowded.

The discovery of the violent universe has expanded astronomers' awareness of weird happenings in hidden and far places. Explosions seem to have marked the nucleus of our Galaxy and others. No one yet knows what generates the energy in quasars. Cosmic explosions indicate abnormal, but perhaps unavoidable, states in the lives of galaxies.

Our universe was born in a big bang. Since then, smaller explosions remind us of the awesome scale of cosmic violence.

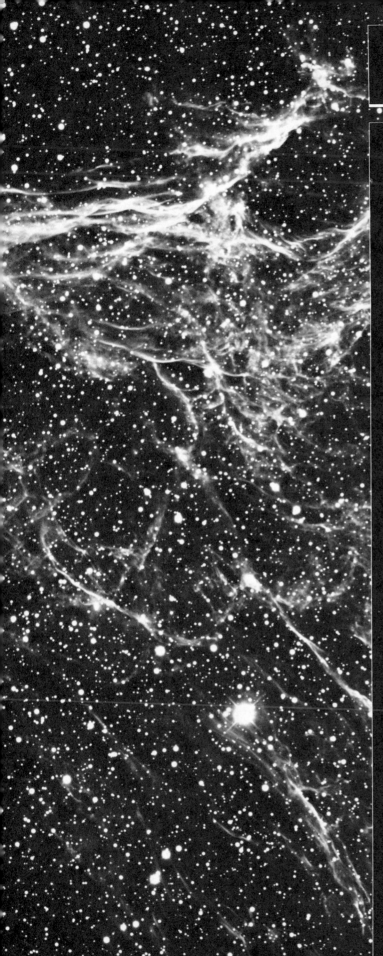

Cosmic Evolution

PART 4

The universe evolves; the whole universe, and all its parts. That is what I mean by cosmic evolution. The universe has a history, and its parts have a history. Unraveling those histories brings insight into the grand scheme of things, and our place in it: the cosmic connections that touch us all.

I'll divide cosmic evolution into three distinct but connected episodes: physical, chemical, and biological evolution. What do I mean by each? Physical evolution relates to the formation and maintenance of mass bound by gravity; this takes place on the astronomical scale. Chemical evolution involves the manufacture of elements by fusion or fission and the making of molecules by chemical bonding. Stars are the places where the physical and the chemical evolution meet. Brought together by gravity, the cores of stars manufacture chemical elements from hydrogen by fusion reactions. When stars explode, they blow these materials back into space. From them, gravity will form new stars. The lives of stars (Chapters 19 and 20) mark a crucial sequence in cosmic evolution.

I return again to cosmology (Chapter 21) to investigate the physical evolution of the universe in the light of stellar evolution. You will see that we have evidence that the universe began in a hot big bang. From it formed the material that ended up in the first stars. It's not clear yet how the universe will end (if it does!), but evidence indicates that the universe may be open, so it will just keep expanding (more and more slowly), forever. The universe has started in a bang, but it may end in a whimper.

Both physical and chemical evolution set the stage for the biological evolution (Chapter 22) that led to the development of us and other living creatures on the earth. Natural processes—simply the result of the nature of matter—result in the formation of complex molecules that are the basis of known organisms. How was the step taken from molecule to organism? That is not yet known. But we *do* live on the earth, so we know that the leap was somehow made once.

Did that crucial episode occur on other planets around other star systems? I'll argue that the Galaxy contains many other planets suitable for life. But I can't go any further than that, for we have no concrete evidence of life outside the earth.

LEARNING OBJECTIVES

After studying this chapter you should be able to:

1. Show how the Hertzsprung–Russell diagram for many stars provides clues about the evolution of individual stars.

2. Describe the physical basis of a theoretical model of a star.

3. Sketch a theoretical scenario for starbirth, emphasizing the conditions of star formation.

4. Trace the evolution of a solar-mass star on a Hertzsprung–Russell diagram, describing the physical changes of the star that result from changes in a star's core.

5. Describe how a degenerate gas differs from an ordinary one, and how degenerate gas can affect a star's evolution.

6. Compare the evolution of a 1-solar-mass star with that of a 5-solar-mass star.

7. Back up theoretical ideas of stellar evolution with observational evidence.

8. List the sequence of thermonuclear energy generation in stars of different masses.

9. Describe the evolution, on an H-R diagram, of a cluster of stars born out of the same cloud of gas and dust.

10. Indicate how mass and chemical composition affect the life of a star.

Under cloudless prairie skies
looking past her lover's shoulders
at the height of it
her eye caught the fine stellar dust.
MICHAEL HELLER: Telescope Suite

The lives of stars
19

The sun whirls majestically around our Galaxy in a spiral arm rich in gas and dust. Here star formation occurs. Gravity has gathered at least 50 percent of the interstellar material in the sun's vicinity into stars. The rest floats as cool clouds trapped in a hotter gas that separates the clouds. Some of these clouds are gigantic—they contain hundreds and even thousands of solar masses of gas and dust. These huge clouds may condense into stars or into planetary systems.

Gravity controls the history of newborn stars. A star survives as long as it can counteract the relentless gravitational crunch. The story of this battle against gravity runs like the aging of a person from birth to death but takes millions to billions of years. To put this span into a human perspective, imagine time speeded up so that one year passes in 1/5 of a second. Then the sun would live only 65 years or so. The sun's birth would be quick; only 4 months would pass from the start of the collapse of the sun's embryonic cloud to its establishment as an immature but full-fledged star. For about the next 60 years the sun would shine calmly as it passed through youth and middle age. Old age would gradually fossilize the energy production of the sun. In about 5 years the elderly sun would slowly expand to almost 100 times its present size; it would become a bloated red giant. Then a sudden burst would blow off the sun's atmosphere, leaving behind a hot core that would cool quickly.

This comparison shows you that during most of its life a star burns hydrogen and converts it to helium in its core. No violent events take place. Those occur when a star begins to die (Chapter 20).

How a star lives and dies depends mostly on how much mass it has at birth. What important stages mark its life and how long each stage lasts relate directly to a star's mass. Those stars much more massive than the sun have short, frenetic lives.

This chapter presents, first, theoretical ideas about stellar evolution from birth to death and contrasts the lives of stars like the sun to those of more massive ones. Second, it offers some observational evidence for these theoretical concoctions. You will see how stars are born, burn, falter, and flame out. Our sun, too, will live and **464** die. And the earth will die with it.

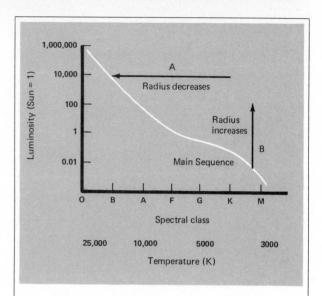

19.1

A schematic H-R diagram. A star's position on the H-R diagram represents its surface temperature and luminosity—and, indirectly, its size. If any of these physical properties change, the star's representative point on the diagram will move. A hypothetical example: Suppose a star's luminosity increases while its surface temperature remains the same. Then its point on the H-R diagram moves vertically (along arrow B). In contrast, if its luminosity remains constant while its temperature increases, its point moves horizontally from right to left (along arrow A). Note that an increase in a star's luminosity while its surface temperature remains the same requires that its radius increase; in the second case, its radius must decrease.

19.1

Stellar evolution and the Hertzsprung–Russell diagram

Contemporary ideas of how stars evolve focus on one general theme: As a star loses energy to space, it must evolve. Stellar evolution is approached from both theoretical and observational points of view. This chapter presents mostly theoretical ideas, because observations of a star's evolution do not come easily. Why? The sun's anticipated lifetime is more than 100 *mil-*

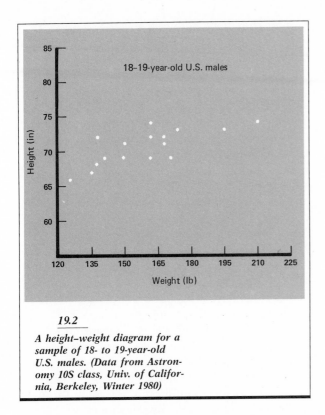

19.2

A height–weight diagram for a sample of 18- to 19-year-old U.S. males. (Data from Astronomy 10S class, Univ. of California, Berkeley, Winter 1980)

lion human lifetimes. So there is no way you could watch a single star, like the sun, evolve. But you can see many different stars at one time. You can organize these stars on the Hertzsprung–Russell (H-R) diagram (Fig. 19.1) if you know their luminosities and spectral types (Section 14.5). Then you can use the H-R diagram of many stars to guess at the evolution of one star. Here's how.

Classifying objects / Suppose you went around and asked all the 18- to 19-year-old males you met for their weight and height. Then imagine you plotted your data as a graph of weight versus height (Fig. 19.2). Note from the results that you find a trend. The points tend to fall along a line (call it a "main sequence") that shows that weight generally increases with height (Fig. 19.2). That result shouldn't surprise you.

Now suppose you did the same experiment, but this time recorded the height and weight of every person you encountered. Plot the data again (Fig. 19.3) and compare with the previous graph. What a difference! You still have a main

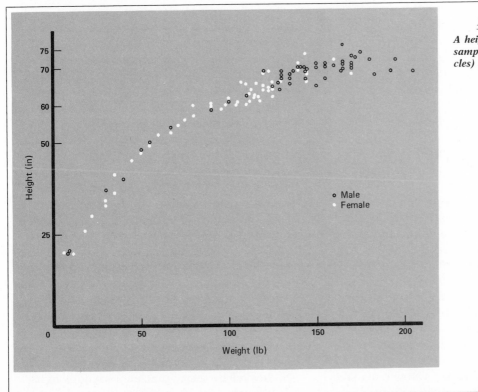

19.3

A height–weight diagram for a sample of U.S. males (open circles) and females (filled circles).

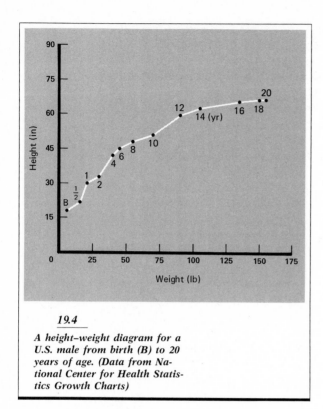

19.4

A height–weight diagram for a U.S. male from birth (B) to 20 years of age. (Data from National Center for Health Statistics Growth Charts)

family. They have gathered together, and you take a snapshot of all them, from the newest baby to the great-grandparents. Now most of the people in the picture are in their middle age (20–60 years old); you have a few infants, some children and teenagers, and a few old people. You have so many middle-aged people because most of your life you will be "middle aged"; you spend relatively less time as an infant, teenager, or old person.

Now suppose you have a collection of any objects that evolve. You believe that the collection spans an evolutionary sequence. Then you can estimate the relative time spent in any evolutionary stage by the relative numbers you find at that stage compared with others. (This argument holds true only if the birth and death go on continuously; if no more people are born, eventually you will see only old people.)

Now go back to the H-R diagram for stars (Fig. 19.1). Recall that it shows the luminosity and surface temperature of the stars. Most of the stars fall on the shallow "S" of the main sequence, so stars found here are going through the longest, most stable stage in their evolution.

Section 15.2 pointed out that the main sequence, from *O*- to *M*-stars, represents a sequence from higher to lower masses. Earlier (Section 13.4) I explained the normal process of the conversion of hydrogen to helium in the sun, which is a main-sequence star. Here's the evolutionary meaning of the main sequence: It marks stars at the stage of converting hydrogen to helium in their cores; stars remain at this stage for the greatest part of their lives. That's why you see so many main-sequence stars now. Other stages—such as becoming a red giant— must be shorter. Why?—because you see far fewer red giants than main-sequence stars.

A star's mass determines how a star will evolve. So you have to examine the H-R diagram to find how stars of different masses evolve. But what is the correct interpretation of the H-R diagram for the evolution of stars? You need hints from the physical nature of stars.

sequence. But you also have other groups that don't follow the original main-sequence trend.

Why the difference exists should be clear to you: The first graph includes people of the *same* age; the second, people at *different* ages.

Now here's a third graph (Fig. 19.4). It's a plot of weight versus height for an average U.S. male at different times in his life, from birth to 20 years old. The line connecting the points has indicated the age from birth to 20 years. It shows you how a *single* person's height and weight changes as he ages. You know how this growth goes from your own experience. Note this evolution graph for one person follows the trend in the height–weight graph of many different people. You can correctly interpret the graph for many people in evolutionary terms *if*, and *only* if, you know how one person evolves. Time was implicit in that graph. In the same way, time and age implicitly play a role in an H-R diagram, in which two essential properties of stars—surface temperature and luminosity— are plotted.

Time and the H-R diagram / How does the H-R diagram tell you about an evolutionary sequence of a star? Imagine that you have a large

19.2

Stellar anatomy

What is a star? A hot ball of gas, mostly hydrogen, heated by thermonuclear reactions in its core. You can imagine a star as a slowly exploding hydrogen bomb! A star does not fly apart

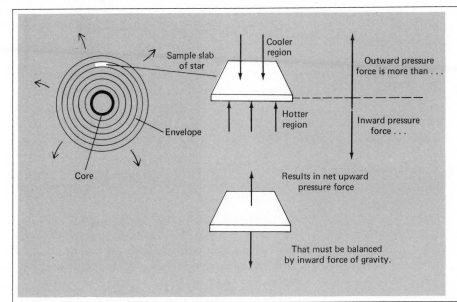

The balance of pressure and gravity in a star. Energy from nuclear reactions in the core heats the star, so, like any hot gas, it wants to expand. The star's gravity, pulling inward, just balances this outward pressure force, so the star does not expand or contract.

Cooler region

Sample slab of star

Outward pressure force is more than . . .

Hotter region

Inward pressure force . . .

Envelope

Core

Results in net upward pressure force

That must be balanced by inward force of gravity.

because gravity persistently pulls it together. All its life a star must withstand the inward squeeze of gravity. How? By being hot. A star consists of gas; a hot gas expands; and this outward force balances the inward gravitational forces.

To picture this, imagine a balloon. If you blow the balloon up, it expands. Place pressure gauges inside and outside the balloon. You find the pressure inside greater than that outside. The balloon doesn't expand because the plastic pulls in against air pressure. So the air pressure inside equals the air pressure outside *plus* the inward pressure due to the plastic's tension. The inward and outward pressures balance. Now picture a star (Fig. 19.5). Pressure gauges inside and outside would register a large difference, for only the vacuum of space surrounds the star. But a star is in balance. The gas pressure inside equals the gas pressure outside (almost zero) *plus* the inward pressure of the star's gravity. This balance must hold at the outermost layer of a star and also each and every layer on the inside. Otherwise the star would not be in balance and it would either expand or contract. If it contracts, it gets hotter and its internal pressure rises. This expands the star until it reaches a stable size.

So gravity keeps a star from expanding and just balances the outward pressure of the hot gases. This balance cannot continue forever. A star loses energy to the cold trap of space. Ther-

monuclear fusion reactions supply the energy to keep it hot. Eventually, it runs out of fuel, runs out of heat, and can no longer balance its gravity. Then it must contract. As long as it can find a means to withstand gravity, a star can survive. When it fails, it dies. How stars survive is a central theme of this chapter.

Star models

What is the theoretical picture of a star? A star emits energy, so it must have an energy source inside. A star is a gas, so as you move deeper inside, the temperature and density—and so the pressure—must increase. Overall, a star must be in balance and must produce, each second, as much energy as it gives off.

In addition, you need to look at how a star transports energy from its core to surface (Focus 32). Basically, three methods are available: *conduction*, *convection*, and *radiation*. In conduction, atoms moving in a hotter region and colliding with atoms in a neighboring cooler region will transfer more energy to the cooler region than the atoms in the cooler region can give back. Net result: Energy flows from the hotter to the cooler region. In convection, a hot gas bubble at the same pressure as a surrounding gas will rise because its density is lower than its surroundings. It carries heat upward. To replace the removed material, a cooler bubble of higher density from the upper region falls and gains some energy. The complete cycle results in a net transfer of energy to the cooler region. In radiative transport, a cooler region emits fewer photons with less energy to a hotter region. It, in turn, emits more photons with greater energy to the cooler region. The net result is a transfer of energy to the cooler region. In most regions of most stars, radiation is the important means of energy flow.

The *opacity* (Section 13.2) of a star's material directly measures its resistance to the flow of radiation. The more opaque a star's material is, the slower is the flow of radiation through it. You can think of opacity acting like insulation in a house in winter. The furnace is generating heat. The greater the house's insulation is, the slower is the flow of the heat to the cold outside. A slow flow keeps the exterior of the house cold and the inside hot. In a poorly insulated house, the outside is warmer and the inside colder than for a well-insulated house. Likewise, if the opacity of a star were suddenly lowered, radiation would escape more easily and the star would become temporarily more luminous. But its inside would become cooler. So the internal pressure would drop, pressure equilibrium would be upset, and the star would contract until equilibrium was regained.

Whether convection occurs at any region in a star is determined by the opacity of the material there. If the opacity is low, energy will flow easily by radiation. If it is so opaque that the radiative energy flow gets bottled up, convective transport will take over and operate instead.

All these conditions combined are not enough to develop a theoretical model of a star. An astrophysicist needs more: what thermonuclear processes produce energy. He or she also needs to specify the mass and chemical composition of the model star. Then a few complicated equations formulate the problem, and these are solved to find the physical conditions in the star from the center to the surface. The catalog of values for important physical properties—such as temperature and pressure—for a specified mass and composition is called a *star model*. (This is not a real star; it's just a list of numbers!)

In practice, the construction of a star model requires much tedious calculation. High-speed electronic computers can, however, complete the calculations for one star model in a few minutes. (See Fig. 19.6 for a model for the sun.) A series of models used to describe the evolutionary sequence of one star may take hours of computer time.

What do such models tell us? They show that as a star evolves, its radius, temperature, and luminosity change in complicated ways. Such changes result in the change in a star's position on the H-R diagram. For example, if a star's surface temperature but not its luminosity decreases, the star's position on the H-R diagram moves horizontally from left to right, with no vertical change (Fig. 19.1). If the luminosity decreases but not the surface temperature, the star's point on the H-R diagram moves vertically from top to bottom, with no horizontal change. Both motions *on the H-R diagram* represent changes in the physical properties of the star.

Note in the first case that to keep the luminosity constant at a lower temperature requires that the star's surface area and so its radius increase. In the second case, with no change in temperature, the star's luminosity can go down only if its surface area and so its radius decreases. You see that a star's surface temperature, luminosity, and radius change together. (*Warning:* What moves around on the H-R diagram is *not* the star but a point *representing* the luminosity and temperature of the star.)

What is so important about making star models? The study of stellar evolution rests on the theoretical construction of physically reasonable models of stars. Model making is how astronomers get evolutionary tracks on the H-R diagram for stars of a specific mass and chemical composition. Models show how *time* enters into the H-R diagram for real stars.

To sum up the basic physical ideas behind stellar evolution:

1   For most of its life, gravity and pressure must balance in a star.
2   That balance depends on the pressure–temperature–density relations in a gas.
3   The core's energy generation rate determines a star's luminosity.
4   Some process must generate the energy; normally it is fusion reactions of some kind.
5   Convection, radiation, or conduction transport the energy from the interior to the star's surface.
6   The opacity of a star's material determines how the energy will flow.

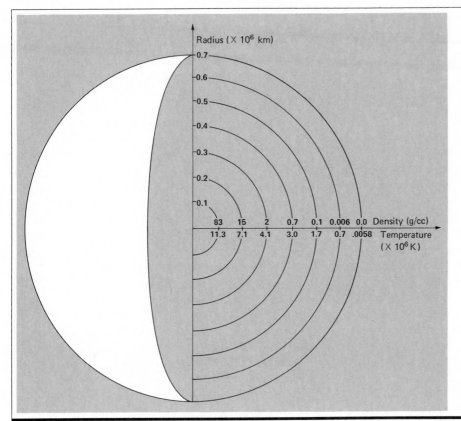

Radius ($\times 10^6$ km)

Density (g/cc)						
83	15	2	0.7	0.1	0.006	0.0
11.3	7.1	4.1	3.0	1.7	0.7	.0058

Temperature ($\times 10^6$ K)

19.6

A theoretical model for the sun. The values for the physical properties here have been calculated by an electronic computer. The central temperature is about 16 million K and the central density is 158 g/cc. This model is calculated for an age of 4.6 billion years, the age of our sun.

19.4

Energy generation in stars

Once an astrophysicist has established a model of a star, how does it *evolve*? The answer lies in the heart of the star. Here thermonuclear reactions cook lightweight elements into more complex ones by fusion reactions that change the star's chemical composition. (Recall the details of energy generation for the sun in Section 13.4). This change in chemical composition and its effects on a star's structure mark another major theme of stellar evolution.

The sun generates energy by the proton-proton (PP) reaction. Here's the essence of this reaction: Four hydrogen nuclei combine to form one helium nucleus and release a certain amount of energy. A minor amount of the sun's energy comes from another sequence, called the carbon-nitrogen-oxygen cycle (CNO cycle). If a star's central temperature is greater than about 20 million K, the CNO cycle produces more energy than the PP reaction. (Both can go on at the same time.) The net result of the CNO cycle is the same as the PP reaction: four hydrogen

$${}^{12}\text{C} + {}^{1}\text{H} \rightarrow {}^{13}\text{N} + \text{gamma ray}$$
$${}^{13}\text{N} \rightarrow {}^{13}\text{C} + \text{positron} + \text{neutrino}$$
$${}^{13}\text{C} + {}^{1}\text{H} \rightarrow {}^{14}\text{N} + \text{gamma ray}$$
$${}^{14}\text{N} + {}^{1}\text{H} \rightarrow {}^{15}\text{O} + \text{gamma ray}$$
$${}^{15}\text{O} \rightarrow {}^{15}\text{N} + \text{positron} + \text{neutrino}$$
$${}^{15}\text{N} + {}^{1}\text{H} \rightarrow {}^{12}\text{C} + {}^{4}\text{He}$$

19.7

The carbon-nitrogen-oxygen (CNO) cycle, a fusion process. Note that the net result is the conversion of four hydrogen nuclei to one helium nucleus; the carbon entering the first step returns in the last.

nuclei are converted to one helium nucleus, with the release of energy (Fig. 19.7).

These reactions take place only in the star's core, where temperatures are high enough to keep them going. Because a star has only a limited amount of hydrogen to burn, the core eventually is all converted to helium, and the CNO and PP reactions cease. What next? If the core's

$$3\,^4\text{He} \rightarrow\,^{12}\text{C} + \text{gamma ray}$$

19.8

The triple-alpha process, a high-temperature fusion reaction. A helium nucleus is sometimes called an alpha particle, and because three are needed in this reaction, it is called the triple-alpha process.

temperature gets up to roughly 100 million K, another reaction can take place: the *triple-alpha reaction*, so named because three helium nuclei (also known as alpha particles) fuse to form one carbon nucleus, with the release of energy (Fig. 19.8).

What happens when the helium runs out? If the temperature increases enough, carbon can be fused into heavier elements. Such processes require extreme temperatures, at least a billion K. Iron, the most stable of all nuclei, ends the sequence of nuclear fusion. To form elements heavier than iron by fusion reactions, energy must be added and absorbed; such reactions occur only under special conditions. When they do, they soak up energy from the core. The steady climb from hydrogen to iron in fusion reactions in stellar cores is called *nucleosynthesis*. This nuclear cementing process makes heavy elements in a universe that otherwise would consist only of hydrogen and helium made in the big bang (Chapter 21).

Hold on! You should be wondering how a star's temperature can go *up* when fusion reactions *stop*. Simple: by gravitational contraction (Focus 28). With no energy from fusion reactions, a star's core can no longer counteract gravity and must contract. As it does, some of the gravitational potential energy of its particles transforms into kinetic (thermal) energy. So the temperature goes up until the ignition temperature of the next fusion reactions is reached. Fusion fires turn on again, and the core contraction stops. This contraction applies to the core; what happens to a star's outer layers will be seen later.

Note that a star's energy generation alternates between gravitational contraction (of the core) and fusion reactions (in the core). The

stages of gravitational contraction are short compared with the stages of fusion. But, inevitably, fusion fuels run out, and the core contracts. As it does, it becomes denser and denser until it attains a bizarre state known as a *degenerate gas*, which dramatically affects how the star evolves.

Ordinary and degenerate gases compared / What's this degenerate gas? Details are in Focus 50; here I'll simply compare the properties of an ordinary gas (Focus 30) with those of a degenerate one. Recall that the particles in an ordinary gas are far apart and free to fly around and collide. When energy is added to such a gas, its temperature goes up, its particles move around faster, and so its pressure also goes up. This increase in pressure with temperature is how a star normally counteracts gravity: If a star's internal pressure is not high enough to balance gravity, the star contracts, heats up, and its pressure goes up until the balance is reached.

When a gas is very dense (greater than about 10^6 g/cc), it no longer behaves in these ways—essentially because its particles are no longer completely free to move around anywhere in the gas. A gas in this state is called *degenerate*. One key property of a degenerate gas: Its temperature no longer has much effect on its pressure; rather, its density essentially determines its pressure. The greater the density is, the greater its pressure will be. Another key property is that degenerate gases *conduct* heat very efficiently. So if a star's core becomes degenerate, it will have the same temperature throughout.

19.5

Starbirth:

A theoretical picture

How are stars born? Astronomers know that stars must condense from interstellar material, but for now the details are hidden. Theoretical calculations done to date rest on a host of simplifying assumptions, so their correspondence to reality may be meager at best. But the general outline, the one first recognized by Newton, is correct: *gravitational collapse*. Here's one possible model for the birth of a sunlike star.

Imagine a huge interstellar cloud of gas—mostly in the form of molecular hydrogen (H_2)—and dust. Also picture that this cloud has sufficient mass to contract gravitationally. As it collapses, material at the cloud's center increases in density faster than at the edge. Because of the density increase, the collapse time at the center is decreased; it collapses faster, grows denser, and so collapses still faster. The rest of the cloud's mass is left behind in a more slowly contracting envelope.

With the rapid infall of material in the core, the hydrogen molecules gain kinetic energy. They bang into each other, and also strike dust grains, stick together, and so transfer kinetic energy to grains. Heated by such collisions, the dust grains radiate at infrared wavelengths. This heat radiation speeds into space. As the core's density goes up, it reaches a critical value at which the cloud traps infrared radiation. The core heats up to a few hundred Kelvins, its pressure increases, and so the core's collapse slows down dramatically.

Meanwhile, the envelope continues merrily falling inward, showering mass on the core. When the infalling material bangs into the core, a shock wave forms. As the matter piles up, it increases the core's mass and temperature. At about 2000 K the hydrogen molecules break up. In the process they soak up heat. The core's temperature drops, its pressure decreases, and gravity takes command again. At the start of this collapse the core's radius is about 4 AU; at the end it will be about the same size as the sun.

When all the hydrogen molecules have broken up, the collapse stops because no more energy is lost this way. Gravitational energy heats the core until, at its center, temperatures reach the ignition point of fusion reactions. A star is born.

But the envelope—still falling in—blocks out this birth from the view of the optical astronomer. This infant star—called a *protostar*—hides in the womb. Dust in the envelope cuts out the protostar's light. However, this radiation absorbed by the dust heats it so that it gives off infrared radiation. So a sign of protostars should be small, intense sources of infrared radiation in or near known clouds of gas and dust. In addition, massive protostars (those that become *O*-stars) emit ultraviolet radiation that ionizes the gas around them. This ionized gas emits centimeter radio waves. So a compact, optically invisible radio source marks the birthplace of a massive star.

Eventually, like afterbirth, the star rids itself of its cloaking cloud, which may all fall onto the young star or be heated and blown off. As the cloud dissipates, you will see a *pre-main-sequence star*, one that is more luminous and cooler than typical for its mass and chemical composition.

Warning: It's still not clear what *triggers* the gravitational collapse that ends up in a star. Perhaps a supernova's shock wave (Section 15.4) does it. Or maybe the shock waves associated with the spiral density waves (Section 16.5) prompt the collapse. Once the gravitational collapse starts, however, the events to follow probably take place along the lines previously outlined.

19.6
Theoretical evolution of a solar-mass star

Gravity instigates the birth of a star. The details of the subsequent evolution are controlled by the star's mass. If the mass is less than 0.08 solar mass, the central temperature never reaches the 10 million K needed to start the PP reaction. (This happened to the planet Jupiter.) But if the mass is greater than approximately 100 solar masses, the outward gas pressure exceeds that of gravity, and the star blows itself apart. Between 0.08 and 100 solar masses, a stable main-sequence star can form. Let's look at the evolution of a star like the sun, a 1-solar-mass star.

Evolution to the main sequence / Gravity pulls together an interstellar cloud of gas and dust. The cloud's density increases; collisions between particles occur more frequently. During the collapse the cloud heats up. Eventually, the temperature reaches about 200 K, and the collapse slows down (point 1 in Fig. 19.9).

The collapsing cloud makes its debut as a protostar. It has a larger radius than it will as a main-sequence star, and the surface temperature is lower (point 2 in Fig. 19.9). However, the protostar has a higher luminosity than it will when it reaches the main sequence. How can this be, if it is cooler? Because it is larger and so has more surface area to radiate energy (Focus 36).

The protostar continues to contract. As it shrinks in size, its luminosity decreases. Its point on the H-R diagram moves vertically to-

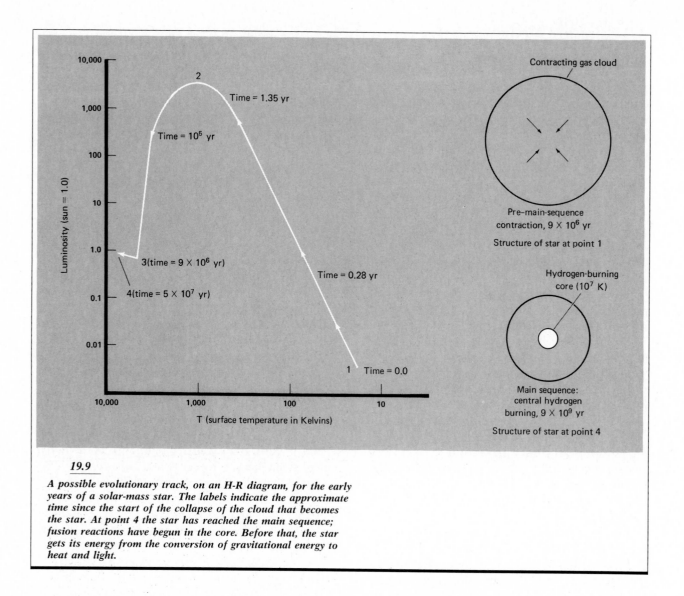

19.9

A possible evolutionary track, on an H-R diagram, for the early years of a solar-mass star. The labels indicate the approximate time since the start of the collapse of the cloud that becomes the star. At point 4 the star has reached the main sequence; fusion reactions have begun in the core. Before that, the star gets its energy from the conversion of gravitational energy to heat and light.

ward the main sequence. Meanwhile the core temperature reaches a few million degrees Kelvin, high enough to start thermonuclear reactions.

When the protostar gets most of its energy from thermonuclear reactions (PP reactions in the case of the sun) rather than gravitational contraction, it achieves full-fledged stardom. It has become a main-sequence star. The star is now called a *zero-age main-sequence* star. It settles down to the longest stage in its life, calmly converting hydrogen to helium in its core. The total time elapsed from initial collapse to arrival as a star on the main sequence is only 50 million years (from point 1 to point 4 in Fig. 19.9).

Evolution on the main sequence / Where the star ends up on the main sequence depends mainly on its mass. The more massive the star is, the hotter and more luminous it is; the less massive the star is, the cooler and less luminous it is. The main sequence consists of a series of stars of decreasing mass (but similar chemical composition), from the upper left-hand corner (*O*-stars with high mass) to the lower right-hand corner (*M*-stars with low mass). A star, like the sun, spends about 80 percent of its total lifetime on the main sequence as it slowly transforms its hydrogen core to helium.

How the star evolves further also depends on its mass. Because massive stars have higher core temperatures, their thermonuclear reactions, which are sensitive to changes in temperature, burn faster than in low-mass stars. As a result, massive stars spend less time on the main sequence, even though they have more fuel to burn because they use it up at fast rates. Such stars are spendthrifts compared with the miserly energy generation of a star like the sun. For example, the sun's time on the main sequence lasts about 10 *billion* years, while the same period for a 15-solar-mass star lasts only 10 *million* years. Why the greater difference? Because of its greater mass, the 15-solar-mass star has a greater temperature in its core than the sun. So its fusion reactions go on at a much faster rate than in the sun—about 25 thousand times faster, because such stars have luminosities about 25 thousand solar luminosities. So even though the 15-solar-mass star has more hydrogen to fuse, it does so at incredibly fast rates. Consequently, its time on the main sequence is much less than that for the sun.

The main-sequence phase ends when almost all of the hydrogen in the core has been converted to helium. During this time the temperature in the core increases as the star contracts slightly. The thermonuclear reactions give off more energy, and the star's luminosity increases (points 1–2 in Fig. 19.10).

Evolution off the main sequence / When the hydrogen in the core is used up, the thermonuclear reactions cease there. However, they keep going in a shell around the core, where fresh hydrogen still exists. At the end of fusion reactions in the core, it contracts and heats up. This, in turn, heats up the layer of burning hydrogen, so the reactions go faster and produce more energy. The luminosity increases. But the layer of burning hydrogen heats up the surrounding part and causes it to expand. So the radius of the star increases and its surface temperature decreases. The star acquires the characteristics of a red giant; its position on the H-R diagram moves to the red giant region (point 3 to point 4 in Fig. 19.10). In about 500 million years a solar-mass star ends up with a luminosity of about 10,000 solar luminosities, a surface temperature of about 4000 K, and a radius of a little more than 200 solar radii. The sun at this stage would engulf Mercury, Venus, the earth, and the moon!

While the outer layers of the star have expanded, the core has contracted, so much that it has become degenerate (Focus 50). And its temperature has been increasing, until it hits the minimum needed to ignite the triple-alpha reaction. Once part of the core ignites, the heat generated by the fusion reaction quickly spreads throughout the core (because it is degenerate) and ignites the rest. If the core were an ordinary gas, this increased temperature would increase the pressure, and the core would expand. Because it is degenerate, the increased temperature does *not* increase the pressure, and the core does *not* expand. Instead, the increased temperature drives up the rate of the triple-alpha reaction, which generates more energy and a higher temperature. This out-of-control process is called the *helium flash*. It ends when the core becomes hot enough so that it is no longer degenerate. The helium flash takes little time—perhaps only a few minutes!

After the helium flash, a Population I star's radius and luminosity decrease a little, and the star's point on the H-R diagram moves slightly downward and to the left. (For a Population II star with fewer heavy elements than in a Population I star, the radius and luminosity decrease more.) Its point on the H-R diagram moves near the horizontal branch (point 5 in Fig. 19.10). The star quietly burns helium in the core and hydrogen in a layer around the core.

Evolution to the end / Eventually the triple-alpha process converts the core to carbon. The reaction stops in the core but continues in a layer around it. This situation—core shutdown, but thermonuclear reactions going on in a layer—resembles that when the star first evolved off the main sequence. The physical processes force the same evolution; the burning layer makes the star expand. The star again becomes a red giant (point 6 to 7 in Fig. 19.10).

Because the rate of the triple-alpha reaction is very sensitive to changes in temperature, the helium-burning layer causes the star to become unstable. Here's how: Suppose the star contracts a little. The temperature and energy production in the layer increase; the pressure also increases. However, the increase in pressure more than compensates for gravity; the outer parts of the star expand. The expansion decreases the temperature, the pressure, and—

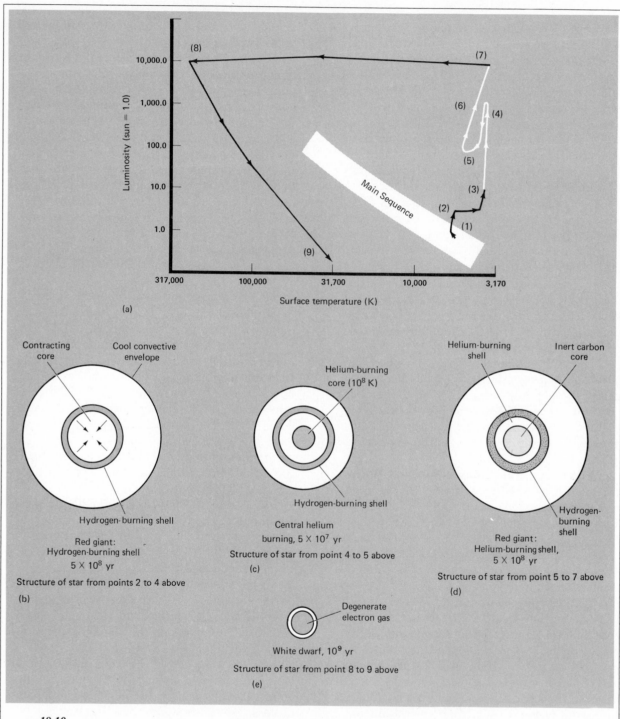

19.10

The evolutionary path of a solar-mass star off the main sequence (point 1). The star's luminosity increases as hydrogen is depleted in the core (points 1–2). When the core runs out of hydrogen, it burns hydrogen in a shell (3–4). Gravitational contraction heats the core until it gets hot enough to burn helium (4–5). When it runs out of helium, the star makes energy in a hydrogen-burning and a helium-burning shell and becomes a red giant again (5–7). The star becomes unstable, throws off its outer layers (7–8), and becomes a white dwarf (8–9).

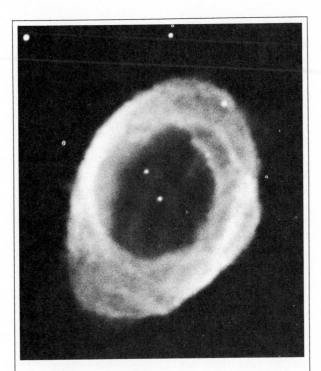

19.11

A typical planetary nebula. The central blue star was once the core of a red giant. The nebula, which looks like a ring but actually forms a spherical shell, was the outer layers of that red giant. (Courtesy Lick Observatory)

more dramatically—the energy generation rate. Gravity takes command: The star contracts, the energy generation increases a lot, the star expands, and the cycle repeats. The star pulsates rapidly.

The pulsations gradually grow larger. Finally a violent one rips off the cool outer layers of the star (point 11 in Fig. 19.7). A hot core is left behind. The expelled shell forms a planetary nebula, and the leftover core becomes the central star (Fig. 19.11). The nebula keeps expanding until it dissipates in the interstellar medium. What happens to the core? It contracts. For a star of 1 solar mass or less, the core never reaches the ignition temperature of carbon burning. The ash contracts quickly, fed by gravitational energy. In about 75,000 years it forms a white dwarf star, composed mostly of carbon (point 9 in Fig. 19.10). Without energy sources the

white dwarf slowly cools to a black dwarf, the dark culmination of a 10-billion-year biography.

Lower mass stars / The evolution of stars of lower mass than the sun is similar to that for the sun, with two exceptions. First, few stars that are less massive than the sun have had time to evolve off the main sequence. The universe simply isn't old enough. A star of mass 0.74 solar masses, for example, will have a luminosity about 0.37 that of the sun, according to the mass-luminosity law, and hence, will have a main-sequence lifetime of 20 billion years, longer than most estimates for the age of the universe (Chapter 7).

Second, if the mass of a star is less than about 0.08 solar masses, it will not even reach the main sequence. Gravitational contraction does not heat it very effectively. Before it gets hot enough to start nuclear reactions, the density has risen so high that the matter becomes degenerate (Focus 50). Then the pressure of the degenerate gas supports the star and keeps it from contracting any further. If gravitational contraction cannot heat the star, the nuclear fires can never be lit, and the star simply cools off to become an invisible black dwarf or (if the mass is *very* small) a planet, like Jupiter.

19.7
Theoretical evolution of a 5-solar-mass star

Now to examine the history of a star more massive than the sun—a 5-solar-mass star. (Regulus, the bright star that marks the heart of Leo the Lion, is a 5-solar-mass star.) A larger mass does not change the general flow of stellar evolution; but the details (such as energy generation) do change. Massive stars differ in their evolution from less massive stars because they can reach higher temperatures in their cores. The greater temperatures have three important consequences: (1) While on the main sequence the star burns hydrogen by the CNO cycle; (2) the main-sequence lifetime is shorter; (3) the higher temperatures may kindle carbon and heavier-element fusion in the core.

Evolution to and on the main sequence / A 5-solar-mass star evolves to the main sequence along a track of roughly constant luminosity. The star is hot enough so that its opacity is low enough for radiative transport to be more effec-

focus 50

DEGENERATE GASES

When matter is packed to very high densities (greater than 10^6 g/cc), it no longer behaves in ordinary ways. In a normal gas the particles are widely separated and rush helter-skelter into one another and rebound away. In highly compressed material little space exists between particles. The matter is so jammed together that the electrons on the outside of the atoms are, in a sense, touching each other. The nuclei no longer can hold electrons in their usual energy levels, and the electrons move among the nuclei. But there's not much space for moving about.

Electrons also abide by a quantum property called the Pauli exclusion principle. It states that no two electrons can be together in exactly the same energy state. In contrast to a low density gas where many energy levels are available for occupation, a very dense gas has far fewer levels available.

What happens if you try to cool down this dense gas by letting electrons give up ki-netic energy? They can't lose very much kinetic energy, because all the lower energy levels are already occupied. So no heat can be extracted from these electrons (in a sense, their available heat energy is zero). Yet they exert a great pressure because they move with high speeds.

A gas in this state is called a degenerate gas and the pressure from the exclusion principle in action is called the degenerate gas pressure. Unlike an ordinary gas where the pressure is directly proportional to temperature, degenerate gas pressure is nearly independent of the temperature.

Electrons become degenerate at densities of about 10^6 g/cc—such densities occur in stellar cores after main-sequence hydrogen burning, and also in white dwarfs. When electrons are degenerate, they conduct heat very efficiently and temperature variations are quickly smoothed out. So degenerate cores have the same temperature throughout. A high enough temperature can relieve the electrons of their degenerate condition—this requires a temperature of some 350 million Kelvins for electrons.

tive than convection. The conversion of gravitational energy powers the star; it contracts and heats up. As it does, its opacity falls and energy flows out more easily. So its luminosity increases a bit as the star contracts and its core temperature climbs. In about 50 million years the star's point on the H-R diagram moves almost horizontally to the left (Fig. 19.12).

First, the PP reaction ignites in the core. But when the core's temperature rises to about 20 million K, the CNO cycle produces more energy than the PP reaction. The exhaustion of hydrogen causes the core to shrink, its temperature to go up, and thus its luminosity to increase. Stoked by the high core temperature, the CNO cycle uses up the core's hydrogen in about 60 million years, while the star's luminosity becomes twice as large (points 1 and 2 in Fig. 19.13).

Note that a 5-solar-mass star ends up farther to the left on the main sequence than a solar-mass star. Regulus, for example, is a *B*-star. Obviously, less massive stars fall to the right side of the main sequence.

Evolution to the end / When the central fusion fires are exhausted, the star contracts. New hydrogen falls to the inner regions and ignites in a shell around the burnt-out core (point 5 in Fig. 19.13). The luminosity increases as the radius expands, so the surface temperature drops. The star becomes a red giant. Meanwhile the core contracts until it gets hot enough to ignite the triple-alpha process (point 7 in Fig. 19.13). In contrast to a solar-mass star, the core does *not* become degenerate. So no helium flash occurs when the triple-alpha process ignites. (Stars with greater than 2.25 solar masses do not develop degenerate helium cores because they do not become dense enough, from gravitational contraction, before helium ignition takes place.)

The star burns helium in its core for about 10 million years. When the helium runs out, the star again contracts (point 11 in Fig. 19.13). Now

TABLE 19.2 *Stages of thermonuclear energy generation in stars*

Process	Major products	Approximate temperature (K)	Approximate mass (solar masses)
Hydrogen burning	Helium	$1 - 3 \times 10^7$	greater than 0.1
Helium burning	Carbon	2×10^8	1–1.4
	Oxygen		
Carbon burning	Oxygen	8×10^8	1.4–5
	Neon		
	Sodium		
	Magnesium		
Neon burning	Oxygen	1.5×10^9	5–10
	Magnesium		
Oxygen burning	Magnesium to sulfur	2×10^9	10–20
Silicon burning	Elements near iron	3×10^9	greater than 20

SOURCE Adapted from a table by A. G. W. Cameron.
Note The last column gives the *minimum* mass needed for the fusion process in the first column to occur.

Central stars of planetary nebulas / In the scenario for the evolution of a solar-mass star, when a red giant pops off its outer layers, it leaves behind a hot, dense core. This cinder cools to form a white dwarf.

If this picture is correct, you'd expect that the central stars of planetary nebulas should fall along the evolutionary track after the red giant stage. Well, they do (Fig. 19.24)! Some central stars are extremely hot and luminous; others are hot, but not so luminous. Their positions on the H-R diagram fall neatly above that for white dwarfs. So the stars of planetary nebulas mark a transition between the core of a red giant and a white dwarf. This observation nicely confirms that stars of about the sun's mass evolve from red giants to white dwarfs.

19.10
The synthesis of elements in stars

In order to survive, a star must fuse lighter elements into heavier ones and so generate energy. Gravitational contraction provides the initial heat to get fusion reactions going. The more mass a star has, the greater is the central temperature produced by gravitational contraction and the heavier the elements it can fuse. From the ignition temperatures of fusion reactions, you can set limits on the heaviest elements that a star of a certain mass can fuse (Table 19.2). For example, our sun can burn helium to carbon but will never get hot enough to fuse carbon.

Table 19.2 summarizes the principal stages of nuclear energy generation and nucleosynthesis in stars. Note that the products (or ashes) of one set of reactions usually become the fuel for the next set of reactions. What a beautiful scheme for energy production in the universe!

Also note in that table that only very massive stars (those with greater than about 5 solar masses) can produce elements heavier than oxygen, neon, and sodium. Few stars in our Galaxy have this much mass, and so many stars come to the end of their nuclear evolution without having manufactured some important elements. This fact emphasizes the importance of massive stars in the scheme of cosmic evolution—they fuse heavy elements *and* throw some back into the interstellar medium in supernovas.

SUMMARY

This chapter has described the contemporary concepts in the life histories of the stars. Here's a summary of the major themes:

1 Stars are born—most likely in groups—when a dense interstellar cloud fragments and these pieces collapse gravitationally. Different fragments of the cloud form stars at different times. As a star forms, the dust in the cloud hides it from view.

2   *A star's evolution depends mainly on its mass; more massive stars have higher core temperatures and so higher luminosities. They evolve faster and live shorter lives. Their higher core temperatures allow them to fuse heavier elements. They are likely to die in supernova explosions.*

3   *During its life, a star constantly struggles against gravity. It resists gravitational collapse by pressure from heat in its interior. Fusion reactions in the core provide this heat; they are first ignited by the heat from gravitational collapse. A star must fuse heavier and heavier elements in order to withstand gravity.*

4   *Stars recycle some material back into the birthplace of stars—the interstellar medium—but have changed its composition by the addition of heavier elements. Some of the material stays locked in a star's corpse, never to participate in cosmic evolution unless the universe collapses and restarts again.*

The stars form the *crucial evolutionary links in the chain of cosmic evolution. They produce light and warmth vital to life on any planets around them. Previous generations created the elements out of which those planets were made. How? By fusion reactions. What ignites these reactions? Gravitational contraction. Gravity, the driving force of the astronomical universe, literally squeezes matter into heavier elements in the hearts of stars.*

STUDY EXERCISES

1   A star like the sun consists completely of an ordinary gas. Why doesn't it suddenly collapse gravitationally? (*Objective 2*)

2   Present calculations indicate that a solar-mass protostar is much more luminous than the sun. Yet it's much cooler at the surface. How could the protosun be much cooler and yet more luminous than the present sun? (*Objective 4*)

3   How can you tell from an H-R diagram that the stars in the Pleiades cluster are younger than those in the Hyades? (*Objective 7*)

4   Why are massive stars able to fuse heavier elements than less massive stars? (*Objective 6 and 8*)

5   What evidence is there that red giant stars become white dwarfs? (*Objective 7*)

6   What is one main difference between the evolution of a 1-solar-mass star and a 5-solar-mass star? (*Objective 6*)

7   After a star fuses helium (helium burning), what element can it fuse next, if its core gets hot enough? (*Objective 9*)

8   In a few sentences, describe how the evolution of a Population I star and a Population II star of the same mass *differ* on an H-R diagram. (*Objective 10*)

9   Explain how the helium flash occurs in solar-mass stars. (*Objective 5*)

10 A 5-solar-mass star has more fuel to burn than our sun, yet it lives a shorter life. Explain. (*Objective 6*)

BEYOND THIS BOOK. . .

For good background material on star formation, try "The Birth of Stars" by B. Bok in *Scientific American*, August 1972, p. 48. Let me warn you that some of his material is already dated.

I. Iben describes the evolution of Population II stars in "Globular Cluster Stars," *Scientific American*, July 1970, p. 26.

An advanced, technical article—but very readable—is S. Strom's "Star Formation and the Early Phases of Stellar Evolution" in *Frontiers of Astrophysics*, edited by E. Avrett (Harvard University Press, Cambridge, Mass., 1976).

For more details on one aspect of starbirth, read "The Birth of Massive Stars" by M. Zeilik in *Scientific American*, April 1978, p. 110. For another view, try "Bok Globules" by R. L. Dickman, *Scientific American*, June 1977, p. 66.

> *I believe a leaf of grass is no less than the journey-work of the stars.*
> *WALT WHITMAN: Song of Myself*

LEARNING OBJECTIVES

After studying this chapter you should be able to:

1. Compare the physical natures of white dwarfs and neutron stars and describe their place in stellar evolution.

2. Argue, with observational support, that pulsars are neutron stars.

3. Describe a black hole in terms of an escape velocity and the speed of light.

4. Describe what happens to an observer who falls into a black hole from the standpoint of the infalling observer and that of an outside observer far from the black hole.

5. Indicate the place of black holes in the context of stellar evolution.

6. Describe and evaluate the observational evidence to date for the existence of black holes.

7. Contrast the observed features of a nova and a supernova.

8. Outline a possible model for a nova that involves a binary star system.

9. Outline a possible model for a supernova explosion.

10. Cite observational evidence that the Crab Nebula is a supernova remnant.

11. Place supernovas in the grand scheme of cosmic evolution.

How do most stars die? Violently, say contemporary astrophysicists. Imagine, as in the previous chapter, that one year equals one-fifth of a second, so the sun would live 65 years. Then in this speeded-up time you would see about 25 stars in our Galaxy wink out every second. These deaths are signaled by a violent ripping off of a star's outer layer. These discarded shells replenish the interstellar medium that has been depleted by the formation of stars and planets. The dead star's remnant core cools. Locked tight by gravity, it forms a cinder in space. What are these remains like? In some instances—as the sun will do—the burnt-out core becomes a white dwarf star, a solid carbon crystal. In others the core becomes a neutron star, a smooth, spinning sphere of nuclear matter. In still others—perhaps for many stars in the Galaxy—the core may disappear through a warp in spacetime as a black hole.

What paths do stars take to these strange deaths? Astrophysicists do not all agree on the details of the final stages of stellar evolution. But how a star comes to its final fate does depend on its mass at the end of its life. With less than 1.4 solar masses, a star's corpse will be a white dwarf. For up to about 5 solar masses, the end is marked by a neutron star. With a greater mass, a star falls into a grave marked by a black hole.

Although the details are uncertain, observations do imply that almost all stars throw off mass before they meet their ends. A supernova is the most destructive example of mass loss. But a supernova is constructive too; in its immense explosion the heavy elements of the universe are made and thrown to the currents of space.

20.1
White dwarf stars

The evolution of a 1-solar-mass star (Section 19.6) illustrates the constant battle of pressure and gravitational forces. Because gravity never lapses the way thermonuclear reactions do, the final state of any star depends only on the physical properties of matter at high densities and the total mass of the star. When all the thermonuclear reactions cease, what pressure can support the star?

Recall what happens to the core of a solar-mass star as it evolves off the main sequence. It contracts, growing denser, until it becomes so dense (about 10^6 g/cc) that it is no longer an ordinary gas but a *degenerate* one (Focus 50). Now, one important property of a degenerate gas is that, by and large, its pressure does *not* depend on its temperature. Rather, it depends on the number of particles and how tightly they are crammed together. So denser degenerate gases exert greater outward pressures. This degenerate gas pressure can support the star against gravity.

Theory of white dwarfs / In 1935 Subrahmanyan Chandrasekhar applied the physics of a degenerate gas of electrons to a model of a star. He found that the pressure exerted by the electrons could resist the force of gravity for stars less than 1.4 solar masses at a density of 10^6 g/cc. Such a star at the end point of its thermonuclear history is a *white dwarf*. A star this dense with the sun's mass would be about the size of the earth (Fig. 20.1)! No more thermonuclear reactions go on; no heavier elements are fused, no energy produced. How does a white dwarf fend off gravity? By the outward pressure from the degenerate electron gas. The nuclei in a white dwarf form a crystal structure embedded in a degenerate electron gas. If the expulsion of the outer layers of the star left a carbon core, the white dwarf would be a solid carbon crystal containing a degenerate electron gas.

The small radius and high density of a white dwarf can be traced to the behavior of a degenerate electron gas in a gravitational field. Chandrasekhar found this result: The more massive the white dwarf is, the *smaller* is its radius.

A crucial point is reached when the mass of the white dwarf is about 1.4 solar masses; such a star has the highest density and smallest radius possible. (This contrasts to normal stars, where the more mass a star has, the larger it is.) How does this come about? More mass means more gravity. To balance gravity requires internal pressure. In a white dwarf the pressure does not come from internal heating from thermonuclear reactions. Instead, it arises from the nature of a degenerate gas, where greater pressures are a response to closer packing of the material (greater density).

Add a bit more mass and the gravitational forces overwhelm the degenerate electron gas pressure. The star collapses. It cannot be a

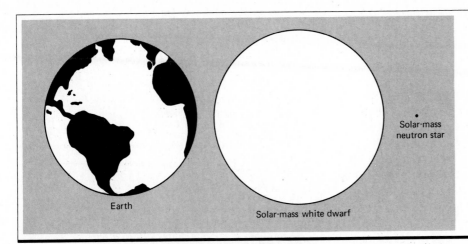

20.1

A comparison of the relative sizes of the earth, a solar-mass white dwarf, and a neutron star.

Earth

Solar-mass white dwarf

Solar-mass neutron star

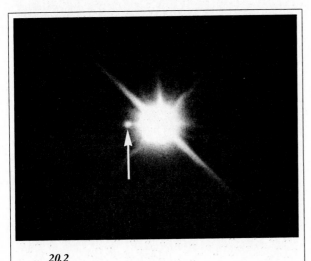

20.2

Sirius B (arrow), a white dwarf star. The sizes of the stellar images in this photo bear no relation to the actual sizes of the stars, only to their brightnesses. The brighter star is Sirius A. (Courtesy Lick Observatory)

luminosity, a high surface temperature (about 29,500 K), and so a small radius, around 7×10^{-3} the sun's radius. Given its size and mass, Sirius B must have an average density of about 3 million grams per cubic centimeter!

Most white dwarfs seen so far are actually white, but a few are yellow, and some are red. Until now, about 300 stars have been identified as white dwarfs. Because of their low luminosities, white dwarfs are hard to see. Although this makes it hard to estimate the number of white dwarfs in the Galaxy, they may comprise 10 percent of all stars.

Recently, Harry Shipman has investigated the radii and masses of over 100 white dwarf stars. Most of these show hydrogen lines in their spectra; that is, their spectra resemble those of *A* stars, but they are white dwarfs. Shipman finds that the radius of these sample stars ranges from 0.0103 solar radius for 0.75 solar mass to 0.0127 solar radius for 0.55 solar mass. (Note the more massive stars are smaller in size.) Typical values for the physical properties of white dwarfs are 0.8 solar mass for the mass, 0.01 solar radius (7×10^6 m) for the radius, and 10^6 g/cc for the density.

How often do white dwarfs form in the Galaxy? White dwarfs probably originate from stars with between 1.4 and 6 solar masses while on the main sequence. Such stars burn hydrogen to helium until they produce a hydrogen-exhausted core of about 0.7 solar masses—just the average mass of known white dwarfs. Obviously, these stars must lose mass at the end of their lives (usually as red giants) before they become white dwarfs. It is estimated that the

stable white dwarf. This amount of mass, 1.4 solar masses, is called the *Chandrasekhar limit* and signals the point at which electron degenerate matter is crushed by gravity. The degenerate gas pressure can no longer support the star.

Observations of white dwarfs / In 1862 the American optician Alvan Clark observed Sirius B (Fig. 20.2), the faint companion to Sirius (Focus 39). Later, this star was found to be a white dwarf of about 1 solar mass. Sirius B has a low luminosity, about 3×10^{-3} times the sun's

rate at which white dwarfs are born from their more massive progenitors is one every 4 years.

20.2

Neutron stars

What happens to stars with more than 1.4 solar masses of material at the end of their evolution? Strange things happen. Gravity crushes the star to higher and higher densities. At about 10^{10} g/cc the inward pressure has increased to such a high value that inverse beta decay occurs (Fig. 20.3). (*Inverse beta decay* is the process of putting an electron and proton together to form a neutron and neutrino; an electron is sometimes called a beta particle.) At this density electrons and protons are forced together to form neutrons and neutrinos. At around 10^{12} g/cc the neutrons begin to drip off the nuclei and to form a separate gas. At 10^{14} g/cc the nuclei suddenly fall apart into a gas with 80 percent neutrons, 10 percent electrons and 10 percent protons. At this density the neutrons become degenerate in the same manner that electrons become degenerate in a white dwarf star. The degenerate neutrons provide a degenerate gas pressure and so balance the inward pull of gravity. This pressure holds off gravity and allows the formation of a stable *neutron star*, a star composed mainly of neutrons. Its diameter will be about 10–20 km, depending on its mass. (See Fig. 20.1.)

A neutron star is a weird beast compared with an ordinary star. In a typical neutron star model (Fig. 20.4) with a diameter of about 15 km, the inner 12 km consists of a neutron gas at such high densities that it is a fluid. The next 3 km out from the center is a mixture of the neutron fluid and neutron-rich nuclei, which are arranged in a solid lattice. The crystal structure is a crystalline solid similar to the interior structure of a white dwarf. In the outer few meters, where the density falls quickly, the neutron star has an atmosphere of atoms, electrons, and protons. The atoms are mostly iron.

Because a neutron star is so dense, it has an enormous surface gravity. For example, a solar-mass neutron star with a radius of 12 km has a surface gravity 10^{11} times greater than that at the earth's surface! Such an enormous pull means that "mountains" on a neutron star won't be very high—a few centimeters at most. This intense gravitational field also results in a

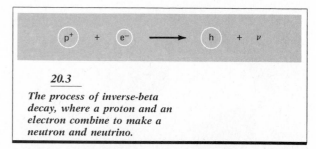

20.3

The process of inverse-beta decay, where a proton and an electron combine to make a neutron and neutrino.

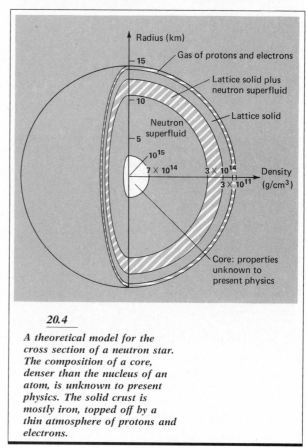

20.4

A theoretical model for the cross section of a neutron star. The composition of a core, denser than the nucleus of an atom, is unknown to present physics. The solid crust is mostly iron, topped off by a thin atmosphere of protons and electrons.

huge escape velocity—as much as about 0.8 the speed of light. Objects falling onto a neutron star from a great distance have at least the escape velocity when they hit, which means that even a small mass carries a fantastic amount of kinetic energy. For example, a marshmallow dropped onto a neutron star from a few AU's out will bang into the surface with a few *megatons* (TNT equivalent) of kinetic energy!

An ordinary star with a mass at the time of collapse greater than 1.4 solar masses probably ends up as a neutron star. Theoretically, a stable neutron star with a mass less than 1.4 solar masses can also form. These low-mass neutron stars are probably made in the pile-driver compression of a supernova explosion, as are most neutron stars.

Because the neutron gas is degenerate, a neutron star has the same mass–radius relation as a white dwarf star: The greater the mass is, the smaller is the radius. In an analogy to the Chandrasekhar limit, a mass limit for neutron stars is reached when the gravitational forces overwhelm the degenerate neutron gas pressure. This limit—not exactly known, but about 5 solar masses—signals the next crushing point of matter by gravity.

Warning: Do you think neutron stars really exist? Notice that I haven't presented evidence for their existence yet. What I've sketched out are *theoretical* ideas about neutron stars, which were first worked out in the late 1930s. Evidence for the reality of neutron stars didn't crop up until almost 40 years later. That evidence involves cataclysmic explosions of stars—supernovas—and rapidly pulsating radio sources—pulsars (Section 20.5).

20.3
Stellar explosions: Novas

Aristotle asserted that the heavens were unchanging. Throughout the Middle Ages this precept required that the number of observed stars remain constant. This deeply ingrained principle received a hard knock in 1572 with the discovery of a new star, or *nova* (Latin for "new"), which was observed carefully by Tycho Brahe. Just a few years later Kepler kept a close watch on another nova that burst into view in the constellation of Ophiuchus in 1604. With the advent of photography and large telescopes in the nineteenth century, astronomers discovered larger numbers of novas scattered throughout the sky. By the beginning of this century a nova was no longer considered an actual new star but, rather, the sudden eruption of light from an existing star (Fig. 20.5).

Astronomical investigation of spiral galaxies revealed occasional flare-ups when a star would briefly surpass the entire galaxy in brightness. These cataclysmic explosions spew out energy in such extraordinary amounts—about 10^9–10^{10} times the sun's luminosity at their peak—that

20.5
A nova, Nova Herculis. These are photos of the star before (top) and during (bottom) its outburst. (Courtesy Lick Observatory)

they are classed as *supernovas* to distinguish them from ordinary novas. Both the new stars observed by Tycho and Kepler were supernovas. Since the supernova of 1604, no such grand explosion has been seen in our Galaxy. Supernovas are such rare events that only six have been visible and noted in our Galaxy during recorded history (Table 20.1).

Astronomers now believe that both novas and supernovas represent explosions of stars.

TABLE 20.1   Supernovas observed by the naked eye

Date (A.D.)	Constellation	Apparent brightness	Distance (kpc)	Observers
185	Centaurus	Brighter than Venus (−6)	2.5	Chinese
369	Cassiopeia	Brighter than Mars or Jupiter (−3)	10.	Chinese
1006	Lupus	Brighter than Venus (−5)	3.3	Chinese Japanese Korean European Arabian
1054	Taurus (Crab Nebula)	Brighter than Venus (−5)	2.	Chinese, Arabian Southwestern Indian (no European)
1572	Cassiopeia	Nearly as bright as Venus (−4)	5.	Tycho and Many Others
1604	Ophiuchus	Between Sirius and Jupiter (−2)	6.	Kepler Galileo Many others

SOURCE   Adapted from a table compiled by W. C. Straka.

For ordinary novas, only the outer layers of the star participate in the explosion. But for supernovas, the interior regions are also involved.

Ordinary novas / In a typical nova outburst, a star in just a few days increases about 7000 times in brightness. It stays up at peak brightness for several hours; then the nova's light slowly declines in a few hundred days to an inconspicuous level—usually brighter, however, than the star's prenova brightness. A plot of a nova's rise and fall in brightness (or luminosity) is called its *light curve* (Fig. 20.6). All novas have the same general shape for their light curves: a sharp rise with a gradual decline.

A typical nova hits a peak brightness of greater than 10^5 solar luminosities. All told, a nova emits during its flare-up and demise some 10^{37}–10^{38} J or about as much energy as the sun generates in about 100,000 years—emitted, instead, in a few hundred days!

A nova's spectrum undergoes pronounced and complicated changes during its outburst. Generally, the prenova star's spectrum has broad dark absorption lines with weak or no bright emission lines. At maximum, the nova has absorption lines like an *A* or *F* supergiant star. Some time after maximum, the nova's spectrum develops emission lines similar to those from H II regions, such as the Orion Neb-

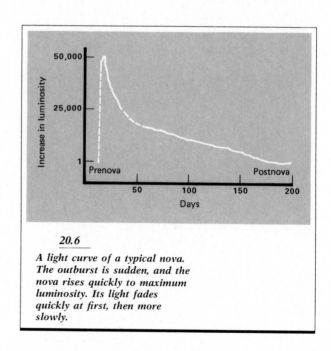

20.6

A light curve of a typical nova. The outburst is sudden, and the nova rises quickly to maximum luminosity. Its light fades quickly at first, then more slowly.

ula. The Doppler shifts of these lines range from a few hundred km/sec in some novas to a few thousand km/sec in others.

What does the evolution of a nova's spectrum tell about the outburst? Several things can be learned from the changing strengths and Doppler shifts of the lines. First, the star's pho-

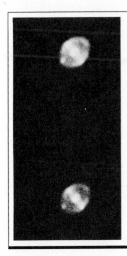

20.7

Nova Herculis, photographed in red light in 1951. You can see the shell of material blown off in the nova explosion. This shell is expanding rapidly into the interstellar medium. (Courtesy Palomar Observatory, California Institute of Technology)

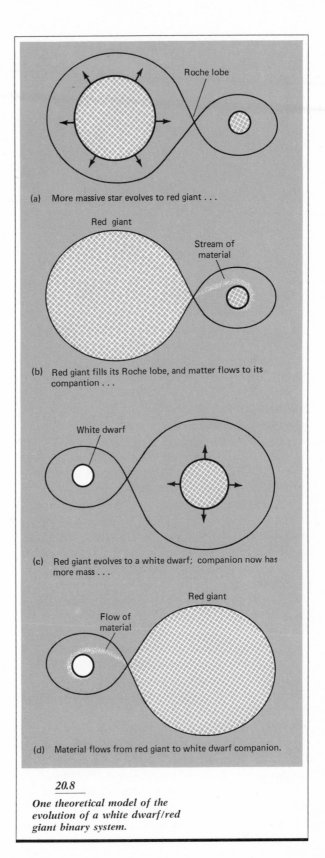

(a)   More massive star evolves to red giant . . .

Red giant

Stream of material

(b)   Red giant fills its Roche lobe, and matter flows to its companion . . .

White dwarf

(c)   Red giant evolves to a white dwarf; companion now has more mass . . .

Red giant

Flow of material

(d)   Material flows from red giant to white dwarf companion.

20.8

One theoretical model of the evolution of a white dwarf/red giant binary system.

tosphere dramatically expands in size, to 100–300 solar radii. Second, the photosphere then collapses back onto the star. Third, a shell of material is blown off the star and rapidly expands away from it (Fig. 20.7). Overall, a typical nova spurts off about a 10^{-4} solar mass. Because some evidence indicates that the prenova star has about 1 solar mass, the ejected material makes up only a small fraction of the total.

A possible nova model / What causes a nova to explode? One major clue: Observational studies indicate that almost all novas occur in close binary systems, that is, binary stars with short periods, such as spectroscopic binaries (Section 15.2). In such systems the two stars are so close that matter may flow from the larger companion to the smaller one.

Astronomers now picture that a nova may occur as part of the the natural evolution of binary stars consisting of two stars of much different masses. At the end of its life the more massive star (which evolves faster) becomes a white dwarf. Remember that a white dwarf has relatively little hydrogen. In order to ignite hydrogen fusion again, it needs fresh hydrogen fuel.

Where might such material come from? In a close binary star system the material can come from the companion star. How? Around each star is a region of space where its gravitational force dominates (Fig. 20.8). The edge of this region is called the *Roche lobe;* any matter within the Roche lobe is gravitationally bound to the star and cannot escape to the other star.

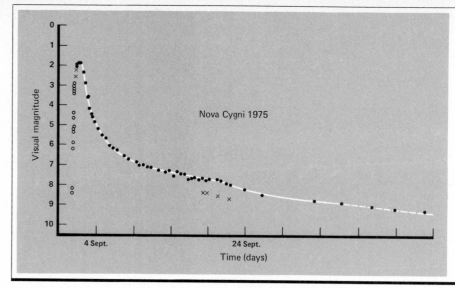

20.9

A light curve for Nova Cygni 1975. (From work by P. Young, H. Corwin, J. Bryan, and G. de Vaucouleurs in the Astrophysical Journal, copyright © 1976 by the American Astronomical Society)

But there is always one point where the Roche lobes touch and join—where the gravitational pull from one star just cancels that from the other. This means that a gravitational highway exists for the flow of matter between the stars.

But in order for the mass exchange to happen, material from one star has to get out to the Roche lobe. How? When stars like the sun reach old age, they become red giants before ending up as white dwarfs. Therefore when the less massive companion star to a white dwarf finally evolves, it bloats up as a red giant (Fig. 20.8), so that its atmosphere swells up and reaches its Roche lobe. Material then flows from the red giant to the white dwarf.

As the matter falls toward the white dwarf, it forms a disk around it. Called an *accretion disk*, the material gathers in a disklike structure from the conservation of angular momentum (Focus 26). The matter spirals into the white dwarf's surface from the accretion disk. Fresh hydrogen gradually accretes on the white dwarf's surface, forming a virgin envelope. Additional material piles on, compressing and heating it. When the temperature at the bottom of the accreted layers reaches 10^6 K, hydrogen fusion reactions ignite. Because the gas here is degenerate, the ignition is explosive (just like the helium flash in red giant stars). The runaway fusion reactions heat the entire layer to some 10^6 K; the gas loses its degenerate state. Then the material expands. Both explosive shocks and pressure blow the accreted material into space. A buildup of as little as 10^{-6} solar mass prompts the nova outburst.

The result is that it doesn't take a large rate of mass infall to set up and ignite runaway reactions in a reasonable time. For a typical nova in a binary system, just a 10^{-8}–10^{-7} solar mass a year suffices. Some studies have shown that a mere 10^{-13} solar mass a year will do the trick. This low rate can even be supplied by accretion from the general interstellar medium rather than from a companion star. That's one way a single white dwarf can become a nova.

Nova Cygni 1975—A recent nova / I moved to New Mexico toward the end of August 1975. My department had a picnic in Corrales, on the west bank of the Rio Grande. It was a beauty of an August day, with the Sandia Mountains turning watermelon-pink at sunset. As I gazed up at the darkening sky, I sensed something wrong with the stars. Then I saw it. A bright new star in the constellation Cygnus near Deneb. For a moment I was stunned. Then I recalled hearing about the discovery of this nova. But in the hustle and hassle of getting set up in a new place and at a new job, I had forgotten about it. The shock of my personal discovery brought home to me the strangeness of a *nova stella* in the sky.

Nova Cygni 1975 peaked at apparent magnitude 1.8. Its light curve (Fig. 20.9) showed a nova's typical sharp rise and decline. But note there's less steep rise before the nova's light shot up to its peak. This part of a nova's light curve had never really been seen before. Fortunately, some photos of Cygnus—such as those by Los Angeles amateur astronomer Ben Mayer—caught the star before it exploded (Fig. 20.10).

Prior to its nova outburst, the star had a magnitude of less than 20 on old photos. So it increased at least 16 million times in luminosity. That's unusually luminous for a nova. Yet Nova Cygni 1975 had a spectral evolution that followed the typical nova's pattern. So this out-

20.10

A unique set of photos showing Nova Cygni 1975 before, during, and after its outburst. The photos have been specially processed to match different negatives. (Courtesy Ben Mayer)

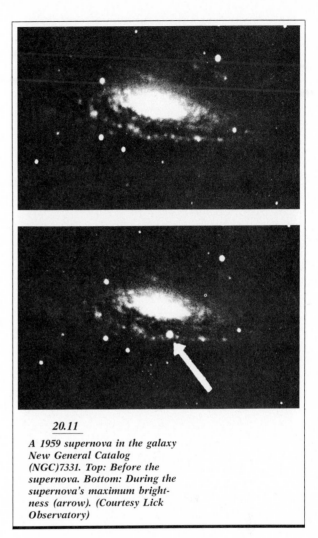

20.11

A 1959 supernova in the galaxy New General Catalog (NGC)7331. Top: Before the supernova. Bottom: During the supernova's maximum brightness (arrow). (Courtesy Lick Observatory)

burst was a regular nova, but an extremely violent one.

So far, there's no indication that Nova Cygni 1975 is a member of a binary system. It may be one of those infrequent cases where a star becomes a nova from the accretion of interstellar material.

In summary, novas may occur when material accretes onto a white dwarf. The infall heats the material, igniting runaway thermonuclear reactions that blow off the outer layers. Most novas are members of binary systems, with a red giant companion. Matter flows from the red giant to the white dwarf to set up the nova explosion. A few novas may be white dwarfs by themselves, accreting interstellar matter.

20.4
Supernovas: Cataclysmic explosions

As violent as novas may appear, they cannot match the fierce destruction of a star in a supernova. These cataclysmic explosions spew out energy in extraordinary amounts—about 10^9–10^{10} times the sun's luminosity at their peak (compared to a nova's 10^5 solar luminosities). According to contemporary ideas, a supernova usually signals the death of a massive star.

The name "supernova" was coined by Fritz Zwicky and Walter Baade for the extraordinary novas discovered in our own and other galaxies. Over 300 supernovas have been found in galaxies outside the Milky Way (Fig. 20.11). Only a few dozen remnants have been detected in our Galaxy.

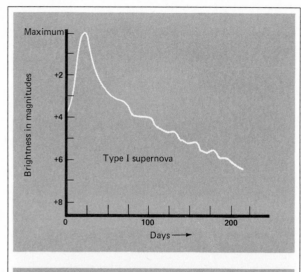

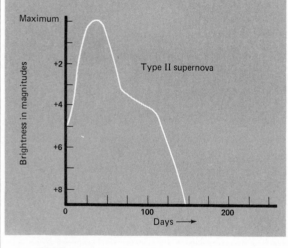

20.12

Representative light curves for Type I (top) and Type II (bottom) supernovas.

TABLE 20.2 Properties of supernovas		
	Type I	*Type II*
Ejected mass (solar masses)	0.5	5
Velocity of ejected mass (km/sec)	10,000	5,000
Total kinetic energy (joules)	5×10^{43}	10^{44}
Visual radiated energy (joules)	4×10^{42}	10^{42}
Maximum absolute magnitude	-19 to -20	-17
Frequency	1 in 60 years	1 in 40 years

SOURCE "The Interaction of Supernovae with the Interstellar Medium," by R. A. Chevalier, *Annual Reviews of Astronomy and Astrophysics*, vol. 15, 1977.

Astronomers classify supernovas by the shape of their light curves in two general categories (Table 20.2): Type I, which exhibit a sharp maximum, about 10 billion solar luminosities, and die off gradually; and Type II, which have a less sharp peak at maximum, about a billion solar luminosities, and die away more sharply than Type I (Fig. 20.12). The total energy output from any supernova is stupendous: 10^{44} J, or approximately as much energy as the sun produces in its entire lifetime of 10 billion years. At its brightest, a supernova shines with the light of *10 billion* suns!

How often this kind of cosmic violence takes place is still debated. The rate of occurrence in any one galaxy is low, but the vast number of visible galaxies ensures that a few supernovas will be observed every year. From the rate in other galaxies, astronomers estimate that a Type I supernova bursts forth in a galaxy, on the average, once in 60 years. Type II are more frequent; one explodes in a galaxy roughly every 40 years. Some astronomers argue that the true frequency must be greater because we do not observe all supernova events. A reasonable estimate is a supernova once every 50 years in a galaxy.

What kinds of stars go supernova? Recall (Chapter 19) that massive stars—*O* and *B* spectral types—probably end their lives in a supernova explosion. Now, Type II supernova occur in spiral galaxies, but not in elliptical ones. This fact implies that massive Population I stars in spiral arms make Type II supernovas.

Type I supernovas are still a mystery. Astronomers used to believe that, because Type I supernovas appeared in elliptical galaxies, they came from old, low-mass Population II stars. A vague model developed in which Type I explosions arose in binary systems with accretion onto a white dwarf—essentially an enhanced nova explosion. But recent work indicates that even elliptical galaxies have some star formation occurring (but at much lower rates than in spiral and irregular galaxies). And that Type I supernova are actually more frequent in spiral and irregular galaxies than in elliptical ones—an indirect indication that they come from young stars whose masses are greater than about 2 solar masses. But from exactly which stars and how is not yet understood.

Both types of supernova violently eject a large fraction of the original star's mass at speeds of about 5000–10,000 km/sec. At maximum brightness, a supernova has reached a size about that of the solar system—a few light hours in diameter.

Supernova remnants / A supernova bangs out a blast wave into the interstellar medium. Traveling at supersonic velocities, the shell of material creates a shock wave that plows through the interstellar gas and dust. The shock wave's collisions with the cool clouds of the interstellar medium can excite the interstellar material into glowing. The Loop Nebula in Cygnus (Fig. 20.13) looks spherical—a shell produced by the interaction of the interstellar medium and a supernova shock wave.

A similar feature in the southern sky—the Gum Nebula (Fig. 20.14)—extends over 50° in

20.13

A supernova remnant in Cygnus. Note how the bright wisps appear to almost make a circle, as if material has been blasted out from a central point. (Courtesy Palomar Observatory, California Institute of Technology)

20.14

A part of the Gum Nebula, another supernova remnant. Again, note how the filaments form circular arcs. The entire nebula is more than 2000 light years in diameter. It was created by the blast shock wave from a supernova. (Courtesy B. Bok and Steward Observatory)

20.15

The relative sizes of the Gum Nebula and the Galaxy. The edge of the Gum Nebula closest to the sun is only a few hundred light years from us and moving toward us at thousands of kilometers per second. A large fraction of the Galaxy's interstellar medium may consist of supernova remnants, with a few as large or larger than this one. The circle labeled "earth" indicates its position, not its size. (Courtesy NASA)

the sky. The Gum Nebula has a diameter of about 2300 ly, its closest edge being only 300 ly from the sun (Fig. 20.15). This nebula was created by the pulse of ultraviolet radiation and X-rays generated by a supernova some 11,000–20,000 years ago. An X-ray source—named Vela X—lies almost in the nebula's center. It is a prime suspect as the supernova site. The discovery of a pulsar (see the next section) at the same location as the Vela X source supports its nature as a supernova remnant. (Pulsars are believed to be formed in the turmoil of a supernova.)

Radio astronomers have a significant advantage over optical astronomers in the hunt for galactic supernova remnants: They can observe low-density excited gas that has no detectable optical emission but does emit radio (Fig. 20.16). Radio astronomers can label supernova remnants by a special property of their radio spectrum: The intensity plotted versus frequency

displays a *nonthermal spectrum* (see Focus 47 for a discussion of the difference between thermal and nonthermal spectra). If a radio source is observed at a variety of frequencies, the shape of its spectrum distinguishes between a possible supernova remnant (nonthermal) and an ordinary H II region (thermal).

X-ray astronomers can also observe young supernova remnants directly; over 30 have been observed so far with the Einstein X-Ray Observatory. These huge shock waves plow through the interstellar medium at speeds of hundreds of kilometers per second; they compress and heat the interstellar gas to temperatures of at least a few million Kelvins in the zone just behind the blast wave. This gas emits X-rays. The X-ray pictures of Type I remnants, such as Tycho's supernova (Fig. 20.17) typically show symmetrical shells with variations in brightness around their rims—a possible indication of the patchy structure of the interstellar medium.

The Crab Nebula—A supernova remnant / The supernova seen in Taurus in 1054 marks an event of continuing interest since its sighting. Chinese astronomers termed temporary celestial objects, such as novas or comets, "guest stars." The Chinese history *Shung-Shih* refers to the report of a guest star that did not move, so it must have been a star rather than a comet. The dynasty dates the event well: The guest star entered the sky on July 4, 1054. Close study of Chinese and Japanese accounts of this visitor confirms that the star remained visible to the unaided eye for over 650 days in the night sky. It was visible in daylight for 23 days! The position noted by the oriental astronomers placed the event in the constellation Taurus.

In 1731 the amateur astronomer John Brevis discovered a faint nebulosity just above the Bull's horns. Much later, in 1928, Edwin Hubble measured the expansion rate of this nebula, which had become known as the Crab. He deduced that its expansion began about 900 years earlier. Hubble concluded that since the Crab Nebula was near the position given for the Chinese guest star, that explosion was the source of the nebula. The Crab Nebula became the first identified supernova remnant in our Galaxy (Fig. 20.18). It is only 6500 ly away.

The systematic observation by Chinese and Japanese astronomers of the supernova that produced the Crab Nebula contrasts sharply

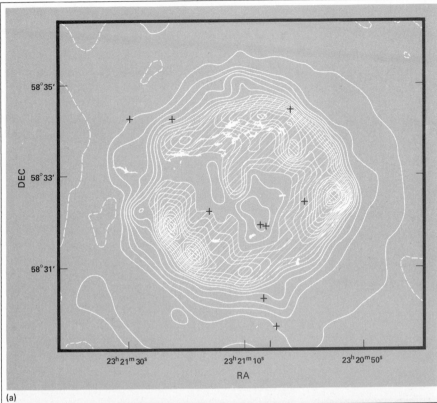

(a)

(b)

20.16

(a) *A radio map of a supernova remnant that appears to have been the "nova" observed by Tycho Brahe in 1572. The map shows a shell of gas expanding out through the interstellar medium. (Based on observations by M. Ryle, B. Elsmore, and A. Neville.)* (b) *An optical picture of the same region of the sky, taken by the 200-inch telescope in red light. The only indication of the supernova remnant are a few faint wisps, which you can see grouped in the top center of the picture. (Courtesy Palomar Observatory, California Institute of Technology)*

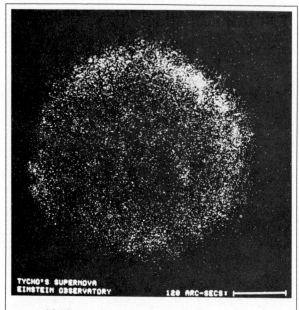

TYCHO'S SUPERNOVA
EINSTEIN OBSERVATORY   120 ARC-SECS!

20.17

An X-ray image of Tycho's supernova remnant, taken by the Einstein X-Ray Observatory. (Courtesy of P. Gorenstein, and F. Seward, Center for Astrophysics)

with the utter lack of comment by European astronomers at the time. Recently, a near-Eastern account of the supernova has been found in a journal kept by a physician named Ibu Bultntan, who lived in Constantinople. His record implies that the sudden appearance of a "spectacular star" took place in the summer of 1054 A.D.

Although unrecorded in Europe, the supernova may have been observed and recorded in the southwestern part of North America. One good example is a painting on a rock in Chaco Canyon, New Mexico, which may represent the predawn conjunction of the waning crescent moon and the supernova (Fig. 20.19). The Anasazi (Section 1.6), who lived in Chaco then, may have made this painting to commemorate the event.

The material blown off in the explosion should still be expanding today. Indeed, the Doppler shift of the expanding filaments indicates—if the expansion rate has been constant—that they began expanding at around 1132–1148 A.D. That's close to the actual date of the explosion. The fact that it is later may mean that the velocity is now higher than the average; that is, the expansion has been accelerating.

20.18

The Crab Nebula, photographed in red light that shows its filamentary structure. It looks like an explosion. Doppler shift measurements show that the hot gas is expanding away from the nebula's center. (Courtesy Lick Observatory)

20.19

A drawing in Chaco Canyon, New Mexico, that might represent the Crab supernova. The view here is looking up at an outcrop of rock from the canyon's southwest wall. The hand symbol indicates that something extraordinary is pictured here. Below it is a crescent, moon-shaped symbol. To its left, a starlike symbol is found. On the morning of July 5, 1054 the supernova—which was brighter than Venus—rose close to the crescent moon. This rock drawing may represent that spectacular dawn. (Photo by M. Zeilik)

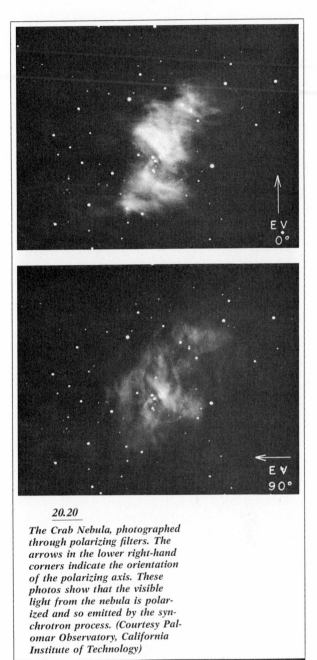

20.20

The Crab Nebula, photographed through polarizing filters. The arrows in the lower right-hand corners indicate the orientation of the polarizing axis. These photos show that the visible light from the nebula is polarized and so emitted by the synchrotron process. (Courtesy Palomar Observatory, California Institute of Technology)

In 1953 J. Shklovsky resolved in part the enigma of the Crab Nebula's radio and optical emission when he suggested that the synchrotron process produced it (Focus 47). Synchrotron radiation requires a magnetic field and a source of energetic charged particles (such as electrons). Such emission is usually polarized and has a nonthermal spectrum. Shklovsky's argument was clinched in the following year, when Russian astronomers found that the optical emission was strongly polarized (Fig. 20.20).

If all the radiation from the Crab nebula is generated by the synchrotron process, then this emission should be polarized at all wavelengths. The Crab Nebula also emits X-rays. Are they polarized too? The problem in making such an observation is that the pulsar in the Crab Nebula also gives off X-rays, so the two different sources of the X-rays—the pulsar (next section)

and the gas of the nebula—are mixed together (Fig. 20.21). Recently the polarization of the X-rays from the Crab Nebula has been measured without interference from the pulsar's X-rays. It shows that the X-rays are polarized about 19–20 percent, which confirms that the X-rays must be produced by the synchrotron process.

The solution to one puzzle posed another one even more vexing: What is the source of

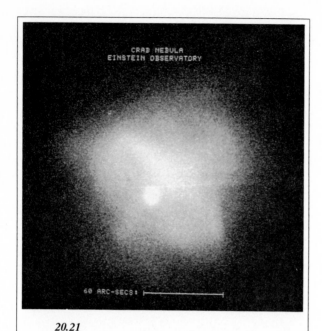

CRAB NEBULA
EINSTEIN OBSERVATORY

60 ARC-SECS

20.21

*An X-ray image of the Crab
Nebula, taken by the Einstein
X-Ray Observatory. The bright
point at the center is the pul-
sar, strongly emitting X-rays.
(Courtesy of F. R. Harnden, Jr.,
and H. Tananbaum, Center for
Astrophysics)*

the energetic electrons? (Same problem as in
active galaxies!) As these electrons spiral
through the magnetic field emitting synchrotron
radiation, they rapidly lose energy. For the electrons producing the optical emission, half their
energy would be drained off in only 70 years.
So the supply of electrons must be continuously
replenished. The problem of the electron's
source became even more acute when X-ray
emission was discovered in 1963. The electrons
that produce synchrotron X-ray emission have
higher energies than those that produce optical
emission. They also deplete their energy faster,
losing half in only seven years! The Crab Nebula emits about 100 times more energy in the
form of X-rays than as radio or optical emission, so a large amount of energy must be
added to the nebula over a time of only a few
years.

The energy problem disappeared in 1968
with the discovery of a pulsar in the Crab
Nebula.

20.5

Pulsars:
Rapidly rotating neutron stars

Do neutron stars exist? Models of supernovas
suggest that a neutron star may remain as a
corpse of the exploded star. A neutron star
found in a supernova remnant would clinch this
argument. But how would a neutron star be visible? In a way not anticipated by astronomers:
as *pulsars*, accidentally discovered in the summer of 1967 by an English radio astronomy
group headed by Anthony Hewish.

The pulsar detection ranks high on the list
of those marvelous accidents of scientific discovery. The Hewish group was mapping the sky
at radio wavelengths in an attempt to find quasars. A search of the entire sky necessitated a
special radio telescope: 2048 antennas covering
4.5 acres of a field.

Jocelyn Bell, then a graduate student in
charge of the preliminary data analysis, noticed
a strange signal that suddenly disappeared, only
to reappear three months later. The Hewish
group concentrated on this unusual signal and
found radio pulses occurring at a remarkably
regular rate, once every 1.33730113 sec. Flushed
with excitement, the radio astronomers searched
the sky for any similar signals and discovered
three more objects emitting radio bursts at different rates. The Hewish group concluded that
the objects must be natural phenomena and
named them *pulsating stars*, or *pulsars*.

Observed pulsar characteristics / To date, a
total of about 150 pulsars have been studied in
detail. About an equal number have been recently discovered in a special pulsar survey, for
a total of roughly 300.

For a given pulsar, the time period between
pulses repeats with very high accuracy, better
than 1 part in 10^8. The amount of energy in a
pulse, however, varies considerably; sometimes
complete pulses are missing from the sequence.
Although the intensity and shape vary from
pulse to pulse, the average of many pulses from
the same pulsar defines a unique shape (Fig.
20.22). The average pulse typically lasts for a
few tens of milliseconds.

For the well-studied pulsars, pulse periods
range from 0.03 to 4.0 sec, with an average
value of 0.65 sec. In the cases where accurate
radio observations have been made, periods

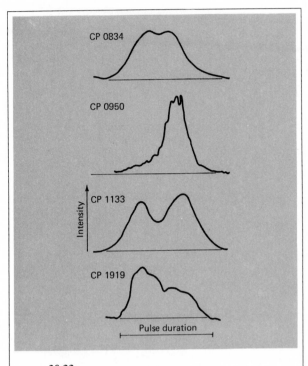

20.22

Average shapes of radio pulses from four different pulsars. The pulse durations are very short—only about a few thousands of a second. The actual shape of a pulse from the same pulsar varies some from pulse to pulse, but many pulses averaged together provided a unique radio "fingerprint" for each pulsar.

have been noted to increase in a regular, but very gradual, fashion, typically about 10^{-8} sec per year.

Radio observations indicate that the distances to pulsars ranges from 300 to 60,000 ly. They tend to lie in the galactic plane—which implies that they are most likely from Population I objects.

These observed general properties of pulsars provide clues to the possible physical properties of these precise cosmic clocks. The pulse duration indicates an upper limit to the size of the bodies emitting the radiation. How? Suppose that you could switch off the sun. Due to the finite velocity of light, it would take slightly more than 2 sec for the entire solar disk to appear dark, and then another 2 sec to regain its original brightness if quickly turned on again.

This is because the part of the sun seen when you look at the edge of the visible disk is at a greater distance (halfway around the sun) than the part at the center of the disk. So if the sun is turned off, you won't know that the edge is dark until about 2 sec after you see the center become dark. So an object the size of the sun, an average star, is too large to be a pulsar, as the pulse durations amount to a few hundred milliseconds or less. The region emitting these pulses must be less than roughly 30,000 km in size (the light travel distance during the pulse's duration). The more typical pulse durations of a few tens of milliseconds imply sizes of roughly 3000 km or less.

What stellar objects exist at this size or smaller? Also, what objects can contain the large quantities of energy that pulsars emit? A dense object rotating rapidly acts as a storehouse of kinetic energy. This clue points to either white dwarfs or neutron stars as the candidates for pulsars.

Physical characteristics of pulsars / Immediately after the discovery of pulsars, some theoreticians were inclined to consider white dwarfs as the source of their radiation. The reason was quite simple: Many white dwarfs had been observed, whereas no neutron star had ever been sighted. But problems arose in trying to fit characteristics of the white dwarf models to the observations. These ideas did not match the observed characteristics of pulsars well.

Here's the basic trick: Pulsar models must account for the precise clock mechanism of pulsars, that is, the extremely regular repetition of pulses. Basically, three clock mechanisms are available: orbital revolution, pulsation, and axial rotation. Consider each in turn.

First, revolution. Two very close, compact bodies can orbit with short, regular periods. But a pair of white dwarfs even in *contact* cannot orbit each other faster than once every 1.7 sec; many pulsars are known with periods shorter than this. Two neutron stars can whip around each other with shorter periods, but here a different problem crops up. According to the general theory of relativity, two massive bodies in short-period orbit should lose energy in the form of gravitational radiation. With this energy loss, the two objects come closer together and their period *decreases* (following Kepler's third law). Eventually, the two bodies would collide. But pulsar periods are known to *increase*, not decrease. So scratch orbital revolution as the clock mechanism.

Second, pulsation. Imagine a white dwarf or neutron star expanding and contracting regularly, with one expansion and contraction equal to a pulse period. How fast a spherical mass can pulsate basically depends on its density. Denser objects can pulsate more rapidly. That should seem reasonable. Imagine standing above the surface of a white dwarf star and pulling it outward. Release it; gravity pulls it in, and it pulsates about once a second. Now try the same imaginary experiment with a neutron star. Because it is denser, its surface gravity is greater and so its surface is pulled in more rapidly than a white dwarf's surface. The least massive, least dense neutron stars can pulsate no slower than once every 0.01 sec. That's faster than the fastest known pulsar, which has a period of 0.033 sec. Pulsation doesn't work. White dwarfs can't pulse as fast as the fastest pulsars, and neutron stars pulsate too fast.

Third, rotation. Consider one rotation equals a pulse period. Can rotation of white dwarfs explain the fastest pulsars? No. Here's the basic physical argument. If a spherical mass rotates rapidly enough, gravity will not be able to hold it together, and material will fly off from the equator. For a typical white dwarf, the fastest it could spin without losing mass is about once every 4 sec—that's slower than the typical pulsar pulsation interval of 0.65 sec and much slower than the Crab's rate of 0.033 sec. In contrast to white dwarfs, neutron stars are much denser and can withstand much faster rotational rates without losing mass—as fast as once every 0.001 sec; fast enough for even the fastest pulsar. (Of course, a neutron star can rotate more slowly.) So a rotating neutron star can provide the clock mechanism for pulsars.

Pulsars and supernovas / The idea that pulsars are neutron stars would be clinched if an observation made the connection. Theoretical models predict that neutron stars are made in supernova explosions. So you need to look at supernovas or their remnants to connect neutron stars to pulsars. Fortunately, there are two examples to date: a pulsar in the Crab Nebula and another in the Gum Nebula, both supernova remnants.

The Crab Nebula pulsar (Fig. 20.23) is called PSR 0531+21. It has the distinction of being the pulsar with the fastest period: 0.033 sec, or 30 pulses per sec! The Crab pulsar has other outstanding features. It was the first pulsar discovered to emit optical pulses as well as radio ones (Fig. 20.24); the optical and radio pulses were found to have the same period. Remarkably, the star emitting these pulses was picked out by Walter Baade and H. Minkowski in 1942 as a possible candidate for the stellar remnant of the supernova! Although this star is now known to be the pulsar, astronomers had observed it for years without noticing the optical blinking; a flicker of 30 times a second is just beyond the frequency that the eye can detect, and photos combine all the pulses into one image.

Two other important features of the Crab pulsar: First, it is the only pulsar discovered so far to pulse in the infrared, X-ray, and gamma-ray regions of the spectrum (Fig. 20.25), as well as at radio and optical wavelengths. The total rate of energy emitted in the pulses is about 10^{28} W. Second, the Crab pulsar was one of the first to exhibit a definite slow down in pulse period, at a rate of about 10^{-5} sec per year—fast for pulsars but less change than your electronic watch shows in a year.

The discovery of the Crab pulsar seems to solve the energy problem of the Crab Nebula. At all wavelengths the Crab Nebula emits about 10^{31} W. What is the source of this energy? If the pulsar is a rotating neutron star, its slowdown in period gives a change in rotational energy of about 5×10^{31} W. That's enough to power the nebula—if the rotational kinetic energy of the neutron star can somehow be converted to kinetic and radiative energy of the nebula.

If the Crab pulsar were the only one associated with a known supernova remnant, it might be written off as a chance coincidence. But astronomers know of another one: the pulsar in the constellation Vela, near the center of the Gum Nebula (Fig. 20.26). This pulsar is called PSR 0833-45.

In 1976 astronomers finally observed optical pulses from the Vela pulsar (Fig. 20.27). It took 8 years since the discovery of the pulsar because the optical pulses are very weak—their

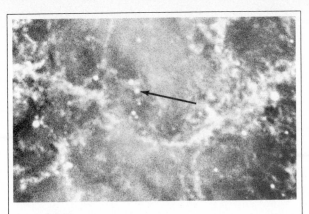

20.23

The location of the pulsar (arrow) in the Crab Nebula. (Courtesy Lick Observatory)

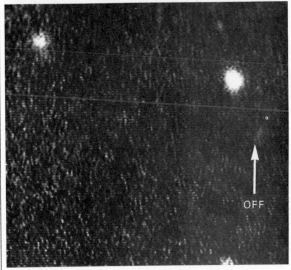

20.24

The Crab pulsar turning on (top) and off (bottom) at visual wavelengths. (Courtesy Lick Observatory)

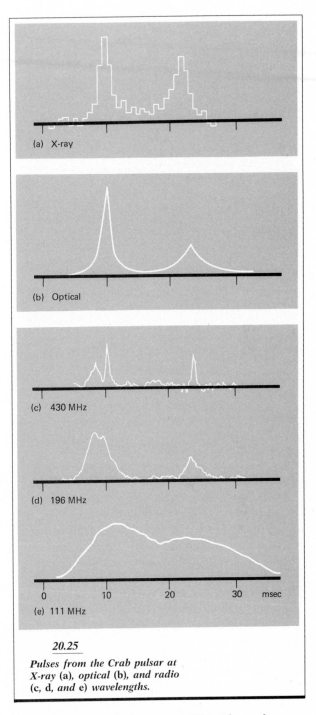

(a) X-ray

(b) Optical

(c) 430 MHz

(d) 196 MHz

(e) 111 MHz

20.25

Pulses from the Crab pulsar at X-ray (a), optical (b), and radio (c, d, and e) wavelengths.

average magnitude is a mere 25.2. The pulses come every 80 msec and have two peaks, separated by about 22 msec. Also, gamma-ray telescopes have detected pulses from Vela (Fig. 20.27). So this pulsar resembles the Crab pulsar in many ways: Both are rapid, both emit pulses over a wide range of the electromagnetic spec-

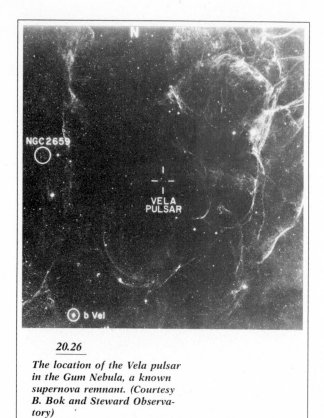

20.26

The location of the Vela pulsar in the Gum Nebula, a known supernova remnant. (Courtesy B. Bok and Steward Observatory)

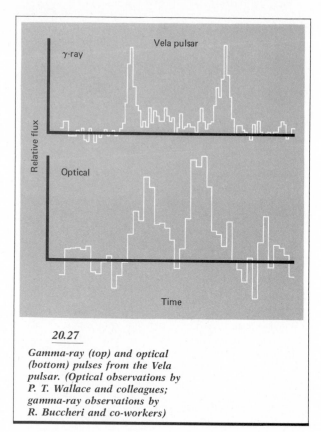

20.27

Gamma-ray (top) and optical (bottom) pulses from the Vela pulsar. (Optical observations by P. T. Wallace and colleagues; gamma-ray observations by R. Buccheri and co-workers)

trum, and their gamma-ray pulse profiles are very similar.

The lighthouse model for pulsars / Now to try to tie these observations together in the accepted basic model for pulsars—a rotating, magnetic neutron star—otherwise known as the *lighthouse model.* The model has two key components: (1) The neutron star, whose great density and fast rotation ensures a large amount of rotational energy, and (2) a dipole magnetic field that transforms the rotational energy to electromagnetic energy.

The big picture is this (Fig. 20.28): The magnetic axis of the pulsar is tilted with respect to the rotational axis (just like the earth). As the pulsar spins, its enormous magnetic field induces an equally enormous electric field at its surface. This electric field pulls charged particles—mostly electrons—off the solid crust of iron nuclei and electrons. The electrons flow out above the neutron star where they are accelerated by the rotating magnetic field lines. The accelerated electrons emit synchrotron radiation

(Focus 47) in a tight beam more or less along the field lines.

You can now see how a pulsar pulses without actually pulsating. If the magnetic axis falls within the line of sight, each time a pole swings around (like the spinning light of a lighthouse) you see a burst of synchrotron emission. The time between pulses is the rotation period. The duration of the pulses depends on the size of the radiating region. As the pulsar generates electromagnetic radiation, the drag of accelerating particles in its magnetic field slows down its rotation. This slowdown is observed.

Sounds good, doesn't it? Well, I've outlined one possible model from the many available. A big problem with all models remains with the exact method by which a pulsar converts its rotational energy to electromagnetic energy. Models to date have limited success in explaining the abundant observational data. The basic clock mechanism seems right, but the detailed emission mechanism is not clear.

Binary radio pulsars / Most stars in the

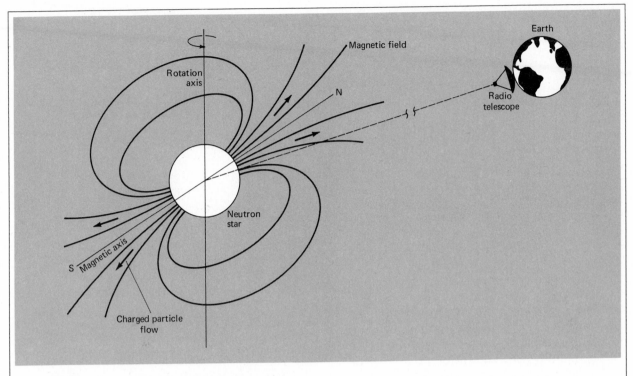

20.28

A schematic model of a pulsar as a highly magnetic, rapidly rotating neutron star. In this lighthouse model the magnetic axis is tilted with respect to the spin axis. Charged particles from the neutron star's surface flow out along the magnetic field lines and so escape most easily out along the north and south magnetic poles. These particles emit synchrotron radiation, which we see as pulses each time a magnetic pole spins across our line of sight.

Milky Way are members of binary or multiple star systems. Even after one member of a binary becomes a supernova, the pair usually remains intact. So a radio pulsar could exist in a binary system.

In fact, one has been observed. It's called PSR 1913+16 and was discovered by R. Hulse and Joseph Taylor in July 1974 during a search for new pulsars. This pulsar at first looked interesting because its pulse period was only 0.059 sec—shorter than any known pulsar except the one in the Crab Nebula. When Hulse and Taylor reobserved PSR 1913+16 in September 1974, they found that its period went through a large cyclical change in a period of only 7.75 h. What was going on? Such regular changes would naturally come about in a binary system of the pulsar and a companion with an orbital period of

7.75 h. What was seen was a Doppler shift in the signal produced by the orbital motion of the system. When the pulsar is moving away from us, its pulses are spread out and come at longer intervals. (Each pulse originates farther away and so takes longer to reach us.) When it is moving toward us, the pulses are pushed together and come at shorter intervals.

PSR 1913+16 lies about 15,000 ly away. Visual and X-ray observations have so far failed to detect either the pulsar or its companion. The radio observations indicate that the pulsar and its companion have an orbital semimajor axis of only 7×10^5 km—that's only the sun's radius! Their combined masses are 2.8 solar masses, so if the pulsar has a mass of about 2 solar masses (a typical neutron star), its companion has about 0.8 solar mass; it might be a white dwarf.

There are other pulsars in binaries, seen with X-ray telescopes, which you'll meet in the next section.

20.6
Black holes:
The ultimate corpses

A significant minority of stars in the Milky Way have masses greater than the neutron star limit of about 5 solar masses. Assume such stars do not lose enough mass during their evolution to go below this upper mass limit for a neutron star. Further assume all thermonuclear reactions have ceased, so there is no pressure to support the star. Now ask the question: Will there be any barrier to the collapse of this material with mass greater than 5 solar masses?

There is no barrier to collapse. The crush of gravity overwhelms all outward forces, including the repulsive forces between particles with the same charge. No material can withstand this final crushing point of matter. The collapse cannot be halted by any known force; the volume of the star will continue to decrease until it reaches zero. The density of the star will increase until it becomes infinite. (Neither of these events can be true of a *real* object in this universe.) This theoretical collapse to a singular point of zero volume and infinite density, or a *singularity*, marks a crucial limitation in our understanding of the physics of the universe. Because a singularity grows out of the general theory of relativity, its theoretical existence signals a possible flaw in Einstein's grand scheme.

Before a mass becomes a singularity, bizarre events occur. As the density increases, the paths of light rays emitted from the star are bent more and more from straight lines from the star's surface. Eventually the density reaches such a high value that the escape velocity from the star is greater than the speed of light. The photons are trapped by the intense gravitational field in an orbit around the star. Any additional photons emitted after the star attains this critical density can never reach an outside observer (Fig. 20.29). The star is engulfed in a *black hole*.

The Schwarzschild radius / Let me describe the meaning of *black* in black hole in terms of escape velocity (Focus 13). Having watched rocket launches, you probably realize that for an object to leave the earth permanently it must

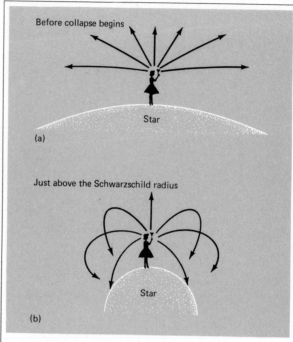

20.29

The trapping of light by the collapse of a mass into a black hole. Imagine a person standing on the star's surface with a wide-beam flashlight (a). When much larger than its black hole size (Schwarzschild radius), the mass has a low enough gravitational field so that the light leaves the star on straight-line paths. As the star collapses, the intensity of gravity at its surface increases so that the light paths are bent. When the star is just a little larger than its Schwarzschild radius (b), all the light paths—except for the one straight up—are bent enough so that the photons fall back to the star's surface. When the star is smaller than its Schwarzschild radius, even that straight-up photon returns. (Adapted from a diagram by W. Kaufmann)

leave the earth's surface with a minimum velocity—the escape velocity from the earth, about 11 km/sec. Imagine that you could squeeze the earth so that it would become smaller and denser. Its escape velocity would increase. Imagine the earth compressed until its escape

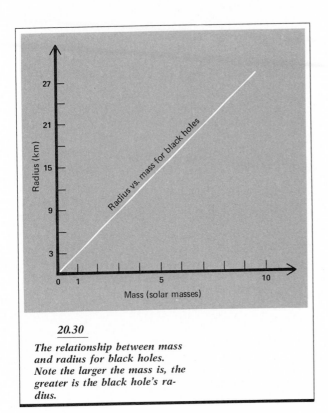

20.30

The relationship between mass and radius for black holes. Note the larger the mass is, the greater is the black hole's radius.

velocity equaled the velocity of light. Then nothing—*not even light*—emitted at its surface could escape into space. Nothing gets away, so the earth appears black to an outside observer.

How small must a mass become to be dense enough to trap even light? Einstein's general theory of relativity provides an answer. Just after the general theory's publication, the German astrophysicist Karl Schwarzschild (1873–1917) calculated this critical size, now called the *Schwarzschild radius*. For the sun the Schwarzschild radius is about 3 km—very much smaller than the typical sunspot! When compressed to this size, the sun would have a density of about 10^{16} g/cc. (Present physics cannot tell us the properties of matter at this density.) The mass of any object, in *solar masses*, directly gives its Schwarzschild radius. For 1 solar mass, it's 3 km; for 2 solar masses, 6 km; for 10 solar masses, 30 km; and so on (Fig. 20.30).

How can a star get as small as its Schwarzschild radius? Two ways are possible. First: runaway gravitational collapse. If you put together more mass than 5 solar masses, it must eventually squeeze itself into a black hole. Nothing

known—not even the hardness of matter itself—can stop this final crushing. Second: a supernova. A star's self-destruction can crunch matter into a size smaller than its Schwarzschild radius, even if its mass would otherwise allow it to be a white dwarf or neutron star.

That's how black holes may form. Once a black hole forms, what happens to the matter that makes it? Einstein's general theory predicts that the matter keeps collapsing gravitationally inside the black hole until it has *no volume*. But it still has mass, so its density is infinite. This theoretical end to runaway gravitational collapse is called a *singularity*. The matter has literally squeezed itself so that it occupies no space. Yet it's still there. What a paradox! How can matter *not* take up space? The general theory of relativity points to the formation of a singularity, cloaked in the center of a black hole, as the natural end of gravitational collapse.

Journey into a black hole / Put aside the puzzle of the singularity for a moment and consider the theoretical properties of a black hole, both inside and outside. Keep in mind that a black hole marks a weird region of spacetime. A person falling into a black hole meets a fate an outside observer cannot ever find out about—unless the outside observer drops in, too. (One way you can find out if a singularity exists in the center of a black hole is to jump in. Unfortunately, you'll never be able to come back to tell others what you've found.)

Just for fun, take an imaginary journey into a black hole. You'll follow the adventures of a crazy astronaut who takes the plunge and compare this trip with what an outsider observer sees of it.

You and a friend start out in a spaceship orbiting a far distance away from a 10-solar-mass black hole (Fig. 20.31). Nothing peculiar here. The ship orbits the black hole in accordance with Kepler's laws, as it would any ordinary mass. In fact, Kepler's third law and the spaceship's orbit permit you to measure the hole's mass. But if you look hard for the mass, you won't see anything.

Your friend volunteers to hop in. She takes with her a laser light and Accutron watch. You and she synchronize watches. Once a second, according to her watch, she will send a laser flash back to you.

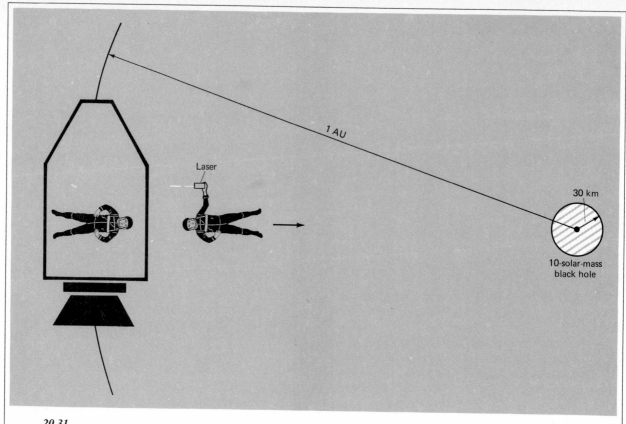

20.31

Orbiting a 10-solar-mass black hole. The black hole itself has a radius of about 30 km. At a distance of 1 AU you could not see the black hole. Your orbit would be the same as that around any object of 10 solar masses at a distance of 1 AU. That is, you can use the period and distance with Kepler's third law to infer the mass of the black hole.

Down she goes! For a long time as she falls toward the black hole, nothing strange happens. But as she gets closer, stronger and stronger tidal gravitational forces (Focus 25) stretch her out (if she falls feet first) from head to toes. Also, another tidal force squeezes her together, mostly at the shoulders. (You feel such tidal forces on the earth, but they are too weak to bother you.) Near a black hole, tidal forces grow enormously. An ordinary human being would be ripped apart about 3000 km from a 10-solar-mass black hole. Suppose your friend is indestructible, so she can continue her trip.

Down she drops. The tidal forces get stronger fast and make her more uncomfortable. But nothing strange has struck her. Every second on the dot she sends out a blast of laser light. Peering down, she can just make out a black region in the sky. (A 10-solar-mass black hole has a radius of only 30 km.) Then it happens—she crosses the Schwarzschild radius! But nothing new happens to her. No solid substance, no signs mark the edge of the black hole. However, no amount of energy can push

her out of the black hole; she has crossed a one-way gate in spacetime. The trip now swiftly ends for your foolish friend. Quickly—in about 10^{-5} sec after she crosses the Schwarzschild radius—she crashes into a singularity (if it exists!) Crushed to zero volume, she is destroyed. Even if a singularity does not lie in the black hole's center, the mass that made the black hole probably does. So she would smash into it. End of friend's trip.

But what of your view, back in the spaceship, of your friend's adventure? You would *never* see her final destruction; in fact, you'd not even see her fall into the black hole. As she dropped closer to the black hole, you'd notice that the light from her laser was red-shifted, with the shift increasing as she fell closer to the black hole. (The light must work against gravity to get to you, so it loses energy and increases in wavelength—Focus 49.) Also, you notice that the time between laser flashes increases. What's happening? Compared with your watch, your friend's watch appears to slow down as she gets into regions of stronger gravity. Your watch and

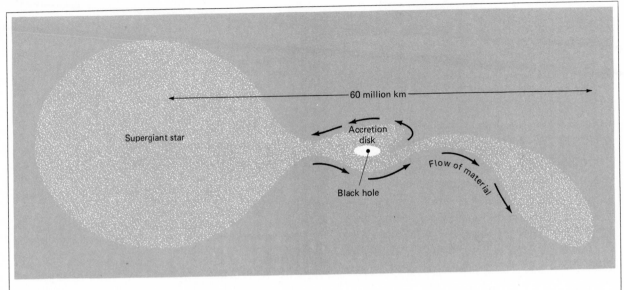

20.32

A model for a black hole as an X-ray source. The key point is that the X-ray source is part of a binary system, with a black hole coupled by gravity to a supergiant (or giant) star. Material from the supergiant star flows to the black hole, where it is caught in an accretion disk around the black hole before it plunges into the hole and out of this universe. As the material falls into the disk, it heats up to temperatures of millions of Kelvins and emits X-rays. (Adapted from a diagram by K. Thorne)

hers disagree about how long it takes her to travel to the black hole.

As she comes closer to the Schwarzschild radius, the watches get more and more out of synch. The times between your reception of her flashes stretches out. In fact, that last laser burst sent out just as she crossed the Schwarzschild radius would take an *infinite* time to reach you. To you, her fall would seem to grow slower and slower as she got closer to the black hole, but she would never appear to fall into it. Time slows down so much that, near a black hole, it seems to be frozen. In addition, the light gets more and more red-shifted until you can no longer detect it.

A black hole practices cosmic censorship. It prevents you from seeing your friend even fall into it. Light—our only astronomical communication medium—is cut off by the black hole. You never know the fate of your friend inside.

How can you see a black hole? / With difficulty! Light emitted inside cannot get out. Light sent out close by is strongly red-shifted, so it's hard to detect. In addition, a black hole is

small, only a few kilometers in size. So you'll have a hard time seeing an isolated black hole.

But a black hole surrounded by clouds of material might be visible. Any matter falling into a black hole gains energy and heats up. (It's also squeezed by tidal forces.) Heated enough, the atoms are ionized. Gravity accelerates the ionized gas, and it emits electromagnetic radiation. If heated to a few million Kelvins or so, the gas can emit X-rays. As the material flows toward the maw of the black hole, it piles up into a disk of material around it—called an *accretion disk*. In a fatal whirlpool the material in the disk swirls around the black hole, slipping in closer until it is finally swallowed up. Before the plunge, X-rays emitted by the material in the accretion disk can escape into space (Fig. 20.32). So X-ray sources are good candidates for black holes.

The Uhuru satellite, launched in 1970 and designed to observe X-ray sources, detected about 160 strong X-ray objects (Fig. 20.33). Some of these X-ray sources are prime candidates for black holes because they are binary—

516

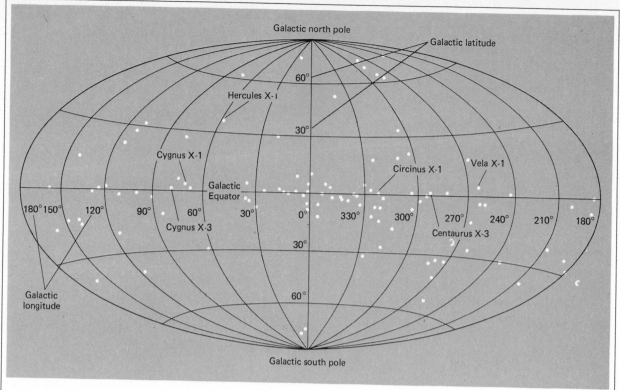

20.33

A map of the location in the sky of strong X-ray sources detected by the Uhuru satellite. Note that many of the sources are concentrated in the galactic plane, an indication that they are in the Galaxy. The strongest sources are named. (Adapted from a diagram by H. Gursky)

TABLE 20.3   Some binary X-ray sources

Name (constellation)	Binary period (days)	Characteristics of X-rays	Characteristics of visible star
Cygnus X-1	5.6	Varies in duration from 0.001 to 1 sec	Blue supergiant of about 20 solar masses
Centaurus X-32	2.087	X-ray eclipses with duration of 0.488 day	Blue giant of about 16 solar masses
Small Magellanic Cloud X-1	3.89	X-ray eclipses with 0.6 day duration	Blue supergiant of about 25 solar masses
Vela X-1	8.95	X-ray eclipses with 1.7 day duration; flares lasting a few hours	Blue supergiant of about 25 solar masses
Circinus X-1	longer than 15	X-ray eclipses lasting about a day	Not yet found
Hercules X-1	1.7	X-ray eclipses lasting 0.24 day	Companion HZ Her about 2 solar masses
Cygnus X-3	4.8	4.8-h variations, no eclipse	None visible; infrared source with 4.8-h variation

SOURCE   Adapted from tables by H. Gursky, E. P. J. van den Heuvel, S. Rappaport and P. C. Joss.

the X-ray source and a normal star orbit a common center of mass (Table 20.3).

Why are *binary* X-ray sources most suspect? Imagine a black hole orbiting with a giant or supergiant star. Suppose they are very close together so that their orbital period is a few days or so. The star has a huge, distended atmosphere—perhaps a thousand times the size of our sun—and material from this atmosphere can be sucked up by the black hole (Fig. 20.32). Falling around the black hole, the material emits X-rays. Only a small region around the black hole gives off X-rays, and because the material may fall in sporadically, you might expect the intensity of the X-rays to vary quickly. Also, imagine the black hole and star with their orbital plane in our line of sight. When the black hole went behind the star, its X-rays would be cut off. In this case you would see an eclipsing X-ray binary system.

Warning: I've used a black hole as the X-ray source. But *any* superdense object into which material is falling will emit X-rays, for example, a neutron star.

So a sign of a possible black hole is a rapidly varying X-ray source, which may be eclipsed at regular intervals. Have we seen such variable X-ray sources? Yes! (See Table 20.3). But are any of them *really* black holes?

Is Cygnus X-1 a black hole? / So far I've treated the *theoretical* properties of black holes. But these might be no more than gleams in the eyes of astrophysicists. To prove the reality of black holes you need to observe one. To date, the most likely candidate is Cygnus X-1, a strong X-ray source in the constellation Cygnus (Fig. 20.34).

Cygnus X-1 emits about 4×10^{30} W in X-rays. Observations have shown that Cygnus X-1 flickers rapidly, in less than 0.001 sec. This observation indicates that the X-ray emitting region must be less than 0.001 light second in size (less than 300 km). In 1971 radio astronomers discovered radio bursts from Cygnus X-1 and were able to pin down its location better than the X-ray astronomers. In the most likely place for Cygnus X-1 lies an *O*-supergiant star, that is, a hot, blue star (Fig. 20.35).

Optical astronomers got into the act and found that the dark lines in the spectrum of the blue supergiant went through periodic Doppler

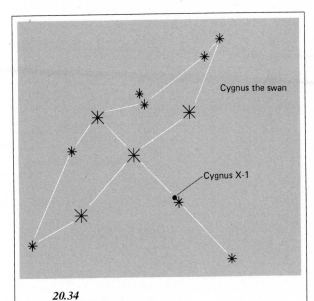

20.34

The position of Cygnus X-1 in the constellation Cygnus, the Swan, sometimes called the Northern Cross.

20.35

The arrow indicates the blue supergiant star (called HDE 226868) about which the X-ray source Cygnus X-1 orbits. (Courtesy J. Kristian and Palomar Observatory, California Institute of Technology)

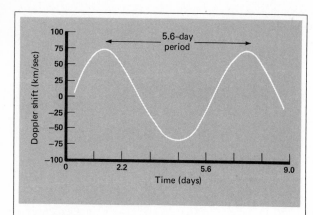

20.36

The orbital period of Cygnus X-1, inferred from the Doppler shift in the spectral lines of the blue supergiant star about which Cygnus X-1 orbits. Both the X-ray source and the supergiant star revolve around a common center of mass once every 5.6 days. This orbital motion results in a Doppler shift that can be measured with a spectroscope. (Based on observations by C. Bolton)

shifts in 5.6 days (Fig. 20.36). So the supergiant orbits with the X-ray source about a common center of mass every 5.6 days. The supergiant has a massive but optically invisible companion—Cygnus X-1.

Recall that only for binaries can you directly find the masses of stars (Focus 39). But you need to know the orbital period *and* the separation of the stars from the center of mass. The distances from the center of mass can be worked out correctly only if you know the orbital tilt with respect to the line of sight. In this regard the mass of Cygnus X-1 is hard to find out, because it has not been found to eclipse, so you can't pin down its orbital inclination.

The best you can do is make reasonable estimates. Blue supergiant stars are typically 15–40 solar masses. The orbital period and the Doppler shifts (from which the orbit's size is inferred) give the sum of the masses of the supergiant and the X-ray source, uncertain by the amount of orbital tilt. A study of the brightness of the supergiant indicates that it varies a little in 5.6 days. If due to partial eclipses, this leads to an inferred orbital tilt of about 30°. If true,

then Cygnus X-1 has a mass of at least 4–5 solar masses, possibly as great as 14 solar masses, and most likely about 9 solar masses. If so, Cygnus X-1 must be a black hole, provided the limit for a neutron star is 5 solar masses.

Many astronomers feel that there is strong evidence here for a black hole. To sum up the chain of inference:

1 Cygnus X-1 must be a small, dense object onto which matter is falling.
2 The blue supergiant is the star about which Cygnus X-1 revolves.
3 From the Doppler shift of its spectral lines, the blue supergiant (and so the X-ray source) has an orbital period of 5.6 days.
4 The blue supergiant has a mass of 15–40 solar masses.
5 If the blue supergiant has a mass of 20 solar masses, Cygnus X-1 has at least 4–5 solar masses and more likely 9–14 solar masses.
6 A small object with a mass greater than about 5 solar masses is a black hole.
7 Therefore Cygnus X-1 is a black hole.

Not all astrophysicists accept this conclusion. Note that the evidence is very indirect. For example, if the blue supergiant has a larger share of the mass, then Cyg X-1 could be an ordinary neutron star.

Is Centaurus X-3 a black hole? / Cygnus X-1 may be a black hole. What about the other X-ray sources?

Take a close look at Centaurus X-3 (abbreviated Cen X-3). The Uhuru satellite showed that this X-ray source pulses every 4.84 sec (Fig. 20.37). Also, long-term observations revealed that X-ray eclipses take place every 2.087 days and last about 0.5 day. So for Cen X-3 the orbit is tilted so that its plane lies in our line of sight. In the summer of 1973 Vojtek Krzeminski, a Polish astronomer, found a faint star at the X-ray source position that varies in light in the same period as Cen X-3. The star turned out to be a blue giant about 25,000 ly away.

This information all falls into place with a simple model for the Cen X-3 binary system (Fig. 20.38). Cen X-3 itself moves in an almost circular orbit around the blue giant star at 415 km/sec. Its orbit has a radius of about 11 million km—closer to the blue giant star than Mercury is to our sun. At this close distance,

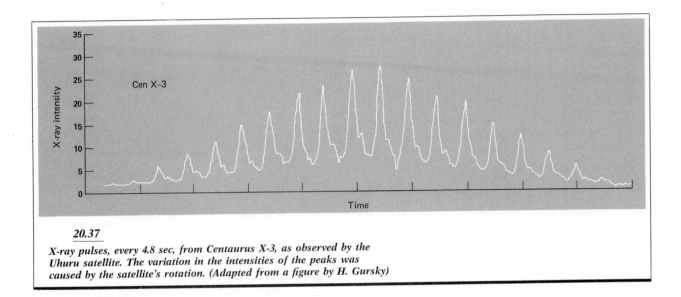

20.37

X-ray pulses, every 4.8 sec, from Centaurus X-3, as observed by the Uhuru satellite. The variation in the intensities of the peaks was caused by the satellite's rotation. (Adapted from a figure by H. Gursky)

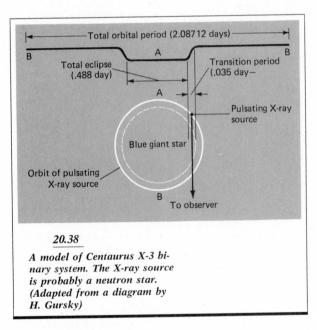

20.38

A model of Centaurus X-3 binary system. The X-ray source is probably a neutron star. (Adapted from a diagram by H. Gursky)

mass flowing from the giant star is picked up by the X-ray source. About every 2 days the X-ray source orbits behind the giant star as seen from the earth, and an X-ray eclipse happens.

Is Cen X-3 a black hole or a neutron star? That depends on its mass. Because Cen X-3 eclipses, you can pin down its mass more definitely than that of Cygnus X-1. Yoram Avni and John Bahcall have concluded that Cen X-3 has a mass between 0.6 and 1.1 solar masses—so it is not a black hole. The only real option is a neutron star.

The fact that Cen X-3 is an X-ray pulsar also supports a neutron star model, in analogy with the model of radio pulsars as magnetic neutron stars. The X-ray pulses might arise from accreting matter channeled into the magnetic polar regions by the intense magnetic field.

The evolution of binary X-ray systems / How to end up with an X-ray source—black hole or neutron star—in a binary system? One answer relates to the basic fact of stellar evolution: The more massive a star is, the faster it evolves (and so the shorter its lifetime). With this fact in mind, I'll examine some facets of one possible model for the evolution of a binary X-ray system.

Start with an ordinary binary containing a 20-solar-mass star and a 6-solar-mass star (stage 1 in Fig. 20.39). The more massive star evolves faster, becomes a red supergiant star, and fills its Roche lobe (stage 2). Matter streams from the more massive star to the less massive one. When the flow stops, the stars have switched roles (stage 3)—the 6-solar-mass star is now a 20.6 one, the other, a 5.4-solar-mass star which is essentially the core of the former 20-solar-mass star. This core supernovas (stage 4); it leaves behind a neutron star or a black hole (stage 5). The other star now evolves rapidly (because of its increased mass). It first loses matter by a stellar wind. Any of this material falling onto the black hole generates X-rays (stage 6). Later, the star expands until it fills its Roche lobe (stage 7). Material can then flow

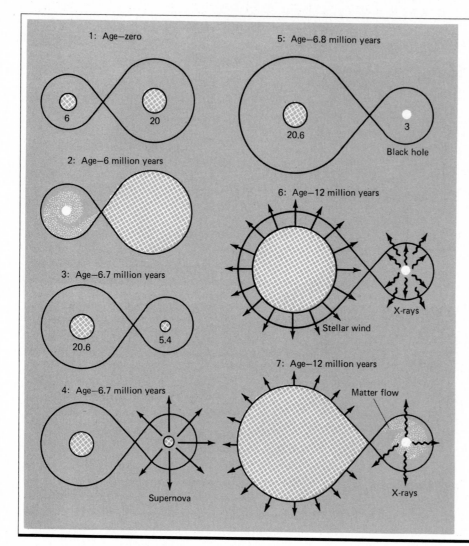

1: Age—zero

6   20

2: Age—6 million years

3: Age—6.7 million years

20.6   5.4

4: Age—6.7 million years

Supernova

5: Age—6.8 million years

20.6   3

Black hole

6: Age—12 million years

Stellar wind   X-rays

7: Age—12 million years

Matter flow   X-rays

20.39

A model for the evolution of a close binary system with massive stars. Imagine a binary system starting out with 20- and 6-solar-mass stars. The more massive star evolves quickly and expands in size, and material from it flows to its less massive companion (1 and 2). This companion gains the bulk of the material and becomes the massive star (20.6 solar masses) in the system (3). Meanwhile, the hot core of the other star supernovas (4) to leave behind a black hole (5). The companion then evolves, expanding to a supergiant with a strong stellar wind. Matter flows from the supergiant star to the black hole, and X-rays result from the infall of material into the black hole (6 and 7). (Based on calculations by E. P. J. van den Heuvel, C. de Loore, and J.-P. de Greve)

along the gravitational bridge to the black hole to emit X-rays.

What next? The massive supergiant should also supernova. That leaves a binary black hole system or binary neutron star system or binary black hole-neutron star system. In all these cases the matter is locked up. So the binary no longer emits X-rays. Note that the X-ray emitting stages don't last long—at most a few million years or so.

X-ray bursters: Active black holes or neutron stars? You have seen that X-ray astronomy played a key role in uncovering black hole candidates. But the story does not end with Cygnus X-1. In fact, it has gotten more curious since the discovery of *X-ray bursters.*

As you might guess from the name, X-ray bursters are set apart from other X-ray sources by their emission of brief but powerful bursts of X-rays (Fig. 20.40). The bursts may peak for several seconds. Some bursters repeat their X-ray blasts at more or less regular intervals of a few hours or a few days. Others fire off in a rapid sequence like a machine gun, shooting off several thousand bursts in a day. A 10-second burst carries as much X-ray energy as the sun gives off in a week at *all* wavelengths! Here's the story of two X-ray bursters.

The *Uhuru* X-ray sky survey detected a source, called 3U 1820-30 ("3U" means the Third *Uhuru* catalog) that lies near the center of the globular cluster NGC 6624. In 1975 astronomers

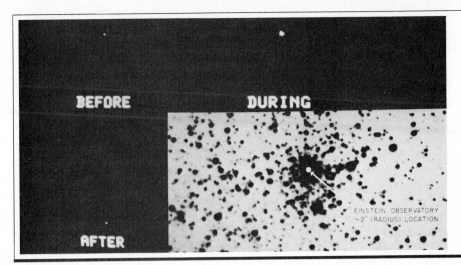

20.40

X-ray burst (before, during, and after) from a globular cluster (Terzian 2), observed by the Einstein X-Ray Observatory. (Courtesy J. Grindley, Center for Astrophysics)

discovered a brief burst of X-ray from NGC 6624. Other X-ray satellites examined the source and confirmed its position very close to the core of NGC 6624. X-ray astronomers then looked at some new and old data to find bursts that lasted about 10 sec. Remarkably, the bursts seemed to recur every 4.4 h.

A photograph of the core of NGC 6624 taken with the Cerro Tololo 4-m telescope shows a dozen or so red supergiant stars in NGC 6624 crowded into a region only 1 ly in diameter (Fig. 20.41). If you assume for every supergiant the cluster contains roughly 200 stars too faint to show in the photo, you end up with 2000 stars packed into a region 1 ly in radius—a million times the density of stars in the sun's neighborhood!

Meanwhile, X-ray astronomers at MIT, headed by Walter Lewin, discovered a more curious burster, called MXB 1730-335 ("M" stands for MIT, "XB" for X-ray burster). This burster pumps out blasts in rapid-fire succession as fast as every 10 sec. With the position of MXB 1730-335 known, the Cerro Tololo 4-m took infrared photos of the region. (Why infrared? To cut through the dust in the Milky Way.) It showed a vague blob of stars at the burster's position. Meanwhile, extensive infrared observations at the burster's position indicated that the source was a distant (30,000 ly away) globular cluster with a highly concentrated core. (At this distance each burst emits about 10^{31} W.) The cores of NGC 6624 and the cluster containing MXB 1730-335 looked much the same.

What do these observations mean? Both bursters just described lie in globular clusters. That fact presents a problem. Globular clusters

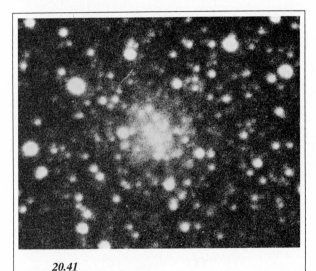

20.41

An infrared picture of NGC 6624. (Courtesy W. Liller and J. Gindley, Center for Astrophysics)

contain little gas and dust compared with galactic clusters. So the material needed to feed a condensed object to produce X-rays by accretion around a condensed mass is not so available as it is in other parts of the Galaxy. Many models have been proposed for X-ray bursters in globulars. Some use black holes, others, neutron stars. One pictures the condensed object in a binary system with a low-mass red giant star. Matter flowing sporadically from the red giant generates the X-ray burst.

To date, it appears likely that neutron stars fit best to explain bursters' X-ray characteristics, which are: rise to peak in less than a second, duration of about 10 sec, interval between bursts

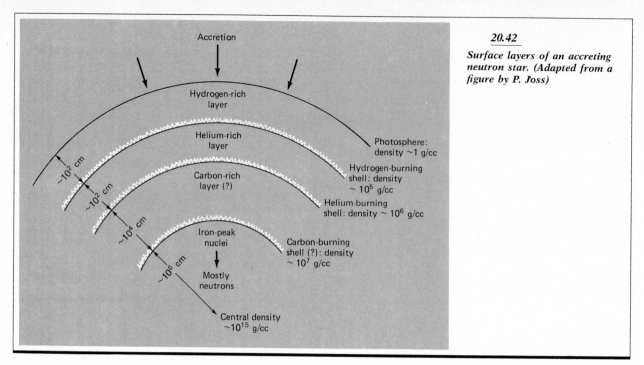

20.42

Surface layers of an accreting neutron star. (Adapted from a figure by P. Joss)

Accretion

Hydrogen-rich layer

Helium-rich layer

Carbon-rich layer (?)

Iron-peak nuclei

Mostly neutrons

~10^2 cm

~10^2 cm

~10^4 cm

~10^6 cm

Photosphere: density ~1 g/cc

Hydrogen-burning shell: density ~ 10^5 g/cc

Helium-burning shell: density ~ 10^6 g/cc

Carbon-burning shell (?): density ~ 10^7 g/cc

Central density ~10^{15} g/cc

of 10^3–10^4 min (about 2 h), a blackbody effective temperature at maximum of about 3×10^7 K. The bursters appear concentrated near the galactic center; if they are 30,000 ly away, one burst has a luminosity of a few times 10^{31} W. An effective temperature of 3×10^7 K requires a blackbody of roughly 9 km radius to produce 2–3×10^{31} W. This hints circumstantially that bursters are neutron stars.

Paul Joss of MIT has developed a model of helium-burning flashes on an accreting neutron star that accounts for a good number of burster properties. He starts out with a neutron star, whose mass is 1.41 solar masses and a radius of 6.57 km. He lets hydrogen and helium fall onto the neutron star at a rate of roughly 10^{17} g/sec to build an envelope on the neutron star (Fig. 20.42). As the matter accretes, the temperature rises to 2×10^9 K at the base of the helium layer. The helium ignites in a flash (Fig. 20.43), producing some 2.5×10^{31} W just 0.2 sec after the fusion reactions begin. With continual accretion, the flashes can recur every 15 h. These calculated characteristics are much like those observed. The model does not rely on any special source for the accreted material; it may come from a binary companion. This model is similar to that for novas (Section 20.3). The differences are: the material falls onto a neutron star, not a white dwarf, and the temperatures are higher, so that the energy comes out as X-rays, rather than as visible light.

Beyond the black hole / Does a singularity lie in the center of every black hole? Must it?

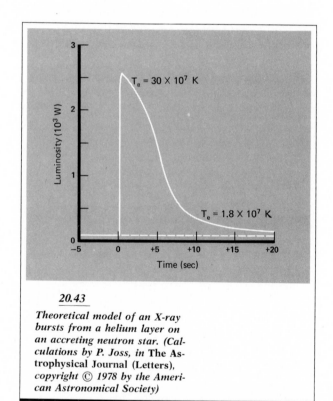

20.43

*Theoretical model of an X-ray bursts from a helium layer on an accreting neutron star. (Calculations by P. Joss, in **The Astrophysical Journal (Letters)**, copyright © 1978 by the American Astronomical Society)*

Einstein's theory says "yes." Yet a singularity rubs physicists the wrong way. How can *something* end up in no space? People have taken the prediction of the singularity as a sign of the breakdown of the general theory of relativity. Efforts are being made to fix the theory up.

Roger Penrose, a British theoretician, has developed a theorem of the possibilities of what happens in black holes. Three ends are pre-

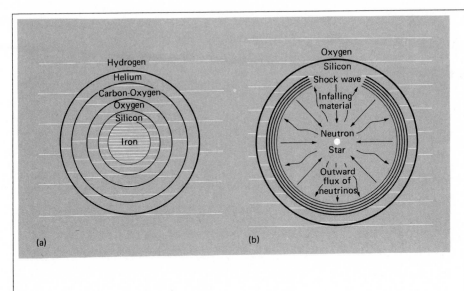

20.44

A possible model of the structure of a massive star as a supernova. This diagram shows just the very central regions, not the entire star. Just before it becomes a supernova (a) the star's core consists of layers that come from thermonuclear burning in shells. The core's center is iron, which may suddenly disintegrate into helium. This process soaks up energy and causes the star to collapse rapidly (b). The collapse heats up the central region, causing explosive ignition of a variety of fusion reactions that blasts off the star's mass in a tremendous shock wave. The very center implodes to form a neutron star. (Adapted from a diagram by C. Wheeler)

dicted. One, the singularity *does* form. Two, a black hole joins its local region of spacetime with another region of spacetime in our universe via a tunnel in spacetime. Three, the black hole connects our universe with "another universe." These three fates are theoretical (we're not completely certain that black holes exist!), but they do derive directly from general relativity, not science fiction.

20.7
The manufacture
of heavy elements

A massive star dies in a supernova. The blast can leave behind a neutron star or a black hole. So a massive star digs its own grave. Does any good come of its death? Yes. For without massive stars dying violently, neither you nor I nor the green, green grass would be here.

An extravagant claim? Not really, if you investigate where the elements in the universe are made. Start off with hydrogen (which comes from the big bang). Recall (Chapter 19) that ordinary stars fuse hydrogen to helium by the PP reactions and CNO cycle in their normal lives. After that, a solar-mass star converts helium to carbon by the triple-alpha reaction. But there, for our sun, thermonuclear reactions will end. The sun's core will not grow hot enough to burn carbon.

Notice that in the sequence of thermonu-

clear energy generation (look back at Table 19.2) the ashes of one set of reactions become fresh fuel for the next. Each step up in the fusion chain requires higher temperatures to overcome the greater repulsive electrical force of nuclei with more protons. These fusion reactions—carbon to oxygen, neon, sodium, and magnesium; onward to silicon burning—can fire only in massive stars. The end to the fusion chain comes with iron, the most tightly bound of the normal nuclei. Iron rests at the bottom of an energy well. To split iron into lighter elements takes energy. To fuse it to heavier ones also needs energy put in. So nuclear reaction naturally stops at iron in very massive stars—greater than about 20 solar masses.

But the elements we know do not end at iron (Appendix G); many are heavier. Where and when are they manufactured? A supernova explosion acts as nature's workshop for forging some elements heavier than iron.

Here's one possible model of how a supernova happens (Fig. 20.44). Imagine a very massive star with a core of iron. Its interior temperature decreases from the core outward. Because of this temperature decline, you expect the star's interior to be layered. Around the iron core is a silicon layer; here temperatures did not get high enough to fuse iron. Around that layer is one of oxygen; here temperatures were too low to fuse oxygen to silicon.

focus 51

HEAVY ELEMENT SYNTHESIS IN SUPERNOVAS

In the periodic table (Appendix G), the isotopes fall into three basic classes: (1) those that have equal numbers of protons and neutrons, (2) those that have more neutrons than protons (called neutron-rich*), and (3) those that have more protons than neutrons (called* proton-rich*). These isotopes were probably formed by different processes, or combinations of processes—especially the elements heavier than iron. And in a supernova, conditions are ripe for heavy-element synthesis.*

Before this description, recall that a neutron by itself is not *a stable particle. It disintegrates (in about 17 min) into a proton, an electron, and an antineutrino. This process is called* beta decay, *because at one time electrons were called beta particles. Unstable isotopes with many neutrons can undergo beta decay, usually within a few hours of their formation. When an isotope beta decays, it essentially loses a neutron and gains a proton; so it is transformed into another element.*

Back to heavy-element synthesis. Two basic processes involve neutrons. In one, called the rapid process, *neutrons are captured by nuclei* faster *than the beta-decay rate, so nuclei are formed that are more and more neutron-rich. In the other, called* slow process, *nuclei capture neutrons* slower *than the beta-decay rate; essentially, protons are added to the nuclei. In either case, the capture of neutrons is relatively easy because neutrons have no electric charge and are not, like protons, repelled by nuclei.*

A supernova explosion generates huge amounts of high-energy neutrons, which bombard any remaining nuclei. Neutron-rich isotopes are then built up by the rapid process. This rapid process buildup produces heavy elements such as uranium and thorium.

A specific example: transforming lead-206 (^{206}Pb) to other isotopes of lead and finally to bismuth-209 (^{209}Bi). See Fig. 1. Sock ^{206}Pb

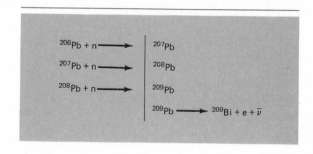

$$^{206}Pb + n \longrightarrow \; ^{207}Pb$$
$$^{207}Pb + n \longrightarrow \; ^{208}Pb$$
$$^{208}Pb + n \longrightarrow \; ^{209}Pb$$
$$^{209}Pb \longrightarrow \; ^{209}Bi + e + \bar{\nu}$$

1

The synthesis of isotopes of lead and bismuth by neutron capture and beta decay.

with a neutron; it becomes ^{207}Pb. Hit it with a neutron, and so on, up to ^{209}Pb. Each heavier isotope of lead is less stable than the previous one, and ^{209}Pb is so unstable that it decays rapidly (by beta decay) to ^{209}Bi (and an electron and an antineutrino). Then the ^{209}Bi can absorb neutrons and build up to isotopes and the next element, and so on.

This process can produce neutron-rich nuclei. Proton-rich nuclei, which are in the minority, cannot be produced in the same manner. How is not clear. One possibility: Protons may reach high enough energies in supernovas that they can overcome electrical repulsion and penetrate some nuclei.

Once the core ends up as iron it must contract, for the fusion fires have failed. Relentlessly the core attains higher temperatures and densities. When the core gets to about 5 billion K, the photons there have so much energy that they can penetrate the iron nuclei and break them down into helium. As the iron disintegrates into helium, large amounts of heat are used up. The core collapses suddenly. But you should know by now what this will mean: The gravitational contraction pumps heat into the material.

Two important events occur in this collapse. First, protons and neutrons released by the disintegration of nuclei in the core pelt and penetrate remaining nuclei. These can capture neutrons and be transformed to heavier elements (Focus 51). Second, all the elements lighter than iron fall into the core and heat up. Suddenly, ignition temperatures of many fusion reactions are reached. They turn on explosively. A blast shock wave from this explosive ignition bullies its way outward from the core (Fig. 20.44). It carries material with it into the interstellar medium—material enriched with heavy elements. This material will form new stars and planets.

What about the remaining core? Hammered by the explosion, it probably forms a neutron star.

Because of the emphasis on nucleosynthesis in supernovas, you might think that *only* supernovas make elements heavier than iron. That's not the case. Red giants can also make some of these during their normal lives. While a red giant undergoes helium shell burning, small numbers of neutrons are produced and added at slow rates to iron to make heavier elements. Although this process is slow, the red giant stage lasts long enough (100,000 years or so) to synthesize an appreciable amount of heavy elements. Nucleosynthesis in red giants generates many of the elements lighter than lead but heavier than iron. Supernovas are required, however, to synthesize elements heavier than lead, such as uranium and thorium.

Now to support the claim about you, me, and the green, green grass. Life as we know it (Chapter 22) is built on carbon atoms. Stars like our sun can fuse carbon, *but* it remains locked in a corpse after death—a white dwarf. The material flung out by the sun after it becomes a red giant comes just from its outer layers. Here

TABLE 20.4 Death of stars

Mass (solar masses)	Normal life	Death
0.1–0.5	M-stars	White dwarf
0.5–4	K–A-stars	Red giant, mass loss, white dwarf
4–10	A–B-stars	Red giant, supernova, neutron star
10–20	B-stars	Red giant, supernova, neutron star or black hole
20–60	O-stars	Supernova, black hole or neutron star

SOURCE Adapted from tables by A. G. W. Cameron and J. C. Wheeler.

no fusion reactions have gone on. So this material has pretty much the same composition it started with. Only a massive star in a supernova spews into the interstellar medium newly made heavy elements. So if all stars had about the sun's mass, no carbon would get out into the interstellar medium to end up in living organisms on a planet. Your body (and mine) is mostly recycled stardust. So is the grass under your feet.

Stars die to seed new life. That I find the most incredible connection of cosmic evolution.

SUMMARY

How a star dies depends on its mass at its time of death (Table 20.4). If its final mass is less than 1.4 solar masses, its corpse takes the form of a white dwarf. If it is greater than 1.4 but less than roughly 5 solar masses, gravity crushes it to a neutron star. In either case gravity does not defeat the star completely. But if it has greater than about 5 solar masses, gravity wins out absolutely and forms a black hole. (Keep in mind that the minimum mass needed to form black holes is not accurately known now.)

Astronomers have observed two of the three possible stellar corpses: white dwarfs and neu-

tron stars. White dwarfs are seen directly with optical telescopes; they signal their presence by their high surface temperatures and low luminosities. Neutron stars are seen in their guise as pulsars, some as X-ray binaries, and possibly as X-ray bursters. The evidence for black holes is not so good. But Cygnus X-1 presents a strong case as a black hole in a binary system.

Violence marks the death of stars. For stars of about 1 solar mass, the death rattle involves only a small fraction of the star's mass. For massive stars, almost all the star participates in the cataclysm of a supernova. This destructive violence has constructive ends. Heavy elements are made and sent into the interstellar medium from which stars and their planets are born. So stars go from dust to dust again.

STUDY EXERCISES

1   In a short paragraph describe the primary characteristics of a white dwarf. (*Objective 1*)

2   In a short paragraph describe the chief features of a neutron star to a friend who has not studied astronomy. (*Objective 1*)

3   What observational evidence do we have for the actual existence of neutron stars and white dwarfs? (*Objectives 1 and 2*)

4   In what way does a black hole practice censorship? (*Objectives 3 and 4*)

5   What evidence leads some astronomers to believe that Cygnus X-1 is a black hole? (*Objective 6*)

6   If a black hole is "black," how can it give off X-rays? (*Objective 5*)

7   Look around you. Of the items you see, what would *not* be there if supernovas didn't occur? (*Objectives 9 and 11*)

8   Compare and contrast a model for a nova and an X-ray burster. (*Objective 8*)

9   If you were to observe a nova and a supernova with an optical telescope, how would their characteristics differ? Be similar? (*Objective 7*)

10   Why can't you find out what happens inside a black hole? (*Objectives 3 and 4*)

BEYOND THIS BOOK . . .

For an advanced article on the deaths of stars, try "Endpoints of Stellar Evolution" by A. G. W. Cameron in *Frontiers of Astrophysics*, edited by E. Avrett (Harvard University Press, Cambridge, Mass., 1976). In the same book you'll find "Neutron Stars, Black Holes, and Supernovae" by H. Gursky; it's rather technical.

K. S. Thorne describes "The Search for Black Holes" in *Scientific American*, December 1974, p. 32.

H. Gursky and E. P. J. van den Heuvel present a comprehensive picture of "X-Ray Emitting Double Stars" in *Scientific American*, March 1975, p. 24.

We haven't had a supernova in our Galaxy recently, but we do see them in others. See "Supernovas in Other Galaxies" by R. P. Krishner, *Scientific American*, December 1976, p. 88.

You can find more information about black holes in relativity theory in *The Cosmic Frontiers of General Relativity* by W. J. Kaufmann III (Little, Brown, Boston, 1977).

For an up-to-date view on X-ray bursters, read "The Sources of Celestial X-Ray Bursts" by W. Lewin, *Scientific American*, May 1981, p. 72.

LEARNING OBJECTIVES

After studying this chapter you should be able to:

1. State the basic assumptions of cosmology.

2. Present, in a short paragraph, basic observations that have cosmological import.

3. Compare and contrast the big-bang and steady-state models, especially the assumptions made for each and the ability of each to explain fundamental cosmological observations.

4. Describe briefly the *observed* properties of the cosmic background radiation.

5. Present at least one argument for ascribing a *cosmic* origin to the background radiation.

6. Describe how matter can be produced from radiation.

7. Discuss the importance of the cosmic radiation for both big-bang and steady-state models.

8. Outline the process of element formation in the standard big-bang model, and cite at least one observation that supports theoretical ideas.

9. Outline a history of matter and radiation from the time they both stopped interacting strongly to the present.

10. Describe a simple model of galaxy formation from the big bang, and pinpoint problems with this model.

The universe unfolding

21

Some 20 billion years ago the cosmic bomb exploded. Perhaps you have seen movies of an H-bomb blast. Split seconds after detonation, an awesome fireball rips violently through the atmosphere. Our universe was born out of a similar fireball—but this was a cosmic fireball, the big bang, in whose violence all we see now was created (Fig. 21.1).

That, in a nutshell, is a picture of our universe's creation accepted by many astronomers today. But before I discuss its history, how can *the universe* be defined?

If an astronomer considers all that can be seen with various telescopes, he or she is considering the *observable universe*. Yet this cannot be *all* of the universe; there are objects too faint and too far to be seen, and regions of the spectrum to which we and our instruments are so far blind. Other objects may be detected by their gravitational effects, such as the dark companion in a double-star system. So there is more than the observable universe: a *physical universe* that includes directly observable matter and those objects we detect by effects described by the laws of physics. The reality of the physical universe rests on the assumption that local physical laws apply to the rest of the universe.

Cosmology—the subject of this chapter—is the grandiose (but human) study of the physical universe's nature and evolution. You can't talk about the evolution of the universe by simply describing what happens to each part; you must consider the universe as a unique whole. That's one of the problems of cosmology: We have only one cosmos to look at! In contrast, we can tell a lot about stars simply because so many stars are around.

Cosmologists have been fed on a meager diet of observational facts about the universe. They make up for this lack by dreaming up models of the universe. Some of the models have been quite bizarre, but only two have gathered a substantial following: the steady-state theory and the big-bang theory. I—and most astronomers—believe that the present evidence indicates that the universe began in a big bang.

21.1

Fundamental assumptions of cosmology

To practice cosmology does not require a large telescope to scour the skies for observations of

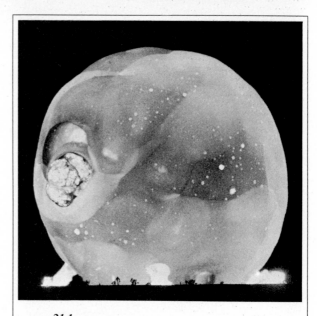

21.1

A terrestrial analog to the cosmic big bang. This photo shows a nuclear fireball, fractions of a second after the bomb's detonation. For a very brief time interval, the temperature, density, and pressure in the fireball correspond to that in the big bang. (Courtesy Harold E. Edgerton, Massachusetts Institute of Technology)

cosmological import. One fact about the cosmos can be found in the simple observation that the sky is dark at night (Focus 52). This observation requires that the universe *evolve*, that it be dynamic, not static. To go beyond this fact to discuss the universe's evolution in detail requires a few fundamental assumptions.

First, the *universality of physical laws*. This assumption covers both local (the earth and solar system) and cosmic regions. It means that you can apply the physical laws uncovered here to all localities and to the universe as a whole. A few observations support this assumption: For example, the spectra of distant galaxies contain the same atomic spectral lines as those produced by elements found on the earth. So other galaxies are made of the same elements as here, put together in the same way. When applied to double stars, Newton's law of gravitation correctly describes their motion. Kepler's third law applies to part of the whirlpool motion of galaxies.

focus 52

OLBERS'S PARADOX

In 1826 the German astronomer Heinrich Olbers (1758–1840) asked himself why the sky is dark at night. Recall that Newton, in a dramatic split with ancient traditions, conceived that the universe was infinite in extent. Olbers took up Newton's infinite universe, filled it with stars, and concluded that the night sky should be as bright as the sun. But it is not. This observation is at the heart of Olbers's paradox.

Olbers tackled a seemingly simple question: What is the total amount of starlight striking the earth? He assumed that (1) the universe was infinite; (2) it was uniformly populated by stars similar to the sun; (3) no interstellar material blocks out any of the stellar light; (4) the light diminishes as the inverse square of the distance; and (5) the universe (and the stars in it) does not evolve. Because this static universe is filled with stars of the same luminosity, an observer sees differences in the brightnesses of stars only if they are at different distances from him or her. Recall that the brightness depends only on the inverse square of the distance (Focus 34). But as you look at fainter stars, you see deeper into space, and the number of stars increases directly as the square of the distance. The diminishing intensity (inverse-square law) is just balanced by the increase

in number of light sources (direct-square law). Net result: The total light striking the earth is equivalent to that from one average star placed so close that it completely fills the sky.

Another way to see it: Every line of sight must end at a star if space is infinite and the stars are uniformly scattered. All fused together, these individual images blend into a uniformly bright surface.

The actual night sky, however, is not a luminous blend of stars but a dark expanse dusted by sparks of light. This gross discrepancy between theory and observation suggests that one or more of the initial assumptions are false. Olbers required the universe to be static. The light from distant stars can be reduced if the universe expands and stars are uniformly receding from the earth.

Consider that each star emits the same number of photons of the same energy each second. If the stars are receding from the earth, the number of photons reaching the earth each second is reduced, compared with the static case. Because the wavelength increases, the energy of each photon is also reduced. So the total energy reaching us from the stars is diminished. If the expansion is uniform (so that the more distant stars have the greatest velocities), the light from the farthest stars is suppressed the most. One possible escape from Olbers's dilemma is that rather than a static universe, the cosmos is expanding.

Second, the universe is assumed to be *homogeneous* (Fig. 21.2). This means that matter and radiation are spread out uniformly, with no large gaps or bunches. You know that this assumption is not strictly true, for clumps of matter, such as galaxies and stars, do exist. But the cosmologist assumes that the size of the clumping is much smaller than the size of the universe. It's like looking at the earth from space: Bumps, such as mountains, are too small to be seen, so the globe looks extremely smooth.

The third assumption is that the universe is *isotropic* (Fig. 21.3). This idea is a bit more abstract than that of homogeneity; it relates to a quality of space itself, rather than to the matter in it. Here's how to think of it: Space has the same properties in all directions. So no direction or place in space can be distinguished from any others. The universe has no center in space, because there is no way to tell if you are there. No direction in space provides special rewards when taken; for example, your mass does not increase as you travel in one direction or decrease when you go another way.

These assumptions can be summed up in one phrase: the universe is *uniform*. All irregularities are ironed out. As the cosmologist Edward R. Harrison has quipped, the result is like

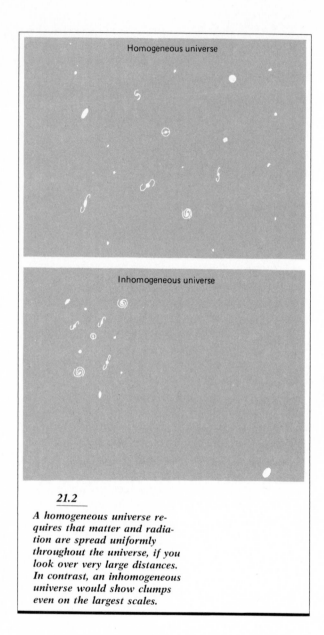

21.2

A homogeneous universe requires that matter and radiation are spread uniformly throughout the universe, if you look over very large distances. In contrast, an inhomogeneous universe would show clumps even on the largest scales.

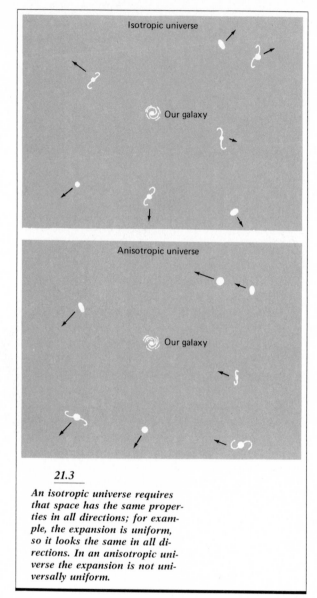

21.3

An isotropic universe requires that space has the same properties in all directions; for example, the expansion is uniform, so it looks the same in all directions. In an anisotropic universe the expansion is not universally uniform.

that of the vanishing Cheshire cat in *Alice in Wonderland:* Everything is wiped out except the grin. As a result, cosmological models that rest on the preceding assumptions ignore the structure and substance of planets, stars, and galaxies. Galaxies are considered, but only as tiny particles like a gas filling the universe. This gas is the cosmic grin. Such a mental simplification has real dangers, for like the Cheshire cat, what lies behind the grin may be crucial. The universe may not obey the laws we laid down for it; observations must validate our assumptions.

21.2

A brief review of cosmology

Chapter 7 outlined the rise of relativity and its impact on cosmological ideas and presented some fundamental cosmological observations. These observations did not fall into a grand scheme until explained by Einstein's general theory of relativity.

What *do* we know about the universe? First, the universe *evolves;* it is not static. This conclusion is recent; as explained in Part I, people originally conceived the universe as eternal and unchanging. Einstein's ideas changed that view in this century (although his first model was static).

Second, matter in the universe is *grouped*. Elementary particles (whatever they are) make up protons and electrons, which make up atoms. You know that atoms make up gases (molecular and atomic) and dust particles, which form stars, planets, and us. Stars come in clusters of stars, which are found in galaxies. And galaxies are grouped in clusters of galaxies, which in turn may congregate in clusters of galaxies. Beyond them, as far as is known, is the universe.

Third, the universe is *expanding*. Hubble and Humason (Section 7.4) observed red shifts in the spectra of other galaxies; they made the important discovery of cosmic expansion. The rate of expansion now is about 50 km/sec/Mpc. Einstein's theory of general relativity relates the rate of expansion to the average density of matter (and energy) in the universe. This average density, in turn, determines the overall geometry of spacetime. Two possibilities exist for this geometry: (1) closed, the cosmos being finite but unbounded in space and finite in time; and (2) open, the universe being unbounded in space and time. Observations to date imply that the universe has an open geometry; the question is still unsettled. (Einstein has an aesthetic preference for a closed universe. I personally prefer an open one.)

Finally, you can estimate the ages of celestial objects. From the Hubble constant you find that the universe has been expanding for no more than 13 billion years (Focus 20). Radioactive dating places the earth and the moon at an age of about 5 billion years. Astronomers estimate our Galaxy's age at some 8–12 billion years. These estimates, in spite of uncertainties, are amazing: All are less than the presumed age of the universe, and they fall in a natural evolutionary sequence, from the universe to the earth. Here's a hint that the universe was born at a finite time in the past and evolved in a sequence set by known physical laws.

21.3
Contemporary cosmological models

Over the past 70 years, ingenious theoreticians have devised a bewildering array of cosmological models. Almost all fall into one of two categories: (1) the *big-bang model*, which is the standard model based on Einstein's general theory of relativity, and (2) the *steady-state model*, which requires some changes in standard relativistic ideas. (The oscillating model—in which the universe expands, then contracts, only to expand again—is a big-bang model. You can think of it as a "bang-bang-bang . . ." model.)

The observational bases for the big-bang and steady-state models are the same, but the interpretations of such observations have crucial differences. These differences arise from different philosophical and aesthetic grounds for each model. This section describes the two basic models of modern cosmological thought. (Keep in mind that most astronomers now favor the big-bang model.)

Steady-state model / Cosmological models rest on the assumptions that the universe is isotropic, homogeneous, and describable by the same physical laws everywhere. These assumptions taken together are sometimes called the *cosmological principle;* they can be summed up by saying that the universe appears uniform to all observers at every location. Now add another restriction: that the universe appears the same not only at *all locations* but also at *all times.* This statement is often called the *perfect cosmological principle.* It is the aesthetic basis for steady-state models of the universe. This principle does not mean that the universe does not change. Galaxies condense, stars ignite and flare out, but the cosmos retains the same features. No matter *where* you are or *when* you are, the universe looks similar in its most general characteristics. *Warning:* This principle does *not* mean that the universe does not evolve. The universe evolves in the steady-state model, but so that it has a similar appearance in all places at all times.

In the light of Humason's and Hubble's observation of an expanding universe (Section 7.4), you might think that gaps of matter must appear as the galaxies spread apart (Fig. 21.4). So you could date different times in the universe's history by watching the average density of matter decrease. How does the steady-state model get around this dilemma?

Simple: It allows the continual creation of new matter to fill the gaps resulting from ex-

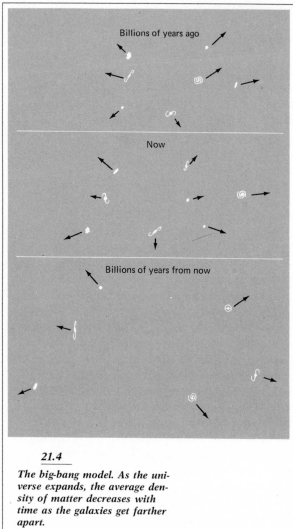

21.4

The big-bang model. As the universe expands, the average density of matter decreases with time as the galaxies get farther apart.

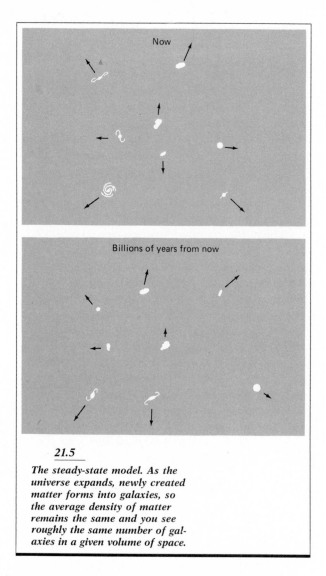

21.5

The steady-state model. As the universe expands, newly created matter forms into galaxies, so the average density of matter remains the same and you see roughly the same number of galaxies in a given volume of space.

pansion. Not much matter needs to be created to keep up with the expansion: only a single hydrogen atom per liter every billion years. As originally envisioned by Herman Bondi, Thomas Gold, and Fred Hoyle, the created matter is new and is not recycled from other matter or energy. The matter springs forth everywhere, newborn from nothing. The continuous creation of matter marks a primary difference between the steady-state and the big-bang model. You can see how it gets its name: Regardless of where and when you look at the universe, its state is the same (Fig. 21.5). If the universe is expanding, matter must be created to save the perfect cosmological principle.

***Observational problems with the steady-state model* /** The steady-state model presents a

pleasant picture of a fulfilled, eternal cosmos. Nasty questions—such as how the universe began—do not arise. But how well does this model stand up to observations?

Consider first the age of matter in the universe. Three possibilities exist for its age: (1) It is infinitely old; (2) it has a finite age because it was all created in a single event in the past; (3) different particles of matter have different ages because they were created at different times. How can you tell which possibility is correct? It is impossible to tell the age of any one particle, such as a proton. So you must look at matter in bulk. As gravity squeezes matter together, hydrogen transforms to heavier elements in a one-way process. If all matter were infinitely old, most of it would no longer be hydrogen. But observations show that the matter in the universe is mostly hydrogen. So the choice is between incremental creation (steady state) and instantaneous creation (big bang).

The trouble (or virtue!) with instantaneous creation is that you can date it. Before 1952 the big-bang model faced the following dilemma: The age of the universe estimated from the Hubble constant was only 2 billion years. But the age of the earth was estimated at 4 billion years, that of the sun at 10 billion years, and the ages of the oldest stars near 20 billion years. The universe appeared younger than the objects it contained! Steady-state supporters took this discrepancy as evidence for their model. Since 1952 the Hubble constant has been redetermined (to smaller values), and the age of the universe estimated from it has increased enough to include the oldest stars, now believed to be 12–16 billion years old. So a major thorn has been taken out of the side of the big-bang model, and the steady-state model has lost one of its main props.

The steady-state model has received some hard knocks from recent observations. For example, it predicts that as the galaxies spread apart, new galaxies are born. So young galaxies must be clustered among the old, and this age pattern for galaxies must be observable everywhere. But galaxies in a cluster of galaxies appear to have roughly the same age. They all have old stars, which indicates that they formed at approximately the same time.

Second, the shape of the Hubble plot for galaxies can be specified in the steady-state model. It dips far below the Hubble plot for a flat universe. That is, the steady-state model requires an open universe. However, the observed Hubble plot for galaxies does not match that predicted by the steady-state model (Fig. 7.17 and 7.18).

Third, in the steady-state model everything, on a large scale, must remain similar, even the Hubble constant, H. The universe is expanding, however, so d for any galaxy must increase. To keep H the same, v must also increase. The steady-state model must put in a mysterious force to accelerate galaxies to higher velocities as they move apart. Many astronomers find this necessity objectionable, and it is another argument against the steady-state model.

Fourth, the distribution of quasars in space and time (Section 21.7) indicates that more quasars existed in the past than do now. This is contrary to the steady-state model, which requires that the number of quasars be the same at all times.

The final blow, however, came from an accidental observation made in 1965. It dropped a bomb in the minds of cosmologists: the discovery of the still-resounding echoes of the big bang.

The big-bang model / The universe is now expanding. Imagine it running backward. The galaxies and all matter within and without them eventually come tightly together. The extreme compression heats (just as any squeezed gas heats up) both matter and radiation together to a very high temperature—high enough to break down all structure that was created previously, including all the elements fused in stars. The atoms break down into protons and electrons. In addition, the density of matter is so great that photons can travel only a short distance before they are absorbed. (They are then reemitted, only to be absorbed again.) As a result, the entire universe is opaque to its own radiation. A similar situation occurs in the interior of a star: Here matter and radiation interact so often that the inside of a star is opaque.

Now, when matter is opaque to all radiation, it acts like a blackbody (Focus 31). The radiation from a blackbody exhibits a characteristic shape when you study the variation of the intensity with wavelength (Fig. 21.6). In an early, dense, hot state, the universe acts like a blackbody radiator. If you could have been there, you would have seen a bright fog all around, like sitting in the sun's interior.

Imagine the universe expanding from this infernal state. It is so hot that it expands in a rush like an explosion; hence the name *big bang* for this picture of the universe. As the universe expands, its overall density and temperature decrease. (This is true for the expansion of any gas. Have you ever suddenly let a gas out of a container? If so, you noticed that the gas suddenly became cold as it expanded.) Eventually the temperature drops low enough so that protons can capture electrons to form neutral hydrogen.

This event—the formation of neutral hydrogen from an ionized gas—marks a crucial stage in the evolution of the universe. No longer ion-

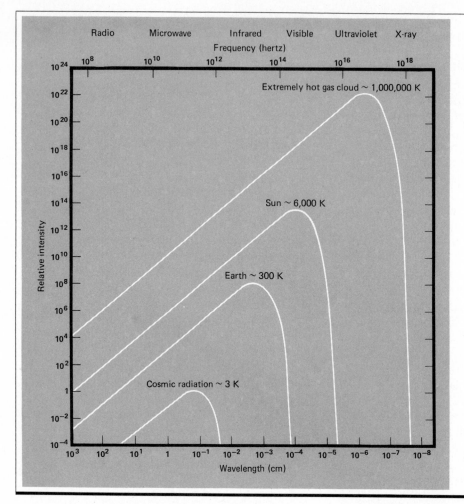

Radio   Microwave   Infrared   Visible   Ultraviolet   X-ray

Frequency (hertz)

Extremely hot gas cloud ~ 1,000,000 K

Sun ~ 6,000 K

Earth ~ 300 K

Cosmic radiation ~ 3 K

Relative intensity

Wavelength (cm)

21.6

A comparison of the spectra of blackbodies at different temperatures. Note that radiation at about 3 K peaks in intensity at microwave-infrared wavelengths, so these are the best wavelengths for trying to observe blackbody radiation at this temperature.

ized, the universe becomes transparent to its own radiation. The radiation freely speeds throughout space, and the expansion dilutes it. As it is diluted, the radiation cools because it is red-shifted, just like the light of distant galaxies. (The photons act like the particles of a gas, and when a gas expands, it cools as the energy of its particles decreases. As they are red-shifted, the energy of the photons decreases, so the radiation's temperature goes down.)

If the universe *did* begin in a hot big bang, debris (both matter and radiation) from the explosion must now lie all around us. The matter's pretty obvious—you can see planets, stars, galaxies, and the unformed matter among all of these. But what about the radiation produced in the big bang? It's been red-shifted to a fairly low temperature. Because of its low temperature, the radiation's wavelength would be long compared with that of visible light. And if the universe expanded uniformly, the graph of the radiation's intensity versus wavelength should show the telltale blackbody shape.

Have astronomers seen such a cosmic radiation? Yes! And its discovery verifies the hot big-bang model.

The cosmic blackbody microwave radiation / In 1964 Robert H. Dicke, P. James E. Peebles, Peter G. Roll, and David T. Wilkinson at Princeton University were pursuing the question of the possible existence of leftover radiation from a big bang. The Princeton group attacked this problem: What would happen if the universe went through a hot stage, so that a high temperature decomposed any heavy nuclei into elementary particles? If a primeval fireball occurred, cosmic blackbody radiation should survive today. Peebles made a calculation that this fossil radiation should have a blackbody temperature of roughly 10 K.

21.7

Arno Penzias (right) and Robert Wilson (left) standing near the horn antenna (back) with which they discovered the cosmic background radiation. (Courtesy Bell Laboratories)

Just as Roll and Wilkinson were building apparatus to detect the radiation, Arno Penzias and Robert Wilson, scientists with Bell Telephone Laboratories in New Jersey, detected an annoying excess radiation with a special low-noise radio antenna (Fig. 21.7). They intended to do a sensitive study of the radio emission from the Milky Way. The excess noise they found would affect their results, so they set about to try to eliminate it.

They tuned their radio receiver to 7.35 cm (4080 MHz), where the radio noise from the Galaxy is very small. Even then they picked up the static. Penzias and Wilson further discovered that the noise did not change in intensity with direction in the sky, the time of day, or the season. Perplexed, they examined the antenna again and found a pair of pigeons roosting inside. These pigeons, oblivious to radio astronomy, had coated a part of the antenna with their droppings. Perhaps the coating could supply the excess noise? The birds were moved, their droppings cleaned out. But still the excess noise persisted, with an intensity at 7.35 cm equivalent to that of a blackbody at 3.5 K.

Penzias called Bernard Burke, a radio astronomer at MIT, to discuss matters other than the excess radio noise. Burke asked about the experiment, and Penzias explained the problem. Because Burke had heard about Peebles's work,

he suggested that Penzias call the Princeton group. Penzias did. When he made contact, the Princeton group quickly concluded that the excess noise came from the cosmos—radiation left over from the big bang.

This intuitive, risky leap needed verification. After all, the Penzias and Wilson measurement was at a single wavelength (Fig. 21.8). But to establish the radiation as truly Doppler-shifted from a hot, dense stage in the universe's past, more observations were needed to confirm the characteristic blackbody shape of its spectrum and its uniform intensity in the sky. Soon Roll and Wilkinson (Fig. 21.9) added another point at another wavelength (3.2 cm), corresponding to a 2.8 K temperature, close to that observed by the Bell Labs pair. Other experimental groups later contributed additional evidence to the blackbody nature of the radiation. The points crept up the long-wavelength side of the (hopefully) blackbody curve to the hump of the turnover point. An observed point on or over the hump would clinch the argument, but at infrared wavelengths observations are notoriously difficult to make because of absorption by the earth's atmosphere.

Far-infrared observations made above most of the earth's atmosphere have confirmed that the spectrum of the cosmic radiation turns down at short wavelengths (to the right of the peak in Fig. 21.8). You can see this turnover more clearly in Figure 21.10, where observations by a Berkeley group are indicated by a band, other observations (points) are by a group at Queen Mary College, London. The different results seem in good agreement for such difficult observations. The blackbody temperature of the Queen Mary College result is 2.94 K; that of the Berkeley group, 2.99 K. Other observations to date averaged together give a blackbody temperature of 2.89 K.

In my opinion, the observations so far fit a blackbody spectrum pretty well—but not perfectly. For convenience, take the radiation's blackbody temperature as simply 3 K.

To confirm its cosmic origin further, the radiation should be isotropic—that is, have the same measured intensity from all directions in the sky. If the radiation were from a hot primeval state, the isotropy of the universe at that time would fix the isotropy of the radiation. (Recall that we *assumed* isotropy—that the uni-

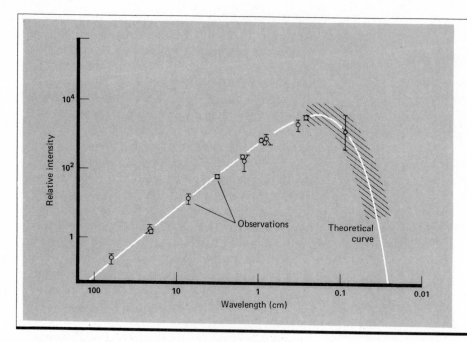

Actual observations of the cosmic microwave radiation. The points and the box show measured intensities at radio and infrared wavelengths; the curve corresponds to a blackbody of 3 K. The shaded region on the short wavelength end corresponds to recent observations by P. L. Richards and co-workers. (Adapted from a diagram by P. J. E. Peebles)

21.9

The Princeton antenna for measuring the cosmic background radiation; it provided the next data point after Penzias and Wilson. (Courtesy of D. Wilkinson, who is visible at right under the platform)

verse looks the same in all directions—without experimental confirmation.) The Princeton group also made some of the first observations to determine the isotropy of the radiation; they searched for a variation in the radiation's intensity, scanning the sky. After a year of collecting data, they concluded that the variation was no more than 0.5 percent.

This result suggested both that the radiation originated from the early universe and that, in fact, the newborn universe was very nearly isotropic. The lack of a regular variation also ruled out a local solar system or galactic source of the radiation. The evidence—equal intensity from all directions in space—implies that the radiation is cosmic, existing everywhere in space, so that it arrives at the earth uniformly from every direction. If so, it fills all space at all times. The isotropy observations clinch the interpretation of the radiation as cosmic.

This background radiation is usually given the long-winded name of *cosmic blackbody microwave radiation.* "Cosmic" because it comes from all directions in space; "blackbody" because of its spectral shape; and "microwave" because its spectrum peaks at centimeter–millimeter wavelengths. Its discovery forces cosmological models to account for its properties.

First, it has direct cosmological significance that rules out the steady-state model, for it contradicts the perfect cosmological principle. The argument goes like this. The radiation is now blackbody in character. That means it must have been emitted by an opaque, dense gas. The universe is not *now* opaque and dense. So it must have been different in the past, which is

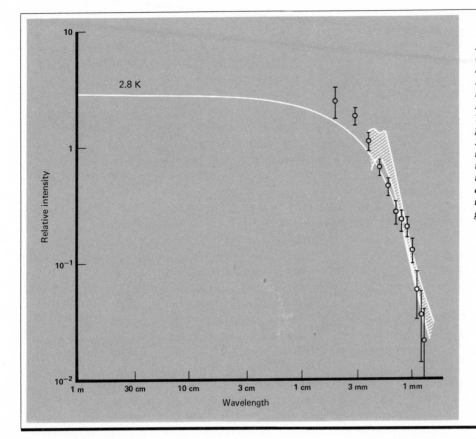

21.10

A comparison of measurements of the cosmic background radiation by the Queen Mary College group (open circles) and the University of California, Berkeley group (shaded region). The solid curve is the emission from a theoretical blackbody at 2.8 K. Note that both sets of measurements curve down in the infrared—a drop necessary to prove that the observed radiation is, in fact, a blackbody in nature. (Adapted from a diagram by P. Clegg)

contrary to the assumption of the steady-state model.

Second, the radiation enables astronomers to glimpse the raw, young universe. They conclude that the initial universe was indeed quite homogeneous and isotropic.

Third, the present temperature, about 3 K, and the isotropy of the radiation set severe limits on the thermal history of the universe, that is, the change of the temperature of matter and radiation with time.

Fourth, the radiation's presence establishes an important marker for galaxy formation. Until the radiation and matter stopped their interaction, matter could not form any clumps of large size. Only after the ionized gas recombined could matter form clumps that eventually became stars and galaxies.

To sum up: The discovery of the cosmic blackbody microwave radiation has a significance for cosmology as great as that of the discovery of the expansion of the universe. Its presence eliminates the simple steady-state

model; its measured uniformity backs up the assumptions that the universe is isotropic and homogeneous; and its present measured temperature (about 3 K), combined with Einstein's equation of general relativity, allows you to work out the evolution of the universe as its temperature changes. The details of this evolution will be traced out in the next section: The standard big-bang model has reasonable support from present observations.

Is the cosmic background radiation perfectly isotropic? Early observations indicated that, within experimental error, the cosmic background radiation was isotropic. That is, its measured temperature and spectrum is the same in all directions in space. This observation implies that at the time the universe became transparent, it was expanding isotropically and the matter was distributed homogeneously. If so, you can use the cosmic background radiation to define a reference against which to measure motion. In other words, if you take the cosmic radiation to be "at rest," then the earth's motion around the sun, plus the sun's motion around the Galaxy, plus the Galaxy's motion in the local group, plus the local group's motion in the local supercluster—all these motions together should show up as a Doppler shift. In the direction of the summed up motions, you'd see a blue shift, so the radiation would appear hotter. In the opposite direction you'd see a red shift, so the radiation would appear cooler. The temperature would appear slightly anisotropic.

Astronomers have detected an anisotropy of a mere 3.5×10^{-3} K with the hottest spot in the direction of the constellation Leo, and the coolest, 180° away in the direction of Aquarius. They interpret this anisotropy as due to a motion of the earth relative to the radiation of almost 400 km/sec. Other measurements have confirmed this result, with an average value of 360 km/sec.

What might account for this motion? Recall (Section 17.3) that the local group moves at 480 km/sec in the direction of the Virgo cluster. The anisotropy measurement, after taking out the motion of the solar system and of the Galaxy, results in a local group velocity of 540 km/sec in a direction about 35° away from Virgo. The part of the motion toward Virgo is then 440 km/sec. The reasonable agreement of these results (which have experimental errors of roughly 50–75 km/sec) implies that the anisotropy arises from motions in the local supercluster unconnected with the expansion of the universe.

21.4

The primeval fireball

Since the discovery of the cosmic microwave background radiation, most astronomers accept a hot big-bang model for the beginning of the universe. With the addition of experimental and theoretical knowledge on how matter behaves under hot, dense conditions, theoreticians have been able to develop step-by-step details of what can happen in a big bang.

Warning: Please *don't* picture the big bang as happening in the "center" of the universe and expanding to fill it. The big bang involved the *entire* universe; every place in it was *at* creation, which was an event marking the beginning of time and space.

The hot start / Although the present temperature of the cosmic radiation is low, the amount of energy it contributes to the universe is large: Each cubic centimeter contains 4×10^{-20} J, equivalent to about 4×10^{-37} kg. For comparison, if you take the material contained in visible galaxies and spread it uniformly around the universe, each cubic centimeter would contain 4×10^{-34} kg. So for each kilogram of galactic matter there are approximately 10^{+14} J of cosmic radiation. If the energy in the radiation could be used to heat up the matter, the temperature would be greater than 10^{12} K. Here is one clue about how hot the early universe might have been.

From Einstein's equations of general relativity we find that a temperature of 10^{12} K corresponds to a time of about 10^{-4} second after the actual beginning of the present expansion. At that time the universe had an average density of 5×10^{13} g/cc (almost as dense as an atom's nucleus).

This hot, dense start to the universe is sometimes called the *primeval fireball*—the cosmic explosion in which space, time, and all matter began.

The high temperature drives such a rapid expansion that the temperature and density drop rapidly. The contents of the universe (Table 21.1)—initially a flood of energetic light and heavy particles, such as protons, and their respective antiparticles—change with the temperature and time. The possibility that nucleosynthesis might occur on a cosmic scale motivated George Gamow (1904–1968) to investigate the situation for which he coined the term big bang. Only very limited but very important nucleosynthesis occurred in the early universe: the formation of helium and deuterium and a little bit of other light elements.

I will sketch a scenario of the early universe in which temperature plays a crucial controlling role. Each period of time since the beginning can be matched with a corresponding temperature. Roughly, the universe's thermal history divides into four eras: (1) a heavy-particle era when massive particles/antiparticles dominate; (2) a light-particle era; (3) a radiation era when most particles have vanished and radiation is the main form of energy; and (4) a matter era, in which you now live, when matter is the dominant form of energy.

Here's an outline of what follows: The universe in a few minutes after creation expands and reaches temperatures and densities suitable for the formation of deuterium and helium. The

TABLE 21.1 *Particles that play a role in cosmic nucleosynthesis*

Particle (antiparticle)	Symbol	Charge	Comments
Neutrino, antineutrino	ν, $\bar{\nu}$	0	Massless(?) particles that travel at light speed; stable(?)
Proton, antiproton	p, $\bar{p}$	+1, −1	The proton is a hydrogen nucleus; stable
Electron, positron	e^-, e^+	−1, +1	Electrons surround the nucleus of an atom; stable
Neutron, antineutron	n, $\bar{n}$	0	Free neutron decays to a proton and an electron in about 1000 sec
Photon	γ	0	Packet of radiation
Deuteron	^{2}H	+1	Nucleus of deuterium, or "heavy hydrogen"; contains 1 proton, 1 neutron; stable
Helium-3	^{3}He	+2	Nucleus of an unusual type of helium; contains 2 protons, 1 neutron; stable
Helium-4	^{4}He	+2	Nucleus of ordinary helium; contains 2 protons, 2 neutrons; stable
Lithium-7	^{7}Li	+3	Nucleus of the most abundant type of lithium; contains 3 protons, 4 neutrons; stable
Beryllium-7	^{7}Be	+4	Nucleus of the most common type of beryllium; contains 4 protons and 3 neutrons; unstable

big-bang model predicts a helium abundance of 25–30 percent (by mass) and very little formation of heavier elements. (These are made later in stars.) If the big-bang picture is correct, this abundance is the *minimum* amount of helium you should find in the universe. About a million years after the time of helium's formation, electrons and protons get together to form neutral atoms (almost all hydrogen and helium). At this time matter can clump to form the first stars, galaxies, and quasars. The radiation no longer plays a dominant role in the universe's evolution. (See Fig. 21.11 for a graphical summary of this history.)

Warning: Whenever I say the universe was "smaller" or "larger," I mean that the distance between a pair of objects is smaller or larger. The universe itself may be finite or infinite. Its overall geometry does not affect what I'll say subsequently about the big bang.

Creation of matter from photons / Before the story unfolds, you need a little background about one key part: the creation of matter and antimatter from photons.

At some time in the past of the primeval fireball the density and energy of photons (in essence, their temperature) must have been so high that photon collisions produced matter. This process occurs when the energy contained in the colliding photons equals or exceeds the mass ($E = mc^2$) of the particles produced.

Sounds bizarre? Yet the concept of matter creation from photons comes directly from Einstein's relation between matter and energy: $E = mc^2$. Note that this relation says nothing about the *direction* of the transformation—matter can become energy, or energy can become matter.

The creation of matter from light happens in a special way, for it involves both matter and antimatter. Antimatter is made of antiparticles. For example, an antiproton (Table 21.1) has the same mass as a proton but an opposite charge; likewise for a positron (antielectron). So an antimatter hydrogen atom consists of an antiproton for a nucleus and a positron orbiting it.

When matter and antimatter get together, they annihilate each other and convert to pho-

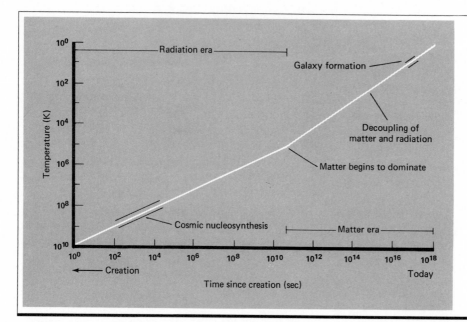

The history of the universe in the standard big-bang model. This graph shows how the temperature of the dominant material (radiation or matter) changes with time. The cosmic history falls into two general periods: the radiation era and the matter era (in which we are now). If the universe is closed and collapses, the temperature will increase, more or less following this graph in reverse.

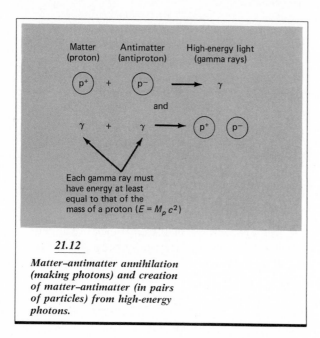

21.12

Matter–antimatter annihilation (making photons) and creation of matter–antimatter (in pairs of particles) from high-energy photons.

tons. The reverse process can also happen. If two photons with enough energy hit each other, they can convert into a particle–antiparticle pair (Fig. 21.12). How much energy must the photons have? At least the energy equivalent of the masses of the particle–antiparticle pair they form. So to make a proton and an antiproton takes photons with more energy than that required to make an electron and a positron, because protons are more massive than electrons.

For example, the energy equivalent of the masses of an electron and antielectron is about 1.6×10^{-13} J, which corresponds to a radiation temperature of 1.2×10^{10} K. Protons and antiprotons have masses 1800 times greater than that of electrons and antielectrons. Their masses have an energy equivalent of 2.9×10^{-10} J, which corresponds to a temperature of about 2.2×10^{13} K.

One other point. To make large numbers of particles–antiparticles from photons, you need sufficient energy and also must have an extremely high density of photons. Why? So that photons will collide frequently enough to create matter–antimatter.

The conditions in the primeval fireball just fit this requirement of great densities of energetic photons. So matter and antimatter must have been made then.

Temperature greater than 10^{12} K, time less than 0.0001 sec since the creation / Photons create pairs of particles (Fig. 21.13) and antiparticles. Annihilation also takes place, and the balance between annihilation and creation fixes the density of particles and antiparticles for the next stage. At this time the universe has such a high temperature that photons have very large energies—about that of gamma rays. So very massive particles, such as protons, are created. This marks the heavy-particle era.

A critical difficulty with the model here is

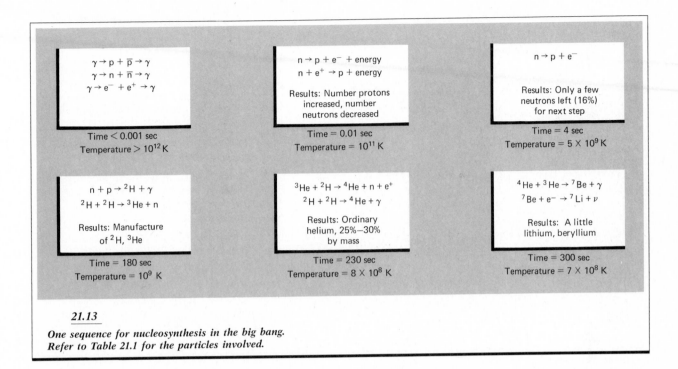

21.13

One sequence for nucleosynthesis in the big bang.
Refer to Table 21.1 for the particles involved.

that the average density predicted by relativity is greater than 10^{14} g/cc—and physicists really do *not* know how matter behaves at such extreme densities. But whatever happens in detail, heavy particles can be created at this stage.

So at the earliest times for which the present physical theories are valid, the universe is a smooth soup of high-energy light and massive particles.

Temperature from 10^{12} to 5×10^9 K, time from 0.0001 to 4 sec / Annihilation of heavy particles with their antiparticles continues. The remaining photons, however, lack the energy to create new heavy particles. Only light particles—electrons and antielectrons—can be made, because these need less energy for creation. The universe enters the light-particle era.

The present imbalance of matter over antimatter requires that a few extra protons remain; that is, the early universe contained a slight excess of protons over antiprotons. (Why is a baffling mystery.) Protons and electrons interact to generate equal numbers of neutrons and protons (Fig. 21.13). As the temperature decreases, the number of neutrons falls while the number of protons rises. (This imbalance of protons and neutrons is important later in the formation of helium.) When the temperature falls to 5×10^9 K, photons can no longer make elec-

tron-positron pairs. This temperature marks the end of the light-particle era and the beginning of the radiation era. The universe still expands, but less rapidly.

Neutrons, totaling 16 percent of the particles, can no longer be produced by interaction with electrons or positrons. The neutrons are now free to decay into protons and electrons.

Temperature 10^9 K, time from 4 to 180 sec / In this crucial period the remaining neutrons and protons react to form nuclei that can survive the still-high temperatures. The most important reaction involves the combination of a neutron and a proton to form deuterium. All neutrons, except those that have decayed, end up in deuterium. Once the deuterium is produced, a proton-proton reaction creates normal helium (Fig. 21.13) and also a little tritium (^{3}H) and ^{3}He. As a consequence of the still-rapid expansion, the density and temperature drop so fast that almost all the neutrons end up in helium. The net result is 25–30 percent of helium by mass. A little bit of beryllium and lithium is created by the combination of deuterium and tritium (Fig. 21.13). Some deuterium is left over. Extremely little of the heavier elements is made.

The final helium and deuterium abundance depends on the rate of the universe's expansion. If the expansion rate were any faster, less time

TABLE 21.2 *Sequence of events in the big-bang model*

Event	Time	Density (g/cc)	Temperature (K)	Comments
Creation	0	?	?	Not province of present science; general relativity fails
Heavy-particle era	10^{-44} sec	10^{94}	10^{33}	Photons make massive particles (such as protons) and antiparticles
Light-particle era	10^{-4} sec	10^{14}	10^{12}	Photons have only enough energy to make light particles and antiparticles, such as electrons and positrons; protons and electrons combine to make neutrons
Radiation era	10 sec	10^{4}	10^{10}	Few particles left in a sea of radiation; these partake in nucleosynthesis of deuterium, helium, lithium, beryllium
Matter era	7×10^{5} years	10^{-21}	3000	Ionized hydrogen recombines; cosmic radiation and matter decouple
Now	2×10^{10} years	10^{-34} (radiation)	3 (radiation)	Astronomers puzzle about creation

would have been available for neutrons to decay, and more helium would have been produced. On the other hand, if the expansion rate had been very much slower, the neutrons that would have formed helium would have had a longer time to decay, so less helium would result. Helium, once formed, is tough to destroy. So the present helium abundance in the universe rests on a cosmologically (rather than stellar) created base and sets severe constraints on the expansion rate and density of the early universe. The helium abundance also serves as a test for the big-bang cosmology. It predicts that no celestial object can have a helium abundance of less than 25–30 percent. (Because stars form helium, the abundance can be greater than this number.)

Temperature 3000 K, time 21 $\times$ 10^{12} sec / So far the temperature has been so high that all atoms in the universe have been ionized. After about 700,000 years since creation, the radiation's temperature has plunged to only 3000 K. The nuclei begin to capture electrons to form neutral atoms. This recombination process happens quickly; the matter becomes transparent to the radiation. Suddenly light breaks through the now transparent universe. The matter and radiation are no longer locked together.

Freed from this interaction, the radiation merrily expands with the universe. The matter, however, follows a different course because of little local bumps in the generally smooth distribution of matter. A local region of slightly higher than average density does not expand so fast as the rest of the universe, owing to its self-gravity. Consequently, a local blob increases its density contrast and expands even more slowly than the cosmic rate. Clouds of matter condense out of the primeval fireball. The radiation era ends, and the matter era begins. The universe has a density of 10^{-27} g/cc. Material condensation could not happen until the radiation and matter uncoupled as the atoms recombined. This event flags the time when galaxy formation could begin (see next section).

For a summary of these events, see Table 21.2.

The evidence for the big bang / How do you know that the contemporary big-bang cosmological picture is not mere speculation? The scenario for the hot early universe pushes our knowledge about matter and gravitation to shaky limits. What observational evidence supports such a stretching of present ideas?

First and foremost, observations indicate that the blackbody radiation pervades the universe. Open the window to your room and reverberations of the primeval fireball stream in. Within the limits of observational errors, measurements confirm a blackbody spectrum with about a 3 K temperature. Measured in many directions of space, the radiation comes into the earth with uniform intensity. The background radiation has all the attributes expected of a cosmic, hot origin.

Second, the theory predicts that primeval helium was formed in the first 5 min of the universe's history and that the helium/hydrogen abundance should be 25–30 percent by mass. The big-bang model sets this helium abundance as the basement level; any observation of a substantially lower amount calls the theory into question. Because helium is formed in stars and once formed is difficult to destroy, the present helium abundance is probably larger than 25–30 percent.

Unfortunately, you can assess the present cosmic helium only indirectly. You can examine material from the earth, moon, and meteorites directly, but any initial helium has escaped into space because these bodies do not have sufficient gravity to hold down helium—the second lightest element. Satellites have sampled the solar wind to find that 15–30 percent is helium nuclei by mass. As pointed out in Chapter 13, the solar photosphere is not hot enough to excite helium lines for direct viewing with a spectroscope. The chromosphere's higher temperatures do excite helium atoms to emission, and the observational abundance there is 28 percent. Theoretical models of stellar evolution place the helium abundance in the sun's interior at 17 to 28 percent. Similar calculations for Jupiter yield a helium abundance of roughly 20 percent.

Population I *O*- and *B*-stars exhibit helium absorption lines that imply a helium abundance of approximately 30–34 percent. H II regions surrounding hot stars have helium emission lines at optical and radio wavelengths that give abundances from 26 to 29 percent. Planetary nebulas also have strong helium emission lines that imply a helium abundance of greater than 30 percent.

The best objects to search for primeval helium are the oldest stars now surviving, the Population II stars. Unfortunately, most Population II stars are much too cool to excite helium lines in their atmospheres. However, indirect evi-

dence indicates that these stars have helium abundances of about 30 percent.

I find it remarkable that the helium abundance for a variety of celestial objects falls so close to the number predicted by the hot big-bang model. The evidence for the compatibility of observations with theory is good but not conclusive, and as is usual in astrophysics, no one observation clinches the affair. But the accumulation of evidence is impressive.

Finally, the creation of the universe in a primeval fireball requires that the universe expands. And it does.

21.5
The end of time?

So much for the universe's past. What about its future? Recall (Chapter 7) that Einstein's general theory of relativity allows the cosmos to have one of two general geometries: open or closed. If open, the universe will expand forever, and time will never end. If closed, however, the universe must eventually collapse, running backward through the history outlined in the previous section.

Which fate will be what will be? Chapter 7 mentioned observational tests that indicate that the universe is open. First, the measured value of the Hubble constant ($H = 50$ km/sec/Mpc) and Einstein's theory give a critical density for a closed universe; it's about 5×10^{-30} g/cc. If the actual average density of the universe is greater than this value, the cosmos is closed. Luminous matter in the universe has an average density of 4×10^{-31} g/cc; so, on the surface, this evidence implies that the universe is open. Second, the Hubble graph for distant galaxies can indicate the universe's geometry. This Hubble test is tough to do, but so far, very weak evidence points to an open geometry.

The standard hot, big-bang model provides another, stronger test. The test rests on the observed present cosmic abundance of deuterium.

How can the abundance of deuterium tell whether the universe is open or closed? To do big-bang model calculations, you need to put in the *present* value of the Hubble constant, the *present* temperature of the cosmic radiation, and the *present* average density of the universe. The first two items are reasonably well known, but the third is not. However, the amount of helium

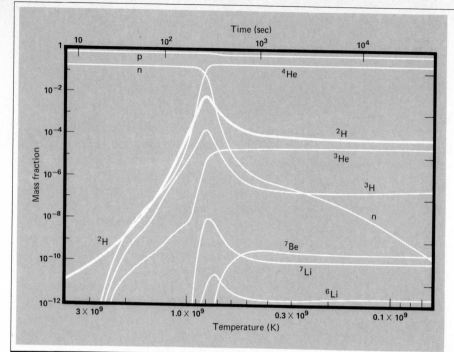

21.14

Details of the formation of light elements in the big bang. Along the top axis is given the age of the universe since creation; the bottom axis gives the temperature; and the vertical axis gives the abundance in terms of the fraction of the total mass. Note that all the nucleosynthesis takes place in a sharp blip between 100 and 1000 sec. Deuterium is ²H. (Based on theoretical calculations by R. V. Wagoner)

to come out of the big bang does not depend very much on the value used for the present density of the universe (Fig. 21.14). But the amount of deuterium that theoretical calculations predict does depend very sensitively on the value used for the present density of the universe (Fig. 21.15). So you can use the theory to turn the argument around. If you can measure the present cosmic abundance of deuterium, then you check this number against that predicted by the big-bang model (Fig. 21.15). The model then gives the present average density of the universe, and you can compare that number with the critical density.

As usual, there's a hitch to this beautiful procedure. Unlike helium, deuterium is very easy to burn up in fusion reactions in stars. So you can't look at stars to find the deuterium abundance. Even if you look for deuterium in the interstellar medium, you have to estimate how much of that has been processed by stars.

Enough for the complications. How to observe deuterium? The Copernicus satellite carries an ultraviolet telescope that can observe spectral lines emitted by the molecules H_2 and HD. Both have been detected, so a value for the D to H ratio of the interstellar medium is about 2.0×10^{-5} by mass.

Now to estimate how much original deuterium has been burned up in stars. Beatrice Tinsley estimates about half, so the original deuterium abundance was about twice that observed by the Copernicus satellite, or 4×10^{-5}.

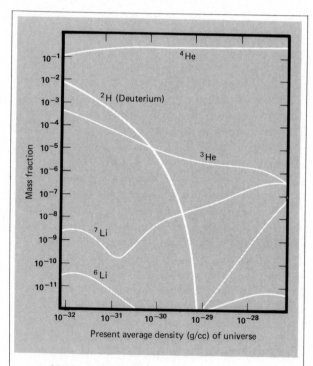

21.15

Theoretical calculations of the abundance of light elements formed in the big bang as related to the average density of the universe now (horizontal scale). Note how sharply the abundance of deuterium (²H) varies with the different present average densities. (Based on theoretical work by R. V. Wagoner)

Look at the big-bang calculation (Fig. 21.15). A deuterium to helium ratio of 4×10^{-5} implies a present cosmic density of 4×10^{-31} g/cc.

Conclusion from this test: The universe is open. Time will *not* end.

21.6
From big bang to galaxies

Up to 700,000 years after creation, gravity could not clump matter into stars and galaxies. Why not? The universe was opaque to radiation, so light and matter interacted strongly. Pressure from the radiation itself inhibited gravitational collapse. But once protons and electrons recombined, the universe became transparent to radiation, and no longer could radiation pressure stop gravity from doing its natural work. This is called the time of *decoupling*.

Because the cosmic background radiation now arrives very uniformly from all directions in space, you know that at the time of decoupling the matter and radiation in the universe must have had a very uniform distribution.

But that's not the situation now. Look around the universe with a large telescope. You find the matter clumped in planets, stars, clusters of stars, galaxies, and clusters of galaxies. Even the most spread-out of these systems of matter—clusters of galaxies—have average densities about 100 times greater than the average density of the universe.

So here's the crucial question: How did an originally very smooth universe become clumpy? From the uniform mix of gas and radiation in the primeval fireball, how did stars, galaxies, and clusters of galaxies form? This is a tough question to answer because only gravitationally bound systems with a wide range of masses developed from the big bang. This range includes galaxies—from 1 million to 10^{12} solar masses—and the largest clusters of galaxies, which contain about 10^{15} solar masses. On the low end, it may also include globular clusters, which have about 100,000 solar masses.

So one important requirement that a model must meet is that the physical processes involved must account for the formation of masses from about 10^5 to 10^{15} solar masses. Any model also faces another critical hurdle; it must operate effectively in at most a few billion years. Why this limitation? Remember that be-

cause light travels at a finite speed, when you look at very distant galaxies you peer back in time to when the universe was billions of years younger. To date, astronomers have seen objects as far as some 12 *billion* ly away. So the matter from the big bang must have formed into large clumps well before this time.

I'll describe the general models that astronomers have devised to explain the formation of galaxies, but be warned that many of these ideas are mostly earnest speculations. In a few years our present concepts will probably change, but the central problem will very likely still be there.

Gravitational instability / What makes matter form large clumps? The process involved is called *gravitational instability*. Imagine a very uniform, static gas. Picture a disturbance taking place so that a small, spherical region becomes slightly more dense than its surroundings. Its gravity increases. The disturbed patch attracts more matter to it and also condenses. These actions increase both the patch's density and gravity. So it attracts more matter to it and . . . well, you can guess what happens. The particles in the disturbed region (and those added to it) condense to form a gravitationally bound object.

Some three centuries ago Sir Isaac Newton first dreamed up the general process of gravitational instability and collapse. Early in this century Sir James Jeans showed that internal pressure plays a critical role in the development of gravitational instability. Imagine again a disturbed patch of gas. It has a higher density than its surroundings, but it also has a higher internal pressure. Like the gas inside a balloon, this pressure tends to push the condensed region apart.

Which wins out, the inward pull of the gravity or the outward push of pressure? Jeans discovered that the outcome depends on the size of the disturbed region. If the patch is too small, pressure overcomes gravity and makes the patch expand. If the region is large enough, gravity wins and the region condenses. The minimum size a disturbance must have to contract gravitationally depends on the pressure (and so the temperature) and density of the gas; it is called the *Jeans length*. If the disturbance is as large as or larger than the Jeans length, gravita-

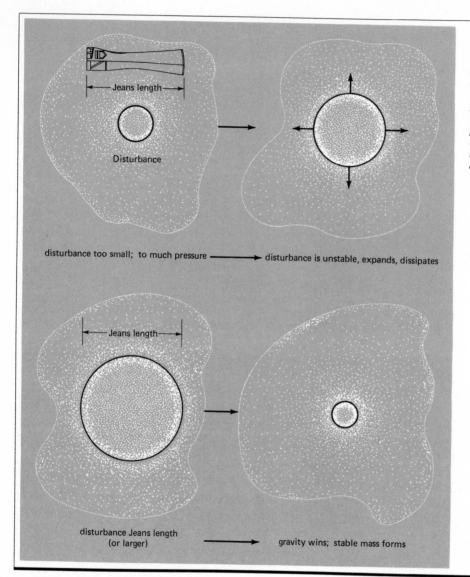

Jeans length

Disturbance

disturbance too small; to much pressure ——————→ disturbance is unstable, expands, dissipates

Jeans length

disturbance Jeans length
(or larger) ——————→ gravity wins; stable mass forms

21.16

Gravitational instability and the Jeans length. The size of the Jeans length depends on the temperature and density of a gas. If a disturbance is smaller than the Jeans length, internal pressure dissipates it. If larger, the disturbed region has enough mass to overcome pressure and collapse gravitationally.

tional collapse must follow. If smaller, the disturbance simply results in the compression of the gas like a sound wave. Such waves eventually dissipate, as you know sound waves in the atmosphere die out if you turn off the source of the waves (Fig. 21.16), such as a set of stereo speakers.

Jeans found that the temperature and density of the gas affected the Jeans length in the following way: The higher the temperature and the lower the density, the larger the Jeans length becomes. This fact has important consequences for the formation of galaxies. As the universe expands, its density and temperature decrease. But the density decreases at a *faster*

rate than the temperature does. So as the universe expands, the Jeans length gets larger, which means that bigger and bigger disturbances are needed to ensure gravitational collapse. As the universe ages, it becomes harder to make disturbances that can result in the formation of galaxies.

Relativity and instabilities / In 1946 the Russian physicist Eugene Lifshiftz applied Jeans's analysis to disturbances in a model of the expanding universe that used Einstein's theory of general relativity. He discovered that Jeans's ideas applied virtually unchanged. Lifshiftz ran into a disturbing problem, however: The predicted rate of growth of gravitational instabilities into bound masses was very slow—so slow that galaxies could just *barely form by now* from small disturbances in the young universe.

Lifshiftz made his analysis before the discovery of the cosmic radiation by Penzias and Wilson. The observation of this radiation forced astrophysicists to consider what happens to disturbances in a hot, dense universe filled with matter and radiation. They found that, before decoupling, the radiation played a powerful role to inhibit the growth of disturbances. Recall that internal pressure has a crucial effect on instability. A dense patch in the early universe will have a high internal pressure because the radiation adds to the pressure force. Only very large disturbances would have any chance of growing so long as the matter and radiation interacted. Small disturbances would just create sound waves that would not grow in size or density but would eventually fade away. The radiation pressure dissipates disturbances that have masses of 10^{12} solar masses (or less) up to the time of decoupling. So before the decoupling of the matter and radiation, disturbances that contained roughly the mass of a galaxy could not grow.

Just after decoupling, it's a new show (Fig. 21.17). The radiation and the gas no longer interact, so radiation pressure no longer helps out in the battle against gravity. Small disturbances amounting to only 10^5 solar masses can condense out of the gas, along with disturbances of greater mass. This result gives some hope, for the large gravitationally bound masses seen now range from 10^5 to 10^{15} solar masses (clusters of galaxies). Disturbances of this size range can grow just after decoupling. So the time of decoupling, roughly 700,000 years after the big bang, marks the time when the galaxy formation could take place in the young universe. This result is reassuring, for it allows ample time for the galaxies to form and evolve, approximately 5 billion years.

So far, so good. But here's one real weakness in these ideas, and that is Lifshiftz's results. Even though disturbances can be permanent, they grow slowly, so slowly that the galaxies could hardly have formed by now, according to the model.

But galaxies have formed and did so early in the history of the universe. If gravitational

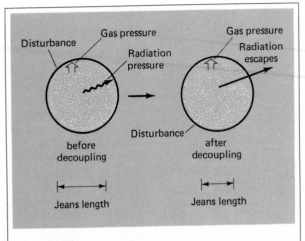

21.17

Before decoupling, radiation pressure added to the internal pressure of a disturbed patch because the gas was opaque to the radiation and held it in. After decoupling, the gas is transparent and the radiation escapes, no longer contributing to the internal pressure. The Jeans length decreases, and the region can now collapse.

instability alone did not do the trick, what helped the process out? One contemporary answer, favored by a few astrophysicists, pictures *turbulence* as the critical aid to galaxy formation. This idea pictures the big bang as producing not only matter and radiation but also turbulence, which speeded up the growth of galaxies.

You are probably familiar with turbulence. As smoke rises from a smokestack, it breaks up into whirling cells of material called eddies, which die away after a while. This fading away happened because of friction between the particles in the eddy and those outside of it.

Picture the young universe, before decoupling, filled with whirlpools of photons and gas particles. This turbulence was generated very early in the big bang, perhaps in the first few minutes. The largest eddies contain 10^{12} solar masses and greater. Remarkably enough, these huge whirls experience very little friction and so persist for a long time—all the way up to decoupling. After decoupling, they end up quickly forming clusters of galaxies. The fate of smaller eddies has not yet been worked out.

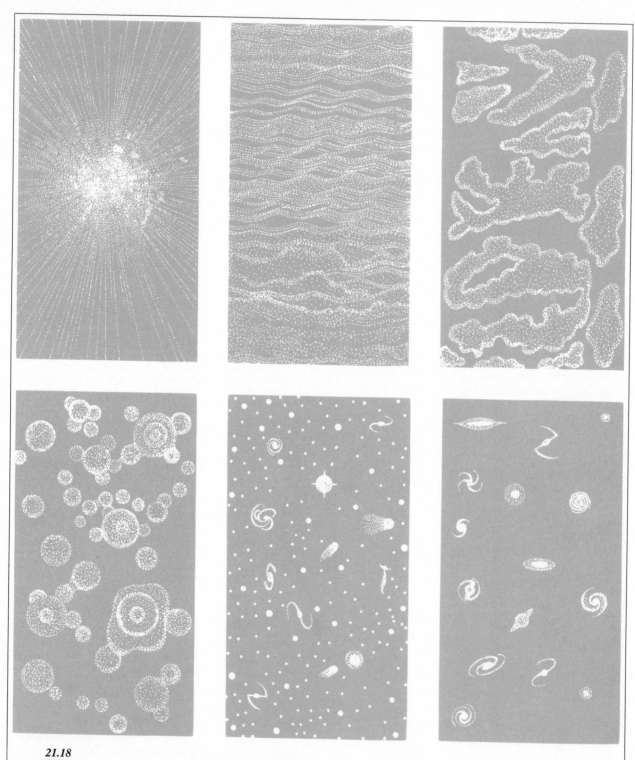

21.18

*A complete time strip of the sequence from the big bang to
now, highlighting galaxy formation. Aided by turbulence, irregularities in the big bang eventually condense by gravitational instability to form the variety of galaxies seen today.*

Despite this vagueness in the model, whatever survives decoupling grows swiftly into gravitationally bound masses, spurred on by the turbulence (Fig. 21.18). This development may have been helped out by the generation of shock waves after decoupling. Shock waves help to compress material. Also, large eddies may collide, cause shock waves, and break up. The smaller blobs of matter broken off in the crashes then form into galaxies.

You may have noticed that I skipped over an important issue: How do eddies and disturbances with greater than 10^{12} solar masses end up as *clusters* of galaxies, rather than as individual galaxies? That's still an unanswered question.

The origin of the Galaxy / Let me sketch a possible scenario for the formation of one special Galaxy, our own Milky Way. Assume at decoupling a disturbance occurs, large enough to condense finally into the Galaxy. This disturbance would have to have a mass of at least 100 billion solar masses. Picture this disturbance forming a cloud that first expands with the universe. But as gravity pulls the material in the cloud together, the rate of expansion slows down. The cloud reaches a maximum size—about 160,000 ly—and then rapidly falls together. This collapse takes place about 1 billion years after the big bang. Meanwhile, other clouds like the one that will form the Galaxy also reach their maximum size and then condense. All these clouds interact with each other gravitationally and set each other spinning slowly.

The spinning is important. As the Galaxy's cloud condenses, it spins faster and faster. The material making up the cloud is pulled together along the direction of spin but not so much at right angles to the spin axis. The cloud flattens out from an originally spherical shape into a pancake with a dense central condensation. During this collapse, parts of the cloud become gravitationally unstable and fragment into stars. Whatever material did not get caught up in this first phase of star formation makes up the disk of the young Galaxy and then later becomes stars.

You can view the process of fragmentation in terms of the Jeans length. Applying this analysis to the temperatures and densities expected in the young Galaxy, you find that the disturb-

ances that were able to condense were very large, at least a few hundred solar masses. (These masses are large because the temperature is high, approximately 1000 K.) The first bound masses to form in the Galaxy could not have been ordinary stars, which typically have about 1 solar mass and do not exceed 100 solar masses. According to present ideas, these superstars evolved quickly (in a few million years), were blown up as supernovas, and formed black holes or neutron stars. So if they ever existed, you can't see them now. In their explosive deaths, the superstars fling heavy elements into the material from which the next generation of stars form. The addition of these heavy elements cools off the remaining gas, and so the Jeans length becomes smaller. A disturbance of only a few solar masses can grow. This stage of starbirth probably formed the oldest stars seen now, the Population II stars.

Whatever material did not make up the second generation of stars fell into the disk. Turbulence in the disk, perhaps whipped up by supernova explosions, helped to form the third generation of stars, which are old Population I stars. After these stars our sun formed, and the gravitational collapse of the cloud that formed the sun also resulted in the formation of the planets, including the earth. This important starbirth took place about 5 billion years ago, roughly one-third the time since the beginning of the universe.

With each subsequent stellar generation, more heavy elements feed back into the interstellar medium. The continued enrichment permits the formation of stars with lower and lower masses. These low-mass stars do not eject much material. As the Galaxy ages, more matter is trapped in low-mass stars and is lost from the interstellar medium. The process is a one-way street; with each recycling of the material between stars and the interstellar medium, less and less matter takes part in the process of evolution.

The general processes of formation and evolution for other types of galaxies probably ran much the same as in the Milky Way. The details are obscure, however, and most ideas about galaxy formation are speculative. Recall that elliptical galaxies have little gas and dust and few young stars, in direct contrast to spirals. The lack of hot stars and of an interstellar medium falls into the outline of the preceding scheme. Because of their short lifetimes, hot stars are present only if they are continually formed from the interstellar medium. A sparse amount of gas between the stars ensures the formation of few new stars.

Why do galaxies come in different types? This is a most vexing question about galaxy formation. One good idea is that the forms are related to the initial angular momentum of the protogalaxies. For example, irregular galaxies have little angular momentum; so their parent clouds must have had little spin. In contrast, spiral galaxies—becuase they have flat disks—have much more angular momentum; their parent clouds must have had considerable initial spin.

21.7

Speculations on quasars and active galaxies

How do quasars and active galaxies fit into this gravitational instability model for the formation of galaxies? Not very well, because there aren't clear ideas about the evolution of quasars and active galaxies, and what physical processes link them. If quasars' red shifts arise simply from the expansion of the universe, then quasars must be among the firstborn from the primeval fireball.

You can infer something general about the evolution of quasars by observing the most distant and so the youngest ones. The trouble here lies in the fact that the limited light-gathering power of telescopes permits seeing only the most luminous of the high red shift quasars. In a study of quasar evolution Maarten Schmidt has concluded that quasars evolved rapidly when the universe was young. About 8–9 billion years ago approximately 100,000 times more quasars marked the heavens than exist now. And only 5 billion years ago, at about the time the earth was formed, the abundance of quasars was about 100 times greater than now.

From his calculations Schmidt concluded that 15 million quasars, visible to the largest telescopes, dot the entire sky. The majority, however, are so far away that during the long time required for their speeding photons to reach the earth, the quasars themselves have already expired. Like fireballs blasted from a display sky-rocket, quasars bloomed brilliantly many years ago; and like the fireballs, which are extinguished before they hit the ground, most quasars are now played out.

In this view quasars do not live much longer than several hundred million years. Then, if quasars are the youthful phases of the typical evolution of a galaxy, this hyperactive quasar stage lasts but a few hundred million years. Although short (by comparison to the ages of normal galaxies), a quasar phase still poses a severe problem: the energy machine. For instance, the total amount of energy emitted by 3C273 over 100 million years would be about 10^{55} J—equivalent to the energy released if 10^8 suns were *completely* converted from matter to energy.

I've hedged so far in describing models for the power sources of quasars in any detail. Here, in some depth, is one popular and fruitful model—supermassive black holes.

The overall picture is a simple one and related to binary X-ray sources that may be black holes (of ordinary stellar mass). Imagine a supermassive black hole—roughly 10^8 solar masses—in the core of a young galaxy. Such a core may have had a very high density so that the first stars to form may have been very massive (hundreds of solar masses or more). They evolved quickly and left behind massive black holes; these attracted more material and perhaps each other. Collisions of black holes might have occurred, and a supermassive black hole eventually formed. It would have a radius of only some 3×10^8 km—only twice the size of the earth's orbit around the sun.

The tidal forces close to this supermassive black hole would be stupendous—a human body would be ripped apart only a few hundred AUs from it. Stars passing close enough would also be ripped apart. Peter Young, Gregory Shields, and Craig Wheeler have worked out such a model in detail. They pictured that the stellar material forms an accretion disk and radiates as it spirals into the black hole, thus powering the quasar. The model calculations show that luminosities of 10^{12} solar luminosities, about that of bright quasars, are possible. To feed the black hole requires at least a solar mass of material a year. As the black hole feeds, it uses up nearby material in the core. The rate of mass infall slows down. Then the quasar becomes less active, emits less energy, and evolves into an active galaxy (such as a Seyfert), then a normal one.

From Schmidt's work it seems that the quasar stage of a galaxy's evolution began only 1 or 2 billion years after creation and lasted at most a billion years. A galaxy goes through an active galaxy phase for a few billion years. Then somehow the active phase ends, leaving a galaxy with a monstrous black hole in its nucleus!

One natural consequence of this idea: Most (all?) galaxies—active or normal—harbor a supermassive black hole in their cores. If so, you should see these black holes indirectly—for instance, by the emission of X-rays from a very small nuclear source; or perhaps the nucleus will show an intense, pointlike source of light (from a concentration of stars around the black hole), stars orbiting the center should have high velocities, and emission lines with high Doppler shifts might be visible from the infalling matter. Observations of such effects have been reported by two research groups: One has found a high-luminosity spike in M87's nucleus (such a spike is not found in the nucleus of normal elliptical galaxies), and the other has discovered a dramatic increase in the velocities of stars in the nucleus compared to those outside the nucleus. A model consistent with these observations is one of a 5×10^9 solar mass black hole hiding in the inner 300 ly of the nucleus. The black hole would cluster the stars in the nucleus closely around it, and they would orbit at high velocities.

What about our Galaxy? In this model it, too, should have a nuclear supermassive black hole. Does it? Maybe—from the radio and infrared line observations that indicate rapid rotational motions near the Galaxy's core. Here it appears that the rotational velocities increase closer to the core. The rotational velocities are so high that a huge concentration of mass is needed to hold all that speedy gas together. For example, if the Galaxy's core simply contained a cluster of stars, you expect the rotational velocities to decrease toward the core because as you get closer in you have less mass to bind the moving materials gravitationally. To account for the rapid rotation requires a mass in the core of 4–6 million solar masses—all lumped together in a region only 0.13 ly in diameter!

What form might this mass have? One possibility—and it's very hard to come up with another—is that the mass is locked up in a black hole. If it were in the form of, say, solar-mass stars, these stars would be separated on the average only 1–2 AU from each other. That seems unlikely, because stars so close, especially if many of them were red giants, would collide rather frequently—and form a black hole!

Note that this model resembles that for binary X-ray sources (Section 20.6). And so, you'd expect X-rays to be emitted by the hot gas in the accretion disk around the black hole. But so far X-ray telescopes have *not* detected a strong X-ray source at the position of the Galaxy's nucleus. This lack poses a serious problem for a model of a supermassive black hole in the core of the Galaxy.

If supermassive black holes power active galaxies, what is their connection with the observed radio and optical jets that spout from some nuclei? That's not clear in detail, but here's one idea. Look close up at a black hole surrounded by an accretion disk (Fig. 21.19). Note that where the material actually flows into the black hole, it is pinched into a very narrow stream. Here the walls of the accretion disk rise sharply, forming a central funnel around the black hole. The funnel centers about the rotation axis of the black hole and accretion disk. The gas in the funnel is hot—so hot that material blows off of the accretion disk. The funnel acts to channel the blown-off material pretty much parallel to the rotation axis. (Material streaming at an angle will hit the sides of the funnel or fall into the black hole.) The oppositely directed streams of hot gas blow out the funnel and make the jets seen close to the nuclei of some active galaxies.

The great advantage to these black hole models is that the energy conversion (from gravitational to other forms, such as radiative) happens with high efficiency—so large luminosities can be produced over long periods of time.

Is the evolutionary connection of quasars and active galaxies correct? Finding black holes in nearby galaxies (such as our Galaxy and M87) would provide evidence for it. But be warned that even though the black hole models may be the best buy in terms of a conventional physics understanding of quasars and active galaxies,

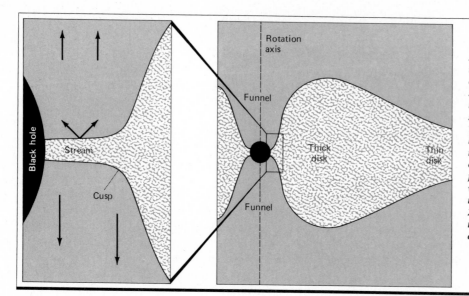

21.19

A possible model for a super-massive black hole powering a quasar or an active galaxy. A sharp funnel forms where matter in the accretion disk streams into the black hole. The disk is hot, and so gas blows off it. The funnel directs this gas along the rotation axis of the black hole. (Adapted from a diagram by M. Abramowicz, M. Calvani, and L. Nobili, the Astronomical Journal, vol. 242, p. 772, copyright © 1980 by the American Astronomical Society)

the models are hard to test observationally. Martin Rees, a theoretician, has expressed the optimistic view: "The energy source in these galaxies will be shown to be a black hole, I think, even though it may take 100 years before we have proven it."

SUMMARY

This chapter emphasized theoretical ideas concerning the universe by spending more time with cosmological models than with observations. The two main models presented were the steady-state model and the big-bang model.

The discovery of the cosmic blackbody microwave radiation boosted the big-bang model to its present status as the "correct" model for our universe. The isotropy of the radiation implies that our assumptions of isotropy and homogeneity are reasonable. The present temperature of the radiation and the universe's expansion imply that the universe was hot and dense in the past. The model also shows the variation of the temperature with time. This permits an outline of the history of the universe that describes the interaction of radiation and matter.

The universe begins as a cosmic fireball. It expands in a big bang, and the high-energy radiation creates matter. The matter interacts to form helium nuclei, about 25–30 percent by

mass. The universe expands more slowly; eventually nuclei capture electrons to form neutral atoms. At this point matter can be brought together by gravity to form stars and galaxies.

The broad outlines of this history do not depend strongly on the details of the big-bang model. For example, whether the universe is open or closed does not affect the general conclusions for the universe's past. The universe still has a hot big bang and about the same amount of helium is produced as in early times.

Whether the universe is open or closed does significantly affect the future of the big-bang model. The first possibility demands the same end: no end at all. The expansion continues, and the temperature of the cosmic radiation goes down. Eventually most of the matter is locked in dark stars and black holes. No more nuclear fires flare up. Cosmic evolution stops.

More acceptable aesthetically is a closed, oscillating universe, which collapses on itself at a finite time in the future, just as it sprang from itself at a finite time in the past. As pleasing as this idea appears, it has problems. It requires that the universe be closed. But the universe appears open from observational evidence to date.

A "bang-bang-bang . . ." model also runs into theoretical problems. Like a black hole, the universe should collapse into a point of zero volume and infinite density, a singularity. This is physically meaningless, so theoreticians assume that the universe somehow avoids collapsing into a singularity. Maybe it bounces out and expands again. Here Einstein's equations offer no help; at such incredible densities they have no physical meaning. Even the single-bang model has this unanswered question: What was the universe like before the cosmic fireball?

STUDY EXERCISES

1 State in one sentence how the philosophical basis of the steady-state model differs from that of the big-bang model. (*Objectives 1 and 3*)

2 Make a list of the fundamental cosmological observations. (*Objective 2*)

3 Interpret the observations in exercise 2 in the framework of the standard big-bang model. (*Objective 3*)

4 Give *one* observational argument for asserting that the microwave background is cosmic in origin. (*Objectives 4 and 5*)

5 How does the discovery of the cosmic microwave background radiation "disprove" the steady-state model? (*Objective 7*)

6 List the elements that can be made in a hot big bang, and give one reason that no elements heavier than lithium/beryllium are manufactured. (*Objective 9*)

7 What evidence do we have that backs up the standard big-bang model? (*Objectives 3, 5, 7, 8 and 9*)

8 Describe the origin of matter in the hot big-bang model. (*Objective 6*)

BEYOND THIS BOOK . . .

D. Sciama in *Modern Cosmology* (Cambridge University Press, Cambridge, England, 1972) gives a clear but fairly technical and mathematical presentation of contemporary ideas.

J. Singh looks more at the philosophical base of cosmology in *Great Ideas and Theories of Modern Cosmology* (Dover, New York, 1970).

For a short introduction to relativistic ideas, try *Relativity and Cosmology*, 2d ed., by W. Kaufmann III (Harper & Row, New York, 1977).

P. J. Peebles and D. Wilkinson discuss the discovery of the cosmic background radiation in the "The Primeval Fireball," *Scientific American*, June 1967, p. 28. An update can be found in "The Cosmic Background Radiation" by A. Webster, *Scientific American*, August 1974, p. 26.

J. R. Gott III, J. E. Gunn, D. N. Schramm, and B. Tinsley present an excellent discussion on "Will the Universe Expand Forever?," in *Scientific American*, March 1976, p. 62. They answer "yes."

For a more comprehensive exposition of the origin of the universe in the standard big-bang model, read *The First Three Minutes* by S. Weinberg (Basic Books, New York, 1977).

Robert Wilson presents a personal history of the discovery of the relic radiation in "The Cosmic Microwave Background Radiation," *Science*, vol. 205, p. 866, August 1979.

A good recent exposition of cosmology and the origin of galaxies is contained in *The Big Bang* by Joseph Silk (Freeman, San Francisco, 1980)

For a discussion of the imbalance of matter over antimatter in the universe and the connection to particle physics, read "The Cosmic Asymmetry Between Matter and Antimatter" by F. Wilczek, *Scientific American*, December 1980, p. 82.

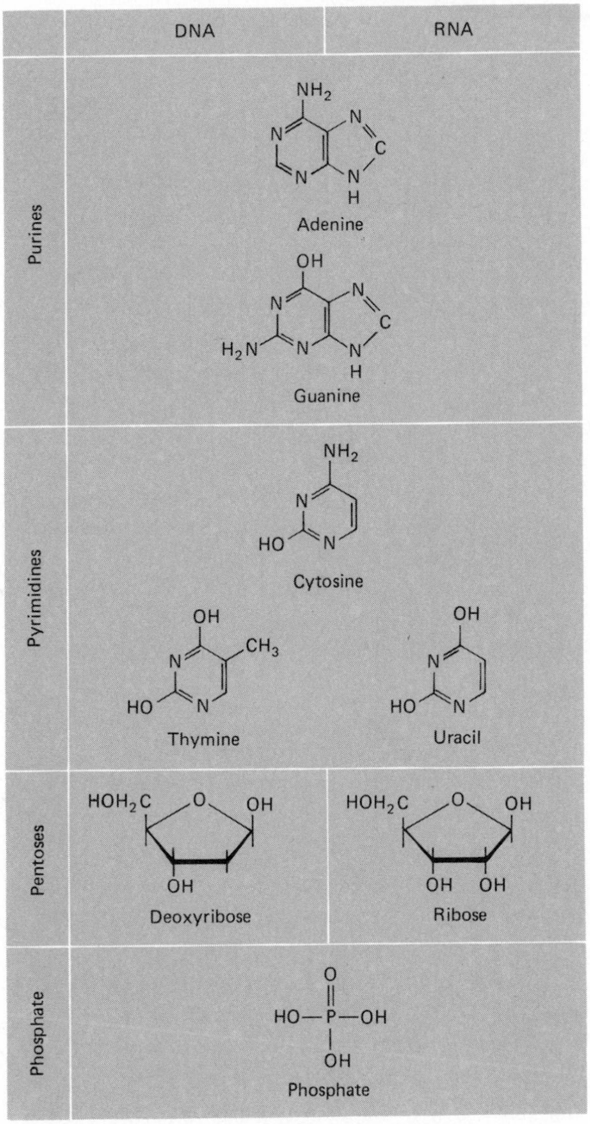

	DNA	RNA
Purines	Adenine / Guanine	
Pyrimidines	Cytosine / Thymine	Uracil
Pentoses	Deoxyribose	Ribose
Phosphate	Phosphate	

2

The chemical building blocks of the nucleic acids DNA and RNA. Five chemical bases are involved: adenine, guanine, cytosine, thymine (in DNA), and uracil (in RNA). These bases are linked in pairs by interlocking chemical bonds and connect to a backbone chain of phosphates and deoxyribose (in DNA) or ribose (in RNA), which are sugars. Note that phosphorus (P) is the most complex atom in the molecule.

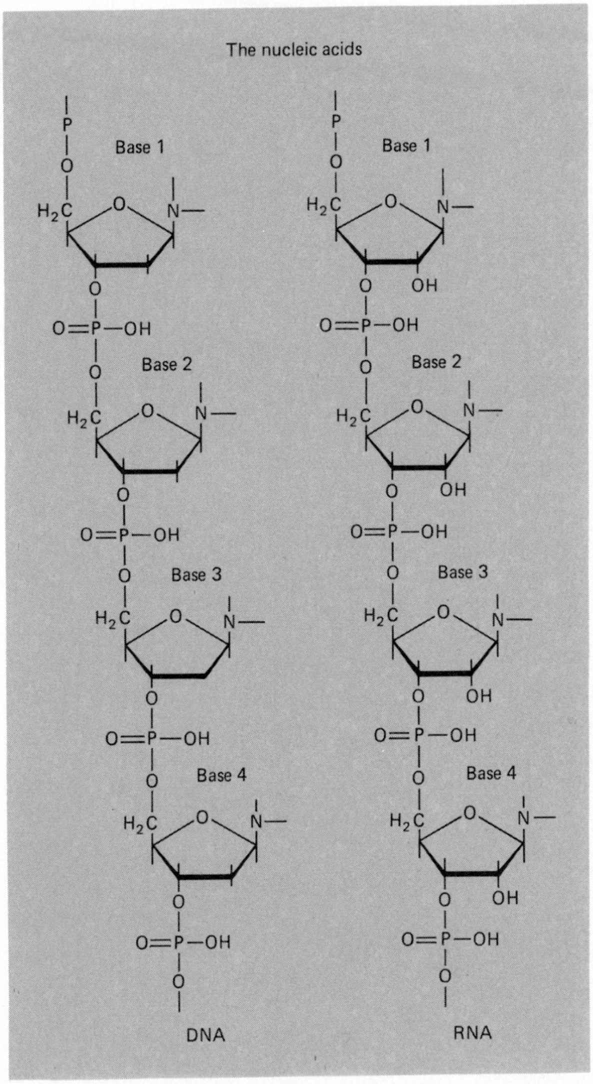

The nucleic acids

3

Schematic diagrams of the chemical construction of one-half of DNA and RNA strands. A complete DNA molecule consists of two such strands, in a spiral, cross-linked by pairs of adenine, guanine, thymine, and cytosine. These cannot pair at random; only adenine with thymine and guanine with cytosine. The nonrandom ordering of these bases permit the DNA molecule to code information—the basis of genetics.

(higher) organisms with the passage of time. This progression from lower to higher forms presupposes some primeval life form to start the process of biological evolution. At some point biological evolution began, but chemical evolution must have preceded it.

An aside about mutations: How are mutations triggered? Among the known processes are chemical changes in the genes induced by natural radioactivity and cosmic rays. Now, recall that one source of cosmic rays (Section 15.3) is supernovas. And heavy elements, such as the uranium in the earth, are synthesized in supernova explosions. So mutations are driven in part by stars, and we are made of starstuff. These facts highlight the crucial role played by stars in cosmic evolution.

Clues from geology / Fossils in rocks provide the essential traces of biological evolution on the earth. Radioactive dating techniques (Focus 23) permit the dating of the ages of fossils.

Until recently, the fossil record faded at the hazy border between Cambrian (beginning about 600 million years ago) and Precambian times because extremely primitive life forms did not possess structures that could be fossilized (Table 22.2). Careful microscopic inspection of ancient rock samples has revealed the remains of bacteria and algae from 1 to 3.5 billion years old that provide clues to life's evolution on earth.

The oldest region of rocks, the Fig Tree formation, lies on the border between the Republic of South Africa and Swaziland. A strontium-rubidium clock dates these rocks at about 3.2 billion years. The rocks contain two distinct life forms: rod-shaped structures resembling modern bacteria (Fig. 22.2) and round cells similar to modern blue-green algae.

Bacteria and blue-green algae both have a simple cell structure devoid of a cell nucleus and specialized components. They reproduce by simply splitting in two. The lack of specialized cellular and genetic structure indicates that these fossils are on the lowest rungs of the evolutionary ladder.

These first self-sustaining organisms must have been able to manufacture food from inorganic substances. Photosynthesis provides the simplest chemical mechanism for freeing the organism from dependence on its environment to produce food, and many modern bacteria

Era	Age (millions of years)	Life
	Now	*Homo sapiens* dominates earth
Cenozoic	2–4	*Homo sapiens* appears
	58	Mammals appear
	63	End of dinosaurs
Mesozoic	135	Flying reptiles
	181	First bird
	239	Dinosaurs appear
	280	First reptiles
	400	First amphibians
Paleozoic	410	First land plant fossils; first insect fossils
	460	First fish fossils
	550	First plant fossils
	3200	Oldest possible fossils
Precambrian	3800	Oldest rocks
	4600	Formation of earth

TABLE 22.2 *Simplified geologic time scale*

and all modern blue-green algae are photosynthetic. So the Fig Tree fossils appear as a crucial junction in biological evolution, about 1 billion years after the formation of the earth.

Recently, scientists have announced the discovery of a new microfossil collection at North Pole, western Australia. These rocks are a bit older than the Fig Tree formation, about 3.5 billion years old. They contain spheres of carbon, which have shapes similar to the fossils in the Fig Tree rocks. The carbon spheres may be biogenic in origin. At another location in Australia a rock was found, also dated at 3.5 billion years, which contains layered structures thought to be built by colonies of bacteria. These observations suggest that early life may have been more widespread than generally thought.

Evidence for the next evolutionary step comes from the Gunflint formation along the shores of Lake Superior in western Ontario, Canada, for which radioactive dating sets a maximum age of about 2.4 billion years. Many of the fossils here show characteristic algal structures (Fig. 22.3) similar to modern photo-

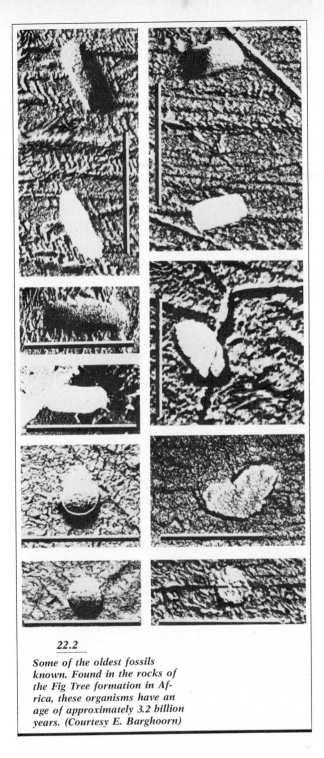

22.2

Some of the oldest fossils known. Found in the rocks of the Fig Tree formation in Africa, these organisms have an age of approximately 3.2 billion years. (Courtesy E. Barghoorn)

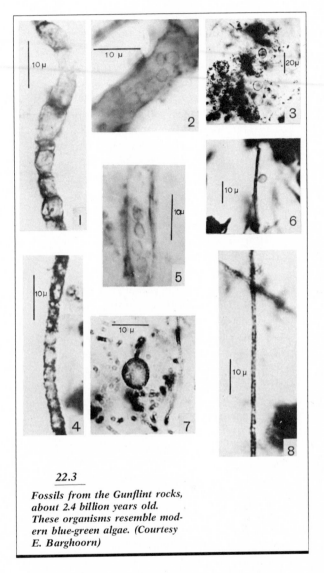

22.3

Fossils from the Gunflint rocks, about 2.4 billion years old. These organisms resemble modern blue-green algae. (Courtesy E. Barghoorn)

synthetic blue-green algae. Even more striking are structures suggestive of a cell nucleus. With the advent of definite genetic structures in the nucleus, a cell gains a greater potential for mutation and rapid evolution. The Gunflint fossils show that this level may have begun about 2 billion years ago.

The final document of the lower rungs of biological evolution comes from the Bitter Springs formation in the Northern Territory of Australia. The rocks found here are approximately 1 billion years old. Three of the fossils

appear to resemble modern types of green algae. Unlike the simpler blue-green algae, the green algae contain complete cell nuclei, the necessary parts for sexual reproduction. The Bitter Springs fossils definitely display the capacity for sexual reproduction. Two billion years of evolution passed before cells attained this potential. Once this happened, biological evolution accelerated, because the mixing of genetic material from two cells made possible many new genetic combinations.

So the fossil hunters have unearthed vital clues in the biological evolution of life. The fossil discoveries imply that (1) the evolution of LAWKI takes a long time (*billions* of years) and (2) chemical evolution must have been completed on the primeval earth about 1 billion years after the earth formed in space, for DNA and proteins must exist before cells form. What must have been the conditions on the young earth for chemical evolution to take place?

Hints from astronomy / Step back a moment to reconsider the physical evolution of the cosmos. The universe began in a big bang at most 15 billion years ago. The big bang produced hydrogen and helium. The other elements up to iron were produced in the cores of massive stars. When massive stars explode, heavier elements are made, and the star-manufactured materials are blown into space. So at least one generation of massive stars must have died before the elements necessary for life were available.

The sun is probably a third-generation star, formed about 4.6 billion years ago. The birthdates of the earth and moon, inferred from radioactive-dating methods, are close to that of the sun. This coincidence reflects the fact that the formation of the sun, earth, and moon occurred in a common event out of the same cloud of gas and dust.

The sun reflects the average chemical composition of material in our Galaxy. The earth ended up with a composition quite different from that of the sun (Table 22.1). How did this happen?

Recall (Chapter 12) that the earth formed from the accretion of planetesimals. The earth's bulk composition and the chemical condensation sequence imply that the temperature in the solar nebula at the earth's position was around 600–700 K.

This condensation temperature presents a problem for depositing carbon—the essential element of life—in the earth. The condensation sequence predicts that carbon, in the form of methane, condenses at 120 K. So the planetesimals making up the earth should contain little methane, and the earth little carbon. But that's not the case.

As yet this carbon deposition problem is unsettled, but here's a possible way out. At high temperatures carbon combines with oxygen to form carbon monoxide (CO). Under the proper conditions carbon monoxide combines with hydrogen to form large hydrocarbons, such as those found in tar. If such reactions went on in the solar nebula, the tars would form on the grains that made up the protoearth. (This reac-

tion—carbon monoxide plus hydrogen to make hydrocarbons—is used commercially to make gasoline.) In addition, if ammonia and water are present, the chemical reactions result in the formation of organic molecules, such as amino acids. This process—formation of carbon molecules on grains—is one way carbon might have been incorporated in the earth.

Finally, consider again the earth's primitive atmosphere (Section 8.8). Recall that outgassing from the hot earth supplied the atmosphere with carbon dioxide, water, methane, ammonia, and hydrogen sulfide—the compounds found in volcanic gases today. So the early earth's atmosphere lacked free oxygen, which is so abundant today. In other words, the primitive atmosphere was hydrogen-rich and nonoxidizing.

The stage was set for chemical evolution on the young earth.

22.3
The spark of life

In 1924 the Russian biochemist Aleksandr I. Oparin proposed the idea that life on the earth was the result of gradual chemical evolution. He also recognized that the atmosphere for such evolution must have contained hydrogen compounds. Oparin's work was not published in English until 1938. Before this happened, the English biologist J. B. S. Haldane had written in 1928 an article in which he proposed that ultraviolet light acting on a mixture of hydrogen-rich compounds could build up simple organic compounds. This crucial idea has been supported by laboratory experiments.

In 1953 Stanley L. Miller and Harold C. Urey experimented with hydrogen-rich atmospheres. They sparked a natural soup spiced with various hydrogen compounds, such as ammonia, water, and methane (Fig. 22.4). An analysis of the products turned up a slew of amino acids, including four commonly found in terrestrial proteins. Ultraviolet light instead of spark discharges as the energy source was found to have a much lower efficiency for organic molecule production. *Result:* As long as the gas was composed of hydrogen-rich materials (such as methane and ammonia), organic molecules were produced.

Subsequent experiments with gases, liquids, and solids (such as silica, pure sand) naturally produced *most* of the amino acids common in

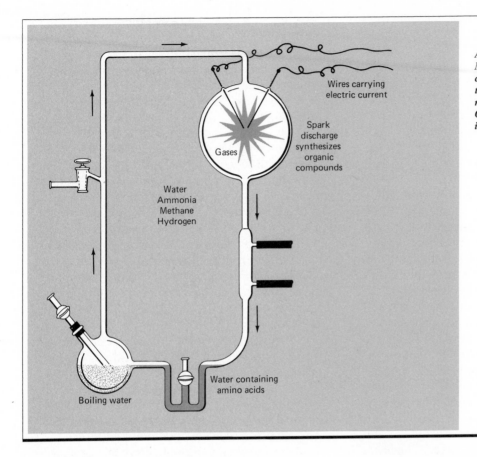

Wires carrying
electric current

Gases

Spark
discharge
synthesizes
organic
compounds

Water
Ammonia
Methane
Hydrogen

Water containing
amino acids

Boiling water

22.4

A schematic diagram of the Miller–Urey experiment. Electrical discharges were fired through a gas of water, ammonia, methane, and hydrogen. Output collected at the bottom included amino acids and fats.

protein and *none* of the amino acids *not* found in modern proteins.

Experiments to simulate the primitive synthesis of DNA have not been so successful. They do indicate that in hydrogen-rich gases and liquids—powered by free energy from sparks or ultraviolet light—some of the basic units of DNA naturally form.

So lab experiments back up the basic model for the beginning of chemical evolution on the earth. All require the input of energy to drive the basic reactions. What was the source of this energy on the young earth?

One possibility is ultraviolet radiation from the sun. Theoretical studies of the sun indicate that the total solar energy striking the earth would have been about 25 percent less 4.6 billion years ago. Solar ultraviolet at wavelengths less than 2200 Å is especially important because it is absorbed by complex molecules and can cause the formation of still more complex ones. (The ozone layer now filters out most of the ultraviolet radiation. Because of the lack of free oxygen, the earth's primitive atmosphere, that

produced by outgassing, did not form an ozone layer.) As a pre-main-sequence star, the sun's surface temperature was less than now. So you would expect that in the past it emitted less ultraviolet, as a fraction of its total energy, than it does now. Estimates are 5–40 percent of the present values at 1500–2500 Å at a time 4.4 billion years ago—smaller than now, but still important.

Radioactive decay can also release free energy. The rate now is about 1/100 the energy input from solar ultraviolet. But 4.6 billion years ago the fraction of radioactive isotopes in the earth would have been greater than now— roughly 3 times more. So radioactive energy might have been comparable to solar energy on the early earth.

Heat from the earth's crust—lava from active volcanoes—also can drive chemical reactions. This energy source now generates little energy compared with radioactivity and sunlight. More volcanic activity probably existed just after the earth's crust solidified than now— perhaps 10 times as much. But the total energy available from this source would still only be a fraction of that from solar energy and radioactive decay.

I should mention two other possible energy sources. (1) Cosmic rays from both the sun and beyond the solar system. The earth's magnetic field deflects the low-energy cosmic rays, so if the young earth had little or no field, the intensity would be greater than now. If the sun were more active in the past, the cosmic ray intensity might have been higher still. On a relative scale, that intensity still wouldn't amount to much compared with other energy sources. (2) Electric discharges, especially as lightning. Today, lightning accounts for almost as much free energy as short wavelength ultraviolet. Before the earth cooled enough for rain to fall, probably little lightning occurred near the earth's surface. Why? Because contemporary research shows that the regions of thunderclouds that generate the electric charges for lightning are in the ice zone—below 0°C. The turbulent circulation of the ice crystals somehow produces the huge accumulation of the charge needed for a lightning bolt. So before the first rain, any lightning flashed at much higher altitudes than now. After a great primeval rain, lightning storms possibly raged widely over the earth's surface. Then the energy from lightning probably had at least the relative importance it does now.

Note that all these energy sources have the capacity to destroy as well as to help synthesize molecules. The balance between creation and destruction determines the number and kinds of molecules that could exist.

To sum up: Energy put into a hydrogen-rich gas or liquid naturally promotes chemical reactions that produce the building blocks of proteins and nucleic acids. These conditions existed on the young earth.

Notice that little was said about how these simple molecules get together to form known proteins, DNA, and RNA—which are both large in size and precise in architecture. The how is not yet clear, and laboratory studies so far have yielded meager results.

22.4

Amino acids from space

Meteorites provide some evidence to support the theories of natural synthesis of organic compounds. Of the three main classes of meteorites

(Section 12.1), the minority (about 1 percent) are carbonaceous chondrites, which contain a relatively high percentage of carbon (2 percent). Only 36 carbonaceous chondrites have been known to fall to the earth. People have regularly speculated that some of the carbon contained in these meteorites might be organic in nature.

The first indication that this might be true came in 1961, when Frederick Sisler and Walter Newton analyzed fragments from a stony meteorite that fell in Murray, Kentucky, in 1950. The specimen was sterilized, crushed, and placed in a nutrient solution. After a few months Sisler and Newton identified an unusual, elongated bacterium growing in the culture. Other scientists were not able to repeat these results, and suspicions arose about the possible contamination of the meteorite during the long time that elapsed between its landing and its analysis in the laboratory.

In the same year scientists at Fordham University conducted a careful investigation of a meteorite that fell at Orgeuil, France, in 1864. They discovered simple organic molecules. Opponents, however, pointed out that this meteorite also incurred a long delay before analysis and might have been contaminated by terrestrial carbon compounds. In 1963 the Orgeuil meteorite yielded the first meteoritic amino acids. Doubt was cast on these results because the most abundant amino acid found is also the most abundant amino acid in human fingerprints.

The best chance for the discovery of extraterrestrial organic materials occurs when the sample undergoes analysis in a scrupulously clean environment as soon after its fall as possible. That chance came in 1969, when a meteorite fell in Murchison, Australia, on September 28, about 11:00 A.M. This meteorite, a carbonaceous chondrite, was rushed to the Ames Research Laboratory of NASA and analyzed by a team of scientists headed by Cyril Ponnamperuma. During the analysis of a 10-g sample cut out from the interior, the NASA research group discovered five amino acids common to living protein. The quantities were small, only a few micrograms of amino acids in each gram of the meteorite.

Some skeptics scoffed at this as nothing more than another example of the ease of contamination of extraterrestrial samples by earthy materials. However, the Ponnamperuma group rebutted this claim. Organic molecules exist in two distinct forms: right-handed ones and left-handed ones, depending on the direction of the twist of the linkage of the atoms. Almost all terrestrial organic molecules are left-handed (for an as yet undiscovered reason), so earth-based contamination is expected to be left-handed. The Murchison meteorite contained just about equal quantities of right- and left-handed molecules, the left-handed forms predominating a little. This evidence strongly points away from terrestrial contamination and toward an extraterrestrial, nonbiological origin of the Murchison organic molecules.

A further hint for the presence of organic material has cropped up in a new analysis of the Murray meteorite, by John Cronin and Carleton Moore of Arizona State University. Their study indicates an amino acid content similar to that of the Murchison meteorite.

Edward Peltzer and Jeffery Bada have analyzed new samples of the Murchison meteorite and have found amounts of hydroxy acids comparable with previously measured amounts of amino acids. (Hydroxy acids are formed when hydroxyl, OH, is added to a hydrocarbon in a particular way.) Amino acids can be formed by electric discharges in a mixture of ammonia, hydrogen cyanide, and aldehydes. Such discharges can also produce hydroxy acids from hydrogen cyanide and aldehydes. How much hydroxy acids are produced compared with amino acids depends on the amount of ammonia around; the more ammonia there is, the more amino acids and the fewer hydroxy acids there are. The detection of the hydroxy acids in the Murchison meteorite backs up the idea of electric discharges forming the organic compounds—a nonbiological origin.

The glut of complex molecules discovered by radio astronomers lends further credibility to nonbiological formation of organic substances. Of particular importance to interstellar organic chemistry are the molecules such as formaldehyde, hydrogen cyanide, cyanoacetylene, formic acid, methyl alcohol, and methylacetylene. Each molecule in this sequence has greater complexity and nonhydrogen composition. For example, cyanoacetylene has a core of three carbon atoms that is the heart of many organic substances. The presence of cyanoacetylene

strongly suggests the presence of acetylene (C_2H_2) as one of its forebears. Acetylene is an active compound with a tendency to form complex molecules, especially benzene (C_6H_6). The benzene ring provides the necessary links for many amino acids and for the nucleic building blocks of DNA. Also, formaldehyde and hydrogen cyanide can be chemically combined to make amino acids.

The interstellar medium seems a breeding ground of preorganic compounds. The important conclusion is: The chemical evolution from simple compounds to complex organic substances occurs so naturally that it takes place even in the hostile environment of space in a nonbiological way.

22.5
From molecule to organism

The previous two sections have explained how chemical evolution naturally—and perhaps inevitably—leads to the making of complex organic compounds that are the building blocks of protein and nucleic acids. These are both needed to join together in a cell. But how was the first cell made?

We don't know the answer. Fossils cannot give information about this crucial time. They do show that organisms populated the earth about 1 billion years after this planet's formation. What happened in between remains something that at present can only be guessed at.

Cells are at the very base of the evolutionary tree. But they are not simple structures! Much of the activity of a cell depends on the fluid nature of its protoplasm, which consists of small particles suspended in water. The characteristics of the protoplasm provide some hints about the formation of the first cells.

Large protein molecules have the ability to surround themselves with a shell of water. By doing so the protein is concentrated in a smaller volume, but the water allows it to interact with other molecules. A number of protein molecules can unite, making a supermolecule encased in water. This resembles the protoplasm of present cells.

Another suggestion for the grouping of molecules comes from the ability of chains of amino acids to form little spheres when dissolved in water. These spheres might clump together to form larger organizations.

These ideas are speculations. In any case the first cells might have formed at the surface of water (such as in a small pond) or at the interface of water and solid material (such as on rocks in a tidal pool). Although we don't know the details about the origin of the first cells, we do know: Organisms appeared on the earth within a billion years after its formation.

These first organisms must have relied on food that was already present in their environment. They must also have been protected from the ultraviolet radiation streaming down to the earth's surface. Remember that little oxygen existed in the atmosphere at this time, so no ozone layer existed to cut out the ultraviolet radiation. Ultraviolet light penetrates only a few centimeters of water, however, so the early molecules could survive if they were below the surface of ponds, lakes, or oceans. They probably formed at the surface and then sank down. Gradually the action of the ultraviolet light on water released some free oxygen to the atmosphere. The ozone layer began to build up. This process cut off more and more of the ultraviolet radiation and so cut down on the synthesis of organic compounds. The first organisms had their food supply cut off at this point. Millions probably died. But a few survived—those that were able to use photosynthesis to manufacture their food. More oxygen was added to the atmosphere, and finally the ozone layer was thick enough to shield almost all the ultraviolet radiation.

Life exploded on the earth (Table 22.3).

This section brings us back to the biological evolution for which we have fossil records. I've taken you back in time and then forward. Let me recap the events so far (Fig. 22.5).

The physical evolution of the cosmos takes us up to the formation of the earth, along with the sun, from a cloud of interstellar gas and dust. The raw materials for life are available: the hydrogen from the big bang, the heavier elements made in the generations of massive stars that preceded the birth of the sun. The process of the fusion of hydrogen in the sun's core guarantees that the earth will receive sunlight for a long time. About 10 billion years have passed since the beginning of the universe.

The scene shifts to chemical evolution on the earth. In a hydrogen-rich atmosphere, simple hydrogen compounds form. With the addition of some energy—mostly ultraviolet radiation from the sun—chemical evolution proceeds to make simple organic molecules. These eventually link up to make more complex ones, such

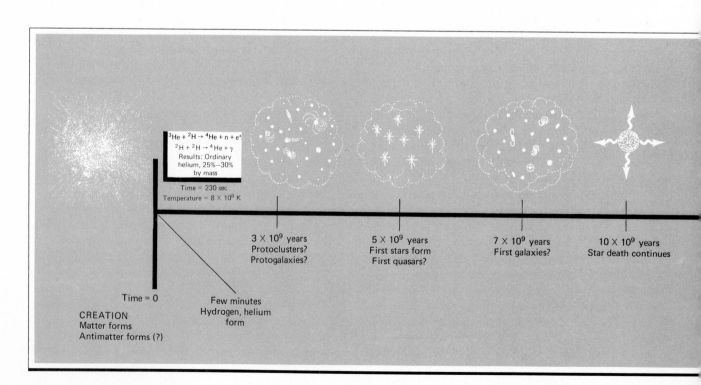

$^3He + {}^2H \rightarrow {}^4He + n + e^+$
$^2H + {}^2H \rightarrow {}^4He + \gamma$
Results: Ordinary helium, 25%–30% by mass

Time = 230 sec
Temperature = 8×10^8 K

Time = 0
CREATION
Matter forms
Antimatter forms (?)

Few minutes
Hydrogen, helium form

3×10^9 years
Protoclusters?
Protogalaxies?

5×10^9 years
First stars form
First quasars?

7×10^9 years
First galaxies?

10×10^9 years
Star death continues

as proteins and nucleic acids. Then it happens. Somehow these molecules get together to form the first organisms. Biological evolution begins—about 9 billion years since the universe began. It culminates with the advent of human beings only a few million years ago.

I'll admit that the "somehow" that led to biological evolution is not clearly known. But we do know that it *did* happen. With this scheme in mind, let me turn to the solar system and the Galaxy to investigate the possibility that we have cosmic neighbors.

22.6
The solar system as
an abode of life

So far we know of only one planet in the solar system with carbon-based life—our earth. Given the environmental conditions on the other planets, LAWKI could not survive on them, with one slim exception—Mars. I'll discuss the red planet first and then turn to some speculations about the Jovian planets as prebiological worlds.

Mars: The best chance / The fate of Martian LAWKI hinges on the abundance of surface water. The Viking missions found an atmospheric composition of about 95 percent carbon dioxide. The surface pressure is about 7.5 mb—

less than that on the highest mountains on the earth's surface. At this low pressure, liquid water cannot exist on the surface. As evidenced by the polar caps, both water and carbon dioxide are in solid ice form. Even in these regions, abundant liquid water needed for LAWKI probably does not exist. Mars is a very, very dry planet: Even in the "wet" polar regions, the water vapor in the atmosphere, if all condensed, would form a layer only 0.1 *mm* thick on the surface.

Water probably flowed on Mars in the past. East of the volcanic ridge dominated by Olympus Mons stretches the series of channels that may have been carved by the erosive action of liquid water. A possible source of water is a frost layer below the ground, because the temperature is always below freezing a short distance below the surface. Alternatively, some astronomers imagine that at an earlier epoch Mars had a denser atmosphere capable of holding water vapor to generate rainfall.

This speculation ties in with past volcanic activity. On the earth, volcanoes spew out large volumes of carbon dioxide and water vapor. Possibly the violent geologic episode that spawned the volcanoes (Fig. 22.6) at the Tharsis Ridge also injected a significant amount of

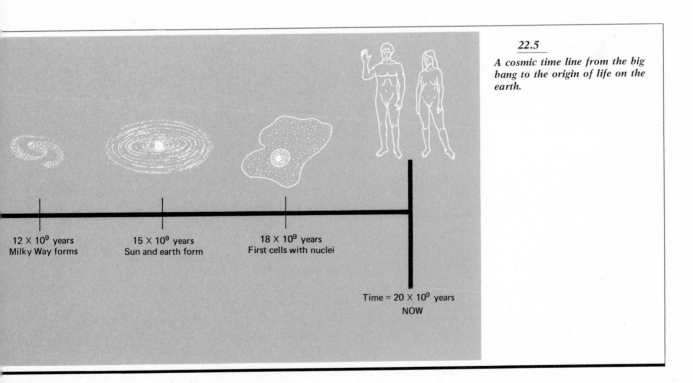

22.5
A cosmic time line from the big bang to the origin of life on the earth.

12×10^9 years
Milky Way forms

15×10^9 years
Sun and earth form

18×10^9 years
First cells with nuclei

Time = 20×10^9 years
NOW

TABLE 22.3 *Possible timetable for biogenesis on the earth*

Time (billions of years)	Events
4.6	Formation of earth; loss of primordial atmosphere
4.5–3.5	Internal melting from heat of radioactive decay of short-lived isotopes; core and mantle form; magnetic field forms
	Outgassing creates second atmosphere of hydrogen-rich compounds; no free oxygen; continents and ocean basins form; no ozone layer, so intense UV radiation strikes surface
3.8	Oldest known rocks form
4.0–3.5	Prebiological chemical evolution driven by solar UV light; biogenesis of simple life that must get food from its environment
3.2	Oldest possible fossils; continents growing; water increasing in ocean basins
2.4–1.8	Oxygen release increases, approach 0.1 percent of present level in atmosphere
1.8–1.0	Carbon dioxide rapidly decreases, carbonate rocks form; first cells with distinct nuclei develop
1.0–1.7	Ozone layer begins to form, sheltering earth's surface from UV
0.7–0.6	Oceans reach present salt level animal life in seas; flowering plants on land
0.5–now	Explosion of life leading to *Homo sapiens*

SOURCE Adapted from A. N. Strahler, *The Earth Sciences*, Harper & Row, New York, 1971.

gases into the Martian atmosphere. An increased atmospheric pressure would have allowed water to flow on certain regions of the surface and to cut the meandering channels. That water may now be frozen below the surface or locked up in surface minerals.

Recurring deluges or meltings (from higher temperatures) may explain the origin of the laminated terrain found in the polar regions (Fig. 22.7). There, stacks of thin plates of crustal material stand about 10 km tall and up to 200 km across. Because they exist only in the polar regions, where carbon dioxide and water ice form annually, the plates may be related to the influx and outgo of these substances. A time of a denser atmosphere may have produced the laminated terrain along with the eroded channels.

An eruption of interior gases may also have been combined with astronomical effects to change the Martian environment in the past. Owing to the gravitational attraction of the other planets, Mars's orbit varies in its average distance from the sun. As a consequence, the average amount of sunlight and its peak amount vary over 2-million-year periods. The variation in solar energy input affects the size of the polar caps. It is possible to imagine large polar caps accumulating during the colder periods and melting during the warmer ones, adding carbon dioxide and water to the atmosphere. Perhaps during the warm spells, Martian life developed.

This optimistic speculation should not cloud the direct test for Martian LAWKI: the Viking landers' biology experiments (Focus 54). Unfortunately, the results were negative—in the soil sampled, LAWKI does *not* exist on Mars now.

Why such a negative view? First, and I think most important, both landers contained an instrument called a mass spectrometer, designed to detect and measure organic molecules—the complex chains, secured by carbon, that characterize LAWKI. At both landing sites, *no large organic molecules were found.* The samples gave off some carbon dioxide and water vapor—that was all. The instruments had the sensitivity to detect organic compounds in a concentration of just a few parts in a billion. That's about 1 million bacteria (dead or alive) in a sample—far below the concentration found in desert soils on the earth.

In light of the lack of complex molecules in the soil, the landers' biology experiments (Focus 54), when they gave apparently positive results, can all be explained by *chemical* reactions rather than by *biological* ones. *Warning:* These

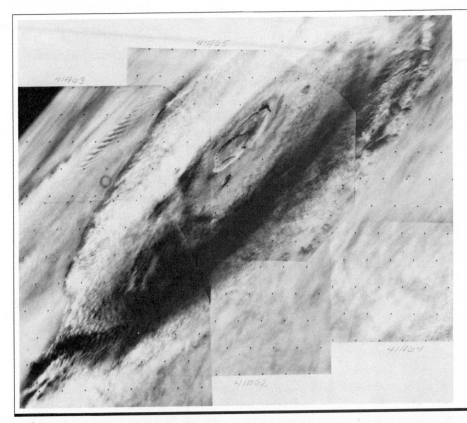

22.6

The giant Martian volcano Olympus Mons, 24 km high. Clouds wreath the volcano up to an altitude of about 19 km. These clouds may be water ice that condenses from the atmosphere when it moves up the slope of the volcano and cools. (Courtesy NASA)

22.7

Laminated terrain on Mars near the south pole cap. These formations may contain water ice. (Courtesy NASA)

focus 54

VIKING BIOLOGY EXPERIMENTS

Each lander contains a biology instrument package that has three miniature laboratories designed to analyze soil samples for signs of life. Each lab operates on a different principle relating to LAWKI.

The gas-exchange experiment / The basic idea is simple but most earthlike in its assumptions. Any living organism alters its environment by eating, breathing, reproducing, and other life activities. Changes in the atmosphere around the creature may indicate whether any such activities are going on. For example, we breathe in oxygen and emit carbon dioxide.

For this experiment, a soil sample sits partially submerged in a complex food solution in an atmosphere of helium, krypton, and carbon dioxide. Every few days the gas is sampled to look for traces of such molecules as oxygen, carbon dioxide, and methane.

The major drawback to this experiment is that Martian organisms might not like the food we've sent them or the amount of water with it.

The pyrolytic release experiment / This device attempts to look for Martian life in its normal, arid conditions. The goal is to look for microorganisms taking in carbon dioxide from the atmosphere. An example of carbon assimilation on the earth is photosynthesis:

Sunlight powers the conversion of carbon dioxide and water into organic material and oxygen.

A soil sample incubates for a few days in a normal Martian atmosphere to which radioactive carbon monoxide and carbon dioxide have been added. Simulated sunlight, with the ultraviolet taken out, bathes the sample. Martian life might take in the radioactive carbon from the atmosphere. The chamber's atmosphere is flushed out at the end of the incubation period to remove all the radioactive carbon not eaten by living organisms. The sample is then heated to about 900 K to vaporize any organic material, and the released gases are then checked for radioactivity. A positive result indicates that carbon assimilation has occurred.

The labeled-release experiment / This test rests on some crucial assumptions: (1) Microorganisms are present in the Martian soil; (2) biochemical reactions take place in a fluid—water; (3) microorganisms take in material from their environment and discharge gases; and (4) Martian life is carbon based.

The experiment takes a soil sample and adds just a little water and some food containing radioactive carbon. The sample incubates; during this time microorganisms can eat the food and release radioactive carbon. The system senses any radioactive carbon in the released gas.

experiments presumed certain characteristics about Martian life; these assumptions may be wrong.

First, the gas-exchange experiment. This analysis aims for changes in the atmosphere around a soil sample to indicate possible life processes. As microorganisms eat, they grow and reproduce, so the gas they let off should increase with time. Two gas changes were observed: (1) The amount of carbon dioxide first increased rapidly and then *decreased* with time. (2) When water was added to the sample, oxygen was rapidly released and then leveled off in about 24 hours. The rapid output of carbon di-

oxide and water suggests that the results come from simple chemical reactions. Carbon dioxide can be contained in the dry Martian soil; when exposed to water vapor, the soil releases the carbon dioxide and takes in the water.

Second, the labeled-release experiment. Here a small amount of radioactive food was added to a soil sample, and sensors looked for the release of radioactive carbon dioxide gas. For the result to be of biological origin, the decomposition of food to gas should be sensitive to high temperatures. When heated to about 430 K for a few hours, the soil sample should stop its gas release, if that is derived from organisms (the high temperature should kill any microorganisms). The results: Without heating, the sample in the nutrient gave off carbon dioxide. With heating, the gas output stopped. These results were the same at both landers.

Finally, the pyrolytic-release experiment, which was designed to measure the synthesis of organic material under Martian conditions. Curiously enough, seven of the nine tests yielded positive results, although the amount of organic matter needed to explain the result is small: only 100–1000 bacteria. However, when samples were heated, the gas output dropped but did not cut out completely. This heating test points to a chemical interpretation, for any Martian organisms should have been killed by the high temperatures. So the pyrolytic-release experiments may yet have a biological explanation, but a chemical one is more likely.

Despite this one positive clue, the results—taken as a whole—strongly imply the disappointing conclusion that LAWKI does not inhabit the top layers of the soil of Mars (Fig. 22.8). At the International Astronomical Union meeting in Montreal in 1979, a NASA biologist declared that he didn't think there's life on Mars. Our best extraterrestrial search for terrestrial life has so far failed.

Jovian planets: Prebiological worlds? At first glance, the giants of the solar system do not appear amenable to life. Their cold temperatures and sunlike compositions seem to be inhospitable to LAWKI. Yet the cold guarantees that even hydrogen has not been depleted from the atmospheres of the Jovian planets since their formation. The retention of atmospheric hydrogen implies the retention of all heavier elements, such as carbon, nitrogen, and oxygen. The natural expectation, supported in part by observations, is that the Jovian planets are engulfed by extensive atmospheres rich in hydrogen compounds such as water, methane, and ammonia. These compounds are the prebiological components of the earth's atmosphere. I'll treat Jupiter in detail—partially because we know more about it than the others.

Jupiter appears stamped by a striking set of zones and belts (Fig. 22.9), the result of atmospheric convection powered in part by the outflow of internal heat. The belts and zones are distinctly colored, usually yellowish and occasionally white. Some observers have noted pas-

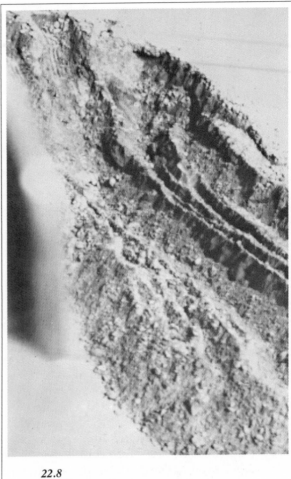

22.8

A deep hole dug by Viking 1 in an attempt to get soil samples from below the surface. (Courtesy NASA)

tel shades of pink, red, and blue. What is the proper mix of chemical compounds to match the observed coloration (Color Plate 12)?

Infrared and ultraviolet spectroscopy, both from the earth and from the Pioneer and Voyager spacecraft, have identified numerous kinds of molecules in Jupiter's atmosphere, including water, methane, ammonia, and molecular hydrogen, as well as acetylene, ethane, phosphine, and germane. Carl Sagan and his co-workers have investigated theoretically the expected abundances of large carbon molecules constructed of the known compounds. Hydrocarbons with appropriate color appear possible under Jovian conditions. These organic molecules might be produced locally by spark discharges in the various cloud layers. Lab experi-

22.9

A view of Jupiter looking down on the polar regions. (Courtesy NASA)

ments find that spark discharges through a mixture of methane and ammonia at room temperature result in a carbon compound with a deep red color; and ultraviolet light shining on a mixture of methane, ammonia, water, and hydrogen sulfide at room temperature and pressure results in slush with a brownish-yellowish color. Other experiments have produced similar results: energy added to a Jovian-like atmosphere promotes the manufacture of colored organic compounds.

The production of such compounds requires a fair amount of energy. Where can it come from? Jupiter receives a mere 0.1 W on a square meter of upper atmosphere from solar ultraviolet radiation. From this energy source the efficiency of organic molecule production is low, so the total amount formed would be small. Shock waves are much more effective production mechanisms; two possible sources on Jupiter are thunder and meteorite impacts. The Voyagers' confirmation of lightning in the Jovian atmosphere makes the scene look even more like that expected on the primitive earth. The flow of internal heat upward through the atmosphere might also provide some of the energy needed to synthesize large carbon molecules.

Traditional arguments against the existence of life on Jupiter have appealed to the harsh temperatures, the crushing pressures, and the poisonous gases. But our present poisons may well have been our chemical ancestors. Although the upper atmosphere is cold (150 K), the temperatures in the Jovian atmosphere just below the cloud tops are not much different from the earth's (about 300 K); and high pressures do not significantly affect the genesis and survival of life. A layer of liquid ammonia that might exist about 50 km below the layer of frozen ammonia is a possible alternative solvent to water, particularly at temperatures below freezing. However, the Pioneer flybys found intense radiation close to Jupiter; this energetic radiation might inhibit the development of any life forms. Also, the continuous convection in the atmosphere probably carries any organic compounds down to lower, hotter regions where they would decompose.

Jupiter appears to be in a state of chemical evolution that is prebiological, but we have no idea if creatures of any kind exist now or will eventually develop.

22.7
The Milky Way as an abode of life

Although the question of the existence of life in the solar system (outside the earth) has not yet been answered "yes," some scientists have already turned to the Milky Way for footprints in the stellar sand. The huge number of stars in the Galaxy—over 10^{11}—argues for the existence of planets elsewhere, in the context of the nebular model of planetary formation. Even if the probability of the genesis and survival of life is indeed slim, the number of possible habitats is so large that some extraterrestrial creature has viewed the dawn of its day. If life developed from the natural evolution of the inorganic, these processes must have also operated in realms beyond the solar system. This is the central idea of modern biology: Life arose from nonlife. The elements of life are the most abundant in the cosmos, so there is no lack of the proper ingredients. All that is required is the proper construction. This forming takes physics, chemistry, and—most important—time.

Cosmic prospecting / To declare that extraterrestrial life exists is not enough to begin the search. You might argue in a similar fashion about the existence of gold in the grains of sand on all the beaches of the world: the uncountable number of sand grains requires some gold grains to be mixed in. This reasoning is not of much help to the gold prospector, who wants to know that gold exists and also *how much* exists and *where* is the best place to hunt for it. We want to try to answer the same two questions concerning life in the Galaxy.

Civilizations of living creatures must evolve; that's part of cosmic evolution. So the number of intelligent civilizations in the Galaxy changes with time. At any one time the number of civilizations depends on the rate at which these civilizations are born and how long they last.

Suppose you are locked in a dark room filled with candles; a friend gropes about and lights a certain number of candles per hour. If you know the average lifetime of a single candle, you can anticipate the number you will see burning at any one time. If your flame-bearing friend lights four candles per hour, and if the average candle burns for one hour, you expect to see four lighted candles in the room at any one time after the first hour. If the candle burns for only half an hour, you see two; if eight candles are lighted per hour, you see four flames. You conclude that the number of observed candles is equal to the rate of candle lighting, R_c, times the lifetime of one candle, L_c, or

$$N_c = R_c L_c$$

So if you know the average lifetime of one candle and the rate at which they begin burning, you can estimate the number lit at any time.

The same reasoning applies to the number of civilizations aflame in the Galaxy at any one time: If R_{ic} is the rate of formation of intelligent civilizations and L_{ic} is their lifetime, then

$$N_{ic} = R_{ic} L_{ic}$$

This relation may be broken down into more specific factors, loosely independent of one another:

$$N_{ic} = R_* P_p P_e N_e P_l P_i L_{ic}$$

Radio astronomer Frank Drake first put together this equation (in a somewhat different form); so it's often called the *Drake equation.*

The meaning of each of these factors relates directly to important facets of cosmic evolution. R_* is the rate of star formation averaged over the age of the Galaxy; P_p is the probability that once a star has formed it will possess planets. The next factors, P_e and N_e, are the probability that some of the planets will lie in the ecosphere and the number of planets in the ecosphere. P_l is the probability that a planet in a star's ecosphere will develop life, and P_i is the probability that biological evolution will lead finally to intelligent life. The final term, L_{ic}, is the lifetime of this intelligent civilization. Note that these factors group into three categories: R_*, P_p, P_e, and N_e relate to astronomy and physical evolution; P_l and P_i relate to biology and chemical/biological evolution; and L_{ic} derives from what I call speculative sociology.

Astronomical factors / The Galaxy contains a few times 10^{11} stars. These stars have formed over at least 5 billion years. So the average birthrate of stars from these figures is about 20 per year. However, the initial burst of star formation delivered a first generation composed mostly of massive stars that quickly spent their energy stores. Their violent ends ejected heavy elements into the currents of space. The next stellar generation acquired these elements and formed in a greater range of masses. Some of the second-generation material was also flung into space, but some of it remained, trapped by gravity to become white dwarfs, neutron stars, or black holes. A third generation of stars (our sun, for example) was born at a much more leisurely rate than the first two generations. The slowdown of the birthrate pushes the initial estimate down to perhaps 10 stars per year. Adopt this value for R_*.

What is the chance that one of these stars will develop a planetary system? Nebular models (Chapter 12) imply that many planets exist in the Galaxy. A collapsing gas and dust cloud must form either a star with a planetary system or a multiple-star system, perhaps also with planets. More than 50 percent of the stars in the Galaxy are in binary or other multiple-star systems. A planet in a multiple-star system may not have a stable orbit, so exclude these from consideration. If planetary system versus a multiple-star system is an either–or proposition, then P_p equals 0.5.

A star's *ecosphere*—the zone in which planets must lie to have conditions suitable for life as we know it—depends primarily on the temperature of the star. The hotter the star is, the farther out the habitable zone starts (Fig. 22.10).

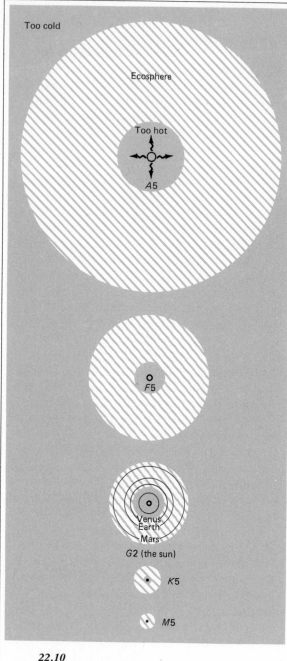

Too cold

Ecosphere

Too hot

*A*5

*F*5

Venus
Earth
Mars
*G*2 (the sun)

*K*5

*M*5

22.10

The size of stellar ecospheres for stars of a few different spectral types. Note that the cooler the star, the smaller the ecosphere and the closer it lies to the star.

The width of the ecosphere is also greater for hotter stars and thinner for cooler ones. The ecosphere must also persist long enough to allow the genesis and evolution of life.

Luminous *O*- and *B*-stars live out their normal lives in about 10 million years, a time much shorter than the 3–4 billion years that elapsed while life evolved on the earth. By our standards, these energy spendthrifts are inconstant parents. So it seems unlikely that attendant planetary systems would have the breathing time to develop life for short-lived stars. Therefore consider only stars whose life spans at least equal the sun's—spectral class *G* or lower, a choice that fortunately includes 98 percent of all the normal stars in the Galaxy. Unfortunately, for stars cooler than spectral class *K*, the ecosphere is small. If you throw out these cool stars, only about 8 percent of the total remains, so P_e equals 0.08. These stars are good suns for nurturing life.

Michael Hart has emphasized that because a star's luminosity changes with time, the ecosphere evolves too. His calculations indicate that the thickness of a *continuously* habitable ecosphere is very small. (He defines the ecosphere as the zone in which an earthlike planet will neither suffer from a runaway greenhouse effect early in its history nor a runaway glaciation after it develops an oxygen-rich atmosphere.) From this evolutionary viewpoint, Hart finds that for the sun the inner edge of the ecosphere lies at 0.958 AU, the outer edge at 1.004 AU, for a thickness of a meager 0.046 AU. Essentially, no ecospheres exist for *K*- and *M*-stars; the maximum thickness, for F9 stars (about 1.1 solar masses), is 0.069 AU. So P_e may be only 0.01 or less. These specific numbers probably shouldn't be taken too seriously, for many poorly known factors go into Hart's models, but you should realize that the continuously habitable ecosphere is probably significantly smaller than might be thought at first.

How about the number of planets in the ecosphere, N_e? Here we have only the unique example of our solar system: three planets—Venus, Earth, and Mars—lie in that zone. (Hart would argue that only the earth does.) If the planetary formation processes in the nebular model are universal, you'd expect other planetary systems to more or less resemble the solar system. Is this belief reasonable? Some years ago Stephen Dole attempted to computer model the results of a nebular-style formation that results in a spacing law for planets. The planets consist of a Jovian-terrestrial mix. And a few planets orbit at the magic ecosphere distance of a solar-mass star. So N_e may range from 1 to 4 or so; use 3.

Biological factors / Here's another either–or proposition. Either the existence of terrestrial life is unique and the probability of life elsewhere is zero, or the earth is typical, the normal result of cosmic evolution, and the probability of any planet's developing life once the astronomical conditions are favorable is 1.

Appealing to the presumed uniformity of physical laws, assume we are typical. Scientists strongly believe that the physical laws as they have been unraveled locally apply to the rest of the universe. This *belief* is expressed in the cosmological principle (Section 21.1). Unfortunately, we have only ourselves as the proof of this supposition. However, laboratory experiments have shown the natural start of chemical evolution. With these as a guide—along with a feeling that the nature of the universe makes the start of chemical evolution inevitable, choose P_e equal to 1.

But beware. It's easy enough to produce organic molecules but much harder to put them together to form an organism. The step from molecules to the Fig Tree fossils is a huge one!

It is extremely difficult to estimate the probability of the evolution of intelligent life once life has developed on a planet. In *Homo sapiens* the mark of intelligence, our huge forebrain, is the single most powerful biological adaptation capable of coping with the struggle for survival. Our brain blossomed on the stem of our spine recently in geological time, not much farther back than the time when the first great ice cap pushed southward. The cycle of the ice ages led to widespread extinctions as animals and plants died under the cold crush of the ice. In the frantic clawing at the threads of survival, *Homo sapiens* emerged as the victor, our emblem of superiority is the brain encased in our expanded skulls. The adaptive powers of a thinking organism appear so great that if at all possible, intelligence may be the ultimate result of genetic natural selection. So choose P_i equal to 1.

Speculative sociological factors / How long can an advanced, technological civilization survive? Is intelligence flexible and complex enough to cope with adverse aspects of its technology? What happens when the fragile net of the environment is pushed beyond its breaking point? These questions demand immediate attention as a growing humanity requires energy and food at the edge of our capabilities to provide them.

Two tacks appear possible to navigate through these winds of doom. The optimistic one views the heavy winds as short gusts that only momentarily hinder the course to the technological golden age. The pessimist peers at a gloomy, unrelenting storm ahead in which present civilization will soon founder. By our own example, the lifetime of an intelligent civilization may be only a few thousand years. If it is possible that every advanced civilization steers clear of its problems, then it should survive as long as the parent star. For civilizations encircling a *G*-type star, their lifetimes could be about 10^{10} years. Their lifetimes may be much, *much* shorter.

The numbers game / As you have progressed through the astronomical, biological, and sociological factors needed for a rough estimate, the footing has become shakier. I have also ignored some important factors in the analysis, such as the upper and lower limits to the masses of planets that can support life and the possible stable planetary orbits in a binary star system. My purpose was not to reach definite conclusions but reasonable exclusions in the enormous range of values each element might take. My personal biases also affected the discussion; I hope I made them clear.

Excluding L_{ic} momentarily,

$$N_{ic} = 10 \times 0.5 \times 0.08 \times 3 \times 1 \times 1 \times L_{ic}$$
$$\sim 1.0 \, L_{ic}$$

If I use the smaller value, $L_{ic} \sim 10^3$, then $N_{ic} \sim 10^3$; on the other hand, with $L_{ic} \sim 10^{10}$, then $N_{ic} \sim 10^{10}$, and almost every star in the Galaxy has fostered an intelligent civilization!

The weakness of this approach is that it is basically speculation. Each step creaks along on some assumption, and the result should be taken skeptically. It is difficult to talk of the probability of untested possibilities and heap one upon another and expect any substance. Furthermore, I have delineated each of the values of the life factors in a reasonable and yet ultimately arbitrary manner. Our own example, life on the earth, may be more special than I have been willing to admit. The genesis of terrestrial organisms moved in a crooked path through the junctions of geological time. At each crucial point, one path was chosen out of many, one history written out of many potential ones. At each moment, conditions were uniquely set in the historical stream and then passed by. The long flow of time can be retraced, but it cannot be repeated.

22.8

Neighboring solar systems?

What evidence exists of other planetary systems? Because a planet shines by reflected light from its parent star (and also because planets are small in size), the light from a planet near any star in the solar neighborhood would be too weak to detect from the earth. Also, a planet is not likely to be very far from its local sun. Even if the planet were just visible, the angular separation of the planet and the star, as seen from the earth, would be so small that the planetary gleam would be lost in the stellar glare. So astronomers cannot *directly* observe other planets outside the solar system.

Instead of searching for the light from very large planets, you can hunt instead for the motion around the center of mass of the planet–star system (recall the earth–moon system's motion about its center of mass, Section 9.1). As a result of this seesaw effect, the visible star wobbles from side to side from the center of mass as a massive planet orbits it (Fig. 22.11). From the observed stellar wobble and an estimate of the stellar mass, you can estimate the mass of the invisible planetary companion by the same method used to measure binary star masses (Focus 39).

Planetary companions? Barnard's star, the second nearest to the sun, appears to exhibit such a corkscrew motion in its proper motion across the sky. In 1963 Peter van de Kamp of the Sproul Observatory concluded that a planet about the mass of Jupiter could account for the size of the wobble. Later he proposed an alternative interpretation, which allows two planets, one about 80 percent the mass of Jupiter and

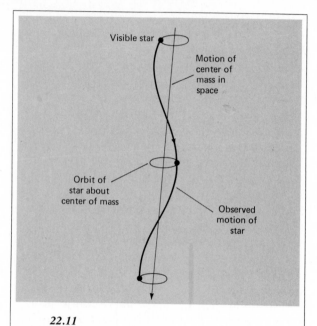

22.11

The path of a star in space with motion about a center of mass. Barnard's star appears to display such a motion, so it may have at least one dark companion.

the other 10 percent larger than Jupiter, to encircle the star. The lesser mass would be about 2.8 AU from the star, and the greater mass, approximately 4.7 AU.

Barnard's star is the only one to display certain telltale signal of invisible comrades. However, some nearby stars of solar mass may display similar motions. If these result from dark companions, most of these are greater than the minimum mass of a star—about 0.06 solar mass. But a few (Table 22.4) may have less than this minimum mass.

Warning: The observations required to detect planets around nearby stars are *extremely* difficult to make. The wiggles sought for are only about 0″.01, or about one one-hundredth the size of a star's image on an astronomical photographic plate. Such minuscule changes are dramatically affected by changes in the telescopes themselves, whether by self-aging or conscious effort (such as cleaning). George Gatewood of Allegheny Observatory has analyzed the errors in such observations and concluded that *no* good evidence supports the existence of Jovian-mass planets. The possible exception is

TABLE 22.4 *Selected stars that may have invisible companions with less than stellar mass*

Name	Distance (light years)	Suspected companion's mass (Jupiter = 1.0)
ε Eridani	10.7	6–50
61 Cygni	11.0	8
Barnard's star	5.9	1.1, 0.8
BD + 43°4305	16.9	10–30

SOURCE Peter van de Kamp, "Unseen Astrometric Companions of Stars," *Annual Reviews of Astronomy and Astrophysics*, vol. 13, 1975; and George Gatewood, "On the Astrometric Detection of Neighboring Planetary Systems," *Icarus*, vol. 27, p. 1, 1976.

Barnard's star, for which the observations from three different observatories seem to show the necessary wiggle.

A curious fact emerges from such investigations: The sun is the only star you know *for certain* that does have a planetary system and does not have a companion star. This raises a key question: What fraction of stars like our sun in the Galaxy have stellar companions?

Recently, 123 sunlike stars (within 85 ly of the sun) have been searched in an effort to find out whether or not they have companions. The technique aimed at detecting regular Doppler shifts in the spectra of these stars. Results: Over half (57 percent) of their stars had at least one stellar companion. What about the others? By inference, roughly one-sixth to one-fifth could have planetary companions (but none were directly observed). This argument, if true, implies that the Galaxy contains 15–20 billion stars with planets—and many of these stars resemble the sun.

Nearby good suns / Of the few hundred stars fairly close to the sun, three stand out as exceptionally good candidates for possessing planets suitable for life (Table 22.5). These nearby systems are consistent with the range of numbers developed in the preceding section for the probability of extraterrestrial life. The first is the star system closest to the earth, Alpha Centauri, a multiple system with a life-bearing-planet probability of 0.1. So if Alpha Centauri is encircled by the same number of planets our solar system possesses, one is likely to shelter life. Such a planet would be a true interstellar neighbor, because Alpha Centauri is only 4.3 ly from the sun. Next in line, at a distance of 10.8 ly, is the *K*-star Epsilon Eridani. Its long main-sequence lifetime, greater than 10^{12} years,

TABLE 22.5 *Stars within 20 light years of the sun that could have habitable planets*

Name	Distance (light years)	Mass (sun = 1.0)	Spectral class	Probability of a habitable planet
α Centauri A	4.3	1.08	G4	0.054
α Centauri B	4.3	0.98	K1	0.057
ε Eridani	10.7	0.80	K2	0.033
τ Ceti	12.2	0.82	G8	0.036
70 Ophiuchi A	17.3	0.90	K1	0.057
η Cassiopeiae A	18.0	0.94	F9	0.057
σ Draconis	18.2	0.82	G9	0.036
36 Ophiuchi A	18.2	0.77	G9	0.023
36 Ophiuchi B	18.2	0.76	K2	0.020
HR 7703 A	18.6	0.76	K2	0.020
δ Pavonis	19.2	0.98	G7	0.057

SOURCE From S. H. Dole, *Habitable Planets for Man*, American Elsevier, New York, 1970.
Note For this study, a habitable planet was defined as one on which a person could now survive without extensive technological aid. The probability in the last column means, for Tau Ceti for example, that if the star has 10 planets, the probability of an inhabitable one is 0.36.

enhances the opportunity to create life but decrease the size of the habitable zone. At almost the same distance (11.8 ly) is the *G*-dwarf-star Tau Ceti, which has physical characteristics much like the sun's. These three stars are the most likely of those nearest to us to have planets with LAWKI.

22.9
Where are they?

The previous section may have whetted your mental appetite for speculation about extraterrestrial civilizations and searching for them. This natural impulse founders on one sticky question: Where are such civilizations?

So far we know of only one—us. Whether or not we should search for others depends on how many technologically advanced civilizations exist in the Galaxy *now*. (For this discussion, take "technologically advanced" to mean creatures who can manipulate their environment at least to the extent that we can, so they have electricity, radios, telescopes, and so on.) If the number is large, then on the average such civilizations must be closer together than if the number is small.

As I pointed out, the key element in estimating this number, N_{ic}, is the *lifetime* L_{ic} of technological civilizations. For example, if the lifetime is about 100 years (which is about how long we've had a technologically advanced human culture on earth), then the average distance between galactic civilizations is roughly 10,000 ly. That makes conversation practically impossible. Why? If you tried to signal by radio, for example, by sending out a message just at the moment our technology permitted, the civilization would have died while the words were still in transit. Communication with extraterrestrials is possible (under known physical laws) if the number of civilizations is large and their lifetimes are long.

Note that N_{ic} is *not* a fixed number. It changes with time as the Galaxy and the objects within it evolve. For instance, for the first billion years of the Galaxy's existence, N_{ic} was probably zero, because life had not yet had time to evolve. So estimates for now need not apply to the past or future.

How far to our galactic neighbors? If we are it, we don't have any neighbors within 10^5 ly (the size of the Galaxy). That's for N_{ic} very small.

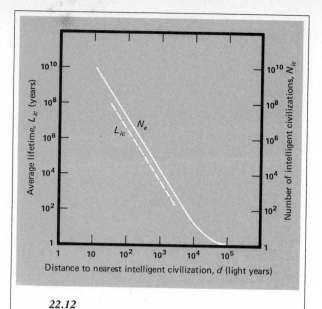

22.12

The relationship of the average lifetimes of intelligent civilizations (L_{ic}), the total number of such civilizations in the Galaxy now (N_{ic}), and the distance to the nearest intelligent civilization now (d). (Adapted from a diagram by R. N. Bracewell)

If N_{ic} is very large, say 10^9–10^{10}, then our neighbors are only a few tens of light years away (Fig. 22.12).

If N_{ic} is 10^6—a compromise guess—then our neighbors live a few hundred light years away (Fig. 22.12). They are then just within reach.

Note that each of these choices implies a value for L_{ic} (Fig. 22.12). If N_{ic} is very small, L_{ic} is at most a few hundred years. We are then probably on the verge of extinction. If N_{ic} is very large, L_{ic} is 10^9–10^{10}. Civilizations then last as long as their suns. If N_{ic} is 10^6, then L_{ic} is roughly 10^5–10^6, and we still may have some time on the planet earth. (But recall, L_{ic} is only an average, not necessarily the most probable lifetime. Maybe civilizations last *either* a very short time, *or* an extremely long time, depending on whether or not they survive the crisis of atomic technology. In such an either–or situation, there might be none that actually last the average time.)

To sum up: We have *no* direct evidence for any other advanced civilization in the Galaxy. But based on the ideas of cosmic evolution, you expect them. So the key question remains unanswered: Where are they?

At a session on extraterrestrial life at the 1979 Montreal meeting of the International Astronomical Union, the discussion revolved around the so-called "four facts" of extraterrestrial intelligence:

1 We are here—but we don't know for how long.

2 No LAWKI has been found on Mars.

3 No positive results have resulted from radio searches.

4 No aliens are here now.

Those four facts were used to support pessimistic views about the abundance of life in the Galaxy.

I certainly agree with the first three "facts." But what about number 4? We have conducted fairly careful extraterrestrial searches for terrestrial life. But we've been very lax in mounting a terrestrial search for extraterrestrial life.

The speculation (and this is *really* speculation) goes like this: If other beings are advanced technologically, they could send observers here. Those might be robots, which might be biologically engineered rather than mechanically constructed. The observers might be here to find out when we've reached the cultural maturity to take the shock of contact. Of course, they work hard to remain undetected.

That sounds like science fiction, but it is one way of answering the question: They *are* here but in *disguise!*

22.10
Communication with extraterrestrial intelligence (CETI)

For the sake of speculation, assume we have cosmic neighbors within a few hundred light years of the sun. How might we communicate with them?

First, traditional space travel is impractical. Despite the popularity of *Star Trek*, the distances involved are too far, the energy needed too great, the cost too expensive, and human lifetimes too short.

Second, focus on the possible *tools* of communication—the hardware involved (rather than the form or content of the message). Arguments have been made for a number of techniques, from superlasers to cosmic postcards (which have already been sent by Pioneer and Voyager). I won't detail these technical arguments. They do imply that the best method to use today is *radio*, essentially the same equipment as large radio telescopes (Section 6.3). The most sensitive telescopes could communicate with a twin some thousand light years away. (To have at least one civilization with a similar technol-

ogy within communicating distance requires a lifetime of at least a thousand years.) One astronomical advantage of radio communication is that it is little impeded, at centimeter wavelengths, by interstellar gas and dust.

The devices for CETI seem clear. What about the technique? What should the communication strategy be? This question brings up a host of hard questions, such as: How to encode the message? What language is the message in? What to say? Fortunately, physics and astronomy point to how to cope with some of these problems.

For instance, do you send or listen? The answer appears: *listen*. Then once you catch a signal, send your own. Here's the argument: If technological civilizations live at least a thousand years, then we are mere infants. Most of them will be technologically superior, with better facilities for sending and receiving. Since sending is technically more difficult than receiving, you use your resources most efficiently to listen. For CETI, it is better (at first) to receive than to give.

Okay, so you listen, but at what frequency? After all, the radio band of the electromagnetic spectrum (Fig. 5.13) covers the range from a few Hertz to hundreds of gigahertz. The choice of station hinges on what part of the radio spectrum has the least background of natural noise, because when we listen we will be trying to detect weak signals. (Noise is, for example, the incessant jumble you hear when you tune your AM radio to a spot between stations.) Astronomy and physics naturally define a low-noise band (Fig. 22.13). At the low-frequency end (0.1–1 GHz), noise from the Galaxy (mostly synchrotron emission from high-speed electrons) dominates. At the high-frequency end (100–1000 GHz), noise in radio receivers, which comes from the quantum nature of matter and so cannot be eliminated, picks up. Between these two noise hills lies a valley of relative quiet (filled in a bit by the 3 K cosmic radiation, Section 21.3) from 1 to 100 GHz—part of the *microwave* region of the radio spectrum. The earth's atmosphere fills in this microwave noise valley above 10 GHz. So the low-noise range from the earth's surface lies between 1 and 10 GHz.

That's still a wide band of frequencies. Accidentally, the 21-cm line (Focus 42) from neu-

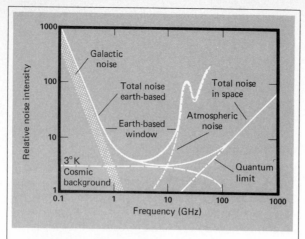

22.13

Background noise in the microwave region of the electromagnetic spectrum. At the longer wavelengths, most of the noise comes from synchrotron emission from throughout the Galaxy (labeled "galactic noise"). At very short wavelengths, the noise comes from the atomic nature of the materials that make up the radio receivers ("quantum limit"). Over most of the radio wavelengths, a little noise arises from the 3K cosmic background radiation (Section 21.3). The earth's atmosphere also produces background radiation. Adding all these noise sources together leaves a low-noise dip (called the "earth-based window") in the frequency range from 1 to 10 GHz. This is the best region to search for signals from extraterrestrial civilizations. (Adapted from the Project Cyclops report)

tral hydrogen (1.42 GHz) falls in this band, as do strong emissions from hydroxyl, water, and carbon monoxide. Astronomers have argued that these indicate natural frequencies for communication, because any civilization with radio astronomy would find them. I don't consider this argument all that persuasive and believe that the entire low-noise range must be searched. This attitude presents a technical problem: The range to be probed is wide (it has many channels), and radio telescopes now receive only a few channels at a time. However, recent advances in electronics will permit receivers to tune into as many as a *million* channels at one time. So the project can be made feasible.

In what directions do we listen for signals? A sphere of space a thousand light years in radius includes about one million stars. A radio telescope dish looks at only a certain part of the sky at one time—roughly a circle a few arcminutes in size. You can imagine that when a radio telescope points at some direction in space, it can pick up signals from a huge cone, extending far into space, with its tip at the telescope and its cross section larger at greater distances. The telescope must be pointed at a certain object so that it falls within this cone. In addition, the emission from a celestial object decreases as the inverse square of the distance (Focus 34). So although the expanding cone from the telescope picks up more objects at greater distances, their signals will be weaker. One search strategy then would be to point at *nearby* stars of spectral types K, G, and M (Section 22.7).

This search has actually been carried out sporadically by astronomers in the United States and the USSR since 1960. A few hundred stars have been observed, mostly at 1.42 GHz. *No extraterrestrial signals have been detected to date.* Of course, we may have been listening at times when no signals were coming in.

Suppose life exists around nearby Epsilon Eridani and has evolved intelligence, how might you communicate with this alien culture? The rapidity of communication is limited to the speed of light. A regular coded message transmitted continuously might be detected by the Eridanians if they decided to search in our direction at the wavelength on which you were transmitting. Such a coincidence does not seem likely, yet they may be scrutinizing us for the same reason we peer at them: the wiggle in the proper motion of the sun.

Suppose we do make contact. And suppose we can convince each other that we are intelligent by adopting a logical code to transmit and decipher information. Each exchange of signals would take about 22 years; in a human lifetime, only three round-trip communications could take place and would require great patience at both ends. Assume the nearest intelligent civilization is three times the distance to Epsilon Eridani; then one greeting and response would span a human lifetime.

Space and time effectively quarantine us from contact with our neighbors. Even if the Galaxy teems with life, each planetary system is a solitary unit fenced off by vast volumes of space. We are very much alone.

22.11
Cosmic speculation

Before the sun dies, we probably will have left our home planet—perhaps for others, perhaps not for planets at all. Predicting the future is always a dubious enterprise, but I feel certain that we will have to leave the earth; maybe long before the sun ages.

Why? Because the Spaceship Earth is a finite resource. If we do not achieve a stable population for the human race—for moral, ethical, or political reasons—we have no choice but to leave the earth.

Growth / The problem here is one of growth, growth that looks small on a yearly basis but adds up quickly—*exponential growth*.

Steady doubling characterizes exponential growth. It leads to rapid increases in numbers, even for small fractional growth rates. A rule of such growth is that the doubling time, T (in years), for a growth rate P, of percent in a year, is approximately

$$T = \frac{70}{P}$$

For example, if P is 10 percent a year, the doubling time is 7 years. In 1975 the growth rate of the human population was 1.9 percent a year. So the doubling time is roughly 37 years. That doesn't sound like much, but *if* the rate remained constant, the mass of people would equal the mass of earth in only 1600 years!

Constant doubling results in the rapid use of finite resources. Consider bacteria that double every minute. Suppose we place a bacterium in a bottle and note that the bottle is full up at 12 noon. When was the bottle half full? One doubling time (one minute) earlier: 11:59. When was it one-quarter full? Two doubling times earlier: 11:58. Suppose at this time some far-sighted bacteria leaders got together and intensively searched for more living space. At 11:59, they find an empty bottle on the shelf, which doubles their total living room. When will that new bottle be filled? *12:01.* When consumption grows exponentially, even enormous increases in resources are consumed in short times.

The earth is a finite resource—a small planet. Even if zero population growth were achieved tomorrow, our resources would be consumed at present rates in only a few human lifetimes. We will need to leave our home planet: for space, for energy, and for natural resources.

Space colonization / Where to go? The traditional science fiction view had us journeying to and colonizing other planets in our solar system. With the possible exception of Mars, the other worlds in the solar system are not habitable planets. Even if they were, don't forget the lesson of the bacteria in the bottle. Human population growth now doubles roughly every 40 years. Suppose we fill the earth to the limit. How long would it take us to fill another planet—say, Mars? Right—*one* doubling time, 40 years or so, if our present growth rate continues. In only 1500 years (37 doubling times), we would have enough people to populate 10^{11} planets, one for every star in the Galaxy.

But there's no good reason to restrict ourselves to living on planets at all. This fact has encouraged Gerard K. O'Neill to revive and develop an older idea (some aspects were foreseen by the Russian physicist Konstantin Tsiolkowsky almost 100 years ago): human habitation in space, often known as *space colonies*. O'Neill has aimed at making the dream of space colonization a reality with available technology.

I won't detail his plans here, but will sketch the broad outlines. Stripped of luxuries, people need energy, air (oxygen), water, land, and (probably) gravity to live a comfortable life. With space colonies in orbit around the earth, somewhere between the earth and the moon, all these are available: energy from the sun, oxygen and raw materials from the moon, and water from the earth. (Water might also be collected from the asteroids or moons of Jupiter and Saturn.) What about gravity? It can be simulated by rotating the space colony.

Key to this vision is harnessing solar power. A satellite solar power station has many advantages over a terrestrial one: no weather to worry about, no cycle of day and night, a zero-g environment in which it is easier to build large physical structures, less upkeep and so a longer life for the photovoltaic cells that convert sunlight into electrical energy. Overall, a space environment has about 10 times more solar energy falling on a square meter than does the earth—roughly 10 kW/m². So a collecting area of 10^6 square meters (1 km by 1 km) can gather

10^7 kW. If the photovoltaic cells operate at 10 percent efficiency, the system develops one MW.

How to transmit this power? By microwaves. In a household microwave oven there is an electronic device that converts electricity to microwaves; the same can work in a solar satellite power station. The receiving end—whether on the earth, moon, or in space—requires the reverse conversion. Such devices have been built but aren't very efficient yet.

The first space colonies and solar satellite stations would be built with resources from the earth. Expansion to many colonies requires breaking the mother earth's umbilical cord. For raw resources for development, we can turn to the moon and mine it. The moon's surface contains abundant aluminum, titanium, oxygen, and silicon. (It lacks water; so we'd have to bring hydrogen from the earth to combine with lunar oxygen to make water.) A solar power station can support mining activities. Then a reliable, inexpensive way is needed to transport the lunar materials to the colonies' orbit. O'Neill and others envision the use of a magnetic linear accelerator that would boost payloads to lunar escape velocity (about 2 km/sec) with accurate aim to the space colonies' vicinity. Here they would be caught in a huge net, and then used for manufacturing. It is critical to this concept that the space colonies break economically from the earth. They could bankroll themselves by selling power (beamed by microwaves) to the earth.

What might a space colony look like (Fig. 22.14)? The simplest design is a cylinder. One some 3 km in diameter and 32 km long could support upward of 200,000 persons on its inner surface. Spinning once every 2 min to simulate gravity, the inside would alternate strips of land and windows. The windows would have shutters to simulate the seasons and day and night by controlling the influx of sunlight. The colony craft would be constructed of aluminum and titanium from the moon.

How long will this high frontier accommodate our population growth? At present growth rates, the earth–moon space could handle 400–500 years of population doubling. That may appear long, but it's only about 7 human lifetimes. And continued population growth will eventually fill it up. For example, imagine we fill all the space between the sun and the earth with people jammed together. How long will it be until this region is saturated? In about 3000 years, at present rates.

The moral of this extrapolation is that the human race will leave the solar system a few thousand years from now, or we will be forced to limit population growth.

Beyond the solar system / Space colonies—"cities in space" as science fiction writer James Blish called them—could convey people between stars at speeds of 0.01 *c*. Imagine that we send colonies out across the Galaxy. When each arrives at a suitable star, they could build a new colony ship from local resources and send it out to the next star. A few centuries might elapse from arrival to the next departure; and then a few centuries to glide to the next star. How long does it take to travel across the Galaxy at 0.01 *c*? It takes 100,000 ly for the diameter of the Galaxy. Then at 1/100 the speed of light, the time in years is 100 times the distance in light years, or 10,000,000 years. This star-hopping process could carry people across the Galaxy and colonize it in roughly 10^7 years.

Ten million years is short compared with the age of the Galaxy and the time needed for life on the earth to evolve intelligence. So we could fill the Galaxy quickly, in cosmic terms. And so could any civilization that has achieved a technological level similar to ours.

This view brings up again the question of the number of technological civilizations in the Galaxy. If colonization can happen so swiftly, and if L_{ic} is long, then it probably has happened, and "they" are everywhere. But to take seriously the evidence of "their" absence, then L_{ic} must be very short, at least less than 10^7 years. But suppose we ignore that argument. If L_{ic} *is* 10^7 or so, some 10^3 waves of colonization have rippled through the Galaxy since its formation.

Such a picture of galactic colonization raises again the hard question: Where are they, or, where have they been? We have *no* undeniable evidence of any artifacts that may have been left behind by galactic colonists.

Enough speculation. I sincerely doubt that I can say with any certainty what the future evolution of the human race will be. I will predict that the future that unfolds will be wilder than any that you and I can dream of today.

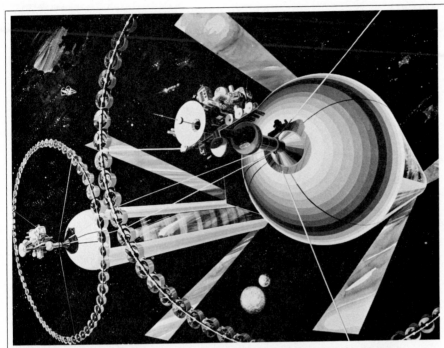

22.14

(a) *One possible model of a space colony, as suggested by G. K. O'Neil. This colony consists of twin cylinders, each 32 km long and 6.4 km in diameter and housing 200,000 people. Windows and mirrors control the input of sunlight. Each cylinder rotates about its axis once every 2 min to create an earthlike gravity on the inside wall.* (b) *Interior landscape of such a space colony. (Both courtesy NASA)*

(a)

(b)

SUMMARY

Assume that LAWKI is typical in the sense that it has arisen naturally in the course of cosmic evolution. Then you are forced to find the trail of that evolution, which falls into three interconnected stages: physical, chemical, and biological evolution.

You can hunt down the traces of biological evolution on the earth. Fossil evidence implies that with time, life has grown more complex on the earth and that the origin of life took a long time—about a billion years to get to the first cell.

To search for evidence of the chemical evolution that preceded the biological is hopeless. Here you rely on general theoretical ideas and some crucial laboratory experiments. These show that if the **primitive atmosphere of the earth was rich in hydrogen compounds,** *then the addition of energy (solar ultraviolet, lightning) naturally results in the formation of basic organic materials, such as amino acids. Complex molecules in space and amino acids in meteorites support the idea that such molecular formation is not a freak accident.*

Astronomical ideas underlie the understanding of physical evolution. For LAWKI you need a planet (earth), a star (the sun), and the proper elements (hydrogen, carbon, nitrogen, oxygen, and some others). Where did these come from? The earth, from the dust of the interstellar medium; the sun, from the gases. All from the material lost by earlier stars, mostly in their violent ends. These explosions and normal fusion reactions in stars manufactured the chemical elements—except for hydrogen and helium. These were made in the first few minutes of the big bang.

This sequence in general seems appropriate for all the observable universe. So if LAWKI is typical, then it must be common. I believe that statement is true. Our Galaxy and the entire universe may teem with life because we are part of cosmic evolution.

STUDY EXERCISES

1   Life on earth revolves around carbon. Where did the carbon come from, and how did it get to the earth? (*Objectives 1, 2, and 3*)

2   What is the crucial role played by supernovas in the origin of LAWKI? (*Objectives 2 and 3*)

3   How good are the chances for LAWKI in the solar system? (*Objectives 6 and 7*)

4   *O*-stars have the largest ecospheres around them. Yet they are not good suns for fostering life. Why not? (*Objective 8*)

5   Criticize the book's estimate of the number of intelligent civilizations in the Galaxy. (*Objective 9*)

6   Suppose radio astronomers tomorrow announced the discovery of amino acids in interstellar molecular clouds. How would that effect the general ideas of this chapter? (*Objectives 1–10*)

BEYOND THIS BOOK . . .

The Cosmic Connection by Carl Sagan (Dell, New York, 1973) is an expansive view of life in the universe.

The classic is *Intelligent Life in the Universe* by I. S. Shklovshii and C. Sagan (Holden-Day, San Francisco, 1966).

You can find a technical, comprehensive discussion of chemical evolution in *Molecular Evolution and the Origin of Life* by S. Fox and K. Dose (Freeman, San Francisco, 1972).

A dated but classic book is *Origin of Life* by A. I. Oparin (Dover, New York, 1953).

For a more detailed account of the Viking lander biology results, see "The Search for Life on Mars" by N. Horowitz, *Scientific American*, October 1977, p. 52.

Carl Sagan and Frank Drake discuss SETI in "The Search for Extraterrestrial Intelligence," *Scientific American*, May 1975, p. 80. More details can be found at NASA special report SP-419 (1977) with the same title, edited by P. Morrison, J. Billingham, and J. Wolfe.

The Search for Life in the Universe by D. Goldsmith and T. Owen (Benjamin/Cummings, 1980) is an up-to-date book on the subject.

Interstellar Communication: Scientific Perspectives edited by C. Ponnamperuma and A. Cameron (Houghton Mifflin, Boston, 1974) is an excellent source of a wide range of aspects of CETI. It contains a huge bibliography.

I got into astronomy when I was very young—I can't remember exactly when, but it was around the second or third grade. By accident I found a book in the school library that showed how to find and identify constellations. I used it. In a year I came to the stage where I could spot all the major constellations that could be seen from Stratford, Connecticut.

Since then I have looked at the sky many times, sometimes in working earnest, most times in a casual glance. The stars have never lost their familiarity to me since I have made their acquaintance. One lonely night I recall gazing out of a bus window as it lurched its way down the backroads of New Jersey. In the spaces between the dark trees I spotted Orion—fending off Taurus—climbing the sky again. The winter patterns were born again. Suddenly I felt a warm smile grow inside me. In spite of all my confusion and longings, I saw a pattern in the deep cosmos and felt a part of it. That feeling of calmness and peace I treasured then, and I value even more now.

Astronomy teaches that we are creatures of the universe, children of the stars, offspring of the interstellar clouds. We are products of cosmic evolution. We are also part of the process of cosmic evolution. Perhaps we are the universe's way of becoming aware of itself. You and I and the other living creatures in the cosmos—when we look into space, we see the source of ourselves. And to those wide-open spaces we add hope, fear, imagination, and love.

Thank you for coming this far with me. I have tried in this last part to show you the cosmic connections that touch us all. Reading this book, you have touched me. Remember that when you touch your sister, brother, parent, lover, friend—you touch the stars.

. . . we will conquer the earth, the sun, all space, and the stars . . .
J. BREL: If We Only Have Love

Do you think you can take over the universe and improve it?
LAO TSU: Tao Te Ching (# 29)
(Translated by Gia-Fu Feng and Jane English)

585

Saturn Update

When Voyager 2 swung past Saturn at the end of August, 1981, it sped past the rings at greater than 10 km/sec. Despite problems with its camera platform, Voyager 2 did accomplish most of its goals and so provide new clues—and puzzles—about Saturn.

First, the rings. A special instrument on board Voyager 2 (that had failed on Voyager 1) was able to record the light from a star through the many ringlets that make up the ring system (Fig. 1 and Color Plate 23). The flashes of starlight indicated that the ringlets number in the hundreds of thousands—not just in the thousands seen in regular photos. Also, the ringlets seemed to have a wavelike structure; that is, rather than each ringlet being a distinct entity that lasts some length of time, they may be short-lived structures formed by waves passing though the ring system. (An analogy are the density waves that create spiral arms—Section 16.5).

Second, the upper atmosphere. In the Voyager 1 photos, Saturn's upper atmosphere looked bland compared to Jupiter's. By chance, the TV camera of Voyager 2 was much better than the one on Voyager 1. It showed much more detail in the structure of the upper atmosphere (Figs. 2 and 3). These photos imply that the weather on Saturn has changed enormously in a time equivalent to a week on the earth. Large storm systems have changed shape, but still remained visible—a hint that Saturn's storms, like Jupiter's, are long-lived compared with the earth's storms.

The Voyager 1 photos indicated that the upper atmospheric wind flow of Saturn was quite different from Jupiter's—winds blowing all eastward at equatorial speeds four times those found on Jupiter. The Voyager 2 results show that the pattern does follow an east–west flow alternation (as found on Jupiter) but only at the higher latitudes. And the wind velocities for both planets fall off rapidly away from the equator. But Saturn's atmospheric bands do not mark jet stream flows as they do on Jupiter.

Finally, the satellites. Titan, still in its smog shroud, had lost its dark polar hood—it had changed into a ringlike collar around the pole. Voyager 2 was able to get a close-up look at the mysterious Iapetus, which ground-based observations have shown to have a bright and dark hemisphere. Indeed, this difference was

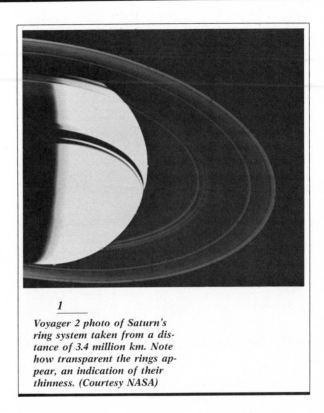

1

Voyager 2 photo of Saturn's ring system taken from a distance of 3.4 million km. Note how transparent the rings appear, an indication of their thinness. (Courtesy NASA)

seen in amazing contrast—the light side of Iapetus is some 15 times more reflective than the dark side, a difference like having clean snow on the light side and soot on the dark one. The reason for this difference is still unknown. Also, Voyager 2's pass of Iapetus permitted a measurement of its size and mass, and so its density—1.1 g/cc. This implies that it is basically an icy body.

The real surprise with Saturn's moons came with the images of Hyperion. They revealed it to have the shape of an oblate disk—something like a thick hamburger—200 by 300 by 100 km thick. And strangely enough, Hyperion rotates on an axis tilted some 45° to the plane of its orbit—a very unnatural, unstable situation. It may in fact be tumbling around in a cockeyed fashion.

A milder surprise came with the photos of Rhea, Dione, Enceladus, and Tethys. These icy bodies, on the basis of their small size, were thought not to have undergone internal heating or crustal movement. Not so! Especially for Enceladus, the surfaces have fissures, canyons, and areas wiped clean of primeval craters—all indications of internal heating and crustal deformation.

587

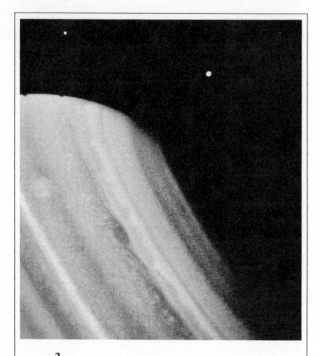

2

Flows in Saturn's upper atmosphere. North is to the upper right. The two moons above the planet are Dione (right) and Enceladus (left). The smallest visible features in the clouds have sizes of about 300 km. Note the similarity of the flow pattern here to those in Jupiter's atmosphere (Fig. 11.3). (Courtesy NASA)

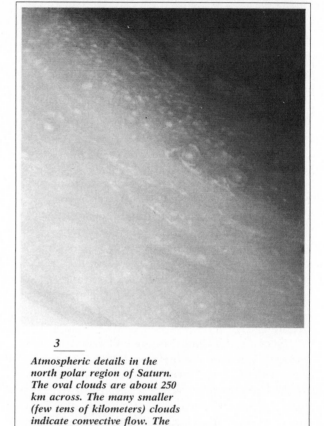

3

Atmospheric details in the north polar region of Saturn. The oval clouds are about 250 km across. The many smaller (few tens of kilometers) clouds indicate convective flow. The linear, wavelike features at the top may mark the northernmost east-flowing jet stream in Saturn's atmosphere. (Courtesy NASA)

Voyager 2 is now aimed at Uranus (1986) and Neptune (1989). It might not make it in working shape. Its primary radio receiver failed in 1977 and its back-up one is faltering. The problem with the camera platform may recur—space is a harsh environment. I hope for the best, since no new missions are planned. But the odds for success are no better than 2 to 3. This Saturn trip may well be the last planetary picture show.

Appendix A
Units

Powers of ten

Astronomers deal with quantities ranging from the truly microcosmic to the macrocosmic. It's very inconvenient to always have to write out the age of the universe as 20,000,000,000 years or the distance to the sun as 149,600,000,000 meters. To save writing time, powers-of-ten notation is used instead. For example, $10 = 10^1$; the exponent tells you how many times to multiply by ten. As another example, $10^{-2} = 1/100$; in this case the exponent is negative, so it tells you how many times to *divide* by ten. The only trick is to remember that $10^0 = 1$. Using powers-of-ten notation, the age of the universe is 2.0×10^{10} years, and the distance to the sun is 1.496×10^{11} meters.

The English and metric systems

You are familiar with the fundamental units of length, mass, and time in the English system: the yard, the pound, and the second. The other common units of the English system are often strange multiples of these fundamental units, such as the ton (2000 lb), the mile (1760 yd), the inch ($\frac{1}{36}$ yd), and the ounce ($\frac{1}{16}$ lb). Most of these units arose from accidental conventions and so have few logical relationships. Most of the world uses a much more rational system known as the metric system, with the following fundamental units:

Length:
 1 meter (m)

Mass:
 1 kilogram (kg)

Time:
 1 second (sec) or (s)

This is the meter-kilogram-second, or mks, system. A slightly older system often used by astronomers is the centimeter-gram-second, or cgs, system, with the following fundamental units:

Length:
 1 centimeter (cm)

Mass:
 1 gram (g)

Time:
 1 second (sec) or (s)

All of the unit relationships in the metric system are based on multiples of ten, so it is very easy to multiply, divide, and use powers-of-ten notation.

The contemporary standard for the meter uses the wavelength of orange light from krypton 86. The meter is defined as 1.65076373×10^6 times this standard wavelength. Any efficient laboratory can set up such a standard and use it accurately.

The multiples of the metric system and their associated prefixes are:

$$\frac{1}{1,000,000} = 10^{-6} = \text{micro-} \quad (\mu)$$

$$\frac{1}{1,000} = 10^{-3} = \text{milli-} \quad (\text{m})$$

$$\frac{1}{100} = 10^{-2} = \text{centi-} \quad (\text{c})$$

$$\frac{1}{10} = 10^{-1} = \text{deci-} \quad (\text{d})$$

$$10 = 10^1 = \text{deca-} \quad (\text{da})$$

$$100 = 10^2 = \text{hecto-} \quad (\text{h})$$

$$1,000 = 10^3 = \text{kilo-} \quad (\text{k})$$

$$1,000,000 = 10^6 = \text{mega-} \quad (\text{M})$$

Some relationships between the metric and English system are:

Length:
1 kilometer (km) = 1000 m = 0.6214 mile
1 meter (m) = 1.094 y = 39.37 inches
1 centimeter (cm) = 0.01 m = 0.3937 inch
1 millimeter (mm) = 0.001 m = 0.03937 inch

 1 mile = 1.6093 km
 1 inch = 2.5400 cm

Mass:
 1 metric ton = 10^6 g = 1000 kg
 $= 2.2046 \times 10^3$ lb

 1 kilogram (kg) = 10^3 g = 2.2046 lb
 1 gram (g) = 0.0353 oz = 0.0022046 lb
 1 milligram (mg) = 0.001 g = 2.2046
 $\times 10^{-6}$ lb

 1 lb = 453.6 g
 1 oz = 28.3495 g

Temperature scales

Scales of temperature measurement are tagged by the freezing point and boiling point of water. In the United States the Fahrenheit (F) system is the one commonly used; water freezes at

32°F and boils at 212°F. In Europe the Celsius (formerly the Centigrade) system is the common temperature system; water freezes at 0°C and boils at 100°C. The Kelvin system is based on the idea of absolute zero, the temperature at which all random molecular motion ceases. Since 0 K is at absolute zero, water freezes at 273 K and boils at 373 K. Note that the size of the degree is the same in both the Kelvin and Celsius systems (100 between the freezing and boiling points of water). To convert between the systems, recognize that $0 \text{ K} = -273°\text{C} = -459°\text{F}$ (the Kelvin system never measures negative degrees) and that the Celsius and Kelvin degrees are larger than Fahrenheit degrees by the factor $180/100 = 9/5$. Then the relationships between systems are:

$$K = C + 273$$

$$C = \frac{5}{9}(°F - 32)$$

A comparison of the three temperature scales is seen in Fig. A.1.

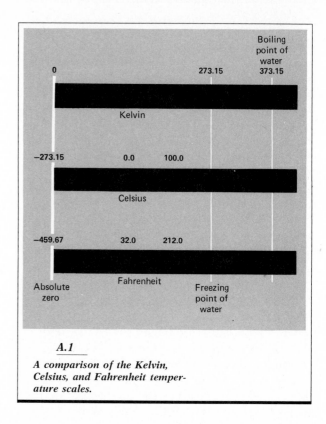

A.1

A comparison of the Kelvin, Celsius, and Fahrenheit temperature scales.

Astronomical distances

Although astronomers do use the metric system, they encounter distances so large that other measures are often used. In the solar system the natural distance is the Astronomical Unit (AU), the average distance of the earth from the sun. The AU equals 1.496×10^8 km.

Beyond the solar system the AU is even too small to be convenient. So astronomers then use the light year or the parsec. The light year (ly) is the distance that light travels in one year. It equals 9.46×10^{12} km. A parsec (pc) equals 206,265 AU, or 3.09×10^{13} km, or 3.26 ly.

Beyond the Galaxy, astronomers often talk in multiples of parsecs. A thousand parsecs is called a kiloparsec (kpc), and a million parsecs is termed a megaparsec (Mpc). Two units not commonly used by astronomers but sometimes found in this book are the *kilolight year* (kly) and *megalight year* (Mly). Based on the discussion of metric units at the beginning of this appendix, what would you guess the kly and Mly to be equivalent to? Right: a kly is a thousand light years and a Mly is a million light years.

Other physical units

Another important unit you will encounter is the speed of light (c), which equals 2.9979×10^5 km/sec.

The unit of energy in the cgs system is called the erg. A mass of 2 g traveling at 1 cm/sec has an energy of 1 erg. To illustrate how small an erg is: If you place one foot up one stair, you have expended about a billion ergs. In the mks the energy unit is a joule (J), which equals 10^7 ergs. It takes about a joule of energy to lift an apple from the floor to a table.

Power is the amount of energy coming from an object per second, so it is measured in ergs per second. (Astronomers use the word *luminosity* to describe what most physicists would call power.) A convenient and familiar unit for power (or luminosity) is the watt (W), defined as 10^7 ergs/sec, or 1 J/sec.

This book uses the *gauss* (G) as the unit of magnetic field strength (rather than the SI unit of *telsa*, which equals 10^4 G). To give you a feel for a gauss, keep in mind that the earth's magnetic field is about 0.5 G.

Appendix B
Planetary Data

Planetary rotation rates

Permanent natural markings on the surface, seen through a thin atmosphere, provide a simple means to measure a planet's rotation rate. Such markings are plainly visible on the Martian surface. The dense, opaque atmosphere of Jupiter, however, completely obscures the surface; only the top of the cloud layers is visible. Semipermanent irregularities in the upper clouds persist long enough to allow us to determine the rotation rate of the cloud layers. Some planets, such as Venus, do not have easily discernible atmospheric markings, and others, such as Mercury, do not have readily visible surface markings. In these circumstances the rotation rates are measured by the Doppler shift, which is produced by the relative velocities of the opposite edges of a planet toward and away from the earth.

If the planetary surface is visible, the measured rotation rate is that of the surface; if the visible disk is actually composed of high atmospheric clouds, the rotation rate is that of the cloud layer. Although opaque to visible radiation, cloud layers may be transparent to other wavelengths in the electromagnetic spectrum. If an atmosphere is transparent at radio wavelengths, radio astronomers can measure the rotation rate by bouncing a signal off the surface and determining the Doppler shift of the signal on return to earth. Table B.1 gives planetary rotation rates, inclinations of rotational axes, and method for finding the rotation rate.

Planetary distances and diameters

The distance between a planet and the earth can be calculated by triangulation from various points in the earth's orbit. The distances of the planets from the sun can be computed from observations of their synodic periods, transformed to sidereal periods and slipped into Kepler's third law. These methods give distances in relative terms of the earth–sun distance (the Astronomical Unit); to find the distance scale in kilometers or miles is a more difficult task. To determine the distance scale for the solar system in kilometers requires only that one segment be measured. For example, suppose you were given a map of the United States with no distance scale but with all locations laid out correctly relative to one another. Now you hop in your car and drive—keeping close track of the miles—between two points on the map. You then know the distance between these two points and so have established a scale for the entire map.

To find solar system distances poses the same kind of problem. You have the relative spacings of the planets in AU's. Now you need to find the distance in kilometers between any two known points on the solar system map. The modern method of finding the distance scale uses radar beams bounced off Venus. From the measured return time and the accurately known speed of light, you calculate the distance in kilometers; it is the return time, divided by two, times the speed of light. Table B.2 lists the planetary distances and periods.

TABLE B.1 *Planetary rotation rates and inclinations of rotation axes*

Planet	Rotation period (equatorial)	Inclination of equator to orbital plane	Method of measurement
Mercury	58.65 d	Less than 28°	Radar Doppler shift
Venus	243.16 d (retrograde)	3°	Radar Doppler shift
Earth	23 h 56 m 4.1 s	23° 27′	Star transits
Mars	24 h 37 m 22.6 s	23° 59′	Optical features
Jupiter	9 h 50.5 m	3° 05′	Optical features
Saturn	10 h 14 m	26° 44′	Optical Doppler shift
Uranus	12–23 h	97° 55′	Optical Doppler shift
Neptune	18–22 h	28° 48′	Optical Doppler shift
Pluto	6.39 d	?	Optical light variations

TABLE B.2   *Distances, periods, and orbital velocities of the planets*

	Semimajor axis of orbit[a]		Sidereal period		Average orbital velocity
	(AU)	*(× 10⁶ km)*	*(years)*[b]	*(days)*	*(km/sec)*
Mercury	0.387	57.9	0.240	87.97	47.9
Venus	0.723	108.2	0.615	224.7	35.1
Earth	1.000	149.6	1.000	365.26	29.8
Mars	1.523	227.9	1.881	687.0	24.1
Jupiter	5.203	778.3	11.86	4,333	13.1
Saturn	9.540	1,427	29.46	10,759	9.7
Uranus	19.18	2,869	84.10	30,685	6.8
Neptune	30.07	4,498	164.8	60,188	5.4
Pluto	39.44	5,900	248.4	90,700	4.7

[a]Same as average distance from sun.
[b]Tropical years, that is, the year of seasons.

TABLE B.3   *Dimensions of the planets*

Planet	*Nature of measurement*	*Radius (km)*	*Radius (earth radii)*	*Method of measurement*
Mercury	Average radius	2,439	0.38	Radar/optical
Venus	Upper cloud layer	6,110	0.95	Optical
	Equatorial radius	6,050		Radar
Earth	Polar radius	6,356	1.00	Satellite
	Equatorial radius	6,378		
Mars	Polar radius	3,394	0.53	Optical
	Equatorial radius	3,407		
Jupiter	Polar radius	66,550	10.8	Optical
	Equatorial radius	70,850		
Saturn	Polar radius	53,450	8.9	Optical
	Equatorial radius	60,330		
Uranus	Polar radius	24,700	4.0	Optical
	Equatorial radius	25,400		
Neptune	Average radius	25,100	3.9	Optical
Pluto	Average radius	1,500	0.24	Inference from albedo

Once the actual distances have been measured, you can calculate a planet's diameter if you are able to measure the apparent angular size with a telescope. With these two pieces of information you can compute the actual diameter of the planet. Table B.3 provides a summary of planetary dimensions.

Planetary masses

To determine a planet's mass requires either Kepler's third law or Newton's law of gravitation. If the planet has a natural satellite (or if an artificial one can be placed in orbit around it), the orbital period and the semimajor axis, incorporated into Kepler's third law, give the sum of the masses of the planet and satellite relative to the sun (Focus 12). If no satellites are available, the gravitational perturbations that any planet produces on another planet, a passing asteroid, or a passing space probe are needed to derive the mass from Newton's laws. Table B.4 lists the masses in the solar system and the method of measurement.

TABLE B.4 *Masses of the planets*

Planet	Mass (earth masses)	Mass (kg)	Density (g/cc)	Measured by motions of
Mercury	0.0553	3.32×10^{23}	5.44	Mariner 10
Venus	0.815	4.87×10^{24}	5.24	Mariner 2 and 10
Earth	1.000	5.974×10^{24}	5.517	Mariner 4
(Moon)	0.012	7.35×10^{22}	3.34	Ranger series
Mars	0.1074	6.42×10^{23}	3.96	Mariner 4, 6, 7
Jupiter	317.9	1.899×10^{27}	1.33	Satellites and asteroids
Saturn	95.7	5.69×10^{26}	0.68	Satellites
Uranus	14.56	8.69×10^{25}	1.60	Satellites
Neptune	17.24	1.03×10^{26}	1.65	Triton
Pluto	0.0022	1.3×10^{22}	~1	Charon

Planetary temperatures

The heating of a planetary surface depends primarily on three factors: the planet's distance from the sun, its albedo, and the occurrence of a greenhouse effect. The inverse-square law for electromagnetic radiation requires that the intensity of sunlight striking a planet decreases as the inverse square of its distance from the sun. A square meter of the surface of Jupiter, for example, receives only about 1/27 the amount of sunlight hitting an area the same size on the surface of the earth. How much of the surface area heats up also depends on how much sunlight is reflected and how much is absorbed. Only the absorbed energy contributes to the heating. A planet's albedo indicates how much of the sunlight is reflected; the rest must be absorbed. The earth's albedo is 0.39 (it absorbs 0.61 of the incident light). Because the earth and the moon are at the same distance from the sun, the moon would be hotter than the earth if all other factors were equal. (They are not, because the moon has no atmosphere, so does not have a greenhouse effect.)

Outside the earth's atmosphere, incident solar radiation carries energy at the rate of roughly 1370 W per square meter. A planet's albedo and distance from the sun allow astronomers to calculate the theoretical solar heating and the temperature produced by it. The theoretical temperatures can be compared with the actual measured temperatures. The presence of an atmosphere or a slow rotation rate causes the measured temperature to be higher than the theoretical one. In particular, if the atmosphere contains ample carbon dioxide and water vapor, the greenhouse effect creates a higher temperature than the predicted one.

Planetary atmospheres

The crucial data needed for the identification of

TABLE B.5 *Most abundant atmospheric gases*

Planet	Gas
Mercury	Helium, hydrogen, argon, neon
Venus	Carbon dioxide, carbon monoxide, hydrogen chloride, hydrogen fluoride, water, nitrogen, helium
Earth	Nitrogen, oxygen, water, argon, carbon dioxide, neon, helium, methane, krypton, nitrous oxide, ozone, xenon
Mars	Carbon dioxide, carbon monoxide, water, oxygen, ozone, argon
Jupiter	Hydrogen, methane, ammonia, water, carbon monoxide, helium, acetylene, ethane, phosphine
Saturn	Hydrogen, methane, ammonia, ethane, helium, phosphine
Uranus	Hydrogen, methane
Neptune	Hydrogen, methane
Pluto	Methane

Note The results listed are a combination of ground-based and satellite observations.

atmospheric gases come from a planet's spectra. Because all the planets reflect sunlight, the absorption lines of a planet's atmosphere will be superimposed on the solar spectrum. The absorption lines in the solar spectrum are produced under physical conditions different from those producing planetary absorption lines, and the two are easily distinguished. For the ground-based observer, the situation is confounded by the earth's atmosphere. Our atmosphere's absorption features blot out absorption lines of common gases (such as carbon dioxide, water, and oxygen) coming from another planet's atmosphere. The difficulties of ground-based planetary spectroscopy can be overcome by sending a planetary probe equipped with a spectroscope. Table B.5 lists the known atmospheric compositions of the planets.

Physical properties of planets' satellites

All the techniques described in the previous sections can be used to find out about the physical natures of the satellites in the solar system. Because satellites are usually small, they are faint and difficult to observe so flybys give us the most detailed information. Tables B.6–B.10 give information on the satellites as far as can be observed or reasonably estimated. (See Table 11.4 for Pluto's moon, Charon.)

TABLE B.6   Satellites of Mars

Satellite	Mean distance from center of planet (10^3 km)	Sidereal period of revolution (days)	Dimensions of satellite (km)	Mass (planet = 1)	Bulk density (g/cc)	Discovery
1 Phobos	9.4	0.318910	$14 \times 11 \times 20$	3×10^{-9}	2	Asaph Hall (1877)
2 Deimos	23.5	1.262441	$8 \times 6 \times 6$	6×10^{-10}	2	

TABLE B.7   Satellites of Jupiter

Name		Distance from Jupiter $\times 10^3$ kilometers	Jupiter radii	Orbital period (days)	Mass (planet = 1)	Bulk density (g/cc)
Adrastea	J14	134	1.76	0.30	—	—
Amalthea	J5	181	2.55	0.49	2×10^{-9}	~3
1979J2	J15	222	3.11	0.67	—	—
Io	J1	422	5.95	1.77	4.7×10^{-5}	3.5
Europa	J2	671	9.47	3.55	2.6×10^{-5}	3.0
Ganymede	J3	1070	15.10	7.15	7.8×10^{-5}	1.9
Callisto	J4	1880	26.60	16.70	5.6×10^{-5}	1.8
Leda	J13	11 110	156	240	5×10^{-13}	—
Himalia	J6	11 470	161	251	8.5×10^{-10}	—
Lysithea	J10	11 710	164	260	10^{-12}	—
Elara	J7	11 740	165	260	4×10^{-11}	—
Ananke	J12	20 700	291	617	7×10^{-13}	—
Carme	J11	22 350	314	692	2×10^{-12}	—
Pasiphae	J8	23 300	327	735	8×10^{-12}	—
Sinope	J9	23 700	333	758	2×10^{-12}	—

TABLE B.8 Satellites of Saturn

	Mean distance from center of planet (10^3 km)	Sidereal period of revolution (days)	Radius (km)	Mass (planet = 1)	Density (g/cc)
Mimas (S1)	186	0.942422	195	6.6×10^{-8}	1.2
Enceladus (S2)	238	1.370218	250	1.5×10^{-7}	1.1
Tethys (S3)	295	1.887802	525	1.1×10^{-6}	1.0
Dione (S4)	377	2.736916	560	2.0×10^{-6}	1.4
Rhea (S5)	527	4.517503	765	3.2×10^{-6}	1.3
Titan (S6)	1,222	15.94552	2560	2.4×10^{-4}	1.9
Hyperion (S7)	1,481	21.276665	155	2×10^{-7}	?
Iapetus (S8)	3,560	79.33082	720	4×10^{-6}	1.2
Phoebe (S9)	12,930	550.45	~70	5.2×10^{-8}	?
S10 ⎫ (co-orbiting	⎫ 151		~100	?	?
S11 ⎭ satellites)	⎭		≳65	?	?
S12 (Dione B)	377		~40	?	?
S13 ⎫ (shepherding	142		~125	?	?
S14 ⎭ satellites for F-ring)	139		~100	?	?
S15 (near the edge of A-ring)	138		~50	?	?

TABLE B.9 Satellites of Uranus

Satellite	Mean distance from center of planet (10^3 km)	Sidereal period of revolution (days)	Radius (km)	Mass (planet = 1)
1 Ariel	191.8	2.52038	800	1.5×10^{-6}
2 Umbriel	267.3	4.14418	550	6×10^{-6}
3 Titania	438.7	8.70588	1000	5×10^{-5}
4 Oberon	586.6	13.46326	900	2.9×10^{-5}
5 Miranda	130.1	1.414	300	10^{-6}

TABLE B.10 Satellites of Neptune

Satellite	Mean distance from center of planet (10^3 km)	Sidereal period of revolution (days)	Radius of satellite (km)	Mass (planet = 1)
1 Triton	653.6	5.87683	3600–5300	2×10^{-3}
2 Nereid	5,570	365	300	10^{-6}

Appendix C
Physical Constants, Astronomical Data

Physical constants

Gravitational constant
$$G = 6.673 \times 10^{-11} \text{ newton-m}^2/\text{kg}^2$$

Speed of light in a vacuum
$$c = 2.9979 \times 10^8 \text{ m/sec}$$

Planck's constant
$$h = 6.62618 \times 10^{-34} \text{ J-sec}$$

Wein's constant
$$\sigma_w = 0.0029 \text{ m-K}$$

Boltzmann's constant
$$k = 1.3806 \times 10^{-23} \text{ J/K}$$

Stefan-Boltzmann constant
$$\sigma = 5.6697 \times 10^{-8} \text{ W/m}^2\text{-K}$$

Electron mass
$$m_e = 9.10956 \times 10^{-31} \text{ kg}$$

Proton mass
$$m_p = 1.6726 \times 10^{-27} \text{ kg} = 1836.1 \, m_e$$

Neutron mass
$$m_n = 1.6749 \times 10^{-27} \text{ kg}$$

Mass of hydrogen atom
$$m_H = 1.6735 \times 10^{-27} \text{ kg}$$

Astronomical data

Astronomical Unit
$$AU = 1.4959789 \times 10^{11} \text{ m}$$

Parsec
$$pc = 206264.806 \text{ AU}$$
$$= 3.2616 \text{ ly}$$
$$= 3.0856 \times 10^{16} \text{ m}$$

Light year
$$ly = 9.46053 \times 10^{15} \text{ m}$$
$$= 6.324 \times 10^4 \text{ AU}$$

Sidereal year
$$y = 3.155815 \times 10^7 \text{ sec}$$

Mass of sun
$$M_\odot = 1.989 \times 10^{30} \text{ kg}$$

Luminosity of sun
$$L_\odot = 3.827 \times 10^{26} \text{ W}$$

Solar constant
$$S = 1373 \text{ W/m}^2$$

Radius of sun
$$R_\odot = 6.96 \times 10^5 \text{ km}$$

Mass of earth
$$M_\oplus = 5.9742 \times 10^{24} \text{ kg}$$

Equatorial radius of earth
$$R_\oplus = 6.37814 \times 10^3 \text{ km}$$

Mass of moon
$$M_M = 7.34 \times 10^{22} \text{ kg}$$

Radius of moon
$$R_M = 1.738 \times 10^3 \text{ km}$$

Appendix D
Stars Within 13 Light Years

Name	Parallax (arcsec)	Distance (ly)	Spectral type	Proper motion (arcsec/y)	Apparent visual magnitude	Luminosity (sun = 1.0)
Sun			G2 V		−26.7	1.0
α Cen A	0.750	4.3	G2 V	3.68	−0.01	1.6
B			K0 V		1.3	0.45
C	0.772	4.2	M5e		11.0	0.00006
Barnard's star	0.552	5.9	M5 V	10.30	9.5	0.00045
Wolf 359	0.431	7.6	M8e	4.84	13.5	0.00002
Lalande 21185	0.402	8.1	M2 V	4.78	7.5	0.0055
Luyten 726-8A	0.1387	8.4	M6e	3.35	12.5	0.00006
B(UV Ceti)			M6e		13.0	0.00004
Sirius A	0.377	8.6	A1 V	1.32	−1.5	23.5
B			wd		8.7	0.003
Ross 154	0.345	9.4	M5e	0.74	10.6	0.00048
Ross 248	0.314	10.3	M6e	1.82	12.3	0.00011
ε Eri	0.303	10.7	K2 V	0.97	3.7	0.30
Luyten 789-6	0.302	10.8	M7e	3.27	12.2	0.00014
Ross 128	0.301	10.8	M5	1.40	11.1	0.00036
61 Cyg A	0.292	11.2	K5 V	5.22	5.2	0.083
B			K7 V		6.0	0.040
ε Ind	0.291	11.2	K5 V	4.67	4.7	0.13
Procyon A	0.287	11.4	F5 IV–V	1.25	0.4	7.65
B			wd		10.7	0.00055
Σ 2398 A	0.284	11.5	M3.5 V	2.29	8.9	0.0028
B			M4 V		9.7	0.0013
Groombridge 34 A	0.282	11.6	M1 V	2.91	8.1	0.0058
B			M6 V		11.0	0.00040
Lacaille 9352	0.279	11.7	M2 V	6.87	7.4	0.013
τ Ceti	0.273	11.9	G8 V	1.92	3.5	0.45
BD + 5° 1668	0.266	12.2	M5	3.73	9.8	0.0015
L725-32 (YZ Ceti)	0.262	12.4	M5e	1.31	11.6	0.0002
Lacaille 8760	0.260	12.5	M1	3.46	6.7	0.028
Kapteyn's star	0.256	12.7	M0 V	8.79	8.8	0.0040
Kruger 60 A	0.254	12.8	M4	0.87	9.8	0.0017
B			M5e		11.3	0.00044

SOURCE Based on a table by A. H. Batten in the *Observer's Handbook* (1980) of the Royal Astronomical Society of Canada.

Note An e after the spectral type indicates emission lines in the spectrum.

Appendix E
The Twenty Brightest Stars

Star	Name	Apparent visual magnitude	Spectral type	Absolute magnitude	Distance (ly)	Proper motion (arcsec/y)
1. α CMa A	Sirius	−1.46	A1 V	+1.42	8.7	1.324
2. α Car	Canopus	−0.72	F0 I–II	−3.1	98	0.025
3. α Boo	Arcturus	−0.06	K2 III	−0.3	36	2.284
4. α Cen A	Rigil Kentaurus	0.01	G2 V	+4.39	4.3	3.676
5. α Lyr	Vega	0.04	A0 V	+0.5	26.5	0.345
6. α Aur	Capella	0.05	G8 III (?)	−0.6	45	0.435
7. β Ori A	Rigel	0.14	B8 Ia	−7.1	900	0.001
8. α CMi A	Procyon	0.37	F5 IV–V	+2.7	11.3	1.250
9. α Ori	Betelgeuse	0.41	M2 Iab	−5.6	520	0.028
10. α Eri	Achernar	0.51	B3 V	−2.3	118	0.098
11. β Cen AB	Hadar	0.63	B1 III	−5.2	490	0.035
12. α Aql	Altair	0.77	A7 IV–V	+2.2	16.5	0.658
13. α Tau A	Aldebaran	0.86	K5 III	−0.7	68	0.202
14. α Vir	Spica	0.91	B1 V	−3.3	220	0.054
15. α Sco A	Antares	0.92	M1 Ib	−5.1	520	0.029
16. α PsA	Fomalhaut	1.15	A3 V	+2.0	22.6	0.367
17. β Gem	Pollux	1.16	K0 III	+1.0	35	0.625
18. α Cyg	Deneb	1.26	A2 Ia	−7.1	1600	0.003
19. β Cru	Beta Crucis	1.28	B0.5 III	−4.6	490	0.049
20. α Leo A	Regulus	1.36	B7 V	−0.7	87	0.248

SOURCE Based on a table compiled by Donald A. MacRae in the *Observer's Handbook* (1980) of the Royal Astronomical Society of Canada.

Appendix F
Understanding Contour Maps

Many of the figures in this book are *contour maps,* pictures of how the intensity of some kind of radiation (radio, visible, infrared, etc.) varies over some region of the sky. Such maps show a lot of wavy, connected lines. What do they mean?

Here's an analogy you are familiar with: a weather map (Fig. F.1). This is a map of atmospheric pressure across the United States, with high (H) and low (L) pressure systems indicated. What do the contours here tell you?

First, consider how a pressure contour is drawn. The weather stations around the United States report their local pressures. Each is put on the map. Then a contour line is drawn that connects all stations giving the same reading, *providing* that it does *not* cross a station of higher or lower reading. Then another contour (of higher or lower pressure) is drawn in, and so on. Notice that contour lines *cannot* cross. Why? Because if they did, it would mean that the *same* place has two *different* pressures—and that's impossible!

Second, note that there are places where the pressures hit a maximum (high) or a minimum (low). At the center of each is a last contour surrounding the region of highest or lowest pressure. The center of a high, for example, you can imagine as the peak of a pressure mountain. The contours around the peak tell you how the pressure falls from the peak. If the contour lines are close together, the pressure drops quickly over a short distance—the fall-off is steep. If the contour lines are spread out, the pressure drops off slowly—you have a kind of ridge.

The same analysis applies to an intensity contour map (Fig. F.2). Instead of pressures, the map shows the intensity of radiation—in this case, radio waves of 2 cm from an H II region. Note that there is one main peak where the radio intensity hits a maximum. To the right and below it lies a secondary peak. Between the peaks the intensity does not fall off as quickly as it does moving away from either one.

To help you see this better, I've plotted the same intensity map in a three-dimensional way (Fig. F.3). The height of the contours here indicates the intensity. Notice that the H II region looks like a mountain! The peaks and the steep sides stand out. This kind of image should pop into your mind when you see an ordinary contour map.

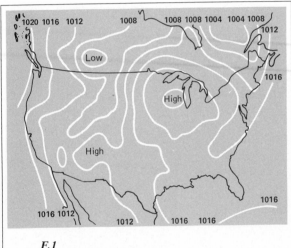

F.1

A weather pressure map over the United States. The contour lines connect regions with the same pressure readings. (Courtesy U.S. Weather Service)

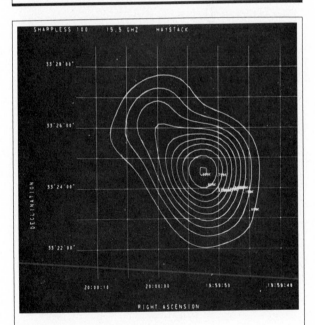

F.2

An intensity contour map of the radio emission from an H II region. This region is called Sharpless 100; its position in the sky is indicated by the coordinates "Right Ascension" and "Declination." Observations were made at a frequency of 15.5 GHz or a wavelength of about 2 cm. Each contour is a 0.1 unit lower in intensity than the inner one. (Observations made by M. Zeilik at Haystack Observatory)

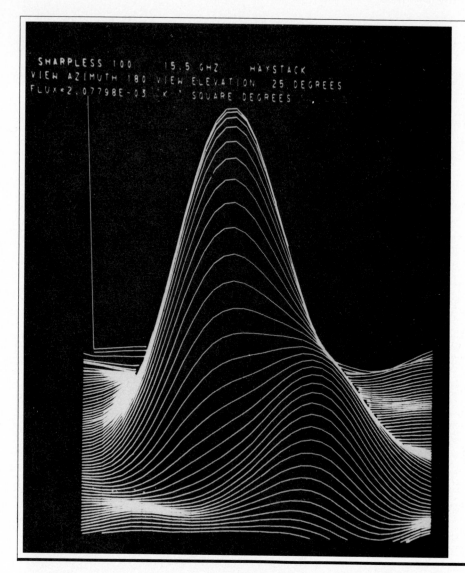

The same observations as in Fig. F.2 plotted here so that height represents relative intensity. The view is from an observer positioned at the top of Fig. F.2 looking down at an angle of 25°. (Observations and data reduction by M. Zeilik at Haystack Observatory)

With the basics in mind, you can try to visualize such maps in terms of brightness, as if your eye could detect radio waves. The peak appears to be the brightest. From it, the brightness falls off to the edges of the source—faster where the slope is steeper and slower where it is gradual—just like a contour map of slopes on the ground.

natural selection the process by which individuals with genes most well adapted to their environment have greater genetic representation in future generations.

nebula (Latin "cloud") a cloud of interstellar gas and dust.

nebular theories a model for the origin of the solar system, in which an interstellar cloud of gas and dust collapsed gravitationally to form a flattened disk out of which the planets formed by accretion.

neutrino an elementary particle with no mass or electric charge that travels at the speed of light and carries energy away during certain types of nuclear reactions.

neutron a massive subatomic particle with no electric charge; one of the main constituents of an atomic nucleus. It is made of a proton and an electron.

neutron star a star of extremely high density and small size that is composed mainly of very tightly packed neutrons.

nonthermal radiation emitted energy that is not characterized by a blackbody spectrum; usually used to refer to synchrotron radiation.

noon midday; the time halfway between sunrise and sunset when the sun reaches its highest point in the sky with respect to the horizon.

Norma arm a segment of a spiral arm of our Galaxy. It lies about 11,000–13,000 ly from the sun toward the center of the Galaxy in the direction of the constellation Norma.

north magnetic pole one of the two points on a star or planet from which magnetic lines of force emanate and to which the north pole of a compass needle points.

nova (Latin "new") a star that has a sudden outburst of energy, temporarily increasing its brightness by hundreds to thousands of times. This term was used in the past to refer to some stellar outbursts that modern astronomers call supernovas.

nuclear fission a process that releases energy from matter. In this process a heavy nucleus hit by high-energy particles splits into two or more lighter nuclei whose combined mass is less than that of the original.

nuclear fusion a process that releases energy from matter by the fusion of nuclei of lighter elements to make heavier ones.

nucleic acid a huge spiral-shaped molecule, commonly found in the nucleus of cells, that is the chemical foundation of genetic material.

nucleosynthesis the chain of thermonuclear fusion processes by which hydrogen is converted to helium, helium to carbon, and so on through all elements of the periodic table.

nucleus (of an atom) the massive central part of an atom, containing neutrons and protons, about which the electrons orbit.

nucleus (of a comet) small, bright, starlike point in the head of a comet. It is believed to be a solid, compact (a few tens of kilometers) mass of frozen gases with some rocky material.

nucleus (of a galaxy) the central portion of a galaxy, probably composed of old Population I stars, some gas and dust, and a concentrated source of nonthermal radiation for many galaxies.

objective the main light-gathering lens or mirror of a telescope.

occultation the eclipse of a star or planet by the moon or another planet.

Olbers's paradox the statement that if there were an infinite number of stars distributed uniformly in an infinite space, then the night sky should be as bright as the surface of a star, in obvious contrast to what is observed.

opacity the property of a substance which hinders the passage of light through it; opposite of transparency.

open cluster see galactic cluster

open geometry see hyperbolic geometry

opposition the time at which a celestial body lies exactly opposite the sun in the sky as seen from the earth.

orbital angular momentum the angular momentum of a revolving body; the product of a body's mass, orbital revolution velocity, and distance from the system's center of mass.

orbital inclination the angle between the orbital plane of a body and some reference plane; in the case of a planet in the solar system, the reference plane is that of the earth's orbit; in the case of a satellite, the reference is usually the equatorial plane of the planet; for a double star, it is the plane perpendicular to the line of sight.

organic relating to that branch of chemistry concerned with the carbon compounds of living creatures.

Orion Nebula a prominant H II region only 1500 ly away, found in the constellation Orion.

Orion spur a small branch of the Cygnus arm in which the sun is located.

ozone layer a layer of the earth's atmosphere about 40–60 km above the surface, characterized by a high content of ozone, O_3.

parallax the change in an object's apparent position when viewed from two different locations.

parent meteor bodies small solid bodies, a few hundreds or thousands of kilometers in size, believed to be the source of nickel-iron meteorites. They formed early in the history of the solar system and then broke up by collisions.

parsec the distance an object would have to have

from the earth so that its heliocentric parallax is 1 sec of arc; equal to 3.26 ly.

perfect cosmological principle the statement that the universe appears the same to an observer at all locations at all times.

perigee the point in its orbit at which an earth satellite is closest to the earth.

perihelion the point at which a body orbiting the sun is nearest to it.

period a time interval for some regular event to take place; for example, the time required for one complete revolution of a body about another.

periodic comets comets that have elliptical orbits around the sun.

periodic variable a star whose light varies in a regular fashion with time.

period-luminosity relationship a relation between a variable star's average luminosity and the time period over which the luminosity varies. For cepheids, the greater the luminosity is, the longer is the period.

Perseus arm a segment of a spiral arm that lies about 10,000 light years from the sun in the direction of the constellation Perseus.

phases of the moon the monthly cycle of changes in the moon's appearance as seen from the earth.

Phobos the larger of the two moons of Mars.

photodissociation the breakup of a molecule by the absorption of light with enough energy to break the molecular bonds.

photon a discrete chunk of light energy.

photosphere the visible surface of the sun; the region of the solar atmosphere from which visible light escapes into space.

pitch angle the angle between a spiral arm's direction and the direction of circular motion about the Galaxy.

planet any of the nine (so far known) solid, large bodies that revolve around the sun; traditionally, any heavenly object that moved with respect to the stars.

planetary nebula a thick shell of gas moving out from an extremely hot star. It is believed to be the outer layers of a red giant star thrown into space, the core of which eventually becomes a white dwarf.

planetesimals asteroid-sized bodies that, in the formation of the solar system, combined with each other to form the protoplanets.

plasma a gas consisting entirely of ionized atoms.

Polaris the present North Pole star; the outermost star in the handle of the Little Dipper.

polarization a lining-up of the planes of vibration of light waves.

Population I stars stars that tend to be luminous, hot, and young, concentrated in the disk of a spiral galaxy, especially in the spiral arms. They have a heavy element abundance similar to the sun (about 2 percent of the total). An old Population I is found in the nuclei of spiral galaxies and in elliptical galaxies.

Population II stars stars that tend to be found in globular clusters and the halo of a galaxy; they are somewhat older, less luminous, and cooler than Population I stars and also contain fewer heavy elements.

positron an antimatter electron; essentially an electron with a positive charge.

potential energy the ability to do work due to position. It is storable and can later be converted into other forms.

PP chain see proton-proton chain.

precession of the equinoxes the slow westward motion of the equinox points in the sky relative to the stars of the zodiac because of a wobbling of the earth's spin axis.

primary the brighter of two stars in a binary system.

primeval fireball the hot, dense beginning of the universe in the big-bang model, when most of the energy was in the form of high-energy light.

principle of equivalence the equality of inertial mass and gravitational mass so that gravitational forces can be made to vanish in a small region of spacetime by choosing an appropriate accelerated frame of reference; the fundamental idea in Einstein's general theory of relativity.

proper motion the angular change in the position of a star in a year due to its motion relative to the sun.

protein a long chain of amino acids linked by hydrogen bonds.

protogalaxies clouds with enough mass that they are destined to collapse gravitationally into galaxies.

proton a massive, positively charged elementary particle; one of the main parts of the nucleus of an atom.

proton-proton chain (PP chain) a series of thermonuclear reactions that occur in the interiors of stars. Essentially, hydrogen nuclei are fused into helium; believed to be the primary energy production process in the sun.

protoplanet large masses formed by the sticking together of planetesimals; the final stage in the formation of the planets out of the primeval nebula.

protostar a collapsing mass of gas and dust out of which a star will be born (when thermonuclear reactions turn on) whose energy comes from gravitational contraction.

pulsar a radio source that emits signals in very short, regular bursts. It is believed to be a highly magnetic, rapidly rotating neutron star.

quanta discrete packets of energy.

quasar an intense, starlike source of radio waves that is characterized by large red shifts of the lines in its visible spectrum.

radar mapping the surveying of the topographic features of a planet's surface by the reflection of radio waves from it.

radial velocity the component of relative velocity that lies along the line of sight.

radiation usually used to refer to electromagnetic waves, such as light, radio, infrared, and so on; sometimes used to refer to atomic particles of high energy, such as electrons (beta radiation), helium nuclei (alpha radiation), and so on.

radiative energy the capacity to do work that is carried by electromagnetic waves.

radioactive dating a process that determines the age of an object by the rate of decay of radioactive elements in it.

radioactive decay the process by which an element fissions into lighter elements.

radio galaxy a galaxy that emits radio signals generally characterized by two giant lobes of emission situated on opposite ends of a line drawn through its nucleus.

radio jet a small spike of radio emission emerging from the nucleus of a radio galaxy.

radio line emission sharp energy peaks at radio wavelengths, usually caused by low-energy transitions of atoms.

recombination the joining of an electron to an ion; the reverse of ionization.

recombination line sharp energy peaks caused by photons emitted when an ion recombines and the captured electron falls to lower energy states.

reddening the preferential scattering of blue light by small particles, allowing more red light to pass directly through.

red giant a large, cool star with a high luminosity and surface temperature of about 2000–3000 K.

red shift an increase in the wavelength of the radiation emitting by a receding celestial body as a consequence of the Doppler effect; a shift toward the long-wavelength (red) end of the spectrum.

reference frame a set of coordinates attached to the observer that goes wherever he or she goes.

reflecting telescope a telescope, invented by Isaac Newton, that has a curved mirror as a primary light gatherer.

reflection nebula a bright cloud of gas and dust that is visible from the reflection of starlight by the dust.

refracting telescope a telescope that uses glass lenses to gather light.

resolving power the ability of a telescope to separate close stars or to pick out fine details on celestial objects.

retrograde motion the apparent *westward* motion of a planet with respect to the stars.

Roche lobe in a binary star system, the edge of the region of space where the gravitational force of one star dominates the other.

rotation the turning of a body, such as a planet, on its axis.

RR Lyrae stars a class of giant, pulsating variable stars with periods of less than 1 day.

Sagittarius arm a portion of spiral arm structure of the Galaxy that lies about 5000–6500 ly from the center of the Galaxy. It appears in the constellation Sagittarius as seen from the sun.

satellite a smaller body that revolves around a larger one.

scarp a long, vertical wall running across a flat plain.

Schwarzschild radius the critical size that a mass must reach to be dense enough to trap light by its gravity; that is, to become a black hole.

second of arc $\frac{1}{60}$ of a min of arc, or $\frac{1}{3600}$ of a degree.

secondary the fainter of the two stars in a binary system.

seeing the unsteadiness of the earth's atmosphere that blurs telescopic images.

seismic waves sound waves traveling through and across the earth that are produced by earthquakes.

seismometer an instrument used to detect earthquakes and moonquakes.

sexigesimal system a counting system based on 60, such as 60 minutes in an hour or 60 min of arc in a degree.

Seyfert galaxy a galaxy whose bright nucleus shows broad emission lines; often a strong radio and infrared source.

sidereal month the period of the moon's revolution around the earth with respect to a fixed direction in space or a fixed star; about $27\frac{1}{3}$ days.

sidereal period the time interval needed by a celestial body to complete one revolution of another with respect to the background stars.

signs of the zodiac the 12 equal angular divisions of 30° each into which the ecliptic is divided. Each corresponds to a zodiacal constellation.

silicate a compound of silicon and oxygen, very common in rocks at the earth's surface.

singularity a theoretical point of zero volume of infinite density to which any mass that becomes a black hole must collapse, according to the general theory of relativity.

solar day the time from noon to noon.

solar eclipse an eclipse of the sun by the moon, when the moon passes in front of the sun.

solar mass the amount of material in the sun, about 2×10^{30} kg.

solar wind a stream of charged particles, mostly protons and electrons, that escape the sun's outer atmosphere at high speeds and stream out into the solar system.

solstice the time of year when the day or night is the longest. In the Northern Hemisphere the summer solstice occurs around June 21 and is the longest day; the winter solstice occurs around December 21 and is the shortest day. On the summer solstice, the sun is highest in the sky at noon for the year; on the winter solstice, the lowest.

south magnetic pole a point on a star or planet from which magnetic lines of force emanate and to which the south pole of a compass needle points.

space a three-dimensional region in which objects and events occur and have relative direction and position; the final frontier.

spacetime looking at the universe with space and time unified; a continuous system of one time coordinate and three space coordinates by which events can be located.

special theory of relativity Einstein's theory describing the relations between measurements of physical phenomena as viewed by observers who are in relative motion at constant velocities.

spectral line a particular wavelength of light corresponding to some energy transition in an atom.

spectroscope an instrument for examining spectra.

spectroscopic binary two stars revolving around a common center of mass that can be identified by periodic variations in the Doppler shift of the lines of their spectra.

spectroscopic parallax the distance found by comparing the apparent brightnesses of stars with their actual luminosities, as determined by their spectral class.

spectroscopy the analysis of light by separating it by wavelength (color).

spectrum (plural "spectra") the array of colors or wavelengths obtained when light is dispersed, such as by a prism; the amount of energy given off by an object at every different wavelength.

spherical geometry an alternative to Euclid's geometry, constructed by G. F. B. Riemann on the premise that no parallel lines can be drawn through a point near a straight line. The sum of the angles of a triangle drawn on a spherical surface is always greater than 180°.

spin angular momentum the angular momentum of a rotating body; the product of a body's mass, rotational velocity, and radius.

spinar a highly condensed, spinning object that may be the energy source of a quasar.

spiral arm a structure in a spiral galaxy composed of gas, dust, and young stars that winds out in a plane from a galaxy's center.

spiral galaxy a galaxy with spiral arms; the presumed shape of the Milky Way.

spiral tracers objects that are commonly found in spiral arms and so are used to trace spiral structure; for example, Population I cepheids, H II regions, and OB-stars.

spontaneous generation the natural origination of living from lifeless matter.

stadium an ancient Greek unit of length, probably about 0.2 km.

standard candle see distance candle

star model a table of values of the physical characteristics (such as temperature, density, and pressure) for a star with a specified mass and chemical composition, calculated from theoretical ideas of the basic physics of stars.

steady-state model a theory of the universe based on the perfect cosmological principle, in which the universe looks basically the same to all observers at all times.

stellar spectral sequence a star sequence classification that ranges from hot stars to cooler ones, the sequence runs OBAFGKM from hotter to cooler stars.

stones meteorites made of light silicate materials.

stony-irons meteorites that are a blend of nickel-iron and silicate materials.

stratosphere a layer in the earth's atmosphere in which temperature changes with altitude are small and clouds are rare.

summer solstice the longest day of the year (in the Northern Hemisphere); the day on which the noon sun reaches its highest point in the sky for a year.

sunspot a temporary cool region in the sun's photosphere. It has a strong magnetic field.

supercluster a group of clusters of galaxies.

supergiant a massive star of large size and high luminosity.

supernova a stupendous explosion of a massive star, which increases its brightness hundreds of millions of times in a few days.

synchrotron radiation radiation from an accelerating charged particle (usually an electron) in a magnetic field. The wavelength of the emitted radiation depends on the strength of the magnetic field and the speed of the charged particles.

synodic period the interval between successive similar lineups of a celestial body with the sun.

temperature a measure of the average speed or energy of the particles in a substance.

terrestrial pertaining to the earth.

thermal radiation electromagnetic radiation due to the fact that a body is hot. Under equilibrium conditions, it is characterized by a blackbody spectrum.

tidal force the difference in gravitational force affected by one body's gravitational attraction on various points of a second body, which causes the second body to be deformed.

time a measure of the flow of events; beyond the final frontier.

Titan Saturn's largest satellite. It was the first satellite detected to have an atmosphere.

transition (in an atom) a change in the electron arrangements in an atom, which involves a change in energy.

transverse wave a sound wave that moves in an up-

82 83 84 85 86 1 2 3 4 5 6 7 8 9